"And I Was There"

BOOKS BY JOHN COSTELLO:

The Battle for Concorde (with Terry Hughes, 1971)
D-Day (with Warren Tute and Terry Hughes, 1974)
The Concorde Conspiracy (with Terry Hughes, 1976)
Jutland 1916 (with Terry Hughes, 1976)
The Battle of the Atlantic (with Terry Hughes, 1977)
The Pacific War (1981)
Love, Sex and War—Changing Values 1939–45 (1985)

BOOKS BY ROGER PINEAU:

A Picture History of the Pacific War (with Robert Sherrod, 1952)
Midway, the Battle That Doomed Japan (with Mitsuo Fuchida, Masatake
    Okumiya and Clark Kawakami, 1955)
The Divine Wind (with Rikihei Inoguchi and Tadashi Nakajima, 1958)
Japanese Destroyer Captain (with Tameichi Hara and Fred Saito, 1961)
The End of the Imperial Japanese Navy (with Masanori Ito and Andrew
    Y. Kuroda, 1962)
*The Japan Expedition, 1852–4: The Personal Journal of Commodore
    Matthew C. Perry* (Ed., 1969)
"Isoruku Yamamoto" in *The War Lords* (Ed. Sir Michael Carver, 1976)

"And I Was There"

Pearl Harbor and Midway—
Breaking the Secrets

by Rear Admiral Edwin T. Layton, U.S.N. (Ret.),
with Captain Roger Pineau, U.S.N.R. (Ret.),
and John Costello

WILLIAM MORROW AND COMPANY, INC.
NEW YORK

In recognition of the unsung heroes
of radio intelligence
in the United States Navy

Library of Congress Cataloging-in-Publication Data

Layton, Edwin T., 1903-
  "And I was there".

  Bibliography: p.
  Includes index.
  1. Layton, Edwin T., 1903-   . 2. Pearl Harbor
(Hawaii), Attack on, 1941—Personal narratives, American.
3. Midway, Battle of, 1942—Personal narratives,
American.   4. United States. Navy—Biography.
5. Seamen—United States—Biography. I. Pineau,
Roger, 1916-   . II. Costello, John. III. Title.
D767.92.L39   1985   940.54'26   85-18960
ISBN 0-688-04883-8

Printed in the United States of America

First Edition

1 2 3 4 5 6 7 8 9 10

BOOK DESIGN BY BERNARD SCHLEIFER

Acknowledgments

COMPLETING THE PROJECT that the late Admiral Layton began so many years ago in the densely packed handwritten pages of his notebooks has required the assistance and cooperation of many people. Foremost of them are his surviving wartime colleagues and his widow, Miriam. She not only encouraged her husband to make the decision to commit his story to print and assisted with the preparation of early manuscript drafts, but after his death continued to sustain his collaborators by making available all his research notes and papers in addition to providing them with gracious hospitality. Mrs. Layton has also read the final manuscript and provided insightful comment on it.

Admiral Arleigh Burke, who has initiated so many significant projects, inspired Admiral Layton and us to undertake the writing of this book. We have benefited from his sound advice and encouragement. Others strongly supportive of this project have been Rear Admiral John Butts, U.S.N., Rear Admiral P. W. "Pete" Dillingham, Rear Admiral William C. Mott, Rear Admiral L. Robert Schulz, Rear Admiral Robert H. R. Weeks, all U.S.N. (Ret.). Captain Raymond P. Schmidt, U.S.N.R., with his knowledge of radio intelligence history, has contributed greatly to this work and, with his wife, Roberta, devoted many hours to a critical reading of the manuscript.

Friends and colleagues of Admiral Layton who have given generously of their time and knowledge are many. We are especially grateful to the late Captain Thomas H. Dyer, his naval academy classmate, cryptologist, and mathematician par excellence; and Captain Wesley A. "Ham" Wright, who has shared with us his acute recollections, lively humor, and vast cryptanalytic lore.

Others who shared with us their wartime Cincpac experience and memories of Admiral Layton include Rear Admiral D. M. "Mac" Showers; Captains John G. Roenigk, Arthur L. Benedict, Forrest R. "Tex"

Biard, Allyn Cole, Robert E. Hudson, Wilfred J. Holmes, Willis L. Thomas, and Gilven M. Slonim, all U.S.N. (Ret.); Brigadier General Bankson Holcomb and Colonel Alva B. Lasswell, U.S.M.C. (Ret.); and Commander H. M. Anthony, U.S.C.G. (Ret.). We are also indebted to Rear Admiral Kemp Tolley; to Captain H. Arthur Lamar, wartime aide to Admiral Nimitz; to Pauline Birtley, widow of Captain Thomas B. Birtley; and Mary Lee Watts, widow of Captain Ethelbert Watts, for information each provided.

The book has benefited from the insights provided by Phil Cate, Eunice Willson Rice, and Fred C. Woodrough, Jr. These former civilian employees of OP-20-GZ have perceptively helped to flesh out the archival record.

We are grateful also to Captain Thomas Kimmel (son of Admiral Kimmel) and his son Tom Kimmel. They have given us access to many of the admiral's papers and provided informed advice. Mrs. Janet Elerding, daughter of Captain Joseph J. Rochefort, generously made her father's private document collection available, as did the Dyer family. We are grateful to Commander Howard McCollum, son of Admiral McCollum, for placing useful papers and records at our disposal.

Professor E. B. Potter and John Lundstrom have generously made available their correspondence with Layton and his critiques of key issues. Keiji Miyoshi, formerly an intelligence officer in the imperial Japanese navy, has been an unstinting source of answers to many questions. Robert Haslach and James Rushbridger have magnanimously shared with us the fruits of their respective research into the Dutch and British intelligence services. Paul M. Stillwell has kindly made available records from the U.S. Naval Institute's comprehensive oral history program.

Although the interpretation of the recently declassified documentation is that of the authors, we are grateful for the advice and help given by Professor Warren Kimball of Rutgers University, Professor Forrest C. Pogue of the Eisenhower Institute, Dr. John W. Chapman of Sussex University, Dr. Martin Gilbert of Oxford, and Dr. David Reynolds of Cambridge University. Professor Raymond G. O'Connor, formerly of the Naval War College and Stanford University; Professor Gerald Wheeler, formerly of San Jose State University; and Bill Williams, latterly with *The Washington Post,* have given valued professional critiques of the final manuscript.

The staffs of many federal archives have responded promptly and helpfully over the years to many requests for documents. They include: the National Archives in Washington, D.C., and its subsidiary repositories at Suitland, San Bruno, and Laguna Niguel; the National Personnel Records Center, St. Louis; the Franklin D. Roosevelt Library, Hyde Park, N.Y.; and the Naval Historical Center and the Self-Defense Force Historical Center in Japan.

The Naval Security Group and the National Security Agency have released vast quantities of wartime intelligence material and both Admiral Layton and his co-authors have been privileged to have received invaluable assistance from the members of the historical departments at these organizations.

In these massive and seemingly impersonal organizations we have discovered helpful friends who have made our research easier by the personal interest they have given this project. To name some is to risk omitting others who are equally deserving, but we are particularly grateful to Michael Anderson, B. F. "Cal" Cavalcante, Fred Close, Martha Crawley, Robert Cresswood, Charles R. Haberlein, Jr., Terri Hammet, Richard von Doenhof, Deborah Edge, Hisao Iwashima, Rose Mary Kennedy, Raymond E. Lewis, William H. Lewis, Barbara A. Lynch, Sally Marks, Katherine Nicastro, Diane Nixon, Neal Petersen, Robert Parks, Edward Reese, John C. Reilly, Jr., Lieutenant Commander Robert J. Schultz, U.S.N., John Taylor, Jim Trimble, and John E. Vajda.

The Public Records Office, England; the New Zealand National Archives, Auckland; the Australian War Memorial, Canberra; the Imperial War Museum in London; the Bundesarchiv, Frieberg; the Admiralty Library, London; and the Military History Section of the Royal Netherlands Army have also been the sources of new documentation. The staff of the Library of Congress, especially the Japanese section of the Orientalia Division, has answered our many calls on their expertise with promptness and precision.

Admiral Layton would have wished us to extend a particular express of gratitude to the librarians of the U.S. Navy Postgraduate School, Monterey, for all the assistance they gave to his researches. The New York Public Library and the Columbia University Library have also served as valued sources of published material. The University of Wyoming Library afforded us information from its Archive of Contemporary History.

Others who have helped with this project are those with special knowledge, wartime experience, or authors of important source works. Friends and relatives of Admiral Layton and his two co-authors have assisted with information and translations, or have generously contributed to logistical support. Our gratitude is extended to Captain Edward L. Beach, U.S.N. (Ret.), Joan and Richard Bergsund, Patrick Beazely, Clay Blair, Jr., William C. Bodie, Commander Masataka Chihaya, Robert T. Crowley, George M. Elsey, Admiral Sir Morgan Giles, Dr. Ruth Harris, Douglass Hubbard, Henry and Julianne Hubbard, Stephen Hubbard, Gerald P. Jantzi, Ernest Kroll, Andrew Y. Kuroda, "Red" Luckenback, Catherine Magistretti, Richard and Virginia Morrall, Kenneth J. Nichols, Captain Wyman Packard, U.S.N. (Ret.), Lawrence Pratt, Commander Ernest Saftig, U.S.N. (Ret.), Robert Sherrod, Charles A. "Sandy" Sims, Riley Sunderland, Anna Del Valle, Robin and Julia Wight, and Thomas F. Troy.

The copy-editing and production staff of William Morrow have met impossible deadlines with graceful competence, and we are especially grateful to assistant editor Elizabeth Terhune. We should like to thank

Victoria Klose and freelancer David Falk for their judicious copy editing, Bernard Schliefer for designing the book, Cheryl Asherman for her striking cover, and Richard Natkiel of London whose cartographic skills provided the maps.

Maxine Pineau earned our gratitude for having let World War II be waged again on her home front in the 1980s. She not only kept Layton's collaborators nourished but her expertise with the word processor greatly facilitated the production of the final manuscript.

A very special category of our appreciation must be reserved for two friends without whose help this book would never have been realized in its present form. One is Bruce Lee, prescient editor extraordinaire, who inspired and guided the project to its successful conclusion. The other, though his name appears in these pages, has requested anonymity. That request is honored, but we want him to know that his comments and suggestions, based on deft command of our language and thorough knowledge of communications intelligence, have contributed greatly to the authority and accuracy of Admiral Layton's story.

In the quarter century of our life together, my husband relived over and over the events of his naval career, particularly the period of duty as intelligence officer for Admiral Nimitz. I became almost as familiar with the day-to-day happenings as if I had been there—and in the retelling his memory remained fresh.

He fairly seethed with pent-up emotions surrounding the trauma of having gone through all but one of the Pearl Harbor investigations and of hearing some of his fellow officers verbally coerced into testifying falsely. Our countless evenings of conversation fulfilled his need to give vent to his outrage at the cover-up in Washington, and at the sacrifice of Admiral Kimmel and General Short.

Time and again Edwin was urged to write his experiences. Though he was reticent, he finally came to the conviction that he owed one more contribution to his country. The gradual release of top secret documents in the National Archives helped persuade him to reveal the true version of events. Proof of his statements was assured via copies of actual messages as more and more papers were freed. He felt history required that he produce a record of what really happened as only he could tell it because he was there, living it all.

With two friends whose professional qualifications he respected and admired, my husband agreed to recount, tape record, and write his experiences for the benefit of historians and the future generations of Americans who will love their country as much as he did.

—MIRIAM P. LAYTON

Carmel, California
July 1985

Contents

"And I Was There"

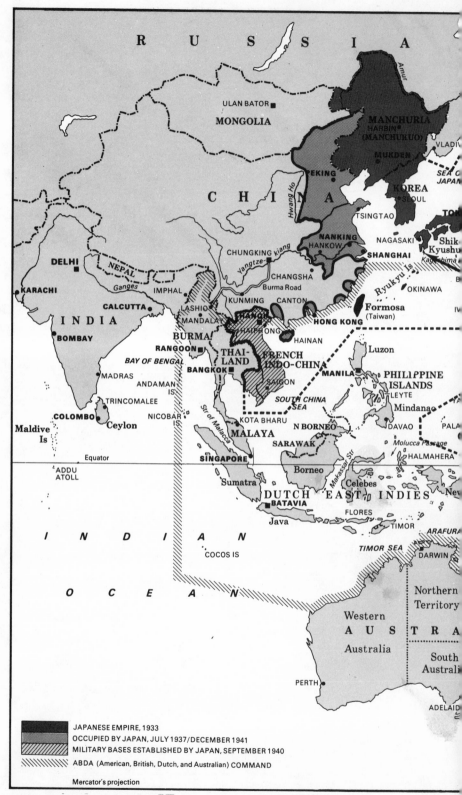

THE PACIFIC WAR—1941: The Japanese Conquest

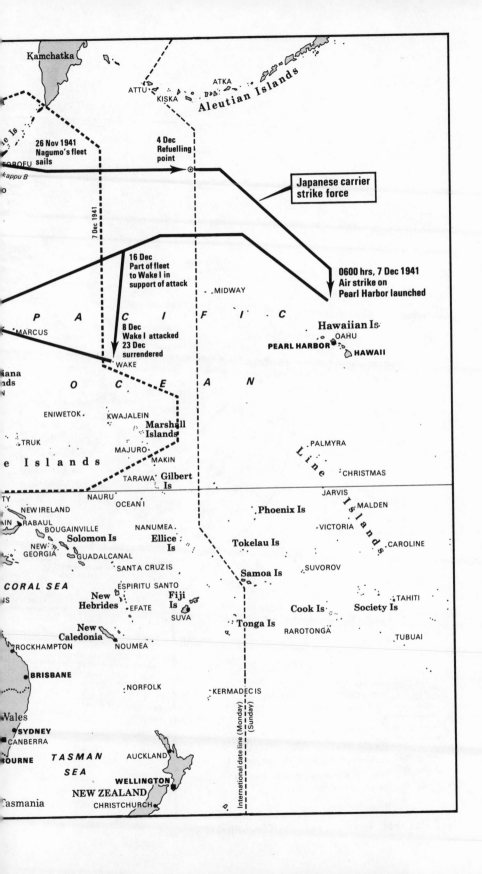

Kamchatka

ATKA
ATTU   Aleutian Islands
KISKA

26 Nov 1941
Nagumo's fleet
sails

4 Dec
Refuelling
point

Japanese carrier
strike force

ETOROFU

Kappu B

7 Dec 1941

16 Dec
Part of fleet
to Wake I in
support of attack

0600 hrs, 7 Dec 1941
Air strike on
Pearl Harbor launched

MIDWAY

P   A   C   I   F   I   C

MARCUS

8 Dec
Wake I attacked
23 Dec
surrendered

Hawaiian Is

OAHU
PEARL HARBOR
HAWAII

WAKE

iana
nds

O   C   E   A   N

ENIWETOK   KWAJALEIN

TRUK

Marshall
Islands

Line

PALMYRA

e   Islands

MAJURO   MAKIN

TARAWA   Gilbert
Is

CHRISTMAS

NAURU   OCEAN I

JARVIS

Islands

MALDEN

TY

NEW IRELAND

Phoenix Is

VICTORIA

RABAUL
BOUGAINVILLE   NANUMEA

AIN

NEW
GEORGIA   GUADALCANAL

Solomon Is

Ellice
Is

Tokelau Is

CAROLINE

SUVOROV

SANTA CRUZ IS

Samoa Is

CORAL SEA

ESPIRITU SANTO

New
Hebrides   EFATE

Fiji
Is
SUVA

TAHITI

Cook Is

Society Is

New
Caledonia

ROCKHAMPTON   NOUMEA

Tonga Is

RAROTONGA

TUBUAI

BRISBANE

NORFOLK

KERMADEC IS

Wales

SYDNEY
CANBERRA

OURNE   TASMAN
SEA

AUCKLAND

International date line (Monday)
(Sunday)

WELLINGTON
NEW ZEALAND
CHRISTCHURCH

asmania

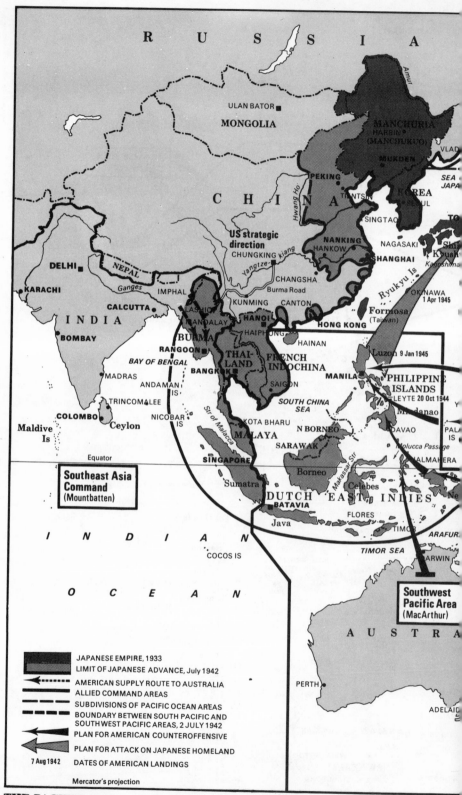

THE PACIFIC WAR—1942-45: The Allied Offensives

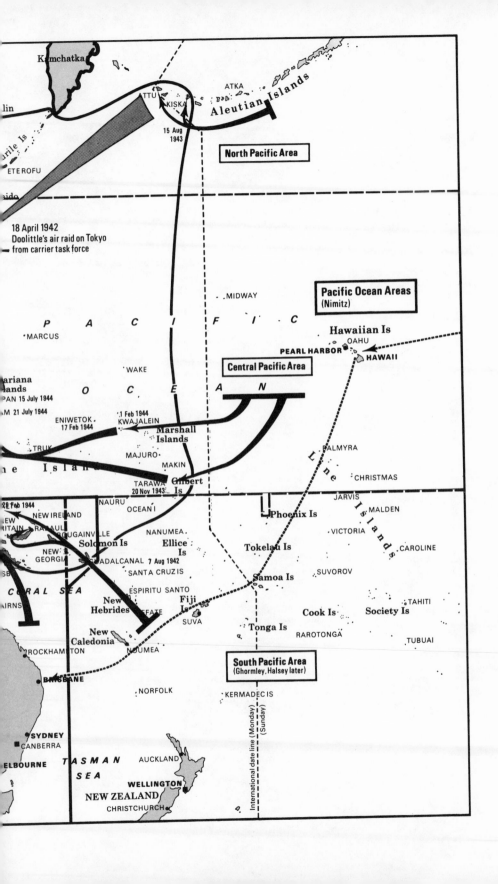

Kamchatka

ATKA

ATTU

KISKA

Aleutian Islands

15 Aug 1943

North Pacific Area

lin

urile Is

ETEROFU

ido

18 April 1942
Doolittle's air raid on Tokyo
from carrier task force

MIDWAY

Pacific Ocean Areas
(Nimitz)

P A C I F I C

MARCUS

Hawaiian Is
OAHU

PEARL HARBOR

HAWAII

WAKE

Central Pacific Area

O C E A N

ariana
ands
PAN 15 July 1944
AM 21 July 1944

ENIWETOK
17 Feb 1944

1 Feb 1944
KWAJALEIN

**Marshall
Islands**

TRUK

MAJURO

MAKIN

Line Islands

PALMYRA

CHRISTMAS

ne   Islan

TARAWA
20 Nov 1943

**Gilbert
Is**

JARVIS

MALDEN

28 Feb 1944

NAURU

OCEAN I

Phoenix Is

VICTORIA

CAROLINE

NEW IRELAND

RITAIN RABAUL

BOUGAINVILLE

NANUMEA

Solomon Is

**Ellice
Is**

Tokelau Is

SUVOROV

NEW
GEORGIA

GUADALCANAL 7 Aug 1942

SANTA CRUZ IS

Samoa Is

SB

ESPIRITU SANTO

**New
Hebrides**

**Fiji
Is**

Cook Is

Society Is

TAHITI

RAL SEA

EFATE

SUVA

AIRNS

**New
Caledonia**

NOUMEA

Tonga Is

RAROTONGA

TUBUAI

ROCKHAMPTON

South Pacific Area
(Ghormley, Halsey later)

BRISBANE

NORFOLK

KERMADEC IS

SYDNEY

CANBERRA

TASMAN

AUCKLAND

ELBOURNE

SEA

WELLINGTON

NEW ZEALAND

CHRISTCHURCH

International date line (Monday)
(Sunday)

1

"I Was There"

"**P**EARL HARBOR is under air attack, sir."
That Sunday morning telephone call from the duty yeoman in my office at Pacific Fleet headquarters was the most stunning message of my life. At my home near Diamond Head, fifteen miles east of Pearl Harbor, there had been no sound of planes, bombs, gunfire, or any other indication that Japan had brought war to the Hawaiian island of Oahu.

"I'll be right there," I replied, and began pulling on my clothes of last evening. Almost immediately an expected phone call came from my Kalanianaole Highway neighbor Lieutenant Paul Crosley. He was flag secretary to Admiral Husband E. Kimmel, commander in chief of the United States Pacific Fleet, and I was fleet intelligence officer. "Be out front, Eddie," he hollered. "I'll pick you up in three minutes."

Mrs. Crosley was driving as the huge roadster paused at the curb and I jumped into the rumble seat. We roared off in their striking blue sixteen-cylinder Cadillac, with its white-sidewall tires. We must have been doing sixty as we flew into the eastern outskirts of Honolulu. The scene was eye-catching enough to attract a motorcycle cop who overtook us with his red light flashing.

Before he could say a word about our speeding, I yelled that Pearl Harbor was under air attack, we were fleet staff officers, and we needed his help to get out there immediately. At that moment the policeman's radio blared news of the air raid. He motioned us to follow, flipped on his siren, and shot ahead, leading the way along the hill route skirting the city. As Crosley later recalled, "We must have been the only private parties who ever drove through the Punchbowl area at eighty miles an hour."

Smoke billowed skyward as we approached the naval base. At the Schofield barracks intersection, traffic was completely blocked. Our cop-

17

guide veered off the highway and led us bumping and bouncing over a rough stretch of terrain and into the navy yard just as the second wave of Japanese planes came screaming in.

I dashed into the submarine base administration building and leaped up the stairs toward my second-floor office. Several officers were conferring in the corridor. Captain Willard Kitts, the staff gunnery officer, spotted me and called out, "Ah, here's the man we should have been listening to all along."

The middle of an air raid, with the rat-a-tat-tat of machine guns on the submarines in the slip below our windows, was hardly a moment for philosophic reflections. As fleet intelligence officer, my job was to keep the commander in chief informed of when, where, how, and in what strength a potential enemy attack might be anticipated.

Until that very Sunday morning we had not known the whereabouts of the main Japanese aircraft carriers. On the 2 December intelligence sheet I had written "Homeland waters?" for their location. This prompted an exchange with Admiral Kimmel which, in the event, was a dreadful irony.

"What? You don't know where the carriers are?" Kimmel had erupted.

"No, sir," I replied.

"You haven't any idea of where they are?"

"No, sir. That's why I have 'Homeland waters' with a question mark. I don't know."

"You mean to say that you, the intelligence officer, don't know where the carriers are?"

"No, sir, I don't."

"You mean they could be coming around Diamond Head, and you wouldn't know it?"

"Yes, sir, but I hope they'd have been sighted before now."

"I understand." Kimmel said, with a twinkle in his eye that kidded me for losing track of a substantial part of the Japanese fleet.

I have since worn a hole in the seat of my trousers kicking myself for not reminding Kimmel then and there about the translation I had given him several months earlier. It was from a Japanese book, *When We Fight,* published in 1933, and it had predicted that in the event of war with the United States, the Japanese fleet would attack Pearl Harbor.

The numbing memory of those terrible first hours of the Pacific war came flooding back to me during the measured ritual of the formal surrender ceremony on board battleship *Missouri* the morning of 2 September 1945.

Scudding gray clouds swirled over the long lines of Allied naval vessels that crowded Tokyo Bay. The early morning mists had lifted by the time that General Douglas MacArthur came on board *Missouri* shortly after 0800, but a sullen sky continued to threaten the anchorage. The waters of the great bay were eerily still and black, dancing with reflections of the lean hulls of 260 assembled warships, an awesome demonstration of the military might that had been marshaled to defeat Japan.

At the appointed hour of 0900, an American destroyer bearing the eleven-man Japanese delegation closed the battleship's starboard side. The emperor's burden of capitulation appeared to weigh heavily on the shoulders of the foreign minister. It was impossible not to feel sympathy for this frail figure in frock coat and top hat who labored so painfully up the companion ladder. Mamoru Shigemitsu had lost his left leg to a Communist bomb years before, and we watched in agonized silence as he limped across the quarterdeck below number two gun turret. Alongside him stood General Yoshijiro Umezu, the chief of the imperial general staff, whose stony detachment betrayed a warrior's distaste for submitting to the ultimate military indignity.

When MacArthur called on them to "conclude a solemn agreement," the minister and general were the first to sign, followed by the supreme commander and the officers representing all the Allied nations. The final surrender document had been laid out before the Japanese delegation on an old mess table that, to one observer, seemed to have been transformed by a green felt cloth into an altar of peace. In an auspicious epilogue to MacArthur's final prayer for world peace, the sun burst through the cloud layers just before hundreds of Allied planes roared overhead.

Many diverse elements had conspired to ensure that I was one of the few people to be present at both the opening and closing events of the war in the Pacific. Although I had labored long and hard in the intervening four and a half years to help America win that war, I still felt a curious sympathy for Japan and its people. From the day I first arrived in Japan sixteen years earlier, their proud nationalism had impressed me, even though it had led them into horrific wartime deprivations and the finality of a bitter defeat.

My view of the actual moment of surrender was obscured by ranks of senior officers crowded in front of me. Still I counted myself very fortunate to be present as the personal guest of Admiral Chester W. Nimitz, whom I had served as fleet intelligence officer throughout the war. But my personal relief that Japan and the United States were finally at peace was rudely shaken by another memorable event that day. Unlike the surrender ceremony, this experience was intensely personal and bitter—and totally unexpected.

As a member of the Pacific Fleet commander's official entourage, I was quartered on board his flagship *South Dakota*. That evening, after we had finished dinner and were relaxing with a game of acey-deucey in the wardroom, Admiral Richmond Kelly Turner, another personal guest of Nimitz, strode in.

The war had made "Terrible" Turner a naval legend. As commander of Nimitz's amphibious forces, he had executed all our landing operations from Guadalcanal to Iwo Jima with brilliant distinction. But few who worked closely with him in these operations could forget—or forgive—his stormy temper, overbearing ego, and celebrated bouts with the bottle. From the manner in which he entered the wardroom that evening, it was evident that he was stoked up. He soon galvanized the wardroom with the reason for his celebration.

"Did you see the navy department's release about the findings of the Pearl Harbor court of inquiry?" he demanded, his booming voice stopping all conversation. "They said that goddamned Kimmel had all the information and didn't do anything about it. They should hang him higher than a kite!"

Turner continued to hold forth. Time and again he said, "Kimmel was given all that information and didn't do anything about it."

I sat there stunned. I knew that what he was saying was not only untrue, but a monstrous slur on my former commander in chief.

Turner's gloating denunciation was not the first venting I had been exposed to of the internecine feud that had flared up time and again in the upper reaches of the navy. Its ramifications were to divide a generation of senior officers and help fuel a mounting political and historical controversy over who was to blame for the events leading to the disaster at Pearl Harbor on 7 December 1941.

The feud was rooted in the classic power struggle that has been endemic in military organizations since men first answered the call to arms: the struggle over who should control military intelligence. The resurgence of the old fight had caused divisions in the navy department, between the office of naval intelligence (ONI) and office of naval communications (ONC), during the critical year between the spring of 1941 and the early summer of 1942. Not only had it made a major contribution toward ensuring that the Japanese succeeded with their surprise attack, but had almost cost us the battle at Midway. In truth it had plagued our military commands throughout World War II—and it is still going on today.

It was ironic that on the first night of official peace I found myself walking into the flames of another such controversy. Having been Admiral Kimmel's fleet intelligence officer on 7 December 1941, and having testified at all but one of the secret wartime inquiries into Pearl Harbor, I knew that Turner's bald assertions were scandalously untrue. Admiral Kimmel had been a victim of circumstances and became a convenient scapegoat in order to cover up navy department derelictions.

Responsibility for this failure bore heavily on Turner who, in his capacity as chief of war plans, had been the forceful junior member of the triumvirate who virtually ran the office of naval operations throughout 1941. He had arrogated to himself many of the traditional functions of the office of naval intelligence and to protect his errors of judgment and conceal the collective culpability of the most senior officers in the navy,

Turner had played a leading part in the campaign to pillory a fellow officer and fine commander of the fleet.

Turner repeated his rant: "They should hang him higher than a kite!" And I, boiling with indignation, had to correct him. "Admiral," I said, "I'm sorry. But Kimmel did not have that information. You say that he did. I know that he did not, and I was there."

"Who are you?" demanded the four-star admiral, with the fury of a bull stopped in mid-charge. I identified myself as Kimmel's intelligence officer at the time, saying that I knew what had happened and why. Before I could finish, Turner came roaring across the room bellowing, "Are you calling me a liar?" He grabbed at my throat. We were stopped from fisticuffs only by the swift intervention of *South Dakota*'s skipper, Captain Emmet P. Forrestel, who parted us. Later I pondered the incongruity of four stripes mixing it up with four stars.

For all his lustrous war record as an amphibious commander, Admiral Turner that evening had lived up to his other reputation as an opinionated, stubborn fool. There he was, hanging Kimmel by his fingernails, when the truth—as we both well knew—was that Turner had failed to relay to the fleet commander at Pearl Harbor the vital intelligence that might have averted the disaster. Despite his loudmouthed bluster in the wardroom of *South Dakota,* the former director of war plans was later obliged to admit under oath that his assertion was wrong,[1] but he was never to concede his own errors of judgment. It was already too late to rectify the harm done to Admiral Kimmel. His reputation had already been sacrificed in order to placate the wartime outrage of the American people and save the prestige of United States military leadership.

Turner's behavior was unforgiving—and unforgivable. One of the first things I learned on entering the navy was the primary principle of command, that an officer bears personal responsibility for ensuring that his orders are carried out. Turner, instead, blamed his subordinates, maintaining that they had assured him that Admiral Kimmel was "receiving the same decrypted information" available in Washington.[2] A simple check of his own signal logs would have revealed that we had *not* received some of the most essential and important pieces of intelligence that became available to the navy department during four months preceding the Japanese attack.

Military commanders seldom if ever receive enough intelligence—evaluated information on which they can rely when making strategic and tactical decisions. Yet, by any objective measure, Admiral Kimmel was cheated. Intelligence is always a matter of trying to assemble a jigsaw puzzle with missing pieces. But my task in the weeks before 7 December 1941 had been frustrated because Washington had failed to relay to us vital pieces of the intelligence jigsaw that we at Pearl Harbor were still missing. Had those pieces arrived in time, they would have provided us with clues that the impending Japanese attack was a probability rather than a remote possibility.[3]

We had no way of knowing that much additional information was being denied us.[4]

I had been personally assured in May 1941 by the office of naval intelligence in Washington that we would be sent every piece of pertinent information. So when I eventually learned the truth, I was shocked at the extent to which we had been shortchanged. That discovery raised serious questions in my mind about who in the navy department knew what and when they knew it, questions that had to remain publicly unanswered until the declassification of wartime intelligence records made it possible to break the inside secret story of Pearl Harbor and Midway.

Intelligence is a perishable commodity. Battles are won and lost and campaigns decided often on the basis of which side is most proficient in the use of intelligence—that is, the acquisition, evaluation, *and* dissemination of military information in time for commanders to act upon it. No matter how accurate the information, it is militarily useless if it is not *made available* soon enough for command decisions.

The Japanese attack on Pearl Harbor succeeded not just because of their audacious planning and skillful execution, but also, as we shall see, from a dramatic breakdown in our intelligence process.

That breakdown was related directly to feuding among high-level naval officers in Washington. The 7 December catastrophe should have served to quell the feuding and provide a lesson against such failures in the future. It is therefore shocking that, within six months of the Pearl Harbor disaster, continued feuding in Washington almost caused us to lose the tide-turning battle at Midway in June 1942. It is indicative of the extent and seriousness of those failures that the full details in both instances have been so successfully concealed from public scrutiny and understanding for so long.

2

The Undeclared War

WHEN THE IDEA OF a naval career struck me, like most boys I saw myself only on the bridge of a battleship, where a sailor belongs, never deskbound as a pen pusher. The idea surely arose during my early childhood in the river town of Nauvoo, Illinois. Holiday boat trips on the Mississippi with my grandfather heightened my early nautical interests. Like most aspiring midshipmen, I could not imagine swerving from the notion that a sailor's proper place is at sea. The gallant image persisted during academy years, and after my difficulties in getting there, I was not about to buck tradition.

In high school my favorite writing topic was Annapolis and the naval academy. My determination to go there was influenced by natural rivalry with my older brother, Clyde, who always talked of going to West Point. Each November we bet part of our meager allowance on the Army-Navy football game. Army usually won, but that did not put me off the navy. When Clyde enlisted in the army right out of high school, I determined to get into the naval academy as soon as possible.

On the recommendation of our congressman, a family friend, and a customer on my newspaper route, I took the competitive examination in 1920. I was seventeen, a year younger than the four other Illinois candidates. It wasn't very competitive because the others failed to show up. All that I had to do was to pass the written exam, or at least that's what I thought. Naval regulations also required a physical examination, however, and I was rejected for being underweight. I went to Washington to apply in person for a waiver so that I could try again.

While I was sitting in an office of the navy department waiting for them to straighten out my qualifications, an old pharmacist's mate gave me some good advice. "Son, I've got a word for you," he said. "They aren't going to do anything about this until your congressman calls to say he'd like to have them fix it. I've seen your report, you just haven't got

your weight up. Before you take the physical again, eat a few pounds of
bananas."

So I telephoned my father, who telephoned our congressman, and
then things happened. I ate a dozen or so bananas, put on two and a half
pounds, took another physical examination, and got the waiver.

I expected discipline and regimentation at Annapolis and was not disappointed, but it was a far cry from Illinois home life. I became acquainted with classmates from all parts of the country: Tommy Dyer from
Kansas, Tom Huckins from Wisconsin, Dan McCallum from Idaho, and
Bertie Watts from Pennsylvania all were friends throughout undergradu-
ate years, and our careers became interwoven in intelligence. Also in our
class of 1924 was the bookish Hanson G. Baldwin who left the navy to
make his name as a historian and military correspondent for *The New
York Times.* A year ahead of us was Arleigh Burke, who wrestled in
school as a lightweight but was an unquestioned heavyweight in wartime
destroyer squadrons, and went on to become an outstanding chief of
naval operations.

Younger and smaller than most of the class, I did not go in for athlet-
ics any more than was necessary, but Dyer and I were both in the Radi-
ator Club, which, instead of engaging in strenuous sports, was devoted to
sitting around on chilly days on warm radiators swapping dirty stories.
Dramatics interested me, and being slight of build, I won a lead role as
the vamp in one of the annual productions. Classmates never let me forget it. But as it turned out the role playing was good experience for a
couple of counterintelligence assignments later in my naval career.

We all learned how to give orders, the hard way, by taking them for
three years from upperclassmen, and then having a glorious year of being
first classmen ourselves. Among all our varied studies in those four years,
one subject never covered was naval intelligence. Surprising as that seems
today, when so much emphasis is placed on intelligence, it was never
even mentioned in any academy class. Intelligence was something that an
aspiring midshipman of my day never thought about. In a navy in which
war college tactical courses were largely devoted to refighting World War
I engagements, like Jutland with its nineteenth-century principles, intelligence was ignored by officers striving for flag rank.

My first awareness of anything remotely connected with naval intelligence did not come until six months after I was out of the academy.
Upon graduation in June 1924 I was delighted and proud to be assigned
to duty in battleship *West Virginia.* The following January we steamed
into San Francisco Bay with two other new battleships to serve as hosts
for the annual visit of Japan's cadet training squadron.

It was at first incongruous to me that we would send three of our
newest and biggest battleships as hosts to three old armored cruisers,
survivors of the Russo-Japanese War. Then I realized that it was done to
overawe and impress our visitors with the might of the United States.

As a lowly ensign I was among the junior officers detailed to escort our opposite numbers, who had just completed four years at Etajima, the Japanese naval academy. I had never met any Japanese. These eager and friendly young men surprised me by their command of English, which they spoke with ease and fluency, not at all in textbook fashion. The few who didn't know English could converse in excellent French. I was embarrassed to realize that not one of our officers could speak a single word of Japanese, and it dawned on me what it means to "lose face." The United States might have more and bigger warships, but I was more impressed by the discovery that the Japanese could communicate in our language.

That did not prevent us from having a good time. My Japanese companion was eager to visit a speakeasy and a nightclub, so I took him to one of each. At the nightclub, he produced from his raincoat pocket a bottle of genuine scotch, literally "just off the boat." This, at the height of the Prohibition era, won the hearts of the nightclub manager and staff, and the visitor from Japan was soon made the center of attention by the entertainers.

By the time the Japanese squadron was steaming out through the Golden Gate, I was writing to the navy department. My brash letter suggested that on such visits we should have someone present who spoke Japanese; and that if there was no such policy there should be. I even volunteered to learn Japanese myself.

Back came an official letter pointing out that there already existed a Japanese language program for officers who had completed five years of sea duty. I later learned that it had been started in 1910 and, after wartime interruption, resumed in 1920, and that an average of two officers a year entered the program, including a marine every third year. Then and there, it became my goal to get into that program. After battleship duty and four years in four-stack destroyer *Chase,* my assignment to the Japanese language program came through in June 1929.

In my youthful enthusiasm, it did not even occur to me that naval intelligence was not a stepping-stone toward advancement. Alternating tours of sea duty with the fleet and staff assignments ashore was still the traditional way up the naval ladder. Intelligence duty was suitable for reservists and dilettantes, but it was just marking time for career officers for whom gunnery and navigation were surer routes to flag rank.

This attitude had prevailed even after World War I had demonstrated how the revolution in communications had changed the nature of military intelligence. Until the development of electrical transmission in the nineteenth century, military orders and reports were sent by couriers or visual signals. Messengers were still being waylaid during our Civil War campaigns, as they had been since the days of the ancient Greeks, for the secrets they carried could have decisive influence on the outcome of battles. The basic principle remained the same when military organizations adopted the new systems of transmission. Telegraphs and telephones were tapped—anyone within range could pick up wireless transmissions—multiplying the opportunities for waylaying secret messages.

In the context of naval operations, radio solved the age-old problem of how to direct widely scattered forces at sea, which, until World War I, had relied on flags and scouting vessels for relaying orders and collecting intelligence. But electronic communications introduced new problems. For the first time it became possible for admirals ashore to intervene directly in fleet operations, and complex ciphers and codes were needed to protect radio transmissions from hostile listeners.

Because the terms *cipher* and *code* are not always clearly understood or precisely used, a simple definition of the two words may be appropriate. A rule of thumb used by Captain Wesley A. Wright, one of the navy's noted World War II cryptanalysts, is that the cipher changes the text "letter by letter," and a code makes the change "idea for idea."[1]

As codes and ciphers became valuable adjuncts of communications and intelligence-gathering, there developed a tremendous need and demand for breaking them. There also developed the arcane science of *cryptology* (from the Greek *kryptos,* "hidden," and *logos,* "word"), which deals with methods of secret communications, and *cryptanalysis,* which is its application. Cryptology includes signal security (protecting one's own communications) and signal intelligence (acquiring information by nullifying the enemy's signal security). *Cryptography* is the process of encoding (or enciphering) messages intended to be decoded (or deciphered) only by those to whom they are addressed.

Cipher systems involve cryptographic treatment of textual units of constant and equal length, usually single letters, but sometimes pairs or three-letter sets. The two basic classes of ciphers are those created by transposition (rearrangement of the plain-text letters without changing their identity), and those created by substitution (replacement of the plain-text letters without change in their sequence). When number groups are used in substitution, a further variation of the system can be achieved by the superimposition of a set of prearranged additives, making the solution more complicated for eavesdroppers.

In diplomatic and military communications, where secrecy is of the utmost importance, a message may be protected by a combination of encoding and enciphering, or superencipherment. Identical code books listing the equivalent number or letter groups are held by the legitimate communicators, who also possess the "key," which identifies the method they are using to encipher their message. Before a third party can break into their communications, the key used to encipher their code must first be identified. The more frequently it is changed, the more secure the system of communications.

Even when the contents of an intercepted communication cannot be read by cryptanalysis, it can be made to yield important intelligence by means of a process called traffic analysis. This involves making deductions from an analysis of messages transmitted—on the basis of from whom each message was sent and to whom it is addressed—a process that often does not require knowledge of the cipher key since the originator and designee are usually transmitted in a simple code to facilitate identification. Further, radio direction finding can pinpoint the location of transmission, and other factors such as a transmission's length, its routing, and the volume of traffic can also yield important clues to the general nature and contents and precedence of a message.

The Japanese navy has the distinction of having first made use of radio traffic analysis as a technique in war. In 1904, during the Russo-Japanese War, radio-equipped Japanese warships intercepted a message sent by a squadron of the czar's Vladivostok fleet, which was cruising secretly south of Tokyo Bay.[2]

World War I proved that, even with modern technology, there was still nothing like "intercepting the messenger," be it human courier or invisible radio waves. "We found, in the enemy's communications, information which was always truthful, obtained without risk of human lives, without expense, with a speed and surety that no other intelligence organization was able to equal" was the evaluation of Colonel Marcel Givierge, chief of the French army's cipher division in World War I.[3]

The interception and breaking of a potential enemy's codes and ciphers therefore became a vital intelligence function. The advantage of such "radio intelligence" is that it is timely, pertinent, and reliable, and very cost-effective. This was attested to by the successes of World War I. The Russians solved the German naval cipher in 1914, the British applied radio intelligence in the 1916 naval clash at Jutland, and in 1918 the U.S. Army broke into German military communications with a captured trench code.[4]

World War I demonstrated that the key to effective radio intelligence was detailed knowledge of an enemy's communications systems based on analysis of the frequencies, the designators of the addressee and originator of messages, the transmission routines followed, and even the idiosyncrasies of individual radio operators. To be effective such activity requires an extensive and strategically located series of listening posts for interception and direction finding, in addition to the assembly of a team of analysts skilled enough to recognize when an enemy might be sending deceptive messages.[5]

The arcane business of electronic interception, deception, and code breaking was born in World War I, and had its adolescence in World War II when it became known as communications intelligence, or comint. During this time, we were dependent on human ears to pick out radio signals. Enormous applications of time and brainpower were applied to break ciphers and analyze traffic when intercepted messages defied our best efforts to break through their secrets.

After World War II, with the onset of the cold war, comint became sigint (signals intelligence), a term that includes all forms of electronic intelligence emissions, including radar. Today, satellites are used like giant electronic ears hovering out in space providing surveillance of the vast range of global radio transmissions. Some of the world's most powerful computers are employed to sift through the mass of electronic traffic and penetrate the increasingly elaborate cipher systems with which countries try to guard their most sensitive communications.

For all practical purposes the history of American comint activity begins with our entry into World War I, when codes and ciphers were naïve by current standards. Prior to that time neither the army nor the navy had any organization for intercepting foreign communications. The army set up our first organized code-breaking office in June 1917 under Herbert O. Yardley. This cipher bureau, called MI-8, worked with the British and French through the end of the war. Cryptographic techniques were primitive: Ciphers were broken and code values recovered entirely by hand. Starting with just 3 assistants, by 1918 Yardley's staff had increased to 150, with an annual budget of $100,000.[6] To provide suitable recruits for cipher work, 80 officers were sent to Aurora, Illinois, for a crash course of study under William F. Friedman, then in his mid-twenties and already an acknowledged genius at cryptanalysis (he invented the word), who was on the staff of the nearby Riverbank Laboratories. This scientific hothouse had been founded by George Fabyan, an eccentric millionaire, one of whose consuming passions was to demonstrate by comparative word analysis that Francis Bacon was the real Shakespeare.[7]

Russian-born Friedman had joined the Riverbank community as a geneticist but his interests had moved to code breaking and cryptography, which became his life work. The first demonstration of his innate ability came when he worked out the solution to the British army's so-called Plett cipher from a few sample messages. Our army was sufficiently impressed by his ability that it commissioned him a lieutenant and sent him to France in June 1918, where he helped provide the solution of a major German army cipher in time to contribute to the final Allied victory on the western front. When the war ended he returned to Riverbank in April 1919, but by the beginning of 1921 the army had lured him back as a civilian cryptographer with the war department. In Washington, Friedman provided the new code system for the military staff, so when the Signal Intelligence Service was created ten years later in 1931, he was the natural choice to be its first director.[8]

Although radio intelligence had proved its intelligence potential long before 1918, our navy was slow in entering the field. We relied on Great Britain and the pioneering naval code-breakers of the Admiralty led by Captain William R. "Blinker" Hall. Our only comint activity had been to establish a direction-finding network along the Atlantic seaboard to track U-boats. We did, however, build up a code and signal section, an integrated security organization for the compilation, production, distribution, and safeguarding of our own codes and ciphers.

Not until the closing stage of World War I was President Wilson finally persuaded by the secretary of the navy to set up a $100,000 fund for code-breaking operations. The fund—worth more than $1 million in present-day terms—was so secret that it was deposited in a local Washington bank to the personal credit of the director of naval intelligence. Checkbook stubs were the only records kept, and the balance was transferred to the personal custody of each succeeding head of naval intelligence in order to conceal the fund from congressional scrutiny. There was strong distaste at the time for involvement in what many officers regarded as an ungentlemanly profession.[9]

That secret slush fund continued to support our naval code-breaking activities for more than a decade, and it still amounted to $65,000 in June 1931. An acting director of ONI, Captain William Baggaley, stricken by a fit of conscience, prompted by then Secretary of State Henry L. Stimson's 1929 sanction against "reading other gentlemen's mail,"[10] returned the balance to the Treasury. One naval cipher expert characterized the move as "a great mistake," saying, "It is a safe bet that one year hence when he leaves, his reliefs for many years to come will bemoan the fact that their hands have been tied by lack of funds to prosecute urgent secret tasks."[11]

Yardley's postwar cipher bureau, which was financed by the army and the State Department, had to move out of the District of Columbia because the State Department funds could not legally be spent there. It moved to New York City and set up shop as our first permanent code-breaking organization in a four-story brownstone just off Fifth Avenue, and became known as the Black Chamber. Yardley's first major assignment was to break Japanese codes, since we were interested in that country's naval expansion. Yardley had been instrumental in maneuvering Japan into accepting the inferior naval status imposed by the 1921 Washington Naval Conference. By reading Tokyo's secret telegraphic instructions to its delegation, the Americans knew the limits allowed the Japanese representatives and were able to maneuver them into accepting the end of a 5:5:3 capital-ship tonnage ratio with Britain and the United States. This American advantage was the equivalent of knowing the opponent's cards in a poker game, and it enabled us to win an agreement to a naval limitation treaty that sank more battleships than any fleet engagement in history.

In May 1929, Yardley's New York establishment was closed after Secretary of State Stimson's injunction against reading other people's mail. The military intelligence division of the army, which had been subcontracting its cryptanalytic work to Yardley, now transferred this work

and responsibility to the chief signal officer. Civilian cryptanalyst Friedman was placed in charge of a new organization, the Signal Intelligence
Service, which was to set up to combine the duties of the defunct cipher
bureau with those of the Cipher Compilation Service. This was one fore-
runner of our present-day Armed Forces Security Agency and the National Security Agency.

While the United States continued to make steady progress following
a slow start, the Japanese failed to maintain the early advantage gained
by being the first nation to apply comint, and after World War I Japan
found herself at a complete disadvantage in both diplomatic negotiations
and naval intelligence. It was not until 1923, after her Kwantung army in
Manchuria became concerned about the Soviet threat to the extensive
Japanese mining and railway concessions in China, that Japan undertook
a serious comint effort.

Captain Jan Kowalewski, the Polish army staff's code expert, was invited to Tokyo to give a series of lectures on cryptology. (It is interesting
to note that Britain also benefited from Polish cryptographic help that
contributed to the breaking of the principal German cipher systems in
World War II, which relied on the so-called Enigma machine.) His select
group of students consisted of six army and three naval officers, one of
whom was Commander Risaburo Itō, a naturally gifted code breaker.[12]

While serving as communications officer with the Japanese Mediterranean force attached to the Royal Navy in World War I, Itō had singlehandedly broken the Playfair code system used by the British allies as an
army field cipher. That success persuaded the Japanese to upgrade the
security of their own code systems. Itō was also to translate Yardley's *The
American Black Chamber,* which became an instant best seller in Japan.
Later, as head of the communications section of the navy general staff, he
would play an instrumental part in designing the "Red" and subsequently
the "Purple" machines that were to be used for enciphering Japan's most
secret diplomatic traffic.

The natural Japanese predilection for secrecy was greatly magnified in
the armed services, where the zeal for security so dominated communications intelligence as to severely hamper its development. The first organized *tsushintai* (radio intercept unit) was established in the navy ministry
in 1929. This "special chamber" consisted of Lieutenant Commander
Kyujino Nakasugi (a Kowalewski student), two other officers, and three
typists. Not until the mid-1930s was there any large-scale expansion of
radio intelligence work in the Japanese navy, and even six years later the
section was being run by only nine naval staff officers. The entire field of
intelligence in general, despite its importance, was traditionally a hushed
subject in the imperial navy. There was no mention, let alone classroom
discussion, of it at the naval academy, and career officers usually stayed
away from intelligence duty when they could, as it was not considered
useful to advancement.[13]

During these early stages most of the officers assigned to comint had been career men. In the growing wartime establishment, however, the majority of the staff were *yobigakusei* (reserve officers) fresh from colleges, most of whom had majored in foreign languages. By the end of the war, women and nisei were being recruited. When it came to communications intelligence, most regular officers were unaware even of the words for it—*tsūshin chōhō*. The secret clique excluded outsiders to the extent that it was virtually unknown to all but those who worked in it and the very limited number of recipients of its product, who probably numbered no more than a dozen or so in the entire navy.

This obsession with security was not peculiar to the Japanese navy. It also impeded the development of radio intelligence and the proper understanding and use of it in our own navy. Nevertheless, thanks to the dedication and foresight of successive postwar ONI directors, by 1929 our navy finally began to catch up with the British in realizing the importance of communications interception and code breaking. This progress had been achieved through strenuous efforts in cryptanalysis, financed with ONI's secret slush fund, and occasionally requiring resort to burglary. Such involvements made the whole operation suspect in the eyes of many conservative naval officers, especially those who lacked experience in and understanding of intelligence.

As codes and ciphers became increasingly sophisticated, complicating the cryptanalytic efforts of every nation, there was a practical limit to the amount of effort that could be expended in attempting to decipher intercepted traffic. The point was reached where it became desirable, whenever possible, to circumvent the laborious cryptanalysis process by surreptitious means—theft. There was risk involved in such "black bag jobs," as the stealing of foreign codes was dubbed, but the saving in man-hours spent at conventional code breaking justified the risk.

In the decade before the State Department's injunction against reading other nations' code traffic, our navy had become very proficient in this less than gentlemanly activity. In the spring of 1920 the secret ONI fund had financed a major undercover operation that involved not just one but a whole series of break-ins at the Japanese consulate in New York City. The FBI reported that a Japanese naval officer was masquerading there as the vice-consul. A counterespionage squad picked the locks of his office door and a combination safe.

The operation required more than one visit. It was slow going with the cameras of that day to photograph the voluminous code book of the Japanese fleet. It took even longer for ONI to find a reliable and discreet linguist to translate the book. Eventually the director persuaded Dr. Emerson J. Haworth and his wife, both Japanese linguists, to take on the mammoth task. They were paid from the slush fund, which also provided special kana (Japanese syllabary) dictionaries, and grammar books.[14]

The Haworths spent nearly four years translating the code book. That material was updated with more photos taken in a second round of break-ins at the New York consulate in 1926 and 1927. Further translation and retyping resulted in two manageable volumes, bound in red buckram, from which the Japanese code acquired its American color designation, the Red code.

This Red code book was handed over to the Code and Signal Section of the office of naval communications, which managed signal traffic and maintained the security of our own codes and ciphers. In 1924 that duty was expanded to include an effort to break foreign codes and ciphers. Until that time our navy had had no organized code-breaking program. What began as a one-man unit became the nucleus of an operation that was to grow into a radio intelligence organization of more than five thousand in World War II.

A cryptographic section was established late in 1923, not primarily for the purpose of deciphering codes and ciphers of foreign nations, but to analyze our own and suggest improvements. Its original function was "to work side by side with the code desk in a sort of advisory capacity." But in January 1924, Lieutenant Laurence F. Safford was appointed as head of a cryptographic section that comprised one cryptanalyst and two typists. This little group soon realized the possibility offered by the Red Book and began work on intercepted Japanese radio traffic, with "remarkable success."[15] To disguise its true function it was known simply as the research desk.

Safford, who was destined to become the "father" of naval cryptography, was an earnest character whose most remarkable feature was his eyes, which were constantly darting back and forth, as if watching out for some danger. He had been plucked by the sheerest chance of the naval bureaucracy from a humdrum command of a Yangtze River mine-sweeper. Although he had ranked fifteenth in the 1916 class at Annapolis, the communications establishment would always look upon him as an outsider because he did not fit the starched image of a smart naval academy officer. Safford's uniform was always rumpled, as if he had slept in it. According to Mrs. Eunice Rice Willson, a longtime member of the OP-20-G staff, "His hair seemed permanently to be standing on end as if he had been scratching his head in perplexity. He spoke in little bursts, unconnected phrases that unnerved his listeners and brought universal admiration from us for his secretary's ability to produce a coherent memorandum from his dictation."[16] But Safford's natural flair for mathematics and affinity for mechanical devices made him an effective promoter of the navy's nascent code-breaking efforts. He acquired the affectionate nickname "Saffo" and his staff took pride in their boss. "A mad genius" whose eccentricities, according to one of his staff, caused many to laugh and underestimate his abilities, he nevertheless had a "single-minded devotion to duty."[17]

While Safford quickly discovered an innate talent for cryptography, his introduction and grounding in that arcane science was provided by his assistant, Miss Agnes Meyer. She was an enigmatic but brilliant cryptanalyst, who was thirty-two and working as a code clerk in the navy department in 1921 when she solved a sample cipher that cryptologist Edward H. Hebern had considered unbreakable.

Hebern was so impressed by her solution that in 1923 he hired the lady away for his new code-machine business in California. Within a year she left Hebern's employ, married Michael B. Driscoll, a Washington attorney, and was back with the navy, initiating Safford into the mysteries of cryptology. A woman in a man's world, the patrician "Miss Aggie," as friends still called her, was tall, slender, quiet, and extremely dedicated. She not only trained most of the leading naval cryptanalysts of World War II, but they were all agreed that none exceeded her gifted accomplishments in the business. Injuries sustained in a bad auto accident in 1937 required her to use a cane for the rest of her life, but she continued to work miracles, as we shall see, in breaking Japanese and German codes and ciphers throughout World War II.[18]

Safford's tiny clandestine outfit, located in room 1621 of the old navy department building, was charged with the highly sensitive task of using ONI's pilfered code book to open a new source of intelligence on the Japanese navy. The possession of the imperial navy's most secret cryptographic system, in turn, became justification for ONC to encourage Safford's outfit to develop cryptanalytic techniques, and establish a Pacific network of radio intercept stations. With the indulgence of both the director of naval communications and the director of naval intelligence, the research desk thrived under Safford. There was little concern for the day when its jealous parents might vie for their offspring's loyalty.

Safford emphasized the importance of the Red Book as the foundation of our navy's penetration of Japanese naval secrets. "We had only to solve the ciphers used with this code in order to decrypt messages," he wrote. "If we had been faced at the beginning with the task of solving the cipher plus an unknown code, it might have been too much for us and, at least, it would have slowed our early efforts."[19] The daily work load was enough to keep the small staff fully occupied, but there were additional problems. Safford still had to extend an intercept network, develop working methods, acquire a staff of trained cryptanalysts, and find more linguists. He also had to plan against the day when Japan would introduce new ciphers. To acquire further cryptographers, Safford ingeniously circulated practice cryptograms and other puzzles throughout the navy. Applicants who submitted the best solutions were earmarked for duty in his research section as the organization grew.

Safford's day-to-day burdens were eased in 1925 when Lieutenant (j.g.) Joseph J. Rochefort was assigned to the research desk. The newcomer was a lean, intense man whose gentle manner belied a fierce tenacity and independent cast of mind that resulted from competing as an

outsider in a navy dominated by Annapolis men. Unlike most of his contemporaries, Rochefort was not a naval academy graduate, but had enlisted in the navy during World War I after attending the University of
California. He made a fine partner for Safford and both officers learned
the code-breaking skills of the insightful Miss Aggie.

Under the stringent "Manchu" rules of the day, which required officers to alternate duty ashore with service afloat, Safford was sent back
to sea in February 1926, and Rochefort took his place. Before the end of
his first tour, Safford had instituted the first course to train naval officers
in cryptanalysis. One of the earliest students was Ensign Joseph N.
Wenger who recalled as an admiral that he had been selected by his commanding officer because he was the only eligible candidate whose family
lived in Washington and could therefore "afford to live there on an ensign's pay."[20]

Rochefort was in charge of the research desk when the first Red Japanese naval messages were broken, and it was Miss Aggie who was responsible for the initial solutions of the current Japanese cipher key that
unlocked the code. This was no small achievement, because the two-vol-
ume Red Book contained some 100,000 code groups, with as many as 3
groups assigned to each Japanese word or expression. The Japanese instructions for the code stated that it was never to be used without superencipherment.

When the first solution of the cipher used with the Red Book code
was made in 1926, the Japanese employed only one cipher of a relatively
simple nature and each key remained in effect for several weeks. Each
succeeding cipher, however, grew more complex than its predecessor and
the keys began to be changed more frequently. The keys associated with
specific ciphers were often solved by officers under instruction, but
Rochefort's unit was never able to exploit more than a very small fraction
of the messages, because the navy was so desperately short of Japanese
translators.[21]

Safford had returned from sea duty to take over the helm at the research desk when Rochefort left for Japan in the summer of 1929. By the
following year the unit was ready to monitor Japan's naval exercises. The
grand fleet maneuvers that spring saw virtually every ship in the imperial
navy put to sea. The vast operation was nevertheless managed with such
secrecy that not even our naval attaché in Tokyo had any advance warning. The first indication that "something was up" came on 18 May with a
sudden increase in Japanese radio traffic picked up by Guam, one of our
Pacific listening stations.[22] (Others were at Shanghai, Peking, and
Olongapo or Cavite in the Philippines.) But Washington knew nothing of
the Japanese fleet maneuvers until more than a week later when a courier
suddenly delivered hundreds of radio intercepts.

The inefficiency of prewar American naval communications, tragically
to be repeated in December 1941, found the commandant on Guam ne-

glecting to report the Japanese activity because he assumed ONI was so well informed that he did not need to tell them. He even complained that Washington had failed to alert him in advance of the Japanese maneuvers![23]

Safford seized this heaven-sent opportunity to prove to a skeptical navy department the enormous potential of radio intelligence. All hands turned to on the mass of accumulated traffic. Mrs. Driscoll again made the first significant break in the Red code, and other keys then fell out with comparative ease. Our major problem remained not cryptanalysis but translation, since the unit's only linguist at the time was the venerable Dr. Haworth. Many of the routine messages, however, did not require knowledge of Japanese, and much of that work was done by apprentice cryptanalyst Lieutenant Joseph N. Wenger.

The rich intelligence haul made from the intercepts of Japan's 1930 naval maneuvers was officially compared to "exploring virgin territory" since no one in our navy at the time had any idea of the professional concepts, communication routines, or even the battle tactics of the Japanese fleet.[24] By assembling the decrypts, we were able to learn a great deal about how Japan intended to conduct any naval war against us. The capture of Guam and the Philippines were the subject of early "victory" announcements, and the intercepts revealed a mock air raid on Tokyo from American carriers. Their maneuvers concluded that year with what was proclaimed as the "constructive" defeat of the Pacific Fleet, an indication that even in 1930 the imperial navy already considered itself capable of defeating the U.S. Navy in the western Pacific.[25]

After Captain Royal E. Ingersoll, head of the navy's war plans division, had spent six weeks reconstructing the Japanese order of battle, he made "the most astonishing discovery."[26] Their naval intelligence had apparently succeeded in obtaining a very accurate picture of the latest modifications in our war plan Orange. These were current contingency plans for a Pacific war as rehearsed that year by our military war colleges.

The cryptographic section's code-breaking triumph was communicated to the secretary of the navy in a secret memorandum of 31 January 1931, which claimed that we had achieved "as complete ascendency over the Japanese navy in the matter of radio intelligence as the British navy had over the German navy in the World War."[27] Because of the interdepartmental rivalry already stirring in regard to radio intelligence, however, Captain Harry A. Baldridge, the director of ONI, was not made privy to this vital news. Admiral William V. Pratt, the chief of naval operations, outrageously believed he "could not trust" his subordinate and he warned, *"One suspicion on the part of the Japanese would undo the accomplishment of seven years* [emphasis in original]."[28] What misuse Pratt thought Baldridge might make of the information one can only imagine, but it suggests that a bitter feud was already festering in the navy department.

The United States had won a major victory in what Safford was to call "the undeclared war" against the Japanese.[29] Yet this success sparked another undeclared war at home as a long struggle for control of this valuable new source of intelligence began within the navy department. Nominally the research desk was organizationally under the purview of the office of naval communications, but its raison d'être was exploitaion of Japanese naval communications for intelligence purposes. These were accessible only through the Red Book and Japanese linguists, both of which had been funded entirely by the office of naval intelligence.

While the office of naval intelligence had turned over its Red Book asset to naval communications, it had been "with the agreement and expectation that it [ONI] would be furnished the information obtained by the use of this code."[30] But this expectation was not to be fulfilled. A year after its inception the cryptographic section had become the center of an administrative dispute. Soon after Rochefort took charge of the research desk he noted that "several attempts" were made to bring the section over to the office of naval intelligence. The takeover efforts failed because of the "strong opposition" of the director of naval communications.[31]

The result was that by 1930 naval intelligence was being denied the information obtained from the Japanese fleet exercises, because chief of naval operations Admiral Charles F. Hughes sided with the director of naval communications. The rationale offered for ordering the director of naval communications "to show intercepted messages to him[self] and to no other person" was that Hughes "thought he could not trust his director of naval intelligence."[32]

The necessity for keeping the cryptographic section's work a tight secret was undoubtedly a result of several occasions when the Japanese had changed their codes and ciphers, apparently as a result of becoming suspicious of eavesdropping. According to a 1932 memorandum written by Rochefort to Captain Joseph V. Ogan, the acting director of naval intelligence, "several instances of this sort are a matter of record." Rochefort reported that "one happened while I was in the section and the net result was that one year's work went for naught and we were forced to start over from the beginning."[33]

Rochefort's "personal opinion" on the origins of the feud was that "the Cryptography Section has been and is being used by the officers concerned to further their own ends."[34] Nine years before the Japanese attack on Pearl Harbor this warning had identified one of the principal factors that caused us to be so badly surprised at Pearl Harbor: "Instead of handling the information obtained in such a way that the Navy will benefit, they are prone to handle it in order to obtain personal recognition."[35]

The astonishing decision that denied naval intelligence direct access to our most important source of intelligence about the Japanese navy was not rescinded until 1933, when it was agreed that radio intelligence would continue to come under the control of the office of naval communications "at least in peacetime."[36] This made it inevitable that when war clouds began gathering over the Pacific the old feud would be revived. When the war plans division waded in to make the struggle for control of communications intelligence a three-way fight during 1941, its consequences were to contribute to the disaster of 7 December.

3

"Keep the Dogs Yapping"

U NTIL I REPORTED to the flagship in December 1940, I was unaware that the Pacific Fleet had never had a full-time intelligence
officer. The job was normally assigned as additional duty to another member of the staff. To my further astonishment, I found that the
sturdy safe built into battleship *Pennsylvania*'s bulkhead as repository for
the fleet's most secret documents contained just eighteen file folders; and
most of them were empty!

One contained several newspaper clippings from the early 1920s on
South Africa, and three held military dossiers about France, totally unrelated to the Pacific. In only one did I discover *any* information about
Japan. This was ONI Monograph 49, which, although kept meticulously
up to date, provided only the broadest of generalities about the imperial
navy. It had languished in the safe for years protected by its red-stamped
cover, which read, TO BE REMOVED ONLY IN THE EVENT OF WAR.

The discovery that the Pacific Fleet command had been given no up-
to-date military information on Japan was a major disappointment, to say
the least. It was my duty as fleet intelligence officer to brief the commander in chief, Admiral James O. Richardson, on the movements, dispositions, and intentions of the Japanese navy in the Pacific. I realized
that, with the worsening relations between Tokyo and Washington, the
lack of adequate intelligence could leave me sitting on a very sharp spike.

The fact that our intelligence cupboard was so bare spurred my efforts
to remedy the appalling situation. In two tours of duty in Japan I had
become convinced that their armed forces were highly trained, and well
informed about us. Their navy would certainly be a formidable adversary
if and when it came to a fight.

My feeling of apprehension about Japan then was similar to what I
had felt eleven years earlier when I arrived at Kōbe for three years of
language study. As I walked down the ship's gangway and onto Japanese

soil for the first time, it was an unsettling, and at the same time an exciting, experience to be in a totally foreign world.

Until that moment my only naval experience even touching on intelligence had consisted of a few weeks spent at the office of naval intelligence a month earlier, being briefed for my language studies. Fortunately, the other naval officer being sent to study Japanese in 1929 was Joseph Rochefort. Our lifelong friendship began that August on board steamer *President Adams* when the long Pacific crossing gave me the chance to get acquainted with him, his attractive wife, and their infant son. Rochefort was one of only three married officers ever chosen for language study in Japan; his selection came after he had completed a tour of duty as executive officer of destroyer *Macdonough* based in San Diego following two years in the Code and Signal Section in Washington.

Throughout our three years of study in Japan, Rochefort never once mentioned his involvement with the navy's secret code-breaking operations. Not knowing of his experience with Japanese codes and communications, I was surprised at his apparent familiarity with the country. My knowledge of Japan and its people was extremely sketchy. From a tourist magazine I had learned that a woman's hairstyle indicated her marital status. This wasn't much, but it was of vital interest to a young man starting a three-year stay in that strange country.

In Tokyo I reported to Captain James Vance Ogan, the bluff naval attaché. "Layton," he snapped, "I don't know anything about this language, but I understand it's difficult." Looking me square in the eye, he cautioned, "You have only two duties to perform: One, study and master the Japanese language; two, stay out of trouble. If you fail in either, I'll send you home in the next ship. You are not to engage in any spying or other espionage activity. Don't think of yourself as some Nathan Hale or anything like that. Keep your nose clean. Oh, yes, payday is once a month. Other than that, I don't want to see you. Good-bye."

These words were echoed by his assistant, Lieutenant Commander Arthur H. McCollum, who was to supervise our language instruction. He had been born in Japan, and had completed the language course five years earlier, so I took seriously his warning never to "engage in anything that could be construed as intelligence activity." McCollum was a stocky, affable man, the kind who would give a newcomer a cold dry martini and add a warm invitation to dinner.

I appreciated such kindnesses because prewar Japan had a mania about spies, and a foreign naval officer could be very lonely there. The lengths to which the Japanese went to prevent espionage were evident in the extensive areas around military and naval bases designated "fortified zones." On the sandy shore of Tokyo Bay, I was dumbfounded to see at the monument of Commodore Matthew C. Perry a badly done sign, in "Jap-lish," reading PHOTOGRAPHY NO BECAUSE HERE. We were told that any picture of the monument might include beaches that could be used in an amphibious landing.

This national sense of diligence was embodied in the person of our language instructor and closest Japanese contact, Naoe Naganuma, an ambitious young Japanese scholar, our *sensei*—"teacher." He introduced us to the complex language the way a child is taught, through hearing. This was relatively painless, since Japanese is one of the easier languages to comprehend in simple spoken form, although no modern language is more difficult to read and write. The writing, which used Chinese characters, was adopted in Japan and superimposed upon the independently developed spoken language. Each character, or *kanji* (literally, "Chinese ideograph"), has two or more pronunciations in Japanese.

After we were able to understand a little Japanese, Naganuma had us go to a movie house showing American silent films. There a *benshi*—movie interpreter—gave the gist in colloquial Japanese, speaking from a dais adjacent to the screen. Conversation became much easier for us after hearing these shows repeated time after time.

When we had a basic grasp of the language, we went to live away from the capital for a while. My choice was the isolated town of Beppu, in the Kyūshū region; it was four hundred miles southwest of Tokyo, across the Inland Sea. Foreigners, like the Japanese themselves, were kept under constant official scrutiny from the ubiquitous "police box." Nobody passed by without recognition, and it always seemed that the police looked for any opportunity to blackmail foreigners.

Even in remote Beppu I had a "personal" spy who not only dogged my tracks but also pestered my servant, and became a real nuisance. If I went for a walk, my Japanese shadow followed. After a time I began harassing him by going into bars and leaving before he had finished his beer. Then one day I confronted him: "Stop pestering me, and I'll not leave the bar until you finish your beer. But don't hang around my house." The bargain appealed to him, as a beer drinker, and he was less of a bother after that.

While I was living in Beppu, if the Japanese fleet happened to anchor in the spacious harbor it was impossible for me not to observe naval activities, which I did with great interest. The crews came ashore with artillery for exercises, charging up and down the mountains above the beach. It left me with the indelible impression that the Japanese never rest.

Whenever the fleet was in I played a vicarious sort of game with the Japanese officers in the local geisha houses. It was the custom for the proprietor to present an *akagami* (literally, "red paper") naming all available *geisha* ("talented persons") in order of their popularity. I knew that if an officer selected a girl who was already engaged, her patron would have to pay double if he chose to keep her more than an hour. So I would request all of the most popular girls, knowing that they would be busy, in each case causing the patron's bill to be doubled. It always tickled the geisha to see my ruse in action, and they squealed with delight.

My favorite geisha was Ko-ume ("Little Plum"), an excellent conversationalist, full of modern slang, who gave enjoyable company and inexpensive conversation instruction. Occasionally, however, a Japanese officer would *akagami* me by asking for her. It would then cost me double to talk with her after the first hour, but it increased my popularity with Ko-ume.

Such antics with foreigners became noticeably less popular, and suspicion of Americans increased markedly in 1931, after an unsuccessful attempt on the life of Prime Minister Yuko Hamaguchi by ultranationalist Japanese societies. These groups included many junior naval officers who reacted with violence to the government's failure to achieve an increase in capital-ship construction, whereby Japan's battleship strength was constrained by treaty to 60 percent of the tonnage ratio of the American and British fleets.

The nationalists gained support, and popular hostility toward the United States increased after publication of *The American Black Chamber*.[1] Yardley's account revealed how he had apparently tricked Japan into accepting a position of naval inferiority at the Washington Naval Conference ten years earlier. Throughout June, Japanese newspaper headlines blazed with the author's amazing claim that the American government had read thousands of secret official Japanese messages since 1917. Yardley had exacted his revenge for being put out of a job two years early by the State Department's temporary code-breaking ban by revealing details of American cryptanalytic activities. Existing laws made it impossible for the government to prosecute its erstwhile master code breaker for treason, and he profited handsomely from his revelations.

Japan's foreign ministry, which had also contributed to his enrichment, would have been glad to see Yardley tried and sentenced. A secret memorandum circulated within the ministry denounced the book's publication as "a flagrant act of bad faith."[2] It condemned not the United States government, but Yardley himself because the previous year Japan's ambassador in Washington had paid him seven thousand dollars for copies of the Black Chamber cables and methods. The secret bargain had included a stipulation that Yardley would make no public revelation of how the Japanese government had been tricked into the unpopular disarmament straitjacket.

The real cost of Yardley's escapade was not just that it caused the moderate Japanese government to lose face but that he had revealed very precisely how we had broken Tokyo's secret cables. Alerted to American code-breaking successes, the Japanese became more secretive than ever. Not only did they intensify their own code security, but they made their naval call signs more complex by assigning their warships more letters and changing these identifiers more frequently. They were also stimulated to renewed assaults on American cipher traffic.

Our naval systems then became a special target. The Japanese had learned a great deal about our call signs and shortwave transmission systems beginning in 1926 when light cruiser *Yubari* and tanker *Sata* had shadowed our annual naval maneuvers. They had discovered that we had shifted our traffic from medium- to shortwave radio, and they had valuable clues about our fleet organization, call signs, and communication techniques.

Moreover, I saw at first-hand how the furor over Yardley's exploits had increased Japanese xenophobia. Democracy in Japan was already being severely tested in 1932, my final year of language study, as attacks mounted against western-style politicians in the Diet. On 18 September 1931 headstrong generals of the Kwantung army in Manchuria engineered an "incident" on the Japanese railway line at Mukden. Blaming it on the Chinese Nationalists, they used it as an excuse to begin a military takeover of the northern province.

While the League of Nations fumed impotently against Japanese aggression, the Kwantung army moved swiftly to occupy the whole of Manchuria. Secretary of State Stimson called for sanctions, but President Hoover shied from "sticking pins in tigers."[3] Without United States support, the international move against Japanese aggression in China foundered, giving encouragement to other would-be aggressors such as Hitler and Mussolini.

Undeterred by this barrage of diplomatic paper bullets, Japan's mainland adventure accelerated when her naval units moved to occupy the international port of Shanghai in January 1932. Two months later Manchuria became a "made in Japan" puppet state, Manchukuo. It was not enough, however, to prevent the May assassination of Premier Tsuyoshi Inukai. His moderate cabinet had not moved swiftly enough for the ultranationalists in its Manchurian takeover. Succeeding cabinets in Tokyo were committed to supporting the smoldering mainland conflict and the rising mood of military belligerency.

The ominous trends were forcefully impressed on Ambassador Joseph Clark Grew, who had arrived in Tokyo in June 1932 during the final months of my language studies. Grew was an old-school diplomat whose qualifications for the Japan post included a visit there as a child. His wife was a descendant of Commodore Matthew C. Perry, who had successfully opened the door to American-Japanese diplomatic relations in the 1850s.

Notwithstanding his credentials, our new ambassador was not even accorded common courtesy at his maiden public speech in Tokyo, presented to the annual dinner of the America-Japan Society. I was as shocked as Grew must have been by the vice-president's introductory remarks. They were the most insulting words of welcome I have ever heard. He concluded with an abusive demand for "direct answers to my questions on U.S.-Japanese relations, and not just another 'hands-across-the-sea' speech."

Grew earned my instant admiration and lasting respect by his deft response, which he delivered with dignity and incredible restraint. He began by saying that when he was a child, a friend had thrown a fire-cracker at him which had impaired his hearing. "So, since I could not hear anything the vice-president said," he told the audience, "I will not be able to respond to any of his remarks." Grew then returned to his prepared "hands-across-the-sea" speech. It was received with sustained applause by all the Americans and most of the Japanese, for whom rudeness to invited guests is an unpardonable breach of etiquette.

In February 1933, after Japan responded to a sustained chorus of international condemnation by walking out of the League of Nations, Ambassador Grew minced no words in reporting his frank estimate of the national mood. "The military themselves, and the public through military propaganda, are prepared to fight rather than surrender to moral or other pressures from the West," he cabled Washington.[4] When Japan left the league, she did not relinquish control of Germany's former Pacific islands that had been mandated to her "peaceful" custody after World War I.

In the internal upheavals that set Japan on the road to war, I had my own brush with the rising tide of ultranationalist violence. The date, 15 May 1932, is clear in my memory as the night Premier Inukai was assassinated. And that evening I was in Tokyo's Florida Dance Hall. I was standing at the bar having a beer when a Japanese tough swaggered up and deliberately knocked over my glass. The other patrons turned to see my reaction. "You would do well to learn your manners," I said, and ordered another beer.

When it was served, the bully, still at my side, spit in the glass. Infuriated, I whacked him a blow that sent him sprawling. "Do you want to fight now or later?" I challenged, but he just lay there, stunned. So I dropped my calling card on him and went on my way.

Next morning, to my surprise, the police came to my home asking about the incident with a mug shot of a man named Okamura. "You mean, that gangster at the Florida Dance Hall? Sure, I saw him there yesterday evening." They were trying to connect him with the previous night's assassination of the prime minister. As it turned out, I was the bully's alibi, and he later sent me a note of thanks. It occurred to me that my new gangster "friend" might be a useful source of intelligence, but I had been warned against playing spy. After this brush with the authorities I was careful to avoid any further such adventures during my last six months of language study.

In September 1932 I received orders to report for duty at ONI upon completion of my studies, but that was suddenly changed by a cable in early October ordering me to temporary duty in Peiping (the Nationalist name for Peking from 1928 to 1949) as assistant naval attaché at the American legation.

In the past several months the Japanese legation guard had twice marched out of their area (contrary to international rules) on pretext of conducting "night maneuvers," hoping to provoke an incident that would provide an excuse for occupying the city. Our legation had protested the violation of protocol, but the Japanese excuse was that they had no one who spoke English. I was brought in to maintain liaison with the Japanese legation guard and prevent future misunderstandings. As part of this mission, I also called on other legation guard commanders and had an opportunity for intelligence gathering in a trip to Harbin, in Manchuria, which included a visit to the nearby Port Arthur naval base. I made notes of all the details of the docks, repair yards, and facilities, but did not want to carry this compromising information on the rest of my journey. Accordingly, I mailed it by ordinary post from Dairen, addressed to myself in Peiping, affixing something less than the required amount of postage. Having postage due, the package would have to be receipted for by each postal handler until it reached me.

After learning that I played poker, the naval attaché, Cleveland McCauley, gave me the most unusual intelligence assignment of my career: "I'd like for you to sit in on a particular game of poker players. They are the crew of Marshal Chang Hsueh-liang's personal Ford trimotor airplane. Sometimes the marshal himself joins, so I want you to get acquainted, be a part of the game, and keep your ears open. I have no funds for this sort of thing so you'll have to use your own money. What you win is yours, and what you lose is yours, so play carefully."

I got into the nightly game and became well acquainted with the regulars, who played a wide-open, no-limit game that began about eleven in the evening and went on most of the night. Playing in that kind of game on a lieutenant's $175 per month was bound to be exciting.

When Chang Hsueh-liang, the young Chinese warlord who was shortly to demonstrate his independence of Chiang Kai-shek by kidnapping the generalissimo in 1937, played, there was an unwritten rule: One never called his hand. It was OK to raise him, but never just call him, because he might not have the winning hand, and that would cause him to lose face. Then he would be uncomfortable. That taught me more about "face."

In fact, that taught me to develop a rule of my own: Do not even sit in when the marshal is playing. He bet money as if it were nothing at all. The Chinese yuan was not worth very much, but in huge quantities they mounted up. All gambling debts were paid off the following day, in Chinese currency. One time I was paying off the head of the Peking Power and Light Company, and he "rang out" each coin to make sure that it was not counterfeit. If it did not ring true as he dropped it on the table, he would return it for replacement.

I managed *not* to lose my shirt, and the conversation often provided snippets of information that were always of interest and sometimes of use to my mission. After four months in Peiping, where it became increasingly dangerous for westerners as the fighting in Manchuria spread southward, it was a relief to return to the United States in February 1933.

I reported to ONI in Washington during one of the periodic interoffice spats between ONC and ONI. Successive chiefs of naval operations had appeared to encourage the feuding, figuring that it was beneficial to have the two sections fiercely competitive on the principle of "Keep the dogs yapping; they'll go after the foxes better."

Captain Hayne Ellis, then director of naval intelligence, informed me, "Layton, you were scheduled to go to naval communications, where Japanese linguists are sorely needed. They like to have our language students help out their few civilian translators, but we never get any credit for that, so I'm going to put you to work here. We need a study of Japan's electric power distribution network, showing strategic targets; a bombing plot, in the event of war."

I gathered what little information about Japan was then available at ONI, mostly from maps, and added details recalled from my recent duty. My effort was a beginning, but much more was needed, and the work was continued by others with information gathered on strategic industries and port installations. The power-grid work I started developed into a project that eventually was applied in the 1945 strategic bombing raids on Japan.

During my work on the Japanese power-grid system, the interoffice feud cooled off sufficiently for me to be assigned to naval communications. There I received my first introduction to the mysteries of radio intelligence and the intriguing "black chamber" world of cryptanalysis as a translator in the Code and Signal Section then designated as OP-20-G (naval communications was OP-20 and the cryptographic unit was listed alphabetically as G). My new colleagues were all engaged in quiet but frantic activity in anticipation of that summer's annual Japanese fleet exercise. This was to be a crucial test for our expanding Pacific direction-finding network and our ability to read Japan's new naval code system, which had superseded the Red Book at the end of 1930.

It had taken more than three years of incredible mind-boggling work to break a complex code and cipher system by pure cryptanalysis—the hard way. No other code breakers had ever achieved such a breakthrough. This was the greatest challenge and success in the unostentatious but spectacular career of Mrs. Agnes Meyer Driscoll. At the start she and her colleagues had faced the seemingly impossible task of stripping away a two-tier layer of protective encipherment, and then working out the meanings of a code made up of some eighty-five thousand basic groups.

It was a measure of the bad blood left by the interoffice feud that the director of naval communications was determined not to ask for ONI assistance in the form of black-bag jobs, except as a last resort. Instead, the Blue Book solution was to be a test of his cryptanalysts' ability to confront a wartime situation, in which there would be no Japanese consulate to break into. Miss Aggie and the OP-20-G team had "to work out their own salvation" by compiling the new code from scratch.[5] The code groups had to be solved individually, one at a time. These were, and were then entered in the Blue Book (named for the color of its binding), with solutions added by hand in both Japanese characters (*kanji*) and English translations.

The assault on Blue was led by Mrs. Driscoll, to whom it was an article of faith that any man-made code could be broken by a woman! One of her male colleagues marveled at her quiet ability as a "first-class cryptanalyst."[6] She was the first to spot that a new code had been instituted. This occurred in the fall of 1931, six months after Tommy Dyer, my academy classmate, had joined OP-20-G as a trainee to work on solutions to the old Red code. He was not making very fast progress the day that Mrs. Driscoll looked over his shoulder, took a work sheet from his hand, and remarked, "The reason you're not getting anywhere is because this is a new code."[7] The Red Book was a three-kana system, and she recognized through her uncanny grasp of cryptology that the piece Dyer was working on had to be a four-kana system. Even with this discovery, it was slow, painful, laborious work before the code was broken.

While it went on, Dyer and Lieutenant Joseph Wenger, his immediate superior who had recently returned from running the Manila intercept station, looked for ways to improve the situation. Wenger had learned that Remington-Rand had just produced punch-card equipment that could handle alphabetic information, but investigation showed that it did not fill our requirements.

It was Dyer, however, who after five months of pencil-pushing drudgery, came up with an ingenious labor-saving solution. He found a way to use IBM tabulating machines to ease the burden of sifting through the myriad possible solutions of the code group. This was in the biting days of the Depression but Wenger and Dyer managed to talk the Bureau of Ships into providing five thousand dollars to rent the IBM equipment. They were also able to hire two key-punch operators, and things began looking up.

After ten years of pencil-pushing, Mrs. Driscoll was initially unenthusiastic about having her task mechanized until the breakthrough into the Japanese navy's Blue system came in September 1931 after she had worked out the key to the cipher's principal transposition. By then it was clear that although it was a two-part code unlike the predecessor, it used essentially the same vocabulary and phraseology as the old Red Book. The use of the IBM tabulating machine made it easier to keep track of changing cipher keys and speeded up penetration of new systems. Long before the introduction of computers, the sorting techniques that Dyer devised and pioneered enabled the United States to forge ahead of Britain in cryptology; it earned him the accolade "the father of machine cryptanalysis."[8]

In spite of the growing application of machine analysis, however, human errors such as repeated transmissions of the same message still produced the fastest code breaks. "We found we could always trust the Japanese themselves to do something that would assist us in the solutions of their systems," Safford asserted. *"They never failed us!"*[9]

Our experience in breaking the Japanese Blue code was a lesson to us of what is likely to happen if great care is not taken to avoid standard form and phraseology in secret dispatches. That such a fundamental slip was made by Japan was ironic, because it occurred at the very time when they were stepping up their own code-breaking activity in the wake of the Yardley scandal. Their target was not just U.S. communications, but also those of China.

Toward that end an intercept unit, the "X Facility," had been set up within the special naval landing force at Shanghai. With this unit, Lieutenant Commander Tsunezo Wachi and a Lieutenant Yamada, an expert in Chinese codes, succeeded early in 1932 in decryptions that enabled Japanese carriers to make a preemptive strike against Nationalist airfields at Ch'ang-sha. For this achievement, Wachi and Yamada were awarded the Order of the Golden Kite, Japan's highest military decoration. This demonstration of the tactical value of radio intelligence resulted in the naval general staff's establishing a Tenth Section devoted to communications.[10]

This expanded facility concentrated its efforts on the United States Pacific Fleet. Tanker *Erimo* was sent out to spy on our 1932 autumn maneuvers, and reported that the Pacific Fleet was using a Hebern cipher machine—whose system the Japanese promptly penetrated. It was a short-lived triumph, however, because we had discovered for ourselves that the machine's rotary system was too vulnerable to sustained cryptanalysis. It had been abandoned in favor of the so-called strip cipher in which the encipherment, resulting from sliding card strips printed with various alphabetic arrangements, afforded great security because the alphabets could be changed easily and frequently.[11]

The Japanese naval code breakers also paid increasing attention to the United States diplomatic traffic, which was transmitted to the Far East on naval circuits. They tried to penetrate our one-volume State Department Gray code the "hard way." After analyzing the frequency of vowels and key words, they discovered that "NADED" meant "stop," and similarly worked out the groups for words such as "is," "that," "are," and so on, but progress was slow. With help from the Tokyo *kempeitai* (military police), scraps of message tapes were salvaged from American embassy wastebaskets. In this way original State Department telegrams could be compared with the intercepts to permit recovery of a substantial number of cipher keys.[12]

The technique was used not only by the Japanese. Other nations and people had rifled trash heaps throughout history, and ONI received regular shipments of bags filled with scraps from the Japanese consulate in New York. Our linguists worked over these treasures to find many things of interest including travel itineraries of staff members. In one bag salvaged from Japan's New York consulate they discovered details of our design for variable-pitch propellers. But the Japanese appear to have had a special talent for processing scraps of paper, and by the end of 1932 they had recovered some five thousand code groups. To expedite their penetration, the Japanese turned to black-bag jobs, the last resort of the code-breaking fraternity—if you can't break 'em, pinch 'em.[13]

At the beginning of 1933 a certain tailor in Kōbe became a frequent visitor to the American consulate, gaining the trust, as well as the tailoring business, of the staff. He was soon doing other chores for the staff besides making their clothes. No one suspected that he was a *kempeitai* in disguise, or he would not have been allowed free run of the consul's office where the code safe was located. This resourceful "tailor" bribed a staff member to get a wax imprint of the safe key. On a Saturday night in late April, while the American diplomat was celebrating a lovely spring evening at the Gion geisha house, a special squad broke into his office, opened the safe, and photographed the code books.

The operation was so skillfully conducted that there were no traces of the break-in—and the United States' Gray code was thenceforth shared with the Japanese navy's Tenth Section. This success encouraged the *kempeitai* to set up a special unit of safecrackers, photographers, and technicians to cooperate with the navy in breaking into foreign consulates. Squads of judo-men patrolled outside to create diversions if necessary. As a result, the British foreign office's top-secret interdepartmental code was also soon being read in Tokyo as readily as in London, after a clandestine nighttime visit to his majesty's consulate in Ōsaka.[14]

A break-in at the office of the U.S. naval attaché in Tokyo was—fortunately for us—bungled, leading Washington to suspect that the Japanese were pinching American methods as well as our codes, and that the navy's current system—an early version of the strip cipher—had been compromised. Security was tightened and the introduction by mid-1933 of a more complex system sent the imperial navy's Tenth Section back to square one as far as our secret naval communications were concerned. Since no American break-ins had been made to pinch their Blue code, the Japanese did not suspect that we were reading any communications encrypted in their high-level naval command systems.[15]

Before leaving OP-20-G for sea duty in the summer of 1933, I had assisted in the analysis of information obtained from the Japanese naval codes from which we gained "an extraordinarily accurate picture of the organization of all Orange [Japanese] naval forces." According to the report of the Asiatic Fleet commander in chief, the important lesson learned was that "in the matter of training and preparation for war, the Japanese navy was at least equal to our own."[16]

My brief but fascinating introduction into code breaking ended in June 1933, when I joined *Pennsylvania*. For the first of my two tours of duty in the battleship I was a division officer in charge of number four turret. My classmate Tommy Dyer was also to be my shipmate for the next three years and friendly rival as captain of number three turret. Lieutenant Wesley A. "Ham" Wright came on board *Pennsylvania*, fresh from cryptanalytic training in OP-20-G, in 1936. This was shortly before Rochefort arrived, when Admiral Joseph M. Reeves moved his staff into the battleship, which became Pacific Fleet flagship. This curious coincidence brought together in the same ship the four of us who five years later would find ourselves working alongside each other in the critical months leading up to Pearl Harbor and on through the Battle of Midway.

We always looked back on our battleship duty together as an interesting twist of fate. The coincidence was heightened by the fact that *Pennsylvania*'s skipper was Captain Russell Willson, who had been director of naval communications in World War I. Moreover, when Rochefort came on board, in addition to his duties as assistant operations officer, Pacific Fleet, he was also staff intelligence chief. Joe was praised as a "general encyclopedia of information and usefulness" by Reeves, who formally commended him as "one of the most outstanding officers of his rank," whose "judgment and ability are truly remarkable."[17] Although Reeves noted in his report that Rochefort was not a naval academy graduate, he stated that "this makes his ability and performance of duty all the more remarkable" and that Joe was "destined to advance to positions of high rank and great responsibility."[18]

Rochefort had particularly impressed his commander in chief for the acumen he had shown as his intelligence officer. Whenever we were in port Joe had worked closely with the naval district officers to keep track of attempts to subvert enlisted men in local Communist cells, and Japan's increasing espionage efforts. When the San Pedro coast guard reported that the local Japanese fishing boats were sending coded radio messages, Joe put Ham Wright—fresh from the OP-20-G cryptanalyst training course—onto the investigation.

Wright was eager to demonstrate his newly acquired skills and worked through one Friday night with the coast guard. The code came apart before dawn, only to reveal that the Japanese were exchanging information no more sinister than reporting schools of fish. But Ham missed the Saturday morning inspection, arousing the wrath of Captain Willson.[19]

Wright explained how he had become engrossed in breaking the intercepts, only to be given further hell for "fooling around with that stuff." When Ham respectfully reminded Willson that he had once been involved in the business himself, the captain replied, "Yes, but I had the good sense to get out of it."[20] This was symptomatic of the lack of regard for cryptography and radio intelligence in the pre-World War II navy—even from an officer who should have been well informed. It was ironic that his daughter, Eunice Willson, was to be employed as a civilian cryptanalyst in OP-20-G during the war.

Rochefort's many remarkable attributes included his marvelous talent for getting people to help when there was a job to be done. During our *Pennsylvania* days he got me involved on two separate occasions in extracurricular activities that were not only interesting but also turned out successfully.

In the fall of 1934, Joe told me what was on his mind: "There's a Lieutenant (j.g.) Cecil H. Coggins, a doctor, over at Long Beach, who works with Eleventh Naval District and ONI's undercover organization, keeping track of what's going on in the Japanese community. He's just learned that the Japanese naval tanker that came in today has some special film they intend to show to the local Japanese association tomorrow night. We suspect that the film is subversive, and I'd like to have you help the undercover boys in this matter."

The Japanese Citizens Patriotic Society had rented an auditorium in Long Beach from Shell Oil and had the right to deny entry to any non-member—namely me. The auditorium had no projection booth, so the two film projectors would be exposed. Following the suggestion of an ONI agent, I posed as a fire insurance inspector. I took along a fire extinguisher and said that I was there to enforce regulations against smoking in the auditorium during the film show. False credentials provided apparent authority for me to protect Shell Oil interests. Before the meeting I showed the local chairman these papers, feigning no knowledge of Japanese, but he wanted me to clear out. I refused to leave, saying, "Me no here, no movies." By this time some three hundred people had arrived, so I stayed, and I went around telling the crowd to put out cigarettes.

The films were pretty corny, with their strident message that the emperor system was best and democracy was no good. Designed to arouse Japanese patriotism, one showed "brave Japanese soldiers" assaulting Chinese positions, troops atop a wall waving a Japanese flag and shouting "Banzai." Another showed contempt for American democracy, with comedians doing takeoffs of FDR and his mannerisms. An animated cartoon depicted J. P. Morgan pushing a wheelbarrow full of money over the bodies of the poor.

In the course of the evening an inquisitive Japanese seaman from the tanker turned my fire extinguisher upside down and got a face full of foam for his trouble. I had to clean up the mess but received five dollars from the local chairman for my trouble. The doctor, ONI agent, and I drank that up in a Long Beach bar to celebrate the successful conclusion of my first undercover operation.

This exploit led to another counterintelligence mission for me the following year. We were steaming at sea, en route to San Francisco as part of a fleet maneuver, when Joe Rochefort again sent for me. Once his cabin door closed, he briefed me about a Japanese spy operating in the Dutch Harbor area of the Aleutians. Admiral Reeves wanted the spy "out of the way" before he could observe and report on the arrival of our forces for Fleet Problem 16. My orders were to leave ship at Hunters Point Navy Yard, take a train for Seattle, proceed to Bremerton, and there board navy tanker *Brazos,* which was sailing to Dutch Harbor in advance of the other ships involved in the fleet problem.

Early one May morning *Brazos* anchored in Unalaska Bay and, wearing civilian clothes, I slipped ashore at Illilliuk, the civilian community. The naval base of Dutch Harbor is located on a small island in the bay. By prearrangement I went to the postmaster, who was also the federal judge, and presented my credentials. When he had heard my mission, he told me that there was only one Japanese local, a Mr. Shimizu from Seattle. He had to be the man.

We managed to put Shimizu behind bars on a charge of illegally selling me alcohol, along with his prostitute girl friend "contact" by turning up evidence that they were both involved in espionage. I was able to radio a message to the fleet flagship: "For Joe—mission accomplished." Later I learned that when their jail terms were up, Shimizu and the whore were deported from Alaska as undesirable aliens. The cash expenditure for this successful counterintelligence mission was modest by any standard: two dollars for Shimizu's bottle of bad booze and two dollars for a mail orderly to compromise the whore!

The naval authorities approved of my performance in this job, but my Japanese language colleague and friend Forrest R. Biard, who was serving in cruiser *New Orleans* during the fleet problem, reported afterward that there were many disgruntled sailors as a result of my successful mission. As he tells it, during shore leave at Illilliuk the gobs were "doing the town" and learned that the only prostitute was in jail. At least one of the sailors, under a full head of steam, proceeded to the jailhouse and demanded to be permitted to go her bail, shouting that he wanted "some of that Alaskan stuff."[21]

It brought back pleasant memories to recall my shipmates in December 1940, when I rejoined that same *Pennsylvania* battleship as Pacific Fleet intelligence officer. In the earlier tour my turret had won the ship's first E for gunnery excellence. But whereas gunnery is a matter of tactics in which one goes by the book, I had no manuals and no margin for error as I set about to familiarize myself with all available background information on Japan's Combined Fleet.

4

Code Breaking and Kabuki

THE PALM-FRINGED ATOLLS of the western Marshalls were the nearest Japanese territory to our Pearl Harbor base and therefore the
most immediate potential danger to our security. Ever since my
time in Tokyo I had suspected that they were being fortified as military
bases. One of the biggest islands, Jaluit, was just over two thousand miles
southwest of Hawaii and its proximity as a possible enemy base made it a
priority in my intelligence mission to find out what Japan might be doing
in the mandates. The islands of the Japanese mandate, sprawling across
the central Pacific, offered ideal jumping-off points from which their powerful surface and submarine fleet could sally forth to sever our communication lines to the Philippines—or even to raid Hawaii.

As soon as I was established in my new billet, I visited the Fourteenth
Naval District's communications intelligence unit, which was then located
on the second deck of Building No. 1 in the navy yard at Pearl. This was
one of the navy's three prewar centers that specialized in the interception, cryptanalysis, and translation of Japanese radio communications.
Tommy Dyer had started the unit in 1936 as a one-man operation. He
eventually received radio operators and then a language officer, as well as
additional cryptanalysts. Dyer was to remain there throughout the war as
chief cryptanalyst, but the officer in charge of the communication intelligence unit on Oahu, Station Hypo, was Lieutenant Commander
Thomas B. Birtley. He and Lieutenant Ranson Fullinwider were the only
Japanese language officers and it was evident that the outfit was under-
staffed and overworked. I offered to help in any way I could. When Dyer
said that minor systems always needed work Birtley suggested I could try
my hand at solving an auxiliary address cipher. I plunged right in at every
spare moment to assist Birtley work over several hundred intercepts of
what he had designated the WE WE (pronounced WEH WEH) cipher.

It was a simple substitution system and I quickly found that there were altogether too many "soft sound" indicators being used for it to be pure Japanese text. Also "hard sound" indicators were being assigned to kana (the Japanese phonetic syllabary), which in Japanese words never carry those inflections. My analysis showed a presence of the "P" sound in un-Japanese positions in what appeared to be proper names. They appeared to fit with names such as "PA"rao (Palau) and Pona"PE" which were islands in the Carolines and Marshalls.

The cipher continued to break down. As I recovered each new value, specific units were addressed such as the Saipan defense force, Ponape garrison force, Kwajalein submarine base, and Palau landplane base. I plotted each recovery on a chart and, when the picture of a Japanese military buildup became clear, rushed the material to the Pacific Fleet commander in chief. Admiral James O. Richardson was skeptical at first, but after I had explained it in detail, and demonstrated the decryption process, he accepted the validity of this intelligence and recognized its strategic significance.

"Now we know," Richardson said, "that the Japs are secretly violating their mandate for administering those islands. We have been trying to find out what's going on out there for twenty years, and here you've done it in twenty days."

I was impressed with the admiral's quick grasp and flattered by the encouragement he gave me as the "new boy" on his staff. Richardson had relieved Admiral Claude C. Bloch as commander in chief, United States Fleet, in January 1940. It had been a trying year for the rangy admiral from Texas. He was a battleship sailor by training and inclination who—despite a succession of senior shore appointments, including a spell as presidential aide—still firmly believed that "the business of a naval officer is on the sea."[1]

Formerly the Pacific Fleet's battle force commander, Richardson had assumed command of the fleet in a critical year that saw President Roosevelt nudge an isolationist Congress into reluctant support for Britain in the fight against Hitler. The U.S. Navy edged toward an undeclared war against U-boats in the Atlantic while Germany's spectacular spring blitzkrieg through western Europe had acted as a spur to Japan's aggressive intentions in the Far East.

Diplomatic pressure was being exerted by Tokyo to force Britain to close the Burma Road in preparation for an all-out drive against the Chinese Nationalists. Anticipating that this might trigger an American oil embargo, the Japanese government was trying to squeeze massive new petroleum concessions from the Netherlands East Indies. To the British and to the Dutch government in exile in London, the dispatch of a powerful American naval force to garrison the empty fortress of Singapore appeared to offer the only hope of resisting Japan's insistent demands.

Secret talks among American, British, Dutch, and Australian staff officers at Singapore during April 1940 had failed to convince the American chiefs of staff of the strategic necessity, or political advisability, of sending warships to defend European colonial territory in the Far East. But in a symbolic gesture of support for Britain, President Roosevelt directed the Pacific Fleet to conduct its spring maneuvers in Hawaiian waters. Richardson then found that he was ordered to keep the fleet indefinitely at Pearl instead of returning to the west coast.

Japan's growing belligerency in the Pacific persuaded Richardson that his fleet would be less exposed back at San Diego. He felt that the navy was increasingly becoming hostage to the State Department's Far East policy, without considering the danger that provoking Japan would involve the United States in a two-ocean war, when we had only a one-ocean fleet. But when Richardson questioned the wisdom of keeping his ships away from their west coast base "until further notice" and possibly inviting a Japanese attack, Admiral Harold R. Stark, the chief of naval operations, informed him that the fleet was stationed at Pearl as a "deterrent" to Japan.[2]

Richardson, whose determination matched his convictions, flew to Washington in July 1940 to protest that the basing of the fleet at Pearl Harbor "was undertaken under a completely false premise."[3] Stark's polite refusal to rescind the order convinced Richardson that the president was keeping the fleet in Hawaiian waters to satisfy the Far East desk of the State Department who "did not ask their senior military advisers whether it would accomplish such an end."[4]

Richardson's belief that politicians, rather than admirals, were dictating United States naval strategy appeared to be confirmed when he was told that the fleet could not return to San Diego because this would be taken as a climb-down in Tokyo. Nor were his fears eased by the announcement of an American embargo of strategic exports to Japan, including scrap iron.

When the Japanese signed their tripartite pact with Germany and Italy in September 1940, precipitating yet another increase in tension, Richardson took off for Washington again to confront Roosevelt during his October reelection campaign. He had not chosen the best time to force a showdown with a president in the midst of an unprecedented third-term campaign. Roosevelt was facing a strong isolationist challenge and had many political promises to keep, not least of which was to satisfy the strong public demand that there was going to be no sellout of the Chinese Nationalists to the Japanese.

After a "hot and heavy confrontation," according to Richardson, Roosevelt terminated the discussion with an expression of pained surprise, saying, "Joe, you just don't understand."[5]

Richardson nonetheless returned to Hawaii convinced that his forceful presentation had "shocked" Roosevelt into reconsidering his naval policy. It came as a stunning blow, therefore, when Richardson learned in late January 1941 that he was to be relieved. The president had evidently decided to put the demands of diplomacy above those of prudent strategy.

Rear Admiral Husband E. Kimmel, the commander of the battle force cruisers, was promoted to CinC U.S. Fleet over officers senior to him. Handpicked by Roosevelt, who had known him in his years as assistant secretary of the navy, Kimmel had earned the reputation of a hard-driving, conscientious officer, who demanded as much from his staff as from himself. Richardson invited him to flagship *Pennsylvania,* then at sea, for preliminary conversations the last week of January, and it was then that I met Kimmel. We were out on exercises when his flagship, cruiser *Honolulu,* came abeam, and the admiral came over in his whaleboat. The sea was running so heavy that climbing the ship's ladder seemed risky, so *Pennsylvania*'s crane hoisted the whaleboat right on board. After a while, Richardson summoned me and said, "Tell Admiral Kimmel what you told me about Japanese remilitarization of the mandates." I excused myself to get maps from the safe, and returned to give my presentation.

Following the transfer of command, Admiral Kimmel asked to see my mandates charts again. I spread them out in his office for a review of the entire procedure. He was intrigued by the WE WE cipher and wanted the details about how it was broken. I did not know if he was previously familiar with radio intercept material, but his first-rate analytical ability impressed me. He seemed to appreciate the importance of the information, so much so that a week later he had me repeat the briefing for his staff.

What neither Kimmel nor I knew was that the navy department in Washington was still totally ignorant of the full extent of Japan's military preparations in the mandates. At the time of our conference at sea I assumed that since OP-20-G had received the same intercepts they must have made the same evaluation of them. We were to learn nearly three months later that they had completely ignored the WE WE cipher and its important intelligence. That omission alone was a telling indication that the navy department in Washington was not making comprehensive or complete intelligence evaluations of Japanese preparations for war.

Intelligence, as defined by *Webster's Third New International Dictionary,* is "evaluated information concerning an enemy or possible enemy or a possible theater of operations and the conclusions drawn therefrom."[6] That definition is inadequate because it covers only two of the three essential elements of intelligence. It comprehends acquisition and evaluation, but it omits the vital third element—dissemination. Information can be acquired and evaluated until hell freezes over, but it does not become intelligence until delivered to the commanders who can make proper use of it.

Prior to World War II our principal sources of intelligence on the

Japanese navy were the intercepts of their radio traffic made by our network of listening posts and processed in the three cryptanalysis centers.
The Pacific Fleet's communications intelligence unit was code-named Station Hypo after the "H" of Heeia on the east side of Oahu where its
radio intercept towers were located. It had been established in 1936,
twelve years after the first navy intercept station had been set up in the
U.S. consulate in Shanghai.[7] In 1925 a station had been set up to monitor
Japanese diplomatic radio traffic in Peking, the same year that a temporary listening post had been established at Wailupe east of Honolulu.

The first fleet radio intelligence units had been started in 1927 at
Guam and Olongapo in the Philippines under the Asiatic command. Station Cast, as it was designated even before its move to Cavite, was to
establish the units as satellite outposts. When Cast was under the command of Lieutenant Joseph N. Wenger, there had been no staff, or time,
for anything more than intercepting Japanese communications and rudi-
mentary traffic analysis. But in 1934 he had been succeeded by Lieutenant T. A. Huckins whose assistant, Lieutenant E.S.L. Goodwin,
"realized that he was being given a free hand." Goodwin continued the
code-breaking work he had started in Washington. His "remarkable piece
of work" on the Japanese fleet maneuvers was praised in Washington in a
report that noted, "With adequate and capable personnel this unit is capable of furnishing considerable information."[8] Goodwin then established the precedent that led to a 1935 decision by Safford—back from
sea and again in his old job—that the intercept stations should establish
their own cryptanalytic bureaus.

The real front-line warriors in the secret radio war were not the cryptanalysts, however, but the enlisted men who manned the headsets of our
receivers at these intercept stations. This required more radiomen who
were adept at rapidly recording the Morse code equivalents of the Japanese kana characters. This was no mean feat, for the international
Morse code A = (.) was the kana "I," our C = (—.—.) was kana "NI,"
and so on. Two dozen Japanese combinations were unique to kana, although both systems shared Arabic numerals.

In 1924 the navy had only two operators who could carry out this task.
To overcome this obstacle, Safford that same year had persuaded the
Underwood Typewriter Company to develop a special hybrid machine to
his own design. This printed the equivalent Japanese character from the
dot-dash combination, which took care of the twenty-six-letter Roman
alphabet. The other twenty-four unique kana combinations were typed
using the upper-case shift key.[9]

The hybrid kana typewriters, at $160 each, were a high-ticket item for
the time. Only a few could be purchased. Those that were sent out to our
two fleets operating in the Pacific proved that skilled radio operators
could quickly become proficient in recording Japanese Morse. But it was
still necessary to increase the number of radiomen familiar with Japanese

communications and able to take down kana by hand. Commencing in 1928, OP-20-G operated four-month instruction classes for front-line radio operators. They were conducted under conditions of great secrecy in a specially constructed classroom on top of the navy department building in Washington.

The "roofers," or On the Roof Gang (OTRG) as they came to be known, were the "ears" of our radio intelligence system at the chain of naval stations that encircled the North Pacific. The principal listening posts were established over the next decade at Shanghai in China, Guam in the Marianas, Marivele in the Philippines, Heeia on Oahu, and Bainbridge Island near Seattle The roofers manned the headsets and scanned the airways, taking down on message pads the torrent of Japanese Morse. These were relayed—depending on the location of the station—by courier pouch or secure cable line to the three centers where cryptanalysts and translators attempted to break out the messages into plain English. When this was not possible, direction-finding and traffic analysis was applied to extract whatever intelligence could be gleaned from a steadily increasing volume of intercepted Japanese traffic.

The nerve center of our radio intelligence operation was OP-20-G. Code-named Station Negat from the "N" of the navy department building, its maximum prewar staff of sixty civilians and servicemen operated from ten cramped office spaces on the first and second "decks" (floors) of wing number six. The now-demolished three-story World War I complex included the nine wings of the look-alike war department building. Until the Pentagon was completed in 1943, this sprawling four-block-long complex that reached back to the Reflecting Pool from the south side of Constitution Avenue housed the headquarters of our armed services.

Station Negat was my assignment when I returned from China in the early summer of 1936. In June, I took over from Birtley as chief of OP-20-GZ, the translation section. It was my responsibility to see that the decrypts made by OP-20-G were turned into plain English, and my small staff consisted almost entirely of civilian linguists.

My job was not solely translating. In the summer of 1936, I was able to assist with the analysis on a series of decrypts that turned out to be the intercepted radio reports on the postmodernization trials of battleship *Nagato*. To my surprise, these revealed that this rehabilitated World War I dreadnought had made better than 26 knots with her rebuilt turbines. This information also created concern in our war plans division where it was believed that the old *Mutsu* class, to which *Nagato* belonged, was good for only 23½ knots. Our new battleships—then in the blueprint stage—had accordingly been planned for a top speed of 24 knots. Captain Royal E. Ingersoll, from war plans, came down to check our information that *Nagato,* in several full-power runs, had indeed exceeded 26 knots.[10]

This timely intelligence enabled the navy general board to change the design of our *North Carolina*-class battleships to allow for speed of twenty-seven knots—and to provide an even greater margin, with a speed of twenty-eight knots for all later classes. This would give our naval task forces a one-knot superiority over their Japanese opponents. This single piece of radio intelligence gave our new battleships an important tactical wartime advantage. Safford, now promoted to head of OP-20-G, was amply justified in claiming that this coup "paid for our peacetime RI organization a thousand times over."[11] It was during my stint as head of the translation section of OP-20-G that I came to appreciate the magnitude of the contribution being made to our code-breaking effort by Mrs. Driscoll.

I had been warned not to patronize Madam "X," as her colleagues sometimes referred to her, because she was sensitive to her role as a woman in a man's world. Because of this she kept to herself as much as possible and none of us was ever invited to socialize with her and her lawyer husband. While she could be warm and friendly, she usually affected an air of intense detachment, which was heightened by her tailored clothes and shunning of makeup. It was surprising to hear Miss Aggie curse, which she frequently did—as fluently as any sailor whom I have ever heard.

In the navy she was without peer as a cryptanalyst. Some of her pupils, like Ham Wright, were more able mathematicians but she had taught cryptanalysis to all of them, and none ever questioned her superb talent and determination in breaking codes and ciphers. She understood machines and how to apply them. In 1937 she would share the fifteen-thousand-dollar prize granted by the Senate for her contribution to developing a cipher machine with Lieutenant Commander William F. Gresham.[12] But her principal talent was her ability to get to the root of a problem, sort out its essential components, and find a way to solve it. Among her uniformed naval colleagues, she was held in the highest esteem throughout her long career, which continued from the office of naval communications to the Armed Forces Security Agency, and then to the National Security Agency, before she retired in 1959.

My first encounter with Miss Aggie's formidable intellect occurred when she came to me one morning with a large piece of graph paper and asked, "Lieutenant Layton, does this make any sense?" She had marked the paper with zigzag staircases of letters in different color inks. Not being a Japanese linguist, she pointed along the letters on one of the staircases, and asked if it said anything in Japanese. I told her that it did not because there were too many vowels. Then she traced out another zigzag, which read "TO-MI-MU-RA;" I told her that this one made sense. It could be a Japanese name, "Tomimura." When she shook her head at that idea, I suggested that the "mura," which means town, has an alternate reading of "son," so it might also be rendered Tomison, or Thompson. She stopped me later as I was passing her desk on my way to lunch. "Lieutenant Layton, I want to thank you. You helped me solve part of a cipher that has been bothering me for some time. The name is Thompson."

The Thompson, the "Tomimura" whose name appeared in the intercepted Japanese foreign office traffic, after a secret investigation instigated by naval intelligence, was identified as a Pacific Fleet radioman. The American who was his accomplice and referred to as Agent K in the same message turned out to be John S. Farnsworth, a cashiered navy officer. It was he who had masterminded an espionage ring that turned over engineering and gunnery secrets, including the blueprint of the model D-4 bombsight, to Japan. Toshio Miyazaki and Akira Yamaki, the Japanese navy lieutenants who had been their contacts, were legally in the United States as language students.[13]

Farnsworth and Thompson were arrested in 1936. Although the evidence that unmasked Harry H. Thompson and led to the pair's apprehension could never be presented in court, they were convicted the following year of conspiring to violate federal espionage laws and each sentenced to four to twelve years in prison.

The whole affair had underscored the importance of maintaining the closest cooperation between the offices of naval communications and naval intelligence, and relations between the two had been considerably improved—during my eight months in OP-20-GZ, the translation section—by Captain William D. Puleston. Although naval communications still maintained administrative responsibility for OP-20-G, it was ONI that had the responsibility for disseminating the final product of the growing number of intercepted Japanese radio communications.

Like Captain Alfred T. Mahan, the nineteenth-century American naval strategist whom he studied and wrote about, Puleston was a thinking man's sailor. In addition to advocating the establishment of a national war college for senior officers of both armed services, he was one of the moving forces in expanding our secret radio war against the Japanese during his three-year tenure as director of ONI, which began in 1934. He was assisted by Commander Ellis M. Zacharias, his Far East section chief, who was one of the few Jewish naval academy graduates of his generation. Duty as a language student and later as assistant naval attaché in Tokyo had persuaded Zacharias that sooner or later we would have to fight the Japanese for control of the Pacific.

I came to know "Pulie," as we affectionately called him, quite well during the final six months of his productive tenure as ONI director. He was brilliant in addition to being energetic, and my already high respect for him was increased after an incident I witnessed on Christmas Eve 1936.

When Puleston came to offer those of us on duty a seasonal greeting, he found himself barred from access to our section by the armed marine guarding the door to our office, because the DNI's name was not on the official list. Overhearing the rising voices outside, I rushed to his rescue, just in time to find that the marine guard had drawn his pistol. "This gun is aimed at your belt, sir," the guard said. "If you step forward, I'll fire. Those are my orders."

Pulie was standing stock still, livid, and mad as hell. Upon my assurance that this was the director of naval intelligence and that he was authorized to enter, the guard stood aside. But Puleston, not ready to settle for that, took the guard's name and that of his commanding officer. Thereupon his stern manner softened and he congratulated Private Leo S. Schmidt for his diligence, said that he would have put him on report had he done otherwise, and announced that he was going to recommend him for promotion, which he did.

That was typical of Pulie, who was responsible for recommending my appointment as assistant naval attaché in Tokyo, which came through in February 1937.

I arrived in Japan that spring at the height of the cherry blossom season, when most Japanese love to stroll the countryside for *hanami*—flower viewing. That seasonal mood contrasted sharply, however, with the increasing aggressiveness of Japanese militarists and the jingoistic headlines. The army could do no wrong; the Chinese were "insincere and violently anti-Japanese." There was no opposition press to provide any kind of balance.

The invidious effect of the headlines upon the people was plain to see. One day I was sitting on a bench in Tokyo's Shinagawa Station, awaiting a connecting train, when I overheard two men discussing the news.

"I see we are sending troops to China."

"We don't need to send troops over there. All we have to do is send a bunch of boy scouts to kick those Chinese heads in. That would do it."

"I'm not so sure. It might take a little more than boy scouts to do the job."

The last speaker's touch of moderation was a rapidly vanishing trait of the Japanese man in the street. Everyone was being swept up in the extreme spirit of nationalism fostered by the state-controlled press and radio. In June a moderate cabinet fell victim to army factionalism. Prince Fumimaro Konoye's administration tried to reconcile conflicting interests. This was an impossible goal in the face of ultranationalist patriotic societies which championed the wayward army commanders in northern China. Within a month the Kwantung army widened the war in China, and Konoye's policies were derailed.

On 7 July 1937 the young anti-Japanese officers of the Chinese 29th Route Army, dissatisfied with "local agreements," attacked the neighboring Japanese army unit. Their intention had been reported to Washington by the assistant naval attaché at the American legation in Peiping. That message was intercepted by Japanese naval intelligence and reported to Tokyo, where army headquarters ignored the warning.

That same night Chinese and Japanese army units collided at Pei-ping's historic Marco Polo Bridge. The ensuing skirmish was a fuse igniting a full-scale but undeclared war on the mainland. Within three weeks Nationalist Chinese forces and the Japanese army were locked in a series of pitched battles. By August 1937 fighting had spread to Shanghai, and Konoye ordered a partial mobilization for a "war of chastisement." His last-ditch effort to prevent Japan from becoming committed to a continental war collapsed after Japanese army code breakers intercepted Chinese government messages revealing that Konoye was planning to bargain with the Nationalists. The prime minister's emissary was arrested as he was about to set off for Nanking.

The generals got their war. Konoye put the best face on his sandbagged position by claiming that the mainland fighting involving Japanese troops was just another "China incident." Ambassador Grew warned Washington that it was now too late to halt the conflict with "paper bullets." High explosives, however, almost started a real war with real bullets between Japan and the United States on 12 December 1937. That Sunday afternoon Japanese naval planes screamed down over the Yangtze River to bomb and sink U.S.S. *Panay,* which was evacuating the U.S. embassy staff from the besieged Nationalist capital of Nanking.

It was an anxious time for us in the embassy in Tokyo. Ambassador Grew, remembering how the Spanish-American War had broken out in 1898 after the sinking of the *Maine* in Havana Harbor, expected a declaration of war from Washington and ordered his staff to begin packing. The days that followed brought a hectic round of activity in the attaché's office as we tried to ascertain the facts and await the outcome. It was shocking to hear intelligent Japanese friends reveal their sincere and unanimous belief that the whole affair was "Chinese propaganda!" just as the screaming headlines proclaimed. On the other hand, our embassy was deluged with expressions of shame and regret from people of all walks of life. One well-dressed Japanese lady came to Ambassador Grew's office with flowers, made a brief speech of apology, and cut off her hair as a public act of penance.

The Tokyo government quickly moved to defuse the tense situation with a hasty apology, offer of indemnity, and assurances that it was an unfortunate case of mistaken identity. The *Panay* sinking and the savage rape of Nanking caused irreparable damage to Japanese-United States relations. These crises were aggravated, ironically, by the recent success of Japanese naval code breakers.

In 1936 the *kempeitai* had supplied the Japanese navy with codes from the British consulate in Ōsaka. In the fall of 1937, even before the American Brown code had been put into operation, photographic copies of the new State Department cipher together with a military strip system had been secretly obtained from the consulate in Kōbe. The Japanese were therefore able to read sufficient of the diplomatic codes to get the American and British assessments of events. Our secret cables differed dramatically from their official representations and their decrypts of our cables persuaded the Japanese that foreign diplomats were deliberately distorting their reports.

The *Panay* crisis brought an extra chill to the Tokyo winter. Japanese authorities became noticeably more circumspect in their official attitudes and dealings with us. The widening war in China made the gathering of intelligence even more difficult as military mobilization resulted in tighter censorship and security measures. Our sources were reduced to tidbits gleaned from a few military magazines and *gogai* (newspaper extras) sold on the street, and we were still being warned by our superiors to be careful about overstepping the bounds of diplomacy and discretion.

Our Japanese office boy regularly brought in a monthly newssheet issued by his "mobilization center." Once in a while it had squibs of naval news not appearing in newspapers or magazines. Shortly before our 1939 naval maneuvers off the Hawaiian Islands, I noticed an item rescheduling the routing of six Japanese naval tankers to California to load fuel oil. I reported this to ONI by diplomatic cipher, noting that the tankers were probably being diverted to monitor radio transmissions from our maneuvers. When the boy stopped bringing in the newssheets, I asked about them, and he said that they had been discontinued. I did not then know about the *kempeitai* break-in and code theft at Kōbe, and so did not realize that the Japanese authorities had been alerted to the newssheet as an intelligence source by reading my coded cable.

Courtesy calls to the Navy Ministry also became less frequent. I regretted this as I had struck up many friendships during official calls at the old Victorian red-brick building in Kasumigaseki, a district of official ministries and bureaus south-southwest of the imperial palace grounds. There I had met many Japanese naval officers whose names would become well known in World War II. Foremost among these was Vice Admiral Isoroku Yamamoto, who was then naval vice-minister.

We had worked closely with Yamamoto's office during the July 1937 search for Amelia Earhart, a matter in which they cooperated politely, but only halfheartedly. On one visit to naval headquarters I stopped in to greet Yamamoto's friendly aide, Captain Yasuichiro Kondo, who invited me to pay my respects to the admiral.

The admiral rose from the plain wood desk and greeted me cordially with a brisk but firm handshake. I knew he enjoyed chatting with me in Japanese, which my boss, Captain Bemis, did not speak. Yamamoto's manner was poised and cultured, but warm. He motioned me to a chair. The walls of his sparsely furnished office were bare except for a *kakemono* and a large map of the world.

He provided me with a perfect opening: "What can I do for you, Layton-san?"

"Admiral, I've been reading in the newspapers about those naval tankers *Tsurugizaki* and *Takasaki* that you're building."

"Yes. What about them?"

"Sir, I was wondering why their construction is taking so long."

He bristled slightly. "What do you mean by that?"

"Well, sir, yesterday's paper reported that a ten-thousand-ton, twenty-one-knot tanker had been completed by a civilian shipyard in five months and twenty-four days. So I wondered why it was taking so much longer to build naval tankers; I thought they would be completed by now."

I sensed that his initial geniality was fading. This had to be a sensitive matter, but he waved it off, saying, "Oh, I don't know such details. I can't be bothered with things like that." So we dropped that subject and our conversation moved to other things. (I later learned that the two tankers—still on the slipways—were even then being converted into aircraft carriers *Shōhō* and *Zuiho*.)

He asked if I liked kabuki. That highly stylized theater was one of my favorite Japanese entertainments. I told him how seven years earlier, during my language-study years, our *sensei* had taken us to kabuki as part of training. I had acquired a real fondness for it, but found *noh* drama hard to comprehend. Yamamoto said he looked forward to seeing me soon at a theater party he was planning for some of the naval attachés. On that pleasant note I departed.

Soon after our encounter over the mysterious tankers, he invited me to an evening of kabuki. When we were in our places in the theater he indicated adjoining vacant seats, explaining that other attachés were invited, but they didn't show up. That gave me an opportunity to converse with him at great length, but we talked only about theater. He seemed to appreciate my sincere interest in his country, that I had studied its history and its culture as well as the language—just as he had done as a language student and Japan's naval attaché in Washington in 1926. I felt we had a kind of kinship through our work and mutual interests.

Yamamoto asked about my first kabuki of a decade ago, which was still vivid in memory. My initial impression of kabuki had been that it was pretty weird; but it had really moved the Japanese. At thrilling points in the play, people in the audience had stood up and shouted such things as "That's what I'm here for!" "That's what I came for!" "That's what I've been waiting for." I told Yamamoto of the dignified-looking man who had been seated next to me, a complete stranger, who had been so moved at one denouement that he grabbed my shoulder and, cheeks streaming with tears, cried out, "Isn't it saaaad?" Yamamoto chuckled.

My evening with Yamamoto was also memorable for the program which included famed actor Kimburo doing his lion dance. We also saw *Musume Do-jo-ji* (*The Dojo Temple Maiden*), about the dedication of a temple bell. The priest has lustful designs on a maiden who is actually a devil in disguise. She suddenly turns into a devil right there on the stage, all red and fiery, and you think she is really on fire. Yamamoto displayed no emotion during the plays, but he obviously enjoyed them and wanted to know if the burning devil distressed me. It did not, but it certainly moved the audience, who shrieked with delight.

Our next social encounter was in the autumn of 1938 when Yamamoto invited me to a formal *kamoryo* (duck-netting) party. The guests at this were strictly blue-water naval officers. It was held at Hama *rikyū*, a detached palace, about a mile south of the main imperial palace in Tokyo. Part of the grounds had been set aside as a *kamoba*, a series of shallow canals where wild duck, lured by corn and tame decoys, were the quarry of the hunt. The object was to catch them, rather like giant butterflies, by deft use of long-handled nets. A rustic reed-covered hut on the embankment served as a base where the main party drank and played bridge while the hunt was carried on by groups of four. Eventually, when everyone had either caught a duck or given up, we all dined on delicious duck sukiyaki.

After our group had taken our turn with the nets, Yamamoto invited us to join him in a rubber of bridge. He was a skillful player who made clever ruffs and enjoyed winning all three rubbers. He accepted our congratulations and reminded us, mischievously, "Science and skill will always win over luck and superstition."

The favorite drink of senior Japanese officers before the war was John Begg scotch whisky, which was bottled in a squat ceramic jug. At the duck hunt it flowed as freely as the water in the canals outside. But while our host appeared to consume as many glasses as his guests, I later found out that Yamamoto had pulled the old Chinese trick of drinking cold tea.

The foreign naval and army attachés frequently were guests at social affairs, but we were never invited to air displays and army maneuvers, nor were we permitted to visit naval bases, air stations, or dockyards. The Japanese went to extreme lengths to conceal their warship construction. Outside their shipyards they erected huge screens of bamboo and canvas around the ways on which two big new superbattleships and carriers were being built. Every building site and military area was designated a fortified zone, where even casual visitors were often arrested on sight.

One of Japan's most guarded concerns was its trust territories in the mid-Pacific. A cable from the director of naval intelligence early in 1938 directed the naval attaché to obtain information about the possibility that Japan was militarizing these atolls, especially the Marianas, Carolines, and Marshalls, in defiance of the League of Nations' mandate. I was given the assignment and set about to book passage to the mandates, to try to find out whether seaplane and submarine bases had been constructed.

Armed with the schedule of sailings, I repeatedly visited the only steamship line offering passenger service to the islands to secure passage. I was told that each and every sailing was booked solid for the entire year. When I protested the "completely sold out" excuse, the senior passenger agent courteously but firmly informed me that he was under standing instructions "not to sell any foreigners passage to the mandated islands under any circumstances whatsoever."

Despite all Japanese protests to the contrary, American suspicion of clandestine militarization had been aroused as early as 1923 when Earle Ellis, a marine corps undercover agent, had disappeared in the mandates after gaining passage to the islands on pretense of doing nature studies. Japanese authorities had informed our naval attaché only that Ellis had died of unknown causes on the island of Palau, in the western Carolines.

Chief Pharmacist Lawrence Zembsch, of the American naval hospital in Yokohama that had been established in World War I, was sent to investigate the circumstances of Ellis's death. Zembsch returned with the major's ashes, but in a stupor, apparently drug-induced, and suffering from amnesia. He was hospitalized, with some hope that his recovery might clear the mystery. Unfortunately, Zembsch was killed in the naval hospital when it was destroyed in the great earthquake of 1 September 1923.

Although I never got within a thousand miles of the mandates, the authorities, somehow, did not object to my having a summer residence in Hayama, a "fortified zone" south of Tokyo, near the emperor's summer palace. As it happened, my *besso*—beach cottage—was under the aerial path of aircraft making test flights from nearby Yokosuka naval base. The planes flew so close on takeoff and landing that I did not even need binoculars to make out their details.

We had a report from Chungking about a crashed Zero: It was so light that two men could pick up a wing section. Powerfully armed and highly maneuverable, it had shot down many Russian-built I-15 fighters of the Chinese Nationalists. So when I spotted an unfamiliar aircraft overhead I felt immediately that it must be one of the new Zeros. It was also evident from the deft maneuvering of these planes that their pilots were far more skillful and better trained than was popularly believed.

Another advantage of summer living at Hayama for an intelligence officer was that my daily commuter train to Tokyo passed over the big railroad marshaling yards at Shinagawa. From the carriage window I could observe tanks, trucks, artillery, and troops being loaded on railcars for onward shipment to China.

Our commercial attaché and his staff were very helpful when it came to compiling intelligence reports, but we American attachés were never as effective as the British, who had fewer rules restraining their activities and conduct. While I was in Tokyo a new British naval attaché arrived, fully equipped with Leica camera and telephoto lens. When his ship docked at Kōbe, *Chiyoda* was in harbor. He poked his long lens through a cabin porthole and took the first pictures of a *Chiyoda*-class seaplane carrier to reach the West.

On a trip to Shanghai I once missed an excellent opportunity to photograph the new cruiser *Toné.* She was coming in from builder's trials when our passenger liner, *Empress of Asia,* put into Nagasaki for coal. We were held up at the entrance to the harbor to let *Toné* enter ahead of us. She was of the *Chikuma* class, with four turrets forward, and a floatplane-handling deck aft. Our people had never been close enough to obtain accurate information about these hybrid cruisers and it would have been easy to snap pictures of her from my cabin. But I had been officially discouraged from having a camera, "the sure sign of a spy."

The paranoid Japanese concern with security contrasted with the ease with which their attachés and undercover agents were able to operate in the United States. After 1937 the naval staff in Tokyo was faced with having to plan for a war against the United States that might come sooner rather than later. They concluded that more information was needed about their potential enemy.

Reliance on civilian spies had been most unsatisfactory for providing military information about the United States. Their reports included such stupid and useless things as "American warships carry women dressed as men," or "Since these men in the Navy have volunteered in the service just to have a free round-the-world trip, they will take to their heels when a war breaks out."[14] As a result, the naval attaché's office in Washington had been expanded during the 1930s. The Third Section of the imperial navy staff, which directed intelligence operations, had begun recruiting and training navy men as spies and sending them to the United States as undercover agents. Posing as language students, their mission had been to collect technical data about warship construction, radio communications, naval training, and weapons as well as details about American readiness for war.

One of their most successful naval undercover agents was a Lieutenant Commander Togami whose novel mission was to set up a mobile radio intelligence unit and collect detailed operational data on the U.S. Navy. Four years earlier our own office of naval intelligence had attempted a similar operation when four specially trained officers posing as civilian meteorological scientists had spent a year on board American Lines ships making passages to and from Japanese ports in the Far East.[15]

While our first use of mobile radio intelligence units had proved relatively unsuccessful, the Japanese, because they were able to conduct their clandestine operation ashore, had better luck. After sailing from Yokohama for Seattle early in 1937, accompanied by an expert radio operator, Togami spent six months in the Japanese embassy in Washington studying radio intercept methods and exercise routines at American naval establishments. His assistant purchased a high-powered shortwave radio receiver, and they set off on an eighteen-month motor tour—with the set concealed in the trunk of their car.[16]

A carefully planned itinerary took them to our main bases where, from rented houses, they eavesdropped on radio signals sent from ship to shore during maneuvers and routine operations. From hundreds of hours of patient listening, they compiled a dossier on American naval operations that revealed, among a wealth of useful intelligence data, that the American and Japanese navies employed similar fire-control methods, and that U.S. naval ships consumed three times as much fuel in training and were far superior in communications.

The haul of intelligence data, when analyzed in Tokyo, also told Japan's naval planners that the U.S. Navy was weak in night-fighting skills. This was of extreme interest and importance to the planners because for years they had placed considerable emphasis on training in night-battle tactics. Their resultant skill paid great dividends during the first year of the war in the Pacific when Japanese warships repeatedly outfought ours in night actions.

One other most significant observation made by the Japanese naval visitors to American shores pertained to a detail of our annual training schedules. They noted that fighting efficiency in the American fleet reached a peak in June each year, whereas the Japanese navy peaked in December.[17]

This kind of technical information was entirely inaccessible to American naval officers in Japan—and we were not encouraged to try snooping. Our naval attaché, Captain Bemis, frequently warned me in ominous tones, "Keep your hands out of that, boy!" This gave me the impression that we must have extensive undercover intelligence operations in Japan—which I later learned was just not so. The *kempeitai* managed to eliminate every one of our prewar undercover agents. Nevertheless, I contributed some useful intelligence in the fall of 1937 from newspaper communiqués about a Japanese air strike against the mainland. Our assistant naval attaché for air, Lieutenant Commander Frank Bridget, and I were able to determine that the flights had originated in Formosa. His report to Washington emphasized that this brilliant operation demonstrated the strategy of preemptive strikes and showed the capabilities of the Japanese naval air force.

My friend Bridget was an insightful and intuitive man of vast good humor. He enjoyed a drink of good whiskey now and then, which often got him into hot water with our straitlaced naval attaché, Captain Bemis. Frank had undertaken on his own an exhaustive study of the technical ability of Japanese naval aviators. At my recommendation he had taken a house next to mine in Hayama. Together we observed Japanese planes operating from nearby Yokosuka naval air station. We saw type 96 twin-engine bombers after takeoff, on landing approaches, flying singly and in formation, and we knew that their pilots were superbly trained.

Frank's report set out in great detail the skill of Japanese pilots and the performance of their planes. He concluded that men and equipment were superior to our previous reports, and that our own air outfits should know this. Since all his sources of information were public, the report noted that the Bureau of Aeronautics in Washington need not even classify its distribution.

This report proved how wrong were the assumptions current in Washington before the war that Japanese pilots could not fly and shoot straight because of their "weak" eyes. It might have dispelled such racial illusions and have had far-reaching effect on our state of preparedness three years later. But the evening that Bridget presented it to the naval attaché for forwarding to Washington in November 1938, he went out on the town to celebrate, and got drunk. This was reported to Bemis, who was furious. He not only placed Bridget under military arrest, but also gave him an unsatisfactory fitness report—a career blight. Further, in his anger, Bemis refused to sign or forward the report on Japanese naval aviation.

Bridget, in desperation, requested that it go out anyway under his own signature. Bemis refused, saying, "We do not issue reports signed by an assistant," and put the document in his safe. When I left Tokyo five months later, the report was still there, and it never was circulated by the Bureau of Aeronautics. I doubt that it ever reached Washington.

Such bureaucratic foolishness in a naval officer was astonishing, especially in light of the deteriorating diplomatic situation during my final year in Tokyo. Konoye was still struggling to keep his cabinet in power by a political balancing act, trying to bring the China war to a close, eliminate Chiang Kai-shek's Nationalist government, and establish a "new order" in the Far East. The tightrope he walked was already swaying precariously over the chasm of a general Pacific war when I was recalled from Tokyo in the spring of 1939 to assume command of my first ship, minesweeper *Boggs*.

It was during that summer, when *Boggs* put into San Diego, that I ran across Captain Zacharias, who was then running the intelligence office for the Eleventh Naval District. We had become friendly two years before during my spell as OP-20-GZ when "Zach" had headed ONI's Far East desk. As fellow language officers we shared a mutual interest in Japan and now he was anxious to hear the latest news about my time in Tokyo. I also soon discovered that he was talent scouting in anticipation of achieving his ambition to become director of naval intelligence.

We had been casually swapping Japan stories and Zach was squeezing fresh-plucked limes for our daiquiris when, quite suddenly, he asked, "How would you like to be fleet intelligence officer?"

I had never even thought of such a thing, and said so. Zach smiled and, in his conspiratorial way, explained that he had been "talking with people in Washington" about the need for a specialist intelligence officer on the fleet staff at Pearl Harbor. He was convinced that war with Japan was just over the horizon and that the fleet needed an intelligence officer who was a Japanese linguist. Whoever got the job would be the busiest man on the staff when the inevitable conflict broke out in the Pacific.

To my astonishment, Zacharias had already put my name forward for the job, even recommending that I should have an assistant. Had I any ideas about who would be a good assistant? In fact, I had, and named Bob Hudson. A number of us had learned the language, but of all my linguist colleagues, Hudson knew the Japanese people and their psychology best. Zacharias seemed to enjoy my surprise at the whole idea, commended my choice of Hudson, and said that we should keep thinking about it.

I was not surprised, therefore, when the following year orders came for me to report to flagship *Pennsylvania* as fleet intelligence officer. Hudson joined shortly afterward as my assistant. Nor was I surprised to find that Zach had preceded me to Pearl, for sea duty as captain of heavy cruiser *Salt Lake City*. He had no official intelligence function with regard to the Pacific Fleet, but retained his passion for "cloak and dagger" activities. He would drop into my office whenever he was ashore, apparently because he had been given a "commission to continue intelligence work."[18] I sometimes wondered if Zacharias thought that his pushing me for the fleet intelligence billet might provide him with a direct line to Admiral Kimmel. If he entertained such a notion, it was dashed after his one and only attempt to brief Kimmel in April 1941.

Shortly after Zach had brought his cruiser to San Francisco in February he encountered our old friend Admiral Kichisaburo Nomura en route to Washington to become Japan's new ambassador. Later, Zacharias would testify at the 1945 Pearl Harbor congressional inquiry that he had requested a chance to brief Kimmel after this encounter. Specifically he claimed that he had warned Kimmel of the need for long-range air patrols to guard against the dangers of an air strike against Pearl Harbor.[19]

Captain William W. Smith, Kimmel's chief of staff, who was also present at the meeting, testified that there had never been any mention of an air attack. He described Zacharias's sworn recollections as "clairvoyance operating in reverse."[20]

5

"When We Fight"

THREE MONTHS BEFORE I left Tokyo, I had attended a farewell gathering in January 1939 for the British naval attaché, Captain Bernard Rawlings. "I suppose you're a little sad to be leaving Japan?" I said to him when we were making our farewells.

"No, Layton. The next time I see the little yellow buggers, I hope it will be through the sights of a fourteen-inch gun!"

That wish was to be granted exactly six years later. In January 1945, as Rear Admiral Sir Bernard Rawlings, he flew his flag in battleship H.M.S. *King George V* as commander of the British task force sent out to the Pacific to operate with our fleet in the final months of the war.

The seriousness of the British naval attaché's parting salvo did not strike me until nearly two years after I had left Tokyo myself. In April 1941, while assembling a background brief on Japan's fleet for Admiral Kimmel, I came across some translations I had made to keep up my Japanese while skipper of *Boggs*. Among them was a book by the popular naval author Shinsaku Hirata, published in Tokyo seven years earlier. Its title—*Warera Moshi Tatakawaba*—struck me as significant because it translated as not "If" but "When We Fight."

The book included a vivid portrayal of the American fleet commander at Pearl Harbor worrying about the "fearsome" possibility that Japan would send "a fast striking force of cruisers and aircraft carriers" that would be "truly matchless and invincible!" The author's speculative conclusion struck me as remarkably perceptive since it had been drawn from knowledge of our naval exercises:

> Whether such a surprise raid could be organized only the Japanese Naval General Staff knows. During an American fleet problem off Hawaii some years ago, a carrier striking force sent flights of planes to attack after they had penetrated to seventy or eighty miles off

70

Hawaii. Aided by rain squalls these planes were able to surprise the "defenders" and carry out an effective bombardment of Pearl Harbor, theoretically destroying that major naval base.[1]

I was so impressed by Hirata's thesis that, under the pen name Tomomasa Emura, I submitted a translated summary to several magazines in October 1940, with a cover letter that ended, "Whether or not it is a preview of Japanese-American naval warfare is a matter for history to determine." I received the rejection slips philosophically but, after history had indeed determined the matter on 7 December 1941, I could not help wondering if any of those magazine editors remembered my translation and regretted as much as I did their decision not to publish it.

It would be going too far to suggest that *When We Fight* inspired the Pearl Harbor attack, but author Hirata's speculation had been founded on some knowledge of our naval maneuvers in which carrier-based planes had demonstrated it was possible to carry out a "successful" surprise attack on Hawaii. Within three years a Pearl Harbor concept was part of the Japanese naval war college study, "Strategy and Tactics Against the United States."[2]

In the early 1930s the very idea of an assault on Hawaii was enough to raise the eyebrows of Japanese naval traditionalists. While a surprise attack on Port Arthur in 1904 had worked for Japan in the Russo-Japanese War, it did not seem appropriate three decades later against a nation as powerful as the United States. Naval analysts in Tokyo knew that since 1907 America's war strategy—the so-called Orange plan—had envisaged a decisive confrontation west of the Marshalls.

Japan's answer to our Orange plan, which had been drawn up when our Pacific Fleet was numerically superior to Japan's Combined Fleet, was the doctrine of *yōgeki sakusen* ("ambush operations"). This called for their powerful submarine fleet to whittle down our advancing battle line before the final slugging match.[3] But even in 1940 when their battle line exceeded ours, Yamamoto, who knew America better than any other Japanese admiral, saw the strategic weakness of this doctrine. He made no bones about the desirability of avoiding such a confrontation that would result in war with the United States. He knew that if it came to a prolonged fight, the Pacific Fleet would not sortie to challenge the Combined Fleet to "the decisive battle" until we had built up our superiority.

It had been apparent to all observers during the late 1930s that Yamamoto's life was in danger. Being acquainted with him professionally and socially, and feeling a friendly kinship with him through the similarity of our interests, I watched his activities with a special interest. I had seen at first hand how as vice-minister of the navy he had risked his popularity and even his life to steer successive governments away from confrontation with the United States over the war in China. He had been marked by the right wing for his opposition to the tripartite pact, and he had been a stubborn opponent of war with the United States and Great Britain.[4]

During the spring of 1939 and into the summer, reports of plots against Yamamoto became increasingly lurid, and the campaign to drive him out was violent, with some threatening that "if he does not mend his ways he will be got rid of, with explosives or a bomb if necessary."[5]

When, for his own safety, on 30 August he was given command of the Combined Fleet, Yamamoto realized that a clash with the United States had become all but inevitable. Konoye's new-order-for-Asia policy in 1940 had aligned Japan with Germany and Italy in the tripartite pact. The parties were bound by the treaty to come to each other's aid if any one of them was attacked by a power "not involved in the European war or in the Sino-Japanese conflict."

"If we are ordered to do it," Yamamoto had told the prime minister to his face, on the eve of the signing of the tripartite pact on 27 September, "then I can guarantee to put up a tough fight for the first six months, but I have absolutely no confidence as to what would happen if it went on for two or three years. It's too late to do anything about the tripartite pact now, but I hope at least you'll make every effort to avoid war with America."[6]

Distrustful of politicians but loyal to duty, Yamamoto set out to modify the naval staff's *yōgeki sakusen* doctrine into a quick-victory strategy for Japan in the impending naval war. As a young man he had hitchhiked around the United States. He had been mightily impressed with the power manifest in the Pittsburgh steel mills, the Detroit auto factories, the Kansas wheat fields, and above all by the Texas oil fields. More than any other Japanese, Yamamoto had come to appreciate that *Beikoku,* "rice country," their descriptive word for the United States as a land of abundant resources, was correct.

If it should come to war with the United States, Japan's best chance, as Yamamoto saw it, was a quick knockout blow to immobilize the enemy's battle fleet and neutralize American naval power long enough for Japan to secure the natural resources and defenses of southeast Asia and the western Pacific.

Surprisingly, the stationing of our fleet in Pearl Harbor offered the best opportunity for achievement of this goal. The scenario conjured up by Hirata's 1933 tract had been given theoretical shape with a 1936 study at the imperial navy war college of an attack on Hawaii. It became practicable after the impressive demonstration of Japanese carrier planes in the spring naval maneuvers of 1940. But it was the British naval air attack on the Italian fleet in Taranto harbor on 12 November that finally crystallized the concept into a nine-page outline by Yamamoto "Views on Preparations for War," which contains his first formal suggestion of an air attack on Hawaii. He submitted this paper to Navy Minister Koshiro Oikawa in strict confidence on 7 January 1941.[7]

Yamamoto also gave this secret outline to Rear Admiral Takijiro Ohnishi, the tactical genius of Japanese naval aviation, for study and evaluation. Within six weeks Ohnishi had concluded that the operation, though risky, was feasible—but only *if* surprise could be achieved. The working out of operational details was turned over to Commander Minoru Genda, the resourceful thirty-six-year-old tactical aviator on the staff of Vice Admiral Chuichi Nagumo's newly formed First Air Fleet.

Genda, a naval attaché in London at the time of the Royal Navy's successful torpedo plane attacks on the Italian battleships, had made a firsthand study of the techniques employed. If twenty-one British carrier planes could cripple three Italian capital ships, he reasoned, then two hundred Japanese aircraft should be able to put most, if not all, of the Pacific Fleet out of commission.

It took two months for Genda to work up his draft tactical study for the attack on Pearl Harbor. Meanwhile, the secrecy that was essential for any chance of success came perilously close to being blown. On 27 January, Ambassador Grew sent to Washington a report that the Peruvian minister had been told "from many sources, including a Japanese source, that in the event of trouble's breaking out between the United States and Japan, the Japanese intend to make a surprise attack against Pearl Harbor with all their strength and employing all their equipment."[8]

This information was relayed to Kimmel on 1 February, the day when he assumed command of the Pacific Fleet. With it came an assessment by my old boss, Commander McCollum, now head of ONI's Far East section: "Naval Intelligence places no credence in these rumors." Such a casual dismissal, even of cocktail party gossip, was surprising given the current concern of the war plans division that if "war eventuates with Japan, it is believed easily possible that hostilities would be preceded by a surprise attack upon the Pacific Fleet in the naval base of Pearl Harbor."[9]

Admiral Stark had evidently been alarmed enough by this scenario to have the secretary of the navy alert the war department on 24 January 1941 that the "inherent possibility of a *major disaster to the fleet or naval base* warrant taking every step, as rapidly as can be done, as will increase the joint readiness of the Army and Navy to withstand a raid [emphasis added]" The memorandum, which originated from the director of war plans, drew attention to "air bombing attack" and "air torpedo plane attack" as the principal dangers threatening Pearl Harbor, since precautions had already been taken against submarines, mines, and "bombardment by gunfire."[10]

Admiral Turner, the recently installed head of war plans, was to persistently claim—after the event—that he had predicted Japan might attack Oahu with planes launched from "a striking force of carriers." It is all the more astonishing therefore, that Turner authorized a dispatch so dismissive of just such a possibility a week after his memorandum had been circulated.

Whether there had been some kind of a real leak in Tokyo has never been established. It was later learned, however, that the rumor had reached Grew from a Japanese member of the Peruvian embassy's staff who had apparently picked it up from her chauffeur boyfriend. But what was dismissed in Washington as fantastic gossip struck a chord that brought to my mind the Hirata translation, containing his imaginative account of the air attack on Pearl Harbor, that I had tried to get published five months earlier. I was reminded by the Peruvian rumor to show it to Kimmel.

When the admiral returned the translation, we discussed various points about the piece and Kimmel asked if I thought that Hirata had written from an official or semiofficial point of view, and whether the Japanese would consider such a risky undertaking. Considering the Japanese mania for secrecy, I doubted that the author was reflecting official Japanese naval opinion. But I pointed out that the possible would become probable only if they thought that such an attack could succeed. We had to remember that, historically, Japan's actions did not follow orthodox military strategy, and that the Japanese had made a similar preemptive surprise attack on Port Arthur in 1904 during the war with Russia.

Finally Kimmel sent for his war plans officer, Captain Charles H. McMorris, and asked what he thought about the chances of a Japanese strike at Pearl Harbor. Soc (his sobriquet was a tribute to his Socratic wisdom) admitted that, as operations officer at Pearl since 1939, he had considered this possibility. His conclusion was that although it was possible, the Japanese would be deterred by the huge risk involved. But however remote the possibility might appear, he said, we had to admit that the British strike on the Italian fleet at Taranto the previous November had shown that an airborne torpedo attack on anchored ships could be devastating.

Pearl Harbor was not equipped with antitorpedo nets. In January, however, Washington had considered providing them, but the plan had fallen by the administrative wayside. That the Japanese might have in mind a carrier strike against us was an option that we considered. But no information was received subsequent to the dismissive 1 February report from Washington that gave me any grounds for uprating what was only a *possibility* into a *probability*.

Furthermore, in the week before being relieved, Richardson also had expressed his concern about fleet security in the face of "surprise raids on Pearl Harbor," in a report in which Kimmel collaborated.[11] In a letter of 15 February the chief of naval operations told Kimmel that Washington analysts had determined that antitorpedo nets were not necessary since the waters of Pearl Harbor, unlike Taranto, were too shallow for making an effective aerial torpedo attack.[12] Admiral Bloch, commandant of the Fourteenth Naval District, concurred.

Stark's letter had emphasized that his main concern was the threat of enemy submarine attacks and mining at Pearl Harbor, not an air attack. Kimmel, nevertheless, had issued a 15 February order to the fleet which noted that, in addition to these dangers, "a declaration of war might be preceded by:

1. a surprise attack on ships in Pearl Harbor
2. a surprise submarine attack on ships in operating area
3. a combination of these two."[13]

This focus on seaborne threats naturally loomed larger in the minds of surface unit commanders, but bombing and aerial torpedoes were rated a far greater menace in the calculations of air commanders. The vulnerability of Pearl Harbor to a carrier-borne air strike had been demonstrated as recently as March 1938, when Admiral Ernest J. King had launched a successful air strike from *Saratoga,* to conclude Fleet Problem XIX. The alarming ease with which this attack had been executed was still fresh in the minds of Major General F. L. Martin, head of the Hawaiian army air corps, and Rear Admiral Patrick L. N. Bellinger, head of the Hawaiian naval air patrol.

"It appears that the most likely and dangerous form of attack on Oahu would be an air attack," they warned in a joint report of 31 March 1941, which would later appear to be a remarkable piece of prophecy. "At present such an attack would most likely be launched from one or more carriers which would probably approach inside of three hundred miles," they predicted, advising that it would come at sunrise since "in a dawn air attack there is a high probability that it could be delivered as a complete surprise."[14]

Coincidentally, on 1 April (the day after the Martin-Bellinger report was issued) CNO sent a caution to all commands that "past experience" showed that Axis powers preferred to launch attacks on Saturdays, Sundays, or national holidays, and that all commands "should take such steps on such days to see that proper watches and precautions are in effect."[15]

Little did Martin and Bellinger realize that on the other side of the Pacific, Lieutenant Commander Genda's secret feasibility study of the Hawaii attack proposal was reaching identical conclusions. To defend against a dawn raid, the commanders responsible for the air defenses of Hawaii advised that it was "desirable" to organize daily air patrols "as far as possible to seaward through 360 degrees to reduce the probabilities of surface or air surprise." But Martin and Bellinger recognized that the demands of effective defense could not be reconciled with the shortages of aircraft and personnel, both army and naval, in Hawaii. Accordingly, this limited the "desirable" around-the-compass, long-range air patrols to those times when *"intelligence* indicates that a surface raid is probable [emphasis added]."[16]

Despite repeated pleas from Admiral Kimmel and Lieutenant General Walter C. Short, the army commander in Hawaii, Washington refused to make any more planes or other matériel available for adequate long-range surveillance. This is all the more surprising because Admiral Turner would testify at the congressional hearings on Pearl Harbor in 1945 that the Martin-Bellinger report of 31 March 1941 was endorsed at the highest levels in Washington.

"We agreed thoroughly with it, approved it, and it was very gratifying to see that officers in important commands out there had the same view of the situation as was held by the war and navy departments."[17] While this was Turner's position in 1945, it may be asked why he and the other military leaders in Washington did not see to it that Pearl Harbor received the planes and the intelligence that could and should have been sent out to us before December 1941?

This question has two answers. The simple one is that Washington was looking in the wrong direction, toward Europe, and not properly evaluating the Pacific situation; nor were they paying any attention to the advice of commanders in the field. The complex answer is to be found in the breakdown of the intelligence process in Washington in the critical months of 1941 as Japan and the United States drifted closer to war.

Accurate information about our fleet was one of the keys to the success of Japan's attack on Pearl Harbor. It was a tragic paradox that while our intelligence was far more extensive, it still failed to provide us with an adequate warning of the attack. In a sequence of events that bore an uncanny resemblance to a Greek tragedy, our intelligence advantage was thrown away: Washington was doomed, as if by some fatal curse, to ignore, misinterpret, or neglect to relay to Pearl Harbor the vital clues that would have saved the battle fleet. By the same token, General Douglas MacArthur, despite a ten-day warning of the threat of an imminent strike on the Philippines, lost his air superiority in a bombing raid *nine* hours *after* the Pearl Harbor attack.

Never in history had a nation steered into a confrontation with a rival power with more information about the general intentions of the potential enemy than the United States had about Japan on the eve of the Pacific war. But our leaders in Washington gambled on the assumption that our eavesdropping on Tokyo's diplomatic traffic would provide an early warning of their moves—even though we had lost our ability to tap into their army and naval communications.

It is all the more astonishing that such a fundamental miscalculation occurred after Washington had been reading the Japanese diplomatic and naval ciphers for more than a decade. By a combination of code breaking, direction finding, and traffic analysis it had been possible to predict every movement of Japan's fleet until 1940. It was in October that year that the chief of naval operations issued the warning: "During the past year and a half, however, the major Orange naval cryptographic systems have undergone radical changes, resulting in a temporary reduction in the intelligence obtained by cryptanalytical means."[18]

Japan's first counterstrike against our cryptanalysts in the secret radio intelligence war had been made on 1 November 1938 when a new code superseded their eight-year-old Blue Book. The change was apparently a direct response to warnings by Japan's naval commander in China that their high-level administrative code system was no longer secure.[19]

The new cipher system was designated "AD" from its similarity to the "A" version of the Blue Book, but it still meant that all the code values recovered by us over the past eight years had to be scrapped. The entire system—code and new cipher forms, as well as keys—had to be reconstructed from scratch. This required the recovery of the four thousand keys that were changed every four months, in addition to finding the solution of the transposition form that was changed every ten days.

The arduous task was assigned by Safford to Commander Dyer's cryptographic unit at Pearl Harbor. Hypo's staff was increased to four officers to cope, but the problem, according to a contemporary report, was "one of quantity and time rather than difficulty."[20]

After a year's effort, Dyer's team at Pearl Harbor had reached the point in November 1940 that the "AD" system was beginning to produce intelligible text when Japan made another major change in the underlying code. Unlike the first version, the new edition of the code book appeared to have a circulation limited to flag officers. There were comparatively few messages transmitted over the next twelve months and fewer intercepts could be made. Although Hypo continued to concentrate exclusively on what was designated as the "NL" system until the second week of December 1941, it consumed many thousands of valuable hours of cryptanalytic effort for no intelligence return. Only some two hundred intercepts were ever made, a totally inadequate number for the effective penetration of any cipher system.[21]

While the Pacific Fleet's communications intelligence unit was left to wage its fruitless struggle with the so-called flag officers system, navy department cryptanalysts had turned their attention to a new "Operations Code" that had come into use on 1 June 1939. This "AN" cipher, later to be designated JN-25, was radically different from any other so far employed by the Japanese navy. It was a five-numeral, two-part code, consisting of 33,333 groups in the "dictionary book," to each of which were added, by false arithmetic (no borrowing or carrying) a five-digit number selected in sequence according to the start key from a second book of random additives. The resulting encipherment consisted of a series of five-digit numbers divisible by three to provide a convenient check against garbles.

The assault on the three entities that made up the JN-25 system had been spearheaded by the redoubtable Mrs. Driscoll. The three parts of the system were (1) the code itself, (2) the current additive book, and (3) the system of encrypting that was indicated at the beginning of the message, the starting point in the stream of additives.[22] Not until after the initial breakthrough had been made in the fall of 1939 did the most laborious and time-consuming task of recovering the additives and code groups begin. The OP-20-G cryptanalysts under Lieutenant E.S.L. Goodwin labored for a year compiling code book and additive tables in blank ledger books. The columns, five-digit groups, and their appropriate Japanese characters and English translation were entered one by one with medieval patience by civilian linguists Phillip H. Cate and Fred C. Woodrough, Jr.

After the cryptographic section had been "banging its head into the wall over the 5-digit system" the first JN-25 decrypts were finally made two months after Goodwin left in September 1940.[23] By the end of the year the first "A" version of the code, which had by then been in use for eighteen months, had been solved. Then on 1 December 1940 it was superseded by the "B" version. Five successive cipher books had been used during the life of JN-25A, but the fifth was to be in effect during the first two months of JN-25B. This facilitated both the recognition of the change and the rapid recovery of some two thousand values for the new code book. But once the new additives came into use in January 1941, progress slowed until the "difference table" produced by the IBM tabulating machines was used to speed up the recovery process.[24]

Japan's drastic code changes at the end of 1940 left us unable to read anything in their main naval cipher systems until well into 1941. Only their merchant ship code continued to be "99% readable." Even their "Material Code System," labeled "HE," which contained details of naval housekeeping and supply, required six months' work before it could be reread for items of minor importance. Japan's "Intelligence Code System," considered unlikely to be of "any great value as far as current information," was given an even lower priority.[25]

So the critical year of 1941 began with an almost total blackout of Japanese naval intelligence. Safford's five officers and two civilian cryptanalysts were also obliged to divide their labors trying to crack the German naval Enigma used by the U-boats on the Atlantic, while laboring over the machine cipher employed by the Japanese naval attachés. In addition to their main assault on the JN-25 operational code, OP-20-G had to divert efforts to helping the army penetrate Japan's diplomatic traffic.

The army's Signal Intelligence Section led by Colonel William F. Friedman had made their first breakthrough into Tokyo's most secret diplomatic cipher in September 1940 within a week of the navy cryptanalysts' initial decryption of JN-25. This was a remarkable simultaneous feat of cryptography by the two teams, since the Japanese foreign ministry had also introduced its new cipher in February 1939, five months before the navy. Newly released documentation reveals that—contrary to what has previously been written about the army's singular triumph—it was not accomplished without assistance from the navy.[26]

The relatively small SIS team had begun to work on Japan's main diplomatic communications in 1932, after achieving a partial success with the German and Italian government ciphers only three years after the State Department's injunction against reading "other gentlemen's mail." Friedman's special expertise was in machine enciphering systems. He had patented the electrically controlled rotors that became the heart of the cipher machine that was our most secure and widely used coding device throughout World War II. The development of the Sigaba, as the army called the machine, known in the navy as the ECM, was also being paralleled in Japan.[27]

The Japanese navy was evidently spurred to develop an electric coding machine in the aftermath of the revelations of Yardley's book about our Black Chamber. In 1935 its use first became apparent to the OP-20-G cryptanalysts who encountered cipher traffic which Mrs. Driscoll analyzed as having been generated by a machine. She quickly developed a method of manual decryption for "M1," as the Japanese device was named. It involved the use of a graph-paper diagram against which she slid the recovered cipher sequence on a long strip of graph paper, enabling the substitution generated by the machine to be manually recorded. It was by this technique that Miss Aggie had first identified the word "Tomimura," which had led to the capture of our navy spies in 1936.[28] Our cryptanalysts were naturally anxious to reconstruct their own version of the device, none more so than Lieutenant Jack S. Holtwick who had helped Mrs. Driscoll crack "M1." When it became apparent that this traffic was being exchanged with the Japanese naval attaché in Washington, surveillance of his Alban Towers apartment was conducted. This picked up mysterious clicking. On the assumption that this noise was produced by the coding machine, an elaborate break-in was arranged.

While the attaché was being royally entertained by Commander Zacharias and his wife at dinner on an evening in July 1935, Holtwick and a chief radioman called McGregor, posing as electricians, conducted a detailed examination of the Japanese officers' residence-cum-office in the imposing building that dominates the intersection of Massachusetts and Wisconsin avenues. No sign of either an electrical or mechanical coding device was found. So (contrary to what other writers have claimed) Holtwick had to draw on his own ingenuity and Mrs. Driscoll's cryptanalysis in order to design his own version of the machine.[29]

This analog worked well enough to decrypt the Japanese navy's machine cipher until it was abandoned in 1938. But the real value of the "M1" machine was that it gave Friedman's team a headstart in constructing the device that would imitate the "M3" machine, which was then being used by the Japanese foreign ministry in 1935 to encode its most confidential communications. By 1936 it was enabling us to read Tokyo's diplomatic messages on a regular basis. At the suggestion of one of Friedman's staff the colors of the primary spectrum were adopted as identifiers and the "A" enciphering device was thenceforth dubbed the "Red machine"—not to be confused with the Japanese navy's Red code book. The Red machine remained in use for communications between Tokyo and its principal embassies until February 1939. A decrypt late in 1938 forewarned us of an impending change by revealing that a cipher expert named Okamoto was being sent to nine of Japan's most important embassies to install a type "B" machine.[30]

The new encoding device, like its predecessor, had been developed by Captain Risaburo Itō. Designated *97-shiki O-bun Injiki,* or "Alphabetical Typewriter 97," its number was adopted from the year of its invention, 1937, which was the ninety-seventh year of the twenty-fifth century according to the ancient Japanese calendar. It represented a radical departure from the German Enigma and our Sigaba electrical encoding devices because it was not based on rotors, but a battery of six-level, twenty-five-point telephone exchange stepping switches with a plugboard to set up the key. A typewriter keyboard was used to enter the message in kana with a three-letter code for numerals and the enciphered communication was printed out by a second electric typewriter. The millions upon millions of possible cipher combinations made possible by switch and plug settings convinced its inventor—and the Japanese foreign ministry—that the Type 97 code system was unbreakable.

The intercept of a Red message sent from Tokyo on 18 February 1939 announced that the new cipher system would come into operation two days later.[31] Following the precedent set for the Red machine, Friedman adopted the cover-name "Purple" for the new system and immediately launched into an intensive eighteen-month effort to unravel this cipher and construct a new decoding device.

"The volume of messages in the new system gradually increased," according to Frank B. Rowlett, Friedman's specialist on Japanese codes, "until in mid April it was clear that the new machine had virtually replaced the old on the major diplomatic circuits."[32] Because the Japanese continued using the old system after transferring the Red machines to less important embassies around the world, we continued reading part of Japan's diplomatic traffic. This provided important help to Friedman's SIS cryptanalysts, since there was some overlap between the communications sent in Red and Purple. But the most important intercepts exchanged between Tokyo and Berlin, London and Washington piled up unread, and the pressure on Friedman and his team increased as Europe lurched toward war in 1939.

Analysis of this traffic had revealed that while Purple was a more complex encipherment than Red, both were based on a system that divided the twenty-six letters of the Roman alphabet into subsets of six and twenty elements. This was the discovery that provided the key by which Friedman and his analysts began to unlock the new cipher. But recovering the "sixes" proved a slow pencil-and-paper effort that dragged on until August 1940 when Larry Clark, a civilian cryptanalyst recruited by Friedman, hit on the notion that the Japanese had used telephone stepping switches instead of rotors as the enciphering mechanism. Within a month Friedman's team, by a process of trial, error, and mathematical calculation, produced a blueprint for a device that duplicated their conception of the Japanese machine. The first Purple analog was actually built by navy technicians at the Washington Navy Yard. By the second week in September the current keys to the Purple cipher had been recovered and the rat's nest of wiring and chattering relays housed in a makeshift black wooden box finally rewarded the months of ingenious labor by producing the first decrypts of Tokyo's most secret diplomatic messages.

The enormous mental effort put Friedman temporarily in the hospital with a breakdown. But the full measure of his team's remarkable achievement came five years later after the dissection of remains of a captured Japanese "B" machine revealed that of the several hundred connections in their analog, only two were wired differently from the Japanese machine's. The Purple machine, of which five were eventually constructed, also proved more reliable than the Japanese originals in eliminating garbled code groups. The total cost of the hardware in the first two navy-built analogs was $684.65—an investment that was minuscule when measured against the return.[33]

The ability of Friedman's army team to read the high-level Japanese diplomatic communications greatly enhanced their status. As one of its key members, Frank Rowlett, put it, "The chief signal officer liked to refer to us as magicians."[34] This name stuck and the term Magic came into general use with reference to all cryptographic intelligence, even after we had adopted the British practice of formally classifying it as "ultrasecret" information, or simply as "Ultra."

Magic was considered so vital that by the beginning of 1941 it had been hedged with a fetish of secrecy so overwhelming that its value as intelligence began to erode. Apart from the operational heads in the war and navy departments, it was made available only to the president and his secretaries of state, navy, and war. Information derived from the diplomatic intercepts was only sporadically to be sent out to Admiral Kimmel.

Although the army had yet to penetrate any of the Japanese military ciphers, and the navy cryptanalysts were still battling to get back into the Japanese naval codes, the ultrasecret mystique of the intelligence derived from the Purple machine created a sense of infallibility in Washington, as if we possessed a "magic wand" with which to divine Japanese intentions. Control of such a potent source of information in a command setup is never more critical than when it falls into the hands of ambitious and determined officers.

The newly declassified records reveal hitherto unknown details about how this intelligence was abused. It is now clear that ranking officers used Magic to further their own authority at the expense of its proper dissemination as the crisis with Japan worsened. The consequences were disastrous.

6

Pacific Overtures

DESPITE THE MOUNTING TENSION between Washington and Tokyo at the beginning of 1941, on 31 January when Japanese liner *Kamakura Maru* entered Honolulu harbor escorted by two American destroyers, she was roundly greeted. Her distinguished passenger, Admiral Kichisaburo Nomura, was visiting Honolulu for the day en route to his new post as ambassador to the United States. Civilian and military leaders were waiting to greet him when the ship docked at eight that Friday morning. I was with Admiral Richardson because he knew of my friendship with Nomura and had assigned me as his honorary aide for the visit.

I had first met Nomura during my student days in Japan in 1931, when he was director of naval intelligence. We became friends six years later while I was in Tokyo as assistant naval attaché, when he was Japan's foreign minister. Tall, moon-faced, suave, poker-playing, bourbon-drinking, chain-smoking Nomura was a sincere friend of the United States. He had been naval attaché in Washington during World War I, and had many personal friends in America.

His day in Honolulu was busy, and I was at his side throughout the full schedule, which included visits to the governor and flagship *Pennsylvania,* a chamber of commerce lunch at the Royal Hawaiian Hotel, a memorial church service, and a United Japanese Society dinner in his honor at the Sunchoro tea house.

The United Japanese Society had plainly not expected me to be present, but Admiral Nomura's opening words were, "Leftenant Commander Layton here is an old friend and is my guest. I am on my way to Washington to make new friends and straighten out any problems between our two nations. I have asked Leftenant Commander Layton to be present during all my conversations and speeches here because I have nothing to hide from anyone. I want him to know and assure his government that I am honest and sincere."

Despite his tight schedule, we had some opportunities that busy day for friendly conversation, and I was impressed by Nomura's clear sincerity and genuine concern for the drift of events. He thanked me warmly as we parted late that night and he boarded *Kamakura Maru* for San Francisco.

Nomura was one of the few senior Japanese officials I knew who had real affinity for and understanding of the United States. His appointment at this critical time was a signal of Tokyo's attempt to calm American concern. If anyone could have done it, Nomura was that man.

He arrived in Washington on 12 February 1941 and was at the White House two days later to present his credentials and have candid discussions with President Roosevelt on the key issues dividing their two nations. Diplomatically naïve, Nomura was so eager to succeed in his mission to reach a speedy settlement with the United States that he was ready to accept commitments that his cabinet could not possibly have sold to the military. His first meeting was marked by much cordiality and personal friendliness, since the president considered the admiral to be an old navy friend. Even Secretary of State Cordell Hull, who made no bones about his abiding distaste for the Japanese, warmed to Nomura's eagerness to restore friendly relations.

The ambassador reported to Tokyo that Roosevelt was principally concerned that Japan might move into the French Indochina area and that Germany and Italy would force Japan into war by orchestrating another *Panay* incident. The president had reassuringly told him that, provided outstanding differences over Japan's aggression in China could be settled, there was "plenty of room in the Pacific for everybody."[1]

At the beginning of April 1941 the chances for reaching a settlement of long-standing differences between Japan and the United States seemed brighter than they had ever been as a result of Nomura's arrival and the president's favorable reaction to his initial overtures. The Roosevelt administration had a specific reason for welcoming any sign of a thaw in relations with Tokyo. Washington was wrestling with one of America's perennial strategic dilemmas: how to defend the nation and fight a two-ocean war with a one-ocean navy. With Britain having been at war with Germany for a year and a half, our military leaders had adopted a Europe-first commitment that was implicit in their latest "Rainbow 5" contingency war plan.

The army and navy had jointly developed five plans for the principal war contingencies with our foes and allies designated by colors so that Rainbow was chosen as an appropriate code name. By the spring of 1941 it had become increasingly clear that only Rainbow 5, which envisaged dealing with Germany in the Atlantic and holding Japan in the Pacific, would meet the emerging global crisis. Rainbow 5 had itself evolved from an October 1940 memorandum of Admiral Stark that urged the adoption of the navy's Plan D (for dog), which anticipated entering the naval war beside Britain if necessary. This had persuaded the army toward an Atlantic strategy in support of Britain's war against the Axis powers. The logistical balance for this plan had already been set by Roosevelt's ingenious fiscal sleight of hand "to get rid of this silly, foolish dollar sign" by lending the British whatever arms and supplies they needed under a lend-lease bill.[2] It had been fought through Congress against the vociferous opposition of the isolationists, and by March was passed into law.

America's increasing commitment to Britain, however, produced growing German pressure on Japan to launch a diversionary attack against British territory in the Far East. To assure Hitler that this was Tokyo's intention, the pro-Axis foreign minister, Yosuke Matsuoka, undertook the long trans-Siberian railway trip to Berlin in April. He left without being told that Prime Minister Konoye was engaged in a conflicting secret diplomatic initiative to reach an accord with the United States, aimed at nipping in the bud a potential Anglo-American alliance in the Far East.

Konoye's highly unorthodox diplomatic maneuver had begun stealthily in December 1940 with the recruitment of two Roman Catholic priests, Bishop James E. Walsh and Father James M. Drought, of the Maryknoll Mission. While they had been visiting Tokyo just before Christmas 1940, their isolationist anti-Roosevelt sympathies had been skillfully played upon by Colonel Takeo Iwakuro of the military affairs bureau and Tadeo Ikawa, a banker and confidant of Konoye. By the time they left Tokyo the priests had become committed to undertaking a two-man private peace mission whose objective was to strike a deal with Washington that would facilitate Konoye's schemes for a "new order" in Asia without the invoking of American economic reprisals.

Since Japan relied on the United States for more than 90 percent of her oil needs, Konoye's initiative was given a special urgency in January 1941 after Secretary of State Hull threatened her with extensive economic reprisals if Japan went any further toward extending herself in the western Pacific by force of arms. Drought and Walsh returned home to enlist the sympathetic consideration of Postmaster General Frank C. Walker, the leading Roman Catholic in Roosevelt's administration.

Not until the arrival of Admiral Nomura was Walker able to persuade the secretary of state to consider secret negotiations with the new Japanese ambassador. These negotiations were to be based on a "draft understanding" prepared by the two priests that purported to rationalize Japan's aggression in China. This document, which the State Department dubbed the "John Doe Memorandum" was ostensibly formulated by Drought and Walsh. But it had actually been drafted in consultation with Colonel Iwakuro, who had followed them back from Japan in the role of an "adviser" to Nomura.

The intercepted communications of Japan's military attaché in Washington, which were not decoded until the middle of the war, reveal the extent to which Drought and Walsh—who were referred to as John Doe by the State Department—were being manipulated by Konoye's aides and by Taro Terasaki, Japan's spymaster in Washington. "We decided, therefore, first to feel our way from behind the scenes," the military attaché reported from the Washington embassy on 16 April 1941: "In this respect Iwakuro and Ikawa were assigned to sounding out the contacts we made in December [i.e., Walsh, Drought, and Walker] and then have the ambassador confirm the results obtained."[3]

Consistent with Konoye's demands for utmost secrecy, a series of evening meetings took place in late March for which the portly Ambassador Nomura smuggled himself in and out of Secretary Hull's Carlton Hotel suite through the service entrance. These clandestine sessions appeared to Nomura, at least, to have made such progress toward resolving issues that by 16 April he reported enthusiastically to Konoye that an accord was imminent.

The ambassador's optimism was also reflected in that day's report by Japan's military attaché, which acknowledged encouragement given Japan by Charles Lindbergh and his isolationist friends with their antiwar rallies. As a result of their assistance Roosevelt was thought to be "bowing to the pressure" of public opinion.[4] The intercepted communications reveal frequent contacts by leaders of the isolationist lobby with Japanese and Germans, as well as the surprising extent to which the celebrated aviator hero was subject to the influence of intermediaries in the pay of Berlin and Tokyo.[5]

The reports from Washington combined to persuade Konoye that the "John Doe Memorandum" of understanding had been accepted as a basis for opening negotiations. Japan's premier was simply deluding himself. Since the memorandum proposed that the United States recognize Japanese authority over a large part of China, and pressure Chiang Kai-shek to accept a peace treaty, it was dismissed by Secretary Hull as "much less accommodating than we had been led to believe it would be and all that the most ardent Japanese imperialist could want."[6] The State Department's counterproposal was a four-point American demand that Japan respect the territorial integrity of China, support the open-door principle of equal commercial opportunity, abide by the status quo in the western Pacific, and detach herself from the tripartite pact. Hull's "Four Principles," as these demands came to be known, ran diametrically counter to Konoye's proposals.

The rosy April twilight that flooded into Hull's hotel suite during their clandestine evening sessions suffused the conversations between the two men with warm feelings for one another, which disguised the extent of the gulf that separated Tokyo and Washington. Nomura's advancing deafness and his painful determination to maintain cordial relations led him to overstress American willingness to negotiate on the basis of the "draft understanding." For his part, Hull failed to appreciate that Tokyo's pact with Hitler and Mussolini was a major stumbling block, or just how in-

transigent Japan's army leadership was over the China issue. With the
fire-breathing Matsuoka in Berlin cementing Tokyo's alignment with Nazi
Germany at the same time, our State Department was receiving conflicting signals.

After Nomura's early optimistic reports, Konoye hoped to reach an
agreement with Washington before Matsuoka's return to Tokyo resulted
in his pressure for a closer alliance with Germany. But these hopes
foundered when the army refused any concessions over the China issue
and the foreign minister came back with promises to keep to Hitler, plus
a neutrality pact with the Soviet Union. "Japan can straighten out the Far
East and Germany will handle Europe," Stalin had promised the diminutive Matsuoka at Moscow's central station. "Later, together all of us will
deal with America."[7]

After forty years, documents have emerged from the declassified American archives that shed new light on the events of 1941. One of the most
significant must be a Japanese radio intercept of 11 December 1940—not
decrypted until 1945—which reveals an astonishing Axis intelligence coup
that undoubtedly helped precipitate Japan down the road to Pearl Harbor.[8]

The capture of a British steamer in the Indian Ocean by a German
surface raider on 11 November has been a hitherto overlooked incident.
But now its consequences can be seen to have had an important impact
on Tokyo's foreign policy. Although the tripartite pact had been signed in
September, Japan was still hesitant to provide Hitler with all the assistance he was asking for to take the naval war against Britain into the
Far East. Supply ships for the German raiders had been operating from
Japanese ports but the foreign minister wanted far closer cooperation
with Hitler. In this Matsuoka had the support of Nobutake Kondo, vice-
chief of the imperial naval general staff, who forcefully argued that since
the German navy, only one tenth the size of the British, had succeeded in
taking over Norway, then the Japanese navy, with its superior odds, had
little to fear from the Anglo-American fleet in a southward move against
the Netherlands East Indies.

Kondo urged that Prime Minister Konoye must now "openly embrace
the Axis powers."[9] The German naval attaché to Japan reported on 13
September that "a transformation has taken place in the views of fleet
commander in chief Yamamoto, who until now has always taken a pro-
Anglo-Saxon attitude." Rear Admiral Paul Wenneker, an astute observer
of Tokyo politics, ascribed the change to "the continually worsening relations with the USA and the tremendous armament program they have
initiated over there." Wenneker, therefore, predicted Japan would "resolve Far Eastern problems before this has been completed."[10] Hitler
pressured Japan for a more pro-German policy in the Far East, especially
for assistance with commerce raiding on British ships. On 14 November

1940 Admiral Erich Raeder, commander in chief of the German navy, summoned Admiral Yoshikazu Endo, Japan's naval attaché in Berlin, and urged him to cooperate in the submarine war in the Atlantic, bases in the mandates "for use in secret replenishment and repairs of warships operating in the Pacific," and "intelligence regarding movements" of British warships and merchantmen.[11]

Despite Endo's cautioning Tokyo that it would be "advantageous" to give assistance "in utmost secrecy to German naval operations," the naval staff was still uncertain about throwing in its lot with the Axis. They tactfully refused to send submarines into the Atlantic while requesting detailed German plans for secret bases in the Marshalls. But they enthusiastically offered to share intelligence information "to foster the exchange between navies."[12]

The true extent of Japanese assistance to the German commerce-raiding operations in the Pacific is still disputed because "the extent of the help given the German navy is wrapped in a veil of deep secrecy," according to *Senshi Sōsho*, Japan's official war history. "Whatever cooperation between the Japanese and German navies may have been, however, it is certain that it was not such as to have had great effect," it asserts. But this "official" denial is belied by captured German naval records. They reveal that after the fall of 1940 the Kriegsmarine's armed merchant cruisers were regularly using bases in the Marianas, Carolines, and Marshalls for refit and supply.[13]

For the first time, with the release of the Japanese naval attaché intercepts, it is possible to document how close this cooperation must have been, because it brought Tokyo an intelligence bonanza that included Royal Navy and British merchant ship ciphers, in addition to top-secret war cabinet papers detailing the parlous state of Britain's Far East defenses.[14]

This priceless information was discovered in the sixty packets of confidential government mail that the British steamer *Automedon* was carrying from London to Singapore when she was captured by the German raider *Atlantis* on 11 November 1940. The importance of the secret mail was at once appreciated by the intelligence officer of Schiff 16, as the armed merchantman was code-named. At a rendezvous in the mandates it was transferred from *Atlantis* to the Norwegian prize supply ship *Ole Jacob*—contrary to international law, which prohibited regular use of neutral ports by warships. *Ole Jacob* arrived in Kōbe on 4 December when her Norwegian crew was removed in the dead of night to German liner *Scharnhorst* to prevent its contacting any Allied agents and telling of the *Automedon*'s capture.[15]

Couriers from the German consulate general in Kōbe accompanied the large chest of top-secret British documents to Tokyo, and, on 9 December, Admiral Wenneker, the naval attaché, skimmed through them. He at once appreciated the explosive significance of the minutes of a

British war cabinet meeting on the Far East that had been held on 15 August 1940. The papers were sent off that afternoon by special courier to Berlin after Wenneker radioed a summary by a top-secret Enigma cipher that was never cracked by the British.

The importance of the papers as Wenneker read them was that Churchill's cabinet had decided that the British were "unable to send a fleet to the Far East," and so "must avoid 'open clash' with Japan" until military cooperation with the United States was assured. The British would not go to war even if Japan attacked Thailand or Indochina. Instead, efforts would be made to buy off Tokyo with "general concessions"—including abandoning Singapore and making a deal over Malaya.[16]

Four days later, after the material had been evaluated by the naval staff in Berlin, the British documents were passed to the Japanese naval attaché in Germany. He summarized their contents in an 11 December message to Tokyo. Next morning Wenneker handed copies to members of the Japanese naval staff, whose reaction was one of "extraordinary interest."[17] That evening Admiral Kondo sent for the German naval attaché and repeatedly expressed his thanks for such priceless intelligence.

It was not that Japan did not know about the defenselessness of Singapore, but now they were sure that the British government had committed itself to a policy of appeasement if Tokyo stepped up the diplomatic pressure. This sensational intelligence reduced many of Japan's uncertainties about how to proceed with their strategic and diplomatic plans for realization of their "new order" in southeast Asia. Konoye now saw the possibility that diplomacy alone could achieve this goal; but only if an Anglo-American Far East alliance could be prevented. The Japanese navy could then prepare for its southward advance with no opposition from the weak British and Dutch forces. The strength of the Combined Fleet could instead be directed to dealing with the United States Pacific Fleet, when and where it suited Japan.

Konoye's secret diplomacy was intended to drive a wedge between Great Britain and the United States. His plan survived its first test when Churchill responded to the increasingly chill winds blowing from Tokyo by cabling Roosevelt on 15 February that there were "drifting straws" indicating "Japanese intentions to make war on us."[18] His fear was that Australia might be invaded by a Japanese war machine fueled by the oil from the Dutch East Indies. During the round of ABC-1 (American-British-Canadian) staff talks that month in Washington, however, Admiral Stark repeatedly rejected Churchill's call for American warships in Singapore.

General George C. Marshall concurred. Such a move would have been a concession to General Douglas MacArthur's repeated pleas to reinforce the Philippines. The chief of the army was convinced that to reverse the twenty-year-old U.S. policy not to make major defense commitments west of Hawaii would be "a strategic error of the first magnitude."[19] Thus British alarms that Japan was about to move into the East Indies to invade Australia failed to bring about a joint defensive alliance because Roosevelt was advised that their loss, together with that of the Philippines, could be "absorbed without leading to final disaster."[20]

Churchill next sought to tie Britain's Far East interests to those of the United States. He urged Roosevelt to issue a formal declaration that any attack on British or Dutch territory would bring the United States to their defense. This would "inspire the Japanese with fear of a double war."[21] But the president shied away. He needed the backing of American public opinion and his cabinet for such strong talk, and he had neither. Roosevelt, who had deliberately not told Churchill about Nomura's overtures, advised Hull to temporize in the clandestine April meetings and agreed with the secretary of state's suggestion that the navy embark on a series of flag-waving cruises in the Pacific.

Talking softly and carrying a big stick might have worked for Theodore Roosevelt at the turn of the century when our fleet outnumbered Japan's, but four decades later Ambassador Grew was soon warning that a show of naval strength in the Pacific could only increase the risk of war. Admiral Stark reminded the president in February that "the Pacific Fleet is now weaker in total tonnage and aircraft than the Japanese navy."[22] Nevertheless, the president insisted that a squadron of four cruisers be sent to show the flag in Australian waters, and in April he wanted to dispatch another force "to keep them popping up here and there, and keep the Japs guessing."[23] This put additional demands on the Pacific Fleet, whose value as a deterrent was also threatened by the urgent need to reinforce the Atlantic. What Stark termed the "many conflicting and strong cross currents and tide rips" in the policy debate in Washington alerted Kimmel that he might soon lose three of his battleships and their escorts in order to bolster Admiral Ernest J. King's forces on the other side of the globe.

As the Pacific Fleet's commander in chief, Kimmel vigorously protested the proposed reduction of one quarter of his strength. Stark replied that the situation was "critical in the Atlantic," but the president felt that the Far East situation also was sufficiently critical. Therefore, Stark settled for the transfer of only a single cruiser and one destroyer division. He wanted to avoid giving "any signs of seriously weakening the forces in the Pacific" until the outcome of Matsuoka's Berlin visit and Japan's intervention in Indochina became clearer.[24]

That the president and his chiefs of staff were planning a further reduction in Pacific Fleet strength to meet the worsening situation in the Atlantic was not simply because of their commitment to the "Europe first" strategy. When that decision had been made in April, they were also taking account of Nomura's secret negotiations. Although no one in the administration was under any illusion that Tokyo was holding forth an olive branch, the twig proffered by the genial ambassador was at least a sign that the slide to all-out confrontation in the Pacific might be averted by some skillful diplomatic footwork.

The prospect of a thaw in relations between Tokyo and Washington lulled the navy and army staffs in Washington into making a fatal error. Only three months earlier the possibility of a surprise enemy strike at Pearl Harbor had persuaded Admiral Turner and the chief of naval operations to press the war department to approve a plan of "joint readiness for immediate action in defense against surprise attacks."[25] But by April, the director of war plans appears to have revised his strategic opinions.

The about-face by Turner began when he met with Nomura on 12 March and received the ambassador's assurances "against further aggressive moves by the military forces of Japan."[26] Then on 3 April he received an army staff report which painted a very reassuring picture of the strength of our Pacific defenses. According to the army planners, "due to its fortification, its garrison and its physical characteristics," Oahu was claimed "to be the strongest fortress in the world."[27] Sabotage, according to the army, was the main threat to Pearl Harbor because, they predicted, "with adequate air defense, enemy carriers, naval escorts and transports will begin to come under air attack at a distance of approximately 750 miles."[28] Such a forecast was wildly optimistic when the Hawaiian command at the time could muster only a handful of ob-. solescent bombers against an attacking enemy fleet—and none had the range to operate so far from shore. Turner evidently chose to ignore this potentially fatal piece of wishful thinking, nor was it raised by General Marshall when Stimson and he reviewed Pearl Harbor's defenses with Roosevelt in their White House meeting of 24 April.

The chief of staff of the army assured the president that Hawaii was impregnable, whether there were any ships left there or not; that land defense was amply sufficient, together with the air defense, to keep off the Japanese; and that the air defense "could always be reinforced from the mainland of America."[29] How, someone might have wondered, would an island fortress be reinforced and supplied without control of the sea?

Kimmel, however, was not made privy to this astonishing piece of military hyperbole. There was no mention of it in any of the confidential letters he was receiving from Admiral Stark—or he would have been the first to demolish Washington's false premise. He would certainly have responded to the concerns about the security of the fleet, which were raised by Stark's letter of 4 April alerting him to the "tremendous issues at stake," which "at any moment would precipitate action," because "just what the Oriental *really* plans, none of us can be sure."[30]

Yet because we were not being sent any diplomatic Magic, neither Kimmel nor I had any way of knowing what dire intelligence prompted Washington's fears. The chief of naval operations was not merely failing to provide information, but was resorting to platitudes to refer to insoluble strategic dilemmas. Furthermore, Kimmel found himself in the unenviable position of a fleet commander who would be stripped of ships should war break out in the Atlantic.

"I do not know that we have missed anything, but if there is any doubt as to whose responsibility it is to keep the commander-in-chief fully informed with pertinent reports on subjects that should be of interest to the fleet," he had already written to Stark on 18 February, "will you kindly fix that responsibility so that there will be no misunderstanding?"[31]

Kimmel's postscript had reminded Stark to ensure we received "information of a secret nature." In the light of subsequent events, Stark's response, "ONI is fully aware of its responsibility in keeping you adequately informed," turned out to be a hollow assertion.[32] Kimmel was justfiably uneasy despite Washington's assurance. He repeatedly asked me whether I thought that we were receiving all the diplomatic intelligence available to Washington, and I agreed to make my own personal efforts to find out.

I took the matter up directly with my opposite number in the navy department. On 11 March, I penned a personal letter for hand-delivery by courier to my former boss and old associate from the Tokyo embassy, Commander McCollum who was then head of the Far East Section in ONI. I frankly expressed my concern and Kimmel's belief that we were being shortchanged on diplomatic intelligence and urged him to make sure that he sent us intercepted Japanese traffic on a regular basis. As the political situation with Japan was becoming increasingly tense, I also suggested to McCollum that Station Hypo be allowed to retain two of its most experienced Japanese language officers who were "doing exceptionally well," but were coming due for sea duty.

More than a month went by before I received his "Dear Eddie" letter by locked courier pouch on the Pan Am Clipper. Despite its amicable tone, McCollum gave what amounted to a stinging formal brush-off to both my requests. Washington, he maintained, was responsible for "evaluating the political situation" and "matters of security, et cetera, which would be very difficult to solve" made it impractical to send us diplomatic intercepts. As he put it:

> I should think that forces afloat should, in general, confine themselves to the estimates of the strategic and tactical situations with which they will be confronted when the time of action arrives. The material you mention can necessarily have but passing and transient interest as action in the political sphere is determined by the government as a whole and not by the forces afloat.[33]

Washington's decision that diplomatic intelligence was "none of Pearl Harbor's business" was to have fatal repercussions eight months later.

7

"On the Mat"

IN SPITE OF THE REBUFF I received from Washington to my request for diplomatic intelligence, my hopes that it would now be possible to get the full intelligence picture for Admiral Kimmel were raised on 15 May when my longtime friend Joe Rochefort arrived at Pearl Harbor to relieve Tom Birtley as head of Station Hypo. I could not have wished for a better and more understanding colleague in a difficult situation.

My opportunity for close cooperation with Station Hypo at Pearl Harbor had been facilitated in April when Kimmel moved his headquarters ashore from the crowded cabin space in flagship *Pennsylvania*. Cincpac offices were established at the submarine base, on the second deck of the headquarters building. Our office windows looked out on the sub pens below and over to Ford Island with its majestic line of steel dreadnoughts moored at Battleship Row. Across Southeast Loch was the comint nerve center for the Pacific Fleet, housed in the Fourteenth Naval District headquarters building at the naval shipyard. Rochefort was therefore nominally under Admiral Bloch's command, but had special orders also to report direct to Admiral Kimmel.

I visited Rochefort's shop whenever possible, to sound out his opinion and keep abreast of the latest code-breaking developments. Such opportunities were not as frequent as I would have liked, because Kimmel, even after his own headquarters were set up ashore, spent a lot of time at sea. I was shown how the intercepts would be submitted first to traffic analysis by Lieutenant Thomas A. Huckins, my naval academy classmate, or Lieutenant John A. Williams. From its external attributes—the sender of the message and the call sign of its addressee as well as any radio direction-finding information on the transmission—these two officers distilled observations about Japanese naval activities, which were delivered to me each day in summary form.

After traffic analysis, the intercepts were sorted for duplication before being examined to recover additives, code entries, and plain language. The sheets were also scanned for any errors or repetitions made by Japanese radio operators that might aid in our cryptanalysis. The place was jammed with tables of every kind filled with boxes of punched cards and printouts that spewed forth from a row of IBM tabulating machines. These electromechanical sorting devices, the precursors of the modern computer, had somehow been acquired since 1936 by Tommy Dyer, Rochefort's quiet but determined second in command, who ranked as the navy's foremost officer cryptanalyst.

In the interest of security, Rochefort insisted that Hypo's official designation be changed from Communications to Combat Intelligence Unit. When his staff was moved to the underground basement of the headquarters building that summer, an armed guard was posted at its only entrance. "The dungeon" as it was known, did not even have windows, and the air-conditioning system was notoriously temperamental. In the months before war broke out Joe was constantly battling technical problems such as the lack of a teleprinter line to their radio receiving station. Couriers, sometimes even Rochefort himself, had to make the thirty-mile drive to Heeia to collect the intercepted Japanese radio messages. Not until the radio masts were relocated to a site on the west side of Oahu in 1942 was this hand-carried system remedied.

The lack of an adequate and rapid communications link between Oahu, Midway, Samoa, and Dutch Harbor also plagued the operation of the mid-Pacific radio direction-finding (D/F) network, which also came under Rochefort's command. He had complained to Washington that "poor apparatus and lack of suitable control facilities" made our D/F "the weak point of our Communication Intelligence set up." The Pacific D/F capability was so inadequate that Washington had made arrangements with Pan American Airways to requisition their network of stations in the event of war.[1]

The poor performance of Pearl Harbor's direction finding was particularly worrisome because it was the only means we had of pinpointing the movement of Japanese naval vessels while Hypo was still laboring to break into their flag officers cipher. Although a Red machine had been sent out to Hypo, it was not utilized because there was no local traffic in this diplomatic code. Much more serious was that the Purple machine originally destined for Pearl Harbor had been diverted in January to the British. It became part of a trade involving top-secret information in which we received the keys to the German Enigma cipher. Then to add insult to injury, the Royal Navy code breakers in Singapore turned over all their recoveries in the five-numeral system to the Asiatic Fleet. This was especially galling since Station Cast had received a Purple machine. Until 5 March, when the British made the delivery of the keys to unlock JN-25 to Cavite, OP-20-G had retained exclusive right to work on the JN-25 operational code.[2]

When Station Cast informed Washington that they now intended to make JN-25 their first priority, there was a twofold objection. They were told by OP-20-G that their cryptographic unit "was not sufficiently supplied with the necessary statistical machinery," and that it had been intended to "transfer this attack to Pearl Harbor in July."[3] But Cast's claim prevailed over Hypo's. On 24 April, Hypo was the information addressee of a dispatch instructing the rival unit that it should concentrate on breaking the current JN-25 cipher, and that "project will not be transferred to fourteenth as previously planned."[4] Rochefort's arrival at Hypo a month later raised hopes that he might win a reprieve from their fruitless slog against the Japanese flag officers code. But this was dashed by a 2 May order from Washington that his unit would continue exclusively on the admirals system, or AD, as the flag officers code was designated.

The net result of Washington's code-breaking trade with the British was frustration for Rochefort and the navy's best cryptanalysts: Dyer and Wright. It was also ultimately to prove disastrous for the Pacific Fleet. For nine more months the Hypo team would obediently beat their heads against the stone wall of the Japanese admirals code with negative results. They were also cut out of direct access to Japan's high-level diplomatic traffic. There were comparatively few exchanges between Washington and Cast on the dedicated radio network on which the navy's three cryptographic centers swapped technical information using a secure cipher system code-named Copek. Nor was Hypo provided with the current keys for the "J" series of transposition ciphers which were used for the most secret communications by Japan's consulates. The only Japanese diplomatic systems that Rochefort's outfit was equipped for were the low-grade ciphers designated "PA-K2" and "LA," used for routine "housekeeping" traffic.

Just how badly Washington had goofed in dividing its cryptographic resources would become apparent after 7 December 1941. The frantic search for missed radio intelligence clues to the Japanese attack revealed that many of them were contained in the J-19 cipher used by Japan's consul in Honolulu to send Tokyo an ever-increasing flow of ships-in-harbor reports. But even these could not be decrypted by Hypo cryptanalysts only fifteen miles away. Because of the priority given to the Purple traffic in Washington, they had been accumulated unread and for the most part unbroken.

The decision to give the Asiatic Fleet priority over Pearl Harbor for one of the precious hand-built Purple machines reflected Washington's belief that the Philippines were more exposed to the Japanese threat, as well as better placed to intercept Tokyo's radio signals. But the denial of access to Hypo of the main Japanese operational cipher which resulted from the wrangling over JN-25 was a major blunder. With all the other pressures on the cryptanalysts at Washington and Cavite, the JN-25B system was never—as far as our navy was concerned—to yield more than a partial readability before war broke out.[5]

As we shall see, the intelligence that might have been extracted from JN-25 could have been instrumental in forestalling Japan's attack. By the middle of 1941 it had become the Japanese navy's principal operational system. We now know that the "A" version had become readable in little more than a year. Less than five months after being authorized to tackle the "B" version, Rochefort's team was reading enough of the messages to be able to predict the Japanese plan to invade Midway.

If Hypo had set to work on JN-25 as originally intended in July, it is probable that the cipher could have been penetrated in time—especially with the cooperation of the cryptanalysts at Cavite and Singapore—for the course of history to have been changed. This could be why the various Pearl Harbor inquiries dealt only with our ability to read the Purple traffic, and avoided all but the vaguest references to JN-25. It could also explain why not a single American or British JN-25 decrypt made in 1941 has yet been declassified—despite repeated official requests made by the authors and other historians in Washington and London.

At the time, neither Rochefort nor I realized the extent to which Hypo's cryptanalytic resources were being squandered for the greater part of 1941. We received hints from new arrivals from Washington of the huge successes that had been achieved with Japan's diplomatic ciphers. Too late it became clear that the Pacific Fleet's access to important intelligence about our potential enemy had fallen hostage to the running feud that flared and sputtered in the navy department that spring and summer. But it should have been apparent from the decision to put Rochefort in charge of Hypo. Assigning the only naval officer who was fully qualified in both Japanese and cryptanalysis to Pearl Harbor, with the promise of a handpicked team, was an attempt by his old colleague Commander Safford to give the fleet an independent access to radio intelligence, free of the navy department feuding.

Later I was astonished to discover the true extent of the interdepartmental warfare. It actually threatened the second deck of the navy department building in Washington with an incipient mutiny because of the discontent of certain communications and intelligence officers. It shaped the climate of hostility in which intelligence went unevaluated and the special needs of the Pacific Fleet to be kept informed were submerged in furious personal rivalries.

The conflict and jealousy that soured the spring air on Constitution Avenue were not caused by the old feud between the offices of naval communications and naval intelligence for control of the code-breaking product. That had finally been settled. The previous fall Admiral Stark had written an administrative directive that set out, for the first time, the responsibilities of the sections that made up the office of naval operations. The CNO staff manual of 23 November 1940 required that the director of naval communications (OP-20) had to defer to the director of naval intelligence (OP-16), who was charged with securing "all classes of pertinent information pertaining to naval and maritime matters."[6]

The products of OP-20-G's code breaking were therefore clearly "pertinent information" which ONI was authorized to "*evaluate* and disseminate as advisable [emphasis added]."[7] But no sooner had this conflict of interests been settled than a new area of contention appeared. The gauntlet was thrown down by Rear Admiral Richmond Kelly Turner, the recently appointed director of war plans (OP-12), whose own duties were already so extensive that they were divided into two sections—one for "preparing war and operational plans," and the other for developing policies and projects in support of those plans—in addition to preparing directives on a wide range of subjects. Nowhere in Stark's memorandum was there any mention that the war plans division was to evaluate and disseminate intelligence, although both were important collateral considerations in planning for war.[8]

Stark's solomonic division of his staff's authority had not suited Turner, who had been personally selected with promotion to admiral as "the right man" to head the most important section in the navy department.[9] At fifty-five, Turner finally found himself close to becoming the heir apparent to the job of ultimate naval authority, to which he had aspired since he graduated fifth in the 1908 class at Annapolis. Lean and quick-acting and over six feet tall, he cut an imposing figure, with lantern jaw and beetling black brows that gave him a Mephistophelean aspect. Turner was intimidating both in appearance and personality.

"Abrasive as a file" was how a junior navy department officer described the new director of war plans.[10] Turner's competitiveness, which had made him a model midshipman, left him always resentful of having failed to win top place at Annapolis. This drove him to dominate his equals and bitterly resent anyone who opposed him. A relentless taskmaster, he was called "Terrible Turner" behind his back, with good reason.

Stark, however, called him "invaluable,"[11] which provides the best clue to the relationship that Turner quickly established with the chief of naval operations. By relieving Stark of memorandum writing and detailed staff work, he was valued for being a determined "fixer" when it came to getting things pushed through the slothfully bureaucratic peacetime navy department.

Turner was the navy's Patton. They both possessed that amalgam of military brilliance, opinionated paranoia, and instinctive courage that leads men into enemy gunfire; but their immoderate self-assertion soured cooperation down the ladder of command. Like many men supremely confident of their own abilities, Turner made no point of trying to make people like him, but commanded a high degree of respect by the manner in which he had mastered his profession.[12]

Turner had little knowledge of the intelligence process, but rated himself an expert on Japan after visiting Tokyo and the Yokosuka naval base in 1939 as captain of the cruiser *Astoria,* which had borne home the ashes of Ambassador Hiroshi Saito. But as soon as he moved into the war plans division, despite Stark's demarcating memorandum, he conceived it to be the function of war plans to give "the major strategic overall picture for the use of my superiors and disseminate that."[13]

Turner was tapped for flag rank by the December 1940 selection board. But he became the kind of admiral "who could not come ashore in a launch without giving detailed orders to the coxwain."[14] It was the same with intelligence. Although he had no experience in evaluation, the new director of war plans assumed his judgment was superior to the ONI staff's when it came to analyzing and interpreting strategic information. He maintained that the officers in his division were "more experienced than the officers in naval intelligence who generally were more junior, and were trained rather [sic] for the collection and dissemination of information, rather than its application to a strategic situation."[15]

Within a month of his becoming head of war plans, Turner's forceful presentation of his case persuaded Stark to issue a second 1940 Alnav (instruction to all ships and stations) that further undercut ONI's authority: "Certain evaluations can only be made by competent specialists beyond the ability of the division of naval intelligence."[16] The director of war plans then moved swiftly to take advantage of the interregnum existing in ONI when Captain Jules J. James became acting director in December 1940.

James naturally resented the encroachment on his turf. So in addition to preparing the series of fortnightly global naval intelligence summaries that were frequently out of date before they reached the fleet by mail, James continued issuing a weekly digest by radio. This brought Turner storming into his office to demand that "ONI make no estimate of prospective enemy intentions to CNO, but furnish information to war plans who would make the required estimate." James icily reminded him that "existing printed organization instructions of CNO required Intelligence to make these estimates."[17]

This was the kind of interference that the aggressive Turner could not brook. He wanted to do all the roaring and not be roared at by anybody. But he was temporarily diverted from counterattacking by the preparations for the ABC-1 staff talks. In February he returned to the offensive and without any reference to ONI issued a dispatch that predicted that the Japanese were going north to invade Siberia. This forecast contrasted with the latest bulletin sent out by the head of the ONI Far East desk. Captain McCollum's estimate pointed toward a forthcoming Japanese move south into Indochina.

Turner sent for the head of the Far East section to demand an explanation and apology. "I think I made him rather angry when I suggested that maybe he was privy to some intelligence that I certainly didn't have," McCollum recalled of the confrontation, which brought instructions "that hereafter War Plans would do all the evaluating of probable

enemy intentions and that we had to be particularly careful that the director of war plans got all the pertinent information."[18]

An appeal was made to Stark, who according to McCollum accepted
that "it was the function of ONI to talk about intentions; it was in the
manual." But "he thought that in the interests of coordination, Turner
was the man to do the coordinating."[19] Since Turner was already overex-
tended in his duties, he set up what amounted to his own three-man
intelligence section. But the officers he appointed were as inexperienced
as he was in evaluating information. All they did was beat a path down
the corridor to ONI offices, pick the brains of intelligence people, and
carry the word back to Turner, who began distributing his own digests
and summaries.

It was "a futile business" for the officers in ONI. They resented that
Turner's coordinating role enabled him "to keep his hand on our gullets"
and maintain a stranglehold on their output.[20] This was the situation in
March when the battle flared again with the arrival of the forceful new
director of ONI, Captain Alan C. Kirk. Fresh from the exhilarating duty
of monitoring the real war as naval attaché in London, Kirk had been
impressed by the effective meshing of the British navy's intelligence and
war planning organizations in the Combined Operations Intelligence Cen-
tre. He saw no reason why such a joint unit should not be set up in
Washington.

Turner, too, saw the potential of such a clearinghouse for intelligence—but he wanted to run the whole show. The director of war plans
also had the advantage both of rank and of access to Stark's ear, plus the
support of CNO's pliant deputy, Rear Admiral Royal E. Ingersoll.

"Kirk wasn't any weak sister," according to McCollum. "He immediately went in to bat, and he and Turner were on the mat all the time.
The DNI was fighting to maintain the integrity of his section, but losing
out. Every time he'd go in to bat, he'd strike out on it."[21] For the entire
eight months that Kirk remained captain of the ONI team, the struggle
with war plans was to flare and sputter with all the embittered rivalry of a
grudge match, sown by personal venom.

"There was some harassment in this office of mine," Kirk would later
concede with remarkable understatement, "because we had charge of
what was called Magic."[22] So while ONI and war plans battled for control of strategic intelligence, Rear Admiral Leigh Noyes, the communications chief, claimed responsibility for disseminating the actual intelligence
to its limited circle of recipients in the navy department and White
House. Noyes required all his good nature to cope with Turner, who
would often bark his complaints about Noyes "and his God-damn secrets."[23]

When Turner bullheadedly began preparing his own intelligence estimates and sending them out—according to McCollum "without reference
to or consideration by ONI at all"—a showdown with Kirk became inev-

itable. The shootout for control of the intelligence function took place in April 1941. After listening to the stormy confrontation in his office, Ingersoll took the antagonists to Stark where "the points at issue were reviewed." Kirk maintained that "the office of naval intelligence was responsible for interpreting possible enemy intentions after evaluating information received from whatever source." He argued that ONI was "comparable to G-2 in the war department general staff in these respects, and should likewise prepare that section of a formal estimate known as Enemy Intention."[24]

Turner contested this. He argued that "war plans division should prepare such sections of the estimate and should interpret and evaluate *all* information concerning possible hostile nations from *whatever* source received."[25] In a monumental overstatement of the war plans division's role, he insisted that ONI "was solely a collecting agency and a distributing agency, and was not charged with sending out any information which would initiate any operations on the part of the fleet, or fleets anywhere."[26]

Stark had no stomach for refereeing a knock-down drag-out fight on his staff. His exterior affability concealed the fact that he was a shrewd member of the president's inner circle. He had been friends with Roosevelt since 1914 when, as a junior captain, he had demonstrated his independence by tactfully refusing the then assistant secretary of the navy's attempt to navigate his destroyer off the rocky Maine coast. Pink-cheeked, with a mop of white hair, Stark looked like a superannuated schoolboy. His administrative ability and powers of persuasion had won support on Capitol Hill for the president's soaring naval budgets, and he was an astute manipulator in staff conferences. But "Betty" Stark lacked the stern fiber necessary for a battle commander. Secretary of War Stimson regarded him as "a timid and ineffective man to be in the post he holds."[27]

Stark, however, was not so much dominated as impressed with Turner's genuine abilities, which he had demonstrated by reworking Stark's original "Dog" memorandum into the full-fledged Rainbow 5 war plan. Given Stark's admiration for Turner, he had every reason therefore to resolve the feud in the war plans division's favor by fudging the original demarcations that he had established earlier. He therefore let it be known that he had "approved the position" taken by the director of war plans. Kirk had no choice but to admit defeat, and "so advised my principal chiefs."[28]

It was also typical of Stark, the compromiser, that he carefully avoided publicizing his volte-face over the control of communications by revising the staff manual. This created a dangerous area for confusion about responsibility for disseminating directives, which was later described by Turner's official biographer as "an administrative error."[29] It also gave Turner the opportunity to shirk blame for the intelligence failures that left the door wide open for the Japanese attack on Pearl Harbor.

In later years, the maneuvering to avoid responsibility for Pearl Harbor was not confined to the highest levels of the navy department. It extended right down the chain of command. For example, I retained a copy of the 1940 manual titled *ONI 11* that described in detail the function of intelligence. From time to time changes and updates were made and one day in 1944, the fleet's publications officer, a Lieutenant Bidwell, came around saying he had changes for the ONI manual. It was stored in my safe. He made the changes, and I put it back in the safe without examining it, as I was busy at the time. Sometime later I opened it and found that the entire section having to do with "duties and responsibilities" of ONI and fleet intelligence officers had been removed, and no new pages had been added. There no longer was anything on that subject in the manual, and one day in 1943 Bidwell had evidently been acting on instructions from the navy department.

I asked Bidwell about replacement pages. He said none were furnished. I sent him out to see if, by chance, some ship had not yet entered the changes, so I could get the old pages before they were burned (as ours had been). We searched high and low, trying to find one copy, but failed. During the 1945 congressional investigation on Pearl Harbor, where a central issue was who bore the responsibility for the intelligence function, what had previously been on those blank pages could have been important evidence for countering Turner's charges of shirking of responsibility.

When I was called to testify, I originally intended to raise the WE WE cipher affair and the neglect of Japan's fortification of the mandates. The surly CNO message and Kimmel's reply were a good example of how Washington had failed to properly carry out the intelligence function in mid-1941. But I was told by the Judge Advocate General's Office, which previewed my case, that I could not introduce data going back beyond July 1941. This decision, I believe, is another example of the extent to which the navy department went to try to conceal its sorry role in the debacle that overtook the fleet on 7 December.

Certainly Turner had plenty to conceal. He was vehemently unforgiving of officers who defied him. He continued to harass Kirk as he tried to turn ONI into nothing more than an intelligence drop-box. By May 1941 the increasing interference of war plans in what ONI officers regarded as their prerogative in intelligence matters caused deep resentment. One of the fortnightly summaries on which Kirk had handwritten "In my view the Japs will jump pretty soon" had been returned from "coordination" by war plans with the bold scrawl, "I don't think that the Japs are going to jump now or ever! R.K.T."[30]

Turner's confidence in his exclusive ability to forecast Japan's moves, while they provoked Kirk and McCollum to fury, were apparently being taken seriously by the Asiatic Fleet commander. "If Japan starts a war in the immediate future it will be against Russia," Admiral Thomas C. Hart reported back in a dispatch of 25 June.[31] "Success against Russia will be necessary before Japan makes an advance to the south."[32] Kirk ordered his Far East section to invite Hart's attention to a list of the latest intelligence that indicated that if Japan moved it would be southward, not north. "Consider your analysis not now justified in view of these factors," he ended his dispatch—to which Turner appended a petulant "But this does not rule it out as an eventuality."[33]

Such pronouncements vitiated the impact of McCollum's accurate estimates and reveal how Turner tried to dictate strategic intelligence. ONI often found itself in the unenviable position of having no say about enemy intentions, but being accountable if war plans made a wrong evaluation. It left many of those in the junior echelons feeling they had been "robbed" of their main intelligence function—evaluation. The bad blood between the divisions did nothing to encourage the cooperation so essential to the complex function of turning raw data into meaningful intelligence.

Meanwhile, the internal struggle among the CNO staff amounted to a progressive takeover by the abrasive war plans director of many of the functions and responsibilities of Stark himself. "There had grown up in the office of the chief of naval operations a coterie," explained McCollum, who as ONI Far East section head observed the struggle at close quarters. "Stark, Ingersoll, and Turner became a sort of 'triumvirate.' Turner would bring in the ideas and the other two would endorse them—frequently without referring to anyone else on the staff."[34]

As in all triumvirates, one member exerted a dominating influence. In this case it was Richmond Kelly Turner, who aggressively promoted his own intelligence evaluations and made arbitrary decisions on their dissemination, knowing that he could count on Stark to rubber-stamp them. This situation created a climate of embittered indifference and uncertainty in the subordinate divisions of the navy department that was ultimately to prove disastrous for the Pacific Fleet. Shorn of its evaluative function, ONI was unable to heed Puleston's prophetic 1934 admonition that "constant and careful study of the daily course of Orange radio activity cannot be overemphasized in its importance as a barometer of the hostile intentions of that nation."[35]

It was one of the tragic ironies of 1941 that the Japanese were to heed this wise advice more closely than Washington. Although their comint organization was not able to break into any of our ciphered communications, our own observation of the pattern of their radio transmissions had revealed that their communications units doubled as shore-based radio transmitting and receiving stations, as well as radio intelligence intercept and direction-finding stations. Everything was fed into a central control at Owada on the outskirts of Tokyo, where the Japanese navy's cryptanalysis section was located. This was the Japanese naval staff's counter-part of OP-20-G, and it had developed along lines remarkably similar to our own.[36]

Unlike our decentralized setup of OP-20-G, with its two satellite units at Pearl and Cavite, which also carried out decryption and traffic analysis, the Japanese radio intelligence unit relied on the Owada nerve center to exploit both its strategic direction finders and radio intercepts. Its listening-post network extended out from Tokyo like the invisible spokes of a giant wheel which reached south from the Kuriles, along the main islands, down through Formosa, and east out across the mandates.

Just after war broke out in Europe in the fall of 1939, the Japanese had the opportunity to test their radio intelligence operation by monitoring our Pacific Fleet maneuvers then being conducted in the Hawaiian area. They made the most of this chance to snoop data on our operations and tactics by increasing their intercept station staff on Jaluit. They also rerouted seaplane tender *Kamoi* and sent naval tankers to load fuel oil at Los Angeles in order to traverse our maneuver area. From that time on, their radio intelligence organization remained on a combat-ready basis. The large volume of data they gathered throughout 1940 enabled them to update their plan for operations against the United States.[37]

The major difference between Japan's radio intelligence operation and ours was that while our navy department became locked in internal conflict over the control of intelligence, by 1941 their naval staff was gearing up to fight a war.

8

The Biggest Rattlesnake

THERE IS AN OLD cowboy saying: "The nearest rattlesnake is always bigger." It illustrates perfectly how the intelligence evaluations made at Washington and Pearl Harbor differed throughout 1941. The polarity, which had been aggravated by the feud within the navy department, was now further worsened on 27 May when Roosevelt declared a state of "unlimited national emergency" and warned Americans in a radio broadcast that war was "coming very close to home."[1]

To Admirals Stark and Turner, both of whom had played such a leading role in drafting the "Europe first" strategy, compared to the German submarines Japan was a distant menace. The president was calling the U-boats "the rattlesnakes of the Atlantic." They threatened to cut the lend-lease supply line to Britain. But from Admiral Kimmel's point of view the German submarines were less of a menace than a Japanese battle fleet, which could sortie from bases in the Marshall Islands, less than two thousand miles southwest of Pearl Harbor. But if we had known just how closely Axis agents had been studying the Pacific Fleet ever since the early spring, the Japanese rattlesnake would have appeared even larger.

Since February Admiral Yamamoto had been planning and coordinating the massive naval air operation that depended on the skillful application of intelligence in order to realize his strategic gamble for control of the western Pacific. Above his table on board flagship *Nagato* hung a detailed map of the American naval base on Oahu, marked with anchorages, defenses, and fuel-storage depots. In his desk drawer was a weighty volume titled *The Habits, Strengths, and Defenses of the American Fleet in the Hawaiian Area*, a bible of data on warship movements, water depths, and air and sea patrol patterns that were constantly updated by reports from Japanese agents in Hawaii.

Yamamoto's most valuable source of such information was the consulate at Honolulu. On 27 March 1941 the two-story white building on

103

Nuuanu Avenue became the base of operations for the Japanese navy's espionage effort when a junior diplomat known as Tadashi Morimura arrived at the consulate to take up his mission of collecting information essential to the fleet's destruction.

Morimura was the alias of twenty-eight-year-old former Ensign Takeo Yoshikawa. It also literally gave a new lease on life to a naval officer whose career had been terminated by stomach cancer. Yoshikawa had been recruited by the intelligence division of the naval general staff and trained for four years as an undercover agent for American operations. A slim, personable man, with an infectious politeness, he attracted little attention among the many Japanese Americans of Oahu.

At the consulate, however, where "Morimura" was assigned a desk in the vice-consul's office, it was curious—as one of the nisei female clerks was later to admit—that Otajiro Okuda's new assistant paid little attention to his duty of administering expatriate affairs. He was often late arriving for work and was seldom at his desk in the afternoon. Once Miss Kimie Doue saw a map of Oahu spread on his desk, and she often saw him leave the consulate in a taxi driven by John Mikami, who worked out of a stand on Vineyard Street. Another clerk would recall that Morimura sometimes arrived wearing an aloha sports shirt and was driven away in the car of Richard Kotoshirodo, who once admitted that the trips were to "military places."[2]

Although the Honolulu consulate was staked out by both the FBI and the Fourteenth Naval District intelligence office, it was not until after war broke out that interrogation of the taxi driver Mikami and clerk Kotoshirido revealed how extensive had been the assistance they gave to Yoshikawa's espionage activities. Both admitted making frequent trips with him to observe the local airfields, or to the Sunchoro tea house at Aiea Heights and the Punchbowl overlooking Pearl Harbor where they "looked at the view."[3]

During the latter half of 1941 his reports on the movements of the Pacific Fleet would be relayed by the consul in the J-19 cipher to the foreign ministry. To preserve the secrecy of the Pearl Harbor attack plan, neither Nagao Kita nor Yoshikawa was informed of the special importance that was attached to these reports.

In fact every port and naval base in the United States as well as the Panama Canal, the Philippines and the British, Dutch, and Australian territories in the Far East were already under intensive surveillance. By 1941, FBI director J. Edgar Hoover was keeping detailed files on some 342 suspected Japanese agents operating throughout the United States. Their movements were monitored, as it was widely believed that many were engaged in espionage directed from the Japanese embassy in Washington and Japan's main consulates in New York, Los Angeles, San Francisco, and Honolulu. Many of the suspects were nisei on the west coast who belonged to one of the patriotic societies with close links to Tokyo.

Especially close watch was also being kept on those Japanese who met with known Nazi agents.[4]

It was evident by 1941 that there was increasing cooperation between the undercover operatives of the Axis powers, but Hoover was to drop the ball completely when the British sent over to the United States their double agent known as Tricycle, who had been ordered to Berlin to undertake an espionage mission to Hawaii. Dusko Popov—and revisionist Pearl Harbor historians—have made much of the claim that Popov's mission had warned Roosevelt of the Japanese plan to attack the Pacific Fleet. Popov asserted that the straitlaced Hoover underrated the importance of the intelligence concealed in the microdot questionnaire he was given by his German contact in Lisbon. He also clashed with Hoover over his philandering and high-spending ways.[5]

Newly released FBI files, however, reveal that Hoover had more than enough justification for regarding Popov's credentials as suspect. When he had arrived in the United States he had received an unreported eighteen-thousand-dollar payoff from a local German Abwehr agent.[6] Popov did, however, hand over his questionnaire with its misspelled list of Hawaiian military installations drawn up by his German paymasters at the request of Tokyo. But only about a third of the questions dealt specifically with Hawaii; the rest related to general intelligence about United States war production.

Hoover and his aides therefore failed to see any special significance in the document. They were more concerned with claiming credit for uncovering the microdot technique. This formed the basis of Hoover's "Strictly Confidential" report to the White House on 3 September. The president received only the first page of the questionnaire, which did not include any reference to Hawaii. Hoover did not communicate the entire Popov microdot document to either naval or army intelligence, despite a 1940 agreement by which the FBI pledged to cooperate with the military intelligence to counter Axis espionage. His failure represented another American fumble on the road to Pearl Harbor.[7]

The FBI, however, was more diligent in its pursuit of potential Japanese agents, especially the dozens of naval officers who had arrived in the late thirties claiming to be language students or technical experts."[8]

In addition to spying on navy bases and armaments factories by the Japanese, there was another general level of espionage conducted by naval officers posted to the United States to study English. Whereas our own naval officers sent to Japan at this time to study the language numbered about three or four per year, Tokyo was sending them by the dozens to the United States. They reported for a few weeks to the embassy in Washington, where they would be briefed by Second Secretary Taro Terasaki, who by 1941 had become the mastermind of Japan's entire espionage network in the western hemisphere.

Terasaki, whose brother was a ranking official in the Japanese foreign ministry, had studied at Brown University and gleaned valuable information from former classmates who were now in the State Department. We can now see from recently declassified FBI documents, and the signal traffic of Japan's military attachés, just how extensive this espionage was. Terasaki reported to Tokyo that, in addition to the isolationist supporters of Charles Lindbergh's America First campaign, his agents were also cultivating "very influential Negro leaders" in anticipation of stirring up racial discontent "to stall the program of U.S. plans for national defense and the economy as well as sabotage."[9] Special attention was also paid to nisei working in the west coast aircraft factories and to their relatives in the U.S. Army.

Terasaki ordered the naval agents to enroll at universities and technical institutes, principally in the vicinity of west coast ports. The naval attaché maintained a branch office in New York, known as the "inspector's office," where the FBI investigation found that disbursements for the development of intelligence amounted to half a million dollars a month, a staggering sum for those days. Much of this was spent to obtain technical information and to buy aircraft parts, radios, and tools, apparently only for examination. Two officers assigned to the New York inspectorate had been meeting with a German agent, code-named "Steamer," in the Nippon Club where they shared American scientific and technical information.[10]

The major effort was centered on the west coast. In San Francisco, outposts of large Japanese corporations such as the Yokohama Specie Bank, Mitsubishi Shoji Kaisha, and Nippon Yusen Kaisha provided protection and a channel of communications for the imperial navy's undercover agents. The Los Angeles headquarters of the North American branch of the Nippon Kaigun Kyokai (Japanese Naval Association) collaborated with the language officers to obtain information about naval bases and defense plants. In Los Angeles a Dr. Takashi Furusawa and his wife Sachiko (known as the mother of the Japanese navy), members of the Japanese Political Society, ran a clearinghouse for information collected by these undercover Japanese naval officers.

Lieutenant Commander Itaru Tachibana was one of the most active of the "language students." He lived in Los Angeles, used the name Yamato as an alias, and operated a string of brothels for his cover and added income, while spying under orders of Commander Nagasawa, the local representative of the naval attaché.

Tachibana came to the attention of the Eleventh Naval District intelligence office in early 1941 through, of all people, Al D. Blake, also known as Keeno, King of the Robots, from the world record he had set by standing motionless for one hour and twenty-seven minutes. He was a sometime vaudeville performer whose robot act got him occasional jobs at fairs and store openings. He had spent four years in the navy before playing a bit role in Charlie Chaplin's 1917 movie *Shoulder Arms,* where he became acquainted with the star's valet-chauffeur, Toraichi Kono.[11]

When they met by chance again in 1940, Blake was broke and jobless, and Kono was "chauffeur" to Tachibana. Tachibana offered Blake five thousand dollars if he could produce classified naval information. First, however, Tachibana wanted proof of Blake's naval connection and a sample of the sort of data he claimed he could provide. Blake, now realizing that he was beyond his depth, went to the FBI in Los Angeles with this story, saying that he had led Tachibana on out of patriotism, intending to expose him. He confessed that he had no buddy in the fleet, but that he did need money, and offered his full cooperation. The FBI notified the local office of naval intelligence headquarters who cabled Pearl Harbor and asked for cooperation.

Most of Admiral Kimmel's staff wanted nothing to do with this "cops and robbers" caper, feeling that the Fourteenth Naval District could handle it, and seeing no need for Cincpac involvement. Because of my previous experience with undercover operations, I urged that we cooperate. I explained that we could easily arrange for Blake to get faked classified information. That would bolster his position with Tachibana, and at the same time feed bum dope to the Japanese, and perhaps help catch some of their spies. Kimmel approved, saying, "Why not? If we can catch spies, and at the same time lead the Japanese astray, I think it's a good idea. You go ahead with it, Layton."

We arranged for Blake to write to his "buddy Paul Mitchell" in *Pennsylvania,* saying, "We can make a heap of dough if you cooperate." A naval agent in Honolulu posed as "Mitchell" who corresponded on *Pennsylvania* letterhead stationery telling how fed up he was with the navy, how much he needed money, and that he was eager to see his pal Al and hear more about the money. Tachibana was so impressed by the "Mitchell" letter that he booked passage for Blake on *President Garfield,* which sailed for Honolulu shortly after noon on 25 April.

As if Blake was not involved enough, he made shipboard acquaintances of four Nazis and decided to play "boy spy" with them. One of them brawled with Blake, but he got clear of the Nazis when they were arrested after the captain reported the incident to a passing Canadian cruiser 29 April, the night before entering Oahu.

Meanwhile, we had prepared for Blake's arrival. When he stepped ashore and hailed a taxi, a naval agent was at the wheel. They went directly to the Alexander Young Hotel, where a room—specially wired with a recording machine—was reserved. We also had a cover for him, and a cover for the cover. If the Japs tailed him, we'd have a tail on them. At Pearl Harbor, Bill Kitts, the staff gunnery officer, helped me prepare some bait documents on fleet gunfire practices.

Blake spent enough time doing Honolulu with his "buddy" to be seen in the right places, before returning to the mainland with his "delivery." On 15 May, Tachibana, accompanied by another "language student," carried the material to the Japanese embassy in Washington. The naval attaché liked it so much that he authorized a second Blake mission to Honolulu. We had arranged his reception as before.

We were doctoring bait for the second delivery when out of the blue I got a call from the ONI office in Honolulu saying that Blake had blown his cover. He had run across a woman friend from his old vaudeville days, dined her, and got her up to his room. There, midst amours, he bragged of being an intelligence agent. Our microphones had recorded everything he blabbed.

My yeoman, Hedges R. Keene, fetched Blake from Honolulu to my office, where I read him the riot act. I told him his Hawaiian holiday was over, that we knew all about his hotel-room indiscretions, and that he was on his way home. I made it clear that if he created any further fuss, we would notify the woman's husband. Meanwhile, an ONI agent visited her home at Waianae, ensuring her silence in exchange for our not giving her husband a copy of the hotel-room recording.

Back in Los Angeles, Blake made the second delivery to Tachibana, who was arrested by the FBI after it obtained Department of State approval. His property was seized and three of the navy's best translators were rushed to Los Angeles to screen the voluminous papers. Further confirmation of Tachibana's espionage activity came from the code breakers in Washington who intercepted a message from the Japanese consul in Los Angeles asking the embassy in Washington to subsidize Kono and "friends" to the tune of twenty-five thousand dollars "in view of the fact that he might give evidence unsatisfactory to Tachibana."[12]

Among Tachibana's effects was a suitcase belonging to Lieutenant Commander Sadatomo Okada, another "language officer" suspected for many months of being engaged in espionage activities, and who was rounded up for deportation. It contained a great quantity of data relating to national defense in the Pacific northwest: data on antiaircraft defenses for the Boeing aircraft plant in Seattle, details of naval ships under construction, times of warship arrivals and departures, test data on naval aircraft, records of movements of troops at military establishments, production data on national defense factories, and aerial photographs of naval and army bases as well as war plants.[13]

The haul of intelligence material was so extensive and incriminating that Secretary of the Navy Frank Knox wanted Tachibana, Okada, and another language officer named Yamada to be charged with conspiracy to violate our espionage statute. Washington's diplomatic wheels, however, soon began turning and this charge was tempered. Ambassador Nomura personally intervened to request that "the Tachibana incident be dealt with from the standpoint of the current political trend."[14]

On 21 June, escorted by a posse of FBI agents, Tachibana boarded *Nitta Maru* en route to Tokyo. There his talents were to be put to use by the Third Section (intelligence) in supervising and analyzing the flow of information from the consulate in Honolulu. To protect remaining naval agents in the United States, instructions went out from the foreign ministry that they should be appointed naval attachés to give them diplomatic immunity.

The Tachibana case represented the culmination of several years of counterintelligence operations by the navy in unofficial collaboration with the FBI. The headquarters of the Twelfth Naval District at San Francisco was the most active center of these operations. While the detailed counterintelligence files kept by the district intelligence office for the prewar years have been recalled by the navy, station signal logs and the testimony of former staffers confirm that the office was engaged in extensive counterintelligence operations against the Japanese community on the west coast. Not only was it responsible for monitoring all the transpacific telephone calls from a Market Street office adjacent to the main San Francisco telephone exchange, but it was also tapping telephones in offices and hotel rooms used by members of the local Japanese business community.[15]

The evidence of extensive espionage discovered in these and similar operations on the west coast probably influenced Roosevelt when he issued a controversial emergency executive order two months after Pearl Harbor that resulted in the rounding up of Japanese Americans and packing them off to detention camps. Commander Robert E. Lawrance, the deputy intelligence officer for the Twelfth Naval District, was responsible for directing the undercover surveillance of Japan's suspected espionage network. With the promise of a lieutenancy in the naval reserve, he hired William L. Magistretti—a twenty-year-old student of Japanese at the University of California at Berkeley, who had studied at the Imperial University in Tokyo. Lawrance made it clear that the job required illegal entries and break-ins that amounted to burglary, a felony offense, and that if Magistretti was caught in the act the navy would have to disown him. Magistretti patriotically accepted the job, nevertheless, and participated in a number of successful break-ins, starting in 1938. But he finally quit when the promised commission never materialized, joined the office of strategic services (OSS) in 1943, and served in the China-Burma-India theater for the rest of the war.[16]

To assist Magistretti, a civilian named Seeman Gaddis was engaged to pick the locks of offices of Japanese cultural centers, organizations, and businesses in the San Francisco area. An ex-flatfoot known as Soapy, he was an employee of a private detective agency run by Gene Kerrigan, who was under contract to carry out these break-ins for the Twelfth Naval District. In addition to discovering hundreds of pornographic pictures, which many Japanese businessmen kept locked in their desks, the break-ins by Gaddis and Magistretti produced a useful flow of intelligence about the extent of Japan's surveillance of naval and army bases on the west coast.

In 1940 they conspired to obtain a copy of the imperial navy's mobilization codes for the merchant marine from a Japanese ship in San Pedro. During a "customs inspection" Gaddis planted and "discovered" narcotics in the captain's safe, thereby providing an excuse for removal of its contents, over furious protests by the Japanese skipper. Magistretti identified the merchant-ship code book, which was quickly photographed in a dockside warehouse, and the contents of the safe were returned.[17]

Getting the merchant-ship code was a windfall for ONI. Even though the Japanese switched codes as soon as the ship's captain reported that it had been compromised, possessing an entire code was always useful for comparison purposes. This American success, however, was only a drop in the bucket compared with the information Japan's undercover agents like Tachibana were getting in the United States. In contrast to Japan, we were a free country with none of the police-state controls and restrictions that I had discovered made intelligence gathering so difficult when I was assistant naval attaché in Tokyo.

The United States armed services were constitutionally restrained from conducting extensive counterintelligence activities such as phone tapping against civilians. Such operations had to be conducted on an unofficial and ad hoc basis, but it is now clear that enterprising intelligence officers in naval districts such as San Francisco took it upon themselves to organize quite extensive covert surveillance operations with the connivance—if not approval—of the ONI and FBI in Washington.

Once the Pacific Fleet had moved to Pearl Harbor in 1940, it was realized by the local district intelligence office and by the ONI in Washington that that base would certainly become the focus of Japanese espionage. Nevertheless, the monitoring of telephone and cable traffic to and from Honolulu was far less extensive than that conducted in San Francisco.

This was not through any lack of zeal on the part of Captain Irving H. Mayfield, Fourteenth Naval District intelligence officer, but because telegraph companies in Honolulu insisted on hewing to the statutes which made the disclosure of communications a federal crime. On his own initiative Mayfield, in an ingenious bid to bypass the regulations, had enlisted the aid of local telephone authorities. They provided telephone sets modified with live microphones, which were installed in the Japanese consulate by two warrant officers in phone company uniforms who drove up in a phone company truck. The same team used street cables to route the taps on the consulate switchboard to a nearby Nuuanu Heights residence where Mayfield had set up a listening station equipped with recording machines.[18]

The eighteen-month eavesdropping operation on the Honolulu consulate had failed to provide us with any hard evidence of Japan's special interest in Pearl Harbor. It was to be expected that they would be interested in watching our main Pacific Fleet base, but apart from confirming that their diplomats were engaged in a general surveillance, our investigation uncovered nothing that singled out their agent Yoshikawa for special attention by Captain Mayfield's office before December 1941.[19]

Our main concern was with preventing unauthorized snooping at sea. An attempt had been made by the coast guard in 1939 to deprive Japanese nationals from operating fishing boats in the waters off Diamond Head, but the wanderings of one additional Japanese among the 150,000 already living on Oahu attracted no special attention. Using his cover name Morimura, Yoshikawa had set to work promptly and effectively, a professional naval observer who knew exactly what was needed and how to obtain and report it. His casual strolls, auto rides, and even sightseeing plane trips were not as casual as they seemed. All his intelligence data were being channeled to Admiral Yamamoto's planning team.

As the Pearl Harbor attack concept moved from studies by Ohnishi and Genda to full operational treatment by the Combined Fleet staff, details about Pearl Harbor's water depths, ship movements, and fleet routine became increasingly important to the Japanese. The problems were broken down into four categories: operations and supply, communications and intelligence, navigation and meteorology, and air and submarine aspects. By April 1941 a major reorganization was under way that greatly facilitated Yamamoto's still-evolving plan. This was the creation of a First Air Fleet, which saw the effective marshaling of more than two hundred carrier-based planes under a single commander.[20]

The overall plan—designated Operation Z in honor of the signal flag used by Admiral Heihachiro Togo at the Battle of Tsushima—was still known to only a few members of Yamamoto's staff. Serious operational planning could not begin until the imperial general staff resolved differences in strategic policy. The army still wanted a northward advance against the Russians in Siberia and an all-out commitment to conclude the long war in China. The navy argued for a southward assault to seize the oil and other natural resources of the Dutch East Indies, which Japan would need if her expansionist policies led to a severing of trade with the United States. This was the major issue confronting the Japanese cabinet which, by the end of June 1941, still had not authorized the imperial general staff to begin any formal planning for war.

9

Dropping the Ball

W HILE NEITHER KIMMEL nor I yet suspected the danger of the Japanese rattlesnake that was literally "in our backyard" at Pearl Harbor, by the late spring of 1941 we were paying very careful attention to the one that menaced us from the mandated islands. At the beginning of May, I prepared for the admiral and his staff detailed charts of the larger mid-Pacific atolls showing where I believed that Japan had illegally established military installations. The evidence had been provided from monitoring their radio traffic, careful submarine surveillance, and occasional help from Pan American Airways, whose flying boats passed close to the Japanese-held islands on their way across the Pacific. Reports had also been gathered from our agents who solicited information from merchant seamen in ports throughout the Far East.

All this information built up to a disturbing picture. On Kwajalein and Jaluit in the Marshalls there was evidence that seaplane and submarine bases had been blasted out of the coral lagoons. At Ponape in the Carolines, transmitting towers rose high above the palm trees. Airstrips capable of handling long-range bombers had been bulldozed across the cane fields of Saipan in the Marianas. And a deep-water anchorage at Truk offered an advance base big enough to shelter the entire Japanese Combined Fleet.

The most productive source of accurate information on Japanese military activities in these islands had come from radio intelligence as a result of my work on the low-priority WE WE cipher for Hypo. Its revelations had impressed Kimmel, as they had Richardson, and he readily agreed to follow up my inquiry about how Stark viewed the Japanese activity in the mandates when he left at the end of May for conferences in Washington at the navy department. Accompanied by Captain Charles H. McMorris, his war plans chief, Kimmel carried a carefully considered letter that he had written on 26 May. It listed shortcomings in fleet strength and personnel, patrol planes, and antiaircraft defenses.

"No policy today is better than the force available to enforce it," Kimmel cautioned in his letter, adding, "While this is well recognized in principle, it is apparently lost sight of in practice."[1] His sharpest criticism was that with "the rapid developments in the international picture, both diplomatic and military," a "marked improvement" was needed to provide the fleet with "timely information."[2] So Kimmel made it a first order of business to raise the issue of mandates intelligence with the navy department.

On the day Kimmel arrived in Washington, 4 June 1941, a top-secret message was delivered at fleet headquarters, Pearl Harbor, which read:

> It has come to the attention of CNO that the Pacific Fleet intelligence officer has in his possession certain vital information dealing with the militarization of mandated islands by Japan, which he has not seen fit to report to CNO or to ONI. You will immediately send this information to this office in this same cipher system.[3]

Never had I seen such an invidious naval message. But I responded promptly, summarizing all the intelligence I had in three closely spaced pages. The last paragraph noted that *all* of this information came from Station George (Guam) intercepts addressed to CNO (OP-20-G), copy to Station Hypo. Although none of them had been specifically addressed to the commander in chief, U.S. Pacific Fleet, as fleet intelligence officer, I had "examined this material for tactical information of value to the fleet," in accordance with current signal procedure.

It was inconceivable to me that the chief of naval operations might be unaware of the intelligence contents of intercepts sent to his office. But after that dispatch it became clear that no one in Washington had paid proper attention to the Guam WE WE cipher intercepts. Had anyone looked at them, the wealth of intelligence data contained in the originator and addressees would have impelled them to bring it to the attention of OP-20-G, and thence to ONI and CNO. Perhaps even Admiral Turner would have been awakened to the reality of Japan's preparations for a southward advance. But no one in Washington had even bothered to examine the raw intercepts—let alone decrypt, translate, evaluate, and disseminate them.

This failure was just one example of the underlying flaw in the intelligence procedures of the office of naval operations in Washington. During the latter part of May our direction-finding stations, and our analysis of radio traffic, had revealed that Japan was conducting major naval exercises in the mandates. Carrier *Ryūjō*, and possibly *Hiryū*, as well as half the submarine fleet were taking part. Apparently Fourth Fleet had played the role of enemy, attempting to invade the Marshall Islands against defending submarines and land-based planes. After the exercise the ships visited Wotje, Kwajalein, and Jaluit before returning to their normal operating waters by the end of June.[4]

Since Washington appeared to have discounted the importance of these Japanese maneuvers in the mandates, when Kimmel returned I asked him about it, and about my "blast" from CNO. He told me that when the question of the militarization of the mandates came up, Admiral Stark said he had never heard of it. His ONI director, Captain Kirk, and his assistant, Commander McCollum, were summoned. They had to admit that they knew nothing about a Japanese military buildup in the mid-Pacific islands. The raw information was finally found in the files, but nothing had been done with it. Coming hard on the heels of ONI's defeat in the face-off with Turner, Kirk and McCollum were especially irritated to have this new failure exposed to CNO. Their rude blast at me was a cover-up for both their injured pride and the intelligence blunder.

My copy of the Pacific Fleet staff instructions clearly stated that the intelligence officer "directs assembly of enemy information and evaluates the same; disseminating to the various members of staff, indicating where action is required."[5] This is precisely what I had done. There was no way of my knowing that Washington was not properly evaluating the same information when they received it.

The WE WE affair must have been acutely embarrassing for Stark. He had promised to keep Kimmel "adequately informed" and ONI had now been caught on one foot. That OP-20-G had so obviously dropped the ball early in 1941 was indicative of the kind of blunders that accumulated over the coming months into a major disaster.

The WE WE foul-up was just one of a series of jolts that Kimmel received in Washington. Even while he had been en route by air back to the west coast, the first copies of the joint army-navy Rainbow 5 war plan were being circulated to the Pacific naval commands. The policy directive announced that "since Germany is the predominant member of the Axis powers, the Atlantic and European area is considered to be the decisive theater." This meant that American strategy focused now on the Atlantic, and it did not take Kimmel long to discover that it was a course that the navy department intended to hold to at the expense of the Pacific.

"If Japan does enter the war, the military strategy in the Far East will be defensive"[6] was the constraint that the Rainbow 5 plan imposed on Kimmel. In discussions with Turner, he had made no bones about the inadequacy of his assigned fleet for the tasks expected of it. The plan required his fleet to divert enemy strength by undertaking to "capture . . . positions in the Marshalls, destroy Axis sea communications, and protect the territory of the associated powers."[7] But Turner, who was now making contingency plans for a possible American involvement in the naval war against Germany in the Atlantic, could offer no prospects of sending more ships to the Pacific. Kimmel protested that his forces were inferior to the Japanese fleet in every category of fighting ship, and that he lacked the support vessels needed to operate across the vast distance of the Pacific.

To contest a Japanese advance in the Pacific, Kimmel had only one fast-carrier task force, one amphibious task force, and one battleship task force. Twenty-five percent of the fleet's April strength had been whittled away when a carrier, three battleships, four cruisers, and eighteen destroyers had been transferred to the Atlantic in May. The fleet's operating range was restricted by a lack of oilers, a weakness that must have been obvious to the Japanese. Lastly, Kimmel's ships were undermanned, and many more aircraft and antiaircraft batteries were needed to properly defend the Pearl Harbor base.

Such inadequacies, serious though they were, worried Kimmel less than Stark's new and astonishing proposal. Stark was planning to remove an additional detachment of three battleships, four cruisers, two squadrons of destroyers, and a carrier and send them to the Atlantic. Appalled by the prospect, Kimmel had made a vigorous protest against it during his 9 June meeting with Roosevelt. In presenting his views about the fleet's presence at Pearl Harbor, Kimmel had argued, "Once the fleet was placed there, for the assumed purpose of exerting a deterrent effect upon Japan, it was not maintaining a consistent policy thereafter to weaken the fleet, visibly and plainly, by diversion of powerful units to the Atlantic."[8]

Stark and the president took the point. The proposed reductions were canceled. Kimmel had good reason to hope that both the White House and the navy department had now clearly grasped his view of the strategic situation.

While Kimmel's forceful presentation in the White House had prevented any further sapping of his fleet strength, he was unsuccessful in persuading the navy department that there was a pressing need to increase his intelligence input. Our ability to eavesdrop on Japan's diplomatic traffic was not brought up in his meetings with either Turner or Kirk. So Kimmel was to remain ignorant of the scope and limitations of the Magic operation, the surest gauge of Japanese intentions available to his superiors in Washington.

The failure of Turner and Kirk to brief Kimmel on the subject was an indication of the extent to which Magic secrecy had become a fetish by the middle of 1941. This was the result of a series of scares and slipups in handling of the material. These began in March 1941 when the State Department "lost" a Magic memorandum. The same month another one was found in the wastepaper basket of the president's military aide.[9]

The alarm bells rang loudest on 5 May 1941 when message 192 from the foreign ministry in Tokyo to the embassy in Washington was translated: "According to a fairly reliable source of information it appears almost certain the United States government is reading your code messages. Please let me know whether you have any suspicion of the above"[10]

The Japanese military leaders must have reacted with as great a concern as the navy department to the flurry of diplomatic messages from

Nomura. In rapid succession he asked for the "source," assured Japan's minister of his "stringent precautions," promising "investigations" to track any possible leak. It was soon evident from an intercepted message to Japan's Berlin embassy that the "reliable source" was the German foreign minister. The ambassador was requested to find out more information "so that we might take appropriate action."[11]

Forty-eight hours later all Japanese embassies were ordered to put new code routines into operation. Then on 20 May the panic eased after Nomura informed Tokyo, "Though I do not know which ones, I have discovered that the United States is reading some of our codes." The leak had evidently been traced to some source other than Purple, which remained in use. There must have been some residual concern that top-level diplomatic traffic might still be subject to eavesdropping, however, because the ambassador cryptically added, "As for how I got this intelligence, I will inform you by courier or another safe way."[12]

Precisely what codes Nomura believed we were reading, and how the leak occurred, remained a mystery. Nevertheless, Tokyo continued to use Purple for its most sensitive diplomatic communications throughout the war, in the apparent belief that its complex cipher system remained secure. Japan's armed forces, however, committed no important military data to Purple. This was a major blow to our military intelligence chiefs in Washington who apparently maintained an unshaken faith that the diplomatic circuits would provide them with advance notice of the time, date, and target of any Japanese attack.

Piecing together evidence from recently declassified data on both sides of the Atlantic, it emerges that the German warning to Tokyo probably originated from a successful break into one of Britain's cipher systems. A wartime investigation ordered by the foreign office in London revealed that a cipher clerk in the British embassy in Washington on 30 April had made the fatal error of encoding his ambassador's secret bulletin in a low-grade cipher intended for use only by the ministry of aircraft supply. This was picked up by a code-breaking unit in the German embassy, located a mile to the east on Massachusetts Avenue, and relayed to Berlin.

That message to London, which might have blown the whole Magic operation, contained the gist of a Purple intercept. It was reporting a policy accord that Japan had reached four days earlier with Foreign Minister Joachim von Ribbentrop in Berlin. The State Department had sent the Magic report to the British embassy. The irony of the affair was that the British cryptanalysts at Bletchley Park's code and cipher school were already becoming proficient with their recently delivered Purple machine, and had probably broken out the message for themselves.[13]

We Americans were left equally baffled as to the source of these leaks, and our British colleagues were not about to reveal they had dropped the ball. The panic caused by direct evidence that the Japanese, for the first time, suspected that their codes were being intercepted was matched only by our relief when they did not institute an immediate code change. But the incident had prompted a lid to be clamped on the handling and distribution of Magic material. That connection was reinforced after an August report from Ambassador Grew that our State Department codes might be prejudiced. His concern was aroused after a pro-American Japanese foreign ministry official asked Grew to communicate the information he had given in a code that Japan's military cryptanalysts could not read. He advised the astonished ambassador that the embassy had only "one code which is considered unbreakable."[14]

Even before the August scare the army staff had screwed down security. In May they refused to continue accepting responsibility for delivering messages to the White House. Until that point the war and navy departments had rotated this delivery on a monthly basis. Now they resorted instead to presenting only an oral briefing. During the navy's turn, in June, the president specifically asked to see the individual messages, and his naval aide made them available. He continued to do so in subsequent months when the army "sent nothing to the White House."[15]

That the commander in chief could be denied details of vital intelligence for a whole month—a situation that recurred in the fall, according to a formerly secret wartime army report—must once and for all cast doubt on the credibility of the argument that an omniscient Roosevelt had advance warning of the Pearl Harbor attack. It also indicates the extent to which access to Magic was willfully regulated by the officers responsible for its dissemination. This was certainly true for the Pacific Fleet, and it was action by Adolf Hitler rather than the navy department that set in motion the events that resulted in our being sent our first Purple diplomatic decrypts.

The shock of a six-thousand-gun German barrage on 22 June 1941, followed by a tidal wave of tanks and armored vehicles pouring into Russia, plunged Japan into another cabinet crisis. And it started a train of events that set the seal on a secret Anglo-American alliance in the Far East. News of the German attack sent the Japanese foreign minister to the imperial palace to win the emperor's backing for a Siberian adventure. Matsuoka was eager to renege on his two-month-old pledges to Stalin. But the army staff had no intention of taking on Soviet tanks and planes until they could be quite sure of German victory. And the naval staff was dead set against any war in the north, since their planning was now gearing toward a rapid southward thrust to secure Dutch East Indies oil in anticipation of further deterioration of relations with the United States.

Coincident with the German attack on Russia, Roosevelt proposed an offer of lend-lease aid to the Soviet Union, and Secretary of State Hull rejected Nomura's latest diplomatic overture, questioning the good faith of Japan's foreign minister.

Matsuoka took this as a personal insult. He called for termination of all discussions with Washington, radioing Berlin, "Japan is preparing for all possible eventualities as regards the USSR in order to join forces with her [Germany] in active crushing of the communist menace."[16] Japan's ambassador was told to inform Ribbentrop that the "Japanese government have [sic] decided to secure 'points d'appui' in French Indochina to enable Japan further to strengthen her pressure on Great Britain and the United States of America."[17]

The decrypt of this belligerent message aroused the secretary of state to the possibility of war breaking out in the Far East. It concluded, "We Japanese are not going to sit on the fence while you Germans fight the Russian."[18] The Purple traffic on the Tokyo-Berlin and Tokyo-Washington circuits revealed to Washington that Konoye's cabinet was not yet prepared to jump off the fence into war.

Roosevelt could readily imagine the turmoil swirling around Japan's leaders, since he was also having to deal with dissension in his cabinet. Interior Secretary Harold L. Ickes, in his capacity as "Petroleum Coordinator," urged the cabinet on 23 June to initiate an immediate oil embargo because "Japan is so occupied with what is happening in Russia, and what may happen in Siberia, that she won't venture a hostile move against the Dutch East Indies."[19] A week later when Ickes threatened to resign if Japan's oil supply was not shut off, the president chided him, "I think it will interest you to know that the Japanese are having a real drag-down and knock-out fight among themselves for the past week trying to decide which way they are going to jump."[20]

The president apparently believed that any further economic sanctions by the United States might prompt Japan to jump south to grab alternate oil supplies. He reminded his irascible secretary of the interior, "I simply have not got the navy to go around, and every little episode in the Pacific means fewer ships in the Atlantic."[21] Roosevelt's fears were raised by Purple decrypts revealing that the Vichy French were being pressed by Tokyo for air and sea bases at Saigon and Camranh Bay.

On 2 July 1941 the Japanese finally made up their minds. An imperial conference that Friday took the momentous decision for a policy of southward expansion, "no matter what obstacles may be encountered." Konoye's prepared statement of the cabinet position had rejected Matsuoka's advocacy of an immediate attack on Russia in favor of advancing "southward in order to firmly establish a basis for her self-existence and self-protection."[22] A "joint protectorate" with the French in Indochina was to be established. It would provide the army with a base for launching northward against Nationalist China, west against Thailand and Burma, and south to threaten Malaya.

Konoye was still counting on a diplomatic blitzkrieg to influence the British to return to their policy of appeasement. As a precaution, however, two million more troops were to be conscripted and armament production increased. The prime minister left no doubt about Japan's ultimate intention to secure the "liberation of southeast Asia"—by force, if diplomacy failed. "Preparations for war with Great Britain and the United States will be made," he announced, stating that Japan must be prepared to take this ultimate step to achieve her national destiny.

The emperor's assent for Konoye's plan was automatic. But the decision was not acceptable to Matsuoka, who was attracting the tag of "Hitler's office boy." He kept calling for a strike north until he was forced out as foreign minister on 17 July. But if replacing the firebrand Matsuoka with the more temperate Admiral Teijiro Toyoda was intended by Konoye to strike a harmonious note in Washington, it was drowned out by saber-rattling demands revealed in the Magic decrypts of Japan's diplomatic traffic.

Washington's mounting concern at developments in Tokyo became apparent to us at Pearl Harbor ten days before Matsuoka's removal. On 7 July, Kimmel had been sent two messages containing an up-to-date digest of Tokyo's more belligerent signals. Although we knew nothing about the scope of the Magic operations, it was clear to me that this information could have been obtained only by intercepting Japan's most secret diplomatic communications.

This welcome diplomatic intelligence enabled us to keep abreast of the advancing seriousness of the Indochina crisis. The Magic summaries we received clearly set out the timetable of Japan's "determination to get bases" from the Vichy government. A 1 July intercept warned that Japanese cargo vessels in American waters were to be rushed through the Panama Canal by the third week of the month. Intercepts made the following day from the Tokyo-Berlin circuit revealed that "Japan is preparing for all possible eventualities regarding the Soviets in order to join forces with Germany." Broad hints of a possible attack in Siberia reinforced their ambassador's earlier assurance that "Japan will not sit on the fence."[23]

On 15 July another CNO message based on Magic told us that Tokyo had decided "to use force" to get Indochina air and naval bases if the French objected. They wished "to avoid friction with Britain and particularly the United States if possible, but risk is necessary."[24] Two days later another message gave us the full terms of Tokyo's ultimatum, including the deadline, stated as "army planning advance on about twenty July."[25] We received a Purple decrypt of 16 July warning Japan's Hanoi and Saigon legations to "burn codes" and evacuate personnel by sea a week later. Ominously it stated, "Japan intends carry out plans by force if opposed or if British or United States intervenes."[26]

During the July crisis Washington kept Kimmel posted on diplomatic intelligence. We also received other important decrypts directly from Station Cast at Cavite where the Purple machine was used to good effect. On 14 July, following Matsuoka's forced resignation, we were told that Tokyo had advised all consulates, "Although cabinet has changed there will of course be no departure from the principle that tripartite pact forms keystone of Japan's national policy." From the same source, we learned a week later that the Japanese army had "decided to advance [into northern Indochina] regardless of whether demands accepted or not."[27]

We did not know it at the time, but this was the last piece of Purple diplomatic intelligence that Kimmel was to receive for more than four months. We were cut off from Magic, ostensibly for security reasons, a decision that was completely unknown to Kimmel, Rochefort, and me. The lack of this high-level diplomatic information seriously hampered our ability to assemble all the pieces of the intelligence jigsaw puzzle. Having received diplomatic coverage in July, and having been assured that we would be supplied with any information of importance to the Pacific Fleet, we never dreamed that Washington had been collecting Japanese intercepts that would have alerted us to the immediate danger far beyond any warnings of war we received from Washington.

During the Indochina crisis, for example, we received enough diplomatic information from Magic for me to provide Kimmel with a far more accurate picture of the Far East situation than he ever got from Admiral Stark's personal letters, whose intelligence was devalued by both the ten-day-long postal delays and CNO's attempt to disguise the uncertainty of his own evaluations. The chatty style of his personal communications to his Pacific Fleet commander veered wildly among cheerful reassurance, painful obfuscation, and hesitant alarm.

To Kimmel, whose mind worked with a well-ordered precision, the overwhelming vagueness of Stark's communications as the first major Far East crisis of 1941 boiled to a head, was exasperating and unsettling.

On 13 July he had received CNO's letter with Stark's "unmistakable deduction" that "the Japanese government has determined upon its future policy," which "probably involves war in the near future." An advance against the British and Dutch could "not be ruled out," but Stark believed "that Jap activity in the south will be for the present confined to seizure and development of naval, army, and air bases in Indochina."[28]

Stark's vagueness, characterized by an earlier opinion—"What will happen in the Pacific is anyone's guess,"—disturbed Kimmel. It cannot, therefore, have come as a complete surprise, discouraging though it was, when he received Stark's 24 July enjoinder: "Obviously the situation in the Far East continues to deteriorate; this is one thing that is factual."[29] In the circumstances, this must surely rate as some of the most remarkably worthless reading ever to emerge from Washington.

Stark's confusion throughout the July crisis reflected the continuing conflict between the war plans division and ONI in evaluating Japan's likely response to a freeze by the United States on trade with the Axis powers. When the question of economic sanctions was raised, Stark had "opposed it just as strongly as I could." His fear that an oil embargo presented the possibility of a strike at Borneo was reinforced by a frank "admiral to admiral" chat with Nomura on 24 July. "If the Russians are well beaten down, I think it highly probable that they will move into Siberia," CNO wrote, echoing the conviction of the war plans chief that Japan would still strike northward. Stark's 26 July letter concluded with a singularly imprecise "Just where it will all end I do not know."[30]

Stark's underlying pessimism also echoed the alarm sounded in a 19 July memorandum from his director of war plans. "An embargo would probably result in a fairly early attack on Malaya and the Netherlands East Indies, and possibly would involve the United States in early war in the Pacific" was Turner's assessment. His advice that "trade with Japan not be embargoed at this time" was forwarded by CNO to the president with the note "I concur in general."[31]

The day that Roosevelt received this caution from the navy dispatch, he also saw a Magic intercept of 20 July which confirmed that Japan's army had "decided to advance on 24th regardless of whether demands accepted or not."[32] This forewarning of impending aggression persuaded a majority of the president's advisers that they had to force some kind of showdown with Tokyo.

On Monday, 26 July, twenty-four hours after Japanese troops marched across the borders of Indochina, the State Department announced the freezing of all Axis funds in the United States—and therefore trade with the United States. But Roosevelt, heeding State's advice, spoke carefully on the issues involved. To allay the navy's concerns, which were reinforced by Churchill's fears that the American sanctions might force the Japanese to run amok, the president personally reassured Nomura that he did not yet intend the blanket embargo on trade to include oil exports. Nonetheless, Secretary of the Interior Harold L. Ickes and anti-Japanese hard-liners in the State Department (led by Far East desk head Dr. Stanley K. Hornbeck) seized their chance to interpret the freeze order as an oil embargo. This was contrary to the president's assurances to the Japanese ambassador and his remark to Ickes that his intention was only to "slip the noose around Japan's neck and give it a jerk now and then."[33]

The New York Times interpreted the freeze as "the most drastic blow short of war." This view was reinforced by the army's announcement the same day that General Douglas MacArthur was being recalled to active duty as commander in chief of U.S. forces in the Far East. This signaled the beginnings of a major reinforcement of our military strength in the Philippines as a strategic barrier to deter a Japanese southward move to grab the oil reserves of the Dutch East Indies.

It was a move that reversed the strategic doctrines of both the Rainbow 5 war plan and a twenty-year-old policy *not* to make any major commitment of American forces west of Hawaii. As far as the Pacific Fleet was concerned, the Cavite base outside Manila did not have adequate repair facilities or fuel reserves to act as a forward base. So General

MacArthur would be faced with defending the Philippines with untrained troops at the end of an exposed and insufficient ocean supply line.

It was a military commitment that neither the army nor our already overstretched fleet at Hawaii could fulfill. Within four short months the Japanese would prove the point.

By declaring an embargo on the Axis, the president had allowed diplomatic pressures to override the prudent dictates of military strategy. Against the advice of the navy department, a presidential decision had been made to shift our front line of defense five thousand miles westward across the reaches of the Pacific Ocean. This decision invited all the risks attendant on launching a military buildup on the front doorstep of an adversary's intended domain.

10

A Ridiculous Situation

T HE FREEZING OF AXIS FUNDS, which was to cut off Japan's trade
with the United States, was a move that might have precipitated
hostilities in the Pacific. But Washington gave Pearl Harbor only
six hours' notice of the announcement. The message that arrived first
thing that Saturday, addressed jointly to Admiral Kimmel and General
Short, advised them that "at 1400 GCT July twenty-sixth United States
will impose economic sanctions against Japan," and went on to say that
the Philippine militia was to be called to active service, and that American merchant ships would be prohibited from sailing for Japanese ports.
Nonetheless, although "immediate hostile reaction by Japan through the
use of military means" was not anticipated, the Hawaiian commanders
were alerted to "take appropriate precautionary measures against possible eventualities."[1]

No clue whatever was offered to what the "possible eventualities"
might be. As a fleet alert, therefore, the 25 July warning, which it later
emerged had been drafted by Admiral Turner, was full of shortcomings.
It conflicted with an earlier dispatch that Kimmel had received on 3 July.
That was a notification that Japanese merchant ships were to be clear of
American ports within three weeks, when "unusually reliable Chinese
sources" had predicted that Japan would attack Russia. It was beginning
to look to us as though the navy department was crying wolf without a
proper evaluation of the direction, size, and significance of the threat.

"What are you going to do? Be ready to shoot in all directions at
once?" was the angry reaction of Commander McCollum in Washington
when he found that Turner's 26 July alert had been issued without any
reference to ONI.[2] For a month the head of the Far East section, whose
job it was to assess incoming Japanese intelligence, had been disputing
Turner's fixation—based on no good evidence—that the Japanese were
about to abrogate their neutrality treaty and attack Russia. Turner was

apparently "bemused," according to McCollum, by the German attack on the Soviet Union, which had coincided with the alarms flooding in from the Nationalist Chinese. Chiang Kai-shek was claiming he needed more lend-lease aid to meet a supposed Japanese offensive that was about to develop on the mainland.

"Turner had the theory that Russia was going to fold up momentarily, and he figured out that the Japanese would plunge into Siberia," McCollum explained. "This thinking within the navy department tied Japan to Hitler's tail, even though the Japanese never considered themselves as a satellite to anybody."[3] So without referring to ONI, the war plans director had persuaded Stark to fire off his 3 July alert of Japan's impending attack on Russia, with its confused warning that their fleet "is capable of movement either south or north" and "a definite move by the Japanese may be expected during the period."

Turner's insistence on sending out war warnings based on his own hunches forced the navy department into making incorrect evaluations of Japanese intentions. Turner's warnings conflicted wildly with McCollum's more sober estimates, which were sent to commanders in his fortnightly intelligence summary and predicted an imminent Japanese move into Indochina. The arrogant refusal of the chief of war plans to consult with McCollum left ONI officers in the outrageous situation of not having "any information as to what our own government was doing, because we frequently picked it up only as a result of the decoding of the Japanese diplomatic ciphers." As McCollum later observed, "To say that the guy who has the job of trying to figure things out that he [sic] cannot be told what action has been ordered was ridiculous."[4]

It was only because Kimmel had received some dispatches from Washington based on Purple in July that our predicament was not worse. From these gleanings I had been able to assemble a reasonably accurate picture of the immediate Japanese objectives in Indochina and to estimate their probable naval movements. Therefore, I felt confident in briefing Kimmel's Pacific Fleet staff conference on the morning of 26 July with the scenario I had constructed of what Japanese naval forces were at sea that weekend to support Tokyo's diplomatic demands on the French. We had the details of Japan's ultimatum to the Vichy government, so we knew their precise military objectives. That it was clearly a limited military operation was supported by their Magic intercept of 15 July saying that they hoped to make the moves "peacefully with French agreement if possible," and with the express intent "to avoid friction with Britain and particularly the United States."[5]

In contrast to what would happen later, during the weeks preceding the July crisis the intelligence Kimmel received from Magic sources provided us with all the information we needed to keep us abreast of diplomatic as well as military developments. This intelligence put Turner's idiosyncratic viewpoint into perspective. It enabled Kimmel to have the big picture of developments in Washington and Tokyo. At the same time, it provided me with an overall framework within which I could assemble the detailed pieces of data necessary to work out the dispositions of Japanese naval forces.

The diplomatic information was especially valuable because our naval cryptanalysts were still trying for a breakthrough into Japan's fleet code systems. We had to rely on this for our radio intelligence and for the task of identifying individual call signs from more than fifteen thousand designators. This was complicated, because the Japanese navy had made its annual designator changes on 1 May 1941. In less than two months, however, Rochefort's team had managed to find attributions for enough of the two-kana-numeral call signs to make dependable identifications of many units appearing in the radio traffic. We could not track all the important elements, notably the carrier divisions, but we managed to slot together from other sources some key units that were likely to be deployed in the takeover of Indochina bases. We were also reassured to find no new revision of call signs, another indication that Japan was not contemplating an immediate plunge into outright war.

Our main concern was to locate Japan's carriers, since they would provide the best clue to the movements of her naval forces. But the designators for most of the aircraft carrier divisions had not appeared for a week or more as either originators or addressees. This could mean either that the carriers were not at sea or that they were observing strict radio silence to keep their operations secret. By the summer of 1941 we had become pretty familiar with the pattern of their radio transmissions as well as the overall organization of Japan's naval operations. So although we could not read the codes in which their messages were transmitted, traffic analysis and radio direction-finding pinpointed the location of radio sending stations or units, and evaluated message flow for frequencies, volume, and addressees.

The most important intelligence culled from analysis of radio traffic during the weeks leading up to the July crisis were indications that the Japanese fleet was undergoing a major reorganization. Unknown to us, a new First Air Fleet had been created on 10 April 1941, under command of Admiral Chuichi Nagumo. Hints of this new command were first noted by Rochefort's analysts. Its significance, however, was not appreciated until early 1942. There was not sufficient traffic to allow us to reliably plot the pattern of its operations, but we recognized that this air fleet had authority over all eight aircraft carriers and attached units, together with an escort force of at least sixteen destroyers.

The creation of this fleet signified a new Japanese emphasis on naval air power; and because our Pacific Fleet had only three aircraft carriers, this new force presented a formidable threat. While we did not know when the First Air Fleet would operate as a combined force, our analysts determined that it was made up of four divisions having two carriers apiece, with each division having three or four destroyers to guard its planes. We predicted that, in conformity with our knowledge of their current naval doctrine and thinking, the First Air Fleet would play a supporting role in operations with the battle fleets. These were the days in the U.S. Navy when carriers and their planes were still thought of primarily in terms of scouting and reconnaissance. Aircraft carriers had been used on offensive missions in naval fleet problems as early as 1929 and as recently as 1940, before headquarters were moved to Pearl Harbor. But in the summer of 1941 battleship sailors still ruled the waves.

We linked Nagumo, the First Air Fleet commander in chief, with Carrier Division 1, which consisted of flagship *Kaga* and *Akagi,* as being the crack unit. They were Japan's biggest carriers, and operated with Destroyer Division 7. Like our *Lexington* and *Saratoga,* these thirty-thousand-ton flattops had been converted on the ways from a battleship and battle cruiser. Carrier Division 2 was made up of the newer *Sōryū* and *Hiryū,* and was linked with Destroyer Division 23; Carrier Division 3, light carriers *Ryūjō* and *Hosho,* was teamed with Destroyer Division 17. Carrier Division 4, made up of the fleet's newest twenty-thousand-ton carriers, *Shōkaku* and *Zuikaku,* was in tandem with Destroyer Division 3. Two converted merchantmen, *Horyu Maru* and *Kasuga Maru,* constituted what seemed to be an auxiliary carrier force, which we designated Carrier Division 5.[6]

The battleships and cruisers of Combined Fleet we knew were organized into First Fleet, or battle force; and Second Fleet, the scouting force. A Third Fleet, a blockade and transport force, consisted of a light cruiser, a dozen destroyers, tenders, transports, and miscellaneous vessels. So when our analysis of radio transmissions in the weeks leading up to 26 July revealed that, despite the potential power of the new First Air Fleet, two divisions of its carriers were assigned to support First and Second Fleet operations, we were confident that no major expedition was at sea.[7]

Rochefort's daily summaries of intelligence, derived from traffic analysis, indicated that at least one carrier division was with the scouting force in the South China Sea. This became even more of a certainty when we considered what had happened in February 1941, when the Japanese decided to mediate the French Indochina-Thailand border dispute with a show of naval force. At that time the Second and Third fleets, along with their carriers, had been sighted steaming southward. It was therefore a good bet that the Japanese would send a similar force south again in July. Since this time it seemed to be a Second Fleet show, we assumed that Carrier Division 2 would again be part of this operation to cover the occupation of the Indochina bases.[8]

Confirmation that such a task force was under way was evident from intelligence received from our consuls and naval attachés in Shanghai. The concentration of Japanese naval forces was also confirmed by the latest sighting reports from the ONI network of our seventeen undercover observers in Far East ports. A low volume of Japanese naval radio traffic during the second part of July suggested that most of the Combined Fleet was probably still in home waters. *The New York Times* on 8 July supported this with reports from its Tokyo correspondent that most of the fleet was at anchor off Yokohama "without any attempt at secrecy."

Only after the war was the accuracy of our July traffic analysis estimates finally confirmed. Interrogations of Japanese pilots revealed that *Sōryū* and *Hiryū* had spent the two-thousand-mile trip south to Indochina waters and back conducting continual exercises. What we had not guessed was that while Carrier Division 2 was en route back to Japan, it had rendezvoused with carriers *Akagi* and *Kaga* to practice combat maneuvers against Carrier Division 1. These mock attacks were an important operational test of techniques that the same pilots and planes would use for the attack on Pearl Harbor five months later.

The Indochina crisis was also an important test of our own ability to forecast enemy operations in time to be able to meet them. By coincidence, at 0400 that Saturday, 26 July 1941, Kimmel's revised war plan for the Pacific Fleet came into effect. To fulfill the broad directives of the Rainbow 5 war strategy, the fleet would be used to "check any Japanese moves toward the eventual capture of Malaysia (including the Philippines) and Hong Kong," or "the capture of Guam and other outlying positions."[9]

Kimmel developed his plan on the assumption that the Pacific Fleet's numerical inferiority to Combined Fleet would preclude a decisive confrontation. The fleet's principal mission would therefore be "diverting the enemy strength away from the Malay barrier, through the denial and capture of positions in the Marshalls." Until hostilities were imminent, one of our main tasks was to "guard against surprise attack by Japan."[10]

So at his staff conference on the morning of 26 July, although he agreed with the estimates from Washington and from his staff that hostile moves by Japan would be limited to local demonstrations off the Indochina coast by a part of the Combined Fleet, Kimmel agreed with Admiral Bloch on the "advisability" of increasing our long-range air searches. Bloch, the commander in chief of the Fourteenth Naval District, who had preceded Richardson as fleet commander, believed that a surprise attack on Pearl Harbor was a very remote possibility, but he felt it prudent to initiate contingency air defense measures. Planes took off at dawn the next day on a series of long-range patrols five hundred miles to the west-southwest, toward Jaluit, to intercept any Japanese force that might be sneaking in to attack from their secret bases in the Marshalls.

Simultaneously, General Short reacted to Washington's 25 July alert by placing his forces on a "half alert against sabotage."[11] The air reconnaissance continued through the weekend until the absence of "untoward

eventualities" persuaded Kimmel and Short to step down their alert.
Japan had occupied Indochina naval bases at Camranh Bay and Saigon,
and air bases at Phnom Penh, Bien-hoa, and Saigon, but despite Turner's
fears, the Tokyo government appeared to be waiting to test the impact of
American economic sanctions before embarking on any hostile adventures in Siberia or anywhere else.

Kimmel nevertheless continued to regard the Pacific Fleet as being on
a wartime footing because, after 26 July, there was no doubt in our minds
at Pearl Harbor about the ultimate consequence of the embargo. Sooner,
rather than later, Japan would move southward from her newly acquired
bases in Indochina to seize alternative oil supplies from the Netherlands
East Indies and Malaya? The Indochina crisis had, therefore, raised a
number of serious concerns for Kimmel. What would be the role the fleet
was expected to play now that tension between Japan and the United
States had been hiked up several notches by the embargo? What was the
significance of the occupation of bases in Indochina, which shortened the
striking distance between Japanese forces and Malaya?

Kimmel voiced these concerns in a 26 July letter to Admiral Stark. It
stressed the "importance of keeping the commander in chief advised of
department policies and decisions, and changes of policies and decisions
to meet changes in the international situation." Kimmel asked to be informed of what plans Washington had for "mutual support" if Japan attacked British or Dutch territory.[12]

Stark's acknowledgment of 8 August was as brief as it was evasive. He
promised that "we shall go through it paragraph by paragraph" and that
he was "glad to get an occasional check of this sort."[13] Meanwhile, Kimmel's fears about his fleet's strength were exacerbated by another brief
CNO letter, dated 25 July, informing him that the president was considering that "you may be called upon to send a carrier load of planes to one
of the Asiatic Russian ports."[14] It was incredible that anyone in Washington would even consider jeopardizing one of our precious carriers on such
a risky mission. Kimmel fired back at once that the "entire Pacific Fleet"
would be needed to ensure its safety. Moreover, "in the tense situation it
would be tantamount to initiation of a Japanese-American war. . . .

"If for reasons of political expediency, it has been determined to force
Japan to fire the first shot," Kimmel concluded acidly, "let us choose a
method that will be more advantageous to ourselves. Certainly an operation such as that proposed is far less likely to bluff Japan into acquies-
cence or inactivity that it is to disturb her to the point of hostile use of
bombs, torpedoes, and guns."[15]

Kimmel's distaste for what he considered to be Roosevelt's madcap
schemes was increased by the confused "thinking out loud" letter of 31
July addressed by Stark to Captain Charles M. Cooke, Jr., with copies to
Kimmel and Hart. "Savvy" Cooke of flagship *Pennsylvania* had preceded
Turner as Stark's confidant and director of war plans.

The letter was charged with Stark's confusion about whether the embargo would ultimately send Japan charging south to seize the alternative oil supplies of the Dutch East Indies. Roosevelt's erratic course was his main gripe. "To some of my very pointed questions, which all of us would like to have answered, I get a smile or a 'Betty, please don't ask me that,'" Stark complained. He wearily admitted that he had offered to resign more than once. "Policy seems to be something never fixed, always fluid and changing." This also revealed the astonishing degree to which CNO had become dependent on the erratic intelligence estimates of his director of war plans. Turner's incorrect forecast that Japan would soon invade Vladivostok and Russia's maritime provinces was passed on with the comment, "He may be right. He usually is."[16]

It was bad enough being in Pearl Harbor and realizing that the navy department was so confused about what would happen next. But Kimmel was dismayed to learn that Roosevelt was not even confiding in his chief of naval operations. Kimmel knew the president was adept at using affability to sidestep awkward issues and Admiral Stark was not the only senior member of the administration to complain. Supreme Court Chief Justice Felix Frankfurter observed the president's preference for looking at problems through the wrong end of a telescope because "it makes things easier to bear."[17]

Cabinet members did not bear the burden so lightly. They were often exasperated by Roosevelt's penchant for reaching critical policy decisions in long, rambling monologues that went largely unrecorded. It was what Secretary of War Stimson called "the topsy turvy, upside-down system of poor administration" by which the United States was governed.

To the British ambassador, such decision making was more like "a disorderly day's rabbit shooting" than sound government.[18] Lord Halifax's complaint to London about Roosevelt's studied evasiveness is especially revealing. He had been upset because, during the several ABC-1 staff talks in March 1941, the Americans had refused to enter into the most tentative of military commitments in the Far East. Then, despite broad general agreement at joint staff discussions with the Dutch at Singapore in May, the American chiefs of staff still refused to endorse any formal mutual defense pact against Japan. But, as Lord Halifax reported to London, Roosevelt's announcement of 26 July concerning American economic sanctions against Japan had changed all that.

Kimmel was guessing right. To enforce the new sanctions, Washington had to reconsider the desirability of a defensive alliance in the Far East. Some Anglo-American agreement on joint defensive measures to hold the Malay Barrier-Philippine defense line was now not merely desirable, but given Japan's naval superiority and lack of oil supplies, it was essential.

Churchill had appreciated the strategic implications of the American embargo far more clearly than the foreign policy makers in Washington.

With the U-boats in the Atlantic threatening to gnaw through Britain's fuel line to the United States, the prime minister knew just how the Japanese viewed the prospects that their war machine would be drained of its offensive and defensive capability as their planes ran out of gas and their warships were confined to port for lack of fuel. Although the Dutch and British readily agreed to join in with the economic embargo, the prime minister warned Roosevelt that measures were needed to stop the Japanese who were ready to "run amok."[19] Japan had to import all but 12 percent of her oil, 80 percent of it in 1941 coming from the United States. In the year ending March 1941, imports reached an all-time high of nearly twenty-three million barrels of crude, and fifteen million of refined petroleum. The Japanese had been stockpiling oil, but it was calculated that with naval consumption alone running at three hundred thousand tons a month, the reserves on hand would last less than a year even with stringent civilian rationing.

Washington's failure to make this calculation must be counted as one of the major intelligence blunders of history. This was especially true after Magic provided the clear warning in a 31 July Tokyo-Berlin intercept. "To save its very life," Ambassador Oshima was told, Japan "must take immediate steps to break asunder this ever strengthening chain of encirclement which is being woven under the guidance and with the participation of England and the United States, acting like a cunning dragon seemingly asleep."[20] For all its quaint phraseology, this message was a blunt expression of Japan's intention: to advance southward and seize alternative supplies if diplomacy failed to quickly reopen the tap on American oil.

It appears that no one in Washington was alerted by this Magic intercept to the fact that the Japanese government had now been forced onto a deadline for reconciling its national policy objectives. The State Department therefore made a bad miscalculation when it launched into a carrot-and-stick diplomacy in the expectation that the resumption of oil supplies would serve as the reward, while the Anglo-American military buildup in the Far East would provide the threat.

The reality, however, was that our foreign policy toward Japan was now forced into the dangerous posture of allowing diplomatic policy to dictate military strategy. We lacked the military strength to enforce the embargo. To meet the two-ocean Axis menace with a one-ocean navy and avoid the objections of an isolationist Congress, Roosevelt was now forced into a secret commitment to Britain. And this led both nations into a Far East deterrent strategy that was as unfounded as it was to prove catastrophic.

11

Deceptive Deterrents

O N 2 AUGUST 1941 Roosevelt put to sea in the presidential yacht *Potomac*. He was going on a well-publicized "fishing trip." But out of sight of the New England coast, he transferred from the yacht to heavy cruiser *Augusta*, where his military chiefs were already on board. Their mission was to be one of the most consequential, but little understood, meetings in history; it would be held in foggy Placentia Bay on the bleak southern coast off Newfoundland.

Meanwhile, Winston Churchill and his advisers were steaming at high speed westward across the Atlantic on board the Royal Navy's newest battleship, *Prince of Wales*. Still bearing the scars of her gunnery duel the past May with the German battleship *Bismarck*, *Prince of Wales* was relying on Enigma decrypts of U-boat signals to dodge German wolf packs. On Saturday, 9 August 1941, she hove to a short haul from where *Augusta* and her escorts swung at anchor off the village of Argentia and its nearby lend-lease airstrip.

Within hours of the battleship's arrival Roosevelt and Churchill met for the first time as president and prime minister on board *Augusta*. They quickly discovered a strong personal rapport and struck an overall agreement on strategy. The American chiefs of staff, led by General George L. Marshall and Admiral Harold E. Stark, with General "Hap" Arnold and Admiral Richmond K. Turner in attendance, conferred with the British chiefs led by Admiral Sir Dudley Pound and General Sir John Dill, to hammer out what Roosevelt carefully laid down as being "broad principles which should guide our policies along the same road."[1]

During the first round of discussions, the British military leaders found themselves in the same ship but not yet "in the same boat" concerning an agreement on the terms of an overall alliance they hoped for with the United States. Churchill was disappointed to learn that his team could not get an American commitment to send warships into the Mediterranean, or to commence the convoying of Britain's merchant shipping beyond the American neutrality zone all the way across the Atlantic. But when it came to the Pacific it was a different matter. The British delegation was encouraged to find that American military policy against Japan had undergone a complete revision since the strategic stalemate of the May staff conversations in Singapore. They were delighted to discover that Washington's embargo on Axis trade was forcing the American chiefs of staff to accept the need for establishing a powerful military and naval force in the Far East as a deterrent against Japan.

"We are now trying to build up the defense of the Philippines as a direct defense to the Indian Ocean and Singapore," Admiral Stark told a joint meeting on board *Prince of Wales* on Monday, 11 August. "Could the British rearrange their schedules to help out on this?" Marshall explained that the recent American decision to bolster the defenses of Manila and the Asiatic Fleet could be made only if the scheduled lend-lease shipments of antiaircraft batteries and heavy bombers originally destined for Britain could be redirected across the Pacific to General MacArthur.

In the horse trading that followed, Marshall went far beyond the limited commitments to Far East defense which had been agreed to at the ABC-1 staff talks in March and which were the basis of the Rainbow 5 strategic war plan. Pound and Dill fell all over themselves to accommodate the American request. They believed that they were getting the best of a bargain in which bombers and antiaircraft guns were to be traded for a massive American buildup in the Philippines. Visions of the Pacific Fleet in Manila Bay, only three days' steaming from the still-vacant battleship berths at the Singapore naval base, prompted Admiral Pound's enthusiastic endorsement that "a strong defense of the Philippine Islands directly strengthens the defense of Singapore and the Netherlands East Indies."[3] A speedy buildup of MacArthur's forces was also entirely in accord with the sentiments Churchill had expressed in his after-dinner speech on board *Prince of Wales* the previous evening; he had called on the United States to join with Britain and Russia in issuing a final ultimatum to Japan.

Churchill's comments had been received with as much vocal approval by our military staff as by their British hosts. But outside the euphoria in *Prince of Wales*'s oak-paneled admiral's quarters, Roosevelt knew that the full-blooded declaration of mutual alliance that the prime minister sought would not play well with his congressional foes on Capitol Hill.

So the publicly announced result of the conference was restricted to the so-called Atlantic Charter declaration of the British and American agreement to uphold Roosevelt's Four Principles of Freedom that were later to be incorporated into the United Nations Charter. The declaration's euphoric rhetoric, however, camouflaged a more far-reaching military arrangement by the United States, which was not committed to writing. Just what the prime minister and president agreed to in their private sessions was a matter of concern to General Arnold, one of the leading participants in the conference. "I can't make up my mind as yet whether most of us are window dressing for the main actors, or whether we are playing minor roles in the drama," he noted disparagingly, the more so because he had been instrumental in hammering out substantive military details. Alluding to some secret accord, which Arnold termed the "epoch-making" outcome of the conference, he wrote, "What the President and the Prime Minister had to say when together I know not."[4]

The chief of the army air force knew better than anyone that Churchill would not have agreed to release badly needed bombers and anti-aircraft batteries to MacArthur without the quid pro quo that they would indeed be employed as a "direct defense to the Indian Ocean and Singapore.[5] There may have been failure to agree on convoying, or the intended British occupation of the north African French port of Dakar, but when the warships carrying the prime minister and president sailed from Placentia Bay on 14 August, Arnold believed firmly that the military leaders were in total accord on "the handling of Japan if that nation moved farther southward."[6]

The pact on "handling Japan" would indeed turn out to be "epoch-making"—but not in the way the participants intended. The volte-face on strategy in the Pacific resulted in a disastrous strategic miscalculation for the United States, because the belief that a scratch force of American bombers and a few British warships could be transformed by diplomatic bluff into a "big stick" that would force the Japanese to halt their southward advance was a gamble doomed to failure. By embarking on a deterrent policy before the military forces were installed in the Philippines to make it credible, Britain and the United States succeeded in making the concept of a preemptive strike an attractive option to the Japanese.

It was also ironic that the conference should have settled on aircraft rather than battleships as the prescription for dissuading Japan from launching an essentially maritime adventure. But the chiefs of our armed forces had placed their military bets, believing that General Arnold's Flying Fortress bombers were the right strategic chips with which to gamble the defense of Anglo-American territory in the Far East, that the B-17s would be an effective deterrent to Japanese aggression. The long-range bombers, which otherwise would have been on their way to Britain, were accordingly diverted to the Philippines. They were to be backed up by Churchill's pledge to send a squadron of modern battleships and carriers to Singapore.

Getting adequate deterrent forces out to the Far East was going to take many months, so Churchill readily accepted Roosevelt's assurance that the State Department would be able to "baby them [the Japanese] along"[7] until then. Despite foreign office protests that he was making an unprecedented abrogation of British diplomatic independence, Churchill issued instructions that future negotiations with the Japanese were in the hands of the State Department. Did this mean that if the "babying along" failed, the Americans would be committed to fight Japan even if American territory was not attacked first?

In later years it would be a favorite charge by the isolationists that Roosevelt had, indeed, made just such a secret and unconstitutional pact with Churchill at Argentia. Exactly how far the president went in his private sessions with the British prime minister may never be known, but a logical assessment of the situation suggests that some deal was struck that amounted to a de facto Anglo-American alliance against Japan that was never submitted to Congress for ratification. Although Roosevelt would not have run afoul of the constitutional restraints until he was actually called upon to honor the guarantees he had given Churchill, we shall see how he came perilously close to doing just that by 4 December 1941.

Churchill's rejection of a foreign office minute that Britain had abrogated her traditional rights of independent negotiation with Japan, without signing a formal accord with the United States, was one indication of the unwritten alliance. Another was the considerable risk that the prime minister had run in making a seven-thousand-mile round trip across the U-boat-infested Atlantic, which was hardly justified by the idealistic window-dressing of the Atlantic Charter. Noble and inspiring though its ringing phrases were, the document did not amount to any tangible furtherance of Britain's war aims—and it was also unsigned.

The best evidence that the isolationists were right is contained in the minutes of the Joint Army-Navy Board. Chaired by Admiral Stark throughout 1941, the same top military brains that had attended the Argentia conference continued to meet every two weeks, and they were final arbiter of American strategic planning. The minutes of these Joint Board meetings subsequent to August 1941 show how the supreme military council of the United States put a de facto Anglo-American alliance against Japan into effect by making preparations to commit our forces to a war even if it was British rather than our territory that the Japanese struck first. The records now available confirm that the board members were making their plans on the assumption that America would be at war if Japan attacked British, but not United States, territory first.

The nature of the commitments that Roosevelt had given to Churchill were questioned at the first full joint board meeting after Argentia. General Marshall, on 4 September, voiced concern that "the president might direct the British be given a seat on the Joint Board."[8] This unprecedented recognition of the fraternity of Anglo-American military interest was something that the army chief was determined to resist.

When the board next convened on 14 September, Turner outlined the navy's plans for dealing with "offensive operations" by the Japanese— not just concerning the Philippines but taking into account joint operations with British and Dutch forces to defend Malaya. A month later, on

10 October, the board discussed and approved a strategic critique submitted by the British chiefs of staff and agreed to a list of fuel and bomb depots being established at Far East air bases belonging to Britain, Australia, and the Netherlands.

If there was any doubt that a de facto Anglo-American alliance was already in existence, it was removed for the members of the Joint Board at their 3 November session at which Admiral Stark clearly let it be known that we would go to war if Japan launched full-scale offensive operations: "In the case of a Japanese attack against either the Philippines or British or Dutch possessions, the United States should resist the attack. In case of a Japanese attack against Siberia, Thailand or China through Yunnan, the United States should not declare war."[9]

From the context of this statement, there can be no doubt about the true implication of Stark's characteristically euphemistic expression that our forces "should resist" a Japanese attack on the territory of foreign powers with whom at that point we had no congressionally ratified alliance. That there was no question about the board's intentions is evident from Admiral Ingersoll's meeting notes. "Yes" is checked against "War" in only two of five possibilities—that Japan attacked the Philippines and "British or Dutch Malay."[10]

It is now abundantly clear what Roosevelt meant when he told the British ambassador on the evening of 2 December that "we shall all be in it together."[11] The military leadership in Washington was already basing its contingency planning for war on that premise.

That Roosevelt *did* provide Churchill with what amounted to a potentially unconstitutional assurance of alliance became public knowledge six months later. To the consternation of presidential aide Harry Hopkins, on 17 January 1942, the prime minister felt obliged to allude to the agreement in defending himself against a censure motion in the House of Commons. To the charge that Britain's colonies in the Far East had been inadequately guarded, Churchill asserted he had taken care that Britain "should not be exposed single-handed to the Japanese onslaught."[12] Choosing his words with caution lest he let the cat out of the bag and embarrass the president, he insisted there had been no neglect because of "the probability since the Atlantic conference at which I discussed these matters with Mr. Roosevelt, that the United States, even if not attacked herself, would come into a war in the Far East." His "expectation"—as he put it—was "reinforced as time went on" and "one had greater assurance that if Japan ran amok in the Pacific, we should not fight alone." Nor, as Churchill reminded his detractors, had his confidence in the United States been "falsified by events."[13]

The prime minister's 1942 statement that hinted at the true extent of this clandestine military cooperation against Japan set alarm bells ringing in the White House and brought an attack from Senator Burton K. Wheeler who had been one of the most vocal spokesmen of the isolationists. On 21 February, Harry Hopkins sent the president a memorandum warning that "some day soon Wheeler and his crowd may pick it up." They did.[14]

At the 1945 Pearl Harbor hearings it was repeatedly charged that the president had exceeded his constitutional powers in making a secret alliance with Britain. But although considerable evidence was cited, the full records of the Joint Board meetings were not made available to the hearings. As a result the majority determined that no such commitment had been made.

This refusal to release the records was an understandable effort to protect Roosevelt against charges that he had acted unconstitutionally. But the most damaging aspect of the original conference was the failure of Admiral Stark to immediately inform the Pacific Fleet commander of the true implications of the new Anglo-American strategy against Japan. The failure to pass on such a critical bit of information was inexcusable.

In hindsight, it was all the more astonishing because of Kimmel's urgent request of Stark to learn "what arrangements" existed for cooperation with the British and Dutch naval forces in the event that fighting broke out in the Far East. The question was ignored altogether by the chief of naval operations in his 21 August letter which, nonetheless, expressed a growing concern about "the seriousness of the Pacific situation which continues to deteriorate."[15]

Admiral Kimmel was relieved, however, that CNO's first lengthy dispatch since the Churchill-Roosevelt meeting did not request another transfer of Pacific Fleet ships to strengthen our Atlantic naval forces. Nor did it call for sending reinforcements to Admiral Hart's tiny Asiatic Fleet in Manila, although it was now dangerously exposed to Japanese warships, which were operating from newly acquired bases in Indochina.

The events of July had convinced Kimmel that there could be no reining in our preparations for the fleet's assigned mission under the original Rainbow 5 war plan: to conduct a sortie toward Japanese bases in the Marshalls to draw their forces away from the Philippines and the Malay Barrier. There could be no letup in the intensive schedule of training operations needed to bring ships and men up to battle readiness. The problem, however, was more than just keeping men, ships, and equipment in good physical condition and readiness. There were the equally important considerations of morale and spirit. Most of the sailors in Hawaii were long separated from home and loved ones. The fleshpots of Honolulu could offer little more than temporary solace. There was a limit in peacetime as to how long men could be kept on watch-and-watch duty.

Throughout the summer of 1941 Kimmel's hard-driving schedule of operations kept at least one—and often two—of the fleet's task forces at sea. Port calls were necessary for replenishment and crew morale, but it is often forgotten that at no time during 1941 were *all* the ships of the fleet in Pearl Harbor.[16] Maximum security measures, consistent with the

maintenance of the training program, were kept in effect after July. But
to effect the critical transition of the fleet from intensive training to all-
out war measures was a matter of timing. To determine when that moment was at hand, the fleet commander had to rely on the intelligence he
received from Washington.

"When would Japanese-American relations reach the point that all
training should cease and all-out war dispositions should be made?"[17]
That was the question that Kimmel was constantly asking himself, as relations between Japan and the United States worsened.

This was the very time when we needed all the intelligence—especially diplomatic intelligence—that we could lay our hands on. But not
one single piece of the Magic by which Washington was monitoring this
policy of "babying along" Tokyo's diplomats was relayed to us at Pearl
Harbor from August through November. Nor did we know why the decrypts were not sent to us. After Kimmel had received the July Magics, I
had remained confident that ONI's Far East section was living up to their
promise to us the previous April that we would get *all* diplomatic intelligence relevant to the fleet.

Those determined to blame the president for a conspiracy to get the
United States into the war against Hitler "by the back door" claim that
Admiral Kimmel was denied this Magic intelligence on the direct orders
of the White House.

While there can be no doubt now that Roosevelt exceeded the limits
of his executive authority in the assurances he gave Churchill, that the
United States would go to war if British territory in the Far East was
attacked, there is no evidence that any presidential directive was issued
restricting the flow of intelligence to Pearl Harbor—or anywhere else.
The decision to limit the type of intelligence sent to overseas commands,
in fact, appears to have been a bureaucratic one. The reason for it was a
genuine fear that Washington's secrets were leaking to the Japanese.

12

Shortchanged

I N VIEW OF THE fatal consequences of the de facto Anglo-American military alliance against Japan, it was a curious twist of fate that Japan had somehow penetrated our heavy curtain of secrecy in order to correctly estimate the significance of the Argentia conference. This startling revelation emerged from the intercept of Ambassador Nomura's 7 August report to Tokyo that Japanese-American relations were "extremely critical" since "the president accompanied by high army and navy officials is meeting with Churchill."[1]

The Purple decrypt of Ambassador Nomura's report, which had been sent a full *three days* before the first meeting between Roosevelt and Churchill, alerted the foreign minister that the Argentia conference would be proof that "careful preparations are being made to counter our every move." These fears were confirmed the following day by Japan's London envoy. In a cable that was also intercepted, Tokyo was informed that presidential aide Harry Hopkins was accompanying Churchill's party and that Marshall, Stark, and King would participate in the conference in which the Far East was to be one of the principal topics.[2]

The Japanese military attaché in Washington also roused the army's concern with his report that such a high-level meeting could mean only one thing: "closer arrangements for a joint Anglo-American participation in the war."[3] Although this message was intercepted too, it was in a code that could not be read until 1943. But the two Purple decrypts were alarming enough evidence that Japan had advance warning of the Churchill-Roosevelt meeting. So was Tokyo's 9 August instruction to Nomura to press the White House for a meeting with Japan's prime minister "immediately upon President Roosevelt's return."[4] The sources of the leak were never pinpointed, but the incident served to reinforce Washington's security fetish.

When I became Pacific Fleet intelligence officer in December 1940, I had been impressed by my having to swear an oath of secrecy. There were very strict regulations limiting the supersecret comint only to the commander in chief and those few members of his staff who had also been sworn to secrecy. For those other staff members who had not been cleared, I prepared a special intelligence summary that was given an A-1 rating, but no identification as to its source. So great was our concern for these secrets that when Kimmel added his war plans officer to the comint list, I could not brief Captain McMorris on the material until the admiral gave me handwritten authority.[5]

Measures to protect our own communications channels for Magic were every bit as strict. Intercepted Japanese signals, even though they could not be broken, were relayed after reencipherment on a special radio circuit code-named Copek. Messages containing references to radio intelligence used the regular naval communications network. But all such communications had to be sent by our ECM code machines in a special cipher, which could be deciphered only by the command holding the correct rotors for that cipher. The rotors were issued to commands according to rank. A rear admiral (two stars), for example, rated a set that enabled him to read messages sent out for commands of his rank. When such messages were received by the communications office, they could identify only that this was a special cipher. It was then passed to the fleet security officer. At Cincpac, he alone would be responsible for using the special machine and code wheels to break out the message to be hand-delivered to the admiral, his chief of staff, or, if so directed by Kimmel, passed on to me.

The August 1941 security flap in Washington came hard on the heels of a top-secret army inquiry after the State Department reported fears that its codes "had already been broken by one or more foreign governments."[6] Investigation revealed that these fears were groundless, but General Marshall ordered a general tightening up of security where codes and communications were involved.

It was against this paranoid background of investigations and new directives intended to reduce the risk of leakage of our most secret information that the custodians of Magic evidently concluded that even the navy's flag-officer rotor system, which had previously been considered far more secure than the army or State Department code systems, could not now guarantee sufficient protection for their most vital intelligence source. While based on the sound principle of restricting secret information on a "need to know" basis, it negated Magic's informational value as practical intelligence since it was subsequently denied to the Pacific Fleet. Admiral Kimmel was the one overseas commander above all others who had a need to know and act on Magic.

After 7 December, however, no one wanted to acknowledge responsibility for having shut off our Pearl Harbor headquarters from the intelligence that could have saved the Pacific Fleet. At the seven secret wartime inquiries, and again during the public testimony at the congressional hearings held in 1945, a parade of senior staff officers denied any direct responsibility for setting the policy. Such reticence, even in 1945, suggests a realization by these officers that the December disaster might have been prevented if Admiral Kimmel had received detailed intelligence based on Purple diplomatic traffic.

Their testimony was understandably evasive, patently confused, and often conflicting about whether the ban on sending Magic overseas was the result of specific orders, or just a consensus action. But there was general agreement that as relations between Washington and Tokyo grew more strained, increasingly stringent measures had been put into effect by both navy and military intelligence organizations to prevent the Japanese from getting "any inkling" that we could read their diplomatic communications.[7]

Colonel Rufus Bratton, chief of the Far East section of military intelligence, Captain McCollum's opposite number in the army, testified before the congressional committee that orders from the army chief of staff "prevented me from transmitting any Magic to overseas commanders."[8] General Marshall challenged this assertion. He insisted that he could "recall giving no such specific instructions."[9]

Admiral Stark also denied issuing orders preventing transmission of Magic to Admiral Kimmel. He explained that he had tried to incorporate it into his "personal letters." The former chief of naval operations claimed he "would have far rather sent him too much than too little." So great was the secrecy surrounding Magic, and so complete Admiral Turner's control of intelligence, that Stark admitted that he had been led to believe by his chief of war plans that Pearl Harbor could translate, as well as intercept, the Japanese diplomatic messages.[10]

"I inquired on two or three occasions as to whether or not Kimmel could read certain dispatches, when they came up and which we were interpreting," Stark testified, ". . . and I was told that he could."[11] Admiral Turner maintained that this was indeed "my impression at the time" because he had been assured by the director of naval communications in "March or April" 1941 that Kimmel was not only "getting as much as we were" but "he was getting it sooner than we were."[12]

Such oversight on the part of the director of war plans, who was known for poking his nose into everyone's pie, reveals he was either a fool or a liar. This was not in keeping with the character of Turner, who had taken a crash course in music in order to be able to bawl out the band on his cruiser,[13] and whose war plans staff had been used to his raging against Noyes "and his God-damn secrets!"[14] Turner, moreover, not only had access to the daily Magic summaries, but insisted on reviewing all operational intelligence sent to us at Pearl Harbor.

Turner's protested ignorance was essential to his denial of all responsibility for what intelligence was made available to us at Pearl Harbor before 7 December 1941. It put Noyes on the spot when he was sworn as a witness at the secret 1944 naval court of inquiry. At first the former director of naval communications was carefully evasive about precisely what assurances had been given to his buccaneering superior. After re-peated questioning, he eventually conceded that Turner raised the matter of who was getting what in "almost daily" meetings that "continually discussed" the status of decrypting. Turner, therefore, "should have un-derstood."[15]

Under cross-examination Noyes went even further. He testified that it was his remembrance that when the director of war plans "asked what was our setup in regard to intercepted messages," it was "fully explained to him." Pressed whether he had ever given the chief of war plans "any impression that the commander in chief of the Pacific Fleet was getting information of the type contained in the Purple code intercepts," Noyes refused to be budged from his equivocal "Not intentionally."[16]

This refusal to actually blame a brother admiral let Turner off the hook. The former war plans chief maintained his assertion that Kimmel "had everything we had"—as he had so brazenly tried to outface me on the night of the surrender ceremony with his claim that Pearl Harbor could read the Japanese diplomatic traffic!

Four months later, however, on 21 December 1945, Turner was called to answer the glaring conflict in testimony that was revealed when the congressional investigating committee gained access to the secret record of the naval court of inquiry. Then the former war plans chief was forced to admit that he "was entirely in error as regards the diplomatic codes."[17]

Turner then tried to cover up the magnitude of the consequences of his error in a cloud of self-assertiveness that befitted his public stature as one of the heroic leaders of the Pacific campaign. Like a cuttlefish eject-ing ink to escape danger, he blew a bombastic smokescreen that enabled him to dart for cover behind the failures of the intelligence specialists whose function he had so tenaciously usurped in 1941. None of his former subordinates had the courage to take on the fire-breathing four-star admi-ral who had successfully masterminded the navy's wartime amphibious operations. No witness dared to expose the extent to which the director of war plans and his three-man "coordinating" group effectively main-tained a stranglehold on the intelligence that went out to the fleet.

Turner was thereby allowed to escape with his reputation, if not honor, intact by claiming that he "did not know the details at all of the decryption methods or codes." Noyes was supposedly confused or had "misunderstood what I was trying to get at."[18] Turner could not recall whether Noyes had "specified diplomatic intercepts" in their discussion four years earlier, and Turner double-talked at the inquiry, saying that confusion about the actual decrypting process had given them both a false impression about precisely what information Kimmel was receiving.[19]

Turner's deceptive and evasive responses in December 1945 betrayed an ignorance that was highly unlikely, or a deception that was highly obvious. But since none of his former colleagues was going to "spill the beans," he confused the congressional investigators, who tried to chip away at his granitelike composure.

Such confusion of terms might have been excusable in a layman. But it suggests a lack of credibility in a ranking admiral with a formidable reputation for excessive attention to detail. The committee's senior counsel was moved to ask how it was possible for him to have discharged his duty to keep the fleet commanders fully advised of intelligence indicating the possibility of war. "You could not do that," William D. Mitchell asked Turner with deliberate sarcasm, "unless you knew precisely just what they had and what they needed from you. Isn't that so?"[20]

"No, sir; that is not correct. It was not my duty to inform commanders in chief as to intelligence," Turner shot back. "Sending intercepts, or summaries of intercepts, or evaluating them as to authenticity or probability, was not war plans province and we never under any circumstance sent such information out."[21]

To anyone who is familiar with the mutinous conditions provoked by Turner's interference in the intelligence process on the second deck of the navy department throughout 1941, his barefaced denial of any responsibility for its consequences was as outrageous as it was untrue. Not only had he ridden roughshod over the functions and sensibilities of two directors of naval intelligence, but he had sent out false warnings and interfered with estimates without any reference to the very department whose duty it was to evaluate the extent and direction of the Japanese threat. Only because Stark and Ingersoll had resisted making any written change in the naval operations manual was Turner able to outface the charge of culpability for the intelligence debacle that led to disaster at Pearl Harbor.

In 1961 Turner died with his lies caught in his throat. The other officers who, in 1941, comprised the upper echelon of the naval staff in Washington closed ranks to protect his and their own reputations, intending to take the secret to their collective graves. Fortunately, five years after Turner's death, one of them—Captain McCollum—decided that posterity deserved the truth. Then retired, and a distinguished rear admiral, the former head of ONI's Far East desk provided the U.S. Naval Institute with a graphic personal account of the temper and tempests that followed Turner's rise to power as the domineering member of the triumvirate that ran the office of naval operations throughout 1941.

McCollum's chief, ONI director Admiral Kirk, had repeatedly protested this usurpation of their role by war plans. At the height of his battle with Turner in May, it was clear to both McCollum and Kirk that if Turner's arbitrary authority was not formalized, they would be in a position to be blamed for anything that went wrong as a result of the inaccurate estimates that war plans was sending out to the commands without consulting ONI.

Captain McCollum took it upon himself to attempt to resolve the feud between naval intelligence and the war plans division that was poisoning the air on the navy department's second deck, and throttling off the fleet at Pearl Harbor from an adequate flow of properly evaluated intelligence. In a personal interview with Admiral Ingersoll, McCollum sought to enlist his support in persuading Admiral Stark to regularize the procedures Turner was controlling by oral fiat. Ingersoll's deputy was a mild, soft-spoken, thoughtful officer whom Kirk believed to be his only ally in the upper reaches of the naval staff.

McCollum patiently detailed what was going wrong. War plans was sending out its own, often wildly incorrect estimates without any reference to himself or the ONI director. He pointed out the inconsistencies of this conduct with the procedures and responsibilities laid down by the CNO manual. The dangers were self-evident. McCollum reminded Ingersoll of the procedure, similar to the army's, that had been followed by the navy until Turner arrived—for ONI to do the evaluating. Ingersoll was not sympathetic. His hackles rising, he insisted on knowing all about the army practice, but observed that the navy did not do it that way.[22]

"Admiral, if that's the case, how about issuing an order in writing amending that part of the ONI manual?" McCollum ventured. The usually affable Ingersoll was set alight by this apparent attempt by a subordinate to dictate CNO policy.

"Get the hell out of here," roared the admiral. "A verbal [sic] order is enough!"[23]

This abrupt dismissal ended any further efforts by the ONI staff to have the intelligence responsibility of the war plans directorate committed to writing. Since the manual was not amended, Richmond Kelly Turner was allowed to deny his responsibility for failing to keep Admiral Kimmel fully informed with all the pertinent intelligence that was available in Washington. Stark and Ingersoll had knowingly sanctioned Turner's insistence on "coordinating" the final evaluation of operational intelligence. Their tacit acceptance of his role and oral instruction was not on the record. So four years later when the former war plans director professed ignorance of just what intelligence Pearl Harbor received, the opportunity was lost to roast him over the glowing coals of his admitted dereliction.

It was indeed a measure of Turner's influence in the triumvirate that ran naval operations that by the fall of 1941 Stark had been impressed enough by his forcefulness and apparent command of intelligence to let him control ONI's function without need for a written directive. It was a situation that placed McCollum in an unenviable predicament: "We were told in effect, all right, if there's anything wrong with the evaluation, you guys did it, and you guys and not war plans must take the onus [blame]."[24]

Turner, by omission or commission, therefore played a leading part in shutting off Pearl Harbor from the best source of intelligence. He diminished our ability to judge Japan's plans and intentions affecting the Pacific Fleet. The secondhand evaluations sent out by Stark, which he claimed were based on Magic, were more confusing than helpful. They were certainly no substitute for the full decrypts in our efforts to analyze Japan's situation, especially considering the extent to which Stark was influenced by Turner's idiosyncratic views. Moreover, neither Kimmel nor I had any indication that important Magic information that vitally concerned the fleet was being withheld from us after 20 July.

The biggest intelligence loss that resulted from our being denied access to Magic was the opportunity to monitor the traffic in the J-19 code between Tokyo and Japan's Honolulu consulate. Hypo intercepts were forwarded on to Washington unread by Pearl Harbor because of Rochefort's instruction to leave the diplomatic ciphers to Washington. And in Washington they were given a low priority. When they were eventually decrypted, information that would have been very pertinent did not reach us. Evidently Turner and his "expert" three-man intelligence committee did not consider it important for the Pacific Fleet to know that the Japanese consulate in Honolulu was paying unusually close attention to the fleet anchorage and shipping movements in Pearl Harbor.

The intelligence officer on the spot must always assess the scope of the overall picture. In trying to fit together the strategic jigsaw puzzle in the fall of 1941, I had lacked vital information about Japan's diplomatic intentions. I was unaware at the time that these facts were available in Washington or that Magic had uncovered clues that the naval war planners in Tokyo were paying special attention to Hawaii. The tragedy was that even those vitally illuminating pieces of intelligence concerning Pearl Harbor were not passed on to us.

Washington was twice as far away from the uncoiling snake of Japanese military power as we were in Hawaii. When it came to preparing strategic estimates, the vast distances involved in the Pacific induced a dangerous illusion in the minds of the analysts in Washington as to Pearl Harbor's security. They pored over their maps and made neat strategic calculations about where and when Japan was most likely to attack: the Philippines, Malaya, and the Dutch East Indies were obvious targets. In spite of Turner's earlier concerns, Hawaii and not Pearl Harbor did not rate so highly on his danger list after he became convinced that the Japanese would attack Russia in the summer of 1941.

When I found out, a couple of years later, how we had been shortchanged, I was astonished and outraged. Had I been similarly negligent, and willfully withheld information critical to the safety of our fleet, I would have been court-martialed—and would have deserved to be shot!

Yet senior members of the naval staff who bore the real burden for the intelligence failures that led directly to Pearl Harbor were not court-martialed, not reprimanded, not in any way taken to task for their part in the debacle. They all remained on active duty. Indeed, they advanced in rank, prestige, and glory throughout the war. There was no taint or tarnish on their careers. Being in Washington, they were too close to the White House and the rest of the bureaucracy to attract the finger of scorn. Furthermore, and most important, convenient scapegoats were available. It was easier and safer to blame the commanders on the spot at Pearl Harbor: Admiral Kimmel and General Short.

13

"Waves of Strife"

I N THE FINAL MONTHS of peace in 1941, my duty as fleet intelligence officer obliged me to do more than merely be a conduit for strategic information that others sent. It also required predicting where there were gaps that could be filled by collecting intelligence from local sources. My involvement in the Tachibana case, four months before, had taught me that Honolulu, with its large Japanese population rubbing shoulders daily with white hats on liberty, was fertile territory for espionage.

Japan's consulate was on Nuuanu Avenue. The official diplomatic list showed only five assistant consuls. According to the Fourteenth Naval District Intelligence Office and FBI reports, however, it was home base for more than two hundred subconsular agents scattered throughout the territory of Hawaii.[1] At least forty of them were being monitored for espionage activity as they mingled with the 160,000 Japanese-Americans who, besides running most of the fruit and vegetable business of the island, owned more than half the licensed bars in Honolulu, plus many of the legal and illegal brothels that attracted large numbers of off-duty sailors.

Apart from the lure of the Honolulu red-light district, there was a repetitive humdrum to the life-style of the uniformed Americans on Oahu. Off-hours for the enlisted men were usually spent in a service club or in crowded bars and clip joints. These ranged from the few fancy spots at fashionable hotels to a favorite servicemen's hangout like Lousy Lui's at the two-bit end of Waikiki. In this joint there existed an undercurrent of uneasy suspicion that mingled with the tobacco smoke and alcohol fumes. Like many of the bar owners, Lousy Lui was Japanese, but born in the islands, so he was an American citizen. Since his parents were born in Japan, that also made him a citizen of Japan under Japanese law. Rumor had it that he was a military intelligence agent for the Japanese.

Walter Davenport from *Colliers* magazine described the nervous confidence that infused the large service population on the island during its last months of peace:

> The enlisted men grouse about military life, and talk more Jap. Their speculations about war are always on the optimistic side. Oahu is a 604-square-mile fort bristling with eight-, twelve-, and fourteen-inch guns, and the Pacific Fleet is no slouch. Pearl Harbor, Manila, and Singapore know hour by hour where every American and British ship is, between the Panama Canal and the Red Sea. So, militarily we have nothing to be concerned about in the summer of 1941.[2]

While the FBI labored with the near hopeless task of trying to weed the real spies out of a local population of which more than a third was Japanese and potentially suspect, the navy tried to control the sampan fleet. Based at Kewalo Basin, due south of Punchbowl crater, about twelve miles from the entrance to Honolulu harbor, the sampans were sturdy diesel-powered fishing vessels, up to eighty feet long, manned by tough Japanese fishermen. They ranged out five hundred miles to sea in search of tuna, and repeatedly had to be chased from the waters south and west of Pearl Harbor where the fleet exercised. All vessels trespassing within three miles of Diamond Head were stopped and questioned. No Japanese-Americans were permitted to work within naval reservations, but many navy wives had Japanese maids and cooks. So undercover agents for the consulate, like Yoshikawa, probably had little difficulty picking up inside information on fleet movements.

Even with all these precautions afloat and ashore, neither the FBI nor military counterintelligence officers could do anything to bring charges of illegal activity against the Japanese navy's most active spy. Ensign Yoshikawa, under the guise of consulate official Morimura, was able to drive right up to military installations and take air-taxi flights that provided him detailed bird's-eye photographs of our fleet's anchorage. Yoshikawa's phone calls were being tapped as part of the Fourteenth Naval District Intelligence Office's bugging of the consulate. But since we could not read the consulate's enciphered cable traffic, we had no idea of how extensive an espionage operation he was running at the time.[3]

In the midst of the July crisis there had been a flurry of code burning at the Japanese consulate. Mayfield advised General Short that the military police should round up the 217 assistant consuls for violating the act that required the registration of foreign agents. Local FBI agents Shivers and Tillman had already submitted enough evidence to the attorney general's office to commence prosecution against 40 of them with the navy's blessing. But a 25 July letter from the secretary of war halted institution of legal proceedings in favor of a warning. General Short had cabled that "prosecution at this time would unduly alarm the entire population and jeopardize the success [of] our current campaign to secure [the] loyalty of the Japanese population."[4]

Mayfield's concern about Japanese espionage echoed a five-year-old memorandum from the president. On 10 August 1936, Roosevelt had sent a memorandum to the chief of naval operations suggesting that "every Japanese citizen or non-citizen on the island of Oahu who meets Japanese ships or has any connection with their officers or men should be secretly identified" and listed for placement "in a concentration camp in the event of trouble." The memo went on to consider the Japanese population of all the other Hawaiian Islands, and asked for "further recommendations after studies have been made."[5]

The studies revealed the magnitude of the espionage threat, but by 1941 Roosevelt's concern for Tokyo's sensibilities resulted in the administration's blocking efforts by the House Un-American Activities Committee to conduct its planned September hearings into Japanese subversion. The committee's chairman, Martin Dies of Texas, had made headlines earlier in the year with the exposure of German activities. Now he was sounding the alarm about the "potential Japanese spy system" and telling the press that he intended "to rouse the whole American people into a sense of impending crisis."[6]

The State Department, however, was more alarmed that the "exhaustive investigation" proposed by Dies would inflame our critical relations with Tokyo. The president himself intervened to urge Dies to abandon his intention to call fifty-two witnesses to testify about Japan's undercover operations in the United States. This muffling by the White House could not prevent Senator Guy M. Gillette of Iowa from introducing a resolution on 2 October citing "the activities of Japanese consular officials in Hawaii and the western United States" as alarming evidence of the need for a full-scale investigation.[7] Any public hearings would have drawn attention to Tachibana's espionage ring and all its implications. The case would also have raised many difficult questions in the press about the extent to which naval intelligence officers had become involved in surveillance operations against American citizens.

My involvement in April with the Tachibana affair, nevertheless, had taught me that if a broken-down Hollywood actor could be engaged in espionage, Honolulu was obviously ripe for exploitation by agents of Japan. With this in mind, I instructed my yeoman, Keene, to make periodic checks of the downtown streets and bars, wearing old clothes. While his forays as my personal listening resource did not uncover any startling plots, they did confirm that the increasing incidence of brawling and dissolute behavior was an open invitation to Japanese agents.[8] The strain of keeping Pacific Fleet sailors so far from their mainland homes and loved ones was beginning to tell.

Morale was becoming a major concern for Admiral Kimmel. Because of the rigorous sea-training schedule, he demanded that more facilities be provided ashore. A new fleet recreation center, commissioned on 1 August, included an enormous beer bar, ten bowling alleys, eleven pool tables, and a six-thousand-seat arena for boxing matches and movies. A rotation of stateside cruises enabled some sailors to arrange family reunions.

Sustaining the morale of his men was yet another telling indication of the responsibilities and concerns that the Pacific Fleet commander was carrying. It was a burden aggravated by Washington's apparent indifference to his repeated requests for more personnel and escort ships. The fleet desperately needed twenty thousand additional men to bring the crews up to their full wartime complements. "We are ready to do our damnedest," he wrote to CNO Stark on 12 August, but this assurance was accompanied by still another plea that Washington keep him adequately informed. "You will probably have information sooner than I do which will warrant the cancellation of such cruises and I shall of course expect advice or orders from you on the subject."[9]

Although Admiral Kimmel was not given the advice he sought, it was apparent to us that tension was increasing between Washington and Tokyo. An Opnav dispatch had already alerted us that the "Japanese [are] rapidly completing withdrawal from world shipping routes."[10]

The focus of Washington's concern, as I soon discovered, was on the other side of the Pacific. On 26 August the first nine B-17s, which had stopped over in Hawaii, took off to make the long overwater haul via Wake, Midway, and Ocean Island, then south to Australia. Then they would head north to the Philippines. There was considerable apprehension that if the Japanese learned of the flight they might attempt to interfere with this first demonstration that air reinforcement for MacArthur was practicable.

In preparation for the departure of these planes, I was called upon to furnish the army air command on Hawaii with all available information on weather conditions and bases, including some highly secret information we had from the Dutch regarding their air bases in the East Indies. A special watch was kept by Hypo's listening posts for radio transmissions emanating from the Marshalls for any indications of hostile intentions as the bombers flew within range of Japanese air bases there. If Tokyo raised objections, the war department had ready a special press announcement that this was a normal operation involving the replacement of obsolescent aircraft.

It proved to be an unnecessary precaution. All nine Flying Fortresses arrived at Clark Field by 12 September, apparently unspotted by Japan. Secretary of War Stimson was ecstatic. The success of this first flight was seen as giving the army the opportunity "to get back into the islands in a way it hadn't been able to for years." Stimson pressed for an immediate increase in the B-17 production rate. MacArthur was given priority for the bombers, even though they had long been regarded as an essential adjunct of Hawaiian defense. An army air force memorandum of 26 August set quotas for a force of at least 128 Flying Fortresses in the Philippines by February 1942, with twice that number by the end of the year. It was also planned to then begin supplying B-17s for three bombardment groups based on Oahu, to guard against what was prophetically described as a "diversionary" Japanese attack on Pearl Harbor. The same staff paper, however, allowed that the three groups of 204 long-range bombers were the "barest minimum," and that "in the face of a major attack by large forces, it is questionable that this force would be adequate."[11]

The importance of that estimate should have been realized in Washington because it was reinforced by a still more telling report from the Hawaiian air force headquarters that had been issued only a few days earlier. This "Plan for the Employment of Bombardment Aviation in the Defense of Oahu," dated 20 August, had been drawn up on General Arnold's orders. He called for an update of the March study of the island's air defenses, which had been prepared by General Martin and Admiral Bellinger. The new report predicted the threat of an aerial attack, with astonishing accuracy, and estimated that the Japanese "can probably employ a maximum of 6 carriers against Oahu." Underlined for particular emphasis, on page 5, was the forecast that an *early morning attack is, therefore, the best plan of action to the enemy.*[12] A minimum of thirty-six B-17s "would be required to disable and destroy the carriers," but Martin's recommendation was for "immediate consideration to the allotment of one hundred and eighty." This was a "small force when compared with the importance of this outpost," and one that they pointed out could be provided "at less cost to the government than the cost of a modern battleship."[13]

The report from the army's Hawaiian air commanders urged that the planes be made available "as soon as possible."[14] The number of planes General Martin called for was only twenty fewer than the long-range bomber strength recommended for the Hawaiian command by Arnold's own staff, and his report warned that "under no circumstances could the Hawaiian bombardment force be reduced without gravely endangering the security of the Pacific coast."[15]

Yet with every available B-17 being rushed to the Philippines, not even the minimum recommended force of thirty-six was allocated to our local army air command. General Marshall testified that he had "given Hawaii all we could afford to give them up to that time,"[16] but as of November only a dozen of the long-range bombers remained on the island. General Martin had the frustration of seeing airfields, which he believed were critical for the defense of Pearl Harbor, turned into mere refueling stops for bombers heading out to MacArthur's air force.

To the extent that Washington planners were thinking about Pacific requirements at all during the fall of 1941, it appears that they were concentrating on a deterrent force of American bombers in the Philippines. They would not have been so complacent had they known that the main target of this deterrence—Japan's Combined Fleet—was focusing its attention, not on Singapore or Manila, but the Pacific Fleet in Pearl Harbor. On 7 August the naval staff in Tokyo had again considered Yamamoto's plan to attack the Pacific Fleet in harbor as an opening move in a war that most admirals had come to regard as inevitable. Even the more conservative members of navy chief Osami Nagano's staff appreciated the need for attempting a knockout opening blow against the United States. But they postponed the final decision on the Pearl Harbor attack plan until after the concept had been tested on the plotting boards at Combined Fleet's annual war games, which had been delayed, at Yamamoto's request, until the first week in September.

The prospect that their ships, planes, and tanks might be immobilized by fuel starvation galvanized the conference at imperial general headquarters on 15 August. This time it was the navy that called for urgent completion of war planning against Britain and the United States. Four days later the basis of a joint operational plan was established after naval observers participated in army war games which rehearsed the blueprint for military conquest of southeast Asia.

It was masterminded by Colonel Masanobu Tsuji, a brilliant but fanatical member of the army staff, who clearly appreciated the navy's priority for a speedy invasion schedule. Two months were scheduled for the capture of Manila, three for Singapore, and five for Burma. Simultaneous operations were to be conducted against the Dutch East Indies to bring their rich oil fields under Japanese control within the fourth month, between the opening of the war and the occupation of Java.[17]

While imperial general headquarters was fixing mid-October as the deadline for completing war preparations, Konoye was attempting to recover initiative on the diplomatic front. On 18 August, two days after Nomura had advised Tokyo that the Churchill-Roosevelt summit was an indication of Britain's hope for "a Japanese-American war started by the back door,"[18] the prime minister pressed our ambassador for a face-to-face meeting with the president. Grew supported the idea, advising Washington that it was worthy of "very prayerful consideration" because of the "incalculable" benefits that might flow from a Pacific summit.[19]

Still flushed with the success of his Churchill meeting, Roosevelt had not at first ruled out the idea of a Konoye meeting in Alaska or Hawaii in his 17 August talk with Nomura. The ambassador's hopes for pulling off a 15 October tête-à-tête between the president and prime minister at Juneau were soon washed out by the State Department's insistence that a prior condition for any summit would be Japan's agreement to withdraw their forces from China and abandon the tripartite pact.

Konoye believed that such thorny issues should be reserved for a face-to-face meeting. A note of desperation crept into his 26 August instructions to Nomura that he would consider Hawaii as a possible venue for a Pacific summit and self-effacingly he offered to withdraw Japanese troops from Indochina when "a just peace is established in the Far East."[20]

Prime Minister Konoye's hopes that a Pacific summit might halt the momentum of Japan's preparations for war were fading fast. He faced the impatient admirals and generals in a 3 September liaison conference, and they wanted cabinet approval for the Outline Plan for the Execution of the Empire's National Policy.[21] This characteristically Japanese euphemism was the bureaucratic title of the tentative war plan that the army and navy had agreed to weeks earlier. There was nothing euphemistic, however, about the blunt exchanges with which the prime minister was assailed during the seven-hour meeting. Konoye repeatedly stressed the need for more time to arrange his personal meeting with President Roosevelt, but the military chiefs insisted on setting a limit and deadline for negotiations.

"Although I feel sure we have a chance to win a war right now, I am afraid that the chance will vanish with the passage of time," warned navy chief Nagano.[22] Next day the cabinet met to approve the list of "minimum" demands and "maximum" concessions that were intended to severely curtail Konoye's room for diplomatic maneuver. Japan's right to station troops in China or Indochina was nonnegotiable, being essential to her defense. But Konoye could promise not to use them against neighboring areas if Washington agreed to terminate all aid to Chiang Kaishek. The prime minister was to tell the United States that Japan would "guarantee the neutrality of the Philippine Islands," abide by her treaty not to attack Russia, and might even be prepared to interpret her tripartite pact obligations "independently." But the military firmly rejected any other concessions. The crux of the cabinet decision was contained in its opening paragraph, which asserted that Japan, "for the purpose of self-defense and self-preservation, will complete preparations for war." The last ten days of October were set as a tentative deadline for diplomacy, after which Japan "resolved to go to war with the United States, Great Britain, and the Netherlands if necessary."[23]

On 6 September the cabinet declaration was to receive the stamp of irreversible national policy in the conference chamber at Tokyo's imperial palace. The small, bespectacled emperor sat silently on a dais as his ministers and senior officers rehearsed the now familiar arguments in the flat, baleful tones demanded by the solemnity of this formal occasion. Emperor Hirohito heard how the military planned to achieve Japan's national objectives and that they were preparing for "war with the United States, Great Britain, and the Netherlands to expel their influence from east Asia, to establish a sphere for the self-defense and self-preservation of our empire, and to build a new order in Greater East Asia."[24]

In a preconference briefing the day before, the emperor had expressed his regret to Konoye that the cabinet "placed war preparations first and diplomatic negotiations second."[25] Army chief of staff General Hajime Sugiyama had assured the emperor that the "operation in the south Pacific could be disposed of in three months." But when Hirohito pressed Sugiyama about the chances of victory, he would give no guarantee that Japan could be certain of winning. Navy chief Nagano predicted a long war and he foresaw that it would be "impossible to expect a surrender from the United States." The best they could hope for was that a lightning conquest of southeast Asia, and a defensive perimeter of Pacific island bases, could secure an invincible position for Japan, thereby permitting her diplomats to negotiate from a position of strength to bring the war to an end.[26]

Such were the inherent contradictions in cabinet policy that Baron Yoshimichi Hara, in his role as president of the privy council, raised the next morning at the imperial conference. The silent evasiveness of Admiral Nagumo and General Sugiyama, who would not provide direct answers, finally moved Hirohito to break with centuries-old tradition of no direct participation in the council. Suddenly he uttered a shrill demand to know why military action was taking precedence over diplomacy. Then, to the further astonishment of all present, Hirohito drew a paper from his pocket and read in a piping voice a *waka* (or *tanka*, a thirty-one-syllable poem) composed by his grandfather, the enlightened Emperor Meiji:

> *Yomo no umi*
> *mina harakara to*
> *omou yo ni,*
> *Nado namikaze no*
> *tachisawaguran?*

(Since all seas of the world are brothers,
Why do winds and waves of strife rage so violently?)[27]

Hirohito declared that he was only "striving to introduce into the present Emperor Meiji's ideal of international peace." But this unprecedented interruption from the throne brought an awestricken silence that was finally broken by Nagano's expressing his "trepidation" at his majesty's displeasure with the supreme command. He assured the emperor that they recognized "the importance of diplomacy, and advocated a resort to arms only when there seemed no other way out."[28]

When the momentous conference finally adjourned at noon "in an atmosphere of unprecedented tenseness,"[29] Konoye had secured another slender chance to establish agreement with the United States. The prime minister had been given until 16 October to achieve a diplomatic breakthrough.

With less than six weeks in which to overcome the hurdle of Washington's latest demand that "fundamental and essential questions" be resolved, he summoned the American ambassador that very night to a clandestine meeting at the house of his mistress. His case for a summit with Roosevelt made a powerful impression on Grew. He cabled the State Department the next day of the premier's new willingness to "conclusively and wholeheartedly" accept the four principles enunciated by Hull during the secret April talks as a basis for reopening serious discussions.[30]

While not diminishing the obstacles to reaching any agreement, the ambassador warned that Konoye "saw the handwriting on the wall and realized that Japan was on the brink of an abyss and wanted, if possible, to reverse the engines."[31] He reinforced this view in a personal letter of 22 September to Roosevelt warning that the "alternative to reaching a settlement now would be the greatly increased probability of war—Facilis descensus Averno est."[32] The letter with his classical allusion to how easy it was to fall into hell did not reach the White House until after Konoye's cabinet had itself fallen. This well-intentioned bid to assist Konoye in putting the engines of the Japanese war machine into reverse did not succeed, because Roosevelt's attention had been diverted from the Pacific by events in the Atlantic.

On 4 September, America had come close to the brink of war with Germany when a U-boat attacked destroyer *Greer*. Roosevelt promptly accused Hitler of "piracy." Stark dashed off a pessimistic letter that alerted Kimmel to the imminent possibility of war's breaking out in the Atlantic. "We are all but, if not actually in it," he wrote on 22 September (the same day that Grew was writing Roosevelt).[33] So, while the navy battened down to convoy British ships and shoot hostile submarines on sight, Secretary Hull and the State Department hard-liners, led by its Far East specialist Dr. Stanley K. Hornbeck, misinterpreted Konoye's apparent willingness to negotiate as an indication that the American sanctions were biting deeply at Japan's economy. They concluded, wrongly, that it was only a matter of months before the military leaders in Tokyo would be forced to withdraw their forces from the mainland. This mistaken policy was further encouraged by the memory of how stonewalling tactics had succeeded at the Washington disarmament conference twenty years earlier, and it was reinforced by our ability to monitor Japan's diplomatic traffic. But the Purple decrypts, as early as September, were already indicating that, unlike 1921, Japan was in no mood to be bluffed into another retreat.

Yamamoto's strategy to attack Pearl Harbor had been transformed from a staff blueprint into a practical plan. Most of the technical and tactical details were ready by 11 September, when the annual map maneuvers began behind the wrought-iron gates of the naval war college in suburban Tokyo. As colored markers were laid out over large charts of the western Pacific and China Sea, it became evident that this might be their last full-scale dress rehearsal before war. Ten days of intensive wargaming tested all the interlocking naval operations and their ability to effect a swift Japanese takeover of southeast Asia. The staffs of Third Fleet and Eleventh Air Fleet rehearsed the invasion of the Philippines and the conquest of Borneo; the Second Fleet staff practiced moving from the Pescadores to cover the invasion of Malaya; and the Fourth Fleet practiced its attacks on Wake Island and Guam.

Only thirty of more than a hundred staff officers who participated in the map maneuvers were allowed into the college's closely guarded east wing room where the charts of Hawaii were laid out. Yamamoto himself supervised these briefings. Operation Z, as the planned attack was code-named, was conducted under close scrutiny of the still skeptical naval general staff. Admiral Matome Ugaki, Yamamoto's own chief of staff, commanded the Blue Fleet (Japanese) force of two carrier divisions, two battleships, three cruisers, escorted by destroyer flotillas, and tankers, which set out for "Pearl Harbor." On the first run-through he met with disaster during a daylight approach when the Blue force was intercepted by "American" aircraft, which "sank" two carriers. Only minor damage was inflicted on the Red Fleet at Pearl Harbor, while Ugaki's force had paper losses of one third of its air and sea strength.[34]

The umpires concluded that the Hawaiian operation was too risky. This was too quick a rush to judgment for Yamamoto. A second tabletop run-through was held the same afternoon; but this time the Blue Fleet's route was adjusted to bring it within striking distance of Oahu during darkness for launching planes at first light. This time the carrier strike arrived undetected and "sank" four Red battleships. Defending Red planes managed to launch a counterstrike, which the umpires credited with sinking one Blue carrier.[35]

The plotting-table maneuvers underscored both the risks and rewards of Operation Z, leaving the naval staff still in doubt about the wisdom of sanctioning the operation. Even Yamamoto's own staff was not in unanimous agreement. Some tactical details remained to be ironed out, and a few officers doubted that the necessary element of surprise could be achieved. In the few weeks remaining before the mid-October deadline of Japan's war plan, it became a race against time to win over naval staff chief Nagano and solve the problems of how bombs and torpedoes could be modified for maximum effectiveness against Pearl Harbor targets.

The order went out to speed up the development of sixteen-inch shells and bombs to penetrate the thick steel of American battleships. Wooden boxlike baffles were attached to the fins of standard torpedoes to prevent their plunging into the mud of shallow Pearl Harbor. While technical details were being worked out, pilots trained intensively to fine-tune their bombing skills and drop torpedoes low enough and close enough to hit their targets.[36]

In the southern Honshū city of Kagoshima naval planes buzzed in low over Yamagataya department store to make bombing runs on target vessels in the bay. This practice site in the shadow of active Sakurajima volcano was selected for its topographical similarity to Pearl Harbor. Off the nearby naval base of Kanoya, at the tip of Kyūshū, the obsolete battleship *Settsu* was anchored in Ariake Bay as a target for dive-bomber pilots. Safety regulations were ignored, at a cost of at least one plane, in order to perfect steep dives and low-level pullouts and improve bombing accuracy. Off the rocky coast of Shikoku, the smallest of Japan's main islands, the two-man midget submarines practiced making submerged attacks with their temperamental craft.

Midget submarine attacks had been incorporated almost as an afterthought by Yamamoto, against strong argument by some of the Combined Fleet staff that they might prematurely divulge the whole plan. But the objectors were silenced on 9 October, when after five days of map maneuvers on board battleship *Nagato* in Hiroshima Bay, the whole operation was successfully rehearsed with the midget submarines of the Sixth Fleet participating for the first time.

"Some of you may object but, so long as I am commander in chief, I'm intent on going ahead with the raid," declared Yamamoto in an appeal to the loyalty of the Combined Fleet staff officers "on the assumption that the raid is on."[37] This was not easy when his principal critic was the First Air Fleet commander whose carriers were to carry out the surprise attack. Admiral Chuichi Nagumo had sent a delegation with a written plea stressing the inherent risks in attacking Pearl Harbor. He reminded Yamamoto that the eventual necessity of a compromise peace made it advisable "to avoid anything like the Hawaiian operation that would put America's back up."[38]

Compromise was not an issue to be weighed by the members of imperial general headquarters as they prepared to march Japan into war with the United States. For more than a year Japanese foreign policy had been effectively controlled by the military leadership through the "liaison conferences," which virtually dictated cabinet decisions. So as Konoye's diplomatic overtures to Washington stalled, the army faction, led by War Minister Hideki Tojo, lost no time making it clear that they had had enough of diplomacy.

An assassination attempt on the prime minister on 16 September was another indication of how shakily Konoye clung to his office. In a frantic bid for a face-to-face meeting with Roosevelt, he instructed Ambassador Nomura to hold out the chance of a virtual abnegation of the tripartite pact, neutralization of Indochina, and reduction of troops in China. It was an offer born of desperation, since on 25 September Tojo had flatly refused to consider even a token troop withdrawal from China. The war minister's insistence that the "way of diplomacy is not always a matter of concession; sometimes it is oppression," was characteristic of the hardline general whose sobriquet was the Razor.[39]

The State Department was not prepared to back down either. Hull continued to stall the Japanese ambassador. Meanwhile, Nomura lobbied senior officials in the navy department in addition to making his regular diplomatic rounds. The feverish tone of Konoye's instructions to his emissary was plain in the Purple decrypts that reached the secretary of state each day, but its impact appears to have been lost on Washington policymakers. References to the first anniversary of the tripartite pact as a "turning point" and that "the situation is all the more grave" were dismissed along with Konoye's allusion to the pressure he was under from "the advocates of anti-Americanism."[40]

While Washington stalled, Tokyo speculated. It was believed that Secretary Hull harbored strong doubts about the "trustworthiness of Prince Konoye." What the Japanese did not suspect was that Hull's conviction was reinforced almost daily by Magic decrypts. These revealed that Nomura's eagerness to clutch at any straw was getting him sharp rebukes from his foreign minister "not to add or detract a jot or tittle on your *own* without first getting in contact with me."[41]

The Purple decrypts, translated by army and navy linguists untutored in the subtle nuances of diplomatic Japanese, confronted the secretary of state with language that was often far stronger than intended. He paid more attention to these than to Nomura's more studied official representations because Hull was also reading the ambassador's reports, which frequently put too optimistic a construction on the United States' willingness to negotiate. Eavesdropping on the Purple traffic that flashed back and forth between Tokyo and Washington depreciated the normal diplomatic process. The State Department's long-held belief in Tokyo's fundamental duplicity was confirmed by Magic decrypts from Japan's other embassies in the Far East, which revealed the steadily mounting southward momentum of their military buildup in Indochina.

Confident that Magic had betrayed Tokyo's two-faced policy, Hull procrastinated for three weeks before Ambassador Nomura was summoned to the State Department on 3 October. He received an "oral statement" that amounted to a final rejection of Konoye's hoped-for summit. "Since it appears that although Japan agrees with the United States regarding principles, she differs on their application," Nomura cabled the foreign minister dispiritedly. "The United States is doubtful about holding a meeting of the two heads of state."[42]

Tojo denounced Hull's four principles in a stormy liaison conference the next day at which navy chief Nagano joined the demand for "quick action."[43] Konoye had to rein in his ambassador from making any concessionary proposal. Three days later the army high command met and concluded that "war is inevitable."[44]

There was a simultaneous hardening of positions in Washington. After the 6 October meeting of the president's inner cabinet, the secretary of war told Hull that without a troop withdrawal from China "no promises of the Japs based on words would be worth anything."[45] If there was any doubt that another major crisis was boiling up with Tokyo, it should have been dispelled by the diplomatic traffic. On 10 October, Nomura was told that the "decisive stage" of negotiations had been reached "and the situation does not permit of this senseless procrastination."[46] The ambassador's desperation was visible in the Purple decrypt of his reply that "they are not budging an inch."[47] That cable prompted Konoye to summon Grew to tell him that time was running out. Konoye said that the Japanese ambassador in Washington was "very fatigued" and that his replacement was under "serious consideration."[48]

A secret cabinet session was held the next day in the prime minister's home. The navy and army ministers were adamant in their refusal to shift the 15 October deadline for negotiations. After this meeting Konoye sent a final urgent plea to Nomura to do everything to get a breakthrough: "The situation at home is fast approaching a crisis and it is becoming absolutely essential that the two leaders meet if any adjustment of Japan-U.S. relations is to be accomplished."[49]

The polite generalities with which Nomura's last-minute pleading had been greeted by Hull left Konoye with no option but to resign his cabinet on 16 October, when the deadline set by the military expired. The emperor was taken by surprise—as was Washington, where the State Department should have known by the swiftness of Konoye's fall from power that time was now of the essence to Japan's military leadership. If that was not enough, the appointment of the war minister to form a new government was another sign.

By calling on General Tojo to take over, Hirohito was placing responsibility squarely on the army leadership. What Magic did not reveal was that the emperor sternly admonished the new prime minister to make a last effort at a diplomatic solution. The new foreign minister, Admiral Teijiro Toyoda, was accordingly instructed to prepare for a final attempt at opening negotiations with the United States. This brought Tojo under criticism from the navy minister, whose admirals were alarmed by the oil situation. He warned the new cabinet, "The situation is urgent; we must have a decision one way or the other."[50]

The fall of the Konoye government had not been unanticipated in Washington. But its timing was a surprise, because it had not been foreshadowed by Magic. This should have been a timely lesson that the Purple diplomatic traffic would not provide advance warning of every move Tokyo made. The crisis, nonetheless, was judged sufficiently serious for the president to cancel his regular Thursday cabinet meeting. Instead he called an emergency conference of what he liked to call his war council. This consisted of the secretaries of state, war, and the navy; the service chiefs; and his indispensable aide Harry Hopkins. The group's deliberations resulted in another alert message to overseas army and naval commands.

Since the Pacific Fleet command had received no diplomatic decrypts since mid-July, the CNO dispatch arriving on the afternoon of 17 October came as a surprise. It was in our most secure naval code, addressed to Admiral Kimmel with instructions to forward it to General Short. It warned of "a grave situation" created by the resignation of the Japanese cabinet; that there was "a strong possibility" of an attack on Russia; and that, since "the U.S. and Britain are held responsible by Japan for her present situation, there is also a possibility that Japan may attack. . . ." Kimmel was accordingly directed to "take due precautions including such preparatory deployments," but not so as "to disclose strategic intentions nor constitute provocative actions against Japan."[51]

As with the July alert, that Friday afternoon's dispatch left Kimmel at some loss as to just what "preparatory deployments" the emergency demanded. The intelligence picture we had assembled was lacking the diplomatic information that could have provided us with valuable clues about the broad framework of Tokyo's intentions. The only diplomatic intelligence Kimmel had received since July were the vague and often conflicting statements made by Admiral Stark in his letters. Stark had sounded an optimistic note to Admiral Hart in Manila, who was a joint addressee of a 22 September letter, which stated that "the Japanese appear to be making some effort at reaching a satisfactory solution." Yet the following day he wrote informing Kimmel that "conversations with Japan have reached an impasse," and that a "strong warning and a threat of hostile action" would be the "next step" to counter Japanese submarines prowling off U.S. territory.[52] Stark's pessimism was reinforced, as evidenced by his letter to Kimmel of 29 October, after a meeting with Nomura. "He usually comes in when he begins to feel near the end of his rope," CNO warned. "There is not much to spare at the end now."[53]

These Delphic insights into the diplomatic turmoil alerted us at Pearl Harbor to the fact that negotiations with Japan were running out of sand. But they were no substitute for the access we were being denied to the Purple decrypts. There was no way we could judge how likely was CNO's prediction of the "strong possibility" that Japan might attack Russia, or, for that matter, any of our outlying island bases. Instead, we had to take the intelligence we were given at face value. This left us to make our best estimate on the assumption that if Japan was about to make any offensive moves, the targets would be on the other side of the Pacific.

The reaction of the Hawaiian commands to the October alert simply reflected the scenario as Washington relayed it to us. General Short was to testify in 1944 that his second alert in three months of an attack on Russia "weakened as far as I was concerned the probability of an immediate war between the U.S. and Japan,"[54] and so this command merely tightened up "all our guards against sabotage."[55] Kimmel was also under the impression that the threat, such as it might materialize, was on the far side of the Pacific. His principal deployment, therefore, apart from ordering six submarines to be ready to depart for Japanese waters at short notice, was to send twelve more patrol planes to Midway. Additional marines and defenses were also ordered sent to the outlying islands, and the departure of battleship *West Virginia* for refit at Puget Sound was postponed indefinitely.[56]

In a letter dated 22 October, Admiral Kimmel reported his measures taken in response to the alert of the sixteenth. He also informed CNO that he had ordered "some additional security measures in effect in the operating areas outside Pearl Harbor," and that Admiral Pye's battle force was put on twelve hours' notice. Stark acknowledged this two weeks later, saying, "OK on the dispositions you made in connection with recent change in the Japanese Cabinet."[57]

The Pacific Fleet's dispositions might have been dramatically different if Washington had not denied us another vital piece of Magic intelligence. This was an intercepted instruction from Tokyo to the Honolulu consul requesting very detailed reports of the fleet anchorage. It had been circulated in Washington a full week before the mid-October alert. Had we received it at Pearl Harbor at any time before 7 December it would have alerted us to the rattlesnake lurking in our backyard. Tragically, no one on the CNO staff who read it bothered to evaluate its significance.

14

"Affirmative Misrepresentation"

THE WAR GAMES in Tokyo that first tested Yamamoto's daring concept of attacking Pearl Harbor persuaded the naval staff that they needed more detailed intelligence about the status and movements of the Pacific Fleet. The task of obtaining the information fell upon the naval staff's Third Bureau.

Comparable to our office of naval intelligence, its best man was its deputy chief, Captain Kanji Ogawa, a former assistant naval attaché in Washington. His mouselike demeanor concealed an encyclopedic knowledge of the United States that he had acquired through skillful espionage. It was Ogawa who had been instrumental in bringing into the Third Bureau one of his former undercover agents, Lieutenant Commander Itaru Tachibana.

This was none other than the former brothel keeper and Japanese agent in Los Angeles, whose spying had been uncovered in a counterintelligence operation in which I had played a small part. Tachibana's unceremonious expulsion from the United States, instead of being made to stand trial for espionage, was a diplomatic concession to American-Japanese relations that we would regret later. He returned home and put all the information he had garnered to good use, becoming one of Ogawa's principal assistants as an expert on our naval practices.[1]

Because of his expertise, Tachibana had been one of the privileged handful of officers whom Yamamoto had permitted to observe the Pearl Harbor map exercises. And Tachibana subsequently played a leading role in assembling the detailed intelligence that was to make the attack possible. The Third Bureau already knew, from the reports of agents in Honolulu and their traffic analysis of American radio signals, that our task forces usually sortied from Hawaii on a weekly rotation on Mondays or Tuesdays. This schedule indicated that the best opportunity for catching a majority of the fleet in harbor would be on a Sunday. But for

Yamamoto's plan to succeed, it was essential to know not only when the fleet was in port, but the precise locations of where the American warships were berthed or anchored within the harbor.

To obtain the information that the Japanese pilots would need to perfect their bombing and torpedo attack training, Tachibana drafted a dispatch and Ogawa approved it. The "strictly secret" signal addressed to their consul general in Honolulu was transmitted on 24 September by Japan's foreign ministry, at the express request of navy ministry:

> 1. The waters (of Pearl Harbor) are to be divided roughly into five sub areas. (We have no objection to your abbreviating as much as you like.)
> Area A. Waters between Ford Island and the arsenal.
> Area B. Waters adjacent to the island south and west of Ford Island. (This area is on the opposite side of the island from Area A.)
> Area C. East Loch.
> Area D. Middle Loch.
> Area E. West Loch and the communicating water routes.
>
> 2. With regard to the warships and aircraft carriers, we would like to have you report on those at anchor (these are not so important), tied up at wharves, buoys, and docks. (Designate types and classes briefly. If possible we should like to have you make mention of the fact when there are two or more vessels alongside at the same wharf.)[2]

This instruction put an invisible grid over Pearl Harbor. Clearly it was intended as an overlay for planning bombing attack targets—hence it came to be known as the "bomb plot message."

Its significance was immediately appreciated by Ensign Yoshikawa, the Third Bureau's resident agent in Honolulu, who was posing as an assistant secretary at the consulate. Previously, he had been asked only to report the *movements* of the fleet. Now the grid system meant that naval intelligence in Tokyo was interested in having accurate positions of the warships when they were in harbor. Yoshikawa was convinced that this meant that some operation, possibly even an invasion of Hawaii, was being contemplated. Accordingly, five days later Consul Kita cabled a modification that effectively filled in additional grid locators to make the reports even more precise:

> The following codes will be used hereafter to designate the location of vessels:
> 1. Repair dock in the navy yard (The repair base referred to in my message to Washington #48): KS
> 2. Navy dock in the navy yard (Ten Ten Pier): KT

3. Moorings in the vicinity of Ford Island: FV
4. Alongside at Ford Island: FG (east and west sides will be designated A and B respectively)[3]

This second signal was not decrypted by the navy until 10 October, a day after the army had broken out the original bomb plot message. The reason for the long delay between interception and translation was that the navy and army commands on Oahu were responsible only for the collection and forwarding of the diplomatic traffic. The original bomb plot message had not reached Washington for twelve days. Like all the army intercepts it was pouched and sent by mail—in this case the Pan Am Clipper flight had been delayed by bad weather. Then both it and the second message had awaited decryption, because the J-19 consular code in which they had been transmitted had been given a lower priority than Purple.

By a trick of fate as it turned out, the decision of the Japanese foreign ministry not to equip the Honolulu consulate with the Purple system proved to be an unintentional factor in helping to conceal the attack. Five times as many espionage messages were read from Japan's Philippines consulate between September and December 1941 primarily because Manila was transmitting them in Purple.[4]

The downgrading of the Honolulu consular traffic as a potential source of information by Washington might have had less serious consequences if Hypo's cryptanalysts had been assigned to decode the messages Tokyo exchanged with Japan's local consulate. That the "biggest snake is the one nearest you" was, after all, one of the considerations in Washington's sending a Purple decoding machine to Manila.

This meant that the Pacific Fleet, the principal instrument of our military power in the Pacific, was not equipped to monitor the enemy beyond its harbor wall. The situation was all the more surprising because, a month earlier, a Purple decrypt had pinpointed the Honolulu consulate as a potential source of espionage. This information was understandably concealed from the 1945 congressional hearings, and was to remain a secret for more than forty years.

The Purple decrypt in question reveals that, on 2 September, five weeks before the bomb plot messages were decrypted, the foreign ministry had instructed its Washington embassy that the "naval authorities" had made the following request: "They would like to have you insist at this time upon a member of your staff going to Hawaii in the capacity of a courier."[5]

This message was "highly significant," as is pointed out in the hitherto classified 1942 U.S. Navy analysis of the pre-December signal traffic: "If the Japanese Navy demanded a special courier to and from Hawaii at this time, and insisted it be a diplomatic agent rather than a naval officer for better security," there could only be one objective in mind—Pearl Harbor.[6]

That the significance of the courier message was entirely lost, even after another intercept two days later from Honolulu addressed to Captain Ogawa, demonstrates again the poor quality of intelligence analysis that was being carried out in Washington. The message to Ogawa read, "The matter in question should be . . . no later than the end of September. Please advise me."[7] This J-19 message, decrypted in Washington on 26 September, was clear proof of the involvement of the deputy chief of Japan's naval intelligence. It could have been interpreted only as a suspicious espionage operation whose likely focus was the Pacific Fleet.

Neither the Fourteenth Naval District nor our headquarters was ever told about these early signs that Japanese naval intelligence was focusing on Pearl Harbor. Washington's failure to keep the local commands informed of these activities after they had been discovered was tantamount to folly. It was all the more so when the two so-called bomb plot messages were decrypted two weeks later.

The Magic summaries made their rounds of the most senior army and navy staff officers on 9 and 10 October. The first indication that the Japanese had imposed an invisible bombing grid on Pearl Harbor had been asterisked as "an interesting message" by Lieutenant Commander Alwin D. Kramer, who as OP-20-GZ was in charge of the translation section in the navy department. On the gist sheet that he circulated with the daily Magics until the end of the month, when the pressure of work forced him to abandon the practice, Kramer drew attention to the Honolulu signal in a note that read, "Tokyo directs special reports on the ships in Pearl Harbor which is divided into five areas for the purpose of showing exact locations."[8]

Although the second message that circulated the following day was not singled out with an asterisk, it was another example of Washington's lack of concern about Pearl Harbor. Even after the courier messages, neither the director of naval intelligence, nor the chief of war plans, nor the chief of naval operations appreciated that the bomb plot messages were sufficiently worthy of note to relay this intelligence to Pearl Harbor. Their cover-up in public began at the 1945 congressional hearings. They professed not to remember, or assumed that the information was available to us merely because it had been relayed to Admiral Hart at Manila. This was because Station Cast *was* working on Japanese diplomatic ciphers. Kramer, who should have known that Station Hypo could not decrypt J-19, testified that he was under the "impression" that such messages to the Asiatic Fleet were sent "either as an action addressee or information addressee to Admiral Kimmel."[9]

Admiral Noyes, the director of naval communications, was to testify that if Station Cast's cryptanalysts in the Philippines got stuck translating a certain intercept, they had only to radio Washington on the secure

Copek circuit for the translation. But Rochefort's cryptanalysts at Pearl Harbor had been specifically *excluded* from working on any diplomatic intercepts, because Washington evidently believed it was unnecessary to make Rochefort an information addressee of anything to do with diplomatic traffic. Noyes, however, was obliged to concede reluctantly in testimony to the Pearl Harbor hearings that Kimmel was *not* provided this information. He was asked if the consular decrypts had been sent to Kimmel as an information addressee:

"It wouldn't be sent out for information to anybody," Noyes replied.

Nor was the army sending out Magic information to General Short. The army's chief of military intelligence, Major General Sherman Miles, dismissed his G-2 section's failure to acquaint Short with the significance of the bomb plot decrypt by claiming that it was "one of a great number of messages being sent by the Japanese to various parts of the world in their attempt to follow the movements of our naval vessels."[10] But when Miles was challenged and asked to point to any other message that was so specific, he was obliged to admit, "I have not found any, sir, similar to this in the sense of dividing any particular waters."[11]

Colonel Rufus S. Bratton, who at the time was chief of the Far East section of G-2, testified that he believed these two messages indicated the Japanese were showing "an unusual interest in the port of Honolulu." He said he had "discussed this with my opposite numbers in the navy on several occasions."[12] They concluded that the subdivision of Pearl Harbor into areas might be "a device to reduce the volume of radio traffic . . . a plan for sabotage . . . a plan for a submarine attack . . . *or it might be a plan for an air attack.* [emphasis added]."[13]

Why had this vital evaluation of intelligence in Washington not been sent to us at Pacific Fleet headquarters? With the advantage of hindsight this is what both Admiral Kimmel and the 1945 congressional investigators wanted answered. It never was.

Admiral Stark denied ever seeing the bomb plot message. He claimed that if he had, he would have regarded it as "just another example of their [the Japanese's] great attention to detail."[14] Admiral Turner also claimed "no recollection of ever having seen that dispatch of 24 September." And if he had, he said, he would have referred it to the director of naval intelligence rather than "have initiated a dispatch on that subject myself."[15]

Turner's denials increase rather than excuse his responsibility. He had made himself CNO's self-appointed arbiter of what intelligence was relayed by Washington to the Pacific commands. His omission to note the importance of the bomb plot message was compounded because it arrived in Washington at a time when his authority over ONI was undisputed. The usurpation of the naval intelligence function by the director of war plans had finally driven the DNI three weeks earlier to petition the assistant secretary of the navy for a transfer to sea duty.

"We were clashing right along," Captain Kirk would record of his unhappy tenure as DNI.[16] His weeks in office as a lame-duck DNI were not made any easier. His knowledgeable Far East section chief, Mc-Collum, was on duty in London and Kirk had to work alongside his own successor. The new DNI, Rear Admiral Theodore S. Wilkinson, was Admiral Stark's personal choice for the job. His appointment was unexpected, "the penalty of selection" as he wrote to Rochefort. But the appointment was not the "grand job" he anticipated.[17] He was the third officer to be appointed to the embattled ONI directorship in twelve months. He had graduated at the top of his class at the naval academy, which included Kirk, and he was the first officer of his class to make flag rank. Affable as well as brilliant, Wilkinson had received the Medal of Honor for bravery at Vera Cruz in 1914 and, with his accumulated years of naval staff duties, he came to the job with all the right qualifications—*except* firsthand experience in the job. It was experience that was so essential for the proper functioning of the office of naval intelligence.

In contrast to the assertive Kirk, Ping Wilkinson knew how to serve up advice at staff meetings without ruffling feathers. He did this with the same smooth assurance with which he partnered Under Secretary of the Navy James V. Forrestal on the tennis courts of the exclusive Chevy Chase Club. But his lack of intelligence experience was seen by many in ONI as yet another reflection of the lack of respect accorded to their profession by the naval staff. Moreover, he had no doubts that his first duty was to spread oil on the troubled waters between war plans division and ONI.

It was at this juncture that Kirk and Captain Howard D. Bode, one of ONI's most conscientious officers and then head of foreign intelligence, wanted to inform Kimmel of the bomb plot decrypts. So did Commander Safford. He claimed that he actually drafted a message to Rochefort that instructed Pearl Harbor to start decrypting the traffic from the local Japanese consulate. But he was stopped from doing so by Noyes, who told him that he was "not going to tell any district commandant how to run his job!"[18]

Wilkinson was caught in a dilemma. He lacked the necessary specialist's knowledge, and he had no backing from Captain McCollum, who was to return to Washington a week later. So he did nothing. Nevertheless, he was the only member of the naval staff who testified at the 1945 congressional hearings to being aware of a message that, even with his lack of intelligence background, he assumed was "part of a general information system established by the Japanese."[19] He insisted, however, that there had never been any discussion of whether the bomb plot signal should be relayed to the Pacific Fleet because it appeared to him "as an illustration of the nicety of detail of intelligence the Japanese were capable of seeking and getting."[20]

It was indeed this "nicety of detail" that separated the two courier reports, and the bomb plot messages, from those being sent by Japan's consulates in Manila, Panama, and the west coast ports. No other reports divided an American base with such detail into sectors. No other area rated Tokyo's request for couriered information or such precise details as whether two or more vessels were alongside the same wharf or anchored together. And in the weeks that followed, an ominous change in the character of the information requested by Tokyo about Pearl Harbor made it stand out from all the other Japanese espionage traffic uncovered by Magic decrypts. The very specificity of these messages should have drawn careful attention. They were, in their own right, beyond the realm of reasonable suspicion.

Unlike Japan's consulates in Panama, Manila, or Seattle, the one in Honolulu was no longer directed merely to ascertain the general whereabouts of the ships of the Pacific Fleet. Washington knew that the naval intelligence section in Tokyo wanted the locations of our warships when they were in harbor. During the next month, Consul Kita was told that because "relations between Japan and the United States are most critical," his "ships-in-harbor report was to be made twice a week," with "extra care to maintain secrecy."[21] Three days later another area, N, was added to the grid. On 20 November, special reports were asked for about bases "in the neighborhood of the Hawaiian military reservation."[22] Four days later Kita was told to report the exact locations of our warships "even when there are no movements."[23] The tragedy of all this was that only a handful of Kita's reports were even translated before 7 December. This clearly indicates the low priority Washington gave them as intelligence.

As I have said earlier, none of the original bomb plot signals, or any of the decrypts that were made that betrayed Japan's increasing interest in Pearl Harbor, was communicated directly (or indirectly) to Admiral Kimmel or Admiral Bloch, the district commander. It does not require any remarkable foresight to discern the significance of this information. Repeated transmissions of such detailed ships-in-harbor locations could have had no usefulness unless the Japanese were planning to execute an attack on our fleet while it was in port. Why? Such detailed reports lost all value once the ships sailed from the carefully designated berths.

If the suspicions of naval intelligence officers were aroused to this possibility, as Colonel Bratton and Commander Safford's evidence suggests, then the failure of the office of naval operations to ensure that the bomb plot messages were sent to us at Pearl Harbor was blind stupidity at the least, and gross neglect at best.

The tragedy of Pearl Harbor also might have been avoided if only the attempt by the Joint Board to set up a body to coordinate army and navy intelligence functions had been successful. On 26 September, two days after the first bomb plot message had been transmitted, the ranking members of naval and army war plans and intelligence divisions sat down for their first meeting. Their goal was to establish a system for coordinating and handling important strategic and tactical information. But it was shattered by a bitter dispute. Brigadier General Leonard T. Gerow, the army chief of war plans, proposed that the joint committee assume responsibility to "collate, analyze and interpret information with its implications, to estimate hostile capabilities and probable intentions."[24]

Admiral Turner, like many naval officers of his generation, harbored a hearty distrust of his sister service. He disagreed with any proposal for joint evaluation. He argued that the committee be restricted to the "presentation of such factual evidence as might be available, but to make no estimate or prediction."[25] "Admiral Turner was practically Naval Operations," General Miles, the army intelligence chief would testify later. "Neither Gerow nor . . . myself could get very far with him."[26]

So the first session of the committee to coordinate intelligence adjourned in a state of rancorous deadlock that 26 September. It did not meet again until 9 December. But for Turner's bullheadedness, it would have reconvened to "analyze and interpret" intelligence—such as the bomb plot messages—that vitally affected joint commands such as Hawaii. It would have noted the accelerating volume and focus of Tokyo's communications with their Honolulu consulate. And this could have resulted in a proper evaluation and warnings to Admiral Kimmel and General Short.

"Knowledge of these intercepted Japanese dispatches," Kimmel testified, "would have radically changed the estimate of the situation made by me and my staff." Whether it would have enabled us to spring an "ambush on the Japanese striking force as it approached Hawaii"[27] is a matter of debate. But it is difficult to argue that in any recasting of events—*if* we had been alerted to the bomb plot messages—Kimmel would have left his battleships to become sitting-duck targets. One certain result would have been his giving greater priority to interception and decryption of the J-19 messages sent from the Honolulu consulate. (This alone would have changed events.) Or if Hypo had been allowed to participate—as Safford wanted—in decrypting, instead of merely intercepting, the Honolulu consulate's traffic, we would quickly have become aware of the increasing extent, detail, and urgency of the ships-in-harbor reports. It is most unlikely that I, or anyone else on Kimmel's staff, would ever have dismissed this intelligence as being merely a "nicety of detail."

Whatever the reason for the naval staff's dereliction, Washington's failure to relay the bomb plot messages to Pearl Harbor added up to what Kimmel called "affirmative misrepresentation."[28] We had asked Washington repeatedly for all intelligence relevant to the fleet. We had been assured repeatedly that we would have it. We believed that we were receiving it. Our estimates and actions were made on this basis. But the failure to relay these vital pieces of intelligence to us deprived us of essential facts and misled us when it came to our assessing the possibility of a Japanese attack on Pearl Harbor.[29]

15

"Imperfect Threats"

BESIDES BEING DENIED vital information from intelligence sources in Washington, Kimmel faced another handicap. He had to depend on CNO's personal letters for a glimpse into the world of diplomatic news. Unfortunately, these letters were deceptive in their reassuring tone.

For example, on 17 October, Stark wrote to Kimmel, "Personally I do not believe the Japs are going to sail into us and the message I sent you merely stated the possibility," adding that Washington was working "to maintain the status quo in the Pacific."[1] Such a message, which arrived at Pearl Harbor a week after we had been warned about the "grave situation" alert (Stark's letter was written the day after the alert), was hardly reassuring as to the reliability of Washington's alarums.

Kimmel had been surprised by Stark's abrupt retreat from the alert triggered by the fall of the Konoye cabinet. We did not know that Washington's fear of immediate Japanese action had been removed by the Purple decrypt of 18 October in which Tokyo assured Ambassador Nomura, "Regardless of the make-up of the new cabinet, negotiations with the United States shall be continued."[2] And Turner, who had drafted the alert message, was to admit later, "I did not believe that there would be any possibility of war for at least a month."[3]

The only hint of Washington's overview of the new diplomatic situation was Stark's assurance that he saw "eye to eye" with the naval liaison officer at the State Department, who advised Stark not to "overestimate the importance of the recent changes in the Japanese cabinet." Captain Roscoe E. Schuirmann's memorandum echoed the opinion of Dr. Stanley K. Hornbeck, who warned Secretary of State Hull not to be fooled into negotiating "the bill of goods" to save the moderate members of the cabinet in Tokyo. According to Hornbeck's view, Japan's foreign policy was already hostage to military extremists. He believed their next ag-

"AND I WAS THERE"

gressive move was going to be dictated by opportunism, and whether this was north or south would depend on "the course of the war in Russia."[4]

This was the only piece of detailed diplomatic analysis that Kimmel received from CNO in a three-month period, and its impact on him was doubly unfortunate. The memo betrayed the State Department's lack of a sense of urgency and its mistaken assumption that Tokyo's actions would be tied to Hitler's war against the Soviet Union. Its on-again, off-again tone was characterized by its recital of the army's fears that the Japanese might raid Wake Island to disrupt the flights of B-17 bombers to the Philippines. While Stark believed that such an attack was "extremely improbable," he nevertheless cautioned that "a carefully planned raid on any of these island carriers in the Pacific might be difficult to detect."[5]

The implication that Kimmel drew from this letter was that from his depleted resources of men, ships, and planes, he was now expected to provide protection for the army bombers on their way to reinforce the Philippines. It was another galling reminder of the degree to which our strategic priorities in the Pacific had undergone a complete reversal: The United States' front line of defense had effectively been moved five thousand miles westward across the Pacific. Hawaii's strategic priorities had given way to the Philippines. Washington evidently saw Pearl Harbor as being only a way station to ferry B-17s to build up MacArthur's forces. "We turned our endeavor to set up sufficient force in the Philippine Islands to guard the islands to be a threat to any Japanese movement through the South China Sea," General Marshall was to concede four years later. "We turned from the meeting of the demands of Hawaii and fulfilling the Martin-Bellinger request for 190 B-17s."[6]

Admiral Kimmel was never properly advised about this reversal of American Pacific strategy—even though it had been decided at the Argentia summit and endorsed by the Joint Board. The 19 September meeting of what was effectively the supreme war council of the United States had agreed to accelerate the military buildup in the Philippines at the expense of Pearl Harbor. The board "concurred" with the army chief of staff's view that this "would have a profound strategic effect and that it might be the decisive element in deterring Japan from undertaking a Pacific war."[7]

Marshall would later explain the decision, testifying, "If we could make the Philippines reasonably defensible, particularly with heavy bombers in which the air corps had at that time great faith, we felt that we could block the Japanese advance and block their entry into the war by their fear of what would happen if they couldn't take the Philippines."[8]

But we did not know about this decision. Nor did we know that Washington believed that "the Japanese could not dare to attempt to move to the south of the Philippines, or to make a naval attack."[9] Washington's notion of its new Pacific military capability had taken off into a flight of strategic fantasy. And the secretary of war hand-delivered it to the White House on 21 October 1941.

"A strategic opportunity of the utmost importance has suddenly arisen in the southwestern Pacific. Our whole strategic possibilities of the past twenty years have been revolutionized," Stimson enthusiastically informed the president. "From being impotent to influence events in the area, we suddenly find ourselves vested with the possibility of great effective power. Indeed, we hardly yet realize our opportunities in this respect."[10] The "possibilities" that so excited Marshall and the secretary of war were graphically demonstrated by red and blue circles penciled onto an accompanying chart of the Far East. Those that radiated north from the Philippines and south from Vladisvostok implied that by using Russian airstrips, we would bring all the home islands of Japan within reach of aerial attack by the army's four-engine bombers, which had a thousand-mile range.

Stimson's allusion to the possibility of American planes raining destruction over Tokyo actually left Roosevelt "a bit bewildered."[11] But the secretary of war's enthusiastic belief was that the B-17 bomber force "had changed the whole picture in the Asiatic area."[12] Within weeks, even MacArthur was cabling Marshall for target maps for "the location of 600 industrial objectives, in Japan proper."[13]

This was the first time—but not the last—that our military was bemused by the supposed deterrent value of strategic bombing. But in the autumn of 1941 two major flaws ought to have caused Marshall to question this new strategy: The doctrine was untried, and it depended on the Japanese to take no military action until enough bombers had been rushed to the Philippines to put it into effect.

The magnitude of military miscalculation in Washington is apparent in Stimson's memorandum. Its premise was based on the army air staff's calculation that 128 B-17s would be sufficient to defend the Philippines. "Yet even this imperfect threat, if not promptly called by the Japanese, bids fair to stop Japan's march to the south and secure the safety of Singapore," the secretary of war confidently predicted, "with all the revolutionary consequences of such action."[14]

Four years later Marshall admitted the folly of the strategic gamble he had supported: "Although we now think in terms of thousands [of bombers], at that time 100 was a very large figure."[15] Production rates were so low that by the beginning of December fewer than fifty planes could be sent to the Philippines. Yet our military staff had become entranced with the strategic bombing doctrine. It was believed, as Marshall himself was to testify, that only a few score bombers were adequate so "that we would probably deter the Japanese from making an attack."[16]

So Stimson's "strategic opportunity" became, in effect, a monumental blunder. From the time the first B-17 touched down in the Philippines at the beginning of September, until the moment Japan's surprise attack exploded their strategic miscalculation three months later, our leaders in Washington were transfixed by their Far East deterrent strategy. They believed that every B-17 that droned its way from Hawaii to Midway and on via Wake and Samoa to the Philippines would add another nail to the club MacArthur would use to cow Japan. The State Department's "babying along" of Tokyo was focused on the production timetables of the Boeing Aircraft Company instead of the increasing signs of Japanese impatience that diplomacy was failing to yield them results.

"As you well know, however, the final success of the operation lies on the knees of the gods," Stimson had reminded Roosevelt, "and we cannot tell what explosion may momentarily come from Japan."[17] What the secretary of war did not know was that three days before he wrote these prophetic words, the fuse that was to ignite the Pacific explosion had been lit. The naval staff in Tokyo was presented with an ultimatum on 10 October. It was delivered by Admiral Yamamoto's senior staff officer Captain Kameto Kuroshima. He carried the blunt message from the fleet's indispensable commander in chief that either they give their approval to the plan to attack Pearl Harbor with the full force of six aircraft carriers, or they face the prospect of his resignation, along with his entire staff. Navy chief Nagano capitulated. The Pearl Harbor operation was officially made part of Japan's overall war plan. The only proviso was that it must not interfere with the main thrust of Japan's southward offensive.

Yamamoto had played a blackmailing hand to overcome naval staff opposition. It was a measure of his skill as a master poker player and an ominous omen that he now considered war with the United States inevitable. Only a month earlier he had secretly cautioned Premier Konoye that if negotiations with the United States failed, "I can promise to give them hell for a year or a year and a half, but can guarantee nothing as to what will happen after that."[18]

"Yet in a letter of 24 October to the new navy minister, the Combined Fleet CinC struck a decidedly different tone. "When one views the situation as a whole, it is obvious that a collision between Japan and America should be avoided," Yamamoto advised Vice Admiral Shigetaro Shimada, the navy minister. But Yamamoto was a realist who doubted that "now Japan has been driven to its present situation," it might be too late to change course. He insisted that "if the situation is going to force us into action," then the Pearl Harbor operation, conceived though it had been "in desperation," was the only viable strategy. "I feel, as officer in command of the fleet, that there will be little prospect of success if we employ the normal type of operations," he concluded, repeating his threat of resignation.[19]

Yamamoto, however, had no intention of employing normal operations. His victory over the naval staff now secured, he sailed a week later with the Combined Fleet for the broad reaches of Tosa Bay on the southerly island of Shikoku to conduct a final series of maneuvers. While Admiral Nagumo's First Air Fleet completed preparations for a final dress rehearsal of the Pearl Harbor attack on 3 November, Yamamoto was summoned to Tokyo to brief the navy minister.

After the commander in chief left, Admiral Ugaki, his chief of staff, remained on board battleship *Nagato*. He began that day's diary entry on a confident note. "Everything is OK," he wrote. Then, reflecting on the ambition of the undertaking, his self-restraint cracked: "Die, die all of you! I, too, will die for my country."[20]

Under cover of darkness in the small hours of 4 November, Admiral Nagumo's carrier striking force made a high-speed run to the southwest to within two hundred miles of the southernmost tip of Kyūshū before launching planes to make practice strikes against Ariake Bay. While Commander Mitsuo Fuchida led the full complement of aircraft in mock raids against the town of Saeki, Ugaki and the staff on the flagship polished their final drafts of the army and navy agreement for Yamamoto's war plan.

X-day was set for the first week in December. A full moon between midnight and dawn would give the various invasion forces the visibility they needed to get into position to attack. The first Sunday of the month was also considered the ideal time to catch the Pacific Fleet in harbor and unawares. On 5 November the war directive itself was issued by imperial general headquarters: "In the interest of self-defense and survival, the empire is due to open hostilities with the United States, Britain, and Holland in the first ten days of December. Preparations are to be completed for the various operations involved."[21]

The hundred pages of Yamamoto's operational order number 1, which he had submitted personally to the navy staff in Tokyo two days later, was issued the same day. Far more comprehensive than a simple plan for opening hostilities, it was the naval blueprint for the first six months of war. Seven hundred copies were printed under tight security, an astonishingly large number for a top-secret war plan. As a precaution, the final section detailing the Pearl Harbor plan was detached. Copies of it were held under even tighter security for distribution to only the commanders of Nagumo's striking force.[22]

Coincident with the issue of his operational orders, Yamamoto also took care to draw a tight cloak of secrecy around radio communications of the Combined Fleet.

We soon became aware of these new procedures at Pearl Harbor. On 1 November, Rochefort reported that the call signs of all seagoing commands and warships had been changed as of midnight, Tokyo time. This caused us no undue alarm. The last major change had been made in May and the imperial navy routinely revised its call signs every six months. We had been anticipating the switch, because they had introduced new call signs for all shore stations at the beginning of October. But because the Hypo cryptanalysts had still made no progress with the Japanese flag of-

ficer code, and lacked the current keys Washington had recovered to the
JN-25 fleet operational cipher, our ability to track their naval units was
once again curtailed.

The relatively high volume of traffic, however, enabled Hypo's traffic
analysts to make speedy progress toward establishing some key call signs,
of which there were an estimated twenty thousand new warship identifier
codes used in radio transmissions. Within twenty-four hours Rochefort's
daily traffic analysis summary reported "casual identification" of many
units, although the Japanese were evidently using as many as seven call
signs for each major unit.[23]

Despite this effort at concealment, the Japanese could not hide the
signature of certain radio operators. The ears of our On the Roof Gang
manning the Wahiawa listening station had by now become so attuned
that they easily picked out one of the ham-fisted telegraphists on carrier
Akagi who played the Morse key as if he were sitting on it!

On 3 November, Rochefort reported an important discovery. One of
the addressees had been broken out as *Ichi Kōkū Kantai*, literally the
"First Air Fleet." Based upon this, and together with other analyses, Joe
was certain that it indicated "an entirely new organization of the naval air
fleets.[24]

We guessed from the volume of traffic addressed to the Japanese carriers on their tactical circuits that some major Combined Fleet exercise
must be taking place across the Pacific. But there was no evidence in the
radio traffic that they were preparing for an attack on United States territory. Our suspicions might have been aroused had we known more
about the innocent-looking steamer that docked at Honolulu Harbor on
the morning of 1 November. She had just crossed the Pacific undetected,
using the northerly route selected for the Japanese carrier striking force.
The stormy waters to the north and west of Hawaii were empty of our
merchant shipping which, since September, had been routed to the south
of Hawaii as a safety measure. *Taiyo Maru* had proved to the satisfaction
of the naval officers traveling incognito on board that it was impossible to
approach to within two hundred miles of Pearl Harbor without risk of
being spotted by our naval patrol planes.

The ship was staked out by the local ONI and FBI agents as soon as
she tied up. Yet careful monitoring of her visitors did not reveal that
Consul General Kita's frequent visits were for the purpose of relaying
detailed intelligence reports. The naval officers remained on board, carefully making note of the number and direction of daily air patrols.

Our ONI and FBI agents might have been more suspicious about the
role the consul was playing if they had paid more attention to the peripa-
tetic journeyings of his energetic third secretary, Yoshikawa, alias Morimura.

The Fourteenth Naval District had failed to watch closely either
Yoshikawa or one of his resident spies who had been identified as a

"Class A Nazi suspect" by Captain Mayfield's office in July 1940. It was astonishing that such an obvious agent as Fritz Kuehn was overlooked. He had paid frequent trips to Japan after settling in Honolulu in 1936 to run a steel furniture business that soon failed. The former naval policeman and ex-Nazi, who had been jailed twice before leaving Germany, also owned "considerable real estate" and lived well with two homes— one a Lanaikai beach house. Kuehn appeared to have no visible means of support other than his wife's beauty parlor. But his file noted that he had received suspiciously large payments through the local Japanese consulate.[25]

The forty-six-year-old Kuehn, who used the code-name "Jimmie," would later confess to supplying Consul Kita with "perfectitiously information" about the Pacific Fleet. Kuehn had fallen under suspicion the previous year when he began cultivating acquaintances among naval officers. But he was not tailed when he drove his brown roadster up to the Japanese consulate in the fall of 1941 to submit the complex signal system that would enable him to report fleet movements from his beach house by lights and using a radio transmitter. He received $14,000 for his services, the money delivered to his home on an October Sunday by a Japanese contact named Kyogoku, who had come to brief him on the important mission. The mysterious caller was to be identified by Kuehn's stepson as none other than Yoshikawa.[26]

If our counterintelligence operations on Oahu failed to apprehend Yoshikawa and his network it was because their elaborately orchestrated spying had not been detected. Nor had the young Japanese diplomat actually infringed any law that would have enabled the local FBI to bring charges. But there could be no such excuses for Washington's failure to evaluate and alert the overseas commands of the Magic intelligence that clearly indicated Japan's acceleration toward belligerency.

On 2 November a Purple decrypt from Tokyo alerted Ambassador Nomura—and our own military leaders and diplomats—that the cabinet "in a meeting on the morning of the 5th" would issue new instructions for resuming negotiations. "This will be our government's last effort to improve diplomatic relations," it warned. "The situation is very grave. When we resume negotiations, the situation makes it urgent that we reach a decision at once."[27]

This message signaled in unequivocal terms that Japan was about to embark on a final attempt at diplomacy. It had resulted from more than ten days of stormy liaison conference meetings in Tokyo during which Tojo had struggled to reconcile the hard-line militarists—who called for immediate war preparations—with the emperor's instruction to his new premier to "go back to blank paper," to give diplomacy one final chance.

Not until the end of October had the military leaders been persuaded to give their diplomats until the third week of November to arrange a settlement that could lead to the resumption of American oil shipments to Japan. In doing so, the military again rejected Hull's four principles for guaranteeing China's autonomy, as a basis for negotiation. They insisted that there was to be no backing out of their tripartite pact obligations, and refused to remove their troops from Indochina or China until after twenty-five years.

This was the basis of Japan's so-called "A" Proposal, which represented Tokyo's minimum demands and maximum concessions. Tojo continued to argue for a more flexible negotiating position. On 5 November he finally succeeded in wringing cabinet approval for a "B" proposal. This was a *modus vivendi,* a temporary accommodation that was to be put forward only if the terms and conditions of "A" proposal were rejected.

Our ambassador in Tokyo had relayed the information that the new cabinet was being given a stormy ride by its service ministers who wanted action, not more diplomacy. On 3 November, Grew advised the State Department that even Tojo might not be able to hold down the pressure building within his cabinet. His cable warned of "an all out, do or die attempt to render Japan impervious to foreign embargoes, even risking national hara-kiri rather than cede to foreign pressure."[28]

In Washington the next day the senior members of our army and navy staffs wrestled in their 3 November joint meeting with the problem of how to prevent a premature explosion in the Pacific before MacArthur had been adequately reinforced. They considered a toughly worded State Department policy paper that advocated stepping up aid to China and issuing a firm ultimatum to Japan.

"Mr. Hull is of the opinion that there was no use to issue any additional warnings against Japan if we can't back them up," Marshall advised the Joint Board. The army chief reminded the meeting that they still did not have enough military resources in the Philippines to back up any ultimatum to Japan. He reminded the board that it had committed the United States to an Atlantic-oriented strategy. Any flare-up in the Far East would detract from Britain's ability to continue the fight against Germany. Not until mid-December would MacArthur have sufficient bombers to provide the "impressive strength" needed to "have a deterrent effect on Japanese operations."[29]

Admiral Ingersoll was all for rejecting Hull's hard-line policy proposal. He accused the State Department of being "under the impression that Japan could be defeated in military action in a few weeks."[30] The chief of naval operations concurred. Stark also pointed out that it would be impossible to provide enough tankers to support offensive operations by the Pacific Fleet without causing a major fuel crisis in the United States. "Assuming that the fleet could be moved to the Far East," CNO warned, "no repair facilities are available at either Manila or Singapore."[31]

Facing this dilemma, Marshall concluded, "It would take some very clever diplomacy to save the situation." Marshall suggested making "certain minor concessions which the Japanese could use in saving face." The Joint Board therefore resolved to reject the State Department's hard-line proposals. Instead, the board would send the president its own memorandum spelling out the strategic realities and dangers in the Pacific. The board opposed "the issuance of an ultimatum to Japan." Instead it advocated that they "put off hostilities with Japan as long as possible" by suggesting agreements "to tide the situation over for the next several months."[32]

The need to avoid any acts that might provoke Japan into war was stressed throughout a six-point memorandum, over the joint signatures of Marshall and Stark, that went to the White House on 5 November. "The only current plans for war against Japan in the Far East are to conduct a defensive war in cooperation with the British and the Dutch," it declared.[33] The president was advised that the Philippine-based strategic bombers could not become a "positive threat" until mid-December, and they would not reach their projected strength until February or March 1942 when the "potency of this threat will have reached the point where it might well be the deciding factor in deterring Japan."[34]

Meanwhile, Purple decrypts had revealed that Japan's consulate in Manila—paying close attention to every B-17 arrival—was keeping Tokyo posted on the accelerating pace of MacArthur's military buildup. That Japan anticipated Washington might be intending to threaten the home islands from the air was evident in a 4 September circular put out to the Japanese consulates on the west coast from the embassy in Washington asking for investigation of the "possibility the United States is preparing for the eventuality when a considerable bombing force will have to be transferred to the (Siberian?) area."[35]

Their military attaché in Berlin was simultaneously ordered to collect German data on the Flying Fortress raids flown by the Royal Air Force that summer. The Luftwaffe reported the poor performance of the few British B-17s in raiding Berlin. Military analysts in Tokyo were therefore soon able to discount the strategic bombing threat on which our military leaders had placed so much faith as a deterrent.

General Marshall's own staff was also beginning to come to the same conclusion. Their 21 November appraisal entitled "Strategic Air Offensive Against Japan" cautioned that "we are going much too far on the offensive side" for the "smallness of the proposed army air force in the Philippines." It concluded that the inflammability of Tokyo had been "considerably overestimated" in MacArthur's plans for "general incendiary attacks to burn up the wood-and-paper structures of the densely populated Japanese cities."[36]

Hundreds of target maps had already been dispatched to the Philippines, but the limited range of the B-17s necessitated their landing in Russia after bombing the Japanese home islands. Negotiations to land at

Russian airfields around Vladivostok had been dragging on with Kremlin officials since 11 October. And Stalin steadfastly refused to sanction their use by American planes.

Just before Richard Sorge's espionage ring was exposed on 14 November, the Soviet master spy had confirmed to Stalin that Japan was committed to a southward advance. This had permitted Stalin to issue the orders recalling the Red Army's Siberian divisions in time to join the defense of Moscow. With the desperate battle for Moscow looming, the Russians feared that any agreement for our bombers to use their bases might trigger a retaliatory attack by Tokyo across the now weakly guarded Manchurian frontier.

While Stalin's noncooperation was stalling the Anglo-American ability to directly menace Japan, Britain's seaborne contribution to the defense of the South Pacific was also losing its credibility. Churchill had promised to send a "formidable, fast, high-class squadron" to Singapore.[37] But objections by the Admiralty had reduced this to a one-carrier task force.

"There is nothing like having something that can catch and kill anything," the prime minister had nonetheless cheerfully cabled Roosevelt on 2 November, a week after battleship *Prince of Wales* sailed on the first leg of her long haul halfway around the globe.[38] "The firmer your attitude and ours, the less chance of their taking the plunge," Churchill assured the president.[39]

The prime minister's optimism was in no way dampened the next day by the news that the aircraft carrier that had been assigned to the squadron had run aground on a reef off Bermuda. Neither Admiral Sir Tom Phillips, flying his flag in the battleship, nor the prime minister reconsidered the danger to the task force if it proceeded to Singapore without air cover. Phillips, like most Royal Navy gunnery officers of his generation, had repeatedly insisted, as vice-chief of the naval staff, that "bombers were no match for battleships."

When *Prince of Wales* put into Capetown on 16 November, South African Prime Minister Jan Christian Smuts cabled London, "If the Japanese are really nippy, there is an opening here for a first-class disaster."[40] Neither Phillips nor Churchill paid heed to his keen strategic instincts. The veteran Boer general saw the strategic folly of sending a weak force steaming into waters dominated by Japan's overwhelming sea and air supremacy.

The British prime minister's continued expectation that a one-battleship squadron could strike awe into the militarists in Tokyo was yet another link in the fatal chain of strategic illusion. Our own military leaders were blind to the ominous indications that Japan was moving to call the Anglo-American bluff—months before either the sea or air forces became a credible military force. By the end of the first week in November the warnings could be read in almost every line of the Purple decrypts of the messages sent to the Japanese embassy on Massachusetts Avenue from the foreign ministry in Tokyo.

On 4 November, Ambassador Nomura was informed that diplomat Saburo Kurusu was coming to Washington because of the "gravity of the present negotiations."[41] The arrival of a special envoy gave specific warning that this truly was a last-ditch diplomatic effort at negotiation. It removed any doubt that if the current discussions led nowhere, "relations between our two nations will be on the brink of chaos."[42]

In a four-part message the next day, the terms of Japan's "last possible bargain" were spelled out to Nomura. His instructions were that "there will be no room for personal interpretation."[43] "A" proposal for a permanent settlement that was transmitted on 5 November not only contained the very narrow limits within which Japan was prepared to negotiate, but her ambassador was ordered to present it "at the earliest possible moment." He was told, "Speed is an absolutely essential factor."[44]

The cable also contained "B" proposal for a temporary accommodation, which was to be put forward only if there was "a remarkable difference between the Japanese and American views." Nomura was left in no doubt that this was his government's "final step." Time was "exceedingly short," and the situation "very critical." He was told that "absolutely no delays" were permitted, and that it was vital that "all arrangements for the signing of this agreement be completed by the 25th of this month."[45]

Just under three weeks now remained for Ambassador Nomura to pull off what the Japanese foreign minister admitted would be a "difficult order."[46] The ominous drumbeat of impending belligerency was heard in the carefully specified deadline of 25 November, the day appointed by Yamamoto for the striking force to set sail for Hawaii. But even this did not rouse any immediate appreciation of the true dimension of the crisis in Washington.

Magic's forewarnings, it seems, had drained the situation of all urgency. Nomura arrived at the State Department on Friday morning to deliver proposal "A." Hull was cordial, but did not believe that it offered "any real recessions from the position consistently maintained by the Japanese government." The secretary of state did, however, warn Roosevelt's inner cabinet that afternoon that "relations were extremely critical and . . . we should be on the lookout for a military attack anywhere by Japan at any time."[47]

The chief of naval operations allowed only a vague echo of the strident urgency of the Magic decrypts to creep into the message he sent off to Kimmel that same day. "The big question is—what next?" was how Stark began another of his epistles. This one was concerned mainly with turning down Kimmel's recent requests for more destroyers and the new battleships *North Carolina* and *Washington*.[48] He did allow, however, that dealing with Japan "continually gets worser and worser."

Three days earlier we had received notice that Japan was recalling all her merchant ships from the western hemisphere.[49] But no dispatch told us of the most specific intelligence Washington had yet received of

Japan's timetable for war. If Kimmel had been informed of Tokyo's 25 November deadline for negotiations, we might have been more concerned at the sudden disappearance of radio traffic addressed to their carriers.

Instead, Stark sent another of his Delphic warnings that "a month may see, literally, most anything."[50] Considering that this letter was dated 7 November, his prediction, "It doesn't look too good," proved to be one of CNO's more accurate utterances on the situation.

16

"What Will We Do?"

I T WAS A STRIKING incongruity of our naval intelligence setup that while Washington was able to intercept, decrypt, and translate Japan's high-level diplomatic traffic within a day or so, it took more than a week for the letters from CNO to reach Pearl Harbor by mail. So Stark's 7 November letter, with its vapid prediction that "anything" could happen with Tokyo in a month, crossed in transit with Kimmel's urgent question: "If they [the Japanese] do embark on such an adventure and Britain and the Dutch East Indies declare war on Japan, what will we do?"[1]

We believed that the imperial navy was clearly preparing for hostile operations. This was evident from the surge in tactical signal traffic from the Combined Fleet's early November exercises and indications of an acceleration of their military buildup in the mandated islands. Yet it seemed to me that naval intelligence in Washington continued to ignore the growing threat posed by naval and air bases in the Marshalls and Carolines. Remembering how they had neglected the WE WE cipher earlier in the year, on 6 November we sent off our latest analysis of Japanese bases and aircraft in the mandates to the chief of naval operations.

"You will note, of course, that our estimate differs considerably from the one prepared by Washington," Kimmel advised Stark. "I doubt very much if the navy department effort has had the care expended upon it that we have given."[2] Our concern was that Japan had already illegally garrisoned and established facilities for both submarines and aircraft in these strategically located islands.

We know that Truk, with its fine deep-water anchorage, at the heart of the Caroline archipelago, was already in use as an operating base for the Fourth Fleet. My estimates—based on the number of reconnaissance flights being made over Britain's neighboring Gilbert Islands—were that somewhere between 62 and 268 aircraft were operating throughout the mandates.

At the west end of the thousand-mile necklace of coral islands that strategically straddled our Pacific line of communications were the Palaus. We knew that at least two seaplane bases, an airstrip, gun batteries, and barracks had been built there to guard the excellent anchorage. To the east in the Marshall chain was Jaluit, some eight hundred miles south of our highly vulnerable base at Wake atoll. In addition to a pair of four-hundred-foot radio towers that eavesdropped on our communications, Jaluit was equipped with two landing fields, seaplane slips, shore batteries, and antiaircraft guns. The fortification of the mandates, as a launching point for a submarine or surface offensive against our fleet, was a logical strategic move by the Japanese.

One of the basic axioms of intelligence work is to put yourself into the enemy's shoes and try to figure out what he would do. This was how I approached the task of assembling the information on the mandates. And it was the picture of Japanese movements that I gave to Admiral Kimmel in my daily briefing. Also, several times a day I would discuss the latest traffic analysis findings with Joe Rochefort.

During these consultations, I was often reminded how painfully reliant we were on the inexact science of traffic analysis. Hypo was still unable to read any of the major naval code systems. The extent and accuracy of intelligence derived from traffic analysis had certain limitations—as we would learn later—because it was based on the technique of identification by association. To identify an unknown Japanese unit, we monitored its activities on one of the two hundred radio circuits and the traffic—a broad term for communications carried by radio frequency circuits—the unit was associated with.

Japan's unique naval communications system was both a help and a hindrance to this technique. Their commanders did not normally communicate with one another directly, except in tactical situations. Administrative and command traffic was usually transmitted up a chain of command to the nearest shore station, which sent out the signal for all addressees on an umbrella broadcast, usually repeated several times. While our performance in traffic analysis over a long period was pretty good, we were less accurate in divining the details of an opponent's day-by-day moves, especially if new call signs and circuits were introduced, as they had been at the beginning of November.

Yet the peculiar nature of the Japanese communications setup could often yield surprisingly precise intelligence. If for example a carrier division at Kure, in the southwest of Honshū, was ordered to proceed to the northern port of Ominato, it would send a movement report to Kure and another to the navy's main reporting division in Tokyo. A call would then be put out to the naval station in Ominato, which would be rebroadcast by both Tokyo and Ominato. So by comparing the addressees, even though the actual coded message could not be read, it was a simple matter to forecast that the carrier division was proceeding from Kure to Ominato.

I kept an extensive card file in my office listing Japanese naval units and commands. Whenever a new unit appeared on the sheets sent up from Rochefort's outfit, I could thumb through my tickler file on which I noted the latest sightings and radio estimates and pencil in the most likely ship or command involved. Filling in my record cards every day enabled me to draw up a location sheet and chart up-to-date positions and likely movements of the majority of Japanese fleet units.

I had frequent exchanges with Rochefort on call sign recoveries after their November call sign change revealed that certain fleet units had apparently been transferred to other commands. Each fleet circuit—which we called a "mother"—had certain "chickens" under its radio "wing." Some of these chickens no longer turned up with their usual mother, but were calling the mother address of other fleets. This was unusual. When these new commanders began addressing the subordinates of another command, like the First Fleet destroyers that appeared in Second Fleet traffic, it was a sign that they had assumed direct tactical control over them for some impending operations.

A fleet intelligence officer always has to establish a framework for defining the scope of the strategic picture. Within it he can assemble scattered elements to piece together an overall pattern, rather like a jigsaw puzzle. We could never expect to have all the pieces, but that November we had received no Magic dispatches—from either Washington or Cavite. Our attention was, therefore, concentrated on the region bounded by the South China Sea on the west and the Marshall Islands to the east. Those pieces of the puzzle that we possessed fit neatly into this framework. As we saw it, a Japanese offensive move was shaping up against Malaya. It was possible that it was also directed against the Philippines, and there was a strong defensive and offensive capability in the mandates.

Rochefort's communications intelligence summary was delivered to my office each day around 0700. I would take it to Admiral Kimmel an hour later with my own daily briefing. In reading it, he would mark or underline in pencil the items he considered important. The admiral would ask me for clarification or more information, and then initial the paper. His chief of staff, Captain William W. "Poco" Smith, was usually present during my presentation, and if a crisis was building, the senior war plans officer and the senior operations officer would be called in to discuss my reports.

Admiral Kimmel always encouraged his officers to express themselves. I took full advantage of this to offer my opinions. There were also meetings almost daily in which I briefed, so that staff officers did not have to read through the entire material. When our other task force commanders were in port—they usually operated at sea for two weeks and in port for one week—Kimmel had me give them a review of events that had occurred in their absence. There were general discussions covering Japanese intentions and how we could counter them. Particular attention was always paid to the mandates, and General Short was present at several of

the sessions during which we discussed the threat these island bases posed
to Hawaii.

The picture that we constructed in November pointed unmistakably to
a Japanese buildup for naval operations to the south. It was confirmed by
the sightings in November of an increasing number of transports by our
observers in Chinese ports. Our naval attachés and merchant skippers
also added their reports of Japanese troopships departing southward from
Shanghai. Again, this fit neatly into our overall picture formed by our
traffic analysis.

During the first week of November, we discovered that Jaluit radio
activity had increased dramatically, and circuit congestion revealed
"heavy concentrations" in the Marshalls.[3] My discussions with Admiral
Kimmel and his chief of war plans, Captain Charles H. "Soc" McMorris,
increasingly focused on the recent changes in the Japanese tactical organization. It was also evident that a large amount of the Combined Fleet
traffic was appearing, as Rochefort reported, "with secret (tactical) calls
in use."[4] This was another indicator of naval forces making ready for
some major operation. During the second week of November radio activity in the mandates continued at a high level, and the pattern of Combined Fleet traffic continued to point to a major reorganization. On 9
November carrier *Akagi*, flagship of the newly identified First Air Fleet,
was picked up at Sasebo, and transmissions from Carrier Divisions 3 and
4 indicated that they were also heading for home ports after their recent
exercises with the battleships.[5]

Then, during the next five days, there was such a decline in traffic on
the naval air circuits that Rochefort reported that the "carriers remain
relatively inactive."[6] We deduced that the Japanese carriers were probably replenishing prior to operating with the Second Fleet. It remained the
single most active originator of traffic throughout the third week of November.[7] On Monday, 17 October, Rochefort's daily summary confirmed
that the "carriers are mostly in the Kure-Sasebo area, with the exception
of a few which are operating in the Kyushu area."[8] Over the next twenty-
four-hour period several messages were picked up addressed to the carrier divisions from Tokyo, from which we concluded, "No movement
from home waters."[9]

Our estimate was dead wrong! That very afternoon, Admiral
Yamamoto delivered a rousing send-off speech on *Akagi*'s flight deck in
Saeki Bay. As dusk fell, the six blacked-out carriers slipped out to sea
bound for a secret assembly point at Tankan Bay (Hitokappu Wan) in the
foggy remoteness of the Kurile Islands.

Strict radio silence was observed by the Japanese carriers, so our radio intelligence network did not detect the first move of the powerful
force that was to attack Pearl Harbor. The Big Boss—as we called
Yamamoto—continued sending out many messages to Second Fleet,
which we assumed would operate with carriers because on 23 November

Rochefort reported that "Cardiv 3 [carrier division] definitely associated with 2nd Fleet operations."[10]

All our traffic analysis continued to show that preparations were being made for a southward advance through the South China Sea, under cover of Indochina airfields, with Malaya, the Dutch East Indies, and possibly the Philippines being the probable objectives.[11] The Third Fleet was also such a frequent addressee that we believed it must be the main amphibious invasion force, because it appeared prominently in communications with the commander of shore-based air units in Indochina.[12] Station Cast from Cavite estimated Carrier Division 3 could be in the Palaus, but Rochefort and I remained convinced that at least one of its carriers would operate as far east as the Marshalls. I so informed the commander in chief.

We were wrong in our deductions about the Japanese carriers. It was a tragic example of how reliance on traffic analysis alone can lead to error. The pattern of Japanese carrier radio circuits indicated that each division customarily kept its same destroyer division. We therefore assumed that even if their "mother" did not turn up in the traffic, the appearance of her "chickens" would indicate the presence of a carrier division. On 16 November "associations" had been noted by Hypo that indicated carriers were in the mandates as a result of interceptions from the Marshalls of the call sign of a division of destroyers which "has been or is operating with carrier division."[13]

While such analysis did not prove that the mother carriers were with their chickens, we decided they were, because other addressees associated with Japanese carrier traffic had also dried up that week. When Rochefort reported on 23 November that "yesterday a number of dispatches associated Cardiv 3 with CinC 3rd Fleet,"[14] we had no way of knowing that it was actually the small carriers of division 4 that were heading for Formosa. The large carriers of division 3 were already in the Kurile Islands with Carrier Division 1 and were making final preparations for the long voyage across the Pacific to Hawaii.

Twenty-four hours later what appeared to be exchanges between Jaluit and commander carriers persuaded Rochefort there was a definite indication that "one or more Cardivs are present in the Mandates."[16] This was far and away the most potent danger to Pearl Harbor. Again, it fit in with the overall picture of the forces in the Marshalls as being the easterly component of the large task force that was building up to conduct the southward advance and attack the Philippines and Malaya. This conclusion came from an association of the call signs of many Second Fleet warships with the addressees of base commands in Formosa, Hainan, and French Indochina.[17]

By 20 November, Rochefort was convinced that the task force assembling under control of the Second Fleet was so massive that it "will comprise a good portion of the navy."[18]

Although on 24 November, Rochefort was cautioning "no definite indications of location of carriers,"[19] Hypo's traffic analysts predicted that at least one, and possibly two, of the Japanese carrier divisions would probably be associated with the movement and that one might be heading from Japan for the Marshalls. Kimmel was following these reports very closely, the assumption being that wherever the carriers were located would highlight the main thrust of the Combined Fleet.

At my briefing with Kimmel that Wednesday, he told me to ask Rochefort to confirm his estimates of the carrier locations with the other intercept stations. When Joe reported that no one had so far commented on it via the secure cryptographic radio circuit, Kimmel directed me to send a Copek dispatch setting forth his observations and our conclusions drawn from the Hypo summaries. Two days later Station Cast confirmed our general picture that Japan was building up for a southward thrust. They also predicted that a task force was "expected to operate in the Mandates." This included battleships, cruisers, Destroyer Division 23, and at least one unit of Carrier Division 3—*Ryujo*.[20]

The intelligence estimates of the extensive Japanese forces massing on the other side of the Pacific coincided with the arrival that 24 November on Kimmel's desk of the letter dated 14 November from CNO, which equivocally told him "what we will do in the Far East remains to be seen."[21] The letter also included a copy of the Stark-Marshall memorandum of 5 November to the president, which proved to be more unsettling. It was the first indication that a strategic tug-of war was going on in Washington. Kimmel was, however, reassured by their strong plea to the president that "no ultimatum" be sent to Tokyo and the statement that for two months, at least, war "should be avoided while building up defensive forces in the Far East."[22] He took this as a clear indication that the military leadership in Washington hoped to postpone hostilities until the spring of 1942.

The Stark-Marshall memorandum was also Kimmel's first direct confirmation that the Joint Board recognized that because of Pacific Fleet's inferiority it was unable to "undertake an unlimited strategic offensive." Ten days earlier Kimmel had tried once again to explain his predicament to Stark. Kimmel was concerned that the situation in the Pacific was rushing to a showdown, and he put his concerns bluntly: "We must be in a position to minimize our own losses, and to inflict maximum damage to Japanese fleet, merchant shipping, and bases. . . . I must insist that more consideration be given to the needs of the Pacific Fleet."[23]

The measure of reassurance that Kimmel gained from the knowledge that the strategic realities we faced were finally recognized in Washington was diminished by his alarm at the memorandum's confirmation that the United States would go to war if Japan attacked British and Dutch territory, or began a movement into Thailand that threatened to become an invasion of the Malay Peninsula.[24]

That was precisely what our intelligence indicated that the Japanese naval task forces were preparing to do. But Washington's determination to avoid a showdown with Japan, while at the same time committing us to war if Malaya was attacked, exposed a dangerous strategic contradiction. It became a hot topic of "corridor gossip"[25] at headquarters. We could only hope that the State Department would make some accommodation in the negotiations with Japan that would give us the time needed to get the reinforcements Kimmel had requested.

Such hope was not encouraged by an alert flashed out that Monday afternoon from Washington to all the Pacific commands: "Chances of favorable outcome of negotiations with Japan very doubtful. This situation coupled with statements of Japanese government and movements their naval and military forces indicate in our opinion that surprise aggressive movement *in any direction* including attack on Philippines or Guam is a possibility [empahsis added]."[26]

In the absence of any of the diplomatic intelligence, the failure of the warning to specify just what the threat was negated its urgency at fleet headquarters. So did the injunction for observing "utmost secrecy" so as not to "complicate an already tense situation." The dispatch did, however, appear to confirm that the naval staff had made an identical evaluation of the impending southward movement of hostile naval forces. That a warning had been sent at all was also confirmation of my belief that Japan probably would not risk a southward advance if the Philippines or Guam remained free to attack their right flank. It was not in keeping with the historical record of their military operations.[27]

The estimate that I gave the commander in chief that weekend allowed that some aggressive movement might be imminent from the two powerful task forces assembling five thousand miles across the Pacific. Although both were under the authority of the Second Fleet command, it was already clear that the most powerful one was likely to proceed south from the Formosa-Hainan-Bako area into the South China Sea, aiming at the Isthmus of Kra at the neck of the Malay Peninsula in the Gulf of Siam. The other task force was more likely to travel via the Palaus, in the western Carolines, with the intention of threatening the Dutch East Indies. Once such a movement got under way, I felt, it would not be long before they attacked the Philippines. Our growing air force posed a threat to their line of communications if we took action to assist the British and the Dutch.[28]

After my briefing, Kimmel considered the situation sufficiently urgent to instruct me to personally take the alert over to General Short. When I arrived at Fort Shafter shortly past noon, I found him listening to the midday radio news. After reading the dispatch, he quizzed me about Guam's defenses. Apart from the occasional plane, I explained, the navy had dismantled all coast defense guns in accordance with the League of Nations Naval Limitation Treaty of 1922 which did not permit fortification of the island. The meeting ended with the general expressing his disapproval of the consequences of having appeased Japan too much. I reflected on this on my way back to Cincpac headquarters to report my mission had been completed.

General Short's anger would have been still greater had he known that, even as we spoke, our military leadership in Washington was preparing a deal that, on the face of it, appeared very much like appeasement. It would urge the White House to make a temporary accommodation with Tokyo to forestall a possible breakdown in negotiations. Three days earlier a memorandum from General Gerow, the chief of army war plans, had stressed "the grave importance to the success of war effort in Europe that we reach a *modus vivendi* with Japan."[29] The naval staff had also given its support to the *modus vivendi* plan as a way of buying more time to get the fifty more bombers and the troop convoys across the Pacific. Since Marshall was absent from Washington that Monday on a long weekend, Stark had taken the initiative to order the drafting of another appeal to Roosevelt to do everything to continue negotiations despite clear warnings from the Magic decrypts that Tokyo was about to break them off for lack of progress.[30]

The realization that it was going to take more than fifty B-17s and a few thousand more American soldiers in the Philippines to stop Japan from taking the plunge was already beginning to dawn on our military leaders. That Monday, Stark was to dictate a letter that apprised Kimmel of the "gravity of the situation" as viewed by the president and secretary of state. "Neither would be surprised over a Japanese surprise attack," CNO warned. "From many angles an attack on the Philippines would be the most embarrassing thing that could happen to us."[31] And once again Stark watered down the urgency of his warning by confessing, "I do not give it the weight others do."

This letter reached fleet headquarters only four days before the Japanese attack. Stark's final attempt to represent the urgency of the situation as he saw it gave a less than adequate picture as negotiations with Japan entered their final round. But the confusion in his dispatch was symptomatic of the uncertainty of our military leaders as the United States faced a crisis as great as any in our history. Instead of providing Kimmel with a reasoned evaluation of the intelligence that indicated the awesome extent to which American strategy in the Pacific was coming unstuck, the chief of naval operations wrapped his fears in a flurry of conflicting statements: "I won't go into the pros or cons of what the United States may do. I will be damned if I know. I wish I did. The only thing I do know is that we may do most anything and that's the only thing I know to be prepared for; or we may do nothing—I think it is more likely to be 'anything.'"[32]

17

Negotiations On

I N AN UNPRECEDENTED DISPLAY of army-navy unity, General Marshall and Admiral Stark reinforced the Joint Board's warning against any ultimatum to Japan until the Anglo-American force was a credible deterrent. The State Department was obliged to concede its hard-line attitude and the imbalance of United States foreign policy had been redressed by sound military strategy. But it was too late. By the middle of November it was obvious in Washington that Tokyo was not going to endure three more months of diplomatic procrastination while their oil reserves drained away and our strategic bombing force grew strong enough to threaten the Japanese home islands.

Magic revealed the increasingly impatient directions Tokyo was giving its Washington embassy. The assignment of Saburo Kurusu, an experienced diplomat with an American wife, to assist Ambassador Nomura was another sign of the Japanese cabinet's determination to speed up the diplomatic process. Our analysts in Washington had calculated that the Japanese objective must be the restoration of oil supplies by negotiation with the United States, or the seizure of alternate sources in the Dutch East Indies. That Kurusu did not rate his chances highly had been publicized on 10 November. *The New York Times* correspondent in Manila reported the envoy's remark that he was "going to Washington, but [I] have no great hopes for a successful conclusion to negotiations."[1] Tokyo's swift response by cable to Kurusu expressing the foreign minister's displeasure with his comments circulated with the Magics three days after his arrival in Washington on 15 November.[2]

Kurusu's indiscretions did not add warmth to his welcome in Washington; nor did they enhance the State Department's hope for a successful outcome of the new round of negotiations. Although he read Tokyo's protests in the Purple decrypts "that the United States takes this lazy and easy-going attitude,"[3] Secretary Hull had been stalling the Japanese ambassador for a week. Japanese patience was wearing thinner by the day. Two days after Nomura formally had presented the "A" proposal for a full settlement on 10 November, Hull countered with an "oral" statement that prior approval was needed from Chiang Kai-shek before the matter of China could be discussed. It came as no surprise that Nomura reported that this "fell far short of Japanese anticipation,"[4] and Magic eavesdropping revealed the embassy's preparations to begin repatriating diplomatic personnel by sea.

On 15 November, Hull had another hour-and-a-half meeting with the ambassador. Hull held out some prospect of agreement on trade concessions. After offering this small carrot of hope, he insisted on withholding his formal reply to the other two points of the "A" proposal until Tokyo had responded to his demand for recognition of his four principles. The secretary of state then sprang a new, but not unexpected, condition. "If Japan succeeds in coming to an agreement with the United States," he told Nomura, "she would not find it necessary to hold onto the tripartite pact."[5]

Two days later Magic revealed that the American offer of trade concession had not been enough of an inducement for Tokyo to continue negotiations. The decrypt of Tokyo's response to the ambassador's assurance that he would "do my very best with infinite patience"[6] was a brusque reminder that "the fate of our empire hangs by a slender thread of a few days, so please fight harder than you did before." There was to be "no change" in the 25 November "deadline set for the solution of these negotiations."[7]

The day set for the diet (national assembly) to reconvene in Tokyo struck no particular chord of urgency in the minds of the Far East analysts in the State Department. Washington had no way of knowing that 25 November was also the day the Pearl Harbor striking force was due to put to sea.

The foreign minister's 15 November cable did contain Tokyo's instructions to give up on the "A" proposal and present their "B" plan. Once again Magic's forewarning of Japan's fall-back position appears to have reduced, rather than heightened, State Department concern in Washington. Yet it should have been clear that negotiations were now moving toward a climax in the message to the newly arrived Kurusu that expressed exasperation at the "laxness" of the U.S. government's "stalling for time" when "the crisis was fast approaching."[8]

Stalling was precisely what the secretary of state was being requested to do by our army and naval leaders. But Hull's patience was also faltering. So was his health. After eight years of navigating American foreign policy through increasingly stormy waters at home and overseas, the six months of fruitless negotiation with Nomura had left the seventy-year-old Cordell Hull weary of the diplomatic process in general and of Japan's envoys in particular. He took an instant dislike to the portly, bespectacled Kurusu when he arrived with Nomura at the State Department on Monday, 17 November.

If the secretary of state was terse, Roosevelt, who had postponed his annual Thanksgiving trip to the retreat in Warm Springs, Georgia, was at his most affable. For an hour and a half the talk ranged over the three points on which a breakthrough had to be found to end the deadlock: equality in commerce, the tripartite pact, and the evacuation of Japan's forces from the Chinese mainland. Hull's customary denunciation of the Japanese government's "Hitlerian policy of expansion" was interrupted by Kurusu. He sought to inject a note of urgency by warning of an "imminent explosion" unless an accord was reached.[9]

"There is no last word between friends," the president chipped in, offering to remain in Washington through that weekend to further the discussions. The two Japanese envoys seized on this indication of American willingness to cable Tokyo for permission to advance the *modus vivendi* proposal. They dutifully reported that "it seems very clear that they are of a mind to bring about a compromise after making sure of our peaceful intentions," speculating that the new receptivity was because "the United States has turned more and more than ever toward the Atlantic of late."[10]

In this the Japanese envoys were at least partially correct.

The aftershock of the 31 October torpedoing of destroyer *Reuben James,* which sank with 115 crew members, was still being absorbed by legislators on Capitol Hill. Roosevelt had immediately cashed in on the public outrage against Germany to order the arming of all American merchant ships. But our first service casualties of the war brought demonstrators parading in front of the White House railings, with placards calling for the president's impeachment. Isolationist leader Charles Lindbergh was attracting huge crowds at fall rallies that vociferously protested Roosevelt's support for Britain.

The drift into a shooting war in the Atlantic had been another powerful argument for the joint army-navy memorandum of 5 November that urged the president to make concessions to Japan to avert a simultaneous explosion in the Pacific. The strategic logic of Roosevelt's military advisers was endorsed by a 13 November cable from John Hay Whitney, the London representative of Colonel William J. "Wild Bill" Donovan, the coordinator of intelligence for the White House. It succinctly summarized Churchill's priorities for American intervention:

1. every week sooner we come in will reduce the war by one month
2. order of choice:
   a. United States without Japan
   b. United States and Japan both in war
   c. neither at war
   d. Japan without America (this possibility unthinkable!)[11]

After months of ducking the issue, Roosevelt now faced a clear-cut choice between satisfying the demands of either diplomatic principle or military strategy. Against stiff isolationist opposition, the president had successfully nudged the United States into an undeclared war with Germany in the Atlantic, and an unratified mutual defense pact with Britain in the Pacific. But the Joint Board's Atlantic-oriented strategy made it imperative to avoid a military showdown with Japan while MacArthur's forces lacked the strength to constitute an adequate deterrent. Three more months were needed—and Russian agreement—before a strategic bomber offensive could be launched against the Japanese islands. A preemptive strike by the United States against either Axis power would plunge us into a two-ocean war because of the tripartite pact. While this may not have been the worst-case scenario for the British, it was the strategic nightmare that haunted our military leaders throughout 1941.

These were the conflicting demands of military and diplomatic reality that caused the State Department, for the first time in two decades, to reappraise the wisdom of its hard-line stand against the Japanese. At the 17 November meetings, Kurusu, on his own initiative, asked Hull "if the Japanese were now to withdraw their troops from Indochina, could the United States ease their oil and economic pressure to the point of sending small quantities of oil?" That same evening the secretary of state told the British minister in Washington that the idea was "attractive enough to warrant its being tried at least."[12]

In fact the rationale for an American proposal along very much the same lines had already been set out in a memorandum that same morning by the president's confidant, Henry Morgenthau. The forceful secretary of the treasury strongly supported such a plan, and the memorandum, which had been drawn up by Morgenthau's adroit young aide, Harry Dexter White,[13] was entitled "An Approach to the Problem of Eliminating Tension with Japan and Insuring the Defeat of Germany."

The proposal was intended to provide a plan for the release of the Pacific Fleet for operations against Germany in the Atlantic. It envisaged a withdrawal of Japanese troops from Indochina and a phased pullout from China geared to a progressive lifting of America's oil and trade embargo. In effect, it fleshed out Roosevelt's October idea for buying time by offering Japan a six-month truce—"some oil and rice now—more later"—in return for not sending any more troops into Indochina, plus an agreement "not to invoke tripartite pact even if U.S. gets into European war."[14]

The State Department had resisted any compromise with Japan at the beginning of the month. Now the pressures had built to such an extent that Roosevelt was pressing Hull into just such an accord as a means of defusing the dynamite keg in the Pacific. This was evident from Nomura's 18 November cable to Tokyo, which quoted the secretary of state proposing a return to the status quo before July:

I mean Japan should evacuate southern French Indochina, and in return the United States should rescind the freezing order. If the atmosphere remains calm in this manner, there will be no need of sending warships to Singapore or strengthening military facilities in the Philippines. Then we should like to continue talks.[15]

This statement makes it clear that the secretary of state was not simply preempting Tokyo's next diplomatic move. He was also prepared to consider including the Anglo-American deterrent as a bargaining chip to entice Tokyo into another round of negotiations. When he leafed through the Magic summaries three days later, he saw that Nomura and Kurusu had suggested postponing their B proposal to try for "a practical settlement.[16]

But Tokyo would brook no delay. Nomura was told curtly on 19 November to "please present our B proposal of the imperial government and no further concessions can be made." If the American government could not be persuaded to agree by the deadline—now only a week away—"the negotiations will have to be broken off."[17] The ambassador protested that this would "bring about a situation full of dynamite,"[18] but he was given no choice. Reluctantly, therefore, Nomura set off with Kurusu for the State Department on Thanksgiving Day 1941 to present Japan's own *modus vivendi* proposal.

On the morning of 21 November, Hull was careful to give Nomura no indication he had known for over a week the terms of Tokyo's B proposal. According to the Japanese ambassador's report, he was "glad to see both me and Ambassador Kurusu."[19] It was clear that American aid to Chiang Kai-shek was still a major stumbling block. Hull promised to "think over this proposal you have brought me fully and sympathetically." The next day brought further discussions on the general subject of peace. To try to defuse the issue of Tokyo's treaty obligations to Germany and Italy, Kurusu promised that any agreement with the United States would "outshine the tripartite pact." But Hull stressed that Japan must cut its ties with Germany first. He deferred any final decision until after consultation with representatives of Britain, China, and the Dutch government in exile.[20]

Despite Kurusu's complaint that there had been a "complete evasion" of details, Hull had been sympathetic enough to encourage Japan's envoys to anticipate that the weekend would bring a firm American proposal for a temporary accommodation. On the strength of their optimistic reports, Tokyo agreed to extend its deadline four days, despite "reasons beyond your ability to guess why we wanted to settle Japanese-American relations by the 25th."[21] This in itself was a major concession. It indicated that Tokyo was still prepared to seek a diplomatic way out—even after the striking force sailed. But Japan's envoys—and also those who read Magic in Washington—were left in no doubt that they had to get any *modus vivendi* sealed by 29 November. The Magic decrypt read,

"This time we mean it, that the deadline absolutely cannot be changed. After that *things are automatically going to happen.* [emphasis added]."[22]

The third week of November concluded in Washington and Tokyo on a cautiously optimistic note. The State Department was "clutching at straws" in what Hull later characterized the "desperate effort to get something worked out that might stay the hand of the Japanese army and navy for a few days, or a few weeks." Indeed, it appears that that weekend Washington and Tokyo had not given up hope that some temporary accommodation to avert war might be reached.[23]

Working through Saturday and Sunday, State Department officials hammered together a compromise proposal that, while it went against the grain of Dr. Hornbeck's principles, could not be regarded as a sellout of Chiang Kai-shek, or an appeasement to Japanese aggression. The final draft of this compromise proposal was on the secretary of state's desk first thing Monday morning. In return for restoring commercial relations and "a required quantity of oil" for civilian use,[24] Japan would be expected to pull back troops from southern Indochina, set a twenty-five-thousand-man limit to her forces in Indochina, and refrain from further "armed advancement" for three months while negotiations continued to settle the major issues. The proposal stopped short of proposing that lend-lease aid to China be halted, or simply not accelerated. It put forward the Philippines as a site for Sino-Japanese peace talks without direct American involvement. To soothe Chiang Kai-shek's fears of the actual *modus vivendi,* terms were to be accompanied by a ten-point list of the main issues to be negotiated as part of any long-term settlement.

Contrary to the views of some historians, we know now from an unofficially retained memorandum, whose State Department original was destroyed, that Hull regarded the *modus vivendi* as an "important factor in facilitating the conversations and avoiding a breakdown" with Japan. He believed that it would be "giving our army and navy what they solemnly and most urgently represented as an urgent need for several weeks more time in which to get ready to defend on two-ocean fronts."[25]

The secretary of state believed "that to give Japan the privilege for ninety days of purchasing lower grade products in the amount of some two million tons, plus some flour and cotton and certain other foodstuffs, would be in entire accordance with a policy of gradually moving toward a peaceful basis for ninety days in return for a tremendous movement in that direction on the part of Japan."[26]

Hull's willingness to try for a quid pro quo in which the United States made "absolutely microscopic" concessions in return "for what I was asking of Japan," anticipated that Magic would monitor Japan's compliance. As the secretary of state put it:

> It was at this most critical stage with possible war on both fronts threatening that I formally made this proposal in reply to that of the

Japanese. The truth is that the benefits to this government, if the chance for an agreement had been realized—and, of course, it was only a chance—would alone more than have justified the concessions offered to Japan for 90 days.[27]

Given Hull's commitment, as we now know it to have been, the American *modus vivendi* would not have been impossible to reconcile with the proposals already on the negotiating table for Japan. It was ironic, therefore, that the Friday Purple decrypts from Tokyo were instrumental in renewing Hull's fears that the Japanese were about to stiffen their terms. A repetition of the deadline notice heightened the negative impact of a cable reminding Nomura that "cessation of aid to Chiang Kai-shek . . . and at the same time the supply of American petroleum is the most essential condition."[28]

This same decrypt accounted for the lack of optimism in Roosevelt's cable to Churchill informing him of the American *modus vivendi* terms: "This seems to me to be a fair proposition, but its acceptance or rejection is really a matter of internal Japanese politics. I am not very hopeful and we must all prepare for trouble very soon."[29]

Such was the backdrop of tension and uncertainty on 25 November when the president met with the secretaries of war, state, and navy along with the service chiefs. The war council lived up to its name that Tuesday morning—even though the United States was still at peace. Before the conference even started, Hull took care to show the text of the final *modus vivendi* to Stimson and Knox. It had already been approved by both Stark and Marshall, and with the proviso that its presentation would not stop the flow of aircraft and troop convoys to the Philippines.

"It adequately safeguarded our interests," Stimson recorded.[30] Although he had doubts that the Japanese would go along with all the details, he strongly favored any measure that would buy more time for our Pacific buildup. This was evidently the view of the war council, because the main focus of the discussion that Tuesday was not whether America should make an attempt at a temporary accommodation, but what to do if the Japanese rejected it. Stimson's notes reveal that the Far East crisis crowded out any discussion of the Atlantic situation. Roosevelt feared that if negotiations with Japan were broken off after the Friday deadline, "we were likely to be attacked perhaps as soon as next Monday for the Japanese are notorious for attacking without warning."[31]

The "difficult proposition" that would then confront the United States, as the president put it, "was how we should maneuver them into the position of firing the first shot without allowing too much danger to ourselves."[32] This was not necessarily an anticipation of United States belligerence, as some revisionist historians have misquoted it. Roosevelt was more likely expressing an appreciation of the political reality "that in order to have the full support of the American people it was desirable to make sure that the Japanese be the ones to do this so that there should be no doubt in anyone's mind as to who were the aggressors."[33]

Neither Hull's nor Stimson's records indicate that there was any discussion of dropping the *modus vivendi* that day. The secretary of state's prime concern seems to have been how to deal with the Chinese and their supporters. They were already being bombarded by telegrams from Chiang Kai-shek protesting the anticipated deal with Tokyo. (This was in response to the meeting of the previous day in which the secretary of state had patiently justified the proposed ninety-day temporary accommodation in an hour-long briefing with the Chinese, British, Dutch, and Australian representatives in Washington.)

While the other envoys agreed to refer the plan to their governments, only the Chinese ambassador, Dr. Hu Shih, had strongly protested the plan. He argued that five thousand rather than twenty-five thousand should be the limit on Japanese troops allowed to remain in southern Indochina. Hull's conviction that this typified China's selfish attitude and "lack of a disposition to cooperate"[34] was reinforced by the telegrams from Chungking that flooded Washington that day. Hull was deeply affronted by these "numerous hysterical cables to different cabinet officers." He regarded them as an intrusion "into a delicate situation with no idea of what the facts are."[35]

So when the Chinese ambassador arrived for his Tuesday evening meeting, the secretary of state's official demeanor barely concealed his displeasure. Hull wanted to scotch rumors of an impending appeasement. He was equally determined to set out the hard facts justifying the cabinet's decision to go ahead with the *modus vivendi* despite Chiang's "hysterical" protests. Hu Shih was firmly told, "Our proposals would relieve the menace of Japan in Indochina to the whole south Pacific area."[36] Hull stressed the temporary nature of the accommodation's ninety-day time limit and said that "the limited amount of more or less inferior oil products that we might let Japan have during that period would not, to any appreciable extent, increase Japanese war and naval preparations."[37]

According to State Department minutes of the session, Hull warned the Chinese ambassador, "We can cancel this proposal, but it must be with the understanding that we are not to be charged with failure to send our fleet into Japanese water, if by chance Japan makes a military drive southward." Aside from this firm statement of policy, the secretary of state gave no indication that he was even considering abandoning the approved *modus vivendi*—and the ambassador left after promising to send a "fuller explanation" to calm Chiang Kai-shek's fears.[38]

If ever there was a moment in a nation's history that called for a full, calm, and reasoned application of intelligence to guide its interlocked military and diplomatic destiny, that moment dawned in Washington on 26 November 1941.

On that fateful Wednesday an event occurred that caused the president to overrule his diplomatic and military advisers to stop negotiations with Japan dead in the water. Given the previous day's agreement of the war council on the terms for the temporary accommodation, Roosevelt's volte-face was unexplainable. It was tantamount to courting disaster.

What event prompted the president's momentous decision? The evidence has to be examined afresh in the light of newly uncovered documentation that casts grave doubts on the credibility of the versions of events that have been accepted for more than forty years.

18

Negotiations Off

O N THE AFTERNOON OF 26 November the secretary of state quashed any possibility of compromise.

The Japanese envoys had arrived in Hull's office that afternoon expecting to be handed details of an accommodation based on Roosevelt's formula of "some oil now, more later." Instead, they got only an uncompromising ten-point declaration of absolute conditions that had to be met before the United States would consider resuming trade or lifting its oil embargo.

The two ambassadors were "dumbfounded." Hull's declaration left their expectations in ruins. Shaking with frustration and pent-up anger at this apparent reversal, Nomura argued back "furiously." He said that the United States' return to hard-line principles could be interpreted only as an ultimatum in Tokyo. But the secretary of state remained "as solid as a rock."[1] And it was just the type of ultimatum that Marshall and Stark had tried to avoid being sent Japan for at least three more months.

Dropping the *modus vivendi* might not have been an "ultimatum" in diplomatic terms, but in the circumstances it came close. Magic decrypts of Japan's diplomatic communications had already revealed a seventy-two-hour deadline for negotiations to be completed and an accord signed. So the decision to withdraw previously discussed possibilities of a compromise and merely list the issues dividing Tokyo and Washington was not exactly going to assist the diplomatic process. Hull certainly knew this because, around 9 A.M. that Wednesday he had telephoned the war department to alert Stimson that he was about "ready to kick the whole thing over."[2]

In written testimony to the 1945 congressional investigating committee Hull later claimed that it was his decision to abandon the *modus vivendi* because he had come to the conclusion that morning that it was "perfectly evident" even a temporary accommodation with Japan was "not

198

feasible." It would cause the collapse of Chinese morale. In his memoirs Hull claimed that his decision to advise the president against a temporary accommodation had been influenced by the lukewarm attitude of the British as expressed in an overnight cable from London in which Churchill asked, "What about Chiang Kai-shek? Is he not having a very thin diet?"[3]

Churchill's sudden concern for the Chinese was, indeed, a surprise. He was never a noted supporter of the Nationalist Chinese. Recently declassified British cabinet papers indicate that he appeared content to leave negotiations with Japan to the United States. "My own feeling is that we might give Hull the latitude he asks," the prime minister had told the foreign secretary. "Our major interest is: no further encroachments and no war, as we have already enough of the latter."[4]

Confidential British foreign office assessments confirm that "the President and Mr. Hull were . . . fully conscious of what they were doing." Churchill would later try to suppress the 1943 report by Britain's last ambassador to Tokyo, who condemned the way the State Department had handled the negotiations. "I consider," Sir Robert Craigie wrote, "that had it been possible to reach a compromise with Japan in December 1941 involving the withdrawal of Japanese troops from Indochina, war with Japan would not have been inevitable."[5] His views were regarded by the foreign office as a "pretty sweeping indictment of U.S. policy," and they did not please Churchill.

"It is a very strange document and one which should be kept most scrupulously secret," Churchill noted on the report. "A more one-sided pro-Japanese account of what occurred I have hardly ever read. . . . He also writes of the breach with Japan as if it were an unmitigated disaster. . . . It was a blessing that Japan attacked the United States and thus brought America wholeheartedly into the war."[6]

Churchill's reaction is significant. But whether war could or could not have been averted *if* the *modus vivendi* had been presented is less important than the reason for Hull's abandoning it. Policy was reversed overnight. The reversal was so sweeping in its implications that the president must have had a direct hand in it. And the prime minister was quick to distance himself from Hull's suggestion that he might have influenced the fateful decision to drop the *modus vivendi*. "I understood the dangers attending the thought 'the British are trying to drag us into war,'" he wrote in his 1950 memoir. "I therefore placed the issue where it belonged, namely in the president's hands."[7]

Hull's 1945 interpretation of the events of 25 November may have been colored by his fury at Japan's attack. New documentation has come to light, however, that casts serious doubt on the hitherto accepted official version in his memoirs. Far from initiating the dropping of the *modus vivendi,* says an aide who was in his office at the time, the secretary of state was the reluctant executor of a presidential order.

During the critical days before the policy reversal, Landreth Harrison recalls, Hull was summoned to an urgent meeting with the president. He returned to the State Department, which was then housed in what is now the executive office building adjacent to the White House. He returned "very agitated" and muttering that "those men over there do not believe me when I tell them that the Japs will attack us. You cannot give an ultimatum to a powerful and proud people and not expect them to react violently."[8]

Despite what he later recorded for posterity, Hull's reluctance to abandon the *modus vivendi* proposal was evident in a revealing memorandum. He dictated it on 27 November in response to a letter from Dr. Hornbeck, who would later give five-to-one odds against Japan's going to war. Hornbeck had written to Hull to reassure his boss that "in days to come you will look upon the *decision which was made* and the action you took yesterday with great satisfaction [emphasis added]."[9]

Hornbeck's choice of words indicates that the secretary's action had been decided for him by the president. The letter (which was later removed from the State Department records) suggested that the *modus vivendi* had only a "small chance" of success because the Japanese would have balked at what he described as a "not . . . completely honest document" that was intended to "give us more time to prepare our weapons of defense."[10]

Hull did not accept Hornbeck's oily contentions at all. "We differ so entirely, however, that I must in writing offer my dissent," the secretary of state replied. He continued:

> It is no answer to the question of whether this proposal [the *modus vivendi*] is sound and desirable at this most critical period to say that it probably would not have been accepted by Japan in any event; nor to say I would have been widely criticized in the astounding theory of selling China down the river of appeasement. If that sort of demagoguery stuff would be rung into this sort of undertaking, then there could never be a settlement between countries except at the point of a sword.[11]

It is evident that Hull was making a serious effort to reach a settlement with Tokyo until the afternoon of 26 November 1941. Why the *modus vivendi* was called off now becomes of greater historical importance than whether a temporary accommodation with Japan could have averted war.

Apart from Hull's testimony about his professed reluctance to upset Chiang Kai-shek, the generally accepted story about what caused the president's dramatic change of heart was supplied by the diary kept by the secretary of war. While it purports to be an accurate record, it is a carefully typed up reconstruction of events. According to Stimson the key event on the morning of 26 November was Stimson's telephone call to the

White House sometime around nine. This was put through *after* he had called the State Department about the protest he had received from Chiang Kai-shek, only to be told by Hull that "he had just about made up his mind to give up the whole thing in respect to a truce and simply tell the Japanese that he had no further action to propose."[12]

"A few minutes later I talked to the President over the telephone," Stimson's diary continues. "I asked him whether he had received the paper which I had sent him over last night about the Japanese having started a new expedition from Shanghai down toward Indo-china." This was the news of the Japanese convoy of "30, 40, or 50 ships" sighted "south of Formosa." According to Stimson the president was "shocked and at once took it as further evidence of bad faith on the part of the Japanese."[13] His diary paints an even more dramatic reaction: "He fairly blew up—jumped up into the air, so to speak, and said he hadn't seen it and that changed the whole situation. . . . I at once got another copy of the paper I had sent last night and sent it over to him by special messenger."[14]

The "evidence of bad faith on the part of the Japanese" that supposedly played such a large part in influencing the president's decision to drop the *modus vivendi* was an intelligence report that Stimson had found waiting for him the previous afternoon after he had returned from the White House war council meeting. According to his diary it was news that a Japanese "expedition had started" with five divisions of troops arriving at Shanghai. "There they had embarked on ships—30, 40, or 50 ships—and have been sighted south of Formosa."[15]

Stimson's chronology of events depends on Roosevelt's not having received this information on the afternoon of 25 November. Yet it is puzzling that a top-secret report containing Magic information failed to reach the White House. Even more curious is why the notoriously short-fused Hull had not "jumped up into the air" himself that same afternoon when the secretary of war had called him and "told him about it and sent copies to him and to the President of the message from G-2."[16]

The secretary of state did not appear to have considered Stimson's report to be sufficient evidence of Japanese treachery to evoke his sympathy an hour or so later when the Chinese ambassador arrived to protest the decision to proceed with the *modus vivendi*. Nor did Stimson himself consider the intelligence of such urgent importance to call the President directly. Hull made no mention of the Japanese convoy in either his regretful memorandum to Hornbeck or in his 1945 testimony explaining why the *modus vivendi* proposals were abandoned.

What makes it more unlikely that the day-old intelligence was evidence of Japanese treachery alarming enough to shock the president into reversing the course of American diplomacy was the recent discovery of the original message that was sent to the White House. Dated 25 November, it makes reference not to "30, 40, or 50 ships," but to only "ten to thirty troopships." Nor were they at sea. The actual message refers to nothing more explosive than "*a more or less normal movement*" of these transports which were "*in the Yangtse River below Shanghai* [emphasis added]."[17]

Stimson's diary states, moreover, that the convoy movement had been anticipated. Its arrival had been forewarned in a month-old Magic intercept. Enclosed with his letter was the latest British Far East intelligence estimate that predicted nothing more alarming than that "Japan will make a last effort at agreement with U.S.A." The worst scenario was that Tokyo might order troops into Thailand *if* negotiations with the United States broke down.[18]

The message did reach the White House. Attached to it is a cryptic note, dated 27 November from Major General Edwin M. "Pa" Watson, to the effect that he had found it "in the inside pocket of a very distinguished gentleman."[19] The very fact that the message now resides in the recently declassified "Safe File" of the former secretary of war must cast doubt on Stimson's official account. That the president did not know of its contents until the morning of 26 November seems most unlikely. All the indications are that the "very distinguished gentleman" could have been none other than Roosevelt himself.

Stimson's account of the "missing" report seems to have been a cover story for some more important secret information. This seems certain, because his 26 November "duplicate," which was also hand-delivered to the White House, contains an additional line: "Later reports indicate that this movement is already under way and ships have been seen south of Formosa."[20] Yet the actual G-2 intelligence report referred to the ships at anchor below Shanghai, and the penciled notes made by the secretary of war record "no new direct reports of captains at sea—since the five ships capt[ain]s last reported from Shanghai."[21]

Neither the timing nor the implicit threat of Stimson's report is such that it can have been the fateful instrument that caused the president to reverse American policy. But it is equally plain that an alarming piece of intelligence warning of imminent hostile Japanese action must have reached the White House between the evening of 25 November and nine the following morning.

"On November 26 there was received *specific evidence* of the Japanese intention to wage offensive war against Great Britain and the United States [emphasis added]," was how it was described in 1944 by the army board set up to investigate Pearl Harbor. Significantly, however, the army investigators, unable to establish this evidence more precisely, did not link it to Stimson's Shanghai convoy, which was identified as a report of "the concentration of units of the Japanese fleet at an unknown port ready for offensive action."[22]

Such imprecision did not satisfy Admiral Kimmel. At the navy court of inquiry, which sat simultaneously with the army's investigation, he finally won the right to cross-examine Admiral Stark on this critical issue.

Kimmel asked his former chief, "Do you recall whether on or about 26 November you received information from the office of naval intelligence that gave specific evidence of Japan's intention to wage offensive war against Britain and France?"[23] Although the tribunal was sitting in secret, Stark insisted that to answer this question would "involve the disclosure of information detrimental to the public interest." The court came to his rescue by ruling that he need not reveal any "state secrets."[24]

That the former chief of naval operations successfully claimed executive privilege to conceal the precise nature of the catalyst of 26 November was most revealing. It indicates that it was intelligence that did not originate from naval or army sources. Knowledge of whatever information Roosevelt received of Japan's bad faith must have been restricted to the most intimate circle of presidential advisers. If Stark and Marshall knew, they were not saying. Time and again during the 1945 congressional hearings they sidestepped questions, which like Kimmel's a year earlier sought to pinpoint what intelligence had prompted the president to abandon the *modus vivendi.*

Marshall repeatedly had "no specific recollection" of what he had talked about in the flurry of telephone calls put through the White House switchboard that Wednesday morning.[25] Stark admitted, "We were playing for time," but he was "unable to separate and clarify just what happened on the dates around the 25th."[26] Such opacity of memory is surprising. Within a few hours they were framing the warnings that put the armed forces onto a war alert, but four years later they could not recall with any precision what it was that triggered their actions.

There is a further clue that the "missing" intelligence may have reached the White House through the secret channel of the British security coordination organization headed by Sir William "Intrepid" Stephenson. Colonel James Roosevelt, the president's son, was dispatched to Stephenson's New York headquarters that afternoon with a message that resulted in a cable to Churchill in London the next day: "Negotiations off. Services expect action within two weeks." This might have been a response to some vital intelligence that was also received via the same highly confidential channel.[27]

There is another indication that news of Japan's treachery had come to the president directly from Churchill. The cover note to the American embassy in London of 26 November that supposedly enclosed Churchill's "thin diet for Chiang Kai-shek" telegram was marked "Most Secret." It apologized for the "lateness of the hour" of its delivery—around three A.M.—yet nothing it contained, at least as we now see it, can have warranted disturbing the American embassy in mid-slumber. It could have waited until London office hours next morning and still reached Washington at the start of the 26 November business day.

The prime minister's cable, furthermore, specifically refers to a message from Roosevelt "received to-night." If—as the official record would have us believe—this was the "President to Former Naval Person" (as the two familiarly addressed one another) message detailing the final *modus vivendi* proposals, this is a glaring inconsistency. Roosevelt's message had been delivered to Downing Street by the American embassy messenger that morning and the foreign office copy of the same cable was received directly from the British embassy in Washington at 1300 that afternoon.[28]

It is unlikely that Churchill, who set so much store by his direct line to Roosevelt, would have confused information from the White House that was nearly twenty-four hours old with a message that required an immediate response—even to the point of rousing American embassy staff at three in the morning. Yet if there was a second cable, as Churchill's response appears to indicate, it is not in the files.

The evidence points, therefore, to another exchange made that night between London and Washington—for which the "thin diet" cable served as a convenient cover. Especially significant, given this inconsistency in the declassified records, is that Japanese intelligence reports in the prime minister's confidential files remain "closed for 75 years." Repeated requests for their release, or even privileged access, have been repeatedly rebuffed at cabinet level "because it would not be in the national interest at this time."[29]

What can be so secret after forty years that Britain's cabinet continues to deny access to documents that could resolve an important discrepancy in the historical record? Until they are opened there is a strong presumption that the closed files in London concern some additional warning of Japanese "treachery" that reached the White House on the morning of 26 November.

Whatever the intelligence was it had to be specific, credible, and from an undisputed source—such as details of the Japanese army or navy war plans. It must be remembered that seven hundred copies of Yamamoto's operational order number 1 were circulating by the second week in November. Moreover, an even larger number of the army's plans had been sent out—including copies to the Japanese embassy in Bangkok.[30] British or Dutch agents may have gained access to a copy of Japan's war plans.

Soviet agents had tapped the highest levels of power in Tokyo. Their master spy, Richard Sorge, had been arrested a month earlier. But many members of the Communist ring in Tokyo were as yet undetected—including one who was a member of the imperial family. The Russians are also known to have penetrated Japan's Moscow and Bangkok embassies. Moreover, since the German army was poised for Hitler's "final offensive" toward Moscow, it was in Stalin's interest to ensure that Japan became embroiled in a war to prevent another attack in Siberia. It was even more important since the seven Red Army divisions that had been guarding the Nomonhan front against another Japanese attack from Manchuria had been withdrawn for the final defense of Moscow.

It is also interesting to note that Stalin betrayed a remarkable certainty about the imminence of Japan's attack on Malaya to General Sikorski when the Polish military mission visited the Kremlin on 4 December. And General Marshall, in his 1945 testimony, made an oblique reference to secret information the Russians gave exclusively to the British.[31]

It is possible, therefore, that the Russians possessed details of the Japanese war plans. The prime minister might have obtained his information about Japan's impending attack plan from a British penetration of Soviet cipher traffic. There has not been any release of information on any wartime successes in penetrating the Russian cipher code systems. Their ciphers were difficult to break because of their reliance on slow but secure one-time code pads. But if the warning of Japan's treachery had been broken out of some undercover Soviet agent's radio report it would have had the necessary credibility—and that would explain why it is "not in the national interest" for the British government to make the information available.

The British have so far refused to release *any* of their Japanese Ultra intelligence. When combined with the seventy-five-year classification of part of Churchill's records dealing with the Far East, this could mean that the missing intelligence of 26 November is connected with parallel records that also remain classified in the Australian archives. These appear to cover the disappearance of light cruiser H.M.A.S. *Sydney* a week earlier. This celebrated fighting ship, which had outgunned and sunk an Italian cruiser in the Mediterranean, sank with all hands in an encounter with the German merchant raider *Kormoran* off the coast of western Australia."[32] The *Sydney*'s loss has still to be satisfactorily explained, since the *Kormoran* also sank, but most of her crew survived in their lifeboats.

There were also reports of unidentified planes in the vicinity of the action.[33] This raises suspicion that one of the aircraft-carrying Japanese submarines might have assisted in the cruiser's destruction. Churchill would have been reluctant to make the sinking of an Australian cruiser by a Japanese submarine a *casus belli* while America's commitment to war was still in doubt. It therefore would have suited the designs of all sides—including Japan—to hush up the affair.

Information that the Japanese might have been implicated in the sinking of the Australian cruiser, by itself, would probably not have provided sufficient evidence of Tokyo's treachery to prompt Roosevelt to abandon the *modus vivendi*. But it would have been yet another indication of Japan's belligerency. It would have been an even clearer indication of Tokyo's treacherous intent and acceleration of war preparations if taken into account with intercepts of the Japanese navy's main operational cipher.

On the evening of 20 November, Tokyo's main naval radio station transmitted a preliminary war alert that notified all fleets: AT 0000 ON 21 NOVEMBER CARRY OUT SECOND PHASE OF PREPARATIONS FOR OPENING

HOSTILITIES.[34] This message *was* picked up by our navy's radio intelligence network because it has been discovered in among the quarter million recently declassified Japanese naval intercepts. No JN-25 traffic that was actually decrypted *before* war broke has yet been made available and the completely translated version, dated 26 November 1945, provides no real clue about how much of the message might have been broken out in 1941. Although Safford testified that about 10 percent of JN-25 was being read throughout that year, on 1 November the work of the cryptanalysts in OP-20-G and Station Cast had been made more difficult by the introduction of a new additive book.

We now know, however, that our navy was not alone in being able to read the Japanese naval cipher systems. The five-digit operational cipher we knew as JN-25 had also been extensively penetrated by the British and the Dutch. Britain's attack on JN-25 was concentrated at their Far East Combined Bureau (FECB), which was based in Singapore, with an outpost on Stonecutter's Island, Hong Kong. One of the tantalizingly few references to the work of the FECB in the recently published three-volume official history *British Intelligence in the Second World War* notes that "beginning with the Fleet cypher, the new cyphers began to yield" to the interservice code-breaking team in September 1939.[35] Together with the assertion that it remained possible "to keep track of her main naval movements," this suggests that the Royal Navy's successful penetration of JN-25 was equal to, or might even have exceeded, the reading of Japan's main naval operational cipher by our own cryptanalysts.

The Dutch also maintained a remarkably efficient but much smaller code-breaking operation attached to their military headquarters on Java. Under the direction of cryptanalyst Lieutenant Colonel J. A. Verkuyl and his deputy, Captain J. W. Henning, their *Kamer 14* at Bandung was, by 1941, reading the Red diplomatic machine code and the J-19 consular ciphers as well as penetrating the five-digit Japanese fleet system. While Purple intercepts could not be read, they were forwarded to the British code breakers in Singapore under the orders given General Hein ter Poorten, the Dutch commander in chief in the Far East, to cooperate fully with the British.

General ter Poorten, moreover, is on record as asserting that his *Kamer 14* code breakers provided him with intelligence reports that "showed Japanese naval concentrations near the Kuriles."[37] Unfortunately, all the Dutch decrypts were burned in the retreat from Bandung, but according to a civilian member of his intelligence staff, this information was derived from the sailing order to the Pearl Harbor strike force.[38] Since there were no Dutch submarines on patrol so far north, and Nagumo's carriers had been observing strict radio silence ever since they sailed for the secret rendezvous in Hitokappu Wan a week earlier, interception of the message would have been the only source of information that there was a Japanese fleet in the Kuriles.

All Japan's orders to the Pearl Harbor strike force were destroyed at the end of the war, but a reconstruction of events obtained from its surviving commanders in 1945 confirm that such a sailing message was indeed transmitted on 25 November. According to Captain Fuchida's recollection it was worded that "the task force will move out of Hitokappu Wan on 26 November and proceed without being detected to the evening rendezvous point (latitude 40 degrees north, longitude 170 degrees west) set for 3 December where refueling and supply will be carried out as quickly as possible."[39]

The original transmitted message would have given the final refueling point coordinates in a special designator code, so any decryption made in 1941 would not necessarily have revealed that a Japanese task force had sailed for the mid-Pacific. To the Dutch, therefore, the intercept of this message would have indicated that the most likely target of a force assembling in Hitokappu Wan was the Soviet Union. In fact, Ter Poorten's account reveals that his intelligence staff was convinced that Japan might repeat the 1904 surprise attack on Port Arthur with a raid on Vladivostok. As Captain Henning himself wrote: "That war was imminent was clear to us, but I am sure that there has never been talked [sic] directly about an attack on Pearl Harbor."[40]

What is also clear from the JN-25 file in the National Archives is that we evidently did not pick up Yamamoto's 25 November sailing message. It is therefore likely that this vital piece of intelligence could have been passed on from the Dutch only by the British, whose FECB cryptanalysts might also have intercepted it at Singapore. If they did—and the timing appears remarkably coincident—it could have been the final proof that Japan was negotiating treacherously and the evidence that prompted Roosevelt's decision to drop further negotiations with Tokyo. Taken in conjunction with the 21 November message about "opening hostilities," and the suggestion of Japan's involvement in sinking the Australian cruiser, the news that a Japanese task force had been ordered to put to sea on 26 November would have provided the president with a very clear picture of Tokyo's duplicitous intent.

That it was London, not Washington, which was evidently able to assemble these three pieces of intelligence into a war warning would have justified Churchill in sending his "urgent" message around to the American embassy in the small hours of the morning of 26 November. If Yamamoto's sailing order was relayed to the White House—even though it did not give a specific indication that Pearl Harbor was a target—it would explain why Roosevelt's closest aides were so reluctant to be specific about the nature of the "war warning" that reached Washington that same morning.

19

"Future Action Unpredictable"

T HE PRECISE NATURE of the alarming intelligence that arrived in the White House on the morning of 26 November may remain in doubt. But for the detective seeking clues, its impact on the president was obvious to early morning visitors. "He had not touched his coffee," Treasury Secretary Morgenthau noted. "He was talking to Hull and trying to eat his food at the same time, by the time he finished his conversation, his food was cold, and he didn't touch it."[1]

It was a long and agonizing morning for Roosevelt and his war council. The White House switchboard records reveal that the lines were busy as the president consulted with his closest confidants. The dilemma that confronted them was that if they abandoned the *modus vivendi* seventy-two hours before Tokyo's stated deadline for the completion of negotiations, they could force Japan into opening hostilities. Stimson favored a preemptive attack against the Japanese. But the president could not risk such an action because the isolationist opposition in Congress could successfully accuse him of engineering the war.

Yet if Japan attacked after the negotiation of a temporary settlement with Tokyo, Roosevelt would be branded as an appeaser. This would make it more difficult for the president to rally the Congress to fulfill the secret guarantees he had made to the British prime minister. To do nothing except wait for the blow to fall, while it would facilitate winning votes on Capitol Hill to fight Japanese aggression, could expose the president to a charge of dereliction of his duty as commander in chief.

The president and his advisers resolved that there really was no way out of the dilemma. They had to abandon the *modus vivendi* and accept "letting the Japanese fire the first shot," as Stimson put it. To avoid the issue of dereliction if the American bases in the Philippines were attacked, unprecedented steps were necessary to cover up the nature and extent of the warning received by the White House. The charade over the secretary of war's "missing" report, and Stark's and Marshall's inability to recall what they discussed during their busy exchange of telephone calls that morning, were all part of this camouflage operation.[2] The necessity for concealing *any* clue that the White House received any specific intelligence about Japan's intention to go to war was to be intensified by the political aftermath of Pearl Harbor, which overshadowed the disaster that also befell MacArthur in the Philippines.

The message establishing Japan's Friday deadline had threatened that "things are automatically going to happen." So on that Wednesday morning our military leadership had to face a situation in which the Japanese had called their bluff on the Anglo-American plans of deterrence. They were now trapped. Like a chess player who sees no escape from checkmate, they could only hope to gain time. Even if Japan's attack could not be postponed until the end of December, as they had initially calculated, even a delay of a week or two would ensure that the troop convoys steaming across the Pacific, and the B-17 bombers on the west coast, could reach the Philippines before the blow fell.

The prospect of war within a few days galvanized the top echelons of the war and navy departments that morning. At ten-thirty an emergency conference was held in Marshall's office to hear him warn that the president and secretary of state believed that upon the termination of the talks with the Japanese envoys, Tokyo "will soon cut loose" with "an assault on the Philippines."[3] Marshall's principal concern was what instructions should be issued to cover the emergency caused by the breakdown in negotiations, which might not bring an immediate declaration of war. "We know a great deal that the Japanese are not aware we know," Marshall announced, adding significantly "and *we are familiar with their plans to a certain extent* [emphasis added]."[4]

Marshall decided that Tokyo should be warned as soon as possible that if Japanese troops proceeded into Thailand, to the west of a demarcation line 100 degrees east or 10 degrees south, our vital interests would be "imperiled." But this required that MacArthur had to be given a "war warning" on which he could act without precipitating hostile moves that would invite a Japanese attack before reinforcements reached the Philippines.

It was agreed that "prior to a state of war" that MacArthur was to be "directed," not merely "desired," to carry out orders "to attack threatening convoys."[5] He was told to begin the reconnaissance flights over Japanese bases in Formosa, even at the risk of provoking a shooting match. The navy was to be asked to use its two Pacific fleet carriers to ferry pursuit planes from Hawaii to Wake and Midway so that the upcoming flight of forty-eight B-17 bombers could be assured of adequate fighter protection.

After agreement on the need for the war warning, the next priority item was the plan to have the navy rush extra fighters to Wake and Midway. This was discussed at the meeting of the Joint Board that the army chief of staff chaired an hour later, just before he took a plane to observe army maneuvers in South Carolina. It was also agreed that in view of the worsening situation, and recent Japanese flights over our island outposts in the western Pacific, a full-scale aerial reconnaissance must be made of Japan's bases in the mandates. General Arnold agreed to provide two high-flying B-24 bombers to photograph Jaluit and Truk. When the meeting broke up shortly before midday, Stark radioed to Admiral Kimmel, informing him of the impending photoreconnaissance mission and also directing him to arrange for his two carriers to transport the twenty-five planes and ground crews to Wake and Midway "as soon as possible."[6]

That Stark, as well as Marshall, agreed to reduce the fighter strength at Pearl Harbor by half, and to run the risk that "there will be nothing left at Hawaii until replacements arrive,"[7] was in itself evidence that whatever warning of Japan's war moves had been received in Washington, it contained no hint of an attack on Pearl Harbor. There was, however, every indication that some specific warning had been received of an impending attack on the Philippines.

Roosevelt himself dispatched a cabled alert that afternoon to his old friend Francis Sayre, our commissioner in Manila. Admiral Hart certainly took Sayre's alert to be a war warning because, as he noted in his diary, its source was "straight from the horse's mouth."[8] The Asiatic Fleet commander had no doubt about the urgency of the looming danger. A CNO dispatch sent out the same afternoon directed him to begin unrestricted submarine warfare as soon as "formal war eventuates."[9] He was also instructed to begin consultations with British and Dutch liaison officers to coordinate joint operating procedures because the "situation will be far more complex *if hostilities ensue without a formal declaration of war* [emphasis added]."[10]

While this message was another indication of the extent of prearranged Anglo-American military cooperation, it was also a telling sign that the focus of Washington's strategic priorities in the Pacific was not Hawaii. Almost twenty-four hours slipped by and it was well into 27 November before Pearl Harbor received its alert that relations between the United States and Japan were sliding toward a rupture.

According to Stimson's diary, that Thursday began "first thing in the morning" with his phone call to the secretary of state. Hull told him "he had broken the whole thing off," and that he had "washed my hands of it and it is now in the hands of you and Knox—the Army and Navy."[11] The secretary of the navy and the chief of naval operations then hurried over to the war department for consultations with Stimson and General Gerow, who was standing in for Marshall while he was away on maneuvers. They agreed with Stark's proposed draft of a joint army-navy memorandum detailing the reinforcements currently on their way to MacArthur. The memo urged the president that "the most essential thing now, from the United States viewpoint, is to gain time."[12] For the second time that month Roosevelt was to be advised against giving an ultimatum to Japan "prior to the completion of the Philippine reinforcement," and that "military counter-action be considered" only if Japan attacked.[13]

The secretary of war was sympathetic to the memo, but "didn't want it at any cost of humility on the part of the United States or of re-opening the thing which would show a weakness on our part."[14] The more immediate priority was sending "the final alert" to the Pacific commands.

The president telephoned his approval. The war warnings were drafted with General MacArthur and Admiral Hart as their prime recipients. Stimson believed that the Philippines had been put on "quasi alert" the day before, so now all that was necessary was to issue instructions that they be "on the *qui vive* for any attack."[15] The army warning incorporated the latest State Department position subject to the president's constraint that it must be the Japanese who fired the first shot. However, the wording of the army alert, which was sent out late that afternoon, cushioned its urgency and impact.

"Negotiations with Japan appear to be terminated," it began, making no mention of war, leaving open the possibility—albeit a slender one—that "the Japanese Government might come back and offer to continue." It specified no likely targets of attack, merely stating that "Japanese future action unpredictable but hostile action possible at any moment." So while MacArthur and Short were ordered to initiate "reconnaissance and other measures," they were "not repeat not to alarm civil population or disclose intent." The message repeated, no fewer than three times, that Japan had "to commit the first overt act," before "offensive action" was undertaken."[16]

General Short therefore interpreted the dispatch, not as a full-blown war warning, but an alert against Japanese sabotage on Hawaii. It was, according to his testimony, "no more than saying that Japan was going to attack some place."[17]

Stronger terms were favored by the navy department after Stark "pondered almost an entire forenoon" over its wording. To the CNO staff Japanese aggression was "expected" rather than "a possibility," and so they decided on "language which we thought was strong enough to indicate to them that Japan was going to strike."[18]

Admiral Turner, as chief of war plans, was given primary responsibility for drafting the dispatch. Never a man to chop phrases too finely, he put the phrase "war warning" up front "to express the strong conviction on the part of the department that war was surely coming."[19] Furthermore, he was evidently so certain where the first blows would fall that he listed targets on the other side of the Pacific. While this impressed on the Asiatic Fleet commander the immediacy of the danger, it softened the warning's impact for us at Pacific Fleet headquarters, four thousand miles from the scene of the proposed attack.

While minds in Washington that evening were struggling to make the English language convey the complex nuances of diplomatic and military intelligence, the Japanese were having their own communications difficulties. Yet another example of the urgency gripping Tokyo was the foreign ministry's resorting to the transpacific telephone lines to try to clarify the situation. A clumsy group of code words was employed in which the secretary of state became Miss Umeko, the president Miss Kimiko, and the negotiations "matrimonial questions." Kurusu reported that his meeting that afternoon with Miss Kimiko "wasn't much different from what Miss Umeko said yesterday, "and that the 'southward matter' was 'the monkey wrench.'"[20]

American monitoring of this incongruous conversation, during which Ambassador Kurusu broke into laughter at its inanity, yielded one deadly accurate piece of intelligence. Kurusu was told several times that in "the matter pertaining to arranging a marriage—'*don't* break them off.'"[21] This should have alerted Washington that the Japanese government had ordered its envoys to keep up the pretense of diplomatic negotiation as a cover for its preliminary war moves.

While it was evident to the intelligence analysts in the navy department, as it was to us at Hypo, that Japanese invasion and support forces were preparing for a southward advance, there had still been no hint in any of the intercepted communications about the carrier force heading toward Hawaii.

That evening, some eight hundred miles from Japan, out in the northern Pacific, the ships of Admiral Nagumo's *Kido Butai* (literally Mobile Force but more accurately Striking force) were rolling and pitching their way eastward. Despite the rising heavy seas the *Kido Butai*'s oil-hungry destroyers and four carriers had successfully completed their first scheduled refueling operation.

"A good beginning," Commander Tomatsu Oishi noted in his diary. Lookouts had been increased after the Kwajalein radio relayed a report from cruiser *Katori* that an American light cruiser, escorting five transports, had been spotted east of Saipan.[22] This was *Boise* shepherding a convoy of troop reinforcements toward the Philippines—but her captain did not make a sighting report of the Japanese ships until his force reached Manila a week later, on 4 December.

Tokyo naval radio center was also keeping Nagumo posted about the rapidly deteriorating state of diplomatic negotiations. "The striking force hopes the political situation continues until the 8th–9th," staff officer Commander Kikuichi Fujita on heavy cruiser *Toné* confided to his diary. "The activity of the diplomats must not cease because it will cause a relaxation of American vigilance."[23]

Like everyone on board the *Kido Butai,* Fujita appreciated that secrecy and air power were the twin factors on which their do-or-die mission depended. So far both vital elements were intact.

The highly trained First Air Fleet in the six carriers under Nagumo's command counted on their two-to-one superiority in this category to overwhelm the Pacific Fleet, in or out of Pearl Harbor. But if it came to an old-fashioned slugfest, the Japanese would lose their advantage over our carriers. Outgunned by our sixteen-inch shells, against their fourteen-inch projectiles, Nagumo's two escorting battleships, *Hiei* and *Kirishima,* would have only their superior speed to save them from the four-to-one superiority of the Pacific Fleet's battle line. Despite their better torpedoes and speed advantage, his two cruisers and nine destroyers would be outgunned by Kimmel's eighteen cruisers and twenty-nine destroyers.

The *Kido Butai* had to catch the Pacific Fleet in Pearl Harbor. Thus any premature discovery during the first ten days of the mission meant Nagumo would have to abort the mission. He had to count on stealth and surprise. Three large submarines, each with a floatplane in a waterproof hangar, scouted two hundred miles ahead of the striking force, which was restricted to less than fourteen knots speed so that its seven accompanying oilers could keep up. So vital was the preservation of secrecy that Nagumo had given orders that the key of every radio transmitter was to be "sealed or removed" to prevent any accidental radio transmission that might alert enemy listening stations to their approach.[24]

After sailing from Saeki Bay nine days earlier, the *Kido Butai* had had no radio contact, other than listening in on the three shortwave bands and single ultralong wavelength of the number 1 station of the Tokyo signals unit.[25] These were the invisible threads by which the striking force could still be reined back—if a last-minute agreement on the *modus vivendi* was reached with the United States. It was also the link by which Nagumo would be ordered into the final, unstoppable charge to attack Pearl Harbor.

As cruiser *Toné* heaved her long fo'c'sle in and out of crashing gray seas, staff officer Fujita speculated on the odds against the momentous mission of which he was a small part:

> I think this sortie is going to be like going into the tiger's lair to get her cubs. We cannot expect success unless the attack is a total surprise and the enemy is unprepared. It is most important therefore not to encounter any vessel on the trip, either a warship or merchantman of any other nation. That is why a great deal of attention has been paid to the selection of our fleet formation. Still we cannot afford the risk of a chance encounter. The only thing we can do is to pray for heaven's help to prevent this.[26]

Heaven did not answer Fujita's prayers. As it turned out, it was Soviet self-interest rather than divine intervention that let the Japanese striking force reach its target without being detected.

20

"Going to Be in a Fight"

THE SUN WAS DIPPING into the Waianae Hills beyond Pearl Harbor's west loch late in the afternoon of 27 November. That Thursday had been a busy one of coming and going for briefings at the submarine base headquarters of the Pacific Fleet. The CNO dispatch that had arrived overnight brought about almost continuous conferences. In addition to his own staff, Admiral Kimmel met with General Short and his air officers to make arrangements to provide additional fighter cover at Wake and Midway islands to ensure the safe arrival of the B-17s in the Philippines.

Washington's instruction to transfer up to half of Hawaii's P-40 pursuit planes to Wake and Midway was taken by Kimmel as a clear sign that the army and navy staffs "did not consider hostile action on Pearl Harbor imminent or probable."[1] Short insisted on retaining control of all army aircraft, so it was decided to substitute two-Oahu-based marine squadrons so that Kimmel could retain undivided command of the forces garrisoning the outlying islands.

Admiral Halsey's *Lexington* task force was designated to ferry the first mission to Midway. He left the all-day session at 1800 hours, feeling, in his own words, "that we were going to be in a fight." To keep up the appearances of a routine operation, Halsey would sortie with three of the battleships. The slow, old battlewagons would then be detached at the first opportunity. He assured his academy classmate Kimmel, "If I have to run I don't want anything to interfere with my running."[2]

Shortly after Halsey left the headquarters building, I learned that a top-secret and urgent dispatch had just come in. I at once went into the communications office down the corridor and was shown the tape copy of a war warning. As I scanned the smudged tape spewing out of the decoding machine that was reserved for our most secret communications, I was instantly galvanized by the message:

This dispatch is to be considered a war warning. Negotiations with Japan looking toward stabilization of conditions in the Pacific have ceased and an aggressive move by Japan is expected within the next few days. The number and equipment of Japanese troops and the organization of naval task forces indicate an amphibious expedition against either the Philippines Thai or Kra peninsula or possibly Borneo. Execute an appropriate defensive deployment preparatory to carrying out tasks assigned in WPL 46. Inform District and Army authorities. A similar warning is being sent by War Department. Spenavo [Special Naval Observer in London] inform British. Continental districts Guam, Samoa directed to take appropriate measures against sabotage.[3]

When I read "This dispatch is . . . a war warning," it gave me a jolt; I had never seen such a message before. It struck me that there was no mention of Guam as a target this time. Someone else saw this too, and commented, "They probably figured Guam was going to fall anyway, so it wasn't worthwhile putting it in." There was barely time to reread the dispatch, let alone formulate my thoughts about its full implications, before Admiral Kimmel sent for me.

My first reaction to the warning was that it agreed precisely with my own estimates. I believed that the Japanese would continue their push southward and I was apprehensive that they would not risk leaving our Philippine forces on their flank. This was how I summarized the situation to Admiral Kimmel. Our initial discussion was brief, because he wanted the message paraphrased and delivered immediately to General Short.

Recasting the words of top-secret communications was standard procedure to protect the security of our ciphers. It took three attempts before the communications officer and I were satisfied that we had the meaning accurately conveyed. By this time the admiral was in conference and his office door was closed, a do-not-disturb signal that all his staff had learned to respect.

When the door finally opened, I entered and found him deep in conversation with half a dozen of his senior staff. While he interrupted his discussion to satisfy himself that my version of the war warning conveyed the urgency of the original tape, Admiral Bloch's chief of staff arrived. General Short had insisted that no copies were to be made of the army's war warning, which had arrived an hour and a half earlier, and Captain John Bayliss Earle had hand-carried the original over from the Fourteenth Naval District headquarters in Honolulu.

"This is the same dispatch in substance that we have just received," Kimmel announced as he passed it around to his staff for comment. We immediately noted that it was not so strongly worded as the navy's, because of its concluding instruction: "Undertake no offensive action until Japan has committed an overt act. Be prepared to carry out tasks as-

signed in WPL 46, so far as they apply to Japan in case hostilities occur."[4] After some discussion about the similarity and differences in the
two dispatches, Kimmel returned my paraphrase of the navy's warning
and ordered, "Get this to General Short right away."[5]

As I left the office, I chatted with Lieutenant Harold J. Burr, naval
liaison officer at Fort Shafter, who had accompanied Captain Earle. At
their suggestion I gave Captain Earle the paraphrase so that he could
deliver it to the general on his return. It seemed like a good idea at the
time. But it displeased Kimmel when he later found that I had not carried
out his orders precisely. There was never any doubt in my mind that
General Short had received it, however, because on my way home late
that evening I encountered convoys of trucks and troops on the move.

I assumed that the army was going to a full condition of readiness,
and that Short's troops were going to man antiaircraft batteries and set up
mobile weapons around Pearl Harbor and other strategic points. Later I
found out that General Short had only ordered a number 1 alert. Unlike
the navy, which starts with number 3 and builds to a full number 1 alert,
the army's number 1 was their lowest state of readiness and that was a
precautionary deployment against sabotage.

"The danger of sabotage was paramount in my mind, and seemed to
me the chief danger which the war department feared," was how Short
himself later justified his lack of preparedness against enemy air attack or
landings.[6] The same signal had been addressed to all army commanders;
however, Short's emergency staff meeting that afternoon had concluded
that warning of "hostile action" as it applied locally on Oahu could only
refer to the threat of "internal disorder."[7] The morning had been spent
arranging with the navy—at the army chief of staff's direction—the transfer of aircraft from Hawaii to the outlying islands. This in itself was taken
as confirmation that Hawaii was not in any immediate danger, nor had it
been listed as a possible target for attack. In the absence of any other
intelligence to the contrary, General Marshall himself was later to admit,
"We were reasonable in our assumption" in the circumstances.[8]

It was a decision reinforced that evening by another dispatch, specifically addressed to Hawaiian headquarters, reminding Short that "subversive activities may be expected." This second alert, for the information of
"commanding general and chief of staff only," added further support to
Short's decision with its cautionary injunction "not to alarm civil population."[9] Washington was evidently more concerned about possible charges
from Tokyo that Japanese residents of the islands were subjected to undue harassment than defending Pearl Harbor against external attack. So
every effort was made to restrict the antisabotage measures to our bases
and military airfields. Consequently, planes were grouped together to
make them easier to guard with minimum troop deployments, and the
ammunition for antiaircraft batteries was kept locked in the munition
bunkers.

The charges that General Short "must have known" the Japanese would attack without warning, which were leveled against him by Stimson four years later, were grossly unfair. Unfounded too was the statement by the former secretary of war that the Hawaiian command "betrayed a misconception of his real duty that went beyond belief."[10] Indeed, one of the measures that Short took was to order the newly arrived mobile army radar units to begin operations an hour before dawn and continue until 7 A.M.

Stimson's bald assertions appear to have been part of the smokescreen of blame thrown up by Washington to absolve itself of any responsibility. There was never a hint in any intelligence received by the local command of any Japanese threat to Hawaii. Our air defenses were stripped on orders from the army chief himself. Of the twelve B-17s on the island, only six could be kept in the air by cannibalizing the others for spare parts. Hickam Field had been reduced to a refueling station for the long-range bombers on their way to the Philippines. And General Martin's aircrews had been committed, not to long-range defensive patrols, but to pilot training so as to enable the Flying Fortresses to navigate the long ocean-hops to the Philippines.

The secretary of war's bigoted condemnation of a field commander who fulfilled his duty as directed overlooked the war department's own failure to intervene *if* it really had considered Short's reported anti-sabotage efforts an inadequate response to the 27 November alert. General MacArthur had likewise informed Washington that his air reconnaissance had been "intensified and extended."[11] And since General Marshall had seen Short's dispatch confirming that he had been "alerted to prevent sabotage,"[12] Short could presume that Marshall agreed with his state of alert. It was only with the advantage of hindsight in December 1945 that Marshall admitted reproachfully, "That was my opportunity to intervene and I did not do it."[13]

Admiral Stark, even if he had felt differently from Marshall, had no opportunity to intervene. But Stark's director of war plans "did not even consider it necessary" to issue a further warning. Turner was to insist that there was no "possibility of misinterpreting that sentence." But the sentences following "This dispatch is to be considered a war warning" did not rule out further negotiations, and precautionary measures were urged "in order not to complicate an already tense situation."[14]

"We expected all military services and outlying detachments to act in every way as if we were actually at war, except making attacks on the enemy, if encountered, or initiating movements against enemy forces," was how Turner characterized the anticipated response to his so-called war warning.[15] But he appears to have ignored the cardinal rule: Warnings to a field commander are always read and acted upon within the local context.

In sizing up the situation that confronted us at Pearl Harbor in the twenty-four hours following the receipt of the 27 November navy and army war alerts, Admiral Kimmel had neither the advantage of Turner's ex post facto second-guessing nor the full context of the diplomatic intelligence in which the chief of war plans framed his warning.

Only in one respect was the army warning, which was formally relayed by CNO on the twenty-eighth, more specific: It instructed the Hawaiian commanders to "be prepared to carry out tasks assigned in WPL 46."[16] Turner later claimed that his use of the phrase "defensive deployment" should have been interpreted by Kimmel as requiring him to immediately order the Pacific Fleet to carry out its preliminary war plan task of protecting our sea communications "by escorting, covering, and patrolling as required by circumstances and by destroying enemy raiding forces."[17] But Turner's supposedly all-embracing warning omitted any reference to the threats that might be developing within range of the Hawaiian Islands.

The Philippines, Thailand, and the Isthmus of Kra had indeed been identified as "probable" Japanese objectives, with Borneo as the only other "possible" target. All these locations were five thousand miles from Hawaii, which was not even mentioned. The supposedly comprehensive war warning did not even pick up the phrase "an aggressive movement *in any direction* [emphasis added],"[18] which had been used in the alert sent out by Washington three days earlier. Since we received no better information, we assumed that the dropping of this general threat meant that new information must have enabled Washington to be more specific about the Japanese objectives.

With justification Kimmel was later to complain, "The phrase 'war warning' cannot be made the catch-all for all the contingencies hindsight may suggest."[19] Given the intelligence picture, as we had been able to piece it together in the context of the alerts we had received, there was nothing illogical or derelict about his conclusion that "an air attack on Pearl Harbor or anything other than a surprise submarine attack was most improbable."[20]

While our overall picture indicated to Kimmel that "war with Japan was closer than it had been before," there was nothing we had received from Washington or any other source to suggest that it was looming over the Hawaiian horizon.[21] Had we been receiving the Magic intercepts, or even been told about either of the two negotiating deadlines, the dropping of the *modus vivendi,* and the secretary of state's trenchant ten points delivered to the Japanese the day before, the realization that the rupture of diplomatic relations was imminent would have been inescapable.

It was also the third occasion in four months that Washington had flashed an alert to the Pacific Fleet. So, in weighing whether the war would break out in a matter of hours, days—or would again be averted by more negotiations—Kimmel took account of the most recent dispatch from Stark and its enclosed memorandum urging that the president avoid war and that "no ultimatum be delivered to Japan."[22]

Not until the next day, 28 November, with the arrival of our first piece of Magic diplomatic intelligence in four months, did we have any hint that our relations with Japan might be hovering really close to the brink of war. The so-called wind code message on shortwave Tokyo radio was not intended by Tokyo as a war warning per se. Such a message would be an emergency alert to Japan's embassies that there was a "danger of cutting international relations" between Japan and whatever country was specified by a sequence of code words:

1. HIGASHI NO KAZE AME (east wind rain) would mean Japan-US relations in danger
2. KITA NO KAZE KUMORI (north wind cloudy) Japan-USSR relations in danger
3. NISHI NO KAZE HARE (west wind clear), Japan-British relations in danger.[23]

A similar message to "destroy all codes and papers" when "diplomatic relations are becoming dangerous"—also using the same country designators, *Higashi, Kita,* and *Nishi*—was also sent out by Tokyo at the same time.[24] But the importance of this was overshadowed in Washington by the wind code message, because it was decrypted within hours of the expiration of Tokyo's 29 November deadline. That juxtaposition gave many senior staff officers the notion that the receipt of an "east wind rain" broadcast would be tantamount to Japan's declaring war on the United States.

While the crisis was deemed serious enough to warrant sending us some Magic information, it was unfortunate that the opportunity was missed by Washington to provide us with a more informative diplomatic intelligence. Had they done so, it might have prompted us to take more heed of a signal received from British intelligence headquarters at Singapore that "Japan will commence military operations on 1 December against the Kra Isthmus."[25]

This message, which I rated as less than reliable, might have seemed more important had we been given the intelligence decrypted in Washington from Tokyo's message praising the "superhuman efforts" of the two ambassadors. It went on to say that the "humiliating proposal" delivered by Hull was "quite unexpected and regrettable" and that in "two or three days" it was "inevitable" that *"negotiations will be 'de facto' ruptured* [emphasis added]." Nomura and Kurusu were, however, instructed to continue placatory overtures so as not to "give the impression that the negotiations are broken off."[26]

The importance of this message cannot have been lost on Roosevelt and his advisers. They had gathered for their morning session around the presidential bedside to review the "dangerous possibilities." Roosevelt had to decide among three courses of action: "to do nothing; to make something in the nature of an ultimatum again, stating a point beyond which we would fight; third, to fight at once."[27] Stimson was all for fighting, but Marshall and Stark wanted "no immediate action which would lead to immediate hostilities." Their appeal for more time to complete the Philippine buildup had already been overtaken by events.

At noon a more formal meeting of the war council agreed that "if the Japanese get into the isthmus of Kra, the British would fight" and the United States was "committed to join them." The "whole chain of disastrous events," Stimson recorded, would be set in motion if the Japanese expeditionary force, reportedly assembling for a southward advance, "was allowed to round the southern point of Indochina."[28] Hull was of the opinion that the Japanese "might make the element of surprise a central point in their strategy and also might attack at various points simultaneously with a view to demoralizing efforts of defense and coordination."[29] But his point was apparently not taken to heart by the navy or army chiefs. They were evidently still preoccupied with gaining time to reinforce the Philippines. But it was agreed that if the Japanese naval forces advanced past "a certain point, we should have to fight."[30] No ultimatum defining that boundary was to be sent yet to Tokyo.

Halfway around the world a Japanese task force was steaming toward a demarcation line that would have figured prominently in any accounting of American interests: the 180-degree line of longitude that divided the eastern from the western hemisphere.

"Tense since yesterday," staff officer Fujita noted in his diary. "Today we heard from the naval general staff that they had now lost hope for a resolution of U.S.-Japanese relations after America suddenly changed its attitude on 26th and became unyielding."[31]

The ships of the *Kido Butai* were clawing through thick fog. But the greatly increased collision hazard was not the only worry that that day brought Nagumo. Tokyo had radioed "concern that we might run into a Soviet merchant ship bound from San Francisco to the Far East."[32]

This intriguing reference in the official Japanese war history—*Hawai Sakusen* (*Hawaii Operation*) *Senshi Sosho* (*War History Series*) Vol. 10— is confirmed by a firsthand wartime account. But it has been overlooked by every American historian. Investigation of the War Shipping Administration records reveals that the freighter was almost certainly *Uritsky*, which had sailed under the Golden Gate days earlier with a cargo of vital military lend-lease supplies. The steamer's course for Vladivostok would intersect with the *Kido Butai*'s intended track somewhere to the northwest of the Hawaiian Islands.[33]

Just how naval headquarters in Tokyo could have known the precise course of a Russian merchantman raises many intriguing questions. For example, why was Nagumo not ordered to sink the freighter on sight? He had been ordered to dispose of all other vessels. Or, did the information about the *Uritsky*'s course and destination come from the Japanese consulate in San Francisco? Since the route to Vladivostok passed close to waters patrolled by Japan, Tokyo might have been advised, as a precaution and courtesy, of the Russian freighter's imminent passage across the north Pacific. But there is no record in the intercepts of the San Francisco consul's relaying such information. Significantly, however, within hours of the alert's being flashed out to the *Kido Butai,* Tokyo cabled the San Francisco consulate to make "full reports" on the departure of "all" ships that were leaving the west coast and heading into the Pacific.[34] This suggests that Japan's naval staff received news of *Uritsky* from another source and that this prompted the message to San Francisco.

How the Japanese found out about a Russian freighter plowing a lonely course across the vast emptiness of the north Pacific, so that they knew its course and speed precisely enough to predict that it would collide with the *Kido Butai,* becomes an issue of extraordinary significance. It seems highly unlikely that an officer of the naval staff in Tokyo could simply have stumbled across *Uritsky*'s sailing orders. This raises the probability that *Uritsky*'s course must have been given to the Japanese by the Russians themselves. This deduction then leads to the logical assumption that Soviet intelligence *knew* precise details of the course to be taken across the northern Pacific by Nagumo's striking force!

If they did, it would have been logical for Stalin to order that Tokyo be told about the *Uritsky.* He needed to avoid provoking an incident at a critical juncture for both countries. He also had to ensure that the freighter's lend-lease cargo of tanks and planes reached Vladivostok safely so they could be shipped via the trans-Siberian railroad in time for the last-ditch stand to save Moscow.

If the Russians had succeeded in penetrating Japan's tight naval security, then it might well have been Stalin himself—or intercepted Soviet signal traffic—that had been the source of the critical intelligence that had jolted the White House early on the morning of 26 November.

21

"Self-deception"

A T 0800 ON FRIDAY, 28 November, carrier *Enterprise* led the procession of battleships, cruisers, and destroyers that was Task Force 8 into the narrow channel leading out of Pearl Harbor. Once they were in open seas, Admiral Halsey split off the three battlewagons and set course for Wake with three heavy cruisers and nine destroyers. "The *Enterprise* is now operating under war conditions," her captain ordered the carrier's crew. At Halsey's instruction all torpedoes and bombs were armed. All ships in the task force were directed "to regard any submarine seen as hostile and sink it . . . [and] shoot down any plane seen in the air . . . not known to be one of our own."[1]

Admiral Kimmel anticipated that the main danger was attack from Japanese submarines. That morning he issued a fleet directive calling for extreme vigilance. Our warships were to "depth bomb all contacts expected to be hostile in the fleet operating areas."[2] The factor that carried the most weight in influencing his decisions was the directive received from Washington to use his two carriers to ferry fighter reinforcements to the outlying islands. Kimmel could only regard this as a sure indication that "no attack on Pearl Harbor could be expected in the immediate future." Just getting to Wake and back would take a week.

Since speed was essential in this mission, Halsey had elected not to take along the plodding battlewagons. Without carrier air cover as protection against torpedo plane attack, battle force commander Vice Admiral William Pye agreed, it made no tactical sense to keep his battleships at sea. In Pearl Harbor the shallow water, based on studies prepared by the naval staff, was thought to render the danger of such attack negligible. At their berths, the battleships were also expected to be protected by army fighters and antiaircraft batteries.[3]

Kimmel's principal concern was readying the fleet to carry out the assigned mission under War Plan 46, to "prepare to capture and establish control over Caroline and Marshall islands area, and to establish an advanced fleet base in Truk."[4] For months I had been gathering all the information I could on Japanese forces and bases in the mandates. The admiral periodically incorporated my intelligence reports into his daily memorandum: "Steps to Be Taken in Case of American-Japanese War Within the Next 24 Hours."[5]

If a Japanese attack was pointed at Hawaii, then strategic logic and our best intelligence suggested that it would develop from the deep-water anchorage of one of the large atolls in the mandates. Jaluit was slightly more than two thousand miles southwest of Pearl Harbor. We knew from analysis of Japan's radio traffic that a powerful force of submarines was based there, and there were indications that "at least one carrier division unit" was heading toward the Marshalls.[6]

Rochefort and I badly needed confirmation of our suspicions that a powerful Japanese task force was assembling within striking distance of Pearl Harbor. Kimmel was therefore pleased to receive that Friday morning the memorandum describing my conference with General Martin on the army's intended high-level reconnaissance by specially modified B-24 bombers. We had agreed that they were to fly over the Marshalls from Wake on missions that would also cover Truk and Ponape.[7]

Photoreconnaissance was expected to settle the difference between the Hypo and Cast traffic analyses about whether one or two Japanese carriers were already in, or heading toward, the Marshalls. But until the dispute had been resolved, Kimmel had to make his plans on the assumption that the main danger to Pearl Harbor in the event of war was an enemy task force steaming out to make a surprise attack from the southwest. That was the primary focus of our concern. Kimmel's orders to dispatch the carriers to Wake and Midway was seen as fitting neatly in with the need to step up the surveillance of the southwestern approaches to Oahu as well as reinforcing the outlying islands.

"It permitted a broad area to be scouted for signs of enemy movement along the path of advance of these task forces to the islands and their return," Kimmel later explained. "In addition they would be in an excellent position to intercept any enemy force which might be on the move."[8] Although Kimmel was to be severely censured for failing to carry out the basic war plan, the demands of WPL 46 were precisely met by his decision to send Admiral Halsey's Task Force 8 to Wake, and a week later *Lexington* and Task Force 12 (commanded by Rear Admiral John H. Newton) to Midway, while Vice Admiral Wilson Brown's cruisers of Task Force 5 headed south to conduct landing exercises at Johnston Island, which lay a third of the way between Hawaii and the easternmost of the Marshalls.

Each task force was directed to send out air patrols night and morning to scour the southern and western Pacific approaches to Oahu. To increase our surveillance of these waters, which intelligence estimates

showed to be the most logical direction for a Japanese threat to Pearl
Harbor, Kimmel also ordered them swept by two squadrons of PBY-5
patrol planes. On Thursday the unit based on Midway had departed for
Wake to conduct a 525-mile-wide sweep search en route. On Sunday the
patrol wing scheduled to replace them took off from their Ford Island
base and headed south to Johnston Island to refuel before heading northwest to Midway, whence they conducted daily 500-mile deep-ocean reconnaissance.

In the week before 7 December the navy aircraft scoured over two
million square miles of the Pacific without spotting a single Japanese warship. Yet Kimmel was still censured for failing to conduct adequate long-
range air patrols.

Only round-the-compass, deep-ocean reconnaissance, as agreed to in
April 1941 in the Martin-Bellinger report, could have guaranteed Pearl
Harbor adequate advance warning of the approach of hostile forces. But
eight months had elapsed since the plan had been submitted to Washington, and neither Admiral Bellinger nor General Martin had enough aircraft to collectively operate anything approaching a full 360-degree air
patrol on a daily basis.

Only 6 army B-17s were flyable. The navy had only 81 long-range
PBY amphibians. Crew and plane fatigue on the punishing sixteen-hour,
seven-hundred-mile forays cut by one third a patrol wing's effective
strength. It would have required at least 250 PBYs to maintain a comprehensive daily surveillance. This was more than three times the number
Bellinger commanded, and 54 of his 81 planes were new arrivals. Their
partly trained crews had no spare parts for their twin-engine PBY-5 Catalinas.

The Cats, as the crews affectionately called their amphibians, were
less feline than dragonflylike with their large wings and bulbous observation blisters. Ungraceful they were, but each could search an 8-degree
wedge of ocean to a distance of over seven hundred miles. This was more
than enough range to spot an approaching task force a full day before its
carrier planes were within striking distance of Pearl Harbor, but with
fewer than thirty planes available for continuous daily operations, only a
144-degree sector of the approaches to Oahu could be covered, leaving 60
percent of the compass unguarded.

Kimmel's dilemma was not simply which third of the approaches to
cover. He had been ordered by Washington, "not once but twice," to be
prepared to carry out raids on the Marshalls, for which long-range aerial
reconnaissance was an essential precursor of fleet operations. He could
not afford to fritter away patrol plane resources. "Had I directed their
use for intensive distance searches from Oahu," Kimmel was to testify, "I
faced the peril of having these planes grounded when the fleet needed
them and when the war plan was executed."[9]

Wartime inquisitors and postwar historians have repeatedly condemned Kimmel for not conducting more extensive air searches. Their comments reveal little appreciation for the circumstances behind his decision to concentrate his attention mainly on the southwestern sector.

Lack of aircraft and too much geography imposed severe restraints on the Pacific Fleet's operational capabilities. Assume that Pearl Harbor is the center of a circle that represents a compass rose. Directly south of the waters where our warships exercised lay the Line Islands—Palmyra, Christmas, and Victoria—which were some fifteen hundred miles from Hawaii, the same distance that these atolls lay north of Tahiti. Some five hundred miles to the southwest of the Hawaiian chain lay Johnston Island—and fifteen hundred miles southwest of this American sandspit was the easternmost Japanese territory in the Marshall Islands. Just over two thousand miles due west of Pearl Harbor was Wake Island, a vital stepping stone to Guam and the Philippines. Fifteen hundred miles northwest of us was Midway. To the north lay the empty vastness of the northern Pacific, an area of frequent depressions that swept the storms and fogs south from the Aleutian Islands and the rocky Alaskan coastline.

Looking out from the center of the compass at Pearl Harbor it was obvious therefore that our attention would be focused to the southwest. It was the direction of the Japanese bases in the Marshall and Caroline islands. These were the obvious jumping-off points for a Japanese advance toward New Guinea and Australia. They were also a roadblock to our seaborne communications with the Philippines. So when it came to immediate threats, Kimmel had to take into account Jaluit in the eastern Marshalls. It was less than five days' hard steaming away for a fast-striking force. Given the superiority of the Japanese carrier fleet and the signs of the recent buildup in the mandates, it was clear that the Pacific Fleet's first priority was to guard against an attack from the southwest sector.

Kimmel had no precise indication of when war was going to break out, and his air commander was to testify that "any adequate search was impossible for more than a few days."[10] In consultation with his staff, Kimmel determined that the most vital areas for aerial reconnaissance were south from the Line Islands, swinging southwest toward the Marshalls and Carolines, thence westward through Wake to Midway in the northwest. Transposing the compass rose onto a clock face, this meant that while the sectors between 6 and 11 were thoroughly covered by air patrols during the next ten days, the rest were only intermittently searched. The decision to leave the 12 o'clock sector unpatrolled was a calculated risk, taken by professional naval officers acting on the best information that was available to them. Unfortunately, the Japanese either guessed our predicament or knowingly took advantage of it, because they attacked from the north—an area uncovered by aerial reconnaissance.

During the July 1940 alert Admiral Richardson had ordered deep-ocean air patrols to cover the sector from west to northwest. That was the sector from which Pearl Harbor had been successfully attacked during the 1938 fleet problem. But even if Kimmel had repeated his predecessor's action, as his critics later charged he should have, patrols would *still* have missed the Japanese striking force running down from due north.

At no time did Kimmel receive any intelligence, or hint, that there was any threat to Pearl Harbor from any direction but from the southwest. He believed that any Japanese sortie from the Marshalls that attempted an end run to the south or north would have been spotted by the patrol wings of Catalinas dispatched that weekend to Midway, Wake, and Johnston Island. Nor were the remaining forty-nine PBYs unemployed. During the next ten days, in addition to training flights, they mounted patrols to the north and northwest of Oahu as well as executing a daily dawn reconnaissance over the fleet's exercise area three hundred miles south of Pearl Harbor.

"I took account of my probable future needs and of my orders from the navy department," was how Kimmel justified his deployment. "I decided that I could not risk having no patrol plane force worthy of the name for the fleet's expected movement into the Marshalls."[11] Given the information he possessed, the demands of his war plan, the shortage of aircraft, and the geographical constraints he faced, Kimmel could not have made any other decision.

That was the conclusion of the admirals who sat from July to October 1944 as the navy court of inquiry. It was not only a judgment of his professionally qualified peers, but because the court sat in secret session it was not subject to political pressures. Their verdict was a vindication of his decision: "The omission of this reconnaissance was not due to oversight or neglect. It was the result of a military decision, reached after much deliberation and consultation with experienced officers and after weighing the information at hand and all the factors involved."[12]

Such an exoneration of the admiral who had already been publicly made the scapegoat for the Pearl Harbor disaster sat badly with then Secretary of the Navy James V. Forrestal. He suppressed the navy inquiry's report until it had been reviewed by other flag officers. Admiral King, who was then chief of naval operations, found it expedient to leave his fellow admiral in purgatory rather than expose the navy department's blunders.

The facts as we had them at Pacific Fleet headquarters in the first week of December 1941 left Kimmel no choice but to concentrate our sea and air searches to the southwestern and northwestern approaches to Oahu. Throughout that last Saturday and Sunday of peace I worked nonstop to meet the deadline set by the admiral for a comprehensive and detailed estimate of the whereabouts of every major Japanese air and surface unit for his Monday morning staff conference.

Rochefort and I spent a great deal of time comparing notes. But it was clear that despite the best efforts of his traffic analysts there were some big question marks. No further evidence of the carrier division in the mandates had been received since the 27 November communications intelligence summary. Joe was concerned, moreover, that the Japanese might be stealing a march on us. His report the next day stated that *their* radio intelligence network was "operating at full strength," and he had typed in bold capitals, "IS GETTING RESULTS."[13]

On 30 November, as I sat in my office typing up my report, because Yeoman Keene was off duty that Sunday afternoon, I shared Joe's concern that much of the day's intercepted traffic appeared to be repeats of previous transmitted messages. Some were four days old. Two vital pieces of radio intelligence that I confidently incorporated in my report later turned out to be miscalculations. One was to put *Hiei* and *Kongo* in with the southern task force off Formosa, because radio messages addressed to the two battleships appeared to link them with the Second Fleet. The other concerned carrier *Akagi*.

Rochefort's communications intelligence summary for 30 November had noted: "The only tactical circuit heard today was one with *Akagi* and several *marus*."[14] But we did not take these isolated communications as evidence that the other carrier divisions we thought were in home waters were also out because the low power of such transmissions thwarted accurate direction finding by Hypo's shaky system. The report appears anyway to have been a misidentification of call signs. Although *Akagi* and the two battleships were in fact at sea in the north Pacific, the *Kido Butai* was under orders to observe strict radio silence with transmitter switches sealed off—a fact recently reconfirmed by Admiral Genda.[15]

There was no doubt in my mind about the critical importance of the memorandum that I headed "Location of Japanese Fleet Units."[16] The evidence that most of their fleet had been concentrated into two huge task forces was an unmistakable signal that five thousand miles away across the Pacific an unstable powder keg might blow up. The alerts we had received from Washington, our own intelligence picture, and the dictates of geography indicated that the fuse that had been set led directly from the Japanese naval bases in Formosa and Hainan Island to the Isthmus of Kra, Malaya, the Dutch East Indies, and probably the Philippines. But just where the spark would be struck to ignite the explosion was still an open question.

When I reviewed the evaluation that I had worked on all weekend, I was struck by the enormous responsibility I bore for those five typewritten pages. The alarming thought had already crossed my mind that much of the report—which would determine the disposition of the Pacific Fleet in the countdown to war—was nothing more than guesswork. Inspired, perhaps, but it was guesswork nonetheless, because it was founded on analysis of naval signals whose encoded messages we could not decipher.

This was why my estimate was prefaced, "From best available information units of Orange fleet are *thought* to be located as listed below [emphasis added]."[17]

The pattern that emerged from the dispositions of the Japanese fleet—from those pieces that we had been able to lock into place as well as from those that were still missing—was disturbing. This applied especially to half their carrier forces. We could locate them only in the negative sense—that we did not have any confirmation of their precise whereabouts.

The jigsaw puzzle we had assembled at Pearl Harbor by 30 November revealed that two main task forces had gathered under the loose command of the Second Fleet. The previous week's confirmation that had come from Cavite's traffic analysts was that one of these forces, spearheaded by a considerable number of submarines, was heading for the mandates. From there they would be in position either for offensive operations against the Pacific Fleet or to cover the flank of the main force then concentrating for an advance toward Malaya and the Philippines. Although the carriers had not been heard of for more than two weeks, Station Cast agreed with the Hypo analysis that transmissions indicated that at least one division was associated with the force in Formosan ports. Another force was heading for the Palaus. Cavite, however, had not been able to confirm, or discount, Rochefort's estimate that at least one auxiliary carrier was already in the mandates.

So in making my final estimate for Kimmel, I deliberately omitted from my location sheet two Japanese carrier divisions, although I had placed two others in the vicinity of Formosa and I put a question mark beside the placement of the auxiliary carrier in the Marshalls. All the Japanese warship locations in my estimate, with the exception of sightings of transports and light cruisers and the submarines, had been based on nothing more positive than our analysis of the enemy naval radio circuits. Nobody knew better than Rochefort and I that intelligence derived from traffic analysis could be inconclusive, sometimes contradictory, and very often incomplete. Yet barring planned deception—and there was no evidence of this beyond the duplication of previous messages—we believed that traffic analysis had given us a broadly accurate picture.

Contrary to popular myth and the assumptions of many historians, there was no sustained deception plan put into operation by Japan. They did not, for example, reassign carrier call signs to destroyers in the inland sea.[18] It was only assumed that they did by a certain section of the naval staff in Washington, which assumption was given official credence in the navy's secret publication CSP-1494-A as part of the effort to discredit Rochefort in the spring of 1942. *Black Magic in Communications* was the title of this paper. And in the chapter headed "Did the Japanese Paint Us a Picture?" it suggested that the Hypo analysts had been taken in by radio deception.

"The Japs did not even attempt deception," was Joe's angry rejection of the charge that he had been "painted a picture." "There was plenty of deception out here, but it was all self-deception."[19] That self-deception on our part was encouraged by the increased precautions of the Japanese to protect their radio security in the first week of December by using multiple addresses and blanket coverage as well as signals that were addressed to nobody from nobody. The Japanese evidently believed that the overnight change in call signs was concealment enough. Although Rochefort was able to report that within twenty-four hours Hypo had recovered partial identification of "over 200 hundred service calls,"[20] we both knew that having to reidentify nearly twenty-thousand indicators would make positive identification of the "missing" carriers even more problematical.

When all but one of the carriers had vanished from radio traffic after they had returned from the fleet exercises after the first week of November, the logical explanation was that they had returned to port and inactive status, just as they had done for a time in October. It was not unusual for traffic to vanish on the carrier circuits when they were in harbor. Once their planes had been flown off on approach to their home ports—as we ourselves did—there would be no more of the ship-to-air communications that were the giveaway of carriers.

So when Carrier Divisions 1 and 2 air traffic and identifiers dried up in mid-November, the assumption was that they were in port replenishing for operations. As for the other carriers, transmission addressed to the Second Fleet over the previous ten days indicated that at least one other division, and probably two, was associated with the large task force assembling in Formosan waters. We had later to discover that we misidentified the big carriers of Division 3 as the small ones of Division 4. Only the weaker force was in fact participating in the southern operations, because Carrier Division 3 was actually part of the striking force. Identification of call signs from a destroyer division that formerly acted as plane guards led Rochefort to assume that "one or more of the carrier divisions were in the Mandates."[21] But the apparent lack of calls to the four other carriers, including flagship *Kaga,* became a subject of debate in Hypo.

Since the previous Friday an intense watch was being kept by Hypo's listening station to try to find the carrier frequencies. Our On the Roof Gang listeners were by now familiar with the "fists"—the characteristic use of the Morse key—of many radiomen of the Combined Fleet. But there was no traffic intercepted from flagship *Kaga.* Rochefort and I chewed over his 2 December report the next day, which stated that traffic was "at a low ebb" and there was "almost a complete lack of information on the carriers."[22]

Hypo's two traffic analysts were split. Lieutenant Huckins agreed with our conclusion that absence of carrier call signs was because they were tied up at their piers in Japan awaiting orders to sail. But Lieutenant

John A. Williams was sure something was going on.[23] Nobody had any hard evidence, and the lack of any of the other carrier call signs identified with the Second Fleet task forces encouraged the view that Carrier Divisions 1 and 2 were still in harbor at Kure. That is why they were omitted from my 1 December location sheet. But the possibility that they might be involved in the eastern task force in the mandates and ready to conduct offensive operations against Hawaii from the southwest was causing some of us to sprout gray hairs.

We agreed it was possible that the four "lost" carriers had sailed under sealed orders and were observing strict radio silence, as they had during the week they had covered the operations in Indochina that July. Radio silence alone would have been a giveaway *if* they had been identified in the other communication traffic. But when the buildup came during November, they were not addressed. The fact that they were apparently unconnected with the Second Fleet task forces and operating no radio, whether as originators or addressees, led us to the belief, erroneous as it was, that these carriers would not be participating in the forthcoming movements and were preparing for some other operation.

It would have been very different if they had been addressed in *any* one of the thousands of messages sent out from the naval general headquarters in the previous weeks. For if they had been observing radio silence and made no response, it would have been a clear sign that they were at sea. But without such indications, or reliable witnesses to their sailing, our intelligence led us to conclude throughout the next six days that half the Japanese carrier fleet was still in home waters.

While we did not know it at the time, Jack Williams was right. The "missing" Japanese carriers were at sea, observing radio silence—and *were* being addressed. It was just that we did not know what we were looking for. The overnight switch in the two-kana-hyphen-numeral designators made an already difficult task more like hunting for a needle in a haystack—but without even knowing what a needle looked like!

That evening, as the *Kido Butai* crossed the 180-degree longitude line into the western hemisphere, Admiral Nagumo, concerned that they were now within range of American air searches from the Aleutian island of Kiska, flashed a light signal to all ships. Watchkeepers were urged to maintain a "careful lookout for enemy ships including ones that might pursue us from the rear."[24]

We had no way of knowing that the Pearl Harbor attack group that had sailed from Tankan Bay five days earlier was designated as the *Kido Butai*. Since it was not making any transmissions at all, it did not provide us with any signals from which to take a direction-finder bearing, or to compare a "fist," or designator, reference; so we could not make a match with any one of the thousands of new call signs. Hypo's IBM machines and tray of punch cards had been rendered useless by the 1 December change in call signs.

The clues that might have unmasked the striking force's "SU TE 9" call sign had in fact already been intercepted in the JN-25 B fleet code.[25] They had been picked up early on the morning of 17 November by our largest listening facility at Bainbridge Island off the Washington coast. This intercepted message, and another one of 24 November, relayed the latest revisions in the unit identifiers. But the fleet code was unavailable to Rochefort's team.

If Hypo had received the latest recoveries of the JN-25 additives and code book recoveries as scheduled at the beginning of November, Rochefort might have had a slim chance to get into the navy's operational cipher. But the painstakingly handwritten code sheets that he needed for this work lay sealed in the hold of a transport whose departure for Honolulu from San Diego had been delayed by three weeks.[26]

The JN-25 fleet operational code was part of the 90 percent of the Japanese naval traffic that was closed to Rochefort's code breakers. They had continued their fruitless battle concentrating on the flag officers cipher, as Washington had ordered, in addition to the low-grade administrative and weather traffic.

Meanwhile, the Negat cryptanalysts in Washington, and those at Station Cast in Cavite, were breaking into JN-25 B. According to Safford, intercepts in this code were "partly readable" by December 1941, at which time the Japanese introduced a new book of random additives to encipher the five-digit code.[27] Exactly what information was being gleaned from the operational cipher at this stage in Washington or Cavite is difficult to establish.

The recent discovery of a batch of intercepts covering the period from June to November 1941 that were buried amid approximately three hundred thousand wartime Japanese naval messages declassified to date has finally made it possible to see what intelligence could have been recovered *if* Hypo had been permitted to work on the JN-25 traffic.

The translations of the decrypts were reworked in 1945. They do not give a precise indication of what was known in 1941 by our naval cryptographic teams in OP-20-G, Cavite, or the cryptanalysts of Britain's Far East Combined Bureau at Singapore. But they do show which of the Combined Fleet dispatches were picked up and these reveal their enormous *potential* intelligence value as clues to Japan's operational intentions, *including* indications that an attack force of carriers was heading for an unknown target.

All our speculation is based on Safford's assertion of the partial readability of the JN-25 B cipher. According to the estimate of Dyer and Wright, this amounted to about 10 percent. This does not mean that 10 percent of the intercepts in Japan's main operational fleet code were then being decrypted, or even that a tenth of each and every communication in the five-digit cipher was translated into meaningful English. But it does suggest that on average, 10 percent of *each* message that could be broken was yielding some information, even if fortuitous and disconnected.[28]

There can be no doubt that Washington therefore must have had some fragmentary intelligence from the Japanese fleet cipher. What it was or how significant is impossible to assess because, to date, *not one single original decrypt made at the time of any JN-25 message has been found or declassified.* And it should be noted that none was considered or produced by any of the Pearl Harbor inquiries or the 1945 congressional investigations. This does not *necessarily* suggest that an embarrassingly important piece of the intelligence puzzle was missed and therefore has been covered up by Washington. But it is surely another example of how reluctant the naval staff was to reveal that there could have been some additional clues to Japan's intentions from the JN-25 intercepts and that they were either ignored or overlooked like the bomb plot message in the J-19 consular traffic.

The intercepted pre-Pearl Harbor JN-25 signal traffic for the month before 7 December is highly illuminating. The question is how much intelligence was broken out of these messages at the time. Certainly even such a partial decryption as the 10 percent of the traffic claimed by Safford could have provided us with some precise information on those naval movements that led directly to an attack.

The November 1941 JN-25 traffic vibrated with indications of war: On 14 November Japanese merchant shipping is alerted that "wartime recognition signals" will be effective on 1 December.[29] Next day the Combined Fleet is advised of the distribution of new code books;[30] the following day the "Combined Fleet Special Call List for Wartime Use" is announced.[31] On 19 November a destroyer division requests its copy of the "Combined Fleet Battle Plan,"[32] and the same day a cruiser requests its copy of "Striking Force Operational Order No. 5."[33] The next day an oiler reports that she'll finish loading fuel and aviation gasoline by 21 November and join the striking force by the twenty-seventh.[34]

A strict military cordon is drawn around personnel assembling on Hainan Island 20 November "until further notice" because of a "leakage of secret information."[35] On the twenty-first a top-secret Combined Fleet signal is radioed "at 0000 on 21 November, repeat 21 November, carry out second phase of operations for opening hostilities."[36] On 29 November all naval forces in the mandates are ordered to "maintain battle condition shortwave silence."[37]

Even more revealing are the half dozen signals intercepted in the final weeks of November that update the call signs for the commanders about to be involved in the upcoming operations. These allocate the new two-kana-numeral identifiers to all the operational, support, and submarine forces.[38] These list designators for an E Force, an H Force, an M Force, an N Force, an AA Occupation Force, a G Force, an AF Commerce Destruction Unit, as well as the Main Force, an Advance Expeditionary Force, and the *Kido Butai*—Striking Force. The importance of the last is evident, because its flagship is allocated a second call sign, as is its Supply Unit.

The ability to decrypt even 10 percent of this type of traffic in the final weeks of November should have given both Washington and Cavite—not to mention the British—considerable opportunity to uncover some key elements of Japan's naval war plans. Although Safford asserted in 1945 that the "5-numeral system yielded no information which would arouse even a suspicion of the Pearl Harbor raid," it could have provided some indication both of the forces involved and potential targets before the new cipher additives came into use on 1 December.

In 1945 the translator of these messages took pains to note that in 1941 the following was not known: E equaled Malaya; H, the Dutch East Indies; M, Manila (the Philippines); N, Nippon (Japan); AA, Wake Island; G, Guam; and AF, Midway. But to the intelligence officer, the letters chosen by the Japanese indicate a surprising trust in the security of their own codes. With the exception of Wake and Midway they show a direct alphabetic association with their geographic destinations! Even if this self-evident association was not apparent, then merely by allocating the forces on a map, according to their likely targets, could have shown the Japanese strategic objectives in the Far East.

More important, this would have left the targets of the so-called main force of battleships and a striking force which could be presumed to contain carriers, unaccounted for. Since the main force was not allocated any supply units, and the striking force was assigned two of them, it could have been readily inferred that the former would support the E, H, and M operations, which were within range of the naval bases in Formosa and Indochina. The *Kido Butai,* on the other hand, was destined for some long-range operation.

Precisely what its mission was would not have been clear even if the decrypts had been broken in full. But some clues could have been pieced together from the series of ships-in-harbor updates relayed to the *Kido Butai* by Tokyo via Honolulu. The JN-25 intercepts reveal that at least one was picked up and sent to Washington. It was a 27 November report from Consul Kita saying that "4 destroyers left AIO the evening of 16 November."[39] Since none of the operational messages was addressed to individual carrier divisions, this in itself might have been taken as an indication that they were collectively involved with the operational objectives of a striking force that required two support forces. This would have been another clue that the Japanese were planning a strike at some distant American territory, probably in the Pacific, and possible targets included the West Coast, Panama, and our Hawaiian base.

While none of the signals give any *specific* indication that Pearl Harbor was going to be attacked, they contain clear pointers in that direction. They also show the intention of Japan's forces to attack Malaya, Guam, the Dutch East Indies, and the Philippines. What still remains a mystery, until the 1941 decrypts become available, is how much of this was known, or deduced, by the naval staff in Washington. If only a fraction of this had been available to us at Pearl Harbor, it would have answered Kimmel's doubts about the direction of Japan's belligerent intentions and so galvanized the level of the alert at Pearl Harbor.

During that final week one of the main problems that both Kimmel and I faced was having to evaluate evidence when we did not even have the diplomatic background about what Japanese policy really was. It was clear that the bulk of Japan's naval strength was being concentrated into task forces. It was self-evident days before we received the alert from Washington that Japan's probable targets of attack were Malaya, the Isthmus of Kra, Thailand, and possibly the Philippines. It needed no strategic genius to see that. But we knew that the Japanese had a propensity for always trying to get something for nothing. As Kimmel and I rationalized, it was possible that their forces were cover for another operation such as their July takeover of bases in Indochina. This time, it seemed, their objective might be Thailand, knowing that if they got in there and we took no action, they would be strategically well placed for another move southward. The same was true for the Dutch East Indies.

On four or five occasions during that final week of peace, we tried to resolve the uncertainty concerning Japanese objectives. However, the lack of diplomatic intelligence about Tokyo's overall intentions, and our own uncertainty of precisely what action the president would order if British but not American territory was attacked, bore heavily upon us.

"I wish I knew what we were going to do," Admiral Kimmel said to me during our discussions that week.[40] That he repeated this five or six times was a measure of his frustration and worry about being kept in the dark by Washington.

The Pacific Fleet dispositions had been made according to the intelligence picture as I had been able to assemble it. We knew that war was over the horizon—both literally and figuratively. But just how close it was we were never told. What we did know was that the main thrust of the Japanese offensive was going to be directed at Malaya, Thailand, or the Philippines—territories five thousand miles away. Just as Washington was to be mesmerized by the nest of vipers believed to be about to uncoil across the South China Sea toward the Philippines, our attention at Pacific Fleet headquarters was focused on the rattlesnake nearest to Pearl Harbor: the probability that a hostile task force was preparing to strike at us from Kwajalein—less than two thousand miles to the southwest.

We were unaware of the danger that was approaching us from the north. That Washington's collective back remained turned was, in hindsight, an appalling testament of mortal stupidity, shortsightedness, and plain bad luck.

*   *   *

The seeds of the disaster that was about to occur had been sown as Admiral Richardson had predicted the year before, when our foreign policy was allowed to dictate military strategy. This situation had resulted in a disastrous deterrent posture. Our bluff was called when the failure of Tokyo's diplomatic efforts to restore its flow of oil made a preemptive strike an attractive option as a way to save Japan's face. Myopically unaware of the magnitude of its strategic miscalculation, Washington had blundered by failing to keep the fleet adequately informed during the rush of diplomacy. The result was that neither they, nor we, were aware of the extent to which the principal instrument of our power in the Pacific had now become the target for attack.

The stage was set for the attack on Pearl Harbor by 1 December. The final six days were in effect little more than a remorseless countdown to disaster.

22

Countdown to War

1 DECEMBER   *"It May Be Worse Next Week"*

Kido Butai

A RADIO SIGNAL from Tokyo naval headquarters had alerted Admiral Nagumo's *Kido Butai* the previous evening that "AMERICA HAD SUDDENLY CHANGED ITS ATTITUDE ON 26TH AND BECAME ABRUPTLY UNBENDING." A rupture of diplomatic negotiations was therefore inevitable.[1]

After learning of this report, staff officer Fujita in cruiser *Tone* declared in his diary his relief that "the opening of hostilities was inevitable" because they "could now devote themselves to the operation without any anxiety."[2]

Ohnishi noted in his diary after seas moderated enough to permit refueling under cloudy skies that "a divine grace is bestowed on us." The only snag so far was that one of the scouting submarines had developed bearing trouble and had dropped behind during the night. The loss of one of the three scouts required all watchkeepers to increase their vigilance. Binoculars were locked on the gray horizon ahead for any sign of the Soviet freighter that all lookouts had been warned to expect on an intersecting course.

In the small hours they had sailed over the dark ocean's invisible 180-degree line of longitude into the western hemisphere.

"This force has now entered the supposed zone of air searches from Kiska and Midway," Nagumo signaled by blinker lights. The gods were evidently smiling on the *Kido Butai* because southerly winds and calm seas facilitated refueling.[3] Just over seventeen hundred miles to the southeast lay a still unsuspecting Pearl Harbor.

236

Staff officer Fujita's optimism was rising: "The radio signal for the beginning of hostilities has been received, Hawaii intelligence has begun to arrive, and now everything is going as hoped for."[4]

Pearl Harbor

Intelligence about Japanese war preparations reinforced our view at Pacific Fleet headquarters that some assault was imminent on the other side of the Pacific.

Our belief was supported by a relay from Station Cast—the second piece of diplomatic Magic we had received within a week—of the decrypt of a Purple message of 29 November from Japan's Bangkok embassy: "Absolutely reliable agent in Bangkok reports that on 29th conferences were in progress considering plans to force the British to attack Thai at Padang Base near Singora as countermove to Japanese landing at Kota Bharu."[5]

Such clear indications of the imminence of hostilities increased my apprehension as to how Kimmel would react to the lack of information about the Japanese carrier dispositions in my location sheet. So I called Rochefort first thing on Monday to see if anything had come in overnight.

I was concerned to hear that all the Japanese service call signs afloat had changed promptly at midnight. Now we understood why they had been retransmitting so much old traffic in the preceding days; it had been a cover for the switch.

The portents were ominous: First, we had detected their naval exercises in the middle of November; second, we had tracked the formations of the large task forces being formed; third, the call signs had changed again. It all added up to the launching of offensive operations in the very near future.

Traffic analysis indicated that many of the Combined Fleet units were changing their locations. Joe told me to expect more alterations. He suggested I postpone my disposition report one more day so that it would reflect the latest information. I called Kimmel's aide and asked him to inform the admiral that the information he wanted that morning was changing all the time and that my report would be much more meaningful if he could allow me one more day.

The reply was affirmative. I called Joe and told him I would work on it all night if necessary. But he had to get me his latest report first thing in the morning so that I could review my disposition chart before presenting it to the admiral.

As soon as I had Rochefort's latest intelligence summary, I went to see Admiral Kimmel. He shared my concern when he read Joe's assessment: "The fact that service calls lasted only one month indicates an additional progressive step preparing for active operations on a large scale." I witnessed Kimmel's obvious concern. He underlined that sentence as he read it.

The tenseness was also apparent when he noted "No change" in the section dealing with Japan's carriers. He shared my concern that they would be the most dangerous element of a striking force that might already be assembling in the Marshalls for an offensive move against Pearl Harbor. Our concern would have been far greater had we received the intelligence contained in another intercept that had also been broken by army cryptanalysts from a Purple message sent from Tokyo to Berlin only twenty-four hours earlier. It clearly pointed to Japan's being on the brink of war. Its significance could not have been overlooked in the navy and war departments, but it was not considered necessary to inform the Pacific Fleet.

Washington

"Say *very secretly* to them that *there is extreme danger that war may break out* between the Anglo-Saxon nations and Japan through some clash of arms, add that the *time of this war may come quicker than anyone dreams* [emphasis added]," was how Baron Hiroshi Oshima, Japan's ambassador in Berlin, was instructed to present the situation to the Nazi government. He was to reassure the fuehrer that "*by our present moves southward* we do not mean to relax our pressure against the Soviet [Union] and that if Russia joins hands tighter with England and the United States resists us, we are ready to turn upon her with all our might [emphasis added]."[6]

Any doubt remaining in Washington about what Tokyo was about to ought to have been dispelled that Monday by that decrypted message. It had been sent that day to Nomura and Kurusu, and it was broken within hours of its interception by the navy. Nomura and Kurusu had been alerted that the deadline for negotiations had come and gone, yet "*to prevent the United States from becoming unduly suspicious* we have been advising the press and others that though there are some wide differences between Japan and the United States, the negotiations are continuing. The above for your information only [emphasis added]."[7]

The two envoys were told to "make the necessary representations" as a cover for Tokyo's withholding of a response to the United States' rebuff of the *modus vivendi* the previous Wednesday. They dutifully did so at a meeting that day with the secretary of state at which Hull took a firm line and reminded them that the American government was not "going to go into partnership" with Japan's military leaders.[8]

On their return to the Japanese embassy they found a circular cable advising that their "officers in London, Hongkong, Singapore, and Manila have been instructed to abandon the use of the code machines and to dispose of them." The Washington embassy's code machines were to remain intact for the time being. Nomura was advised that when he "faced the necessity of destroying codes," he should contact the naval attaché who had the appropriate chemicals "on hand for this purpose."[9]

A proper intelligence evaluation of these messages would have indicated that Japan's diplomats were being instructed to play for time while Japanese military forces were being deployed for an attack on the United States. But this conclusion does not appear to have been drawn. The decrypt of Nomura's reply was not sent to Admiral Kimmel.

Captain McCollum, however, had already become concerned that Japan was lurching toward hostilities. That Monday morning he had put the finishing touches to his three-page résumé of the outstanding military and political moves made by Japan during the past two months. It summarized all available intelligence about Japan's war preparations. The head of naval intelligence's Far East section reviewed the memorandum with Admiral Wilkinson. Then McCollum accompanied DNI to CNO's office where Ingersoll and Turner were also present, along with Admiral Noyes and Rear Admiral R. M. Brainard, director of ships movements division.

McCollum briefed the admirals from his report, which listed the southward movement since mid-November of Japanese transports carrying veteran troops from northern China to Formosa, Hainan, Haiphong, and Shanghai. These ports were "reported crowded with Japanese transports unloading supplies and men."[10] McCollum drew the attention of those gathered in Stark's office to Japan's recent docking of warships and the requisitioning of merchantmen, the air reinforcement of the mandates, and the air and submarine surveillance of Guam. As additional evidence of the direction and scale of Japan's intended operations, he pointed to the size of the two large naval task groups under the command of the Second Fleet whose CinC "expects to be in Southern Formosa by 3 or 4 December."

McCollum pulled no punches in underlining that Japanese war preparations were nearing completion. Magic had revealed that their consular officials in the Philippines, and in British and Dutch territories, were being evacuated. So were Japanese diplomats and citizens in the United States and Canada. They had been instructed to apply for berths in steamers that were being sent to the west coast to collect them.

The intelligence and espionage section headed by Taro Terasaki in the Washington embassy had also been ordered to pack up in preparation for transfer to Rio de Janeiro, where the government was sympathetic to the Axis. Other Purple traffic had revealed that sabotage agents had been infiltrated into Singapore. The Bangkok embassy had been turned into an undercover military nerve center. And Japan's consul general in Shanghai had "informed his government that all preparations are complete for taking over the physical property in China belonging to the British, American and other enemy nationals."[11]

McCollum knew that he was sticking his neck out by asking whether or not the fleets in the Pacific had been "adequately alerted." But he did so, he later recalled, because he had decided that "war or a rupture of diplomatic relations was imminent." Stark and Turner, he said, both gave him "categorical assurance" that "dispatches fully alerting the fleets and placing them on a war basis" had been sent.[12] This came as a surprise to the head of the Far East section. It was the first he had heard about it. The whole point of McCollum's drawing up his memorandum was to convince the director of war plans that it was high time that war warnings were sent out to the Pacific commands.

After this meeting Stark went to the White House. At Hull's urging, Roosevelt had cut short his brief Thanksgiving break at his Georgia retreat at Warm Springs. The presidential train pulled into the Washington freight yard shortly after eleven that morning. The secretary of state spent an hour discussing the worsening situation.

Magic had revealed a plot by Tokyo to trick the British into making a preemptive occupation of Thailand's territory on the Isthmus of Kra to clear the way for the impending Japanese invasion of Malaya. And Roosevelt was concerned about the commitment he had made to Churchill if the Congress should react negatively to a presidential call for declaring war on Japan before American territory had been attacked. That problems were mounting for Roosevelt was evidenced by his telling Treasury Secretary Morgenthau, who telephoned after his meeting with Stark, to go ahead and float $1.5-billion worth of government financing that Thursday, because "it may be worse next week." The president "could not guarantee anything" and insisted, "It is all in the laps of the gods."[13]

Just how much was "in the laps of the gods" was precisely what the British ambassador wanted to ascertain when he arrived a few minutes later for a working luncheon. The foreign office had instructed Lord Halifax to "ask for an urgent expression" of American views in the event that Thailand was occupied and Malaya invaded.

"You will realize," Lord Halifax was reminded by the 29 November cable, "how important it is to ensure ourselves of American support in the event of hostilities." Churchill had also sent a "Former Naval Person" telegram the previous day expressing his fears about the worsening situation. It was intended to prod Roosevelt to issue an ultimatum to Tokyo: "I beg you to consider whether, at the moment you judge right, which may be very near, you should not say that any further Japanese aggression would compel you to place the gravest issues before Congress."[14]

Roosevelt wanted to delay placing "the gravest issues" before a divided House and Senate. So he told Halifax that he wanted Tokyo's reaction to his formal question about the troop transports heading south from Shanghai before issuing any joint declaration with Britain. The president did, however, discuss the possibility of using the B-17 bombers in the Philippines, in conjunction with Anglo-American naval forces, for a long-distance blockade, "which of course means shooting." But Halifax could report only that Roosevelt, "in an aside," had said "that in the event of an attack on ourselves or the Dutch, we should obviously be all in it together."[15]

A presidential "aside" over the lunch table fell far short of the un-qualified guarantee that Churchill and his ambassador were seeking. As Halifax conveyed it to London, Roosevelt was still far from unequivocal when he stated that Britain "could certainly count on [U.S.] support, though it might take a short time, a few days, to get things into political shape here."[16]

Getting "things into political shape" was interpreted, correctly, as a euphemism for Roosevelt's still having to do some fancy footwork on Capitol Hill in the event that Japan did not fire her first shots simultaneously at the Stars and Stripes when she opened up on the Union Jack. The president sent word to the secretary of state to coordinate with Stimson and Knox on the preparation of a message that would secure congressional backing. This might prove necessary for American involvement should the first Japanese salvos explode on United States territory or ships.

The president retired at eleven that evening of 1 December, unaware that while he slept, his political and military dilemma was about to be resolved for him in Tokyo.

2 DECEMBER   *"Now We Have Come This Far, Will We Succeed?"*

Tokyo

As midnight struck in Washington, it was two in the afternoon of 1 December in Japan. This was the hour appointed for the emperor to ascend the dais in room 1 east of the imperial palace where Prime Minister Tojo was to explain how every effort to bring about "an adjustment in relations with the United States" had failed. The objectives of Japan's national policy made it necessary to go to war. Regrettable though this was, Tojo claimed, the nation was united to the death to break through the crisis. For another two hours wooden rhetoric supporting the prime minister was spoken by the senior members of the cabinet and the service chiefs. This time there was no interruption by the throne. Privy Council president Baron Yoshimichi Hara, speaking for the impassive emperor, accepted the fact that "the proposal before us cannot be avoided in the light of present circumstances."[17]

"At this moment our empire stands at the threshold of glory or oblivion," Tojo declared before adjourning the historic imperial conference with an expression of his "resolve that the nation will go on to victory, make an all-out effort to achieve our war aims, and set his majesty's mind at ease.[18]

Imperial general headquarters was a beehive of activity that evening. Alarming news had been received that a transport plane had crashed that afternoon in Nationalist-held territory in Kwantung province in China. On board was a major who had been carrying the secret war order to the Twenty-third Army headquarters in Canton. If his papers were discovered by Chiang Kai-shek's soldiers, and then relayed to London or to Washington, the British and Americans might launch a preemptive attack on Japan.

With a fatalism characteristic of the Orient, the warlords of Tokyo decided it was too late to do anything except "close one's eyes and pray to the Gods."[19] Next morning the army and navy chiefs went to the palace to formally request the emperor's approval for a war order in his name confirming that X-day was to be 8 December. On that night a full moon would illuminate the intended attack zones from midnight to sunrise.

Imperial authorization was granted. That afternoon, the powerful transmitters of the Tokyo signals unit Station 1 flashed out simultaneously on four different wavelengths the code-message: NIITAKA YAMA NOBORE 1208.

The prearranged signal, which meant "Climb Mount Niitaka on the eighth day of the twelfth month," was picked up by the U.S. Navy's tall antennas on Bainbridge Island in Puget Sound. Precisely how much of the JN-25 message was decrypted that Tuesday is still unclear. But its significance was fully appreciated later by a navy translator in 1945, "This was undoubtedly the prearranged signal for specifying the date for the opening of hostilities. However the significance of the phrase is interesting in that it is so appropriately used in this connection. Niitaka-yama is the highest mountain in the Japanese empire."[20]

Kido Butai

"I have accepted an awesome assignment; with stronger will I might have refused it," Admiral Nagumo confided to his aide. "Now we have come this far, will we succeed?"[21] The chances that they would succeed were looking better every day. They had received a radio message from Tokyo the previous evening that repeated the Honolulu consulate's Friday report on the disposition of the fleet at Pearl Harbor:

Two battleships (OKLAHOMA, NEVADA), 1 aircraft carrier (ENTER-PRISE), 2 heavy cruisers, 12 destroyers sailed. The force that had departed on 22 November returned to port. Ships at anchor Pearl Harbor p.m. 28 November were 6 battleships (2 MARYLAND class, 2 CALIFORNIA class, 2 PENNSYLVANIA class), 1 aircraft carrier (LEX-INGTON), 9 heavy cruisers (5 SAN FRANCISCO class, 3 CHICAGO class, 1 SALT LAKE class), 5 light cruisers (4 HONOLULU class, 1 OMAHA class)

"I pray that the American fleet remains thus on X-day," Fujita noted in his diary.[22]

Pearl Harbor

While Admiral Nagumo was getting up-to-the-minute information on our movements, Admiral Kimmel was getting no intelligence about the Japanese carriers.

"Almost a complete lack of information on the carriers today," Rochefort reported. "Since over 200 service calls have been partially identified since the 1st of December and not one call has been recalled, it is evident that carrier traffic is at a low ebb."[23]

Even as I was reviewing my revised disposition report that morning, Joe called in new changes. I made the alterations and additions in pencil, but there was still no hard information on the two carrier divisions we believed were still in Japan. There was no traffic—or traffic analysis—to or from these carriers or their commanders. Nor were these divisions information addressees of any messages, with the exception of the supply-type signal to *Akagi* two days earlier. Before taking the location sheet to the admiral, I called Joe once again. He confirmed there had not been any direct information on carriers for a long time; therefore he couldn't give them a precise disposition, but the majority opinion of his analysts was that they were still in home waters. So I wrote down, "Unknown—home waters?"

The admiral read my report very carefully. It did not escape his eagle eye that I had left out most of their carriers from my location sheet. His concern became very vocal.

"What! You don't know where the carriers are?"

I explained that I had omitted them because neither carrier Division 1 nor 2 had been identified as an originator or addressee in recent radio traffic.

"Well, where do you estimate they are?"

I explained that there was no recent or good indication of their loca-tions, but that if I had to guess, I would put them in "home waters," probably in the vicinity of the Kure naval base. I admitted that the presumption that they were in "home waters" was based on no hard evidence, but was an estimate deriving from past observations.

"Then you don't really know where Carrier Division One and Carrier Division Two are?"

"No, sir, I do not. I think they are in home waters, but I do not *know* for sure where they are. But I feel pretty confident of the location of the rest of the units."

The admiral then looked at me, as sometimes he would, with a stern countenance and an icy twinkle in his penetrating blue eyes.

"Do you mean to say they could be rounding Diamond Head and you wouldn't know it?"

"I hope they would have been spotted before now," I replied weakly.

Admiral Kimmel was often sharply ironic when he wanted to drive home a point. This exchange, which I recalled during my testimony at the various Pearl Harbor inquiries, was to attract unfortunate accusations of levity on the admiral's part by hostile examiners. But at the time it left me painfully aware that my commanding officer was extremely concerned about this serious gap in my report.

If the continued silence of the carriers created a gaping hole in our intelligence estimate, there was plenty of traffic intercepted from the Second Fleet's tactical circuits. This enabled me to tell Kimmel with some confidence that a large part of the Second and Third fleet units was probably already under way in the China Sea. Since one carrier division was also definitely southbound, and another appeared to be associated with signals exchanged with Tokyo, I estimated, wrongly, that the third carrier division must also be accompanying the fourth division south.

Had Hypo been able to read the Japanese diplomatic traffic and see how closely the local consulate was reporting the fleet dispositions in Pearl Harbor, our estimates would have been different. That Tuesday Rochefort received a hand-delivered envelope marked SECRET from Captain Mayfield's district intelligence office in Honolulu. It enclosed a note from his assistant, Lieutenant Yale Maxon, advising that the office had available "through a very confidential source known to you, rechecks on cables received from time to time by the principal Orange establishment."[24]

Mayfield's cryptic allusion was to the manager of the local RCA cable office who began turning over copies of the consulate cables after he had been ordered to do so by David Sarnoff, the head of RCA. Sarnoff had paid a November visit to Honolulu during which Mayfield had managed to persuade him that it was in the national interest that the navy obtain access to the Japanese consul's communications.[25]

Had Rochefort received notice from Washington of the so-called bomb plot messages with their grid system for reporting the ships moored in Pearl Harbor in October, he would certainly have been alerted to the importance of monitoring the consulate traffic. But Washington had never sent us the bomb plot messages, and had specifically instructed Hypo to concentrate on naval matters.

The basic keys for unlocking the J-19 code were available to Rochefort's unit, but Hypo had not been keeping up with the traffic and did not have the current cipher, because all the intercepted messages had been previously forwarded to Washington. There was also only one member of Joe's outfit with any previous experience in breaking the consular systems,[26] so the offer from Mayfield was not immediately accepted.

The very same day, however, the Japanese consulate was ordered to burn its J-19 code manuals and resort to the PA-K2 code, which was a much simpler system. Then, as chance would have it on the next day, the first cables decrypted were routine consular housekeeping traffic sent in PA-K2, but before the J-19 code had been abandoned.[27] So the first messages to be broken were of "absolutely no value." As a result, the RCA cables were given a low priority in Hypo.

Rochefort's unwitting neglect of a source of potentially valuable intelligence in the final days before the Japanese attack was typical of the comedy of errors that bedeviled our operations. Another was the chance discovery that deprived us of the DIO's "direct line" into the nerve center of Japan's local espionage operation. A lineman of the Mutual Telephone Company of Hawaii making a routine check of the poles outside 1742 Nuuanu Avenue uncovered the two wiretaps, and this was reported to the FBI—who were also independently monitoring the consul's lines.

The DIO was immediately alerted by the FBI. Captain Mayfield's annoyance at the failure of the FBI to inform him that they were eavesdropping on the Japanese was exceeded by his concern that the discovery might trigger an international incident for which the navy would be blamed. Orders were issued to stop the operation immediately. Warrant Officer Ted Emmanuel offered to resign from the navy in order to continue listening in. But at 1600 he had to pull the plugs and "bade adieu to my friend of 22 months' standing."[28]

Actions that Japan might consider hostile also preoccupied Admiral Kimmel. "You will note that I have issued orders to the Pacific Fleet to depth bomb all submarine contacts in the Oahu operating area," he informed Stark in a postscript to a long letter that detailed the steps he had taken to reinforce the outlying islands.[29] After a morning conference with General Short to discuss the construction of army airfields in Fiji and New Caledonia, the admiral was worried that his resources were being stretched too thin.

"Too much diversion of effort for defense will leave us an inadequate force with which to take the offensive," Kimmel warned Stark.[30] The fleet's cruisers were now deployed on convoy duties, and his concluding postscript was a harbinger of disasters to come: "I realize of course that the demands for transpacific escorts may decrease if it becomes impossible to route ships to Manila, but it will still be necessary to supply the Asiatic fleet and our allies in the Far East."[31]

Washington

The problem of how to ensure that Congress would accept the British and Dutch as allies if Japan did not attack the United States continued to nag Roosevelt. The president and his war council dared not risk revealing the extent of the military commitments already made by the Joint Board. So Roosevelt began to plan a speech that would be an appeal for congressional support to warn Japan that offensive operations against British or Dutch territories would be considered a threat to the vital interests of the United States.

The drafting of this critical address began after that morning's White House conference. The secretaries of the navy and war had discussed the latest intelligence report that a Japanese expeditionary force was landing troops near Saigon. Stimson regarded the news as providing "a little respite."[32] Under Secretary of State Sumner Welles, acting as deputy for an indisposed Hull, was directed to send a stiff note to Tokyo demanding an explanation for the "very rapid and material increase" that "would seem to imply the utilization of these forces by Japan for the purposes of further aggression."[33]

Roosevelt knew that more Japanese aggression in Indochina would not win votes for his intended plea to Congress. A public opinion survey taken that week showed that while 69 percent of the nation was willing to risk war to halt Japanese aggression, only 51 percent believed that this would involve hostilities.[34] An assault on American territory or ships was needed to fire up public and congressional outrage.

There was no doubt that Japan must be targeting the Philippines. But Tokyo had shown a preference for step-by-step aggression and might be planning to grab British territory as an opening move that would not rouse the United States. To guard against this eventuality, that afternoon Roosevelt took the extraordinary step of ordering the navy to provide a series of lures for the Japanese tiger.

"The president directs that the following be done as soon as possible and within two days."[35] That was how Stark began one of the strangest orders a chief of naval operations had ever dispatched. His wording was evidently intended to leave Admiral Hart, commander of the Asiatic Fleet in Manila, with no doubt as to the origins of the madcap operation that he was being ordered to arrange.

Charter three small vessels to [sic] for quote defensive information patrol unquote. Minimum requirements to establish identity as United States men of war are commanded by a naval officer and to mount a small machine gun would suffice. Filipino crews may be employed with minimum number of naval ratings to accomplish purpose which is to observe and report by radio Japanese movements in West China Sea and Gulf of Siam.[36]

By quoting Roosevelt's term "defensive information patrol," Stark was disassociating himself from a mission that he knew was foolhardy and unjustified from a military standpoint. In any case, three days earlier, Stark had obtained presidential approval for ordering Admiral Hart to send out aerial reconnaissance to check on the southward movement of the Japanese expeditionary force: "For security of our position in the Philippines desire you cover by air the line Manila-Camranh Bay on three days commencing receipt of this dispatch."[37]

A copy of this dispatch had been sent to Kimmel for information. But Kimmel was not included as an addressee for the dispatch about the "defensive information patrol" by three small vessels. Nor was he made privy to the one that followed it only minutes later that advised Hart that "it is very important that you exchange full military information with the British and Dutch naval commanders-in-chief except in cases where you consider it definitely inadvisable."[38]

The omission of Kimmel from these two signals was another indication of the extent to which Washington kept us in the dark. Understandably, Stark might have been reluctant to let Kimmel in on Hart's "fish bait" operation, whose purpose was apparent from his orders not to risk any naval vessels.

The sacrificial nature of the operation—which required expendable vessels with Filipino crews—was the direct result of the wavering by President Manuel Luis Quezon y Molina to commit the Philippines to fight. If Filipino crewmen were to be killed as the result of Japanese military action, it was assumed that Quezon would have no choice but to support the Americans. Roosevelt's specific instructions as to where the "goats" were to be tethered—with one south of Hainan, another off the Indochina coast, and the third south of Cape Cambodia—intended to ensure that they lay directly in the path of any Japanese naval force advancing south toward Malaya. That the vessels were to sail within forty-eight hours meant that the "bait" was to be laid by Friday.

Hart's response to Roosevelt's subterfuge was less than enthusiastic. He replied that it was "improbable that [we] can start any chartered craft within two days." But since it was a presidential order, the command's steam yacht was selected as one.[39] The very idea that the sleek, two-funneled *Isabel* should be sunk like another *Panay* offended the Asiatic Fleet commander, who used his yacht for weekend cruises around Manila Bay. He informed Stark that "she is too short radius to accomplish much and since we have few fast ships her loss would be serious."[40] With a heavy heart Admiral Hart watched the *Isabel* pull away from the Cavite pierhead on the following day. He was convinced he would never see his "holiday flagship" again.

Two days later *Isabel* was twenty-two miles off the coast of Indochina when she was spotted and buzzed by Japanese patrol planes. When it was clear from her skipper's radio reports that the Japanese were not going to take the bait and attack, Hart recalled her. Meanwhile, at the Cavite naval base two chartered schooners, *Molly Moore* and *Lanikai,* were being readied for their mission with a cannon, World War I machine guns, and a radio set that could receive but not transmit.

Lanikai's skipper was Lieutenant Kemp Tolley, an eager young officer, but neither he nor the Filipino volunteers who had jumped at the chance to don navy uniforms would have been so enthusiastic if they had realized that they were to become fish bait. However, because neither schooner was ready to sail until the morning that war broke out, Kemp Tolley survived.[41]

London

Churchill was unaware of Roosevelt's scheme. The British cabinet's Defense Committee met that afternoon to consider Halifax's report. Evidently, the American president's unofficial assurance that, in the event of an attack upon the British or Dutch, "we should obviously be all in it together" was not a sufficient guarantee of support for the British to issue ironclad commitments to Thailand or the Dutch. Although Roosevelt had told the ambassador that such commitments would have his full support, Churchill needed to be "quite sure of the American attitude."[42]

Lord Halifax was instructed, in effect, to pin the president down by asking if "we would have the armed support of the United States if our action resulted in hostilities with Japan" before the British gave guarantees to the Thai prime minister that they would intervene to prevent the Japanese task force's reaching the Isthmus of Kra to invade Thailand. Until Roosevelt had provided such assurances, Churchill advised the foreign secretary that "settled policy" was "not to take forward action in advance of the United States."[43] This left the suave Anthony Eden with the difficult task of explaining to the Royal Netherlands government in exile that their forces in the Dutch East Indies might have to play the role of fall guy to a Japanese attack.

If only Dutch territory was attacked, the prime minister's memorandum stated, "we should do nothing to prevent the full impact of this Japanese aggression presenting itself to the United States." The Netherlands foreign minister was to be reassured that if the Americans declared war on Japan, "we will follow within the hour." Moreover, if "after a reasonable interval, the United States is found to be incapable of any decisive action, even with our immediate support we will nevertheless, although alone, make common cause with the Dutch."[44]

3 DECEMBER   *"Scary Reports"*

Tokyo

Premier Tojo's cabinet agreed that Foreign Minister Togo's final reply to the United States would be delivered *prior* to the launching of military operations. This was in response to repeated cautions from the emperor that Japan had signed the Hague Convention and must adhere to Article I, which required that "hostilities . . . must not commence without an explicit warning, in the form of either a reasoned declaration of war or of an ultimatum with conditional declaration of war."[45] But the fourteen-part message, whose wording was approved at the next day's liaison conference, made no such specific declaration. Foreign Minister Togo, however, believed it "clearly signified a cessation of peace."

Kido Butai

Some fifteen hundred miles northeast of its objective, Nagumo's striking force had run into the first really big storm since leaving Tankan Bay. A petty officer was washed overboard from carrier *Kaga*; heavy seas ruled out any refueling throughout the day. Nagumo, however, could take some comfort from the fact that the thick weather would also thwart any American air patrols flying south from the Aleutians.

The chances that the *Kido Butai*'s mission would be discovered through interception of any of the signals that were being addressed to it by Tokyo were greatly decreased that day. At midnight the Japanese navy switched over to the new number 8 additive book of random five-digit number groups for its JN-25 fleet code. It is still not clear how much of the system the Washington or British code breakers were able to read even prior to the changeover. But it is possible that OP-20-G had an inkling of the change, since we had intercepted a signal from the navy ministry forty-eight hours earlier directing, "Starting 4 December 1941 additive system #8 of Naval Code D will be used, and additive system #7 will be discontinued."[47]

Pearl Harbor

Once again during my morning briefing I had to inform Admiral Kimmel that we still had no information on the carriers. The extensive use of alternate call signs by the Japanese was taxing the efforts of Hypo's cryptanalysts. There was also activity on the Fourth Fleet circuits in the Marshalls, and Rochefort had a hunch that the Second and Third fleets were already under way. But he did not have any radio intelligence to verify it.

I was in my office that Wednesday afternoon when Kimmel sent for me again. He showed me an Opnav dispatch sent to the Asiatic Fleet and addressed to him for information. This was only the third Magic decrypt that we had received since July. It was an instruction from Tokyo ordering the legations at London, Hong Kong, Singapore, and Manila "to destroy Purple machine." It also advised us that the previous day "Washington also directed destroy Purple."[48]

What was a Purple, the admiral asked? I told him that I didn't know. But after leaving Kimmel, I approached Lieutenant Herbert M. Coleman, the fleet security officer. He had recently come from Washington and was able to tell me that Purple was a Japanese electrical coding machine. I then informed the admiral that the Japanese destruction of their code machines must indicate they were preparing for any or all eventualities. But since most of the embassies, with the exception of London and Washington, were in the Far East, we believed the Magic decrypt was further evidence that Japan was preparing to launch operations in this area. This was confirmed by receipt of another dispatch from Washington quoting "highly reliable information" that the same Japanese outposts had been ordered "to destroy most of their codes and ciphers at once and to burn all other important confidential and secret documents."[49]

The Honolulu consulate was not mentioned. And we did not know if it had one of the Purple machines; but it was not until the next day that I received word from Rochefort that the local Japanese diplomats were also burning their codes. That news was relayed by Captain Mayfield from the FBI who had picked up confirmation on the telephone line they were still tapping to the consulate's kitchens.

When Rochefort called me with the news, I said, "That fits the picture that the Japanese are preparing for something by destroying their codes."[50] I at once gave the information to the admiral. Later, Kimmel was to be accused, unjustly in my view, of failing to let General Short know about the first message about destroying the Purple machines during their Wednesday afternoon conference. But Kimmel was abiding by the strict regulations governing dissemination of radio intelligence and, moreover, was unaware that the army had not informed Short about Purple, either. Anyway, the Purple information did not appear to be "vitally important" because it was not until the *next day* that Kimmel got news of the code burning in the local consulate.[51]

Furthermore, at least two of Short's staff did have the intelligence almost as soon as we did. Rochefort had informed his opposite number in the army that the Japanese were destroying important papers and code books, not only in Honolulu, but everywhere else.[52] I also communicated the same information to Colonel Edward W. Raley at Fort Shafter, although I was careful not to mention the Purple machine to him because this would have meant breaking our strict security regulations.

If both the navy and army commands, in addition to fleet headquarters, failed to make the correct deductions about the code burning, it was because we were becoming immune to what Kimmel called "scary reports."[53] At the time, there were no other clues that Oahu was in danger and the mere fact that there was a bonfire of papers in the embassy was not enough by itself to trigger our apprehension.

Washington

By sending us snippets of Magic out of context, the navy department had overlooked one of the cardinal rules of intelligence: A local commander can only react to information in the context of his immediate situation. Washington had the advantage of construing Tokyo's order to destroy the Purple machine in the broader framework. Stark believed that the message was "one of the most important dispatches we ever sent. We felt that war was a matter of time."[54]

Admiral Ingersoll went so far as to claim that the inclusion of the Japanese Washington embassy in Tokyo's signal clearly indicated that "the first aggressive Japanese move would include us and this was only to emphasize all of the previous dispatches that war with Japan was imminent."[55] Turner was to testify he believed there would be "war within two or three days," because, "the destruction of codes in that manner and in those places in my mind and experience is a sure indication of war with those nations in whose capitals or other places those codes are destroyed."[56]

Yet despite Turner's claim to omniscient farsightedness, the items about Magic reached us as the result of extraordinary circumstances rather than as the result of careful thought on the part of war plans division. McCollum was responsible for drafting the message about "highly reliable information."[57] The wording had been necessarily cautious in order for the director of naval intelligence to be able to issue it on his own authority without risking Turner's wrath.

"We could only send information out, without the approval of War Plans, if it contained nothing but pure facts," Wilkinson was later to explain. "We were prohibited from saying 'Invite your attention that this is a prelude to war.' We could not say that, but we could state a fact. This is what we did."[58]

I later found out that it had been Captain Safford, himself, who was responsible for the dispatch that mentioned Purple. After seeing the original decrypt he realized the importance of the order to destroy the codes. He telephoned McCollum to know what ONI was doing "to get a warning out to the Pacific Fleet."[59]

When Safford sensed from McCollum's tone that the Far East section desk might have difficulty sidestepping Turner, he decided to have a go himself even though it meant that he risked "overstepping the bounds." By drafting his own message, and by incorporating a reference not only to Purple but also giving the Japanese circular number, Safford flouted all the rules of security. He later testified that he had couched the dispatch "in highly technical language" because he knew that Coleman was the one officer at Pearl Harbor who would know its real importance.[60]

Tragically for us, the risks that Safford ran in exposing the extent of our code breaking were to no avail. The true importance of his dispatch was lost on Pacific Fleet headquarters because neither Kimmel nor I had any proper appreciation of the diplomatic intelligence picture.

It was a miscalculation that was compounded by Turner's assumption that Kimmel did know all about Magic. Any further war warnings were unnecessary. "The fact that this was going out in this manner" he considered was "all that was necessary to insure that the commanders-in-chief and the commandants of the fourteenth [Pearl Harbor] and sixteenth [Manila] naval districts thoroughly understood the urgency of the situation."[61]

That understanding, which the navy department and many historians have failed to appreciate, was dependent on the perspective that Washington received because of its daily access to Magic. Admiral Kimmel had been denied this essential knowledge. Meanwhile, the Sixteenth Naval District at Manila had an operating Purple machine. As I have said before, context is an essential factor in transforming information into intelligence.

For those who were eavesdropping on Tokyo's secret communications on a daily basis—such as the naval aide in the White House—it was obvious that the code-destruct decrypt was a sign that war was "going to break out," and that we were "going to be attacked."[62]

"Mr. President, this is a very significant dispatch," was how Captain John R. Beardall, Jr., recalled drawing Roosevelt's attention to these particular messages.

"When do you think it is going to happen?" Beardall inquired after Roosevelt had read the translation.

"Most any time," the president replied.[63]

The indications in Magic that war was looming a matter of days, or even hours, away brought the British ambassador back to the White House shortly after seven that evening. Halifax was under direct instruction from London to nail the president down once and for all on what American support Britain could count on if Japan attacked. Roosevelt finally assured the ambassador, in the presence of Under Secretary of State Sumner Welles, that he really did mean "armed support."

The president evidently felt more comfortable in giving such an unequivocal commitment because of his belief that three small vessels flying

the Stars and Stripes were heading for a collision with the Japanese invasion forces. If this was so, no mention was made to the British ambassador. But Roosevelt did hint that the latest intelligence showed that the
Japanese were heading for the Dutch East Indies and that "action of this
kind would prove more easy of presentation to United States public opinion on the ground of threat to the Philippines by encirclement."[64]

That afternoon the secretary of the treasury had found Roosevelt
buoyed up.

"I think the Japanese are doing everything they can to stall until they
are ready," Roosevelt said. He also advised Morgenthau that he was
"talking with the English about war plans." He was convinced that "the
Japanese were running around like a lot of wet hens" after his formal
inquiry about the increase in their Indochina forces.[65]

The president's speculation about Japan's confusion was probably the
result of an earlier visit from an acquaintance of his, a minister named
Dr. E. Stanley Jones. Like the Maryknoll fathers, the Reverend Dr.
Jones was another cleric trying to bridge the widening chasm between
Washington and Tokyo. Jones had arrived that morning at the White
House, an unlikely emissary of the Japanese embassy. He brought with
him a letter that urged Roosevelt to revive the *modus vivendi* in an ap-
peal directly to the emperor over the head of Prime Minister Tojo.

The plea had originated from special envoy Kurusu, but the letter was
drafted by Hidenari Terasaki. The involvement of the Japanese embassy's
second secretary gave Roosevelt grounds for suspicion. Terasaki and his
American wife were under FBI surveillance as the known heads of
Japan's espionage operations in the United States. Roosevelt nonetheless
told Jones that he was considering the appeal and Jones should tell
Terasaki that "his secret is safe."[66]

4 DECEMBER   *"War Within Forty-eight Hours"*

Tokyo

Roosevelt may have assumed that confusion reigned in Tokyo, but the
only "wet hens" were in the European section of the foreign ministry.
For four days they had been awaiting word from the ambassador in
Berlin that Hitler would accept a reinterpretation of the tripartite pact
that would commit Germany to war providing Japan was the aggressor
rather than the victim.

"Delay regrettable, but unavoidable," Ambassador Hiroshi Oshima
had cabled the previous afternoon. Article 3 of the tripartite pact required the partners to come to each other's mutual aid only if they were
attacked by a foreign power. Mussolini had already agreed to a modification of the article because of the "bullheadedness of the United States

and the meddlesome nature of President Roosevelt." But he did not want Italy left on a limb and he needed to "confer with Germany on this point."[67]

Hitler, however, had neither the time nor inclination to mince legal niceties with the Japanese envoy at a time of great crisis for the Third Reich. He had left Berlin for his advance headquarters to revive the "final" offensive to take Moscow. It was stalling in the snows outside the Soviet capital. His foreign minister was left to handle the politely persistent Oshima.

"As I have told you before," Ribbentrop assured the Japanese ambassador, "we cannot give an official reply until the fuehrer has given his approval."[68] He would only "assume that there will be no objections."

Ribbentrop knew better than to badger the fuehrer with Japan's request at a time that the Wehrmacht's grand strategy was running up against unexpectedly stiff Russian resistance. Hitler's answer would be a sour reminder that the fresh Red Army division blocking his advance on Moscow had been released from border duty in Siberia by Tokyo's decision to advance southward.

With or without the support of her Axis partners, Japan had already taken the decision for war. Admiral Yamamoto that morning was summoned to the imperial palace. "The task facing the Combined Fleet is of the utmost importance," the emperor told him, "and the whole fate of our nation will depend on the outcome."[69] That afternoon the troopships and escorts of the Southern Expeditionary Force sailed from the harbors of Hainan Island. Their destination was the Isthmus of Kra, from where the invasion of Malaya and Thailand was to be launched.

Kido Butai

The Japanese warships had bucketed through another night of heavy rain and stormy seas. It was, as Fujita recorded it, weather "made to order" for not being sighted. On the other side of the coin, "refuelling is impossible and the heavy rolling and pitching of the battleship makes her crew distressed and suffer."[70]

There was some consolation when Nagumo received the Honolulu consulate's Saturday report. The ships in harbor were listed precisely according to the alphabetic designators of the "bomb plot," and it also advised, "No changes to 2 December Hawaiian Time. No signs of any standby condition observed, crews going about as usual."[71]

After eight days on a straight easterly course across the North Pacific, an hour after sunrise that morning the Kido Butai reached "Point C," some one thousand miles north-northwest of the Hawaiian chain and it hauled around onto a southeasterly track to begin its approach to the islands. Akagi's signal lamp blinked out a lengthy message from Nagumo, which began:

Although the opening of hostilities is ordered for 8 December the situation in the Far East is growing increasingly urgent and it is difficult to tell when war will break out. At present we have no impression of a change in the state of alert of the enemy forces in the Hawaiian area. There is no indication that the movement of the *Kido Butai* has been detected and while it is difficult to predict the enemy intentions we shall have to be particularly vigilant.[72]

Within minutes the alert had been relayed to all the ships in the force. It was followed by the latest report of the American ships in Pearl Harbor, an update on refueling plans, and courses to be taken on the return trip after the attack. The clear reception of Hawaiian radio broadcasts not only gave the crews a taste for their prey but provided important weather data and confirmation that the islands were still ignorant of the approaching danger.

Pearl Harbor

The summary that I took to Admiral Kimmel that morning revealed that the Tokyo radio intelligence center had been busily sending out urgent reports to major commanders. We had also observed an important change in the pattern of traffic. The Takao station on Formosa had adopted Radio Tokyo's call sign and was handling fleet traffic on the high-speed circuits. According to Rochefort's "Running Hypo Chronology," which was located recently in his private papers and has never been fully explained, he believed "the large number of high-precedence messages and general distribution might indicate that the entire [Japanese] navy is being prepared for drastic action."[73]

From this evidence, and from the lack of messages originating from CinC Second Fleet, and CinC Third Fleet, we concluded that these forces must have put to sea and were observing radio silence in order not to betray their positions. They were still receiving messages but were not themselves sending. The Japanese had not found out the little trick we used of omitting the originator during operations. We taught them that later in the war after which they dutifully followed it, much to our chagrin because it made tracking an operational force observing radio silence impossible.

On Thursday evening we learned that our naval station at Guam had been ordered to "destroy all secret and confidential publications and other classified matter which is necessary for current purposes and special intelligence." They were also put on the alert to be "prepared to destroy instantly all classified matter you retain in event of emergency."[74]

In isolation this message was not judged by Kimmel as particularly ominous. Guam, which was under command of the Asiatic Fleet, was both indefensible and an anticipated Japanese target. The naval station there was part of our radio intelligence setup and had some very secret code material that Kimmel reasoned the navy department "wanted destroyed because they never should have had them."[75]

Admiral Kimmel might have been more concerned if Washington had informed him that Guam was *not* an isolated recipient of such drastic orders.

Washington

Earlier that day two dispatches similar to the one sent Guam had been sent to our naval attachés in Tokyo, Bangkok, Peiping, and Shanghai, as well as to our observers in Peiping and Tientsin. They were ordered to report the destruction of the code systems "at discretion" with the plain-language signal "Jabberwock" and the burning of confidential papers with the word "Boomerang."

The Japanese had chosen the code word "*Haruna*" as their confirmatory signal, indicating compliance with similar orders. It was the stream of *Haruna*s from their consulates and embassies that had prompted McCollum to ask Safford to draft the code-destruct dispatches for our legations in the Far East.[76]

Safford felt "officially responsible" for stripping ship, but his original strongly worded order to Guam had to be toned down by the over-cautious director of naval communications, Admiral Noyes. He was fearful that Turner might regard it as an action signal and veto its transmission. In a reference to what he termed "the war between war plans and ONI," McCollum noted that even the transmission of these dispatches "was accomplished with some difficulty."[77]

In this way Kimmel was not even made an information addressee for the orders shutting down our entire naval intelligence network in the Far East in anticipation of imminent Japanese attacks. This was a telling revelation that Washington did not regard Pearl Harbor as under any immediate threat.

There can be no doubt that by Thursday even the junior echelons of the navy department knew that war was imminent. At that morning's meeting of the Defense Communication Board, Captain Joseph Redman—Noyes's astute deputy—agreed wholeheartedly with Colonel Sadtler's prediction that "we will have war within 48 hours."[78]

Amazingly enough, it was not Japan's preparations for war but those of America that made the newspaper headlines that day. In a sensational scoop the isolationist Chicago *Tribune* revealed the details of General Marshall's "Victory Program" for committing a ten-million-man army to defeat Germany on the ground in Europe. Some cabinet members wanted the *Tribune*'s owner, Colonel Robert R. McCormick, put on trial for treason. His virulently anti-Roosevelt paper had published the army's documents, which had mysteriously been delivered to Senator Burton K. Wheeler of Montana, one of the leading champions on Capitol Hill of the isolationist cause.

The storm whipped up by the publication of the *Tribune*'s article headlined "FDR'S WAR PLANS" emphasized the magnitude of the president's dilemma. How could he confront the probability of a Japanese attack? Roosevelt reiterated the problem in a late-night meeting with the British ambassador as they discussed the issue of when to send an ultimatum to Japan. Churchill had wanted a parallel warning to include Thailand, Malaya, and the Dutch East Indies. The president, mindful of the address he was preparing for Congress, insisted he must make his declaration first.

"On account of political considerations here," Halifax reported, it was important "that this action should be based on independent necessities of the United States defense, and not appear to follow ourselves." The president also raised with the ambassador the clandestine letter he had received from Kurusu via the Reverend Dr. Jones the day before. Roosevelt felt that an appeal direct to the emperor "would strengthen his general case if things went wrong." While the president confirmed that he had indeed meant what he said about armed support extending to a British preemptive move to prevent a Japanese invasion of Thailand, the "character of this armed support must be decided by the [military] chiefs."[79] But Halifax was concerned about having to report yet again the presidential inclination to postpone the public declaration that would actually put the United States in the same boat as Britain in the Far East.

Time was running out faster than the president appreciated.

Royal Netherlands Navy submarines spotted a Japanese invasion force heading south. The Dutch overreacted when the Java command called on the Australian government to put into operation their joint part in the Rainbow 5 war plan. For twelve hours while the Australian cabinet met to discuss and defuse the situation the American military attaché held off sending the alert message to the Philippines.

5 DECEMBER *"It Could Mean One Thing"*

Tokyo

Late that evening—it was already Saturday across the international date line in Japan—the foreign ministry transmitted the pilot message that alerted their embassy in Washington to expect the final reply to the American ten-point proposal next day. The previous afternoon the vice-chief of the naval general staff, Vice Admiral Seiichi Ito, accompanied by Lieutenant General Shinichi Tanaka, the chief of the army general staff operations bureau, had called on the foreign minister to request a half-hour delay in the delivery of the fourteen-part message breaking off diplomatic relations with the United States.

Without revealing an operational secret they insisted that Togo (who did not know of the Pearl Harbor attack) ensure that their Washington embassy did not deliver the final Japanese message to the State Department until one o'clock the following afternoon in Washington.

Manila

British Admiral Sir Tom Phillips, who had arrived at Singapore forty-eight hours earlier with the *Prince of Wales,* flew in for a council of war. He met with General MacArthur and Admiral Hart to agree on a joint war strategy.

Nothing would please me better than if they would give me three months and then attack me here," MacArthur told Phillips, listing the bombers and troops already on their way across the Pacific. Until then his plan was "in the nature of an improvisation." But the general had "every confidence that we can defend this place." Echoing Churchill's defiant words that he was "going to fight on the beaches" and "fight to the destruction on the shore lines," MacArthur predicted he had "nothing to fear at all" with his 112 tanks, his 125,000-man Filipino army, and his "ace unit" of B-17 bombers.[80]

The British admiral was impressed by MacArthur's vaunted air power. Phillips agreed that Britain's Far East fleet would base itself in Manila, rather than Singapore, for offensive operations against the Japanese. "Clearly, until you have a fleet you can't do much except act on the defensive," the admiral told Hart. "And it is quite clear that to stick your head out where the enemy is with a very inferior force would be foolish."[81]

That afternoon an RAF reconnaissance patrol over the Gulf of Siam spotted a Japanese convoy steaming southwest of the tip of Indochina. The news prompted Admiral Phillips to cut short the conference and make arrangements to fly back to Singapore next day "to be there when the war starts."

Four days later Phillips was to lose his battleship—and his life—in a tragic demonstration of the truth of his words to Hart.

The British report put Manila on notice that a Japanese invasion of the Isthmus of Kra was probably only days away. That same afternoon Admiral Hart received a cable from Captain John M. Creighton, the U.S. naval observer in Singapore, quoting a signal received from London by Air Vice Marshal Brooke Popham, the British commander in chief in Malaya:

We have now received assurance of armed support in cases as follows:

(A). We are obliged to execute our plans to forestall Japs landing Isthmus of Kra or take action in reply to Nips invasion in any other part of Siam.
(B). If Dutch Indies are attacked and we go to their defense.
(C). If Japs attack us [sic] the British.

Therefore without reference to London put plan in action if first you have good info[rmation] Jap expedition advancing with the apparent intention of landing in Kra, second if Nips violate any part of Thailand.

If N[etherlands] E[ast] I[ndies] are attacked put into operation plans agreed upon between British and Dutch.[82]

The apparent guarantees of American military support were a lightning bolt from the blue to Admiral Hart. Forty-eight hours earlier he had been instructed only to "exchange full military information with the British and Dutch naval commanders."[83] This was the first he had heard of any commitment that he would have to fight even if American territory was not attacked.

The Asiatic Fleet commander shot off an urgent cable to the navy department: "Learn from Singapore we have assured British armed support under three or four eventualities. Have received no corresponding instructions from you."[84]

No official instructions were forthcoming. None had been drafted. Until the president made his appeal to Congress for an ultimatum to Japan, the only assistance the navy department knew about was an informal one.

Apparently, the British chiefs of staff in London had jumped the gun or were trying to force Roosevelt's hand. They also sent a similar message to their Middle East headquarters in Egypt. This one was responsible for the warm welcome that Colonel Bonner Fellers was to receive upon his arrival in Cairo.

"Bonner, you will be in the war in twenty-four hours," Air Marshall Sir Arthur Longmore told the American military observer the following morning. "We have a secret signal Japan will strike the U.S. in twenty-four hours." The colonel was amazed. He knew nothing about Japanese-American relations having reached the breaking point. He toyed with the idea of relaying a report to Washington, but did not send it. After thinking it over, he decided that if the British knew about the attack, we also knew about it.[85]

Admiral Hart, however, was better informed, thanks to the Purple machine and Station Cast's cryptanalysts. He had already given the orders the day before to disperse his meager fleet. The cruisers and destroyers were sent south, out of range of Japanese air attacks. The night before, Japanese planes began flying brazenly over the coast of Luzon and he had come to the conclusion that if Japan intended to launch an assault on the British and Dutch, they must simultaneously invade the Philippines.

"My own estimate was that they would not leave us on their flank," Hart was to testify. "Consequently, they would attack."[86] Unfortunately, Kimmel's headquarters was not an information addressee of Hart's signal asking Washington to confirm the guarantees of armed support that had been given the British. Admiral Kimmel had already asked the same question and received no answer.

Kido Butai

Visibility was poor, but the seas were calm that day. Nagumo's meteorologists were having difficulty accurately forecasting the changeable conditions. A leaden cloud base eased the admiral's constant worry about being spotted. Another Honolulu intelligence report, less than a day old, also gave comfort, because it revealed that the Americans were making only "occasional" long-range flights from Oahu.

This reassuring intelligence did not relax the vigilance on the warships. It had been stepped up after Combined Fleet headquarters radioed precise orders on how Nagumo was to deal with any unexpected encounters. These had been relayed by signal lamp to all the commanding officers in the force:

> 1. A warship which sights the enemy or third-nation warships or merchant ships, must recognize the need for concealing our plans and so will immediately render it incapable of signaling and if necessary will attack and sink it.

> 2. Panamanian, Norwegian and Greek ships shall be treated as hostile enemy shipping.[87]

The orders to deal ruthlessly with vessels of countries closely associated with Britain and the United States *excluded* those flying the Soviet flag. It was on this day that the *Kido Butai* finally encountered a "vessel of a third nation," as it was cryptically described by a former Japanese navy intelligence officer.[88]

"Those in command of the task force watched the progress of the ship in question, a merchantman, with an extraordinary degree of tension," Hiroyuki Agawa wrote in his definitive biography of Admiral Yamamoto. "Had it shown any signs of radioing a report on the movements of the task force to anyone else, it would probably have found itself at the bottom of the sea within a few minutes."

Significantly, perhaps, neither Volume 10 of *Senshi Sosho,* the official Japanese history, nor an enlisted man's wartime account, *Southern Cross,* which both refer to the receipt of the alert that a Soviet freighter would be encountered, makes any reference to an actual sighting. That it took a quarter of a century for the Japanese government to publicly confirm the interception is consistent with Japan's reluctance to make any official admission of events that would open new questions about the attack on Pearl Harbor.

Tokyo's instructions to Nagumo suggest that the Soviet Union was the only "third nation" that could be trusted to keep silent about sighting the *Kido Butai.* This can be the only explanation of why this ship was allowed to go on its way. There is no indication that the admiral even considered it necessary to make a precautionary boarding of the ship to remove its radio. That no crew members have ever come forward to tell the story of this remarkable midocean meeting only two days before Pearl Harbor is further confirmation that the ship was from Russia, and not from Peru, which was the only other nation whose ships were still on the North Pacific route to Japan.

The timing and the location of the contact reveal that the vessel sighted by the *Kido Butai* could only have been *Uritsky.* The twelve-hundred-ton freighter had sailed from San Francisco on 28 November and, according to port records, had made a brief stopover at Portland, Oregon, the previous Sunday.[89]

The fact that Tokyo had issued the alert at all and that the *Kido Butai* ran into the Russian ship, which was some nine hundred miles south of the shorter great circle track to Vladivostok from the west coast, suggests that the Japanese had some tipoff. This could only have come from the Russians who were the only ones who knew that *Uritsky* was so heavily laden that their small freighter would be routed on a course unusually far south from the heavy weather off the Alaskan coast. The warning and the contact indicate a hitherto unsuspected degree of collusion between Moscow and Tokyo. If the *Uritsky* did sight the *Kido Butai* that last Friday of peace in the Pacific, her master did not make the customary sighting reports in plain Morse on the recognized international shipping frequencies. They could have been made after the freighter was safely out of range of the Japanese fleet. Although no such reports were picked up, it is probable that the *Uritsky* would have reported such important military intelligence by secret Soviet cipher transmissions outside the standard frequencies.[90]

Mysterious radio signals have even led some into the assertion that the navy tracked the Japanese fleet's advance on Pearl Harbor. While such charges cannot be made to fit the facts, it has been known since the war that the radio operator of S.S. *Lurline* did report receiving messages on the lower marine frequencies on the Matson liner's second and third nights out from Los Angeles on passage to Honolulu. The liner's relatively unsophisticated direction-finding apparatus placed the signals "north and west" of Hawaii. This was also in the general direction of Japan—or Vladivostok. Although the operator positively identified one station call sign as "JCS" Yokohama, it appeared the signals were being repeated by small craft. Their apparent mid-Pacific origination could be explained by atmospheric anomalies—or misidentification of the daily position reports radioed out by *Uritsky*.[91]

If the Russian freighter was the source of these signals, then this would explain why the *Kido Butai* survivors—and the record—deny that the Japanese force ever broke radio silence. It would certainly be astonishing if Admiral Nagumo had permitted a breach of operational orders that could have put the whole operation in jeopardy. But the gullibility of those uninitiated in radio intelligence has been fed by the "revelations" in 1982 of a so-called Seaman Z. He was later identified as Robert D. Ogg, who in 1941 was a seaman first class attached to the Twelfth Naval District Intelligence Office in San Francisco. A year after his story had made newspaper headlines, Ogg provided a detailed deposition to Commander Irwin G. Newman, U.S.N.R. (Ret.), of Naval Security Group Command.[92]

When Ogg's deposition was declassified by the National Security Agency in 1984, it became clear that his recollections were not as specific, or as sensational, as certain revisionist historians had tried to make them out to be. The transmissions were allegedly picked up by commercial radio companies on Wednesday, Thursday, and Friday, 3–5 December and, according to Ogg's statement, contained "no reference that it was a carrier force rather than a fishing force."[93] More important, he conceded that they might not even have been Japanese (Ogg does not speak the language). Under questioning by an experienced naval officer, Ogg admitted that their language was never precisely identified to him at the time and that "they just said these were Japanese and I presumed the language . . . but I'm not sure of that either."[94]

Since the radio signals were on a lower frequency than those which the Japanese used for their transmissions, it is likely that they could have been misidentified. They could have been Russian, because the Soviet Union's merchant ships did not transmit or receive on the standard international bands. It is probable that the bearings "on these odd frequencies" were determined only by an approximate triangulation from shore stations in an "area east of the International date line."[95] This is an enormous expanse of ocean, so it is possible that Russian signals were also picked up from a second Soviet freighter, the *Pavlov Vinogradov*, which was also crossing the North Pacific after sailing from Los Angeles on the sixth of November.[96]

Another bit of circumstantial evidence pointing toward a possible collusion between Tokyo and Moscow suggests that Stalin had a very precise knowledge of how, when, and where the war in the Pacific would break out.

One of the passengers on board the last Pan Am flight across the Pacific was Maksim Litvinov, the newly appointed Soviet ambassador to the United States. He was the Gromyko of his day. Beaming for the photographers, he stepped ashore with his wife from the Boeing flying boat *China Clipper,* which docked at Honolulu that Friday afternoon. That Litvinov managed to reach the west coast safely and arrive in Washington on the very day that war burst upon the Pacific may have been a curious coincidence. But it may be yet another indication that Stalin knew far more about the Japanese strategic plans than he chose to reveal to either Churchill or Roosevelt. It was certainly very much in the strategic interests of the Soviet Union that the Japanese become embroiled in war with the United States.

Pearl Harbor

Our attention that Friday morning at Pacific Fleet headquarters was focused on the western side of the Pacific. Tokyo radio circuits had been sending out messages at a very high rate for the past twenty-four hours. From the continued absence of Second or Third fleet originators in any of the traffic, Rochefort was certain that these forces were already at sea and heading south.[97]

This was the up-to-date intelligence that was given to Rear Admiral John H. Newton who sailed in the morning in *Chicago* to provide the heavy cruiser escort for carrier *Lexington* in Task Force 12. The mission of this task force was to ferry the marine fighter reinforcements to Midway and carry out extensive reconnaissance sweeps of the northwestern approaches to the Hawaiian Islands. Newton, who was the commander of the fleet's cruiser forces, left harbor believing that the "greatest menace" he faced was the threat of submarine attack.[98] It was a concern shared by Admiral Wilson Brown, who later in the day set course for Johnston Island with Task Force 5.

At this point, the disposition of Kimmel's forces was as follows: All the carriers were at sea with specific missions. All the heavy cruisers and more than one half of the fleet's destroyers were at sea protecting the carriers. Only the battle force—the old, slow battleships with their escorts of light cruisers and destroyers—was still at Pearl Harbor.

Meanwhile, our suspicions that the Japanese were concentrating on prowling Hawaiian waters was not considered in itself an especially urgent indication of the imminence of war. Our own boats were on surveillance missions off their home islands. And yet the worry about their submarines had been growing ever since Hypo had detected the easterly movement of Japan's main submarine flotillas toward the Marshalls. The previous night an unidentified submarine had been reported off Hawaii, and that afternoon destroyers picked up two suspicious underwater contacts barely five miles south of Diamond Head.

The newly issued fleet standing orders authorized offensive action against potentially hostile submarines detected in the vicinity of our base and exercise areas. That Friday afternoon the captain of destroyer *Selfridge* had made a sonar contact, but decided not to release any depth charges. As long as we remained at peace with Japan, the prospect of sparking an incident that might ignite war made skippers wary of taking such decisive action.

This was yet another instance of the problems that Kimmel faced when it came to operating a peacetime fleet under what were becoming wartime conditions. His concern was how to effect the transition without provoking an incident that would precipitate hostilities on his doorstep.

Washington

Kimmel would have been more worried had he been informed that intelligence was reaching Washington that convinced some senior officers that hostilities were not a matter of chance, but absolute certainty.

Ever since Tuesday, when Magic had revealed that the Japanese had ordered their diplomatic missions to destroy their code books and machines, Tokyo's winds code alert had assumed a vital new importance in the minds of certain ranking generals and admirals. It was now regarded as the trigger by which Japan would communicate its final decision for peace or war.

All naval radio stations were ordered to institute special watches. The On the Roof Gang operators were instructed to monitor every Japanese weather broadcast for any combination of words that might resemble the "east wind rain" code signal.

One unforeseen result was that OP-20-G's work load increased suddenly and dramatically. Bales of falsely identified winds alerts were relayed to Washington for analysis. This added to the work load of Captain Safford's already overburdened team, and it further diverted his attention and resources from the more critical work of penetrating the Japanese naval code systems.

The pressure was such that Admiral Noyes, the director of naval communications, made a daily check for anything remotely resembling a winds execute message. As Safford put it: "Higher Authority began heckling me as to the possibility of having missed it."[99]

The navy department attached such special importance to the three winds code alerts that they were typed up on small reminder cards that made it clear which country's relations with Tokyo were "in danger."

HIGASHI NO KAZE AME (EAST WIND RAIN) = JAPAN-US
KITA NO KAZE KUMORI (NORTH WIND CLOUDY) = JAPAN-USSR

NISHI NO KAZE HARE (WEST WIND CLEAR) = JAPAN-BRITISH[100]

These prompt cards were prepared at the direction of Admiral Noyes by Lieutenant Commander Alwin D. Kramer who was head of translation in OP-20-GZ. They were intended to be kept in the pockets of the five most senior officers in the navy department. Admiral Noyes, realizing that he would be the person who would flash the word that we were at war, had ordered Captain Safford to have couriers standing by round the clock to get word out to them as soon as OP-20-G translated a winds alert signal.[101]

This is precisely what appears to have happened. It was either that Thursday or Friday. But just which message it was and whether it was a genuine winds alert has been fiercely debated ever since. The debate is related in full in the Notes section of this book, but what is important is that Safford testified at the 1944 naval court of inquiry that an "east wind rain" intercept was received on either 4 or 5 December.

Besides Safford's account, there is a blank page (No: JD7001) in the Japanese diplomatic intercepts file,[102] plus the testimony of Colonel Otis K. Sadtler. This thirty-one-year veteran was a Signal Corps officer, who occupied the same sort of supervisory position in the army signal intelligence operations section as Safford did in naval intelligence. As opposite numbers they had learned to work closely together, forgetting the interservice barrier that so many of their fellow officers failed to surmount. Sadtler's compellingly forthright and precise testimony makes it clear that a winds code alert was received Friday morning, 5 December.

"About 9 or shortly thereafter on Friday, December 5, Admiral Noyes telephoned me to the effect that the message was in," Sadtler asserted.[103] It had to be that morning because the day before he had spent all morning at the weekly Defense Communications Board meeting.

The intercept that prompted Noyes to call Sadtler was, according to a letter written by Safford in 1943, confirmed by Kramer's reply to it, which was written *six months* before either of them was called upon to give any testimony. That it was an intercept from the Maryland Station M appears certain, because it was not a plain-language broadcast, but a kana transmission in Morse.[104]

According to Safford's letter the Japanese naval radio station had broadcast "Higashi no kaze ame. Mishi [sic] no kaze hare."[105] The wording appeared to match exactly the emergency-alert reminder cards that Japanese relations with *both* Britain and the United States were in danger. After the teletype machine had spewed out the message, the watch officer, who was not a linguist, thought it matched the correct wording but "was not sure of it." He telephoned Kramer, who "arrived early in the morning and verified it."[106]

When Safford came into his office shortly before 0800 that morning, he recalled how Lieutenant A. A. Murray had come in "with a big smile on his face and a piece of paper in his hand and said: 'Here it is!' as he handed me the original yellow teletype sheet with the significant Winds underscored and the meaning in Kramer's handwriting at the bottom." Safford immediately had five copies typed up and distributed to the same officers who had been provided with the winds code prompt cards and then went to discuss the matter with Admiral Noyes.[107]

"As I remember it," Noyes was to testify in 1944, before the naval court of inquiry, "we received some outside information which afterwards turned out not to be correct."[108] The director of naval communications subsequently became even more vague, but admitted that the intercept he got that morning "was taken to mean that an execute of this 'Winds Message' had been received."[109]

That was certainly the impression Noyes conveyed in his telephone conversation, as Sadtler recalled it: "I asked him which one, and he told me that it was the word that implied a break between Japan and Great Britain." Sadtler regarded that phone call as "the most important message I ever received." He hurried to the office of the chief of military intelligence to tell General Sherman Miles that "the word is in."[110]

Colonel Rufus S. Bratton was called in. The army's Far East director of military intelligence was told by Sadtler, "Diplomatic relations between Japan and Great Britain are in danger." The head of the army Far East section then pulled one of the navy winds code prompt cards out of his pocket and asked "which one of those words it was."[111] Since Sadtler knew no Japanese, he went back to his office to use his secure navy telephone to confirm that it was not another false alert.

Noyes, who knew no Japanese either and had no time to verify the winds code message because he was on his way to Stark's morning meeting, insisted the intercept "meant Japan and Great Britain." Sadtler went back to Miles and confirmed that the message received was "definitely meaning Japan and Great Britain" and that verification would be given later.[112]

Sadtler did not wait for verification. Although he had not seen the intercept, its indication of the imminence of war was obvious to him. Bratton was also certain that in conjunction with the codes-destruct signals "it could mean one thing, and that was war."[113]

Sadtler knew that Japan's ambassador in the United States had been instructed to keep one of his two Purple cipher machines in operation but that their London embassy had been ordered to destroy both. This was a sure sign to him that relations with Britain were already at an end and that a rupture with the United States was only days, or hours, away. Sadtler regarded the winds alert therefore as further confirmation that "we were going to have war in a very short time."[114]

Filled with concern and apprehension, Sadtler drafted what he considered an appropriate alert to be sent out immediately to the Pacific army commanders: "Reliable information indicates war with Japan in the very near future. Take every precaution to prevent a repetition of Port Arthur. Notify Navy." But General Gerow rejected it because he believed that "the various departments had been adequately warned."[115]

Sadtler's initiative ran out of gas because Noyes never telephoned confirmation that the winds alert was genuine. Meanwhile, Bratton had telephoned McCollum, his opposite number. The navy's Far East section had not yet been told about the intercept.

False or not, that Friday morning call from the navy department sent a current of concern around the war department because everybody, as Sadtler put it, "knew about that winds message."[116] General Miles himself authorized the sending of a dispatch to the Panama command that warned, "U.S.-Japanese relations strained. Will inform you if and when severance of Japanese relations imminent."[117] But it was not given a priority stamp, and so it was not transmitted for forty-eight hours!

Bratton had a nagging concern about the winds alert. He was able to obtain Miles's approval for a signal to General Short's headquarters advising the Hawaiian command's intelligence officer, "Contact Commander Rochefort immediately thru [sic] Commandant Fourteen Naval District regarding broadcasts from Tokyo reference weather."[118] Rochefort was not able to confirm or deny anything, because no warning that a winds alert had been received was ever sent out to us at Pearl Harbor.

Even if Noyes ultimately decided the winds alert was false, it also prompted a Friday morning meeting between admirals Turner and Ingersoll to review the situation. Turner later testified that there was a "50-50" chance of a "heavy raid" on Pearl Harbor. "What more ought to be done?" he claimed to have asked Ingersoll. "Should we send more dispatches or what?"[119]

Ingersoll was of the opinion that this was unnecessary because "everyone" in the navy had expected war with Japan for twenty years. He was prepared to concede, however, that the burning of their codes certainly made it seem more imminent and that he "expected to be at war very shortly."[120]

After Ingersoll, according to Turner, had concluded that "everything had been done covering the entire situation that ought to be done," the two admirals went to the CNO's office. Stark also did not merely "expect," but proclaimed that he "knew," war was a probability.[121] Nonetheless, he "stood together" with Marshall on the need to "gain time" for the reinforcements, already on their way to reach the Philippines. After Stark's flag secretary emphasized the dangers of crying wolf with more warnings, the triumvirate was "unanimous" in the conclusion that their earlier alerts to the fleet were "sufficient."[122]

McCollum, however, did not believe that sufficient notice of Japan's belligerent intent had been given the overseas commands. According to his testimony at the 1945 congressional inquiry and his oral history mentioned earlier, he condensed the indications of war from his 1 December memorandum, into a dispatch and (so Safford claims) added the winds alert and an interpretation for good measure. Then he took his message up to Wilkinson.

"Wilkinson approved the message and discussed it with Admiral Noyes," Safford claimed. He saw the McCollum alert at about 1500 that day. And he was present when Noyes dismissed it as "an insult to the intelligence of the commander in chief [Kimmel]."[123]

"I do not agree with you," Admiral Wilkinson had replied. "Admiral Kimmel is a very busy man, with a lot of things on his mind, and he may not see the picture as clearly as you and I do."[124]

Safford recalled how Wilkinson then left to "get it released by the front office"—meaning Turner, the director of war plans.[125] It was not until two years later that Safford realized while reading the Roberts Commission testimony that McCollum's warning had never been sent. It prompted Safford's search for the missing winds alert and ultimately his crusade to set the record straight by showing how "Admiral Kimmel was a scapegoat from the start."[126]

While McCollum later admitted that he had tried hard to get another war warning sent out on "either 4th or 5th" December,[127] he denied that it had been inspired by a winds alert. He testified that he had used his memorandum for drafting a war warning, which Wilkinson had approved. However, it had stuck in the throat of the director of war plans.

Turner took a dim view of anyone telling him how to perform, especially since his morning conference had been "unanimous" in its agreement that his 27 November warning was "sufficient."[128] McCollum had yet to see this dispatch. Otherwise he might not have continued to press for his own version. Eventually Turner sourly took the new draft. He "made a number of changes in it, striking out all except the informational parts of it."[129] McCollum protested this emasculation. "Finally, I raised so much sand in Turner's office that he showed me the dispatch," McCollum would recall.[130]

"Well, good gosh, you put in the words 'war warning,'" McCollum exclaimed with surprise. "I do not know what could be plainer than that, but nevertheless I would like to see mine go too."[131]

"Well, if you want to send it, you either send it the way I corrected it, or take it back to Wilkinson and we will argue about it," Turner snapped.

Turner later testified that McCollum "tore up his proposed dispatch," saying, "That is enough."[132] It was his contention that the 27 November warning was indeed "covering the entire situation."[133]

According to McCollum, he returned with the penciled draft to try to persuade Wilkinson to reason with Turner about the necessity of sending out an updated message that war was imminent. "Leave it here with me for a while," McCollum said he was told.[134]

McCollum's dispatch was never sent. No copies of his draft survived to show how we might have interpreted it at Pearl Harbor. But it is hard not to believe that his detailed war indications based on Magic, or Sadtler's punchier warning with its reminder of Japan's historic preference for surprise attack, would have directed Kimmel's attention to the imminence of war with Japan.

If a 5 December winds alert was removed from the files, the resulting documentation and testimony it generated indicate two things. First, some army and naval officers doubted the adequacy of Washington's two formal war alerts. Second, other army and naval officers were determined to cover up their efforts to stop another warning's being sent out. So although Safford was left hanging by his unsupported testimony, the navy department had to go to extreme lengths to demonstrate the message's nonexistence.

Charges were made in 1945, and confirmed to the authors recently by a brother officer and neighbor, that Captain Kramer was "persuaded" to modify his testimony about the winds message by the threat of permanent confinement in a psychiatric ward. Then there are affidavits from scores of On the Roof Gang radio operators. Their claims are astonishingly identical, saying they did not know about the winds messages "until I read about it in the newspapers."[135] Such uniformity suggests that their answers might have been dictated.

Perhaps the most telling indication of the rationale behind the official effort to deny there ever was a winds intercept is contained in the recently released waspish memorandum from the naval liaison officer appointed to assist the congressional investigation. On 13 February 1946, after the hearings had been safely concluded, Lieutenant Commander John F. Baecher advised the secretary of the navy that awarding Safford the Legion of Merit for his wartime work was "inappropriate." On the other hand, Baecher maintained, Captain Kramer deserved a higher decoration "because the effect of his testimony was to support the integrity of the higher command of the Navy."[136]

The recent release of the massive amount of the documentation generated by Baecher's office in 1945 is in itself a tangible example of the extent to which the "integrity of the higher command" was felt to be at stake. It also demonstrates how great were the steps taken to conceal the navy department's collective responsibility for Pearl Harbor.

It was also ironic that on Friday, 5 December 1941, the war alarm was sounding more loudly at the navy and war departments than at the Japanese embassy thirteen blocks away on Massachusetts Avenue. The Japanese ambassador and his special envoy still had no real knowledge of their government's commitment to hostilities. This is evident from the two requests they made that day to Tokyo. The first was to "delay for a while yet the destruction of the one code machine,"[137] and the other was to try to postpone the departure of Terasaki, who had been instructed to "leave by plane within the next couple of days."[138]

The requested delay in the second secretary's departure for Mexico had less to do with "the importance of his intelligence set-up" than Kurusu's hope that the White House might yet respond to his personal appeal to Roosevelt. Two days earlier Nomura had advised the foreign ministry about the Reverend Dr. Jones's mission: "Terasaki had Stanley Jones, with whom he is on the most intimate terms, call upon Roosevelt."[139] This message shows that Jones's intervention was neither as disinterested, clandestine, nor unofficial as some recent historians have suggested.

Nomura did, however, confirm that "the president clearly hopes for peace" and was considering some sort of "emergency diplomatic means."[140] That some emergency appeal was needed to break the diplomatic impasse was apparent to both Nomura and Hull when they met that Friday morning at the State Department. The Japanese envoys were to present Tokyo's response to the United States' diplomatic note expressing concern about Japan's military buildup in Indochina. Premier Tojo's curt answer to an "exaggerated" report was that Japanese troops were taking "precautionary measures" in response to "frequent signs" of Chinese movements along the frontier.[141]

Hull dismissed the claim that Japanese troops were in Indochina for purposes solely of defense. A sharp exchange of views concluded with Nomura's plea to Hull that "there must be wise statesmanship to save the situation."[142] To the ambassador's candid observation, "This isn't getting us anywhere," Hull retorted that "we are not looking for trouble, but at the same time we are not running away from menaces."[143]

The acrimonious tenor of the meeting convinced Hull that it was time for the department to instruct our diplomats in the Far East to make preparations for the destruction of secret papers and closing down "in the event of a sudden emergency cutting-off of communications with the department."[144]

Hull's mood of pessimistic resolution was apparent when the secretary of state reported the increasing strain in Japanese-American relations to Friday afternoon's cabinet meeting. "With every hour that passes I become more convinced that they are not playing in the open," Hull told the meeting. According to Secretary of Labor Frances Perkins, the administration's ranking woman, the situation was "ticklish." Navy Secretary Knox then revealed the riveting information that "very secret information" led the navy to believe a Japanese fleet was at sea, heading south and "going to do something."[145]

Singapore was mentioned. The president confirmed that the British base was the "presumed objective," although he could not be certain that they might not also strike elsewhere, even the Aleutians. "What shall we do?" was the question Roosevelt posed to his cabinet. "If they proceed south towards Singapore, what's the problem for the United States? What should the United States do?" According to the Perkins account he wanted a straw poll of their opinions, not a formal policy vote. "It is a terrible problem," the president said as he told them he was "just checking to see how your minds are operating. . . . It's a terrible problem. I hope I won't have to act on it, or settle it, but we may have to."[146]

The secretary of labor was one of those who declared she thought we should go to the aid of the British if Singapore was attacked. But the immediacy of war came as a shock to her. The cabinet came out with a clear majority in favor of standing by Britain if it came to a fight. Roosevelt could take some comfort in the vote. He knew that his critical appeal for congressional support for a full-fledged ultimatum to Japan could not be postponed for long.

That afternoon the secretary of state left with the president a twenty-seven-page draft of the proposed address to Congress in anticipation that he might have to send it up to Capitol Hill as soon as the legislators returned from their weekend break. In reading the recently surfaced document, one can see that its very length and convoluted logic indicate the problem that Roosevelt would face in getting a declaration of war if Japan did not attack the United States.

"I have to report to you a serious danger which is threatening this country and its interests in the Far East," the address began. A dozen pages cataloging and condemning Japanese expansionism, and Tokyo's adherence to the Axis pact, concluded, "Simply stated, what we are confronted with in the Far East is a repetition of the strategy pursued by Hitler in Europe." After attempting to "subjugate China" and invading Indochina, Japan "now threatens with imminent attack various neighboring areas, not excluding the Philippines." After eight months of negotiations the "Japanese government have given no indication of a clear-cut desire to follow the course of peace."[147]

There would be a direct threat to American security and interests if Japan were to become "established in Singapore or the Netherlands East Indies or, were she to dominate China, the lines of communication between the United States, China and other peace-loving nations would be cut." The question that Roosevelt planned to ask in Congress was "whether the United States is or is not to stand by while Japan goes forward with a program of conquest by force." Permitting further Japanese aggression would not only destroy American commercial interests but the "farsighted experiment" of impending Philippine independence. It would "forever terminate the prestige and influence of the United States . . . throughout the Orient." Roosevelt was to remind Congress that "we are pledged to aid those countries," who were defending themselves against "Hitlerism," and express his "full confidence that it is within our capacity to withstand any attack which anyone may make upon us."[148]

Precisely what pledges he had given to the British were left unstated, but they were implicit in his concluding sentence: "As commander-in-chief, I have given appropriate orders to our Forces in the Far East." Whether a majority of Congress would have backed the "appropriate orders" that the president had already issued was never put to the test. But his intention to brand the Japanese as "no better than the Nazi leaders" who asserted their "right to world conquest," to establish "slave states" in a "rule of merciless horror matched only by that of Hitlerized Germany," would undoubtedly have rallied support from the American public.[149]

Whatever rhetorical salvos the president was toying with that Friday, his main objective was still to delay firing them. He knew that his military chiefs needed every day that could be bought to get more reinforcements to the Philippines. Two troop convoys were already in mid-Pacific. The first flight of the forty-eight B-17 bombers, which would more than double General MacArthur's strategic bombing capability, were only twenty-four hours from taking off from airfields on the west coast.

Roosevelt had told his cabinet that Friday that he still had one more diplomatic card to play. This was an appeal to the emperor of Japan himself—the first direct communication from an American president since Millard Fillmore sent his famous greeting of "peace and friendship" with Commodore Matthew C. Perry in 1853. Whether a similar ploy would prove effective eighty-eight years later was much more doubtful. But the president now realized that the time had come to make his final bid to avert war.

6 DECEMBER *"The Japanese Won't Attack Us"*

Tokyo

At 1000 Tokyo time that morning the main naval radio station at Owada relayed Admiral Yamamoto's eve of war message to all the ships under his command. It was the solemn promise given on behalf of his men to the emperor: "I humbly accept your Majesty's order and promise that every officer and man of the Combined Fleet is ready to give his body and soul to achieve the goal of this expedition in answer to the Imperial Command."[150]

Kido Butai

Cloudy skies concealed the noonday sun. Nagumo's force crossed the "last hurdle," as staff officer Fujita called the seven-hundred-mile limit of long-range air patrols from the Hawaiian Islands. But that weekend none of our PBYs was scheduled to patrol north of Oahu. The final refueling of the carrier's destroyer escorts went ahead without a hitch. The last of the accompanying oilers dropped behind and all hands busied themselves with preparations for battle.

Water, which had been rationed to preserve fuel, was now made available for bathing for the first time since leaving Tankan Bay. Each ship held prayer meetings so that their crews could enter into battle clean in spirit as well as body.

Just before dawn a message had been received from submarine *I-72*, which had been scouting off Maui, that the "American Fleet is not in ALL [the code designates for Lahaina Bay]."[151] A final reconnaissance was to be made the following morning to confirm that none of the Pacific Fleet was in its alternative anchorage. Commander Genda prepared for the final aircrew briefings on the assumption that the air fleet would be attacking Pearl Harbor.

That afternoon the *Kido Butai* hauled around onto a course due south and increased speed to twelve knots for the final high-speed night run to the dawn launching point for the air attack. The "D G" code flags were broken out on *Akagi*'s masthead to signify the message that Admiral Togo had flown thirty-seven years earlier at the Battle of Tsushima Strait: THE FATE OF OUR NATION DEPENDS ON THIS BATTLE—ALL HANDS WILL EXERT THEMSELVES TO THEIR UTMOST.[152]

The flagship's crew cheered as they went to battle stations. That evening, the receipt of Tokyo's relay of the Honolulu consulate's latest report indicated there were no unusual American activities or air patrols. Admiral Nagumo finally began to believe that his force had a good chance to emulate Togo's stunning 1904 naval victory.

The overall plans were carefully scheduled to enable the *Kido Butai* to achieve the maximum of surprise by making the first strikes. But that afternoon Combined Fleet headquarters relayed that army pilots flying from Indochina had "shot down a British seaplane to the westward of FGU [the Japanese coordinates for the southernmost tip of Indochina]."[153]

The first blood spilled in the Pacific war belonged to a Royal Australian Air Force pilot from the Kota Bharu airfield on Malaya's north coast. Nevertheless, he had managed to radio a warning that the large Japanese convoy was rounding Cambodia Point heading east before his twin-engine Hudson crashed into the Gulf of Siam.

Pearl Harbor

All the intelligence we had been able to assemble at Pacific Fleet headquarters indicated that the South China Sea was about to become the cockpit of war. It was the focus of my attention that Saturday. At my daily briefing shortly after 0800 I had drawn to Admiral Kimmel's attention that an invasion of Siam or Malaya was imminent. The continued absence of carrier transmission suggested that one or more divisions were tied up in the southward advance.

We had received confirmation early that morning from the Asiatic Fleet that a "25 ship convoy with an escort of 6 cruisers and 10 destroyers" had been sighted off the southernmost tip of Indochina. Not far behind was another convoy of "10 ships with 2 cruisers and 10 destroyers," also on a westerly course. Thirty more transports and a large cruiser had been spotted in Camranh Bay. Admiral Hart's estimate was that "all forces will make for Kohtron"—the narrow of the Isthmus of Kra on the frontier between Siam and British Malaya.[154]

If the Japanese convoys maintained their present course and speed, I calculated, the invasion would hit the beaches early the following day. Siam and Britain would then be at war, and I was concerned that the Japanese might also be planning a simultaneous attack on the Philippines. I did not believe Japan would risk leaving her flank exposed.

After my briefing Admiral Kimmel called in his staff to discuss the situation. Meanwhile, he sent me to get the opinion of Admiral Pye, the battle force commander.

The trip by gig across the harbor to *California* was a welcome break from the mounting tension at the submarine base. It was a glorious day, and the flagship of the battle force was moored in majestic isolation off Ford Island at the head of Battleship Row. I found the admiral, Rear Admiral Pye, and his acting chief of staff on *California*'s quarterdeck. I handed them the dispatch containing the report of the Japanese convoys heading into the Gulf of Siam, and the many naval vessels, including submarines, sighted off the Indochina coast. They both read it and concluded that Japan was probably not going to attack the British but would occupy a position in the Gulf of Siam as an advance base to operate from, probably against the Burma Road.

They asked me what fleet intelligence made of the latest reports. I told them frankly and very definitely that I considered the movement to the Gulf of Siam to be extremely significant. I did not believe that they would stop at the Burma Road. Japan's real objective was farther south, probably the oil of the Dutch East Indies. They might not leave our forces in the Philippines unengaged on their flank. My belief was they would take us out on the way down, and we would be at war.

Pye and his chief of staff were very doubtful about my strategic estimate. "Oh, no. The Japanese won't attack us," Pye told me. "We're too strong and powerful."

After I had returned to headquarters and filed the message, I reported to Admiral Kimmel. He was anxious to know Pye's reaction. When I had explained their confident rejection of my estimate about an attack on the Philippines, he said, "I want you to repeat that again." As I did so the admiral looked straight through me. He then snorted as if disappointed at Pye's response.

Even if Kimmel was inclined to share my fears about an attack on the Philippines, any thought that the Japanese might also hit Pearl Harbor at that time was far from our minds. But while I had been with Pye, Kimmel, after assessing the latest intelligence, had discussed the advisability of sending the battle force to sea as a precautionary measure for commencing war operations.

Kimmel discussed the idea with his chief of staff, Captain William "Poco" Smith; his operations officer, Captain Walter DeLany; and Captain Charles E. "Soc" McMorris, the war plans officer. But they concluded that without the carriers and protective air cover the battleships would be too vulnerable at sea. Moreover, sending the fleet out on a weekend would cause just the sort of alarm that the army war warning had cautioned against. It would also be an unnecessary drain on the fleet's fuel reserves. These were earmarked for long-range operations against the Japanese bases in the Marshalls. Kimmel's primary concern was to have the fleet ready for an offensive sortie as soon as hostilities broke out.

The admiral's extended conference broke up just before 1400. As I was late for lunch at the wardroom mess, I made my apologies to the senior officer present. He happened to be the fleet gunnery officer, Captain Willard A. Kitts, Jr. I explained that I had been delayed because Kimmel had sent me to Pye with an urgent dispatch. During lunch several of the staff asked me what I thought about the news of Japanese troop transports steaming into the Gulf of Siam. I repeated my assertion that they would not leave the Philippines on their flank and that we would probably be at war the next day.

"Ah, Layton and his Saturday crisis," was how Captain Kitts ribbed me, referring to my predictions at the mess lunch a week earlier that a serious crisis was brewing. I assured him that in my view the situation was a lot more ominous this weekend.

Late that afternoon, my conviction that we would shortly be at war was reinforced when Rochefort called to inform me that the Japanese consulate in Honolulu had been burning codes and official papers. Joe explained that Mayfield had gotten the information. While I did not know specifically about the telephone tap on the consulate's kitchen, I guessed that the FBI had a very reliable internal source of information, which Joe liked to refer to as "inside the horse's mouth."

Rochefort told me he had already drafted a cable to advise Opnav: "Believe local consul has destroyed all but one system."[155] But the Fourteenth Naval District Communications Office—in an unwise economy measure—sent the dispatch out "deferred status." In this case, a piece of important intelligence from Honolulu did not reach Washington until after the Japanese attack.

Although I was not sent a copy of the message, I did consider it significant enough to alert Kimmel's duty officer. The admiral was not immediately available, and later he could not recollect whether he had received my report about the code burning. Even if he had been given the message, it was not the first time we had had information that the Japanese consulate was burning codes. Without being able to read it in the context of the increasing number of ships-in-harbor reports being made by Consul Kita, Kimmel testified, he would not have regarded the code burning as "very vital." It merely reinforced what we had already been told by Washington.[156]

What might have proved another vital clue to the impending Japanese attack was also missed that evening, because we had never been alerted to the Kita messages. It surfaced around 1800, when I received a telephone call from Captain Mayfield. He wanted to know whether I would be going to my office on Sunday. When I said that I would be in the next day, he asked me to stop by Fourteenth Naval District headquarters. I asked if I should come down to Honolulu that evening, but was told no. It was apparent that he would not have the information on which he wanted my opinion until the next morning.

It was a year before I discovered that the reason for his call was to discuss the transcript of a transpacific telephone call supposedly made by a Tokyo newspaper to one Mrs. Mori, a Honolulu resident. She was the wife of a local Japanese dentist, who had already come under FBI surveillance. At fifteen dollars for three minutes' time, the two-hundred-dollar cost of the call had aroused suspicions that it must be connected with an espionage operation, the more so since Mrs. Mori had been questioned in code that referred to flowers in bloom and the latest weather conditions. She also supplied information on the movements of the Pacific Fleet and was asked, "Are airplanes flying daily?" and "What about the searchlights?"[157]

When the FBI translated the Mori call that afternoon, the local bureau chief, Robert L. Shivers, was convinced that the call had important "military significance."[158] He telephoned Mayfield's office. The DIO was not there, but when told about the Mori call he decided that it probably was a hidden code. But because all the references were to the Hawaiian Islands he concluded it could not be urgent because "there was nothing in the message in line with previous information indicating Japanese movements."[159] And so he postponed any further action until he could discuss its possible significance with me the next day.

After receiving Shivers's call, Lieutenant Colonel George W. Bicknell, Short's assistant G-2 of the Fort Shafter intelligence section, decided the Mori intercept did warrant immediate evaluation. He drove downtown to pick up a transcript and then persuaded his chief, Lieutenant Colonel Kendall J. Fielder, that it was important enough to delay General Short's departure to a dinner engagement to discuss its significance.

A brief discussion on the porch of the general's quarters was unable to "make heads nor tails of it." Short concluded that although it looked "very fishy" it was "nothing very much to get excited about."[160]

General Short and Captain Mayfield might have become very excited about that Mori message if army or navy intelligence officers on Oahu had known as much as Washington did about the kinds of messages that had been passing back and forth between Tokyo and the local Japanese consulate. Only three days earlier Hypo's cryptanalysts had gotten their first chance to break into that traffic. Unfortunately for us, Rochefort's team had not been assigned the task of cracking any diplomatic intercepts. Unfamiliarity with the consular ciphers and bad luck conspired to keep us from unlocking the potentially vital intelligence they contained.

Warrant Officer Farnsley C. Woodward, the only Hypo cryptanalyst with any experience in the Japanese diplomatic cipher systems, had started on Wednesday with the cables in the low-grade LA cipher. By Thursday afternoon most of these turned out to be routine administrative matters, which he described as "junk."[161] By Friday afternoon Woodward had moved on to tackle the PA-K2 traffic, which the consulate had been using for its confidential messages after burning its J-19 code books that Tuesday.

If Hypo had possessed all the latest key recoveries, the decryption process would have involved about six hours' work to break out the traffic for a whole day. By Saturday Rochefort could have provided me with most of that week's detailed twice-a-day fleet reports that Kita was cabling to Tokyo, and Kimmel—who was already toying with the idea— would almost certainly have sent the battle force to sea.

But Hypo did not have the key recoveries that would have speeded up the process. Because Rochefort was not supposed to tackle any diplomatic intercepts, he could not ask Washington for them without risking a flap. Woodward therefore set to work from scratch and tried to break out the keys himself. This was not a difficult task, given enough traffic. But he also handicapped himself. In the preliminary step of lining up the message text prior to commencing the columnar decoding process, he erroneously set up the messages backward. As fate would have it, four days of wrestling with the seemingly indecipherable messages passed before he discovered his simple error.

So Woodward did not break out a single PA-K2 cable until the Wednesday following the attack.[162] It was yet another human error in a string of similar miscalculations that denied us last-minute intelligence that a Japanese striking force was steaming toward Pearl Harbor. It was a failure that bore heavily on Woodward.[163]

One message that was contained in the first batch Rochefort saw was Kita's 2 December report, which Woodward put aside because he lacked the current key to the J-19 cipher. Instead he turned to the subsequent messages in the simple PA-K2 code. It was a bad mistake because this one report could have proved an even more accurate indicator that the Japanese were contemplating a Taranto-style torpedo plane attack on Pearl Harbor:

> In view of the present situation, the presence in port of warships, airplane carriers and cruisers is of the utmost importance. Hereafter, to the utmost of your ability, let me know day by day. Wire me in each case whether or not there are any observation balloons above Pearl Harbor or if there are any indications that they will be sent up. Also advise whether or not the warships are provided with anti-torpedo nets.[164]

This message was fated not to reach the Washington cryptanalysts until 23 December. With no intimation of the explosive intelligence it might contain, the army communications center at Fort Shafter, which had received instructions not to give priority to J-19 messages, were economists on their cables and so the intercept was sent off by surface mail!

While there is no certainty that this message would, by itself, have changed the course of history, both the loss of this message and Woodward's error denied us access to intelligence that might have sounded the alarm. Any of the Kita reports would, at the very least, have brought an increase in the level of alert on Oahu. Air patrols would probably have been stepped up, and Kimmel might well have reversed his decision not to send the battle fleet to sea.

The first message that could have tipped the balance was contained in a lengthy RCA cable of 3 December in which Consul Kita relayed to Tokyo in PA-K2 cipher the elaborate methods by which Yoshikawa's agent Fritz Kuehn proposed to send his reports to Japanese army intelligence. His proposed system for signaling to a Japanese submarine offshore was a characteristically Teutonic "belt and suspenders" operation. It involved a complex array of prearranged light patterns at night, Roman numerals on a boat sail by day, bonfire signals, and even want ads to be broadcast by a local radio station.

The lights message, as it came to be known, was the first PA-K2 cable that Woodward picked and the one on which he labored so unsuccessfully until 10 December. If he had broken it out, it would have been an inescapable sign of the attention that Tokyo wanted paid to the Pacific Fleet:

MEANING		SIGNAL
Battleship divisions including scouts and screen units	Preparing to sortie	1
A number of carriers	Preparing to sortie	2

Battleship divisions	All departed between 1st and 3rd	3
Carriers	Several departed between 1st and 3rd	4
Carriers	All departed between 1st and 3rd	5
Battleship divisions	All departed between 4th and 6th	6
Carriers	Several departed between 4th and 6th	7
Carriers	All departed between 4th and 6th	8

Kuehn did not know of the impending attack. He had devised his reporting system to be equally applicable to the first week of any month. But if we had seen this cable that Saturday we would have evaluated it in the context of the worsening diplomatic situation and my hunch that Japan would attack the Philippines as well as the Isthmus of Kra. Although not specifically intended to refer to 6 December, the reference to the sixth as the last date the Japanese wanted to know what ships had sailed from Pearl Harbor would have had very special significance that Saturday. It would have exactly tied in with my belief that war would break out the next day, 7 December.

The impact of this lights message as an indication of Japan's focus on the Pacific Fleet anchorage would have been even greater had Hypo's cryptanalysts managed to break out either of the Japanese consul's ships-in-harbor reports made on Thursday and Friday. Any suspicions aroused by the lights message could only have been increased if we had read these messages in conjunction with Tokyo's reminder to Kita that very day to "please *wire immediately* re the latter part of my #123 (. . . . . . .) the *movements of the fleet subsequent to the fourth* [emphasis added]."[166]

The two reports that Kita sent that same day would have opened our eyes to the possibility of an air attack. One answered Tokyo's 2 December request about Pearl Harbor's aerial defenses: "At the present time there are *no signs of barrage balloon equipment.* . . . In my opinion the *battleships do not have torpedo nets* [emphasis added]." It called our attention to the obvious: "I imagine that in all probability there is *considerable opportunity* left to take advantage for a surprise attack." The second message would have emphasized the point because it listed the "9 [sic] battleships, 3 light cruisers, 3 submarine tenders, 17 destroyers and . . . 4 light cruisers, 2 destroyers lying at dock." This final report concluded, "It appears that *no air reconnaissance is being conducted* by the fleet air arm [emphasis added]."[167]

These were vital clues of an impending air attack on the Pacific Fleet. But the information was fated never to become intelligence, because it remained hidden in the PA-K2 code until after the raid. Of greater significance was the fact that Washington had already unlocked information from earlier Kita reports that could have been an equally important harbinger of what was to come. This information was never turned into intelligence, and, instead of being relayed to Pearl Harbor, it joined the accumulating Magic files in the safes of the war and navy departments.

Washington

The terrible irony of the Kita messages is this: The cryptanalysts in OP-20-GZ and the army's Signal Corps special intelligence section had no trouble reading the Japanese J-19 or PA-K2. But the consular ciphers had a low priority and although several had been broken out that week none was relayed to Pacific Fleet headquarters.

Among them was a three-week-old J-19 report of 18 November that listed every major warship in harbor that day. Significantly, it also detailed the speed, procedures, and the time it took—nearly an hour—for five destroyers to enter through the channel and reach their moorings.[168]

On Wednesday, Tokyo's 15 November request for its Honolulu consulate to report "twice a week" and "take extra care to maintain secrecy" was translated by the navy.[169]

On Thursday the army had broken out the 18 November instruction for Kita to "investigate comprehensively the fleet [air] bases in the neighborhood of the Hawaiian military reservation." Twenty-four hours later the readers of Friday's Magics knew that "great secrecy" was to be used to investigate vessels anchored in "Area 'N' Pearl Harbor"; and what was mistranslated as "Manila Bay" was in the context clearly Mamala Bay, which was adjacent to the port of Honolulu itself.[170]

That same day OP-20-GZ read a five-day-old instruction to Kita that should have been seen as an even more explicit clue to Tokyo's increasing concern with Pearl Harbor: "We have been receiving reports from you on ship movements, but in future will you also report *when there are no movements* [emphasis added]."[171] If this had been properly evaluated in conjunction with the other available messages, this was the *one* that was the real giveaway. But apparently no one in the navy department stopped to reflect why Japanese naval intelligence was as interested in knowing what warships were actually *in* Pearl Harbor as they were in those that put to sea.

The failure to relate these recently decrypted messages with the earlier "bomb plot" signal, and so to appreciate what set them apart both in volume and specificity from the espionage reports that were intercepted from the Japanese consulates in Seattle and Manila, was indicative of just how badly the evaluation and dissemination—two of the three functions necessary to turn raw information into meaningful intelligence—had broken down. The extent of this failure was to be recognized by the navy in its own secret analysis, made in September 1942. Understandably, it was not released until nearly forty years after the 1945 congressional hearings.

This report demonstrated how a simple statistical calculation would have yielded the "interesting point" that while Seattle and Panama accounted for only six and eighteen intercepted shipping reports in the months of August through November 1941, fifty-five related to Manila and *sixty-eight to Pearl Harbor*. Naval intelligence's own analysis underscored the magnitude of its failure to see what was staring it in the face for nearly a month before war broke out:

> The significant point is that the Japanese government did not treat the Honolulu and Manila reports as routine matters, but continually kept trying to elicit more information from its representatives. The acceleration of messages from Honolulu and Manila in November was another identification of war preparations.[172]

The lack of any systematic evaluation of Japan's consular diplomatic traffic was not an excuse that justified the subsequent pillorying of Admiral Kimmel and General Short. Their reputations, and the 2,335 servicemen who died at Pearl Harbor, became the victims of Washington's failure to recognize the significance of the Kita messages.

The intelligence breakdown was compounded on 6 December when the intuition of one of OP-20-GZ's newest recruits succeeded in uncovering one of the clues that had been missed by trained intelligence officers and the most senior admirals on the naval staff. The tragedy was that her discovery of last-minute intelligence that might have warned the Pacific Fleet of the incoming attack was not only dismissed, but was ignored until Monday morning.

Mrs. Dorothy Edgers had been working in OP-20-GZ but a few weeks when the Honolulu consulate's three-day-old lights message landed on her desk that Saturday morning. It was part of a batch of diplomatic decrypts awaiting translation into English.

"At first glance, this seemed to be more interesting than some of the other messages I had in my basket," she was to tell the 1944 navy court of inquiry. "I selected it and asked one of the other men, who were also translators working on the other messages, whether or not it shouldn't be done immediately."[173]

The person who gave her permission to go ahead was her brother, Fred Woodrough, who had been one of naval communications' leading

civilian Japanese linguists for more than four years. He had recommended his sister for a translator's job because after thirty years in Japan
she was "much more fluent" in the language.[174] Navy bureaucrats, however, had offered her "practically beginner's pay." But Dorothy, unlike
her quiet and introspective brother, was a spirited extrovert. A "born
salesman," she had successfully argued that her fluency with the language
entitled her to pay equal to the other translators'.

At the congressional hearings in 1945 Dorothy Edgers was to be portrayed as inexperienced and timid by Lieutenant Commander Kramer,
for whom she worked in OP-20-GZ. Nothing could have been further
from the truth. Significantly, Mrs. Edgers was *not* called on to testify
before the congressional committee.

Dorothy was not the kind of woman to be easily brushed aside when
she decided something was important—and that was how the lights message struck her. When she found it contained some garbles, she went off
to find a crippie to straighten them out. The message was not returned to
her desk until around 1230 Saturday and Dorothy could easily have left it
there until Monday, because it was past the hour when civilian translators
ended weekly work.

Dorothy Edgers was not like that. She went to find Kramer and tried
to interest him in the intercept. After a glance, OP-20-GZ told her he did
not think it was of "sufficient importance" to warrant her staying behind
to complete the translation. So she went back to ask her brother's advice.

"What do you think?" Fred recalls her asking. She showed him the
message with its instruction about signal lights and the Pacific Fleet's
movements through the "6th." "I remember reading it quickly and saying, 'Yes, I think you should stay and do this.'" Woodrough recalls, although he admitted he "wasn't about to stay and do it myself."[175]

So Dorothy Edgers stayed behind and completed the first translation,
which she finished around 1400. It made so much of an impression on her
that three years later she was still able to recall all its salient points. The
message revealed "how they were going to communicate from Honolulu
to the parties interested the information on our fleet movements." She
recollected that it had to "do with lights in the window of a certain house,
and there was also something about newspaper advertising."[176]

Kramer was not in the office when Mrs. Edgers left, but since "he
knew I was working on it," she entrusted it to Chief Clerk Harold L.
Bryant, "whose job it was to edit the messages and write them up." But
that was as close as this important information came to becoming intelligence.

"On Monday morning that message was still on Kramer's desk," Fred
Woodrough asserts. "He had not looked at it. It was quite possible that
the English would have had to be smoothed out, but the essential translating work was done."[177]

Commander Kramer, whose responsibility as OP-20-GZ was to review all intercepts for further evaluation, was to deny any recollection of Mrs. Edgers's translation when he was questioned by the congressional investigating committee in 1945. Yet he was obliged to concede that he must have failed to give it proper scrutiny because in the "10 to 15 seconds" that he admitted that he might have studied it that afternoon he decided it was "not materially different from the information we had already." According to Kramer, Mrs. Edgers "was still unfamiliar with the practices and procedures of my office," and he denied that she had ever "invited" his attention to the message that morning. Moreover, he sought to cast doubt on her translation by claiming that he had subsequently to spend three days "clearing and working with this message" before it was readable.[178]

When asked whether he would have considered the lights message an important piece of intelligence, Kramer conceded, "If I had seen it Saturday afternoon, I most certainly would have."[179] That admission explains why his testimony was at odds with that of Mrs. Edgers and the recollections of her brother. Dorothy's original worksheet had disappeared by 1945. The only remaining documentary evidence is Kramer's polished translation of 11 December stamped TOP SECRET ULTRA, which was not sent to Pearl Harbor.

The lights message did not get the attention it warranted from Kramer because it was in a low-grade PA-K2 consular cipher. He appears to have been obsessed with the high-priority Purple traffic that afternoon. As one of Woodrough's staff observed: "Al was not the ideal man for the job at that time." Like many perfectionists he could not distinguish details from important issues. He could never give a short answer and would weigh all the pros and cons. "Sometimes he couldn't give a decision at all—and didn't."[180]

Many of the crippies were first-rate bridge players; it was a skill that went with the job. But when Kramer joined an occasional off-duty game with them, they noticed, he was always the last one to play his hand. He would ponder his cards, trying the patience of his partners, apparently laying out his whole strategy. "If everything went the way he figured, with everyone discarding as he allowed, he would play the next card," Woodrough remembered. "But if there was the slightest variation he would have to go back into his trance again."[181]

During those critical weeks of November and December 1941 the shortage of manpower had been exacerbated by watching for the winds messages. OP-20-GZ and its overstrung chief were under constant strain. The pressure on Kramer was often as imaginary as it was real. "Al would take even the most trivial piece of traffic and devote the same amount of time changing a comma here and a period there, as he would spend on an important message," Fred Woodrough recalled. He often wondered why his boss "got stuck on things" and assumed that the strain of his job contributed to his hospitalization just before the congressional hearings in

1945.[182] Kramer's perfectionism soon came to border on an obsession. It slowed up the whole translation process, because he would not let a message be released until he had personally reviewed it to assure himself it was letter perfect.

Kramer was operating under considerable pressure even before December. Earlier in the year he had participated in several ONI "black bag" operations directed against the office of the Japanese consul in New York. After one of these break-ins early in 1941, Kramer—who had processed the films in his own darkroom—called in Lieutenant Robert H. Weeks, his next-door neighbor and fellow member of OP-20-G, to see the latest haul. When a knock was heard at the door, Weeks recalled how they had to keep the visitor outside while they quickly scooped up the prints of Japanese code books: The caller chanced to be Japan's naval attaché in Washington, with whom Kramer maintained a friendship.

Woodrough observed how on several of the mornings after Kramer arrived in the OP-20-GZ office wearing tennis shoes and looking bleary eyed, a spate of new code breaks had shortly followed. Which ciphers benefited from Kramer's nocturnal excursions in New York are unclear. But the black-bag jobs were evidently sufficiently productive for Kramer to write a revealing confidential memorandum in 1945, in anticipation of his appearance before Admiral H. Kent Hewitt's naval inquiry into the Pearl Harbor attack. "I see no purpose in disclosing the N.Y. period activity that would be pertinent to the investigation," he wrote cryptically. "Such disclosures could only result in compromising the status of certain individuals who contributed, as well as seriously harming [sic] possible further activities in this line."[183]

Kramer, therefore, was overstressed throughout 1941. He put in tough hours and constantly munched on chocolate bars, dropping crumbs around his desk which attracted mice. In spite of being overworked, he was obsessed with achieving perfect translations and would not release even the most unimportant consular decrypt until he had personally satisfied himself that it was absolutely correct. This slowed up the whole process of translating the Japanese naval intercepts and Magics. His lack of organization was evident from his cluttered desk with its piles of partially translated decrypts awaiting his critical analysis and approval.

"When the volume of intercepts was very high, the stuff just piled up in a basket," Woodrough recalled. "Whoever was ready would take the top one and translate it. We picked whichever one had the highest priority, and Purple got top priority."[184] In such circumstances, his sister's translation had only a slim chance of getting past Kramer's supercritical eye during the hectic rush that overtook him during the final afternoon of peace.

That Saturday the navy's cryptanalytic effort was concentrated on the high-priority Purple message that contained Japan's formal rejection of Hull's ten-point proposal of 26 November. The clues that Japan's reply was about to arrive were contained in two pilot messages that had been intercepted by the navy's west coast listening station at Bainbridge Island on Puget Sound at around 0700 that day. As it was an even-numbered date and therefore the army's duty day for translating Purple, OP-20-G routed the intercepts to the Signal Corps Special Intelligence Section in the war department at midday. Two hours later the Purple machine had spewed out the plain Japanese text, which was rapidly translated.

The first pilot message advised Nomura that the "situation was extremely delicate," and that he would receive a communication in fourteen parts, which he was to "keep secret for the time being." The ambassador was to "put it in a nicely drafted form and make every preparation to present it to the Americans just as soon as you receive instructions."[185] It was followed by a second dispatch that instructed, "In the preparation of an aide memoire be absolutely sure not to use a typist or any other person. Be most extremely cautious in preserving secrecy."[186]

When the pilot messages reached the desk of Colonel Rufus Bratton, at around 1400, the head of military intelligence's Far East section realized he faced a logistical problem. Unlike the navy, the army cryptanalysts were not yet on a twenty-four-hour shift. Bratton had to get General Miles's permission to ask the navy to help out. By the time this had been arranged with Safford and Kramer, the intercepts of the first parts of Tokyo's long message were already chattering in on the OP-20-G teleprinters from Bainbridge Island.

Tokyo had begun transmitting its detailed instructions to Ambassador Nomura just after noon. By three that afternoon, all except the final, fourteenth part were being processed by the navy code breakers. Although they were not sent in sequential order, the first thirteen parts had been transmitted in English. There could be no mistaking that this was a final statement of Japan's position because the ambassadors were given no room for misinterpretation.[187]

Typists lent by the army prepared the final copies. All Kramer had to do was to ensure that the message was assembled in logical order. This made it all the more surprising that Kramer did not give proper attention that afternoon to Mrs. Edgers's translation.

Even if the lights message had gotten off Kramer's desk and out to McCollum's analysts, there is no guarantee that it would have reached us at Pearl Harbor in time. It was not just Kramer who was overworked. The whole OP-20-G staff was overstretched and dividing its manpower resources among the Japanese diplomatic messages, the JN-25 naval code, and the tracking of potentially hostile U-boats in the Atlantic.

Two weeks of fifteen-hour workdays had left Safford physically drained and approaching a state of nervous exhaustion as well. An unwelcome new problem had kept him in the office until late the previous evening: An inventory by the Registered Publications Section had confirmed that Wake Island held copies of virtually every secret code and cipher system the navy possessed. Safford, whose responsibilities also included ensuring the security of naval communications systems, labored late into the night checking the list. Before leaving for home in the small hours of Saturday, he drafted an urgent warning to go to the Pacific Fleet commander to order the destruction of all confidential systems "in view of the imminence of war."[188]

When he returned to the office on Saturday morning, Safford took the draft message straight to Captain Joseph R. Redman. But he was unable to persuade the assistant director of naval communications to release a dispatch that warned of war without the approval of his superior, Admiral Noyes. This was despite Redman's prediction the previous Saturday: "If the Japs don't strike us this weekend, I'll eat my shirt."[189]

Admiral Noyes was attending the daily briefing for the secretary of the navy. Stark and Turner were also present when Knox asked, "Are they going to hit us?"

"No, Mr. Secretary," Turner declared. "They are going to attack the British. They are not ready for us yet."[190]

Turner's certainty that Japan would not attack the United States impressed the reticent Admiral Leigh Noyes. Several hours later when Safford went to the director of naval communications to ask why he had still not sent out his warning, according to Safford's testimony a stormy exchange took place in the DNC's office.

"What do you mean by using such language as that?" Noyes shouted, pointing to the message. As drafted, it would have impinged on Admiral Turner's authority because it warned that war was imminent.

"Admiral, the war is just a matter of days, if not hours," Safford replied, standing his ground.

"You may think there is going to be a war, but I think they are bluffing," Noyes snapped back.

"Well, Admiral, if all these publications on Wake are captured we will never be able to explain it."[191]

Safford's point was not lost on his superior. But Noyes, fearful of igniting Turner's wrath, insisted on toning down the dispatch. In deference to the authority of war plans, it omitted all reference to the imminent outbreak of hostilities. Nor was it sent direct to Wake but only to Pacific Fleet headquarters and the Asiatic Fleet command for information.

When it arrived at Pearl Harbor, as a "deferred priority" cable, shortly before midnight, what might have been seen as a last-minute war warning from Washington was shorn of any sense of urgency. It read more like a routine administrative message:

> In view of the international situation and the exposed position of our outlying Pacific islands you may authorize destruction by them of secret and confidential documents now or under later conditions

of greater emergency. Means of communication to support our current operations and special intelligence should of course be maintained until the last moment.[192]

The attempt to goad Admiral Noyes into sending a last-minute alert to Pearl Harbor had been Safford's last effort on a tension-filled day. Secure in the knowledge that the first thirteen parts of the final Japanese message were in the process of being decrypted, he announced at 1630 that he was going home. Safford intended to take a badly needed rest for the remainder of the weekend. He had every confidence that Commander George W. Linn, a proficient cryptanalyst and his "best man on the watch side," would be able to handle all eventualities in OP-20-G.[193]

As Safford joined the exodus of afternoon duty officers on Constitution Avenue, the war department's communications center received a report from their observer in Singapore. Patrols of the Royal Air Force had spotted the two Japanese invasion forces south of Cambodia Point steaming west.[194] Streetlamps were blinking on and the gray shadows of a winter dusk were enveloping the White House when the gaunt form of the British ambassador climbed out of his Rolls-Royce.

Lord Halifax had come to try to get the president's agreement for a preemptive British strike against the Japanese convoys steaming toward the Isthmus of Kra. Roosevelt offered both reassurance and evasion. He told the ambassador, "If we saw Japanese transports steaming west or south west across the Gulf of Thailand [Siam] we should obviously attack them since they must either be going for Thailand or Malaya." But when Halifax indicated that this did not answer the question of whether the United States would respond with immediate armed support, Roosevelt said that "he would not cross that bridge before we came to it, and that you could not tell exactly how the thing was going to start."[195]

After receiving Halifax's cable, Churchill that same evening sent an urgent minute to the foreign secretary and chiefs of staff. It claimed that Roosevelt's answers were "very satisfactory" and that "this removes all political difficulty for initiating Naval or Air action and I agree with [the] President that we 'should obviously attack Japanese transports.' . . . Attack is therefore solely one of naval opportunity and expediency. Admiral Phillips should be made fully aware of all these telegrams from the United States." To nail down Roosevelt's commitment, the prime minister drafted a cable instructing Halifax to advise the president "we should be justified in attacking at sea any Japanese expedition" because "we understand we can rely on armed support of the United States if we become involved in hostilities with Japan. . . ."[196] Roosevelt had now been put squarely on the line. Whether he would have actually honored the guarantees Churchill believed he had given without congressional approval was never put to the test because the Japanese attacked Pearl Harbor before this telegram could be sent.

The uncertainty about what was going to happen charged the president's inner circle in Washington. The latest estimate from military intelligence was that the "most probable line of action for Japan is the occupation of Thailand."[197]

Secretary of War Stimson had earlier canceled a weekend trip to join his wife in Long Island. He had spent the day closeted with General Marshall because the "atmosphere indicated that something was going to happen."[198]

Roosevelt concurred. After receiving a phone call that morning from Secretary Knox reporting the sightings of the Japanese convoy, the president told his budget director, Harold Smith, "We might be at war with Japan, although no one knew."[199] From London the president's special envoy, Averell Harriman, had cabled that in the event of a Japanese attack, Churchill would "postpone taking any action—even though the delay might involve some military sacrifice—until the president has taken such action, as under the circumstances, he considers best."[200]

The prime minister was most anxious not to hurt Roosevelt's chances of persuading Congress to declare war if Japan did not attack the Philippines. Churchill, however, promised that once the president had moved, he would act, "not within the hour, but within the minute."[201] How best to coordinate the moves between the White House and Downing Street was the topic of the half-hour meeting early that evening with the British ambassador. The discussions between Halifax and Roosevelt also included William Casey, Australia's minister for external affairs in Washington.

The Australian cabinet, after a premature precipitation of the joint war plan by the Dutch had been narrowly averted—and when such an outbreak would have spoiled Roosevelt's plans—had confirmed that they would join in issuing an ultimatum to Japan. It had already been agreed that the United States and Britain would issue parallel warnings, but Australia's prime minister insisted that Roosevelt not only approve the text but also give the "signal for actual delivery of the warning."[202] Casey's cable to Canberra that evening set out Roosevelt's carefully plotted moves:

1. President has decided to send message to Emperor
2. President's subsequent procedure is that if no answer is received by him from Emperor by Monday evening (December 8)
   a. he will issue his warning on Tuesday afternoon or evening.
   b. warning or equivalent by British or others will not follow until Wednesday morning, i.e., after his own warning has been delivered repeatedly in Tokyo and Washington.[203]

Grace Tully, the president's personal secretary, was summoned from a cocktail party and Roosevelt dictated his telegram for the emperor. In keeping with the draft agreed upon with Secretary Hull earlier in the week, it opened with a reminder that almost a century earlier one of the president's predecessors had extended the "offer of friendship." Then it detailed the "deep and far-reaching emergency" that prompted a second historic epistle. The president addressed the issues indirectly. Regarding the Japanese military buildup in Indochina, he said it was "only reasonable that the people of the Philippines, of the hundreds of islands of the East Indies, of Malaya and Thailand are asking themselves whether the forces of Japan are preparing or intending to make an attack in one or more of these many directions." Roosevelt compared their situation to sitting "on a keg of dynamite." After giving assurances that the United States had no hostile intentions, "for the sake of humanity" he appealed to the emperor to "give thought in this definite emergency to the ways of dispelling the dark clouds . . . to restore traditional amity and prevent further death and destruction in the world."[204]

"Shoot this off to Grew," the president's note directed Hull. "I think it can go in gray code—saves time—I don't mind if it gets picked up." As he wryly observed to one of Mrs. Roosevelt's dinner guests that evening, "This son of man has just sent his final message to the son of God."[205]

Shortly after eight thirty the Japanese embassy telephoned to Ambassador Kurusu news of the president's cable. He was guest of honor at the dinner being given at Evermay, the lavish Georgetown estate of millionaire industrialist and former U.S. envoy to Poland Ferdinand Lammot Berlin. Among the guests was Colonel William J. "Wild Bill" Donovan, the president's Coordinator of Information. He noted Kurusu's candid reaction to Roosevelt's cable: Kurusu called it "a clever move" that would cause "headaches in Tokyo and more thinking."[206]

The dinner parties at the White House and Evermay were in midmenu that evening when Commander Kramer was finally satisfied with the punctuation in Japan's fourteen-part message. He telephoned Admiral Wilkinson for permission to send it out to the Magic recipients. The director of naval intelligence was also hosting a dinner party, at his Arlington home, for General Miles and Rear Admiral John R. Beardall, the president's naval aide. But Kramer failed to reach Stark or Turner. The chief of naval operations was at the National Theater and the chief of war plans was apparently out exercising the brood of Lhasa terriers that he and his wife raised as a hobby.

According to Kramer's testimony, he crossed them off the navy's distribution list when he made the decision to act as courier himself and deliver the remaining Magic pouches around to the other recipients. He called his wife, who drove over from their Arlington home to the navy department. Their first stop was the White House, at around nine thirty, where Kramer dropped off the locked pouch at the Situation Room. He told Beardall's assistant to deliver it at once.[207]

Lieutenant Lester R. Schulz had been a member of the presidential entourage for only two weeks. Still unfamiliar with the White House routine, he had been alerted, however, to the need to take the Magic pouch immediately to the president, who was expecting it. The president had slipped away from the violin recital that was entertaining his wife's dinner party. He was in his study toying with his stamp collection and chatting with Harry Hopkins. After he was ushered in, Schulz crossed to Roosevelt's desk, unlocked the pouch, and pulled out the papers. Hopkins paced back and forth as Roosevelt pored over the typewritten pages of the first thirteen parts of the message they both knew Tokyo intended to be its last word to Washington.

"The Government of Japan, prompted by a genuine desire to come to an amicable understanding with the Government of the United States," was how Tokyo prefaced statements intended to demonstrate the "utmost sincerity" of the efforts that they had made since April to "insure the stability of East Asia and to promote world peace, and thereby to enable all nations to find a proper place in the world."[208]

Half the document was a self-justificatory analysis of "the China question" as the principal issue in contention and one over which the Japanese government claimed it had "showed a most conciliatory attitude." The United States and Britain were repeatedly accused of conspiring with Chiang Kai-shek to obstruct "constructive endeavors" to stabilize the Far East and "realize the ideal of common prosperity in cooperation with these regions." Washington was accused of being the intransigent negotiator "always holding fast to theories in disregard of realities and refusing to yield an inch on its impractical principles." The American government, moreover, was charged with "scheming for the extension of the war" by "aiding Great Britain and preparing to attack, in the name of self-defense, Germany and Italy, two powers that are striving to establish a new order in Europe."[209]

The president's practiced eye filleted the bones of Japan's position from the obsequious diplomatic phrases. Such a bald accusation of American bad faith could indicate only that Tokyo was intending to rupture relations. Japan's communication concluded: "Therefore, viewed in its entirety, the Japanese Government regrets that it cannot accept the proposal as a basis for negotiation."[210]

"This means war" was Roosevelt's immediate reaction to this clear statement of impending Japanese belligerence. He did not necessarily mean that he thought the United States was going to be attacked, but that we would be at war because of his pledge to support the British in the event of an assault on them by the Japanese. His observation was later to be misconstrued as a dramatic declaration. But it was a low-key reaction given the offensive tone of Tokyo's note, as Schulz's own recollection makes clear: "The President then turned toward Mr. Hopkins and said in substance—I am not sure of the exact words, but in substance—'This means war.'"[211]

The absence of any sensational, sinister intent on the president's part is evident. The presence of the young naval officer did not inhibit five minutes of frank exchange that Schulz subsequently recalled for the congressional investigators.

Hopkins suggested that since war was coming anyway, "it was too bad that we could not strike the first blow and prevent any sort of surprise." Roosevelt was adamant. "No we can't do that. We are a democracy and a peaceful people," he said, raising his voice. "But we have a good record."

There was no mention of Pearl Harbor or of anyplace other than Indochina. Nor was there any indication that war would begin "tomorrow." Schulz's impression was that the president was determined to "stand on that record" and he appreciated that "we could not make the first move."[212]

Schulz was still in the study when Roosevelt tried to reach Admiral Stark only to be told he was at a performance of *The Student Prince*. The president decided not to have him paged because it would cause too much public concern. He announced that he would reach the admiral later, handed the papers back, and Schulz was ushered out.[213]

It was around ten o'clock before the Kramers reached the Wardman Park Hotel in northwest Washington where the secretary of the navy resided. After studying the fifteen pages for twenty minutes in his suite, Knox made "a number of phone calls including Mr. Hull."[214] Security prevented a discussion of Magic on open lines, so it was arranged that they would meet with Stimson in the State Department at ten the next morning to discuss Japan's reply. Kramer was instructed to be there.[215]

Driving from northwest Washington over Memorial Bridge into Virginia took another half hour. It was eleven twenty before Kramer rang the doorbell at the Wilkinson house on Arlington's North Uhle Street.[216] The admiral was entertaining General Miles and Admiral Beardall as well as two Vichy French naval officers, so they discreetly adjourned to the privacy of his study before unlocking the leather pouch. He discussed its contents with Miles and Beardall. But apparently neither navy nor army intelligence head believed the thirteen parts merited immediate action. This must be considered somewhat surprising in view of the president's reaction and their admission later that they had agreed "it certainly looked as though the Japanese were terminating negotiations."[217]

According to Kramer's account, Wilkinson put in a call to the chief of naval operations, who had by then returned from the theater.[218] Later, Stark was to be vague in his recollection of whether he discussed the receipt of the Japanese diplomatic communication with Wilkinson. He was unable to recollect if it was before or after he had received a phone call from the White House. Stark was nevertheless to insist that he would not have regarded it as "anything that required action." Certainly no action was taken—if it was considered—to issue a final war alert that night to the Pacific commands.[219]

Admirals Ingersoll and Turner would both testify later that they recalled reading the thirteen-part dispatch late that evening—and also deciding that no action was necessary. Their certainty was curious, considering that Kramer claimed he had made no delivery to either of them. Their telephones were not answered before he set out on his drive around Washington, and it would have been beyond the abilities of Kramer's car to reach the phenomenal speed required to go out to Chevy Chase, where Turner lived, then on to Ingersoll's house, and to have gotten back to the navy department by half past midnight when the Magic papers were safely back in the OP-20-G safe. After the watch officer assured him that the fourteenth and final part of the Japanese message had not yet been intercepted, Mrs. Kramer was finally able to drive her exhausted husband home to bed around one.[220]

While Kramer had been making the rounds of the navy's Magic recipients, Bratton was discharging a similar duty for those on the army list. A bearlike man of professorial mien, Bratton was one of the most capable G-2 officers and would have made general if he had not heeded the request to remain in Washington when relations with Japan nose-dived that November.[221] In addition to his communications duties, Bratton was also the head of the army military intelligence division's Far East section. It was a post that he was well qualified to fill. He had spent four years in Japan, first as a language student, then in Japan's General Staff College, and later as military attaché at our Tokyo embassy. After commanding an infantry battalion, Bratton was briefly professor of military science and tactics at the University of Idaho before joining the general staff's G-2 section in 1937.

Bratton, therefore, was well informed of the seriousness of the situation. After delivering the pilot message that Saturday afternoon to the secretary of state, the secretary of war, and General Marshall, he had returned to his office to wait for navy to finish decoding and typing up the thirteen parts of the Tokyo message. At the 1944 army court of inquiry, Bratton was to testify under oath, "without equivocation and without qualification,"[222] that around ten that evening he had made another round to deliver the thirteen parts of Tokyo's final message to Generals Marshall, Miles, and Gerow.

"It was my practice to deliver them their copies before I went to the State Department" was Bratton's recollection of his second trip around the war department. He claimed he had given Marshall's locked pouch to Colonel Bedell Smith before leaving the one for Secretary Hull with the watch officer at the State Department at ten thirty.[223] Smith, who was not cleared to receive Magic, was told that the pouch contained an important document that was to go to Marshall straightaway. Bratton thought Marshall's aide had understood the priority because "if it had been otherwise, it would have registered in my memory,"[224]

It was Bratton's testimony that persuaded the army's secret board of investigation in 1944 that General Marshall and his principal aides must therefore have been aware of the contents and implications of the thirteen-part message that evening. This led them to issue their indictment of the chief of staff of the army who "failed . . . to get General Short on the evening of December 6th and the early morning of December 7th, the critical information indicating an almost immediate break with Japan, though there was ample time to have accomplished this."[225]

A year later, however, when Bratton appeared before the congressional investigating committee, he had revised his testimony. He was chased around Germany in 1945 by a staff officer and confronted with affidavits sworn by Bedell Smith, Gerow, and the other former war department staff officers "to the effect that they did not receive these pouches from G-2 on the night of the 6th."[226] Confronted by the denials of his brother officers, Bratton signed an affidavit in a Paris hotel that effectively negated his previous testimony.

There was an evident note of reluctance in Bratton's admission that "in the light of the evidence before me now it seems advisable to modify some of my statements."[227] That "evidence" was the phalanx of his brother officers contradicting his previous testimony. As a member of the West Point class of 1914, Bratton appears to have been influenced by the military academy's code of loyalty, which caused him to put the reputations of brother officers before respect for the truth. The discomfort that this caused Bratton was apparent in the less than convincing rationale for changing his testimony that he gave the probing minority counsel at the 1945 congressional hearings: "I know all of these officers; they are men of honor and integrity, and if they say that they didn't receive the pouches from me or Colonel Dusenbury, or one of my assistants, then my recollection must have been at fault and I so admit."[228]

Yet only a few months later in Japan, Bratton was to assure Colonel Raymond Orr, a fellow officer on General MacArthur's staff, that Marshall *was* more than aware of the implications of the thirteen-part message (see Orr affidavit in Authors' Notes). He explained that he had tried to deliver it personally to the army chief of staff that night. That afternoon, moreover, Bratton had vainly tried to persuade Marshall to issue another alert to the Pacific commands. But Marshall had refused, and he left for his quarters at Fort Myer after telling Bratton that he "did not want to be disturbed."[229]

Whether Marshall was "disturbed"—and by what news—must be a matter for valid speculation. The army chief of staff later demonstrated a surprising inability to recollect where he was, or what he did, in the critical hours of Saturday night and early Sunday morning.

For over a week Marshall's head of military intelligence, General Miles, had "considered war as very probable if not inevitable."[230] It was looming so close that Saturday afternoon when Marshall left the office, he could not have been unaware that it might occur sooner rather than later. The war department had received news that two large Japanese invasion convoys were only hours away from the Malaya Peninsula. Marshall himself had been party to the president's pledges to fight alongside the British. An attack on the Philippines could not be ruled out. Magic had revealed that the Japanese were keeping a careful note of MacArthur's strategic bombers, and the latest diplomatic indications were that Tokyo was about to rupture relations with the United States.[231]

Yet General Marshall's testimony presents a detachment, as the hour of supreme national crisis approached, from this momentous event that was as surprising as it was uncharacteristic of the country's most senior military officer. Under cross-examination, however, the chief of the army conceded that standing orders were "if anything came up at night on which I could act that night, on which it was necessary I should act that night, it should be brought to my attention immediately."[232] Yet Marshall managed to evade admitting whether he had received any information by courier or telephone that evening; he was even uncertain about his whereabouts.

"I think I was at home," Marshall testified before the congressional committee. "I am not certain about that. I had no formal engagement, and we practically did not get out at all, except to the movies." But while he could not even recall which of his orderlies was on duty that evening, he was "certain" that Colonel Bratton had not made a Magic delivery to Fort Myer. Nor, apparently, did anyone else. In fact Marshall agreed that he had gone to bed that night "without any knowledge that the Japs were sending any reply at all."[233]

Marshall, nonetheless, cannot have left the war department in ignorance of the pilot message foreshadowing Tokyo's reply that was circulated in the early afternoon. If Bedell Smith had received the pouch, as it was claimed he did, he would have sent it by courier to Fort Myer. Still more difficult to believe is that if Roosevelt had tried to reach Stark, which he did, he would not have tried to reach Marshall to consult about the thirteen-part message that had caused him to remark, "This means war."

The only possible explanation of why Marshall might not have received the thirteen-part message was given by General Miles. After seeing Admiral Wilkinson's pouch, Miles testified, he had decided that it was of "little military significance,"[234] since Japan's rejection of Hull's ten points plan as a basis for negotiations "had been expected and discounted for some time."[235] Accordingly, Miles "contented himself that night by calling Colonel Bratton at his home about 11:30 P.M., and assuring myself that a full reply would be disseminated next morning on Sunday and that he and I would be in our offices then."[236]

Although he "could not remember exactly what was decided between Colonel Bratton and myself that night," Miles testified, he "saw no reason for alerting or waking up the Chief of Staff." Yet, in apparent contradiction, Miles also admitted that his telephone conversation with Bratton "satisfied me that the messages *were being delivered* or would be delivered early next morning when the complete message was in [emphasis added]."[237] According to Bratton's original testimony he had indeed made his delivery of the Magic pouches to Marshall's aide, and to the secretary of state, nearly two hours earlier!

Such inconsistencies must be considered in conjunction with the affidavits of senior staff officers which deny that Bratton had ever made that delivery. Serious doubt is therefore cast on the veracity of both Miles's and Marshall's stories. Either the army's Magic delivery system broke down that Saturday evening—or General Marshall believed he needed an alibi to deny receiving the thirteen-part message. The latter is more probable, because of the evidence indicating that the chief of the army did not spend the evening at his quarters, or retire to bed too early to be disturbed.

A headline in the Washington *Times Herald* that 7 December reported MARSHALL GOES TO VETS REUNION. It appears that the army chief of staff had attended a reunion dinner of World War I veterans that evening.

This explains why Marshall was so unwilling to recollect that he was actually within a few blocks of the White House that evening, and that he may have been summoned to see the president for a final review of the military situation in the Far East. That possibility appears likely, because of the recent release of a statement by James G. Stahlman, then a reserve officer, who was in naval intelligence and a longtime friend of Frank Knox. Stahlman recalls that on the night that the secretary of the navy returned from his fact-finding visit to Pearl Harbor, a week after the attack, his anger and shock prompted a surprisingly frank admission: "He told me that the following had sat for a considerable portion of the night of December 6 at the White House, anticipating a Jap strike somewhere: FDR, Hopkins, Stimson, Marshall, Knox, with John McCrea [Stark's aide] and Frank Beatty [Knox's aide]."[238]

There is no evidence in the official record that any of the president's war council were admitted to his presence that evening. According to the Usher's record at the White House, Roosevelt retired at a quarter to midnight. But this does not mean that a vigil did not take place. It means only that it was not recorded. It is only logical that Roosevelt would have wanted to take stock of the situation with the key members of his war council.

If the president did summon a late-night council of war, then it was apparently not attended by the secretary of state. This may have been because of his poor health, but it might also have been another indication of the extent to which he was being excluded from Roosevelt's inner circle. The reasons were apparent enough from the confidential report on events prepared a few weeks later by the president's closest aide.

"Hull wanted peace above everything," Hopkins noted cryptically. "It is true that Hull told the Secretaries of War and Navy that he believed that Japan might attack at any moment. On the other hand, up to the very last day, he undoubtedly had hopes that something could be worked out at the last moment."[239] Roosevelt blamed Hull for the "weakness in our policy" and for his inability to "be specific" over guarantees to the British and Dutch. The president had complained to Hopkins on more than one occasion during those final weeks of peace that the secretary of state "always ducked the question" and "would never envisage the tough answer to the problem that would have to be faced if Japan attacked, for instance, either Singapore or the Netherlands East Indies."[240]

Whether Roosevelt and his key aides "deliberately sat through the night of 6 December 1941, waiting for the Japs to strike somewhere" as Stahlman maintained—or just conversed on the telephone, it was clear that the time had come to find that "tough answer." That is why Assistant Secretary of State Adolph Berle wondered in his diary whether that Saturday would go down in history as "the day, when in practice, the war really started."[241] He had spent the morning working on the message that Hull was preparing for the president to send to Congress.

After taking his daughters to see the matinee performance of *The Student Prince,* Berle returned to the State Department around seven. He noted that half an hour later "Army Intelligence reported that they had intercepted the text of the reply which Japan was to make."[242] His 6 December diary entry appears to corroborate Bratton's 1944 testimony that he *did* make his second Magic delivery that evening:

> It was not only a flat turn down, but a coarse and gratuitous and insulting message as well. Bad as this was, the accompanying message, likewise intercepted, was worse. The Japanese envoys were to keep this message locked up in their safe and present it only on receipt of a signal; and during this time the final dispositions were to be completed.
>
> We worked up the text of a message; and I turned in to bed about one A.M., feeling very uneasy. The waltzes of "The Student Prince" seemed like a dirge of something that may have existed once, but certainly had very little relation to anything one knew today.[243]

Berle's reaction to the Japanese thirteen-part message contradicts both the testimony and evaluations made by General Miles and Admiral Wilkinson. Those who burned midnight oil in the State Department grasped, as the president had, its ominous significance. This makes it difficult to understand how the heads of naval and army intelligence could conclude that the decrypts of the Tokyo message were "not of great military significance" without the final, fourteenth part of Japan's final message.[244]

Evaluation of the intelligence that was available to Washington that Saturday night should have revealed that the fuse to the Pacific powder keg was burning down. The war department had been alerted that the British had given orders to their Far East commander for Operation Matador. This was a preemptive occupation of the Isthmus of Kra to forestall the arrival of Japanese invasion forces at the Singora and Patani beachheads. In either event the United States would be sucked into the war because of the assurance that Roosevelt had given, and the contingency plans to which the Joint Board had agreed.[245]

The only two pieces of the intelligence puzzle that the war and navy departments did not have that Saturday night were the precise hour that Japan would commence hostilities—and how soon America would be involved in the actual fighting.

If Japan did not attack the Philippines or some other outpost, the president would have to persuade the nation to honor his commitment to fight. That was why Adolph Berle labored into the early morning hours of 7 December to have the statement for Congress ready for approval of Hull, Stimson, and Knox at their scheduled 10 A.M. meeting that Sunday. That document and its accompanying ultimatum to Tokyo was what consumed the president and his army and naval advisers that Saturday night. So whether he went to the White House on the way home, or conversed in only general terms by telephone with the president, it is improbable that General Marshall went to bed in the blissful state of ignorance to which he testified later.

Contrary to his professed aloofness from the climactic hours of the crisis, Marshall had spoken to General Arnold that afternoon after Arnold arrived at the west coast to get the forty-eight B-17s off to Hawaii on the first leg of their long flight to the Philippines. "These damn fellows don't realize how serious this thing is," Hap Arnold had telephoned.

"Well, you are there and they are your people," his chief of staff retorted. "You start them out."[246]

Arnold did as he was ordered. The first group of unarmed Flying Fortresses took off for Hickam Field, Oahu, that evening.

Marshall's subsequent downplaying of his anticipation that war would break out the next day apparently was an attempt to justify why he took a longer than usual Sunday horseback ride that kept him out of the war department until midmorning that day. His absence from the office was to play a crucial part in the failure to get the last-minute warning to Pearl Harbor and could be construed as a dereliction of duty.

The effort to divert investigators from a collective charge of dereliction against the most senior officers in the war and navy departments appears to have been responsible for the conflicting testimony of the staff officers about how much they knew, or surmised, of Japanese intentions from the intelligence that was in their hands that Saturday evening. Whereas the evaluations made by the State Department pertained to diplomatic and political considerations, Marshall and Stark were the men primarily responsible for keeping the overseas commands informed.

Nor should it be forgotten that the inquiries by both the army and navy in 1944, which weighed all the evidence then available in secret hearings that were free of political manipulation, censured both the chief of naval operations and the chief of the army for their failure to pass on vital intelligence to their Hawaiian commanders. It is also surely significant that Secretary Knox, who never testified and who died before the 1945 congressional investigation began, arrived in Pearl Harbor three days after the attack convinced that another war alert *had* been sent out to our Pacific commands on the evening of 6 December.

In spite of the secretary of the navy's impression, no such warning was received by Admiral Kimmel or General Short. Had such a dispatch been received, it would probably have persuaded Kimmel to reject Admiral Pye's complacency and send the battle fleet to sea. A late-afternoon conference with his chief of war plans and operations officer had revived Kimmel's uneasiness. It led to a discussion about whether he should order a sortie that night at the risk of alarming the local population.[247]

Kimmel's unease was not translated into action. It probably would have been if he had received the warning that Knox assured him and *myself* that he believed had been sent from Washington that night. The failure to send out any eleventh-hour alert on 6 December has been inflated by revisionist historians into a deliberate conspiracy by Roosevelt to deny Pearl Harbor warning so that the nation would enter World War II united and inflamed by the Japanese attack on the Hawaiian Islands.

All the new evidence that has been gathered for this account shows beyond any reasonable doubt that our leaders in Washington *knew* by the evening of 6 December that Japan would launch into war in a matter of hours rather than days. Not a shred of evidence has been uncovered from all the declassified intelligence files to suggest that anyone suspected that Pearl Harbor would be a target. But there was more than enough justification to have sent out an urgent and more precise eleventh-hour war alarm to the Pacific commands. Worse, we shall see how the failure to disseminate even the last-minute intelligence continued to deny us the clues that would have warned of the attack.

Imperial Japan: As language course lieutenants Rochefort (above left) and Layton (above right) in 1931 were attached to the U.S. embassy in Tokyo as McCollum and Zacharias (below second row, right and far right) had been ten years earlier.

The Code Breakers: Laurence F. Safford (above left) was head of the navy's OP-20-G cryptographic unit whose experience of Japanese machine codes assisted William F. Friedman's (above right) army team in constructing the first Purple decoding machine (below) in 1939.

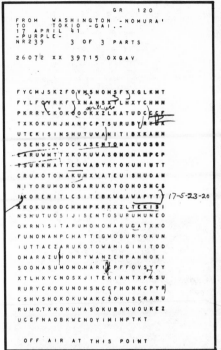

Left (as sent):

```
                GR   120
FROM    WASHINGTON  -NOMURA'
TO        TOKIO -GAI.-
17  APRIL  41
-PURPLE-
NR239      3 OF 3 PARTS

26072  XX  39715  OXGAV


FYCMJSKZFOVHSNOMSFXXGLKMT
FYLFQVRKFXXNANSXTLHXYCHMM
PKRRYCKOKOOOKXZLKATUDCECF
TXKOKUNJNANPCPTSURUBYJR+UK
UTEKISINSHUTUWANITIBXKAMM
OSENSCNODCKASENTONARUOSOR
CARUWMTTXKOKUWASONONAMPCP
TSURKHATTENWABYRYOKUMIUTT
CRUKOTONAKUHXWATEUISHUDAN
NIYORUMONONARUKOTOOHOSNCS
IAKORENITLCSITEBKWGAWAPYT (17-5-23-20
XKOKUNODCHMMNPKRKXZLTEKISI
NSHUTUOSIJISENTOSURUMUNEO
QKRNISITARUMONONARUGATXKO
FUNONANPCHATTEGWOBURYOKUN
IUTTAEZARUKOTOWAMIGINITOD
OMARAZUHONRYWANZENPANNOKI
SOONASUMONONARIHPFFOVSYFY
XTLHXYCNOSXJITEKIANTXPKSU
RURYCKOKUNOHSNCCFHONKCPYR
CSHVSHOKOKUWAKCSOKUSEARU
RUMO.TXKOKUWASOKUBAKUOUKEZ
UCCFNAOBKWENOYIMINPTKT


OFF AIR AT THIS POINT
```

Right (decrypted):

From: Washington (Nomura)
To: Tokyo
April 17th, 1941.

#239.   (Part 3 of 3)

Secret outside the department.

VI. The activities of our two countries in the Southwestern Pacific:

Since there is the danger that an advance southward militarily by our Empire would lead to war between the United States and Japan, it is held that our progress in that direction must be conducted by peaceful means without resorting to the sword. It has been made clear to me that if we do thus, the United States will support our economic penetration thither. I must emphasize that this premise is the one and only basis of the present proposal for an understanding.

VII. The policy of the Two Nations Concerning the Political Stabilization of the Pacific:

Through this clause the countries of Europe will suffer some reverses but our Empire will have all to gain and nothing to lose.

(Message incomplete)

(Copy sent to G-2, 12:00 noon, April 19th)

16448   Trans. 4-19-41 (7)

ARMY

The Purple Code: Japan's top secret diplomatic communications, such as this message to its Washington ambassador as sent (above left) and decrypted (above right), were enciphered on an electric typewriter connected to a Type 97 coding machine similar to the device (below) captured on Guam in 1944.

Anglo-American Deterrent: At the Atlantic Charter summer, Roosevelt, Churchill, and military advisers, including Admiral King, General Marshal, and General Dill (above), agreed to a secret defense pact based on a strategic bomber force in the Philippines.

Marching to Different Drums: General MacArthur (above right) prepared to threaten Japan with preemptive B-17 bomber raids (above left) by 1942 while Secretary Hull (below) babied along ambassadors Nomura and Kurusu. But Tokyo's patience ran out before the deterrent became credible.

Kept in the Dark: Admiral Kimmel and General Short were not informed that the focus of American strategy in the fall of 1941 had shifted from defense based on the Pacific Fleet in Pearl Harbor (below, note prominence of oil storage tanks in upper left) to a strategic bomber deterrent five thousand miles away in the Philippines.

Vulnerable Fortresses: The Pacific Fleet battleships on prewar maneuvers were destined to become floating targets rather than bulwarks of naval power. Too slow to operate with the carriers, the battlefleet was left behind by Admiral Halsey when he sortied in the first week of December 1941 to ferry fighter plane reinforcements to Wake.

A Knockout Blow: Admiral Yamamoto (above left—a posthumous silk painting Roger Pineau rescued from Japan in 1949) believed an air attack on the Pacific Fleet commanded by Admiral Nagumo (above right) was the best chance for Japan's navy—which included powerful 10,000-ton cruisers (below)—to win a quick victory over the United States.

The *Kido Butai*: *Akagi* and three of Nagumo's six carriers shortly before the striking force set sail for Hawaii on 26 November 1941.

The Feud on the Second Deck: Admiral Turner (above left), appointed by Admiral Stark (above center) as director of war plans, fought DNI Captain Kirk (above right) for control of cryptanalytic information. After Admiral Wilkinson (below left) became DNI in October 1941, Turner vetoed all operational dispatches from Commander McCollum (below center) and DNC Admiral Leigh Noyes (below right). NAVAL HISTORICAL CENTER

Missed Clues: Kramer (above left), head of OP-20-G translation section, neglected the true significance of the so-called bomb plot decrypt (below right) and the "lights message" (below left) translated by Mrs. Dorothy Edgers (above right) on the eve of Japan's attack.

From: Tokyo (Toyoda)
To: Honolulu
September 24, 1941

#83

      Strictly secret.

      Henceforth, we would like to have you make reports concerning vessels along the following lines insofar as possible:

      1. The waters (of Pearl Harbor) are to be divided roughly into five sub-areas. (We have no objections to your abbreviating as much as you like.)

      Area A. Waters between Ford Island and the Arsenal.

      Area B. Waters adjacent to the Island south and west of Ford Island. (This area is on the opposite side of the Island from Area A.)

      Area C. East Loch.

      Area D. Middle Loch.

      Area E. West Loch and the communicating water routes.

      2. With regard to warships and aircraft carriers, we would like to have you report on those at anchor, (these are not so important) tied up at wharves, buoys and in docks. (Designate types and classes briefly. If possible we would like to have you make mention of the fact when there are two or more vessels along side the same wharf.)

23260
ARMY

Trans. 10/9/41 (S)

T . C   TOP SECRET ULTRA

From: Honolulu (Kita).
To : Tokyo.
3 December 1941
(PA-K2)

#245 (In 2 parts, complete)

      (Military secret).

      From Ichiro Fujii to the Chief of #3 Section of Military Staff Headquarters.

      1. I wish to change my method of communicating by signals to the following:

      I. Arrange the eight signals in three columns as follows:

Meaning	Signal	
Battleship divisions including scouts and screen units	Preparing to sortie.	1
A number of carriers	Preparing to sortie.	2
Battleship divisions	All departed between 1st and 3rd.	3
Carriers	Several departed between 1st and 3rd.	4
Carriers	All departed between 1st and 3rd.	5
Battleship divisions	All departed between 4th and 6th.	6
Carriers	Several departed between 4th and 6th.	7
Carriers	All departed between 4th and 6th.	8

JD-1: 7370   SECRET   (continued)   (M) Navy Trans. 12-11-41 (7)

TO RA! TO RA! TO RA!: A Japanese Kate (above), armed with a specially modified torpedo, heading in with the second wave to attack an already crippled Battleship Row, while *Nevada* (below center) manages to limp across the harbor.

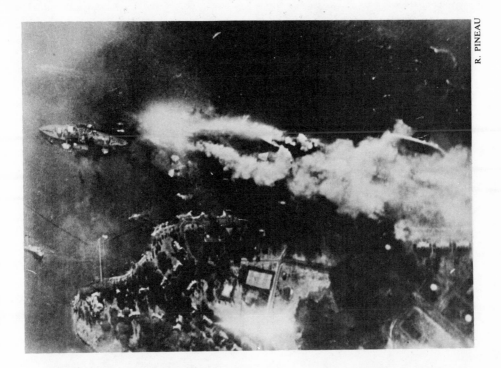

Battleship Row: As seen from the cockpit of an attacking plane (above) and at sea level (below) as *Arizona* blazes after the magazine explosion with *Tennessee* and *West Virginia*.

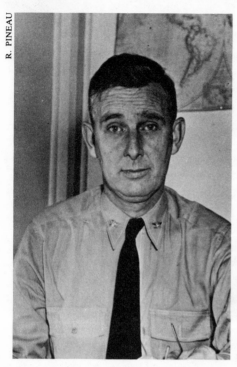

The Men of Station Hypo: The leadership of Rochefort (above left) inspired cryptanalysts like Wesley A. Wright (above right) and the ex-bandsmen of battleship *Maryland* (below), who ran the I.B.M. punch-card machines.

Negat Versus Hypo: The reorganization of OP-20-G by Joseph R. Redman (above left), the new director of naval communications, and his brother, John R. Redman (above right), threatened the independence and integrity of Rochefort and his deputy, Thomas H. Dyer (below, at his pin-up desk).

CAPTAIN DYER USN
G-4

40 1 MAY 1942

82

(1) 810144
Com 14 → COMB. JALUIT RADIO SENT "U.S. RADIO INTELLIGENCE
(0100 1 MAY) REPORT — 14 NAVAL AIRCRAFT HEARD, APPARENTLY
AN AIR PATROL COVERING A SORTIE. COM 14 REPORT —
FOR UNITS SORTIEING. GREATLY INCREASED
INTEREST IN AIR OPERATIONS IN HAWAIIAN, ALASKAN AND SAMOAN
AREA BEING SHOWN BY JAPANESE RECENTLY. ALSO ON 25 APRIL
TOKYO REPORTED THAT FLEET UNITS HAD RETURNED TO PEARL
HARBOR, (FROM DOOLITTLE RAID) AS EVIDENCED BY TRANSMISSIONS
FROM SOME 20 CARRIER BASED AIRCRAFT, INDICATING THEIR RETURN
TO PEARL HARBOR.

011125 — 011138 — 011108   ((C.I. SUMMARY FOR R.I.
Com 14 → OPNAV, BELCONNEN, C.T.F 16. UNIT IN CTF 16.))
(C) ..... "MO" CAMPAIGN NOW UNDERWAY INVOLVES SOUTH EAST NEW
GUINEA AND LOUISIADE ARCHIPELAGO — SUGGEST MORESBY FOR
"MO". FORCES INVOLVED WILL CONSIST OF CARDIV 5, CRUDIV 5 LESS
NACHI, GUNBOAT DIVISION 8, CRUDIV 18 AND DESRON 6 AVAILABLE.
NEW BRITAIN AIR, KNOWN AS 5TH AIR ATTACK FORCE, CONSISTING
OF TAINAN AIR, 4TH AIR, AND YOKOHAMA AIR. FIRST TWO
HAVE LAND BASED BOMBERS AND FIGHTERS, LAST ONE MADE
UP OF SEAPLANES AND FLYING BOATS, TOTAL SHORE BASED AIR
BELIEVED 15 BOMBERS, 18 VP AND UNKNOWN FIGHTERS .... LIGHT
FORCES ENROUTE OPERATING AREA DESPITE MSG. GIVING TOWNSVILLE
AS REFERENCE POINT, DO NOT BELIEVE AUSTRALIA IS TARGET
OF THESE OPERATIONS IN IMMEDIATE FUTURE EXCEPT FOR
SUBMARINES. CINC 4TH FLEET IS IN IMMEDIATE COMMAND OF OPERATIONS.
(D) FIGHTING UNITS IN HOME YARDS PLUS FOLLOWING FORCES ARE
AVAILABLE FOR OTHER OFFENSIVE OR DEFENSIVE TASKS: BATDIVS
1 AND 2 X CRUDIVS 4 AND 7 X KAGA & SORYU & (OTHER CARRIERS
IN YARD ON A 2-3 DAY SAILING-ORDER BASIS) AND AN UNKNOWN
NUMBER OF DESTROYERS. IN VIEW OF GREAT INTEREST
SHOWN BY TOKYO IN PALMYRA, — SAMOA — CANTON AREA RECENTLY,
OF THE PRIMARY AND URGENT RADIO INTELLIGENCE ATTENTION
TO ABOVE AND HAWAIIAN AREAS AND THE RECENT RECONNAISSANCE
OF BAKER-HOWLAND ISLANDS, ESTIMATE PART, OR ALL, OF THE
ABOVE UNITS WILL COVER THE "MO" CAMPAIGN WITH POSSIBLE
RAIDS ON SAMOA AND SUVA AREAS. IN EARLY APRIL THE KAGA
TOLD TO EXPEDITE REPAIRS AS WAS SCHEDULED FOR OPERATIONS IN
THE NEW GUINEA AREA. VARIOUS RADIO INTELLIGENCE STATIONS
HAVE RECENTLY SHOWN INTEREST IN ALEUTIANS. BEST INDICATIONS
OF FUTURE OPERATIONS IS TOKYO'S ASSIGNMENT OF NEW NAME PLACE
DESIGNATORS; LAST JANUARY NEW ONES ISSUED FOR PLACES IN THE
ALEUTIANS, INDICATING THAT AREA FOR FUTURE OPERATIONS. FOR
THAT REASON SECOND CHOICE FOR OPERATIONS OF AVAILABLE FORCES
IS A RAID ON THE ALEUTIANS BUT THIS CONSIDERED UNLIKELY AT
THIS TIME BUT CERTAINLY PROBABLE AT A LATER DATE. CINC
2ND FLEET WILL COMMAND AVAILABLE FORCE. CINC 1ST FLEET IS
STILL IN COMMAND OF SCREENING FORCES IN HOME WATERS"

↳ ALL MESSAGES PRIORITY WHILE UP. ABOVE MSG ARE URGENT

NAVY
REPORT

Coral Sea Action: The Hypo (Com 14) summary of 1 May that predicted the
Japanese naval forces' "MO" operation in the author's reconstruction (above)
of the Cincpac signal log. An enemy pilot's view of the attack on *Lexington*
that cost Admiral Fletcher (lower right) the carrier.

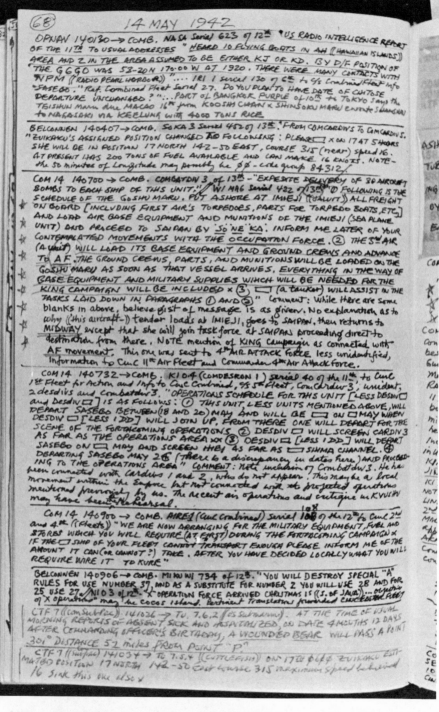

Midway Victory: Hypo cryptanalysts (above, starred) reveal more clues about "AF." But even after the battle began (upper right—a Japanese bomb scoring a direct hit on *Yorktown*) radio intelligence failed to warn that *Yamato* (lower right) was leading the battle fleet into action.

Cincpac Headquarters: The author in the plotting room (above) and Nimitz dining in the Makalapa mess with his staff (below) and Admiral Spruance at the extreme right.

The Winning Team: Admiral Halsey (above left) rotated command of the fleet with Admiral Spruance (center), and Admiral Turner (above right) commanded amphibious operations. The Battle of the Philippine Sea (below) on 14–15 June 1944 was the beginning of the end for the Japanese navy.

Strategic Decisions: The navy's mid-Pacific offensive and devastating sub-marine campaign (above) were defeating Japan by mid-1944. But MacArthur argued successfully for a Philippine invasion at the July conference with Roosevelt and Nimitz (below) at Pearl Harbor.

Victory off the Philippines: The two-day Battle for Leyte Gulf decimated the remaining forces of the once-mighty Combined Fleet. *Yamato* (above), under air attack off Samar, and carrier *Zuiho* (below), sunk off Cape Engano.

Surrender at Tokyo: The author (above), appropriately armed, accompanied Nimitz and Halsey (left) to the Yokusuka naval base the day before the formal capitulation (below) on board *Missouri*—Layton, arrowed, back row.

23

Day of Infamy

Pearl Harbor   *6:30 P.M. local time*
(13 hours 23 minutes before the attack)

I T WAS 1830 in Honolulu, the end of another lazy afternoon, and the
second weekend of low-level alert at the island's army and naval
bases found most service personnel off duty. Enlisted men were flock-
ing as usual to the bars, dance halls, and pinball parlors of the waterfront.
At the officers clubs and the verandahed dining rooms of the Waikiki
hotels, tables were being taken for a leisurely evening.

General Short and his wife attended a charity dinner-dance at the
Schofield Barracks officers club. Admiral Kimmel, more wisely than he
appreciated at the time, had turned down an invitation to cocktails at the
Japanese consulate. Instead, he and his wife went straight to the Hale-
kulani Hotel for a small dinner party hosted by his successor as cruiser
force commander, Rear Admiral Herbert F. Leary.

That evening I was with a group of officers and their wives who gathered to dine and dance in the tropical splendor of the Royal Hawaiian
Hotel. Beyond the terrace, the lights of Waikiki's palm-fringed crescent
stretched away like a Hollywood set. The mood and music almost made
me forget my preoccupation with the events on the far side of the Pacific
that were rushing to shape our nation's destiny. But at midnight the familiar refrain of the "Star-Spangled Banner," which ended the dancing,
brought me back to reality. As I stood to attention I was suddenly overcome with the urge to yell "Wake up, America!"

On that last evening of peace our military installations on the island
betrayed few indications that the island was already on war alert; everything had been carefully concealed to avoid alarming local residents. At
Hickam and Wheeler airfields armed guards patrolled the rows of aircraft
that were parked wingtip to wingtip. The duty air commander had ar-

ranged to pay for radio station KGMB to remain on the air all night so
that its broadcasts would help guide the first flight of a dozen B-17s that
were due to fly in from the mainland at around 0800.

Pearl Harbor was ablaze with light. The main attraction for white hats
without liberty was the band championship at the new fleet recreation
center. Only one officer and a switchboard operator were on duty at the
Naval Control Center on Ford Island, where only seven PBY patrol
planes had been scheduled for dawn antisubmarine patrol off the south
coast of Oahu. The only concession to additional vigilance was the army's
mobile radar trucks on the northern heights of Oahu. They were under
orders to start operating two hours before dawn the next morning.

Yet even if the radars had been reaching out into the dark waters
north of the island during those last hours of peace, their 132-mile
ground-to-air range could not have reached the Japanese warships. They
were still more than 200 miles away. A light cruiser and four destroyers
scouted 3 miles ahead of the main force. The six carriers that bore the
three hundred aircraft that were to deliver the actual strike were guarded
by a phalanx of battleships, heavy cruisers, and destroyers.

Clouds masked the waning full moon through the long dark hours that
the *Kido Butai* charged southward at twenty-four knots. Flight crews
dozed fitfully as mechanics labored with the bombing and arming of the
planes. The first hours of the new day had brought a reassuring piece of
intelligence relayed from Honolulu: "No unusual condition was observed
concerning the fleet."[1]

The fateful race of events that conspired to make that Sunday a day
which would live in infamy were unwinding.

Washington   *7:30 A.M. local time*
              (5 hours 53 minutes before the attack)

When Commander Kramer arrived at OP-20-GZ shortly after 0730 on
Sunday, he found the fourteenth part of Tokyo's diplomatic message,
which had been received an hour earlier. "Obviously it is the intention of
the American Government to conspire with Great Britain," it began, and
continued in the same accusatory vein. It ended with "regrets" that the
Japanese government "cannot but consider that it is impossible to reach
an agreement through further negotiations."[2]

After Kramer discussed the latest message with Captain McCollum, they
together took it to Admiral Stark. The "virulence and tenor of the language" of the entire fourteen parts[3] was a clear indication to McCollum
"that we could expect war."[4] But Stark said, "No, I don't think any further
warning is necessary."[5]

Kramer hurried off on foot to hand-deliver the latest Magics to the
White House and State Department. The president, who had anticipated

the fourteenth part's final rejection, remarked—almost casually—"that it looked as though the Japanese are going to sever negotiations."[6]

Pearl Harbor *3:42 A.M. local time*
(4 hours 11 minutes before the attack)

The moon broke through the patchy overcast shrouding Keanpapuaa Point to illuminate the black waters off Pearl Harbor. The light silhouetted the vertical stalk of a periscope approaching the outermost line of buoys that marked the route into Pearl Harbor. An alert lookout on one of two Channel Entrance Patrol minesweepers guarding the boom defense nets reported the sighting "1 3/4 miles south of the entrance buoys."[7] It was one of the five midget submersibles that had cast off two hours earlier from their mother submarines.

"Sighted submerged submarine on westerly course. Speed nine knots," the minesweeper *Condor* signaled by blinker lamp to the four-stack destroyer *Ward,* which was duty patrol destroyer that night.[8]

Lieutenant William W. Outerbridge swung his ship around onto the bearing, ordered general quarters, and commenced a sonar sweep. An hour later when no contact had been made, the net boom at the channel entrance was opened and the two minesweepers steamed through. They were followed into the protected channel by at least two Japanese midget submarines.

No sighting report reached the Naval Control Center on Ford Island. When no contact was made, the duty officer at the Bishop's Point naval radio station concluded that *Ward*'s report was another false alarm by a jumpy destroyer skipper.[9]

Kido Butai *4:00 A.M. local time*
(3 hours 53 minutes before the attack)

Dawn was less than two hours away when the flight crews were roused. After donning their "thousand stitch," good-luck waistbands, the fliers ate a celebratory breakfast of red snapper and rice, washed down with toasts of sake. Word quickly spread that the one Honolulu radio station that had stayed on the air all night was still playing its soft music. This was an unmistakable sign that their mission would achieve the surprise essential to success.

The *Kido Butai* was still some 230 miles due north of Oahu when aircrews crammed into the dimly illuminated briefing rooms. Even *Akagi*'s "was not large enough for all the men, some of whom had to stand out in the passageway," according to Commander Mitsuo Fuchida, who was to lead the attack. "On the blackboard was written the positions of ships in Pearl Harbor as of 0600 December 7."[9]

Washington   *9:30 A.M. local time*
(3 hours 53 minutes before the attack)

Colonel Bratton arrived at the Munitions Building shortly before nine. He was reading the fourteenth part of the Tokyo message and comparing it with the previous afternoon's thirteen parts when he was handed a much shorter message that had just been decrypted: "Will the ambassador please submit to the United States Government (if possible the Secretary of State) our reply to the United States at 1:00 p.m. on 7th, your time."[10]

"This immediately stunned me into frenzied activity because of its implications," Bratton testified. "The vital factor in my mind was the date and hour of delivery of the 14-part message."[11] That Tokyo would want a diplomatic message delivered on a Sunday was unusual enough, but the specific timing was its real significance. Dawn was an ideal time to launch a surprise attack, and a brief look at a time chart left Bratton "convinced the Japanese were going to attack some American installation in the Pacific Area."[12]

It did not occur to him that Pearl Harbor was at risk because one o'clock Washington time was well after dawn in Hawaiian time. Furthermore, Bratton shared the general belief that the fleet had gone to sea "because that was part of the war plan."[13] The deadline did, however, fall before the sun was due to rise over Guam and the Philippines and he felt strongly that another war warning ought to be sent out. He telephoned his chief of military intelligence at home. General Miles was concerned enough to leave right away for the Munitions Building. There he consulted with Bratton and General Gerow. But while they agreed that an alert should be sent out, neither of them had the authority to issue a command message without approval of General Marshall.

At 0930 Bratton put in a phone call to the chief of staff's Fort Myer quarters. But Marshall was out on his Sunday morning canter along the Potomac. An urgent message was left with his duty officer for the general to call the war department as soon as he returned.

Tokyo   *11:30 P.M. local time*
(3 hours 53 minutes before the attack)

The code clerks at the American embassy had finished decoding Roosevelt's appeal to the emperor. The president's triple-priority telegram had been delayed ten hours by the Censorship Office of the Ministry of Communications. To impress the foreign minister with its importance and make up for lost time, Ambassador Grew asked to be received immediately by the foreign minister. An hour later he was urging Togo to arrange for him to see the emperor. Although he knew that protocol ruled out such an audience, Grew left the foreign minister confident that the president's cable would at least reach the imperial palace that night.[14]

Washington *10:30 A.M. local time*
(2 hours 53 minutes before the attack)

General Marshall finally called the war department. The chief of staff would later not recall speaking with Bratton, who testified that he had offered to make the twenty-minute trip out to Fort Myer to discuss "an important message."[15] According to him, Marshall insisted that it could wait until he came down to the office.[16]

At about the same time, Kramer arrived back in his office, from his brisk walk from the State Department. The decrypt of the deadline message was on his desk. He made a quick calculation "to get a picture of how this 1 o'clock Washington message tied up with the movement of the big Japanese convoy moving down the coast of French Indochina."[17] Kramer decided that it was probably timed to coincide with the beginning of an amphibious operation shortly before dawn on the north coast of Malaya.[18]

Then the watch officer brought him a plain-language intercept. Kramer quickly realized that it was a true winds alert message, which he hastily translated: "Relations between Japan and England are not in accordance with expectations."[19] Later he discovered that he had erred in his translation of the word *higashi* (east), which was their code for the United States.

A correct reading might have sparked a more urgent reaction when he took the message up to Stark's office. Captain McCollum ventured that the 1300 deadline was tied up with some Japanese movement in the southwest Pacific. The message was nonetheless considered sufficiently urgent for Kramer to be directed to take it immediately to the White House and make the army's delivery to the secretary of state. As Kramer set off "at the double,"[20] McCollum pointed out to Stark that 1300 in Washington was "very early in the morning in the Far East."[21] They chewed over the implications of this fact and concluded that "it was timed for operations in the Far East and possibly Hawaii."[22]

Wilkinson, according to McCollum, made the only positive suggestion. "Why don't you pick up the telephone and call Kimmel?" he asked Stark.[23] Considering the security-mindedness of the office of naval operations, McCollum was surprised to see Stark actually lift the receiver. Then he shook his head and said, "No, I think I will call the president."[24]

The White House switchboard regretted that Roosevelt was engaged.

The emergency meeting in Stark's office was over by the time that Admiral Turner arrived at the navy department at 1115. The chief of war plans, surprisingly, testified later that he had not been informed of the deadline message, and that Stark had discussed only matters relating to what the Asiatic Fleet would do in the event that war broke out.

Kramer, after dropping off the morning's Magic pouch for the president, went directly to the State Department, where he found that the secretaries of war, navy, and state were in mid-conference. He emphasized again that the deadline in the Japanese message coincided with "a few hours before sunrise off the north Malayan coast at Kota Bharu."[25]

Kido Butai   *5:00 A.M. local time*
(2 hours 53 minutes before the attack)

The aircrews of the first attack wave, with *hachimaki* headbands tied onto their flying helmets, were clambering into their cramped cockpits. As the battle ensigns were broken out from *Akagi*'s masthead, Fuchida accepted the traditional bandana worn by warriors in battle from the flagship's crew. It bore the Japanese characters for *Hissho*—"certain victory."

At 0530 a pair of seaplanes were catapulted off the two heavy cruisers that were steaming ahead of the carriers. Their mission was to stealthily fly a reconnaissance over Pearl Harbor and the fleet's alternative Lahaina anchorage and radio back positive confirmation of the fleet's position.

For twenty minutes the other aircrews sat in their machines on the pitching decks, waiting for the predawn murk to clear sufficiently to take off. Spray lifted over the decks of the carriers as the force turned into the easterly wind to begin launching just before 0600.

Green signal lamps flashed, engines burst into life, and chocks were pulled to allow the first plane to roll. The crowded decks left the leading Zeros very little room for a takeoff run. After catching their breath as the first plane dipped perilously low over *Akagi*'s bucking bow, cheers rang out as the fighter clawed its way aloft.

During the next fifteen minutes, fighters, bombers, and torpedo planes swarmed up from the six carriers—some barely scraping the spume-flecked waves. Only 1 Zero pilot failed to make the tricky takeoff synchronization and ditched. The other 183 aircraft wheeled overhead as the first attack wave took up its carefully ordered formation.

Five minutes later Fuchida's bomber roared over the flagship's bow to lead the aerial armada, his orange commander's marker light vanishing into the clouds. Setting course due south, Fuchida climbed through the heavy overcast and burst into the dawn sunlight. It flashed off the burnished wings of the forty-nine high-level bombers following in formation. Then came the fifty-one dive bombers, the forty torpedo planes, and the forty-three escorting Zero fighters. Fuchida's navigator estimated that with the help of the strong tailwind they would be approaching their target in just over an hour and a half.

After returning to a southerly course after the first attack wave had been launched, Nagumo ordered his force to head into the wind to launch the second wave. It had taken less than three quarters of an hour to get planes up from the hangars and ready for launching. As the flight deck crews cheered and madly waved their caps, the fifty-four bombers and seventy-eight dive bombers rumbled off into the mile-high cloud base.

As Admiral Nagumo stoically watched their departure, even his confidence was rising that the huge aerial armada of 350 planes really would be able to pull off a spectacular attack.

Washington   *11:25 A.M. local time*
                 (1 hour 58 minutes before the attack)

Nearly two hours had elapsed from the receipt of the deadline message to the time that General Marshall arrived at his office. When Miles and Bratton appeared, the chief of the army insisted on reviewing the full fourteen-part message while they waited impatiently to give him the more urgent decrypt. Only then were they able to explain why they "were convinced it meant Japanese hostile action against some American installation in the Pacific at or shortly after 1 o'clock that afternoon."[26]

MacArthur's forces were seen as the obvious target, although no invasion convoys had been sighted heading south from Formosa and there was some doubt that Japanese bombers had the range to reach Manila. But 1300 Washington time would be an hour before dawn in the Philippines. As a precautionary measure, Miles urged that warnings also be transmitted to all our military commands in the Pacific, including Hawaii, Panama, and the west coast.[27]

Marshall eventually agreed that another alert should be "sent at once by the fastest possible means."[28] On a piece of scratch paper, he later testified, he wrote out the dispatch in longhand before calling Admiral Stark on the White House telephone system to inform him "in a guarded way."[29] But, according to Marshall, the admiral's first reaction was that another war warning would be unnecessary because "we had sent them so much already," and he "hesitated to send more."[30]

After a few minutes' reflection Stark changed his mind. A minute or so later he suggested that a joint dispatch could go out by the naval communications system. When Marshall said he "could get it through very quickly,"[31] Stark replied that the Pacific army commanders should be advised "to inform their naval opposites."[31]

Despite the "awful urgency" about beating the deadline, which was little more than an hour away, for security reasons Marshall did not want to use the scrambler telephone. If he had done so, he testified, he would have given priority to MacArthur, then Panama.[33] As Bratton left with the draft dispatch for the signal center, the chief of the army told him, "If there is any question of priority, give the Philippines first priority."[34]

Time was running out, as Bratton well appreciated. When he arrived at the signal center he was "very much exercised," according to Colonel

Edward F. French who was in charge of the army's signal center.[35] Bratton had to translate Marshall's hastily scrawled dispatch, which read:

> Japanese are presenting at one p.m. eastern standard time today what amounts to an ultimatum. Also they are under orders to destroy their code machine immediately. Just what significance the hour set may have we do not know but be on the alert accordingly. Inform naval authorities of this communication. Marshall.[36]

When Bratton returned to Marshall's office to confirm that the dispatch had been sent, he was told to go back and check with French how long it would take to be delivered to the addressees. Bratton was told by French that it would take "about 30 or 40 minutes."[37] The chief of the army seemed satisfied with this—even though he must have realized that with the decoding necessary the dispatch would not have reached the Pacific commanders until late in the hour before the deadline was due to expire.

Marshall might have changed his mind about using the navy facilities, or his scrambler telephone, to reach General Short if French had reported that heavy static had blacked out the army's radio circuits to Honolulu since 1030. When French learned of this holdup, he decided to send the message to Hawaii using his teleprinter link to the Western Union Washington office. He reasoned that the message would be relayed from San Francisco via the RCA radio station, which had four times the power of the army's and would be able to break through the atmospherics. He also anticipated that this would save time, because he had heard that RCA was installing a direct connection to Fort Shafter.

Unfortunately, the army teleprinter circuit link on Oahu was not yet in operation. This contributed to French's second miscalculation. Because the coded telegram containing Marshall's warning had been inadvertently sent out without a priority designation, when it reached the RCA Honolulu office at three minutes after the deadline had expired in Washington, it was pigeonholed for routine delivery to Fort Shafter.

Task Force 8   *6:00 A.M. local time*
                     (1 hour 3 minutes before the attack)

Approximately the same distance west of Pearl Harbor as the *Kido Butai* was north that morning, carrier *Enterprise* was steaming for home port after delivering the fighters to Wake Island. At dawn Admiral Halsey sent up a search patrol, and a flight of Dauntless dive bombers was being prepared to make the trip to Oahu in anticipation that Task Force 8 would reach harbor that evening.

Pearl Harbor   *6:30 A.M. local time*
                   (1 hour 23 minutes before the attack)

Off the entrance channel the skipper of *Antares,* a supply vessel with a
lighter in tow, spotted what he thought was the conning tower of a small
submarine having difficulty keeping submerged. The highly suspicious object was also sighted by the helmsman on destroyer *Ward.* Roused from
his bunk, Lieutenant William W. Outerbridge immediately had his men
open fire and ordered full speed to ram, while depth charges were hurled
overboard.

"We have attacked, fired upon, and dropped depth charges upon sub
operating in defensive area," Outerbridge radioed to the commandant of
the Fourteenth Naval District.[38] After attempting to ram the underwater
craft and observing a patch of oil, Outerbridge failed to file a detailed
report because he steamed off to chase away a suspicious sampan from
the restricted waters.

The naval radio station at Bishop's Point acknowledged *Ward*'s report, but no alarm bells were rung at Fourteenth Naval District or Pacific
Fleet headquarters. Nor were they set off by a second radio message
received half an hour later from one of the pilots of the dawn PBY patrol
who claimed to have "sunk a submerged submarine one mile off the entrance to Pearl Harbor."[39]

Washington   *12:00 noon local time*
                 (1 hour 23 minutes before the attack)

The conference among the secretaries of state, war, and navy in Hull's
office was breaking for lunch after a grim hour and a half devoted to
polishing the presidential address to Congress. From the Magic reports
whose delivery by Kramer had interrupted their meeting, Hull was convinced that "zero hour was a matter of hours, perhaps minutes" away.[40]
After the Japanese envoys had telephoned to request a meeting, Stimson
noted, Hull was certain that "the Japs are planning some deviltry."[41]

Now the main concern of the three secretaries was "wondering where
the blow will strike." They all agreed that the United States' objective
was "to hold the main people who are interested in the Far East together."[42] To this end Hull dictated a draft of an ultimatum to go to
Japan:

In view of the vital interests of the United States and of the British
Commonwealth and Netherlands East Indies, the movement of any
Japanese expeditionary force into waters in close proximity to the
Philippine Islands or into the China sea south of latitude 10 degrees

north, will of necessity be considered a hostile act directed against the governments concerned.[43]

Fort Shafter *7:00 A.M. local time*
(53 minutes before the attack)

The navy's submarine alert was not communicated to the duty officer at army headquarters. Had this contact been made, more attention might have been paid at Fort Shafter to another contact report that was received by the Information Center shortly after 0700.

The telephone call came from the Opana Mobile Radar Unit stationed at Kahuku Point twenty-eight miles north of Honolulu, where Privates Joseph L. Lockard and George F. Elliott had been operating their primitive radar set since 0400. The radar would have been switched off at the appointed time of 0700 if the breakfast truck had arrived on time.

On the hour Elliott noticed "something completely out of the ordinary on the radar screen."[44] Such a large green blip had flipped up on the oscilloscope of the primitive SCR 270B set that he thought something must be wrong. After a few minutes' checking for possible faults from the flickering green spoke of the oscilloscope he concluded that "it must be a flight of some sort."[45] The two soldiers went to the plotting board to transfer the distance and bearing from the etched Lucite over the screen. It indicated more than fifty planes were bearing down on the island from just over 130 miles to the north.

When Lockard called the Information Center to report "the biggest sighting he had ever seen,"[46] he omitted to pass on his estimate of how many aircraft it represented. As fate had arranged it, the duty pursuit officer to whom the call was routed was inexperienced. Knowing that the flight of B-17s was expected at around 0800, he assumed that this was what the radar operators were tracking.

"Well, don't worry about it," Lockard was told.[47] The irony was that our dozen four-engine bombers were then less than two hundred miles behind the Japanese. Like Fuchida's, the B-17 flight from the west coast was also using the KGMB radio station's music broadcast to home in to the island.

The radar crew nonetheless continued to plot the approach of the incoming planes until they were less than twenty miles off, when the backwave from the mountains scrambled the blips.

In a second breakdown of interservice cooperation that morning, Fort Shafter did not relay the sighting to either naval headquarters. So the last chance to have triggered an alert was lost.

Washington   *12:30 P.M. local time*
(53 minutes before the attack)

At the Japanese embassy Ambassador Nomura impatiently waited for the fourteen-part reply to be typed up so that he could keep his appointment at the State Department. Obedient to Tokyo's instructions not to use an ordinary typist, a diplomatic secretary had been slowly pecking his way through the lengthy message. Nomura realized that he would not now be able to make the deadline, and the embassy called Hull's office to request a three quarters of an hour postponement.

Downtown at the White House, the president was informing the Chinese ambassador of his personal appeal to the emperor. "This is my last effort for peace," Roosevelt told Hu Shih. "I am afraid it may fail."[48]

Fourteenth Naval District Headquarters   *7:15 A.M. local time*
(38 minutes before the attack)

Half an hour of telephone exchanges between Admiral Bloch's and Admiral Kimmel's staff officers failed to resolve whether hostile submarines were attempting to penetrate Pearl Harbor. When he was informed, at 0715, of the sightings, Bloch was inclined to share the opinion of his staff officers that *Ward*'s reported depth-charge run was just another false alarm.

That it took the harbor duty destroyer *Monoghan* only three quarters of an hour to raise steam and get under way was an indication of how swiftly more than eighty vessels could have gone to general quarters even if the alert had been given shortly after seven. The battle force was just awakening to the relaxed routine of another Sunday. Only three quarters of the crews were aboard and many ships had scuttles and watertight hatches unclipped.

It was a situation that Kimmel must have mentally measured as he stood unshaven and undressed and responded to the telephone call from his duty officer. He was inclined to agree with Commander Vincent Murphy, his assistant war plans officer, that it was nothing major. But whatever doubts he might have entertained about the validity of *Ward*'s reports, Kimmel abandoned breakfast and promised to be "right down" to his submarine base headquarters as soon as he was shaved and dressed.

Neither Kimmel nor the duty officer rated the situation as serious enough to rouse the rest of the headquarters staff. I did not discover until much later that awful morning that we had ignored what—in hindsight—were clearly the underwater outriders of the main attack.

The reaction might well have been different if Stark had not had second thoughts and had called up an hour earlier to inform us about the one o'clock deadline. And there would still have been just enough time for a general quarters alert if static and the exigencies of the commercial telegraph system had not delayed Marshall's cable to General Short. At the very least such a warning could have galvanized the island's anti-aircraft and fighter defenses soon enough to have spared the battleships the worst. And in all likelihood they would not even have been in harbor overnight had Kimmel received the warning from Washington that Secretary Knox believed had been relayed to him the previous evening.

Again left in the dark as to the general picture that indicated Japan was about to take the plunge into hostilities, Kimmel had to evaluate in isolation the intelligence concerning a submarine attack. He decided to await verification of the *Ward* and PBY reports and was still hopeful that the flap would blow over in time for him to make his regular Sunday golf date with General Short.

Tokyo   *3:00 A.M. local time*
   (23 minutes before the attack)

An hour after conferring with Prime Minister Tojo on the delicate issue of how to handle a message addressed personally to the emperor from the president of the United States, the foreign minister was driven through the tall gates of the imperial palace. Despite the appalling earliness of the hour, Lord Privy Seal Marquis Koichi Kido had roused the emperor from his bed.

Whether Hirohito knew that the Pearl Harbor attack was scheduled to be already taking place is not certain, but while a melodramatic scene was being played out in the ornate council chamber, the opening shots of the Pacific War were being fired by Japanese warships off the north coast of Malaya.

Kota Bharu   *12:00 midnight local time*
   (23 minutes before the attack)

It was pouring rain at midnight when the most southerly of General Yamashita's invasion convoys arrived off the small fishing port of Kota Bharu. Ahead of schedule, four destroyers and a light cruiser commenced blasting away at the pillbox defenses manned by the 9th Division of the Indian army guarding the beachhead at the mouth of the Kelantan River on the north coast of Malaya.

"Someone's opened fire," the commander of the local airfield told Royal Air Force headquarters in Singapore when he telephoned for permission to scramble his planes.

"Go for the transports, you bloody fools!" was the abrupt reply.

Roused from his bed, the British governor, Sir Shento Thomas, sleepily told army commander General Arthur Percival, "Well, I suppose you'll shove the little men off."[49]

Air Raid Pearl Harbor   *7:35 A.M. local time*
                              (18 minutes before the attack)

Unspotted by any American, the floatplane from the cruiser *Chikuma* winged its way north of Pearl Harbor and radioed back to the *Kido Butai,* "Enemy formation at anchor. Nine battleships, one heavy cruiser, six light cruisers are in harbor."[50] This was followed by a detailed report of the wind and cloud conditions over the target. Simultaneously the *Tone*'s plane signaled from over Maui that there were no American warships in the Lahaina anchorage.

The report was relayed to Fuchida, whose plane was less than twenty-five miles north of Oahu. He was straining through binoculars to penetrate the cloud breaks for a glimpse of the island's peaks. The Hawaiian radio station that had so accurately and unwittingly acted as his guide had just promised a warm, clear, sunny day when he was rewarded with his first sight of the terrain that had become so familiar from intense study of maps and photographs.

"All of a sudden the clouds broke, and a long line of coast appeared," Fuchida was to recall. "We were over Kahuku Point, the northern tip of the island, and it was now time for our deployment."[51] Then came the only snag in the otherwise clockwork precision of the strike.

Fuchida, certain that one flight of torpedo bombers had not seen the flare he fired to send them in to attack an unalerted Pearl Harbor, fired another "Black Dragon." The wing leader of the dive bombers mistook the timing, and thought he had just witnessed the two-flare signal for a diversionary attack on Hickam Field and the naval strip at Ford Island. The dive bombers peeled away, climbed to twelve thousand feet, and came screaming down on our unsuspecting bases. Surprise was so complete that this hitch in the rehearsed precision of the raid was to make little difference.

"Notify all planes to attack," Fuchida ordered his radio operator.

The "TO, TO, TO" signal—an abbreviation for *totsugeki* ("charge")—was flashed out as Fuchida's bomber swung around Barbers Point. Seconds later, at 0753, the prearranged code signal, "TO RA, TO RA, TO RA," was tapped out over the airwaves.[52] It was picked up over five thousand miles away by the aerials of the Combined Fleet flagship in the inland sea.

Admiral Yamamoto was engrossed in a round of *shogi* with his chief of staff. After receiving the message that complete surprise had been achieved, he continued clicking his counters across the hatched game board. The same traditional impassivity was not manifested by his pilots as they swept over the jewel-green checkerboard of Oahu's cane fields and pineapple plantations to rain destruction on the airstrips that were supposed to be the front line of Pearl Harbor's defense.

At Wheeler Field explosions and strafing runs tore apart the rows of parked fighters. On Ford Island bombs plastered the flying-boat slips, sending blazing chunks of PBYs roaring around like comets.

The torpedo bombers with their menacing instruments of destruction crowned by strange wooden boxes came looping in around Ford Island. Peeling off in pairs, they headed toward the line of battlewagons. The raid erupted with such sudden fury that it was vital minutes before those on board the helpless warships grasped what was happening.

Along Battleship Row the forenoon watch had just been piped to breakfast. Smartly drilled color parties were lined up on the fantails awaiting the bugler to signal the hour to break out ensigns. But the calls and the gentler sound of chiming chapel bells drifting across the harbor were abruptly drowned by the rattle of machine gun fire, the whistle of falling bombs, and the sickening crump of torpedo explosions.

The first "Kate" torpedo plane raced in so low over *Nevada* that it shredded the half-hoisted ensign with cannon fire. The sternmost battleship's astonished band continued to thump out a few more bars of "The Star-Spangled Banner" without missing a beat. Like a bloated steel lance the plane's torpedo splashed into the harbor abaft of *Arizona,* which was moored ahead. On board *Maryland* a seaman in the superstructure managed to break out a machine gun belt to open fire on two approaching torpedo planes.

The round of explosions that rocked Ford Island also roused the commander of the 2nd Patrol Wing. He broadcast an alarm from the control tower at 0758: "Air raid Pearl Harbor. This is not drill."[53] Within a couple of minutes the shrill cry of alarm was taken up by the naval radio station, which began flashing it out to the United States.

The Kates attacked in tandem, and moments later torpedoes had slammed into *Oklahoma* and *West Virginia.* High aloft, Fuchida was encouraged by "tiny white flashes of smoke [and] wave rings in the water" as the assault concentrated on the outermost of the three pairs of battleships.[54]

Kimmel was still in his dressing gown at just before 0800 when he took a call from the duty officer reporting that *Ward* had stopped a suspicious sampan. Murphy was still speaking when Kimmel's yeoman rushed in to tell him that the signal tower was broadcasting that the attack was no drill.

Kimmel had not yet finished buttoning his white jacket as he rushed outside. He stood transfixed for a few moments on the neighbors' lawn where he had a clear view of the planes circling over the harbor like angry hornets. "I knew right away that something terrible was going on," Kimmel would recall, "that this was not a casual raid by just a few stray planes."[55]

The first explosions rocked the underground headquarters of Station Hypo where Lieutenant Wesley "Ham" Wright was the duty officer that Sunday morning. The man he sent upstairs to check what was going on was Lieutenant John A. Williams, the only traffic analyst who had argued that the long radio silence of the Japanese carriers meant they were at sea. Williams must also have been the only man at Pearl Harbor that morning who was not surprised to see that the wheeling and diving planes had orange roundels on their wings. "They're Japanese aircraft and they're attacking Pearl Harbor," he came down to tell Wright in a flat voice.[56]

My astonishment was complete when, at about the same time, my yeoman called me with the shocking news. At first I found it difficult to grasp, because the sight and sound of the fury erupting at Pearl Harbor was shut off from my house by the drop curtain of Diamond Head.

Minutes later my neighbor Lieutenant Paul Crosley picked me up in his Cadillac roadster. As we hurtled down into Honolulu, the nightmare grew larger the closer we came to the naval base, which radiated terrible explosions. I remember feeling that this was just a bad dream that could not be true.

Tall columns of smoke were rising from Battleship Row. Prompt flooding of the magazines had saved *West Virginia*. But in the first quarter hour a combined strike by bombs and torpedoes had caught the great battleship astern of her. *Arizona* erupted in a volcanic sheet of flame as her forward magazines ignited.

At the head of the row torpedoes had ripped open *Oklahoma*'s port side. She turned turtle within minutes, entombing more than four hundred crew members.

Waterspouts from bombs and torpedoes continued to burst skyward. Overhead the increasing number of black mushrooms of exploding anti-aircraft shells were a hopeful indication that our gunners had recovered from their initial shock and were fighting back. Fuchida's plane was hit "as if struck by a huge club." A few holes and a severed control cable, however, did not stop the leader's bombing run over *Maryland*. Four missiles plummeted down to become "poppy seeds and finally disappeared just as two white flashes of smoke appeared on and near the ship."[57]

Maryland was saved by her stoutly armored deck. Like *Tennessee* astern, her inboard position also protected her. While far from unscathed, the pair were the least damaged of all the battleships. Not so the battle force flagship. At her isolated forward berth *California* took two torpedoes and was settling by the head. *Nevada*, at the rear of Battleship Row, was struggling to get under way. She had cast off her moorings and every gun that could be trained aloft was firing at the dive bombers that swarmed down on her.

A little under half an hour after the attack began, its fury began to abate when the first wave of planes flew off. Across the harbor, destroyer *Helms* ran down and damaged another midget submarine, which would later beach and a single member of her two-man crew survive to surrender.

During the twenty-minute lull Admiral Kimmel reached his headquarters at the submarine base, while Crosley and I were still fighting our way through traffic with the help of a friendly motorcycle policeman.

Washington   *1:30 P.M. local time*

Just as the first wave of the Japanese attack was beginning to lose its fury, the electrifying news began circulating in Washington.

"My God!" Secretary Knox exclaimed when he was handed the dispatch. "This can't be true, this must mean the Philippines."[58] But Stark himself confirmed it. "No, sir, this is Pearl."[59]

Knox immediately put in a call to the White House. Roosevelt was lunching with Hopkins in his Oval Room study. His aide also believed there must be some mistake: "Surely Japan would not attack in Honolulu?"[60]

Shortly after two the president managed to reach the secretary of state. Hull was shocked. But he agreed to receive the Japanese envoys who had just arrived in his anteroom. Roosevelt advised him not to tell them about the raid but "to receive their reply formally and coolly bow them out."[61]

After he glanced at their copy of the fourteen-part message, Hull's anger burst forth. "In all my fifty years of public service," he told the astonished diplomats, "I have never seen such a document that was more crowded with infamous falsehood and distortions."[62] Nomura and Kurusu, who had not been told of the attack, bowed themselves out in an embarrassed fluster. A department official overheard Hull muttering under his breath as the door closed, "Scoundrels and piss-ants."[63]

At about this time the news that had stunned official Washington was being broadcast to shocked American citizens. From coast to coast, radio stations were breaking into their Sunday afternoon broadcasts to report that Pearl Harbor was under attack by Japanese aircraft.

Pearl Harbor   *8:40 A.M. local time*

While Admiral Bloch was telephoning an eyewitness account of the raid to the secretary of the navy, the second wave of the Japanese attack came winging in over Honolulu.

"He could look through a window," as Knox was to relate, "and see smoke and flames from the ships still burning in the harbor."[64]

The renewal of the raid's intensity coincided with the arrival of the first of the B-17s flying in from the west coast. Unarmed and down to their last gallons of fuel after the fourteen-hour flight, the pilots nonetheless managed to land their bombers by scattering to airfields all over the island.

A hot reception also greeted the eighteen Dauntless dive bombers that had flown off *Enterprise* an hour earlier. One was shot down by our own gunfire, and four by Japanese Zeros.

Not a single navy pilot managed to get aloft as 140 Japanese dive bombers and high-level bombers swept in from the east. Battling fearful odds, a handful of army pursuit planes did climb off from Bellows Field to knock eleven enemy planes out of a sky that was now being punctuated by the puffs of antiaircraft fire.

Retaliation came too late to save the battleships. Kimmel stood by the window of his office at the submarine base, his jaw set in stony anguish. As he watched the disaster across the harbor unfold with terrible fury, a spent .50-caliber machine gun bullet crashed through the glass. It brushed the admiral before it clanged to the floor. It cut his white jacket and raised a welt on his chest.

"It would have been merciful had it killed me," Kimmel murmured to his communications officer, Commander Maurice "Germany" Curts.[65]

Later that day the admiral would show me the bullet and explain that although the practice was to turn over all captured enemy matériel to fleet intelligence, he would like to keep it.

The second wave of the attack was reaching its peak when destroyer *Monoghan* managed to ram a single midget submarine that was coolly firing a torpedo at the tender *Curtiss*, which was moored in the middle loch. The Japanese dive bombers concentrated their efforts on *Nevada* as she crawled past the blazing wreckage of Battleship Row. Her defiance was gamely cheered on by the men waiting to be rescued from the overturned *Oklahoma*.

Some *Arizona* survivors were picked up and helped man *Nevada*'s guns as the defiant battlewagon continued to fight off her attackers. The tugs that hurried out to prevent the listing battleship from sinking and blocking the main channel somehow managed to beach it at Waipo Point. It was the tugs' fire pumps that fought the flames that were threatening to engulf the battleship after her own fire main was knocked out by a bomb.

Nevada's dash for safety drew the Japanese bombers away from *Pennsylvania*, which was helplessly chocked up in the Number 1 Dry Dock. One bomb did penetrate the flagship's boat deck. Another bomb blew the bows off destroyer *Shaw* which was sharing the dock with the battleship and destroyer *Cassin*. The dry dock was flooded to douse the flames, but the intense heat of the burning fuel oil ignited the magazines and torpedo stores of both thin-hulled destroyers.

Ten minutes before this terrific explosion rocked the southern end of the harbor, which occurred just after 0900, Crosley and I roared up to Pacific Fleet headquarters across the loch from the dry dock. Under such terrible circumstances, with antiaircraft gunfire blasting up from the submarines, there was no satisfaction in being greeted as the "man we should have been listening to." I felt numb, and very sick.

The atmosphere was one of general shock and electric wonder about what was going to happen next. Everyone was stunned. Even my yeoman, who was normally as steady as a rock, was jittery as he handed me the intelligence log that he had been keeping. It detailed the progress of the attack and listed the ships hit so far, those that were sinking, and others that were asking for assistance. It made me feel physically ill just to read it.

Looking out of my window, it was even more horrible to see *Oklahoma* upside down and *Arizona* ablaze. Seaplanes were burning like torches on the ramp at Ford Island.

I knew that men were out there dying. Oil was burning on the water and the sky was a pall of black smoke. Such a terrible scene of destruction was impossible ever to forget. There was another pyre rising over the hill from the marine corps field at Ewa. My log said that Wheeler Field had been knocked out and most of its planes destroyed. Kaneohe naval air station on the west side of the island was out of commission and under attack.

Captain McMorris arrived at 0900 and immediately asked to see me. When I entered his office down the corridor I found the chief of war plans with Murphy and other members of his staff. They all looked at me as though it was a court-martial.

"Well, Layton, if it's any satisfaction to you, we were wrong and you were right," McMorris declared.

Of course I had been saying for weeks that Japan was planning aggressive moves, but it had not been my prediction at any time that they would open hostilities with an attack on Pearl Harbor. "Sir," I said, "it is no satisfaction to me whatsoever."

The *Cassin* and *Downes* were exploding in the dry dock as this exchange took place. It made me feel terrible. I excused myself and left to return to my office.

Now that the whole of Battleship Row lay under a billowing black cloud and a big blaze was raging in the dry dock, the Japanese bombers turned their attention to the northern side of Ford Island. During the final phase of their raid they damaged three light cruisers and sank the old battlewagon *Utah,* which was serving as a target ship.

It was during this final round that Ham Wright telephoned me from Hypo to tell me that they had just gotten a direction-finder bearing on radio signals made by the Japanese force. It was a "bilateral," a two-way reading of either 363 degrees or 183 degrees—this could mean that the carriers we had been trying to locate for so long were either due north or due south of us.

I wanted to know why the seventy-five-foot antenna of our top-secret CKK-X direction finder concealed high on a jungled peak to the north of Pearl Harbor could not give us a more accurate fix. "We can't get in communication with them," Wright told me. It later turned out that our telephone lines to it were army circuits. They had pulled the plugs on us when the emergency began and had not given us any warning.

When I went down to the operations room plot to lay down the two bearings, Admiral Kimmel came in. He was white and shaken, but determined to find a way of hitting back without delay. He wanted to know where the Japanese force was, and became uncharacteristically testy when I could not tell him whether the enemy carrier force was north or south.

"Goddammit! We're under attack here, everybody knows we're under attack," the admiral erupted. "Here you are, the fleet intelligence officer, and you don't even know whether they're north or south. For Christ's sake!"

The world had exploded in his face and I could not blame the admiral. If he had known at that moment that Washington had withheld vital intelligence from him, I believe he would have had a stroke then and there. The battleships were burning, ships were exploding, men were dying— and he was the man responsible. He had received no warning and then I was unable to tell him where our tormentors were. It was too much to ask any man to remain calm under such dreadful pressure.

All through the morning we had been receiving confusing and conflicting intelligence. Some army units were reporting an invasion had begun. "Enemy troops landing on north shore. Blue overalls with red emblems" was one message we received. Another reported paratroops landing on Barbers Point. It later transpired that both false reports had been triggered by a mechanic in dungarees who had parachuted to safety after his seaplane had been shot down by the Japanese.[66]

The confusion was awful and inexcusable—and I felt bad about it. We would have been able to resolve our dilemma over where the carriers were if only Fort Shafter had relayed us the bearings plotted by the Opana radar truck. But they did not. The only report in which I had any confidence was Rochefort's. He telephoned me briefly as the raid was in its dying moments to tell me that the *Akagi* was the flagship of the attacking force.

"How do you know it's *Akagi*?" I asked. Joe explained, "It's the same ham-fisted radio operator who uses his transmitting key as if he is kicking it with his foot." But it was not much help to Kimmel that morn-

ing to know that the *Akagi* was two hundred miles away if I could not tell
him whether the Japanese were north or south.

Captain McMorris was of the opinion that the Japanese must have
come from the mandates and were therefore to southward. If so, Halsey's
task force was within striking distance. Accordingly, at 1046 Kimmel radioed Task Force 8: "DF bearings indicate enemy carrier bearing 178
from Barbers Point."[67]

Shortly afterward four army bombers managed to get off from
Hickam Field to begin searching the waters south of Barbers Point. They
discovered *Minneapolis* steaming in the fleet exercise area. Such was the
confusion that the heavy cruiser's report, "No carriers in sight," became
garbled in translation to "Two carriers in sight."[68] That afternoon a PBY
patrol returning from Midway mistakenly bombed a cruiser of Admiral
Wilson Brown's task force, which was also south of Oahu.

Yet despite Kimmel's anger and frustration in his impatience to hit
back, our confused intelligence picture that sent Halsey off on a fruitless
chase to the south undoubtedly saved his force from destruction by the
vastly superior Japanese striking force. This was no comfort to the fleet's
pugnacious fighting admiral who returned to a still-smoking Pearl Harbor
the next day vowing, "Before we're through with 'em, the Japanese language will be spoken only in hell."[69]

Washington   *3:00 P.M. local time*

While the attack on Pearl Harbor was approaching its climax, Stimson, Knox, Hull, Stark, and Marshall gathered for their first real council
of war in the White House. Roosevelt was firmly in command of the
situation, firing off a succession of orders for guarding military installations, grounding private planes, and instructing the FBI to begin rounding up Japanese and German aliens.

Underpinning the brusque confidence of a commander in chief at war
was Roosevelt's realization that Japan's attack had taken him off the strategic and political hook on which his guarantees to Britain had impaled
him. The president knew that whatever the magnitude of the disaster that
had so swiftly and unexpectedly overtaken the Pacific Fleet, the attack
had silenced the isolationists and united Americans in a war fever that no
address to Congress could have achieved.

The president had already decided in favor of a short speech asking
for a declaration of war the next morning when he was interrupted by a
call from across the Atlantic. After Ambassador John G. Winant had
spoken, the gruff voice of Winston Churchill came on the line. Both had
been dining at the prime minister's country retreat at Chequers when the
nine o'clock BBC news bulletin had reported the attack on Pearl Harbor.

"Mr. President, what's all this about Japan?" Churchill asked. "It's quite true," Roosevelt said. "They have attacked Pearl Harbor. We are all in the same boat now." The prime minister told him about the landings in northern Malaya and they agreed that he would make a simultaneous declaration of war against Japan the next day in the House of Commons.[70] (In fact, WSC jumped the gun by declaring two hours before FDR.)

Manila   *4:00 A.M. local time*

It was a full hour since Admiral Hart had been roused with news that Pearl Harbor was under attack. General MacArthur's first reaction had been to exclaim, "Pearl Harbor! It should be our strongest point."[71]

Forty minutes later, as the general was dressing, he took a call from war plans in Washington. General Gerow warned him that he "wouldn't be surprised if you get an attack there in the near future."

At 0400 that morning General Lewis Hyde Brereton, MacArthur's air commander, put his aircrews on standby alert. He also requested permission to send his B-17s on a preemptive strike against air bases in Formosa. Had this raid been allowed to take place, it would have caught Japan's intended dawn strike against Manila grounded by early morning mist. But MacArthur was apparently under the impression that "my orders were explicit not to initiate hostilities against the Japanese."[72]

Inexplicably MacArthur failed to seize the initiative—even after he had been ordered to initiate his war plan, and Japanese carrier aircraft had just bombed a seaplane tender early that morning in the Davao Gulf. His failure to act had a swift retribution in the disaster that overtook the Philippines seven hours after the last bomb fell on Pearl Harbor.

Pearl Harbor   *10:00 A.M. local time*

After the last Japanese bomber had flown off northward, Fuchida's damaged plane continued to circle high above Pearl Harbor photographing the carnage: "I counted four battleships definitely sunk and three severely damaged and extensive damage had also been inflicted upon other types of ships. The seaplane base at Ford Island was all in flames, as were the airfields, especially Wheeler Field."[73]

The pyre of dense black smoke that snaked thousands of feet into the clear sky was an awesome symbol of Japan's tactical victory and our defeat. The acrid stench of destruction haunted us that morning, punctuated by sporadic explosions and the flickering fires of burning ships and blazing oil. Our attackers might have flown off, but the havoc they had wreaked continued to grow as the nightmare translated itself into statistical reality with the ever-lengthening lists of casualties and the bill of destruction.

The final death toll, including 68 civilians, was to reach 2,403—nearly half of them were lost in *Arizona*.[74] All told, some 1,178 were wounded—many of them burn victims whose lives were saved by the doctors who waged a successful battle against infected burns with the new antibiotic sulfanilamide.

The attack had cost the fleet eighteen operational warships. Four battleships and *Utah* had been sunk; four were severely damaged and only two were locally repairable. Three light cruisers, three destroyers, and three auxiliary craft had been put out of action, sunk, or wrecked beyond repair. The navy had lost thirteen fighters, twenty-one scout bombers, and forty-six patrol planes in addition to *Enterprise*'s four dive bombers. The army air force losses were even more punishing: eighteen bombers—including four B-17s—and fifty-nine fighters. In addition there was extensive damage to airfields and installations.

The death and destruction did not end when the bombs stopped falling. Thousands of our men spent the day battling the flames as small craft, captains' gigs, and admirals' barges were pressed into service dodging the pools of burning oil to snatch fuel-blackened survivors from the water. For two days rescue teams and divers waged an agonizing struggle to cut their way into compartments where trapped men could be heard tapping desperately until air ran out. Only thirty-four out of the four hundred entombed in the capsized *Oklahoma* could be extricated alive.

Around 1100 the commander and staff officers of the battle force reported to Kimmel's headquarters. While I was checking the operations plot, I saw a short, heavyset officer with a vice admiral's shoulder flashes, still wearing a life jacket, his whites spotted with fuel oil, his face blackened by smoke and soot. His eyes were almost shut; he looked dazed as he stared off into space, not saying a word.

It was Admiral Pye, who had assured me, almost twenty-four hours earlier to the minute, that the Japanese would not attack us because "we were too strong and powerful."

Fort Shafter   *11:45 A.M. local time*

Tadeo Fuchimaki, the RCA messenger who had been delayed for more than an hour and a half in the panicky traffic jams, finally gunned his motorbike up to the gates of Fort Shafter. General Short's staff was preoccupied with preparing for the possibility of another Japanese air raid and making precautionary deployments against a possible invasion.

The communications staff was flooded with incoming and outgoing reports, so it was almost four hours before anyone thought of decoding the low-priority cable from Washington.

When Short finally saw a copy of Marshall's warning, it was nearly eight hours old. Predictably, he about went through the roof.

Shortly afterward Kimmel angrily crumpled his copy of the dispatch and hurled it into the wastebasket.[75]

Military annals have provided few more glaring examples of information that arrived too late to change the course of history. To his dying day Admiral Kimmel considered the delayed warning of Tokyo's one o'clock deadline as the most shocking example of Washington's mishandling of the whole matter of intelligence. Even if we had known of it that afternoon, I suspect we would have taken little comfort in the fact that the commander of Japan's striking force was also making his own blunder. It would rob the *Kido Butai*—and Japan herself—of the chance of a still more stunning victory.

Kido Butai   *12:00 noon local time*

Fuchida's bomber was the last plane to be recovered by *Akagi,* shortly before 1200. He rushed up to the bridge in his flying gear to deliver an enthusiastic report that four battleships had been sunk and four damaged. Admiral Nagumo wanted to know two things: Had the Pacific Fleet been sufficiently damaged to put it out of operation for six months, and where were the American carriers?

Fuchida estimated the "main force" of the Pacific Fleet would not venture out for six months, but he did not know where the American flattops were. Instead, he proposed launching another strike as quickly as possible to wipe out Pearl Harbor's oil storage farms and dockyard installations.

While the planes were being refueled and bombed up for departure, Fuchida went to the briefing room where his pilots were making their attack reports. Up on *Akagi*'s bridge Nagumo debated the tactical wisdom and strategic necessity of sending out another attack. He believed strongly that he had achieved his main objective of protecting Japan's invasion forces and the mandated islands from a flank attack for at least six months, possibly even longer.

Commander Genda, however, disagreed. He urged another strike, which could deliver a knockout blow to an already stunned opponent. But without knowledge of the whereabouts of the American carriers, Nagumo argued, he would be risking three quarters of the Combined Fleet's carrier strength just to wipe out static facilities. His staff was more conservative in weighing the strategic advantage to be gained against what they saw as the tactical odds against them. Only nine planes had been lost in the first attack wave, but twenty had failed to return from the second wave. Even heavier losses could be expected from antiaircraft and fighter defenses that would be thoroughly alerted to an afternoon raid. Another factor that contributed to Nagumo's decision to cancel preparations for a third attack was his concern that "to remain within range of enemy land-based planes was distinctly to our disadvantage."[76]

"The objective of the Pearl Harbor operation has been achieved" was how Rear Admiral Ryunosuke Kusaka silenced Fuchida, who had dashed back up to the bridge to protest. "Now we must prepare for other operations ahead,"[77] insisted Nagumo's chief of staff.

As far as the imperial general staff was concerned, Nagumo had indeed successfully discharged his part in its master plan for the conquest of the Far East. But other Japanese naval officers knew better. Yamamoto's chief of staff, Rear Admiral Ugaki, compared Nagumo's decision to "the quick pace of a fleeing thief" who was "contented with a humble lot." Commenting on the lost opportunity in his diary the next day, Ugaki observed, "In a situation where we lost only thirty planes the most essential thing is to exploit the achieved results of the attack."[78]

The failure of the Japanese to attack us again, as we expected them to do that afternoon, was their biggest strategic miscalculation since the decision to start the war. Destruction of the huge collection of exposed oil tanks at the southwest corner of the southeast loch would have ensured them a far greater victory than sinking the battleships.

The lack of fuel—and shortage of tankers to resupply the base— would have prevented any of our carrier task forces from operating in the western Pacific for more than six months. As Kimmel himself was to testify, "It would have forced the withdrawal of the fleet to the [west] coast because there wasn't any oil anywhere else out there to keep the fleet operating."[79]

Pearl Harbor   *1:00 P.M. local time*

We were still awaiting another Japanese assault when the afternoon began with news that Guam had been raided by bombers from nearby Saipan. They sank the naval auxiliary *Penguin* in Apia Harbor.

Minutes later came the disheartening news that Wake had been bombed and strafed. The attack cost the marine garrison seven of their newly delivered fighters and a large part of their gasoline stockpile. Pan Am's flying boat, *Philippine Clipper,* however, had managed to escape from the atoll's lagoon with only minor damage. While enroute to Midway the pilot radioed sighting a Japanese cruiser and destroyers that were clearly heading to invade the lonely marine outpost.

News had also been received that Singapore had been bombed and that Britain's colony at Hong Kong had suffered a series of heavy air raids. At Shanghai the Japanese had captured our gunboat *Wake* and imprisoned her crew. There had been two bombing attacks so far on the Philippines—but MacArthur was still refusing to allow his B-17 force to make a counterstrike on Formosa.

As the reports came in to Pacific Fleet headquarters, it was becoming clear that all Japan's attacks had been carefully synchronized with the raid on Pearl Harbor. But it was not until well into the afternoon that I was finally able to tell Kimmel with certainty that our attackers had come in from the north. The information was less vital than it might have been during the morning, because with each hour that passed it was becoming apparent that we were to be spared another strike.

The answer to the question that had caused Admiral Kimmel to flare up that morning was provided by a "plot board" and pilot's navigation sheet that had been recovered from a Japanese plane that crashed into the seaplane tender *Curtiss*. It was marked with the plane's attack course and his return route to the carriers, some two hundred miles to the north of Oahu. Like Marshall's war warning, this information came too late to influence events. But a far more valuable piece of intelligence emerged from this bloodstained package. It was a temporary call-sign card for all the ships that comprised the striking force.

The documents confirmed the report brought back by a dispatch rider sent out to the secret direction-finding station. So when Admiral Kimmel sent for me late that afternoon, I was able to give him the exact composition of the enemy force, which was by then far to the northwest and out of reach of our planes and ships.

It was then that Kimmel apologized to me for blowing up earlier. "I know direction finders are bilateral," the admiral explained. "but I know we had one that gave good bearings and I didn't understand how they didn't get through this morning." I thanked him and explained that he had every right to lose his temper with me, although I regretted that it was the army that had pulled our connections with the direction-finding station.

Washington *8:30 P.M. local time*

The full membership of Roosevelt's cabinet assembled in the White House Oval Room to hear the president give a solemn summary of the day's events. "It was obvious to me that Roosevelt was having a dreadful time just accepting the idea that the navy had been caught unaware," Frances Perkins would recall.[80]

The president drew a historic parallel with Lincoln's cabinet meeting on the eve of the Civil War. He regretted to have to report that casualties "were extremely heavy."[81] Stimson urged that the president use the occasion before Congress to make a joint declaration of war, including Hitler, on "evidence that Germany had pushed Japan into this."[82] But Roosevelt was too shrewd for such a gamble. A double declaration would allow the isolationists to charge that he had engineered the fight with the Japanese. So the cabinet agreed to wait and see whether Hitler carried out the promises made by Ribbentrop to the Japanese ambassador.

At half past nine that evening the Democratic and Republican leaders of Congress were ushered into the meeting. Once again Roosevelt rehearsed the terrible catalog of the day's disasters. Outside the White House portico, which was usually well lighted but now was darkened as a precaution against air raids, the crowd that had been milling around the Pennsylvania Avenue railings all afternoon broke into another chorus of "God Bless America" as the meeting broke up.

One final shock was in store for the president before the day came to a close. A Japanese attack on the Philippines had been looming large in the strategic calculations made by the president and his advisers ever since 26 November. General MacArthur, unlike Kimmel and Short, not only had Purple intelligence, but he had been repeatedly warned that an attack was coming. So when the news arrived at the White House just before midnight that an air raid had wiped out most of the Philippines air force, it fell all the harder on Roosevelt.

It was a reprise of Pearl Harbor. The Japanese planes from Formosa swept in in well-coordinated waves to strafe and bomb Clark Field and the other airstrips north of Manila at lunchtime. General Brereton's planes were swallowed like sitting ducks in a holocaust of exploding bombs and blazing gasoline. In less than half an hour, three quarters of the fighters in MacArthur's command had been reduced to charred skeletons. The only four-engine bombers of his vaunted deterrent force that survived were the seventeen B-17s that had been evacuated south to Mindanao the previous day.

In strategic terms the Japanese raid at midday on the Philippine airfields was a far greater triumph than the attack on Pearl Harbor. At a single blow it had removed our ability to strike back and guaranteed the success of the impending Japanese invasion of the islands.

Roosevelt appreciated these strategic implications as soon as he was handed the dispatch from MacArthur's Manila headquarters. It reached him just after midnight. The president was at the time unwinding from the day's traumas with Edward R. Murrow. The broadcaster was to recall how the president's anger and dismay boiled that so many planes had been destroyed "on the ground, by God, on the ground!"[83]

The president must have wondered whether some terrible curse stalked his commanders in the Pacific to bring off such a Greek tragedy. For while the attack on Pearl Harbor was unexpected and explainable by a breakdown of our military intelligence, it was inexplicable that the thrice-warned MacArthur should have been trapped in the same fate nine hours after the first bombs fell on Pearl Harbor.

"Our general and leaders committed one of the greatest errors possible to military men," observed one of the B-17 pilots, "that of letting themselves be taken by surprise."[84] Why Admiral Kimmel and General Short were to be so publicly and immediately pilloried for a disaster they were powerless to prevent, when General Douglas MacArthur escaped *any* charge of accountability, is a question that has never been satisfactorily answered.

24

"Hard for Us to Take"

A SOMBER MOOD hung over Pacific Fleet headquarters after the attack. Updated casualty reports on Monday morning magnified the enormity of the disaster. Firefighters continued to douse flames that still licked the blackened skeletons of the wrecks, while engineering parties picked their way through the bowels of damaged warships to prepare for a monumental salvage operation. Alongside them rescue parties labored in the reeking hulls to reach survivors still trapped in compartments.

Dense smoke continued to rise from the wrecks along Battleship Row. We were spared the sight; the paint that had been used to hurriedly effect a blackout of the submarine base windows had been applied to the interior surface of the glass, but we had to endure the stifling fumes that intensified the cloying odor of burnt oil that hung over the harbor. This was the depressing setting in which Admiral Kimmel assembled his staff that Monday to announce his plans to commence offensive operations against the Japanese.

Kimmel had not forgotten, even if many of us had, that he still possessed a powerful fleet. The destruction of the battle force as a fighting unit seemed more stunning at the time than it actually turned out to be. This was the result of the prominent role that prewar naval strategists had foreseen for the battleship. Pearl Harbor may have been a disaster, but it was a long way from being the knockout blow that Yamamoto had intended. The Pacific Fleet could still send to battle two task forces with undamaged carriers. Meanwhile, the nucleus of a third task force was steaming at high speed toward Pearl Harbor in the shape of carrier *Saratoga*. Furthermore, a formidable force of nine heavy cruisers had been spared, and all but two of the light cruisers and three of the fleet destroyers had survived. And so had *all* our submarines.

The immediate task facing the fleet was to shake off shock and con-

325

fusion. It still marred the operational efficiency of those units that were at sea that Monday. Admiral Wilson Brown with *Indianapolis* had added his heavy cruisers to Task Force 12. But most of the morning was wasted while *Lexington*'s planes investigated an enemy sighting report that turned out to be heavy cruiser *Portland*. Task Force 12 was recalled to Pearl at noon. But another false report sent Brown haring south again after hearing that Johnston Island was under attack. It, too, was a false alarm.

North of Oahu, Rear Admiral Milo F. Draemel's light cruisers, reinforced by heavy cruiser *Minneapolis,* were spending the first of two days fruitlessly trying to track down the retreating Japanese striking force.

The southwestern approaches of Oahu were being scoured by Halsey's force. After putting in for refueling that evening, Task Force 8 sailed again at dawn on 9 December to continue the search. It was to be two more days before *Enterprise*'s planes caught and sank Japanese submarine *I-70*. Accounting for one of Japan's two-thousand-ton oceangoing submarines was some consolation for Admiral Halsey, whose thirst for revenge had been inflamed by the scene of disaster he had witnessed at Pearl Harbor.

The wild chasing of our tail in the immediate aftermath of the attack may have been excusable, but it was doing nothing to help Kimmel to hit back. I was very conscious of the need for more detailed information about the precise whereabouts of the enemy carriers. Kimmel wanted to know what the prospects were of their launching more attacks, if not on Oahu then on Wake or Midway. The intelligence that I had been able to garner from the Japanese pilot's salvaged logbook convinced me that an examination of an aircraft radio might provide more useful clues about call signs and frequencies.

So I called up Captain Mayfield and told him that we wanted to obtain a radio from one of the downed planes as soon as possible. He sent out one of his work crews to find a suitable specimen. Naturally, I anticipated that the radio set alone would suffice, but Warrant Officer Ernest Saftig, who had been detailed to carry out my request, had more ambitious ideas. After his crew selected a crashed three-man bomber in a cane field not far from Pearl, they loaded it onto a flatbed truck that they borrowed from the sugar plantation, and drove it up in front of the submarine base that morning.

When Saftig came to my office that Monday morning to tell me he had something for me, I asked him where the radio was.

"Outside the front door of headquarters, sir."

"Why the hell didn't you bring it up?"

"Because it's still attached to the plane, sir."

When I got outside, I saw what he meant. The plane had nose-dived into the ground when it crashed, telescoping its forty-foot fuselage into an accordionlike lump of metal along with its three-man crew. The hot

Hawaiian sun had already created a powerful reaction in the compressed corpses and Saftig, a former policeman and FBI agent, wanted to know from which part he should begin digging out the radio and also its documents. He would later prove so adept at such unpleasant tasks that I asked Mayfield to assign him to getting the papers from the midget submarine that was salvaged from the harbor.[1]

While we were standing by the debris, Admiral Kimmel came down and asked what was going on. When I explained my predicament, his face cracked into a grin. It was probably the first time since Saturday night that he had smiled.

In Washington, President Roosevelt had painfully climbed the podium in the House of Representatives on the arm of his uniformed son James, who was a marine captain.

"Yesterday, December 7, 1941—a date which will live in infamy—the United States was suddenly and deliberately attacked by the naval and air forces of the Empire of Japan" was how Roosevelt opened his address. His ringing phrase was to engrave itself not only on the conscience of the nation but forever on this particular page of history. After reciting the solemn litany of the "unprovoked and dastardly attack," the president warned that "there is no blinking at the fact that our people, our territory and our interests are in grave danger." But he promised that "with the unbounding determination of our people we will gain the inevitable victory."[2]

Within an hour Congress passed the war resolution, with only a single dissenting vote. Two hours earlier Churchill beat the United States to the punch with the formal announcement in the House of Commons that Britain was now at war with Japan. Declaring to the war cabinet his intention to visit Washington as soon as possible to secure an American commitment to the Atlantic war, he brushed aside advice that it might be too soon to put such direct pressure on their new ally: "Oh, that's the way we talked while we were wooing her—now that she's in the harem, we can talk to her quite differently."[3]

Roosevelt was reluctant to welcome the British prime minister until the United States was formally at war with Germany. Japan's attack had solved only half the president's strategic dilemma. For three days the two Allied leaders anxiously waited for Hitler to take the plunge and commit us to the global struggle. The fuehrer's declaration of war, when it came on 11 December, was not so much prompted by a desire to honor the tripartite pact—the German general staff saw little military advantage in taking on the United States just to please Japan. But Hitler was determined to beat the hated Roosevelt into the ring. He did so after the German chargé d'affaires in Washington apparently fell for a skillful leak from the White House on 10 December reporting that "within 24 hours the U.S. will declare war on Germany."[4]

The president knew that he could rely on Hitler's pique to avoid a time-consuming debate on Capitol Hill. He had skirted a potentially divisive issue by telling reporters that Germany and Italy already "consider themselves at war with the United States at this moment."[5] But Roosevelt was equally determined not to squander the new mood of national unity. He would not wait for his isolationist opponents on Capitol Hill to cash in on the public outrage over Pearl Harbor by demanding the heads of those who were to blame.

The secretary of the navy was also keenly attuned to the political mood. He resolved on the night of the attack to make a personal visit to Oahu "to determine the extent of the damage and if possible to find out why the Japanese had caught the U.S. forces unprepared." He hoped thereby to avert the "prospect of a nasty congressional investigation."[6] By 9 December he had obtained Roosevelt's approval for a visit. Its principal purpose, according to his aide, Captain Frank E. Beatty, was "for an inspection of the terrific damage with a view to placing the responsibility for the unprepared condition in which the attack had caught our forces."[7]

The navy's first Pearl Harbor inquiry got under way when the secretary of the navy's party boarded a plane for the west coast at the Anacostia naval air station on the afternoon of 10 December. In addition to Beatty, the party included Joseph W. Powell, a vice-president of Bethlehem Shipbuilding Company, and Knox's special assistant, Lieutenant Commander Edward A. Hayes. The ad hoc investigating team was supposed to parallel a similar army inquiry. But the war department's preliminary investigation came to an unfortunate end when a plane carrying Colonel Charles W. Bundy, of the war plans division, crashed into the High Sierras en route to the west coast.

The navy Lockheed, however, made it safely through to San Diego despite severe icing and turbulent winter weather. At the naval base the party transferred to a four-engine PB2Y Coronado flying boat. After his bumpy ride from Washington, the secretary of the navy's confidence in weather forecasts had worn thin. "That's just fine, son, but just you come along with me," he told the base aerological officer, who had just promised a smooth trip across the Pacific.[8] The unfortunate officer had no choice but to comply. He endured having to stand all the way because the giant flying boat was so tightly packed with blood plasma and serum for burn victims on Oahu that it had to make two takeoff runs before unsticking from the water.

Even before Knox's mission was communicated to Pacific Fleet headquarters, Kimmel anticipated that he would probably be relieved of command. It was the old naval principle that defeated admirals were expected to go down with their ship. The first sign that the navy department had lost confidence in him came in the shape of a panicky 9 December dispatch from Stark warning that another raid was imminent. It could "render Hawaii untenable as a naval base in which eventuality it is believed

Japanese have forces suitable for initial occupation of islands other than Oahu including Midway, Maui and Hawaii."[9] It was instructional, rather than advisory. Kimmel was told that "until defenses are increased it is doubtful if Pearl should be used as a base for any except patrol craft, naval aircraft, submarines or for short periods when it is reasonably certain that Japanese attacks will not be made."[10] The message was most certainly not the way Kimmel saw the situation.

According to Commander Safford, who told Noyes that "at a time like this somebody should keep his head," the dispatch had been sent as a result of an overhasty evaluation of the situation by Turner and the war plans division. Safford, as head of OP-20-G, had assured Noyes, the director of naval communications, that the Pearl Harbor attack "was a hit-and-run affair," because the pattern of Japanese signal traffic indicated that now that they had accomplished their objective they were proceeding with the conquest of southeast Asia.[11]

After reviewing the latest radio intelligence with Rochefort, I was able to give much the same estimate to Kimmel. Following my briefing next morning, he tried to correct Stark's pessimistic assumptions by requesting replacement aircraft and assuring him that "our heavy losses have not seriously depleted our fast striking forces nor reduced morale and determination."[12]

Morale and determination, however, were not going to be enough to reverse the tide of the Japanese advance. We realized that fact on Wednesday when we received the news that the British battleship *Prince of Wales* and battle cruiser *Repulse* had been sunk by air attack off the coast of Malaya. Meanwhile, Japanese bombers devastated our Asiatic Fleet's base at Cavite in the Philippines.

Nonetheless, Kimmel worked that afternoon on putting the finishing touches to his revised war plan for beginning offensive operations. It was typical of the admiral that he intended to waste no time in getting the secretary of the navy's approval to hit back quickly and hit back hard with a dispatch to the chief of naval operations:

> With the losses we have sustained, it is necessary to revise completely our strategy of a Pacific war. The loss of battleships commits us to the strategic defensive until our forces can be built up. However, a very powerful striking force of carriers, cruisers and destroyers survives. These forces must be operated boldly and vigorously on the tactical offensive in order to retrieve our initial disaster.[13]

Kimmel had picked himself up, dusted off the ashes of defeat, and was preparing for the next round. The depleted fleet might not be strong enough now—if it ever was—to go steaming across the Pacific to the aid of the Philippines, but it could still project its power to secure those island bases such as Samoa, Fiji, and New Caledonia, which were essential to protect our line of communications with Australia and New Zealand.

To this extent the admiral accepted that Japan's attack had put us on the defensive "and that is hard for us to take."[14] He decided that another raid on Oahu was possible, but not probable, because "the logistic requirements render such an operation unlikely." As Kimmel saw it the principal threat was from submarines and raids by fast-carrier striking forces. He therefore proposed keeping two of his three carrier groups constantly at sea for search and strike operations while the remaining task force guarded the approaches to Oahu or entered harbor for replenishment. The surviving battleships, which were not fast enough to keep up with the carriers (and this was very important but largely ignored by historians), were to be sent to the west coast. This would relieve the congestion in Pearl Harbor and protect the ocean convoy route to Hawaii. Kimmel intended to rely on our submarines to take the war to Japanese waters, and to guard the waters off Wake and Midway. The arrival of new planes and antiaircraft batteries would augment the defense of the fleet base against further raids, with the army and navy sharing an extensive offshore surveillance of the Hawaiian Islands.[15]

The strategy that Kimmel drew up in those first dark days of war was to prove so sound that it governed Pacific Fleet operations for the first six months of the war.

After Guam fell on 10 December and news came that the Japanese were moving south of the Marshalls into the Gilbert Islands, the priority for Soc McMorris and the war plans staff was to draw up plans for sending an expedition to secure Wake Island. An attack there was anticipated to be imminent.

Preparations for the relief of Wake were occupying Kimmel and his staff on 11 December when the secretary of the navy arrived. His Coronado landed at Kaneohe Bay early that Thursday morning. The burned-out hangars and wrecked planes at the naval air station on the northeast coast of Oahu were an unwelcome foretaste for the former newspaper publisher, who had spent most of a wakeful night huddled for warmth in flying gear and blankets.[16] On the drive into Honolulu the ferocity of the Japanese attack was evident from the wreckage of strafed cars and the beached midget submarine.

To preserve the "investigative nature" of his visit, Knox had given orders that "he would not be the guest of any senior officer."[17] Instead the party was driven to the Royal Hawaiian Hotel where they were met by Admiral Kimmel, who escorted them to his submarine base headquarters. Even Knox, the veteran Rough Rider who had charged with Teddy Roosevelt up San Juan Hill during the Spanish-American War, was shocked to his boots by the shambles of Battleship Row. Everywhere Knox looked, he noted men laboring to clear up the debris, removing corpses, and making defenses against another attack.

The loss of three quarters of the battle force was shocking enough, but the heavy toll in American lives was still more disturbing. Knox was told that six hundred servicemen had been buried that morning in a mass grave. On the ferry across to Ford Island he was able to see for himself the oil-soaked bodies being fished from the scorched flotsam drifting in the harbor. The terrible price that we had paid for unpreparedness was measured in the suffering Knox witnessed during his tour of the wards at Hospital Point where some survivors were "so terribly burned and charred as to be beyond recognition." He later confided to his naval aide that "the sight of those men made me as angry as I have ever been in my life."[18]

At fleet headquarters, Knox listened quietly to a thorough review of events by Kimmel. During the course of this briefing, Captain Beatty recorded that a staff officer "made a strong, fervent plea for the dispatch of an expedition to reinforce Wake Island with planes, men and material, but no decision was reached." This first briefing dwelt mainly on the damage the Japanese inflicted, and the secretary of the navy tried to grasp why their attack had taken us by surprise. Knox later commented on "the willingness of those in responsible positions to assume their share of the blame."[19] But when it came to pinpointing responsibility, Kimmel was careful to emphasize that he had received no advance intelligence that he might be under threat of attack.

This appeared to astonish the secretary of the navy. He had carefully studied all the dispatches and background intelligence before leaving Washington. "Did you get Saturday night the dispatch the navy department sent out?" he asked.[20] Kimmel denied receiving any war warning after 27 November. The secretary of the navy declared emphatically, "Well, we sent you one."[21]

Kimmel's denial also surprised Captain Beatty, whose "particular quest was to fathom the failure in delivery of a message ordered sent to Admiral Kimmel."[22] One of the first questions the naval aide asked every staff member from then on was "Did you receive our message of the sixth?"

My first reaction when I heard the question was to think they must be mistaken. Surely they meant the warning sent on Sunday, 7 December, in Marshall's deadline dispatch that did not reach us until after the attack was over. That was also the impression gained by Kimmel's chief of staff Soc McMorris, who was to testify later about hearing Knox make reference to the message.

Poco Smith, like Kimmel and other staff members present, nonetheless distinctly recalled Knox's referring to a "warning message" that was sent from Washington "*on the Saturday* preceding Pearl Harbor [emphasis added]."[23] It does not appear that he was confusing it with Marshall's 1 P.M. deadline warning, because even if it had reached our headquarters it would have given no time for the fleet to have sortied.

Knox's impression that there had been an adequate warning message sent that Saturday night would have been in keeping with the president's

"This means war" reaction to the Magic decrypt of the Japanese diplomatic message earlier that evening. It would also tie in with the claim by Knox's confidant, James G. Stahlman, that the secretary of the navy admitted to him that a late-night council of war took place in the White House on the eve of the Pearl Harbor attack. But if the council had agreed to send out a warning—as Knox's statements that Thursday afternoon appear to indicate—no such dispatch was ever sent out; nor was any trace of a draft to show up in navy department files.

So when Beatty arrived in the intelligence section that afternoon, he quizzed me about the missing war warning. I could only deny that we had received one. I also showed him the photographs of the attack taken by navy photographers, which Kimmel had ordered me to release to no one without his authority.

When Knox came along to look at the pictures, his mood was detached. He showed the curiosity of a not-too-aggressive news reporter who was nevertheless determined to collect all the facts. My impression was that he blustered, but not in an angry way. He was one of those people who wanted to know everything about everything. He insisted on seeing every picture and knowing about each one. How did I get them? Whom did they belong to? Did anybody else have copies? I was sure he was checking to see if any had been released yet and I had the feeling that he would have liked to have them for the *Chicago Daily News*. But the appearance of any single one of them on the front page of a newspaper back home would have done nothing for national morale.

In the course of his brief visit of my office Knox asked me the same question he had asked Kimmel: "Did you get our message?"

"What message?" I asked.

"We sent a message to you telling you to be alert for an attack," he replied.

I could only respond "Sir, as far as I know we never got one; at least I never saw it."'

I remember thinking at the time of this exchange that the secretary of the navy was not so dumb as to be referring to the deadline message of 27 November, or the deadline dispatch of Sunday. He was certainly under the impression that some warning had been drafted the night before the attack. But what it was he did not specify. And it was not my position to ask.

Knox then went off to meet General Short, who had come down to Kimmel's quarters. They had a brief meeting before the secretary of the navy left for dinner at the blacked-out Royal Hawaiian Hotel with the governor, Joseph B. Poindexter. Next morning, Knox went to Fort Shafter for a longer session, which, according to Short, did not "indicate in any way he was not satisfied."[24] That afternoon his party made another stopover at fleet headquarters to collect the photographs, Japanese *hachimaki* bandanas, and spent bullets before departing for Kaneohe where the flying boat was waiting to take them back to mainland.

After just thirty-two hours of "fact finding," which raised more questions than were answered, Knox was confident that he could report to the president. The first remark that the secretary of the navy made to Beatty after takeoff was "Frank, you will be glad to hear that a decision was finally reached and the relief force for Wake will soon be on its way."[25] Then Knox went up to the navigator's compartment to work on the plotting table and prepare the first draft of a document that was to have far-reaching consequences.

"The navy must lead the way. Speed up" was the message that the secretary of the navy had sent to all ships and shore commands three days earlier. That Friday evening, as a blacked-out flying boat droned its way back to the mainland, Knox knew that he was faced with trying to reconcile two conflicting demands: First, he had approved Kimmel's plan for the relief of Wake Island. Second, if the admiral was prematurely removed from his command, it would prejudice the whole operation—which was vital to restoring the confidence of the fleet. Deep though his love for the navy was, Knox was first and foremost a politician. He was well aware of the damage that could be done the administration if the demand for a public accounting of the disaster was not met promptly.

The first hints of a nasty congressional investigation, which his trip was supposed to head off, surfaced while he was traveling back to Washington. The first rumblings had been voiced on Thursday by Republican senators asking why the president had not yet made a full statement of why Pearl Harbor was surprised. There was also the danger of a major interservice fight in the offing.

"We are doing our best to keep from having a row with the Navy," Stimson noted in his diary. "There is bitterness on both sides over the failure at Hawaii and the younger, less responsible—and some of the irresponsible older men—are all trying to throw the burden on the other Department."[26]

While Knox was preparing to take steps to save the administration from a two-front battle, the marines on Wake Island, unaware that their fate would hang on the secretary of the navy's report, were digging in to face a Japanese assault. After surviving a third day of heavy air raids, lookouts on Peacock Point that night spotted the blinking lights of the approaching invasion force. Major James P. Devereux called his five-hundred-strong garrison to general quarters.

Just before dawn the first Japanese shells began exploding on the sandy spit of land, panicking the atoll's population of gooney birds. Seventy-five minutes later the Japanese warships, led by Admiral Sadamichi Kajioka's two light cruisers and four destroyers, escorted four troopships close in to the outer reef to begin loading the landing barges. This miscalculation brought them within range of the active marine batteries. Minutes later *Yubari* was hit. As the flagship cruiser limped off, the gunners on tiny Peale Island at the north of the lagoon landed a salvo squarely on destroyer *Hayate*. After a fierce explosion it broke in two and sank.

Cheering broke out to celebrate the first American sinking of a Japanese warship. "Knock it off you bastards and get back to your guns," bellowed Platoon Sergeant Henry Bedell. "Wha' d'ya think this is, a ball game?"[27] Spurred on by this success, the battery succeeded in hitting another destroyer and setting a transport on fire. As the Japanese invasion force hurriedly withdrew under cover of smoke, Wake's four surviving Wildcats took off. Carrying a pair of bombs apiece, they made repeated shuttle runs and managed to sink another destroyer before Kajioka put discretion before valor and was "temporarily forced to retire."[28]

The news of the victory by the Wake garrison that Friday brought elation to Pacific Fleet headquarters. It raised Kimmel's hopes that the temporary respite the marines had bought would allow him to mount his full-scale relief operation. The knowledge that the Japanese would now probably allocate a much bigger support force for any second invasion attempt was a vindication of Kimmel's original war plan: to strengthen Wake's defenses in order to provide him with the "opportunity to get at naval forces with naval forces."[29]

To turn the temporary Wake victory to our strategic advantage, Kimmel directed McMorris to plan to bring every ship we had into the relief operation. The tiny atoll was to become the bait—just as Midway would six months later—to lure the Japanese into a trap. It was a bold and tactically imaginative scheme. It involved all three carrier task forces: Brown with *Lexington* would make a diversionary raid on Jaluit to pin down enemy air and surface forces in the Marshalls. Halsey's Task Force 8 with *Enterprise* would operate west of Johnston Island as cover for Oahu and long-range support for the actual relief expedition. The expedition itself would be led by *Saratoga*, which would provide the striking punch to ensure that seaplane tender *Tangier*, loaded with ammunition and supplies, could steam in to reinforce the Wake garrison.

The three-pronged operation could not begin immediately. It had to await the arrival of *Saratoga*, which was on passage from the west coast with another marine corps fighter squadron. Rear Admiral Aubrey Fitch, who was flying his flag in the *Sarah*, was the natural choice to lead the critical relief force. But Kimmel, perhaps overconscious of how his own leapfrog promotion to commander in chief had been resented in the fleet, decided to assign the overall command to Rear Admiral Frank J. Fletcher. Although totally inexperienced in conducting air operations, Fletcher was nevertheless the ranking flag officer; his division of heavy cruisers had returned from patrol to Pearl to refuel on 10 December.

The Pacific Fleet's ambitious Wake operation, if it succeeded, might redeem Admiral Kimmel's damaged reputation. Perhaps that is why it was to be doomed by the decisions that were about to be made in Washington.

Knox's plane landed Sunday evening—a week to the day since the Japanese attack. His twenty-nine-page report, which had been prepared on a borrowed portable typewriter during the flight, was taken straight to the White House by the secretary of the navy. The lateness of the hour and urgency that attached to its delivery are attested to by Roosevelt's scrawled notation: "1941—given me by F.K. 10 PM Dec 14 when he landed here from Hawaii."[30]

After his meeting with the president, Knox—according to James Stahlman—unwound from the tensions of his trip to Pearl Harbor by recounting details of the eve-of-war vigil at the White House. The secretary of the navy also confessed that "the damage was so horrendous" that he had not detailed everything in his report for fear of some leak: "He said that if the American people knew what had happened at Pearl, they would panic and the war would be over before we ever got into it."[31]

Knox's assessment of the damage was horrendous enough to knock some stuffing out of the normally resilient Roosevelt. Treasury Secretary Morgenthau found him in very low spirits after he had been closeted with the secretary of the navy "all night and day."[32] With a skillful economy of words, Knox had laid out the facts as he found them. He was carefully evenhanded. He avoided loading all the blame for the disaster onto Kimmel or Short. But he could not disguise his belief that the success of the Japanese attack was due to the "lack of a state of readiness against such an air attack, by both branches of the service."[33]

This unreadiness, as Knox's report made clear, was partly attributable to the denial of much of the Magic intelligence to the local commander, plus their lack of adequate numbers of fighters and antiaircraft guns. Responsibility for these failures could be fixed only in Washington. While his report did not exonerate the Hawaiian commanders, it fell far short of leveling charges of dereliction, which both Kimmel and Short were soon to face.

Knox also submitted his recommendations to the president on the steps that he felt were essential to restore public confidence and the navy's morale. The most important of these was that a board of inquiry be set up to investigate the Pearl Harbor attack. While Knox may have had reservations about replacing Kimmel before the completion of the Wake operation, the report conceded that he would have to go, because his name was linked with the disaster. So while he was reluctant to remove the admiral from his command pending outcome of any investigation, Knox proposed to effect a dramatic reorganization of the navy by removing from Kimmel his administrative responsibility as commander in chief U.S. Fleet. Admiral Ernest J. King—then commander of the Atlantic Fleet—was to be recalled to the navy department as the new commander in chief U.S. Fleet.[34]

Roosevelt endorsed the appointment. This decision diminished Stark's authority, although he remained CNO for the time being. To have replaced him would have made it appear that he was to blame for the Pearl Harbor disaster. The president and Knox were confident that King's reputation as an uncompromising admiral and one of the fleet's most able organizers would help restore public confidence in the navy. After a long discussion at the White House that Monday, it was agreed that both the secretary of war and navy would hold immediate press conferences and release those parts of Knox's report that would not reveal anything of advantage to the Japanese. The objective was to set people's minds at rest by minimizing the extent of the damage, and by providing assurances that the two services shared equal responsibility for the disaster, which would be the subject of a full investigation.

"Knox agrees with me that there had been remissness in both branches of the service," Stimson recorded. His 15 December diary entry emphasized how they were both "very anxious not to get into any inter-departmental scraps, but to keep the thing on a basis of no recrimination but inflexible responsibility and punishment."[35]

That afternoon the secretary of the navy treated the press to a bravura performance, which avoided any suggestion of individual blame. Sticking closely to his agreed brief, Knox admitted only that *Arizona,* three destroyers, and an auxiliary vessel had been sunk besides the target ship *Utah.*

"In the Navy's greatest hour of peril, the officers and men of the fleet exhibited magnificent courage and resourcefulness,"[36] Knox declared. He admitted that the "services were not on the alert against surprise attack." Since it was impossible to reveal his concern that we had been denied Magic intelligence, and would have been imprudent to indicate the lack of anti-aircraft defenses, the impression Knox conveyed in his report to the press inevitably pointed a finger of blame directly at Kimmel and Short.

That was how many newspapers interpreted Knox's report, even though he had announced that the president was immediately going to initiate a "formal investigation" to ascertain *if* there had been "any dereliction of duty."[37] At his press conference Knox had insisted that action against the local commanders was to await "the facts and recommendations made by this investigating board."[38] But the very next day he went back on his word.

The decision to peremptorily remove Kimmel from his command was prompted by pressures put on Knox that evening. The president wanted "to appoint a commission consisting of two army and two navy officers and a civilian to investigate the responsibility for the losses and to make recommendations."[39] This meant that the Hawaiian commanders would be expected to fulfill their war duties while undergoing a full-blown investigation into their conduct. The secretary of the navy also acceded to Stimson's wishes to speed up the process and to accept Justice Owen J. Roberts to head the special commission of inquiry.

Roberts, who had made his reputation in 1923 as the special prosecutor in the celebrated Teapot Dome scandals, was Roosevelt's choice. As an associate justice of the Supreme Court, the president knew, Roberts would have the trust of the public. And since he had been a leading supporter of the pro-interventionist Committee to Aid America by Aiding the Allies, Roosevelt had every confidence that the judge would pay due attention to the need to preserve national unity behind the war effort. The White House was especially anxious to squash the insidious isolationist rumors that Japan had been manipulated into an attack to provide the president with his excuse for joining Britain in the war against Hitler.

When the war council resumed its deliberations in the presidential study at nine the next morning, Stimson had not only won Knox's agreement to Roberts, but had picked his nominees for the commission: Major General Frank B. McCoy, one of Marshall's trusted aides, and Brigadier General Joseph T. McNarney, a ranking air corps officer, who was recommended by the chief of the army. Knox had selected Admiral William H. Standley, a former chief of naval operations, and Rear Admiral Joseph M. Reeves, an engineering officer who had come out of retirement to take charge of the navy's end of lend-lease to Britain. Apart from Standley, therefore, the supposedly independent members of the investigating commission all had ties and owed favors to the administration.

The names of the commission members were not due to be announced until 17 December—the next day. But its mission was prejudiced—some were to say preempted—by the announcement on 16 December that the Hawaiian commanders were to be replaced. Knox's mind was made up at a White House meeting that Tuesday morning, at which the president approved the appointment of Rear Admiral Chester W. Nimitz as the new commander in chief of the Pacific Fleet. Roosevelt stressed the need for urgency.

"Tell Nimitz to get the hell out to Pearl and stay there till the war is won," Roosevelt had directed the secretary of the navy. But when Knox hurried back to the navy department to inform the chief of the bureau of navigation about his new appointment, Nimitz was astonished by the decision.[40] He protested that it would take a week to wrap up his current work. But the secretary of the navy wasted no time in breaking the news.

Simultaneously came the announcement that afternoon from the secretary of war that General Short and General Martin were being relieved. Stimson, who declared he was "side by side with Knox as to the absence of preparedness on December 7th," cited the need to avoid "a situation where officials charged with the responsibility of the vital naval base would otherwise in this critical hour also be involved in the searching investigation ordered yesterday by the president."[41]

The summary removal of the Hawaiian commanders *before* the presidential investigating team had even been formally announced had the effect of branding Kimmel and Short with a public charge of dereliction. It served to draw attention away from any responsibility that Washington might bear for the Pearl Harbor disaster. It smacked of firing the office boys to conceal skullduggery in the boardroom.

25

"Sold Down the River"

T HAT TUESDAY AFTERNOON, 16 December, I was shaken to see a copy of the dispatch informing Admiral Kimmel that he was to relinquish his command "effective 3 p.m. on December 17."[1] I immediately went down to his office. There was no one there except a marine orderly who would only say that the admiral had "retired to his quarters."

At three the following afternoon there was a terse formal handover. Admiral Pye had been designated temporary commander in chief. Each man faced the other, read his orders, and shook hands. Then Kimmel left the headquarters building after quietly bidding farewell to staff. We were as downhearted as he was. Although his dismissal was not unexpected, we all regarded it as premature. We wondered what would happen to the Wake operation. It may be an established American tradition that losing baseball teams have their manager fired, but not during the first game of the World Series.

The choice of Admiral Pye as temporary fleet commander also surprised us—and no one was more surprised than I. It was impossible not to reflect on the part that he had played in the disaster on the eve of the raid by dismissing my estimate with such certainly and saying that Japan would not attack the United States.

While we were apprehensive about Kimmel's departure, we realized that he had been the victim of fate. But none of us expected that he would get the raw deal that was to be meted out to him by Washington. Nor did Kimmel himself.

"Immediately after Pearl Harbor," Kimmel was later to reflect, "I felt that, no matter how hard and how conscientiously I had tried, I had not been smart enough, and to that extent, must accept blame for Pearl Harbor." But he fully expected to be assigned another command. He was assured as much in a sympathetic 29 December letter from Admiral

338

Stark: "Don't worry about our finding duty for you. I value your services just as much as I ever did and more and I say this straight from the heart as well as the head."[2]

But within a month, Kimmel had been forced into retirement. Being made Washington's scapegoat was a fate that a fine admiral did not deserve. "It is an age-old tradition that the commanding officer of a ship is liable if the ship is lost. For this reason, Admiral Kimmel must be held responsible for his losses at Pearl Harbor,"[3] Joe Rochefort was to observe. "However, if these losses were due in part, or in whole, to errors by his superiors, then those superiors must be held responsible."[4]

It was to be several years before the awful truth of Washington's errors began to emerge. When Kimmel discovered how appalling they were, he became fighting mad at the wrong he had been done and the indignity he had been forced to suffer: "Since learning that definite information of the Japanese intentions to attack the United States was in the hands of the War and Navy Departments and was not supplied to me, I now refuse to accept any responsibility for the catastrophe."[5]

At the moment Kimmel stepped out of the submarine base building for the last time on 17 December, the responsibility for the Pacific Fleet passed temporarily to Admiral Pye. Rather than operating through Kimmel's staff, Pye preferred to work with his team, which had become homeless as the result of the damage to *California*. But Pye had to rely on us for intelligence and to operate through the war plans section, which had planned the Wake operation.

It was not a happy arrangement. While Pye could not be faulted for his knowledge of strategy, McMorris and I soon found out that the shock of losing his battle force had shaken his confidence and decisiveness. Kimmel's bold decision to commit all three carrier task forces to the Wake operation rode unhappily with him. It was characteristic of Kimmel to seize the initiative. But Pye was a more cautious commander who preferred to wait and see what the enemy would do before making his moves.[6]

This was a luxury that our temporary commander in chief could not afford. Nor was fleet intelligence in a position yet to predict from radio intelligence, or code breaking, what the Japanese would do, or precisely how many of their warships would be committed in their second attempt to take Wake.

On 17 December, Rochefort had finally been given the go-ahead from Washington to abandon the unbreakable Japanese flag officers code. He was to "commence solution" of the current JN-25 ciphers, but it would be three weeks before the enemy's main operational code began yielding up its secrets.[7]

The task facing Tommy Dyer and Ham Wright was, however, made easier by a message that came in shortly afterward from Station Cast in Manila. This message that the Japanese had inadvertently duplicated in the JN-25 code and again in plain text "confirmed indicator subtractor already recovered by mathematical elimination PM code remains unchanged."[8] This confirmed that the cipher changes ordered in JN-25 on 2 December were limited to the five-figure additives. The main code book was unchanged. And by a happy coincidence, Hypo's copy of the code book recoveries were unloaded that day from a shipment that had been en route from Washington since early November. (The reasons for that slow shipment were typical bureaucratic ones.) Cryptanalysts at Cast transmitted the subtractor and additive recoveries for the current period on the secure Copek line from the Philippines, and Rochefort's team began their assault on JN-25 right away.

Unfortunately, I could give Admiral Pye no assurances the next day about how soon Hypo's code-breaking efforts would begin producing the information he needed so desperately. All I could do was to brief him about the conclusions I had drawn concerning the whereabouts of the Japanese striking force that were based on the documents taken from the bomber that had crashed in the cane field. From them we could be certain that the striking force of six carriers, two battleships, and two heavy cruisers outnumbered us two to one. But my estimate was that most of the enemy force would be returning to Japan for replenishment, and that only one or two carriers would have been detached to ensure the capture of Wake.

Admiral Pye's worry was that instead of springing a trap, to continue with Kimmel's operation could send all our forces steaming into a Japanese ambush. This concern had been raised by Admiral Wilson Brown three days earlier when Task Force 11 was refueling at Pearl prior to sailing with *Lexington* to carry out the diversionary raid on Jaluit. There was a possibility that a powerful land-based air force had already been flown into the easternmost island of the Marshalls. And this had persuaded Kimmel to give Brown the option of shifting his objective to Makin in the Gilberts, or retiring if circumstances dictated. Brown's confidence in the ability of his force to defend itself against planes was further shaken when gunnery practice the next morning revealed that most of the antiaircraft ammunition for his cruisers was defective.

One of Kimmel's final acts as fleet commander was to brief Admiral Fletcher on Tuesday before he sailed with *Saratoga* to make the trip of just over a thousand miles due west to Wake. After Fletcher had departed, Halsey's Task Force 8 entered Pearl Harbor for badly needed refueling and replenishment that was to take four days. The next morning, as the sad transfer ceremony was taking place at the submarine base, Fletcher's force joined up with the oiler *Neches* and seaplane tender *Tangier* which had left Pearl the day before.

Admiral Kimmel had done all that he could. He had disposed his forces for a decisive naval engagement. As we had predicted—but could not confirm—the Japanese were preparing to steam right into the trap that had been set for them by detaching two carriers from their striking force and sending four heavy cruisers northeast from Truk to cover the Wake landing. But while Kimmel was not permitted to remain in charge of his operation, the Japanese gave Admiral Kajioka an opportunity to save face. He was scheduled to sail in command of the invasion force from Kwajalein where his flagship *Yubari* was being patched up. In company with two light cruisers he would escort the transports carrying two thousand battle-hardened veterans of the imperial navy's Special Naval Landing Force on the three-hundred-mile trip north to Wake.

The strategy that Kimmel hoped would provide a badly needed Christmas victory celebration for Americans was shaping up according to plan. But a drama of a very different kind was being arranged in Washington.

That Wednesday morning Justice Roberts held his first informal meeting with Knox and Stimson in the secretary of war's office. In circumstances that must appear highly prejudicial to the objectivity of an impending investigation, guidance was given as to the terms and nature of his inquiry by two of the principal parties. On Thursday morning at ten, without waiting for one of its members, the Roberts Commission got down to business at the war department. That they began work without defining their terms of reference, or waiting for Admiral Standley, who was delayed traveling to Washington, was another sign of how the Roberts Commission was "packed" on the side of the vested interests in Washington. Justice Roberts himself was known to be friendly with the president; Admiral Reeves was beholden to Roosevelt for his lend-lease post; McCoy was a trusted thirty-year confidant of Marshall; and McNarney was an ambitious young member of the army staff in search of promotion. The recorder lacked any court-martial experience. Lastly, a marine corps colonel, without extensive legal expertise, was made provost marshal.

When Admiral Standley finally arrived, he was concerned to find that none of the witnesses had been sworn and that he was expected to serve alongside General McNarney, a ranking member of the army staff whose interests were clearly less than impartial. General Marshall, assisted by the chief of war plans General Gerow, was giving details of the warnings sent to the Hawaiian command. A clubby atmosphere, more appropriate to a mess than a judicial investigation, prevailed. Stark or a member of his team was in attendance during the entire proceedings; they presented their case in the same easy manner that was not conducive to proper cross-examination.

Even if there had been any questioning, no full record was being kept of the questions—or answers. This was too much for the upright Standley. He protested the absence of sworn testimony and a recorder to keep a verbatim transcript. He was puzzled that an associate member of the Supreme Court should permit such informal and ad hoc procedures on an investigation of such importance. After Stark had completed his presentation and withdrawn, Standley pressed for the commission to seek congressional authorization to subpoena witnesses and administer oaths. This was agreed and a special bill hurriedly drafted to go to Capitol Hill.

Yet when Justice Roberts called the meeting to order for the second day on 19 December, witnesses continued to give unsworn testimony and still no written account was taken of the case presented by the heads of naval and army intelligence. Although history was denied a detailed record, perhaps intentionally, Admiral Wilkinson prepared verbatim notes of the proceedings in a "top secret" aide-mémoire. The full text of this memorandum, annotated in Turner's writing and located in his file in the fall of 1984, gives a fuller record of what went on than does the abbreviated summary of the official Roberts Commission report.[9]

The Wilkinson memorandum for the CNO was evidently prepared for immediate circulation that afternoon to Admirals Stark, Ingersoll, and Turner. The document is, in itself, a pertinent indication of the way in which the ranking navy and war department officers were attempting to rig the commission's findings in their favor. It reveals that they sought to divert investigation of their considerable sins of omission by exaggerating the lesser omissions of the Hawaiian commanders.

Wilkinson recounted how he had been accompanied by Captain McCollum to the munitions building where he found General Miles and Colonel Bratton already present in the boardroom. His digest of the evidence of the morning of 19 December suggests that there was a certain degree of collusion and deliberate misstatement in what appears to have been a collaborative effort by army and navy to convey the impression that *no* intelligence had been withheld from Admiral Kimmel or General Short.

"The Commission stated that they wished the Army and Navy intelligence to *cooperate* in their answers" was how Wilkinson reported the opportunity that was given them to line up a unified testimony [emphasis added].[10] This was facilitated because Roberts permitted them to sit in on each other's testimony. Miles, after giving a rundown on the instruction that had been given to the Hawaiian command in the month preceding the attack, "described at some length the events in General Marshall's office, including the sending of the subsequently delayed dispatch to General Short on the morning of Sunday, December 7th."[11]

Speaking from his own experience in the Hawaiian command, Miles said, he concluded "that a successful raid *was possible* against a garrison which *had not been warned,* but was not possible against a garrison that had been warned [emphasis added]."[12] Given the choice between assuming that either the local commands had *not* received adequate warning, or that their commanders were derelict, the majority of the commission chose the latter explanation without questioning it.

Wilkinson was then asked about what information and communications had been sent to the Pacific Fleet in the months before the attack. The discursive reply was intended to convey the impression that Kimmel was as well informed as the navy department: "As to the actual interchange of messages relating to intelligence, in general the sources reported their information to the Commander-in-Chief of the Asiatic Fleet and in forwarding it the Commander-in-Chief Pacific *was usually* advised [emphasis added]."[13]

The chief of naval intelligence then listed the seven-point summary of the indications pointing to war that McCollum had drafted on 1 December. But it was not pointed out that transmission of McCollum's list to Pearl Harbor had effectively been blocked by Turner. Instead, Wilkinson gave the commission the clear impression that the Pacific Fleet was far better informed about the imminence of Japan's intentions to commence hostilities than it actually was. He misled them by listing McCollum's 1 December memorandum—the fact that it was mentioned at all obviously rankled Turner, who struck it through on his copy of Wilkinson's minutes.

In the course of discussing radio intelligence decrypts concerning the two Japanese task groups massing in the South China Sea and the mandated islands, Wilkinson was careful to point out that "nothing in this item made us forecast a movement as far east of the Mandated area as Hawaii."[14] Roberts, significantly, wanted to know how far away these islands were from Hawaii. The director of naval intelligence, perhaps inadvertently, in his answer added two hundred miles (almost a whole day's steaming for a task force) to the distance from Pearl Harbor to Jaluit.

"Without mentioning particular dispatches," Wilkinson told the commission, "we had assured ourselves that all of this information had either passed through the CinC Asiatic and Pacific Fleets or, if not, it had been furnished them from the Department." Such reticence in mentioning diplomatic intelligence was surprising because Wilkinson noted *"the meeting was discussing Magic freely,* but stated that they would be most careful that no mention of it would be made [emphasis added]."[15]

Yet the only "particular dispatches" that Wilkinson made reference to were those of 3 December, relating to the code burning at the Japanese embassies. (This paragraph has also been struck out in Turner's copy of the report.)

Since Wilkinson was aware that the Roberts Commission knew about, and understood, the importance of Magic, his repeated declaration that Kimmel "had as much information as we had" was so misleading as to be a deliberate lie. But he was careful to point out, "I myself could not expect that he and his staff would infer positively a raid on Hawaii any more than we had been able to do from the same information."[16]

What Roberts was *not* told, however, was that the Pacific Fleet did *not* have access to the *same* information that Washington possessed. Wilkinson chose not to reveal that the navy department had ignored the importance of the bomb plot messages and other important Magic intelligence by not relaying them out to Hawaii. His testimony was geared—as had been Stark's and Marshall's the previous day—to reinforcing the contention that the Hawaiian commands had been given all the intelligence available in Washington.

The presidential commission of inquiry was apparently ready to accept the unrecorded and unsworn word of senior officers. Roberts himself was to concede that no attempt was made to examine the actual intelligence records, which would have told a very different story. "The Magic was not shown to us. I would not have bothered to read it if it had been shown to us," Roberts was later to admit. "All I wanted to know was whether the commanders had been advised of the criticalness of the situation. . . . The commission found that they had ample warning."[17]

Justice Roberts, it seems, had made up his mind about where the blame must fall by the time the commission had finished hearing the unsupported statement by the director of naval intelligence. At midday Friday, the inquiry adjourned to pack for their scheduled four o'clock takeoff on the first leg of a two-and-a-half-day flight to Hawaii.

The next day, while the investigators were in mid-flight, Admiral Halsey's Task Force 8 had steamed out of Pearl to guard the western approaches to Oahu. Now the navy began to pay the price for the premature removal of Admiral Kimmel.

On Saturday morning the relief force under Admiral Fletcher was approaching the halfway point of its passage to Wake. Shortly after 1200 on 20 December, Admiral Wilson Brown decided that to press on with his raid on Jaluit might cost him the loss of *Lexington* to air or submarine attack. So he independently exercised the option he had been given to raid Makin as an alternative target. At Pacific Fleet headquarters we had received what turned out to be a greatly exaggerated report of the Japanese forces occupying the Gilberts. Traffic analysis suggested that a big seaplane tender and the Yokohama Corps of the naval air fleet had already reached Makin.[18] Although there was no way of confirming this, I told Admiral Pye that this might mean that anywhere from twenty to two hundred planes were already in a position to threaten Task Force 11. Hypo had also identified the Japanese submarine force commander as being garrisoned at Jaluit. The threat of Brown's force steaming into a possible underwater ambush added to the concern that was swirling around the operation at headquarters.

Admiral Pye, very conscious that he was merely keeping the command seat warm for Admiral Nimitz, decided that he could not risk the loss of any of the carriers. He sent a dispatch ordering Brown north to support Fletcher. At the same time he instructed Fletcher to undertake a refueling operation the next day. Although it was not strictly necessary, Pye wanted to provide a fixed rendezvous point for Brown's force to join up with Fletcher.[19]

The responsibility for this decision to refuel was to be hotly debated. Regardless of whether it was at Pye's or Fletcher's initiative, it disastrously delayed the approach to Wake. Pearl Harbor was receiving urgent cables from the marine commander on Wake that his men were coming under increasingly heavy air attack. One of these reports identified carrier-based dive bombers, which confirmed my estimate that part of the Pearl Harbor striking force had been detached. The news added more fuel to Pye's alarm. He at once informed the chief of naval operations of his revision in the Wake plan in a cable that emphasized his primary concern was the maintenance of the fleet's strength to defend Hawaii. Stark not only confirmed the priority, but cabled that Admiral King—the newly installed commander in chief of the U.S. Fleet—considered Wake Island a liability.

Pye was thereby duly authorized to use his discretion to order an evacuation, rather than attempt a reinforcement. Admiral Kajioka's invasion force set sail the same day from Kwajalein. The next morning *Saratoga* was just six hundred miles northeast of Wake when Fletcher commenced a ten-hour refueling operation that according to ships' logs was unnecessary. If Fletcher had continued a twenty-knot run to Wake, Task Force 14 would have been within range the next day to smash Kajioka's invasion force when it steamed into position to commence its second landing attempt.

The small hours of 23 December, local time, found a much battered marine garrison on Wake preparing to make a final stand in anticipation of reinforcements arriving. A week of repeated air bombardment had knocked out half their gun batteries and cost them all their fighter planes. This time the Japanese landing barges took care to make simultaneous assaults out of the line of fire of the surviving batteries.

At 0250, Wake command flashed out, "Enemy apparently landing." Over the next two hours bitter hand-to-hand fighting erupted. The outnumbered marine garrison was steadily overwhelmed by the numbers of Japanese coming ashore. "The enemy is on the island," Wake command signaled at 0500. "The issue is in doubt."[20]

At Pacific Fleet headquarters, Pye and his chief of staff, Admiral Draemel, were debating with Captain McMorris what to do. Soc McMorris was strongly of the opinion that Fletcher should press the attack and that Brown should steam up in support. But Task Force 14 was still 425 miles northeast of Wake while Fletcher was attempting to top off the bunkers of four destroyers whose tanks were already three quarters full. But heavy swells repeatedly parted the oil hoses. Task Force 11 was twice as far away to the southeast, and Halsey's Task Force 8 was some 100 miles west of Midway, too far away to intervene. It would take twelve hours for Fitch's *Saratoga* to get within range for an air strike. And it would be a full day before *Lexington*'s planes could be brought into the action. McMorris pointed out the tactical advantages of Fletcher's position. Halsey's *Enterprise* could be brought south to assist, or to cover Fletcher's retirement if necessary. But no matter how you viewed it, the Japanese would have been trapped from three sides.

Pye's lack of resolution and his determination not to risk any of his three carriers resulted in a series of conflicting orders to Fletcher. After agreeing with McMorris's plan, Pye's feet got progressively colder about the whole operation. The result was confusion and indecision. It sapped the confidence of the commander on the spot. The first dispatch sent to Fletcher instructed him to make full speed to bring *Saratoga* within two hundred miles of Wake and then launch a search and attack strike. Hardly had that order been received than it was countermanded. Now Fletcher was told that seaplane tender *Tangier* was to make a high-speed unescorted run into the atoll and evacuate its surviving defenders. Within the hour even this halfhearted rescue attempt was canceled.

At 0911, some twenty minutes before the news of Wake's surrender was received at headquarters, Pye sent out an order recalling Fletcher and Brown to Pearl Harbor. Some of the marine fliers on *Saratoga*, who had been destined to fly their aircraft to join their comrades on Wake, were nearly mutinous. Some threatened to get in their planes and fly off regardless. But Fletcher was not cut out for a Nelsonian gesture of "putting the telescope to his blind eye."[21] Those who think he could and should have taken more aggressive action—and who point especially to his refueling delay—have concluded that Fletcher had a yellow streak down his back. They claimed he did not proceed at his task force's best speed, using refueling to wait for a chance to withdraw from the operation. What is clear is that on board *Saratoga*, Admiral Fitch, who probably was the most experienced carrier admiral in the navy, was more disconcerted to be recalled. When during the discussion on *Saratoga*'s bridge it was suggested that Fitch should ignore the dispatch, he retired to his cabin lest his staff should seek to persuade him to defy his orders.[22]

Whether Fletcher intentionally prolonged his refueling or not, it was Pye's apprehension about the Japanese carriers that finally lost us Wake. Pye's decision also ended any chance of delivering a smashing surprise blow against the Japanese naval forces which, as it turned out later, did not suspect that within two weeks of their raid on Pearl Harbor the Pacific Fleet was capable of striking back.

Admiral Pye, who "ordered the retirement with extreme regret," was not prepared to run any risks, however much he tried to disguise it. "The use of offensive action to relieve Wake had been my intention and desire," he was to explain in his report to the chief of naval operations. "But when the enemy once landed on the island, the general strategic situation took precedence, and the conservation of our naval forces became the first consideration."[23]

The tragedy was that Kimmel's strategy had worked perfectly to bring about the conditions for a spectacular American victory. Our three carriers and superior cruiser striking power would have been concentrated against two Japanese carriers and heavy cruisers. But by putting strategic caution before tactical calculation, Pye had deprived the navy of the chance to catch the enemy unawares in much the same circumstances as we were able to do at Midway six months later. A December victory at Wake, moreover, would have been a stunning blow to Japan. It would have been a decisive demonstration that Yamamoto's grand strategy had failed to knock the fight out of the Pacific Fleet for a six-month period as Nagumo claimed. It would have opened the way to a transpacific relief of Corregidor and the Philippines. And it would have rallied the navy and provided a tremendous boost to the morale of the American people who were facing a bleak Christmas.

The lost opportunity at Wake would also have helped redeem Admiral Kimmel's reputation. But the collapse of the operation that he had masterminded, on the very day that the Roberts Commission members flew into Honolulu to begin their investigation, did nothing to enhance the reputation of the former commander in chief.

The members of the presidential investigating commission established themselves at the Royal Hawaiian Hotel on 22 December. That Monday afternoon they began drawing up a list of the army and navy officers they wished to interview. At nine the next morning Justice Roberts began the formal part of his investigation at Fort Shafter. General Short appeared for questioning with no legal adviser, because he regarded himself as "absolutely not guilty in any sense."[24] He had assembled a formidable array of documentation to prove there had been no dereliction of duty as far as he was concerned. Short explained why he regarded the 27 November war warning as an alert against sabotage. Although he conceded that he "made a very serious mistake when we didn't go to an alert against an all out air attack,"[25] he said that it was because he had received no intelligence or any other warning from Washington indicating the possibility of such an attack.

The investigators therefore had to judge the degree to which Short could have been expected to read between the lines to divine the probability of a Japanese raid and to have increased the preparedness necessary to counter it. After the assurances they had received four days earlier in Washington that the Hawaiian commanders were more familiar than they actually were with the overall intelligence picture, it was inevitable that the commission members were less inclined to give either Hawaiian commander the benefit of the doubt.

There was, moreover, a significant shift in the way that Roberts conducted his inquiry. In Washington the witnesses from the war and navy departments had been permitted to sit in during each other's testimony, and were even directed "to cooperate in their answers."[26] But neither Short nor Kimmel was permitted this privilege. This helped foster the impression of a lack of cooperation between the local commands, which compared unfavorably with the impression that had been given by the service chiefs in Washington. The Roberts Commission was to make a great point of this later as a contributory cause of the disaster.

After a break for Christmas, Justice Roberts resumed the chair in Fort Shafter to continue questioning army witnesses. Not until 27 December did the inquiry move to the wardroom lounge of the submarine base to begin a long interrogation of Admiral Kimmel. Unlike Short, the former commander in chief had brought his old friend Rear Admiral Robert Theobald—the fleet destroyer force commander—to assist in the presentation of his case.

"Of course you are not here in the capacity of a defense counsel because you and Admiral Kimmel both understand that no charges have been preferred against him; he is not in the status of a defendant," Roberts assured Theobald. But after the former commander in chief had presented his statement of events, he believed that Roberts's questioning assumed the manner of "a trial lawyer in a lower court."[27]

Kimmel, however much he was reassured to the contrary, could not but see himself in the position of a defendant. To explain and justify the decisions he had made after receiving the 27 November war warning, he had repeatedly to explain technicalities, and justify decisions that were based on these, to a nonnaval inquisitor. Hindsight—and Roberts's assumptions that Kimmel knew as much secret intelligence as Washington—made many of the admiral's decisions appear derelict. Of all his "omissions," none appeared in such a bad light as his belief that the battleships in harbor were not in danger from torpedo attacks, his failure to order round-the-compass air patrols, and to appreciate the significance of the code burning at the Japanese consulate.

Lack of sleep and the strain of having to prepare a full report on the disaster without adequate staff further contributed to the impression Kimmel made as a witness. His pride bristled frequently at having his arguments challenged by a landlubber and the two army members of the commission. "McNarney was a lying s.o.b. who had no more morals than a crawling snake," he would later complain.[28] Admiral Standley, who appears to have been the only commission member sympathetic to the former commander in chief, regarded the fast-talking Admiral Reeves as very antagonistic to Kimmel and Short.

That antagonism surfaced in a nasty exchange when Kimmel, after discovering the inadequacy of the stenographic record—which omitted his entire first statement—asked for permission to correct it. Roberts was very opposed to what he saw as an attempt by the admiral to "interlard things that you did not say."[29] It was the intervention of Admiral Standley that permitted Kimmel to make parallel corrections in the text and append his fully corrected statement as an addendum. According to a memorandum left by Standley, it appears that Justice Roberts and a majority of his fellow commission members had been convinced by what they heard before leaving Washington that the local commanders must be guilty of some major dereliction. Standley did not agree, then or later: "I felt that, with all the information available to them in Washington, Admiral Stark and General Marshall were equally culpable."[30]

I was called before the Roberts Commission on 2 January. The evidence I contributed showed how radio intelligence and traffic analysis left us in the dark about the whereabouts of the main enemy carrier forces, although it had revealed the buildup of the main Japanese forces in the China Sea and the mandates. In my view, I said, the dispatches we had received from Washington "gave rise to the firm belief that some action by Japan was impending" in the Far East, but gave us no specific indication that there was even an indirect threat against Hawaii.[31]

Admiral Standley then raised the question of whether the navy department might have had more information than we had access to. "From my knowledge, they have sir, but I do not know how much," I replied.[32] That was as far as I felt that I could go at the time. Later, I found out that Standley's suspicions and my own were more than justified.

"If that is true, wouldn't they be in a better position to estimate the whole situation than you are here?" Standley followed up.

"That is the way the system is laid," I told him.

But before I could make reference to the efforts that Kimmel and I had made to get access to diplomatic intelligence, the chairman interrupted, "If you are an intelligence officer for the Commander of the Fleet of the United States, you did not expect that anything of value to you as to any important information would be withheld from you by the authorities?"

At that time I had no idea that we had been shortchanged, so could only reply, "No, sir."

"Then why did you say they did not?" Justice Roberts responded with more than a shade of hostility.

"I merely meant that as an answer to a specific question that we were receiving copies of reports."[33] That was the only way I felt able to reply. I did not know whether the commission members had been cleared to hear about our most secret intelligence.

But Roberts persisted. I felt that I could not disagree when asked, "Do you mean they have more incoming matter which they digest, and then send you the gist of it?"

Since I did not know the degree to which the navy department had let us down, I accepted the veracity of Standley's rhetorical question: "You felt sure you would receive all conclusions from naval intelligence that were of any importance to you?" But when General McCoy asked pointedly whether we had been given any warning of the attack, my response was a very definite "No, sir; not here in Hawaii; no, sir. There was no warning that the negotiations were breaking down."

Despite the conflict between my testimony and the repeated assurances Justice Roberts had been given by Admiral Wilkinson about Kimmel's having access to all the intelligence available in Washington, the commission made no effort to follow the points I had raised. Nor did they pursue the further evidence of the discrepancy between the intelligence picture at Pearl Harbor and Washington that surfaced when Justice Roberts, accompanied by Admirals Reeves and Standley, went down to see Rochefort's code-breaking setup and look at the Hypo records. Lieutenant Jasper Holmes, in addition to showing them the reconstructed track of the Japanese attack, also mentioned the messages decrypted from the Honolulu consulate on 10 December. He indicated that if these had been available to us in time, they might have prevented our being taken by surprise.

The presidential commission of inquiry chose, nonetheless, to overlook or ignore the possibility that the navy department might have broken into the consular traffic. No attempt was made to look at the records, or to reexamine Wilkinson under oath, in the two days of questioning that the commission contented itself with after returning to Washington. This may have been because after Roberts left Honolulu on 10 January, he took advantage of the Pullman car that carried the commission members across country from San Francisco to begin writing up his report.

Friday, 23 January 1942, found Justice Roberts putting the finishing touches to the report, after some late-night discussion of his findings three days earlier with Secretary Stimson and Supreme Court Chief Justice Felix Frankfurter. The final draft was not agreed to without some bitter debate between the two admirals on the commission. Reeves was convinced that Kimmel was wholly to blame. Standley believed that this view did not show the whole picture.

Standley admitted years later that he had only agreed not to submit a minority report after being persuaded that such a divisive opinion would threaten the war effort. "The findings as to sins of commission presented true enough statements," he wrote, "but the many sins of omission in the picture were omitted from our findings because the President in his executive order setting up the Commission had specifically limited its jurisdiction."[34]

The Roberts Commission report was written with the intention of keeping Magic, a vital intelligence source, secret. It carefully omitted any mention of Magic. While concealing Washington's sins of omission it exaggerated the errors of commission of the local commanders. So when Roosevelt read through the long report on that Saturday, he was no doubt reassured to find that by shifting the burden of responsibility from the war and navy departments, the commission's findings had not damaged the credibility of key members of his administration. He summoned Marvin O. Macintyre, the White House secretary. Tossing the report onto his desk, he said, "Mac, give that to the Sunday papers in full."[35]

The newspapers drew the inevitable conclusions that Admiral Kimmel and General Short had been found almost entirely to blame. They could hardly do otherwise. The three-part report concluded that the secretaries of state, war, and navy had "fulfilled their obligations." So too, apparently, had the chief of naval operations and the chief of the army. They were credited with discharging their "command responsibility" by warning Oahu. The only criticism leveled at the Washington military establishment was that the war department had failed to "reply to the antisabotage measures instituted by the commanding general, Hawaiian Department."[36]

The blame for Japan's success in attacking Pearl Harbor could not have been more nastily or unfairly attributed. Admiral Kimmel and General Short "in the light of the warnings and directions to take appropriate action" were found "in dereliction of duty" for not conferring with each other "respecting the meaning and intent of the warnings and the appropriate means of defense required by the imminence of hostilities." They had demonstrated "a lack of appreciation of the responsibilities vested in them and inherent in their positions." The Japanese attack achieved its surprise because "they had failed to make suitable dispositions to meet such an attack." The Hawaiian commanders had, moreover, "failed properly to evaluate the seriousness of the situation" and it was these "errors of judgment" that "were the effective causes for the success of the attack."[37]

The press and all but a few of Roosevelt's diehard isolationist opponents on Capitol Hill welcomed the verdict. Without access to the secret intelligence record, there was little that Kimmel or Short could do to challenge the judgment or escape the pillory of public scorn to which they were now subjected. Hate mail poured in. There were the inevitable death threats and proposals that they should be executed for treason.

Short submitted his resignation almost immediately. Kimmel held out for the reassignment that he had been promised, but by 28 January, he, too, submitted a letter to the secretary of the navy offering to retire. The president directed that it should be announced that both officers had applied for retirement and that this had been granted "without condonation of any offense or prejudice to future disciplinary actions."[38]

The implicit threat of court-martial proceedings, when the demands of the war were less pressing, caused Kimmel to protest "my crucifixion before the public" to Stark. "I have kept my mouth shut and propose to do so as long as it is humanly possible," he wrote to the chief of naval operations. "But I think in all justice the department should do nothing further to inflame the public against me. I am entitled to some consideration even though you may consider I erred grievously."[39]

Many of his fellow admirals sympathized with Kimmel's plight. But as long as the demands of wartime required national unity and public confidence in the navy's ability to conduct a successful fight, they held their peace. After the war even the hard-bitten Admiral King would concede that the Roberts Commission failed in its duty of fairly assigning responsibility for the disaster. Not a man to admit errors lightly, "Ernie" King's epitaph on the injustices of the presidential commission might be applied to some extent to all the subsequent inquiries that sought to fix the blame for the Pearl Harbor debacle on the local commanders:

> It seems to me that this committee did not get into the real meat of the matter but merely selected a "scapegoat" to satisfy the popular demand for fixing the responsibility for the Pearl Harbor debacle. For instance, Admiral Kimmel was not asked the important questions nor was he given the proper chance to speak for himself. In fact, he and General Short were "sold down the river" as a political expedient.[40]

Expedient or not, the war had to be fought. Until we were on the road to final victory, Kimmel and Short had to endure in painful silence the opprobrium that fate and political necessity had dealt them.

26

"Heaven's Admonition"

C HRISTMAS DAY, 1941. Despair filled Pacific Fleet headquarters. Following the debacle to relieve Wake, the atmosphere was made more gloomy by the presence of the Roberts Commission investigators, who had just begun their interrogations. It was raining that morning and the weather matched the mood of Admiral Pye and his staff as we waited for the arrival of the new commander in chief, Pacific Fleet, Rear Admiral Chester W. Nimitz. Most of us at what was now to be known as Cincpac headquarters expected to be relieved. We hoped for sea duty as our chance to hit back against the Japanese.

The Catalina flying boat roared in through the gray overcast at 0700 to land in the east loch, the wreckage-strewn waters made even more dismal by the sight of the upturned hulls of *Oklahoma* and *Utah*. The stench of fuel oil still permeated the air. Nimitz, wearing civilian clothes, was greeted by Admiral Bellinger and the chiefs of staff. The party had to remain standing on the way to shore, because the whaleboat was begrimed with oil.

"What news of the relief of Wake?" was Nimitz's first question.[1]

When told the island had surrendered and the relief expedition had been recalled, he fell silent. He stayed that way during most of the trip ashore, which was made more miserable by the bloated corpses that were still surfacing from submerged wrecks.

"This is a terrible sight, seeing all these ships down," Nimitz finally remarked to Poco Smith as the boat pulled into the landing. Admiral Pye, the acting commander in chief, and a somber Admiral Kimmel were waiting to greet him at the submarine base wharf. Nimitz was startled at Kimmel's appearance. "You have my sympathy," Nimitz assured his old friend, who joined them for a working breakfast.[2] Nimitz was to demonstrate the same consideration to Kimmel's staff during the detailed tours of inspection he made in the next few days. Any apprehensions we might have had about him as the new commander in chief were dispelled by his warm manner.

A solemn, thoughtful face framed thin, pursed lips, but it was Nimitz's ready and infectious smile that offered us reassurance. The twinkling blue of his eyes was heightened by a ruddy complexion and boyish mop of sandy-colored hair. But it was his firm jaw line and the incisive thrust of his questions that made it clear that he was steeled for the tremendous task he was to assume.

On Wednesday, 31 December, at 1000, Admiral Nimitz was formally handed command of the Pacific Fleet in a ceremony held on the deck of a submarine. It was uncharitably suggested by some wag in the mess that *Grayling*'s was the only available deck left afloat. But the fact was that Nimitz, as a submariner, chose her to first break out his four-star flag and, throughout the war, the Pacific Fleet flagship was always a submarine.

"We have taken a tremendous wallop, but I have no doubt about the outcome," Nimitz said in a brief address to newsmen and photographers.[3] He spoke in the same spirit to his staff officers that afternoon. Expecting that we would all be reassigned, we were surprised when he told us that as chief of the Bureau of Navigation (the Bureau of Naval Personnel after 13 May 1942), he knew that we had been chosen for our competence and he wished to keep us on. Nevertheless, he promised a sympathetic hearing to any who wanted sea duty.

At first opportunity, I asked Admiral Nimitz to be detached, and have a relief assigned. I said that I wanted to go to sea in command of a destroyer. He smiled understandingly. "You can kill more Japs here than you could ever kill in command of a destroyer flotilla."

Flattered, I was not so sure about his conclusion. But my respect for his enthusiasm and determination to restore the reputation of the fleet was fired up. Morale at Pearl Harbor was at a low ebb. The American military situation across the Pacific was desperate. Two days after Nimitz assumed command, General MacArthur abandoned the Philippine capital city of Manila, and the Asiatic Fleet lost its naval base at Cavite. Within the week a Japanese amphibious force had landed in Borneo; our naval outpost on the island of Samoa was shelled; and Rabaul, Australia's base in New Britain Island, was bombed.

The only American naval power (excluding our submarines) remaining in the central Pacific were the torpedo planes and bombers of the carriers and the heavy cruisers of our three task forces. And they were outnumbered more than three to one by the Japanese. Nimitz's immediate task was to hold the line "at all costs."[4]

This directive had been laid down in one of the first dispatches sent out by Admiral King, who had assumed overall operational command of the navy on 30 December. He chose to be known as Cominch (commander in chief, U.S. Fleet), because he regarded the old Cincus (pronounced Sink us) to be a negative. King, who Roosevelt liked to quip "shaved with a blowtorch," was making a forceful impression at the first wartime Anglo-American staff conference. Churchill had arrived at the Washington meeting determined to ensure that the "Europe first" strategy should be the dominant Allied war priority.

Ernie King was no Anglophile. His prejudices against the overbearing British Admiralty had been forged during World War I when he was chief of staff to Admiral Henry T. Mayo, the commander of our Atlantic Fleet. So King was determined that Britain was not going to dictate the strategic terms of the alliance and promote the Atlantic at the expense of the war in the Pacific. King also realized that winning the war against Japan would depend primarily on naval operations, whereas the army, in its partisan way, believed that Japan could best be defeated *after* beating Hitler in a major land campaign in Europe. When he argued against making the war against Japan the subsidiary theater of operations, King found he was up against more than the British. Admiral Stark supported Marshall's view that "Germany is still the prime enemy, and her defeat is the key to victory."[5]

Even the president endorsed the decision that obliged the Pacific commanders to take second place when it came to allocations of men, ships, and matériel. But King's underlying commitment to the war against Japan was to be a powerful factor in ensuring that Nimitz's requirements were not forgotten. King was a realist. As the Japanese invasion rolled across the Philippines, he saw that MacArthur's predicament could not be resolved by a naval solution. The Pacific Fleet just did not have the strength to battle a relief convoy through to Manila. MacArthur and the army were to bear a bitter grudge against us for letting them down. In the first week of the war it was Marshall and Stimson who reluctantly agreed with Stark to redirect to Australia the convoy of reinforcements that was en route for the Philippines.

King did not enjoy being on the defensive, even though this clearly had to be our first priority in the Pacific theater. His first dispatch to Cincpac outlined Nimitz's twin tasks of "holding the Hawaii-Midway line," and keeping open the sea route to Australia by "covering, securing, and holding the Hawaii-Samoa line, which should be extended to include Fiji at the earliest practicable date."[6]

King's directive made it clear that this was to be no static defense. He instructed Nimitz to conduct raids against enemy forward bases in the Marshall and Gilbert islands besides reinforcing Samoa with a division of marines from the west coast. Implicit in all this was the urgent need to boost general morale.

In three days, thanks to the preparatory studies made for Admiral Kimmel, the Pacific Fleet staff presented Nimitz with detailed proposals for a series of carrier strikes against the Gilberts and Marshalls. These were to be coordinated with the movement of the troop convoys to reinforce Samoa, escorted by carrier *Yorktown,* which had been recalled from the Atlantic.

Nimitz immediately faced opposition from other flag officers at Pearl Harbor. They believed that it was trying to achieve too much with our limited forces. Admiral Bloch, whose responsibility for defending the Hawaiian sea frontier was an essential part of his duty as Fourteenth Naval District commander, argued that it was too risky to attack island bases with carriers whose loss would leave us wide open to a Japanese rampage. Fortunately, this defensive mind set was torpedoed by Admiral Halsey.

Still fuming at the failure of the relief operation of Wake Island, Halsey had returned to Pearl on 8 January. Two days later he arrived at the Cincpac conference to thump the table and call for an end to defeatism and the start of aggressive counterattacks against the enemy. He was the only man in the fleet who could get away with it. Halsey not only enjoyed the reputation of being the navy's leatherbusting carrier commander, but was Nimitz's close personal friend. Nimitz now had his champion. The very next day Halsey's *Enterprise* and Task Force 8 put to sea with orders to join up with *Yorktown.* After covering the Samoan reinforcement, they were to head northwest for strikes against the Gilberts and the Marshalls.

The second American offensive operation of the Pacific war, however, suffered a worse initial setback than the first. *Saratoga* was torpedoed five hundred miles south of Oahu, and the wisdom of Nimitz's decision was thrown open to question. The damaged carrier limped into Pearl, but had to return to the west coast for major repairs. At a single blow, the Japanese had cut our offensive strength by 25 percent. Nimitz demonstrated his mettle by refusing to recall Halsey and cancel the Gilberts raid. But he had to call off *Lexington*'s intended raid on Wake when Task Force 11's oiler, *Neches,* was sunk on 23 January by submarine *I-72.*

No replacement oiler was available. With the U-boats' decimation of our tanker fleet in the blitz on east coast shipping, the fuel situation was to become more critical. This is a measure of how precarious things were during the first months of the war—and it also suggests how much more Admiral Nagumo might have accomplished if he had destroyed Pearl Harbor's exposed oil tanks.

Nimitz's forces were now cut back so sharply that it became more important than ever to know what the Japanese were doing. It was also vital to prevent them from learning about our movements, and on 3 January, Cincpac alerted all commands not to use any codes and ciphers that the Japanese might have captured on Wake Island.

Tense as the war situation was, an easy and informal atmosphere soon prevailed in our daily 0800 intelligence briefing. In addition to the morning session, Nimitz encouraged me to go to his office at any time with new bits of information on a priority basis. Apart from his flag secretary,

I was the only one accorded this privilege. Nimitz clearly appreciated and understood that good intelligence is essential to sound strategic decisions.

"I want you to be the Admiral Nagumo of my staff," Nimitz had told me. "I want your every thought, every instinct as you believe Admiral Nagumo might have them. You are to see the war, their operations, their aims, from the Japanese viewpoint and keep me advised what you are thinking about, what you are doing, and what purpose, what strategy, motivates your operations. If you can do this, you will give me the kind of information needed to win this war."

It was a tall order. We were still breaking into the enemy's main operational code system. But Nimitz would constantly keep me on my toes with questions about possible Japanese reactions to events. My bridge sessions with Admiral Yamamoto and personal knowledge of his staff were useful background, but my main source of information came from Hypo's traffic analysts, who were beginning to get back into their stride with the help of call sign pads salvaged from the downed bombers. This tactical guessing game progressed hand in hand with the efforts that Rochefort and his crippies were making to crack the JN-25 "B" system. First odd words, then phrases, then sentences became intelligible as information was obtained first from the process of decryption of known values, then from cryptanalysis to recover the remaining unknown values. In the case of ciphers, new keys were constantly having to be recovered.

In preparation for the hit-and-run carrier strikes in the Marshalls and Gilberts, Nimitz listed his critical intelligence requirements. We had to track the deployment of enemy carriers and carrier strike forces, the disposition and strength of the Fourth Fleet in the mandates, plus its associated submarine force—the Sixth Fleet. Accurate information was needed on the deployment and strength of the Twenty-fourth Air Force, which was scattered through the Marshalls. Nimitz also wanted to be kept informed of the enemy reinforcements that were likely to reach the area by the end of January.

I was at least able to reassure Nimitz of indications that made another raid on Pearl Harbor seem unlikely. Japan's submarines were being withdrawn from their close-in surveillance and attack missions in Hawaiian waters, and pulled back to distant observation patrols. Our own submarine reconnaissance was producing results by providing some vital intelligence details, for example that there were land-based aircraft operating from Kwajalein's Roi airfield and the auxiliaries massed in the lagoon of the largest atoll in the Marshalls. The move of Vice Admiral Shigeyoshi Inouye's Fourth Fleet units into Truk, 450 miles to the west in the Carolines, was confirmed by radio bearings and traffic routing. Meanwhile, Station Cast reported that the enemy's naval strength in Philippine waters had been reorganized into eastern and western forces, and that a large enemy force was moving southward through the Sulu Sea toward Borneo.

It was inevitable, however, that alternative estimates were made by the three radio intelligence units. The first of these sharp differences of opinion came in January, when Pearl challenged the assumption made by Washington that carriers and battleships were guarding Japan's home islands. Our analysis in Hypo was that the duty had been assigned to vessels that were mostly auxiliaries and patrol craft. Eventually, Rochefort's forecast was proved correct, as was his prediction that the *Kido Butai* was moving in support of the operations in the Dutch East Indies, while the detached Carrier Division 2 was in the vicinity of Truk in support of Admiral Inouye's Fourth (mandates) Fleet.

Positive confirmation of Hypo's inspired traffic analysis came on 16 January when an Australian reconnaissance flight reported twenty naval vessels, mostly destroyers and only a few cruisers, in Truk harbor. Identification of the aerial photographs also provided verification of the specific warship designators in the intercepted radio call signs.

The penetration of the JN-25 code was threatened by the rapidity of the Japanese advances. The British crypto unit had to interrupt its operations briefly and transfer from Singapore to Ceylon to become Station Anderson at Colombo. Station Cast had moved to fortified Corregidor Island's Malinta tunnel before war broke out. By 17 January it circulated on the secure Copek channel some 1,700 new additives, 950 new code group values, and 650 additional indicators. During that week Cast had also been able to provide the outnumbered Asiatic Fleet a warning of the destination, course, speed, and time of arrival of two enemy invasion convoys.

Hypo's dedicated band of crippies, led by Tommy Dyer and Ham Wright, had to rely on the support of only seven language officers to perform the actual translation. The new year did bring additional hands from battleship *California*'s band. When their duty station was sunk, Rochefort and Dyer believed that their musical ability might be useful in working out the chords and syncopations of codes and ciphers.

The bandsmen soon became a vital adjunct of the code-breaking process, taking over the task of running the IBM tabulating machines and transferring the code groups from the intercepts onto punch cards. Their labor was considerable, since each Japanese message required anywhere from seventy-five to one hundred IBM cards, and within a few months they were processing millions of cards every week.

Rochefort sent me up a summary of his daily report, but if there was something of spot urgency or importance, a messenger would bring me a copy of the rough decrypt in its actual state of development with a lot of unfilled blanks. I would then call Joe on our secure telephone line to compare notes on what Japanese words might fit. Whenever possible I would go down to the heavily guarded basement that we called his dungeon to chew over the tidbits that often contributed to the solution of problems.

In mid-January, Hypo was still having to rely heavily on traffic analysis. This formed the basis of Station Hypo's first daily intelligence bulletin that summarized strategic radio intelligence items, and was distributed throughout the Allied commands in the Indian Ocean area. The first issue noted the increase in Truk area radio traffic, coupled with the simultaneous decrease in the Marshalls. This augured well for Halsey and Fletcher, whose task forces were heading for the Marshalls and the neighboring Gilberts. By 18 January, Rochefort estimated that the main strength of an enemy naval force assembling in Truk was preparing to support a movement southward that appeared to be heading toward New Guinea. This key piece of information was derived from a message to a Japanese air unit in the Marshalls—the half-burned call-sign card recovered from the crashed Japanese bomber was again paying handsome intelligence dividends.

At the beginning of the third week in January, Rochefort told me about fragments from three intercepted messages that contained a common code group recovered as *koryaku butai* ("occupation force"). In all three instances the group had been preceded by a code group tentatively identified as the letter *R*, making the fragment "R occupation force." Joe had a hunch that *R* stood for Rabaul, the fine natural harbor at the tip of New Britain. Since the *koryaku butai* code group had appeared previously in messages connected with the occupation of Guam and Wake, it appeared to indicate that the Japanese were about to move south to take over the large island off the southeast coast of New Guinea.

When I reported this to Admiral Nimitz, he realized that although we had no forces with which to frustrate Japan's occupation of Rabaul, neither would they be able to send strong forces in the Marshalls and Gilberts to oppose our carrier raids. Joe, moreover, was right about the *R* meaning Rabaul. On 20 January, the Australians informed us that the Bismarck Archipelago between New Britain and New Guinea was attacked by more than one hundred planes. Carrier Division 1 appeared to be involved, so when the Japanese landings began three days later, we were somewhat relieved to find that the Australian estimate of Japanese forces agreed with our estimates. Admiral King reminded Nimitz of the serious threat that a potential loss of Rabaul posed to our communication line with Australia. King sent a dispatch that urged Nimitz to make sure that the upcoming raid on the Marshalls and Gilberts was driven home hard.

Confidence that we could pull it off increased during the week. Station Cast began sending us the first partially completed JN-25 decrypts. These ordered Carrier Division 2 southwest from the mandates to cover operations off New Guinea.[7] Hypo's traffic analysis, to our relief and joy, also continued to reveal a steady decline in enemy activity in the Marshalls as reports came in from the southwest Pacific of the continued Japanese strikes on the islands off the coast of New Guinea.

Traffic analysis revealed that these operations were being given air support by Carrier Division 2, raising Nimitz's anticipation that the enemy's main striking forces were operating more than two thousand miles away from their bases in the Marshalls and Gilberts. It was even more gratifying to know that the Japanese were about to be caught facing in the wrong direction—just as we had been six weeks earlier at Pearl Harbor.

Japanese army leaders had insisted on carrier support to speed up the southern operations, which were to conclude with the occupation of Java. The generals then wanted to bring their troops north to prepare for a strike against Siberia, since they believed that the Soviet Union was to be defeated by Germany. The naval staff wanted to continue the southward advance by raiding the Australian rear base at Port Darwin so as to cut off the allied forces in Java and "prevent another Dunkirk." The Combined Fleet would then sortie into the Indian Ocean to "draw out, and destroy the British Eastern Fleet."[8]

According to Japan's estimates the attack on Pearl Harbor had forced us to suspend all carrier operations. They considered it safe to send Nagumo's carrier striking force to operate with the Second Fleet to reinforce the landings on the New Guinea coast in the first week of February.[9] Their succession of easy victories had so exceeded expectations that they dismissed the possibility of our undertaking major fleet offensives in less than six months—or even a year.

Because of the speed with which objectives had been achieved, Japanese naval planners were preparing to exploit their advantage by pushing southward toward Australia. The first step in Japan's mushrooming strategic mission was the capture of Rabaul, and the establishment of a base at Kavieng on the adjoining island of New Ireland. Controlling the Bismarck Archipelago would open a northern gateway to the Coral Sea and provide a springboard for the invasion of New Guinea and the Solomon Island chain to the west. Japan would then be in a position to threaten the continent of Australia. Rabaul was the linchpin of this strategy. To ensure its capture, the *Kido Butai* was to sail south to lend its air support to Admiral Inouye's Fourth Fleet, which would sally forth from his base at Truk.

The first symptom of what the Japanese themselves would come to call "victory disease" was their decision to reduce the submarine surveillance of Hawaii and the west coast in favor of attacking Allied shipping in the southwest Pacific. This forced them to rely on radio intelligence for information about our movements. Even with Japan's preponderance of naval strength in the Pacific, they still needed to know what we were doing while their own forces were being so widely spread.[10] Apart from a brief advantage that came from the discovery of some of our ciphers on board the gunboat *Wake,* which they had captured at Shanghai, they had not made any significant penetration of our code traffic.

Meanwhile, concern about the destination of one of our carrier task forces sighted by submarine *I-23* at the beginning of the first week of January had resulted in precautionary alerts to Wake and bases in the Marshalls. An inquiry from the emperor himself sent jitters running through the naval staff in Tokyo, which were increased when a floatplane from another submarine came snooping over Pearl that week to reveal another carrier in harbor.

The Japanese panic subsided somewhat after 12 January, when submarine *I-6* reported sinking *Lexington*. In reality it was the look-alike *Saratoga* that had been torpedoed, but not sunk. Naval intelligence headquarters in Tokyo, however, took the initial report at face value. They assumed we had been reduced to one operational carrier, because they had never discovered that *Saratoga* had been sent out from the west coast. In the absence of any other sightings, and because our two remaining task forces maintained radio silence, naval headquarters concluded that the loss of the carrier had stunned us into canceling all offensive operations!

Tokyo was soon to discover that this was wishful thinking! If Yamato had had an intelligence officer on his staff, instead of relying on estimates made by commanders on the spot, the forces under his control might not have succumbed to such a preposterous assumption. Not until after the lesson had been learned six months later at Midway was the first full-time intelligence specialist appointed to the Japanese Combined Fleet.

Around noon on 31 January, the 6th Communications Unit at Kwajalein transmitted a warning that in recent days there had been an increase of a dozen or so new American radio call signs, a sure indication that some kind of offensive action was imminent. But the naval staff in Tokyo did not believe that this report warranted any general alert. The same complacency evidently infected Rear Admiral Sukeyoshi Yatsushiro at his Marshalls Defense Force headquarters on Kwajalein. That evening he threw a large dinner party.

Admiral Yatsushiro's failure to call an alert cost him his life—although he was posthumously promoted one rank, because he was the first Japanese flag officer to be killed in action in the Pacific war. Afterward, Yamamoto's staff claimed not to have received the warning. This was "horsefeathers" because superbattleship *Yamato* was moored to its buoy in the Hashirajima fleet anchorage, with direct cable, radio, and telephone connections to Tokyo.

Saké was flowing as Yatsushiro toasted his officers that evening and looked forward to his celebratory dinner and Halsey's task force was charging undetected toward the Marshalls at high speed. A unique experiment was also proving its worth. Flagship *Enterprise* carried a radio intelligence unit borrowed from Station Hypo for the occasion. The unit consisted of a language officer, Captain Bankson T. Holcomb, Jr., USMC, and three radio operators. Halsey had asked Admiral Nimitz for this special capability on the chance that they might overhear enemy transmissions helpful to his attack. Late that afternoon Holcomb heard a Japanese pilot from Taroa reporting that he had reached the end of his patrol sector, was heading back to base, and had "nothing to report."

This crucial piece of information, showing that his ships had not been detected, delighted Halsey. With gusto, he dictated a "Thank you for not spotting us" note and addressed it to the commanding officer of Marshall Islands forces.[11] He had Holcomb translate it into Japanese for mimeographed leaflets, which the attacking planes dropped next day, along with their bombs.

When Halsey flashed the news that morning to Nimitz that the attack had achieved complete surprise, it was clear that the Japanese had been caught more completely off guard than we had dared hope. But our intercept stations soon heard Japanese naval radios crackle into action as the American attack began and radio silence was broken. The Owada communications center tried to communicate direction-finding bearings from Japan, adding to the confusion and slowing up the reaction of the local commands.

For nine hours, starting at dawn, Halsey stretched his luck with a succession of air strikes that shuttled back and forth from *Enterprise* to strafe and bomb the Kwajalein anchorage. Transports were attacked, along with shore installations. The exuberance of the American pilots, taking advantage of their first opportunity to fight, was evident from their excited radio talk: "Ease off to the right. That big one's mine. . . . Get that cruiser heading off to the right! . . . Take 'em home, boys, take 'em home! . . . We sure got that big bastard, didn't we, sir?"[12]

The airwaves were alive with our pilots congratulating themselves. Meanwhile, Rear Admiral Raymond A. Spruance's cruisers *Southampton* and *Salt Lake City* hit Wotje, and Fletcher's *Yorktown* task force, to the south, struck at Makin, Mili, and Jaluit.

"Bingo! Bongo! I got one! . . . I'm all out of ammunition. . . . Who has lots of gas and ammo left? . . . Affirmative from Blue. . . . OK, I will go along. I will pick up that guy yet. . . . From Black—I'm out of ammo, request permission to get some more."[13]

Thirteen American planes were lost and Halsey was impressed by the ferocity and accuracy of the attacking enemy planes. A "Betty" twin-engine bomber tried to crash-dive flagship *Enterprise*. Quick helm action and alert machine-gunners foiled the first would-be kamikaze, which nicked the port edge of the flight deck and toppled into the sea. Heavy cruiser *Chester* took one bomb hit before the strike commander issued a characteristically earthy signal: "Haul ass with Halsey!"

During the long night of retirement, radar operators in *Enterprise* tracked enemy planes groping for contacts. Halsey took advantage of a northeast weather front by steering his force into the protection of its cloud cover and low visibility. American pilots celebrated, entertaining the messes with ebullient reports claiming a submarine, auxiliaries, and even a small carrier. None of this turned out to be true; no Japanese ships were sunk. But the psychological impact of the strikes on the Japanese was just as great as the loss of a capital ship might have been.

"This attack was Heaven's admonition for our shortcomings" was how Captain Yoshitake Miwa, Yamamoto's chief of operations, put it. "Our staff could only grit their teeth and jump up and down in frustration."[14] According to the diary of Chief of Staff Ugaki, who grieved the death of Admiral Yatsushiro, his Etajima classmate, their own "carelessness and stupidity" was to blame. "We were asleep at the switch," he lamented. "To be so completely surprised, long after the start of a war, is incredible."[15]

In a frantic bolting of the stable door after all the horses had fled, on 2 February every Japanese radio intelligence station from Tokyo to Jaluit tried to pinpoint Halsey's elusive task force. Heaping chagrin on mortification, Japanese radio operators heard only American commercial radio broadcasts, announcing somewhat exaggeratedly that Pearl Harbor had been avenged.

After such a debacle, the Combined Fleet staff had good reason to grow jittery about the future. "Now, having learned that the defenses of our advance bases are relatively weak, he will probably continue such attacks in the future," observed Admiral Miwa. "Whatever happens, we must absolutely prevent any air attack on Tokyo. . . . Against enemy aircraft carriers, the defensive is bad strategy, and worse tactics."[16]

The first full month of the war had concluded with a classic demonstration of American resiliency and a vindication of the strategy that Admiral Kimmel had shaped after Pearl Harbor. Nimitz had skillfully used our carriers and radio intelligence to deliver the first American counterpunch. At the same time our raids had exposed the inflexibility of our enemy and their failure to make proper use of intelligence to coordinate their far-flung and overambitious Pacific strategy.

27

Where and When?

S IRENS SHRIEKED. Horns and whistles blew. Sailors manned the rail of every ship to welcome *Enterprise* back to Pearl Harbor on the morning of 5 February. Admiral Nimitz was so eager to congratulate his friend Bill Halsey that he did not even wait for a gangway to be secured. A bosun's chair hoisted the Pacific Fleet commander in chief to the hangar deck of the carrier.[1]

Nimitz hopped on board and pumped Halsey's hand, saying, "Bill, it was wonderful, a great job."

Halsey said, "I've got something for you, Chester," handing Nimitz a paper.

"What's this, Bill? It looks like Japanese writing."

Halsey chuckled. "You remember I asked for a language officer. Well, they gave me a marine, and I want you to meet him. Come over here, Captain Holcomb. Tell Admiral Nimitz about this paper."

Nimitz smiled at the account of Halsey's dictating a message to the Japanese commander at Kwajalein, and he doubled up with laughter when he heard how the message was translated, mimeographed, and scattered over the island by our pilots. "Wonderful," Nimitz exclaimed, "a great show all around."[2]

Photographers snapped Halsey's grizzled features, and the press reported his briny remarks. The American public needed a hero, and he was it. His bold strike provided relief from daily headlines, chronicling round after gloomy round of Allied defeat and retreat. Advancing Japanese troops had rolled MacArthur's weary army down the Bataan Peninsula, and invaded Singapore. American and Dutch naval forces were being driven out of the Dutch East Indies.

The morale boost from Halsey's raid was all to the good, but Nimitz knew—from our interception of Japan's own radio reports—that American headlines greatly exaggerated the results. Other advantages accrued from the raid, however. It caused a surge of frantic Japanese radio messages. The increased volume of radio traffic provided our analysts with additional clues toward solving the all-important puzzle of the Japanese geographic designators. Partial recoveries suggested that "A" seemed to represent places in the Hawaiian chain, and "R" prefixed British islands in the South Pacific. The more deeply our naval code breakers unraveled the JN-25 fleet code, the more important became the first two letters when the emerging pattern confirmed that the first letter referred to the territorial area and the second to specific places—it was often the initial of the name or places which had no designators.

"M," from its frequent appearance in radio transmissions originating from units in the Philippines, clearly stood for the whole of that newly conquered territory. We were able to work out that "MM" represented Manila; "MD" appeared to be Davao. Similarly, "R" was Rabaul, "P" the mandated islands; and hence "PP" came out as Palau, "PT" Truk, and "PY" Jaluit. Throughout the spring of 1942 one or more of these geographic designators was being identified almost every day.

Radio intelligence was, of course, a game that two could play, and did. The more Japanese traffic we were able to read, the more we realized that they were making progress identifying our own call signs. This revelation caused a monumental flap. But our best information was that all the compromised calls belonged to shore-based commands, either naval or ones that used adjacent naval base facilities. Admiral Nimitz was particularly concerned about these Japanese recoveries. But I was able to assure him that, from all indications, the enemy had not identified the call signs of any of our seagoing commands. To make the task of Japanese traffic analysts harder, the order went out to cut down unnecessary radio traffic. Shore-based commands that had to issue a great amount of traffic were not to use the same encipherment that was used for highly classified operational traffic.

Nimitz continued to express concern about how much enemy radio intelligence was finding out about us. His questions were always searching, and often led to long discussion of radio communications and intelligence procedures. He insisted that the daily briefings should always tell "who, what, where, when, and why."

Radio intelligence, by its very nature, often led each of our intercept stations to reach differing conclusions. On 5 February, Admiral Stark, who remained chief of naval operations until 26 March, sent a dispatch warning us that Station Negat in Washington had intercepted signals that led the naval staff to believe Japan was planning to attack the New Hebrides, off the southeast coast of Australia.

But Rochefort could find no sign of the move predicted by Washington. My briefing for Nimitz on 6 February, based on the location and currently indicated activities of the major enemy forces, had the main thrust of the Japanese offensives moving toward occupation of Java and

Sumatra. In addition we had discovered a subsidiary operation code-named "MA" for the occupation of airfields and ports in eastern New Guinea and in the Solomons. Their westward shift of submarine forces and a stepping up of activities in the Indian Ocean from a new base at Penang on the northwest coast of Malaya did not suggest any immediate operations in the mid-Pacific.

When I finished this rundown, it came as a big surprise to read the dispatch that Nimitz handed me. Just in from the navy department, this time from Cominch—Admiral King—it confirmed the expectation of an offensive against the Dutch East Indies, but it also alerted us to "expedite dispositions and operations of war forces" to meet "raids against Midway, Oahu, New Hebrides, northeast Australia, and possibly the west coast or the canal."[3]

My reaction was that Washington's evaluation was way off. Perhaps it was prompted by the fear that some spectacular offensive would be launched on 11 February when Empire Day was celebrated to mark the founding of Japan by the Emperor Jimmu. We might anticipate that a few shells could be lobbed ashore from a submarine, but there were no signs of anything as spectacular as a major offense against Australia. King's attitude may well have been colored by the fact that the ANZAC (Australia–New Zealand) area command, established by the Allied chiefs of staff at the Arcadia conference, had been assigned directly to his control. He had activated it on 7 February, under Vice Admiral William F. Leary, after directing Nimitz to send out a heavy cruiser to join the Australian squadron of Rear Admiral John G. Crace, RN.

Nimitz had already sent heavy cruiser *Chicago* and two destroyers to join the Allied force, whose mission was to deter any Japanese moves into the waters west of Australia. But that was not the end of it. King continued to underline the "serious threat to lines of communication with Australia," and at the end of January he ordered Nimitz to send down a carrier task force. Since Halsey and Fletcher were occupied with the Marshalls raid, that left only Admiral Wilson Brown's *Lexington* group free. This move was opposed by most members of Nimitz's staff.

Still Admiral King pressed Nimitz for reinforcements. He sent two more messages on the sixth, warning of an imminent, stepped-up Japanese offensive in the southwest Pacific, accompanied probably by strong raids elsewhere, and calling for Cincpac to take "prompt action to check enemy advance."[4] Before replying to King, Nimitz called a staff conference, at which I repeated my summary of the intelligence situation. The dilemma he faced was how to tell Washington that their intelligence estimate was dead wrong.

The next day Nimitz sent off a tactful but oblique response that "such employment considered inadvisable at present" because our fleet was inferior in all ship types to the enemy and, except for hit-and-run operations, there was little that could be done to "check enemy advance" in the southwest Pacific. Two days later a blistering reply came stating that the "Pacific Fleet not, repeat *not* markedly inferior" because Japan was "committed to extensive operations in the southwest Pacific." Nimitz was ordered by King to review the situation and "consider active operations against Mandates and Wake."[5]

This blast from Washington left Nimitz with limited options. After considering whether to send Halsey's *Enterprise* task force to reinforce Brown's intended strike on Rabaul, he concluded it was tactically sounder to have Halsey join Fletcher's *Yorktown* task force to make another diversionary raid on the mandates. To explain the strategic rationale that prompted his decision and soothe King's ruffled feathers, Admiral Pye was sent posthaste to Washington by navy flying boat.

The spat over the evaluation of radio intelligence, as we were to discover, was the result of changes that were being made in the navy department. Although Stark was to remain as chief of naval operations in an uneasy partnership with King (until Stark's role was absorbed by Cominch at the end of March), King considered he had been given authority by the president and secretary of the navy to make a shake-up that would sweep out the men he considered to be defeatist and whose failures had contributed to the disaster at Pearl Harbor.

The first casualties were to be the directors of naval intelligence and naval communications, who were shortly to be assigned to sea duty. Their memoranda of self-vindication were challenged by Turner who saw eye to eye with King on the need for Cominch to centralize control of the intelligence and code-breaking operation in Washington.

The informal style in which Captain Safford had run the sixty-person OP-20-G organization may have worked in peacetime, but it was less appropriate for coping with the rapid expansion that was necessary in wartime. He wanted to assign even more independence to his friend Joe Rochefort in Station Hypo at Pearl, but this infuriated certain ambitious naval communications officers who, like King and Turner, wanted to keep control of the intercept work in Washington. Foremost among them was Noyes's deputy director of communications, Captain Joseph R. Redman. His brother, Commander John R. Redman, was then one of Safford's deputies in OP-20-G. Their views were shared by Commander Joseph N. Wenger, another high-flying naval communications officer who had been intelligence officer on the Asiatic Fleet staff.

The Redman brothers were adept politicians. They seized on King's arrival to ingratiate themselves by supporting his determination to be master of his own intelligence organization. Safford played into their hands on 23 January when he submitted his proposals to Noyes in response to a directive to all department directors to streamline their organizations. Safford's three-page memorandum, headed "Reorganization of OP-20-G Section," suggested separating responsibility for the security of our code systems from day-by-day cryptanalysis. He also suggested that "certain personnel will be transferred to the CI unit, Pearl Harbor, in accordance with present plans."[6]

Safford's intention to decentralize the intelligence function came under fire three days later. Commander Wenger was convinced that "while security activities can and should be separated from intelligence activities . . . breakup of the latter can only be seriously detrimental to results."[7] It was no accident that the thrust of his proposed reorganization coincided with the ambitions of the Redman brothers and Admiral King.

According to Wenger, the navy department must "assume *active* coordinating control . . . of all intercept stations, D/F nets, and decrypting units [emphasis added]." He proposed a drastic reorganization of OP-20-G, to ensure "a central coordinating authority for all communications intelligence activities," which would restrict Rochefort's Hypo unit in Hawaii. Henceforth, Hypo would "be concerned chiefly with combat intelligence, and . . . the research section in Washington should assist it as much as possible until we can begin to assume the offensive more definitely in the Pacific."[8] To achieve this end, OP-20-G would be reorganized into subsections: Commander John Redman would head a communications combat intelligence section; Wenger would be chief of a communications cryptanalytical section to handle decryption and translation; Safford was to be removed from the day-to-day intelligence process and shifted to an administrative support and cryptographic research role.

Deputy Naval Communications Director Joseph Redman reviewed the conflicting plans on 6 February and gave notice of "a conference on this subject" the following week. But that very day the Redman-Wenger plan was submitted to Admiral King who gave it his immediate approval. Outmaneuvered and outraged, Safford tried to salvage the outfit from dismemberment. In a memorandum eloquent with despair, he conceded the reorganization, but remained adamant in denying that "the senior officers concerned would be utilized to the best advantage."[9] He challenged John Redman's ability for duties beyond the field of his specialization, and proposed that he, not Wenger, be officer in charge of the OP-20-G section.

"I should be logically assigned to cryptological duties as long as I am on active duty," Safford protested, and "respectfully" requested a transfer if his appeal was turned down.[10] It was. Three days later Safford found himself bounced as head of the navy's cryptographic and radio intelligence section, a cause that had occupied most of his thoughts and energies for the past seventeen years.

The relationship of cozy confidence between Negat and Hypo, which depended on the longtime friendship of Safford and Rochefort, was terminated. As the Redman brothers and their supporters moved in to take over OP-20-G, their reorganization made administrative machinery hum more efficiently. But it also destroyed the personal loyalties and relationships that were essential to the creative effort of code breaking. At the same time, the determination of the new regime in Washington to dictate and control the intelligence function brought a clash of jurisdiction and personalities. The result was to exacerbate the inevitable differences in intelligence estimates that emerged with Rochefort at Hypo.

The Japanese were also facing command conflicts in reconciling wartime strategic decisions with intelligence, and were to be repeatedly panicked into wild-goose chases by false estimates they made of our movements. But the alerts ordered for 11 February in both Tokyo and Washington—out of fear that the enemy would make some dastardly attack on Japan's national holiday—proved unfounded. Empire Day passed without any attacks materializing. It was not until three days later that the Combined Fleet was told by Tokyo that the signals announcing the supposed enemy task forces that had brought the most recent panic had been ascertained to be routine radio exchanges between American commercial planes flying west coast routes. Nor was there yet any sign of Cominch's anticipated Japanese offensive in the southwest Pacific.

When Halsey's Task Force 8 sailed from Pearl on 14 February for another raiding operation, Nimitz was relieved to be told that King had finally been won over to our estimates of Japanese strategy. Within hours *Yorktown* was rounding Diamond Head and setting course west for the Marshalls.

Radio intelligence has never been considered an exact science. Interpretations and deductions drawn from it are sometimes incorrect, tending to undermine its otherwise consistent reliability. As with the baseball player, it's the batting average that counts, and while our own was a long way from perfect, the Japanese average was in the cellar. On 14 February the increase in our voice communications from the Hawaii area prompted another Japanese alert. Three days later two American task forces were divined to be west of Midway and northwest of Jaluit, and the emperor was advised by a nervous navy chief that they might attack the Marshalls by the twentieth—or be off the Tokyo coast by the twenty-third.

One of the things that prompted the Japanese confusion was later discovered to be our profligate use of voice radio in the belief that the range of these high-frequency ship-to-air circuits was limited to the horizon. Only later was it discovered that these transmissions bounced up and down from the Heaviside layer and could skip across the breadth of the Pacific. The Japanese were inclined to jump to conclusions and order alerts too readily. Their radio intelligence center at Owada, however, achieved a good record in deducing whenever our task forces sortied from Pearl Harbor from the increased radio activity when they flew on board their complement of planes. Their conclusions were often reinforced by sightings of our submarines, which they correctly assumed were deployed ahead in target areas to provide weather reports, intelligence data, and "lifeguard services" during actual raids.

So while Tokyo was tracking a nonexistent American striking force heading for the Marshalls—or Tokyo—on 19 February, a sighting from Fourth Fleet headquarters in Truk reported that hostile destroyers had been spotted south of the Carolines. Air searches that afternoon and next morning found nothing. Another false alert had to be canceled. But as fate would have it, the Japanese long-range air patrol from New Britain had chanced upon a real carrier task force. Admiral Wilson Brown in *Lexington* was steaming on a northwesterly course to raid the Rabaul naval base. A Kawanishi "Mavis" flying boat reported at 0830, "Large enemy force sighted 460 miles bearing 76 from Rabaul on course 315."[11]

That sighting report—which was also picked up at Pearl Harbor— stirred up a hornet's nest of activity by the Fourth Fleet after Truk head-quarters flashed out immediate orders. Surface ships and submarines were deployed across the line of the American advance, land-based bombers were summoned east from the Marshalls, and Mavis flying boats were ordered to coordinate dawn to dusk torpedo attacks. But because Rabaul's fighters lacked the range, Admiral Inouye had to order unde-fended bombers "to apprehend the attack and annihilate the enemy force."

That afternoon *Lexington*'s fighters and intense antiaircraft barrage from Brown's cruisers made short work of all but two of the Japanese bombers and three of the flying boats. No damage was inflicted on our ships. The action revealed that the large Mavis flying boats had a distress-ing tendency to burst into flames when hit. They were henceforth nick-named by the Japanese as Type I *"Rai-Ta"*—roughly translated as "Zippo lighter."

Admiral Brown, however, had not won the victory, which he had been sent to achieve. Rabaul was now fully alerted. The surprise that was so essential to the success of his mission had been lost. After two fatally hit bombers had tried to crash-dive *Lexington*, he held course northward only until sunset and then ordered a withdrawal. His feint did succeed in a maximum diversionary impact because the Japanese spent two frantic days scouring the seas west of Rabaul for the enemy without result.

Naval intelligence in Tokyo, Admiral Yamamoto's staff, and the com-mander in chief of the Fourth Fleet were now in a state of confusion and uncertainty. Where might the next raid come? It was clear that the carrier force they had attacked southeast of Rabaul could not be the same one that the Owada radio intelligence center had reported as leaving Pearl Harbor only four days earlier. But by 22 February when extensive air patrols had failed to make any sightings, Admiral Inouye cautiously di-rected his forces to resume preparation for their southward offensive against Lae and Salamaua. The assault on these two ports on the north-east coast of New Guinea had originally been scheduled for 6 March, but now had to be postponed ten days because the Fourth fleet warships had exhausted so much fuel and time.

The Japanese garrison on Wake raised another false alarm that day. But it was forty-eight hours later, at dawn on 24 February, that the pilots of Halsey's task force delivered their bombs, while the guns of Admiral Spruance's heavy cruisers bombarded the sandy spits of what had recently been a United States outpost. The half-hour raid dazed the enemy and cost him a patrol craft and three flying boats, and damaged buildings. Halsey withdrew to the northeast, having lost just one plane. He was belatedly chased by a flock of Kwajalein-based bombers that failed to score a single hit.

Admiral Nimitz awoke that morning to the news of another Halsey success. He chided me for having overestimated the effectiveness of Japanese air searches. For the third time in less than a month, our surprise attacks had succeeded against an enemy base.

On board Yamamoto's flagship the same news produced a very different reaction. Had not Wake been alerted against just such an attack? Why had the enemy force not been sighted during its approach? Once again an enemy carrier raid had stirred a massive movement of planes from Truk to the Marshalls. Again the Japanese were caught off guard. Yamamoto's chief of staff once again bemoaned their unpreparedness and promised his diary, "Someday, when he has launched his planes and closed in for gun bombardment we'll get him—the golden opportunity to get him will surely come."[12]

A golden opportunity that Japan did not pass up came three days later when their Third Fleet heavy cruisers smashed the remnants of the joint ABDA (American, British, Dutch, Australian) naval force. The Japanese sent five of our cruisers—one American, one British, two Dutch, and one Australian—to the bottom of the Java Sea. A week later, in the mid-Pacific, Japan was going to be presented with another opportunity. This one, had they been more alert, might have had a devastating effect on our strategy.

When Admiral Nimitz signaled his congratulations to Halsey for the successful Wake strike, he added. "DESIRABLE TO HIT MARCUS IF YOU THINK IT POSSIBLE."[13] This was all the encouragement Bill Halsey needed to begin another charge. After refueling Task Force 8, he turned toward that lonely Japanese outpost, six hundred miles northwest of Wake. Marcus Island, only one thousand miles east of the Japanese home islands, was a forward Japanese base from which air patrols covered an important sector of her eastern early warning and defense perimeter.

Yet again there was no warning of Halsey's predawn attack on 4 March. The first *Enterprise* bombs that morning knocked out the island's radio transmitters and power supply. No report of the raid could be sent until makeshift transmitters were rigged. Once more the Japanese defenses had been caught napping. Yamamoto ordered Carrier Division 5 to join a chase that became even more confused and frantic the next day after a false sighting report that enemy ships were heading for Japan's coast. "Small errors cause big trouble," Ugaki observed. "At this pace, they will surely come to Tokyo Bay next."[14]

Meanwhile, we did not shine brightly in our handling of a Japanese move against Hawaii. It was an operation that was intended to bomb Pearl Harbor by using the new Kawanishi H8K long-range flying boats, which had been designed to make the round trip to Pearl from Japan's bases in the Marshalls. Unfortunately for the plan, however, test flights showed that "Emily," as we code-named the twenty-four-ton, four-engine monsters, could not meet its design range. This meant arranging for an operation of refueling from submarines at French Frigate Shoals, at the extreme western tip of the Hawaiian chain.[15]

We might never have learned of these plans if the Japanese had executed the change in their JN-25 additives that had been foreshadowed in a decrypt by Station Cast of 26 February. New tactical call signs came into effect on 1 March, but no changes were noted in the Japanese service call signs or the cipher system.

On 2 March I was able to give Nimitz the good news that not only was there no change, but that Hypo was able to isolate the two-kana designators for all the Japanese submarine tenders. This meant we had located the general operating areas of their submarines. Rochefort also noted that a movement was under way for a "pending offensive operation." What it was Joe could not yet predict, but his cryptanalysts had succeeded in breaking two intercepts. One, dated 12 February, from CinC Fourth Fleet, addressed to "AA" (which was presumed to be Wake Island), was a request to ascertain the number of ships in harbor in "AK." Wake's reply was also translated, leaving us in no doubt about the identity of these two most important geographic designators.

> Referring to Pearl Harbor, no repairs required. Aviation facilities repairs completed. Three battleships present at Pearl Harbor. Repairs impossible to [?, or, are being investigated with regard to ?] Other battleships have returned to the mainland for necessary repairs. [Midget?] submarine base now being established on land. Prisoner[s] to depart "AA" [Wake] on 3 March by air to Yokosuka.[16]

This Japanese signal confirmed Station Cast's previous identifications of "AA" as Wake and "AK" as Pearl Harbor. The prisoners referred to were two American fliers captured during *Enterprise*'s 24 February raid on Wake, information that was immediately relayed to Admiral Halsey.

Another clue that Japan had something afoot and directed toward Hawaii came from direction-finding bearings that placed two enemy submarines east of Midway. Then there was a reference in another signal to a "pending offensive" scheduled for 5 March, which was designated by "K." There seemed little doubt that the operation was to be directed against Pearl Harbor and this time it did not appear that enemy carriers were involved.

Nimitz remarked that intelligence had produced only the "when and where" portion of the problem. He asked my estimate of the "what." I said that since enemy submarines were still active in the Hawaii area, they might use their deck guns in a night shelling of Pearl's oil tanks and airfields. This would follow the pattern of the recent attack on the Ellwood oil fields at Goleta on the California coast on 23 February. I reminded him that Pearl Harbor had been reconnoitered three times in moonlight by small floatplanes from submarines.

Joe had a hunch about a floatplane raid on Pearl launched from *Chitose*-class seaplane carriers. He added that such planes could carry only a small bomb load at long range. Admiral Bloch accordingly put the Fourteenth Naval District air patrols on alert against the possibility of such raid, which would be made more for propaganda than for its military effect.

On 3 March there were no further clues as to the "what," but we received a dispatch from Cominch that "intercepts concerning these movements be most carefully watched and analyzed."[17] It left us wondering why Washington assumed we were *not* watching and analyzing all pieces of this (and every other) radio intelligence puzzle.

At 2100 that same day Station Cast, which was continuing its outstanding decryption work despite the miseries of the constant bombing of Corregidor, gave us more clues. A garbled intercept from Tokyo naval intelligence was readable enough for it to be seen as a reference to the forces in "AH, AFH, and AF areas" involved in the 5 March operation.[18] Rochefort and I agreed that "AH" stood for the Hawaiian Islands. But although "AF" had appeared before in a fragmentary intelligence-type message, this was the first appearance of "AFH." Since "A" appeared to be the prefix for American Pacific possessions, it seemed clear that "AFH" stood for islands in the Hawaiian group, but we had no clue as to which islands it represented.

Cast's message was studied carefully for new clues. Traffic analysis had shown that the association of a submarine force and air commands as addressees in the same message was not entirely unusual. But one of the two air groups in the Marshalls to which it was addressed was known to operate four-engine flying boats. But we blew it.

Neither Rochefort nor I had spotted the one clue that later seemed so obvious—that the "K" operation was derived from the newly proven designator, "AK," for Pearl Harbor. Hypo would also rework on 5 March a new translation of Cast's 3 March message that made it plain that it was referring to their decrypt of our weather forecast for Pearl Harbor.[19] But the revelation came a day and a half too late.

Operation K revealed itself at 0015 on 4 March. The army radar station on Kauai to the west of Oahu reported, "Aircraft bearing 290 true distant 204 miles from Oahu."[20] As the general alert was sounded, torpedo-laden PBYs took off to attack the ships suspected of launching the raiders. Pursuit planes were sent up to give chase but were foiled by a tropical rainstorm that blanked the harbor area. Just before 0200, the population of Honolulu was awakened by the air raid sirens and minutes later explosions were heard to the west of the city.

The intruders escaped undetected; however, there was no apparent damage except to a cluster of algaroba trees on the slope of Mount Tantalus. Fragments of bomb fins and fuses were later recovered and proved to be identical with those dropped in the raid of 7 December. Admiral Nimitz came to my office to see these exhibits. He was accompanied by his staff air officer, Captain Arthur Davis, who was busily explaining that the Japanese had no planes capable of making a roundtrip from Wake, their nearest base, to Oahu.

Nimitz examined the fragments and was told by the bomb-disposal chief that they were Japanese. When the admiral asked if I had any idea how this morning's bombing had been accomplished, I reminded him of the story "Rendezvous" written by Alec Hudson (the pen name of my friend and naval colleague Jasper Holmes who was then working in Hypo), which had appeared the previous August in *The Saturday Evening Post*. It concerned the refueling of American PBYs by submarine at an isolated atoll to increase their range for a special long-distance operation. I told Nimitz I believed that the Japanese had used this idea to get their flying boats in from Wotje in the Marshalls by landing to take on fuel from submarines at the French Frigate Shoals.

Recent direction-finding fixes had indicated that Japanese submarines were operating in the vicinity of the shoals to the northwest of the Hawaiian chain. That morning Nimitz directed Admiral Bloch to send seaplane tender *Ballard,* a converted destroyer, to the French Frigate Shoals under radio silence, to patrol there and deny their future use for such an operation. Later, he had a defensive minefield laid for the same purpose.[21]

The morning after the raid we were dumbfounded by a "Show immediately to Cincpac in person" message from Cominch. It had obviously been sent before King received our report of the attack. It revised Negat's forecast of Japan's possible 11 March raid. The Johnny-come-lately warning that indications of a raid by the Carrier Division 5 "have some foundation and cannot be ignored"[22] must have brought some red faces in Washington when the next batch of decrypts revealed that these carriers were heading southeast from Japan to chase Admiral Halsey, whose raid on Marcus had taken place that morning.

The next three days were to be filled with alarums and excursions for both sides. The final stage of Japan's takeover of the Dutch East Indies began with the invasion of Java. By 8 March the remnants of the Allied forces had surrendered in Bandung. At the same time our radio intelligence detected a growing concentration of naval forces off New Guinea. This pointed to a resumption of their southward move. Air reconnaissance patrols on 6 March confirmed that enemy invasion forces had sailed from Rabaul and appeared to be heading for the twin ports of Lae and Salamaua on New Guinea's southeastern bight, which borders the Solomon Sea. This appeared to be a first step toward the assault and capture of Port Moresby, the administrative capital of Papua, which was New Guinea's nearest point to Australia.

News that the actual landings were under way on 8 March found Admiral Wilson Brown within striking distance. Two days earlier he had joined up with Admiral Fletcher's *Yorktown* task force to make a second attempt to raid Rabaul. *Lexington*'s pilots were raring to have another crack at the Japanese. To Captain Turner Joy, Brown's operations officer, the opportunity to hit back and disrupt an enemy landing was an "answer to prayer."[23] An all-night conference in *Lexington* weighed the alternate risks of hazarding carriers in uncharted waters off western Papua or sending pilots over the fifteen-thousand-foot Owen Stanley mountain range. The latter option was decided on, and the pilots flew off on the tenth, armed with hastily gathered road maps with which to navigate the treacherous cloud-covered passes and peaks.

The raid was coordinated with an attack by Allied bombers from New Guinea land bases. Tropical rainstorms concealed the approach of our air strikes, which roared in just before 0730 to attack ships of the Japanese occupation force with bombs, torpedoes, and strafing runs. Of the eighteen ships present, four were sunk and thirteen damaged. The Japanese navy suffered its heaviest losses of the war, and the raid forced a badly shaken Admiral Inouye to postpone his assault on Port Moresby from early April to early May because of the need for repairs and for carrier support.[24]

The delay was to cause the first significant hesitation in Japan's southward march of triumph. When Inouye attempted to resume the advance two months later, our forces were in position to turn the hiccup of Lae and Salamaua into a full-blown case of strategic indigestion. Japan's progress toward Australia was halted.

The temporary setback to their New Guinea campaign was a shock to imperial general headquarters. Naval intelligence issued a dispatch that same afternoon forecasting that "in addition to offensive moves against Rabaul and Truk, the enemy plans surprise attack on Tokyo or the Bonin Islands."[25] To guard against this possibility, air and naval units were recalled to defend the approaches to Japan. It also brought a jittery series of alerts as the naval headquarters in Tokyo responded to fears of the national disgrace should American carrier planes manage to drop a single bomb on the sacred soil of the home islands.

Rochefort was soon reporting that radio intelligence showed that the Japanese were reacting to the increase in our patrol activity in the

Hawaiian area. Decrypts of the messages flashed out by their Owada center indicated their concern that "an enemy force has sortied," and the presence of our submarines in Japan's coastal waters suggested "that the enemy is planning something aggressive, possibly an air attack on Japan's home islands." Combined Fleet units raised steam "to take appropriate measures to cope with the situation."[26] Carrier Division 5 was recalled to assist.

The streams of such urgent anticipatory messages between Japanese naval commands were being intercepted by Station Hypo, decrypted, translated, encoded in our secure communications channels, and disseminated within six hours of Japanese transmission. It was a dramatic demonstration of the progress that Rochefort's team had made in penetrating the enemy's operational ciphers. We were puzzled by the flood of messages that showed the increase in Japan's air and submarine searches and the concentration of naval forces in the approaches to Tokyo Bay. Joe observed that this renewed concern with the defense of their home waters was "creating more panic than seems reasonable." Admiral Nimitz was intrigued by Rochefort's theory that our carrier raids were paying such unexpected dividends that the Japanese were redeploying their forces against a "nonexistent force."[27]

The diary of Yamamoto's chief of staff confirmed that Rochefort's analysis was correct. Ugaki was complaining that it was "irksome" to be on the defensive in the midst of victory. "Today Japan is celebrating the fall of the Netherlands East Indies," Ugaki wrote on 12 March while units of the Combined Fleet screening force sortied to defend Tokyo against another imaginary American raid. "I can't help but shudder at the thought of enemy aircraft attacking masses of our rejoicing people celebrating a great victory."[28]

The overreaction of the Japanese navy's radio intelligence center, and the consequent wild-goose chases by the Combined Fleet, wasted enormous reserves of fuel. It also caused unnecessary wear and tear to the machinery of their warships and to their morale and self-confidence. All this had been achieved at little cost to us. The damage we had inflicted may have been military pinpricks, but each attack put mounting pressure on the Japanese to turn the tables and "make face" for previous failures.

A major reason for the success of Nimitz's strategy was this: In just three months we had established a reliable basis for tactical and strategic intelligence to support the Allied war effort in the Pacific. It was our ability to intercept and break significant portions of the enemy's operational traffic that gave us the edge.

What was to turn out to be the most significant bit of intelligence of all—though we did not appreciate it at the time—was uncovered in a 9 March message from Tokyo addressed specifically to air group commanders in the mandates. It gave a two-day forecast of wind force and direction at "AF." Since the local submarine commander was not an addressee of this message as in the previous ones, Rochefort interpreted the intended targets of Japanese air attack as being our island bases within range of the Marshalls. It was our very first inkling that "AF" could be Midway.

28

"A Bungling Attack Is Better Than the Most Skillful Defense"

O N 11 MARCH 1942, the day after Halsey's task force had returned from the raids on Wake and Marcus islands, Admiral Nimitz received another alarm from Admiral King. A secret and personal dispatch warned "that recent enemy air and submarine activities may well indicate another full-scale effort against the Hawaii-Midway line with the likely principal objective of crippling or destroying our vital base at Pearl Harbor."

King's "strong" belief that an attack requiring Nimitz's "unremitting supervision of readiness" was the result of naval intelligence putting two and two together and making five—again.[1] It appears that Captain Redman and Commander Wenger had linked a decrypt about the intended changes in the JN-25 additives with a misreading of Rochefort's "AF" weather decrypt. The result was their belief that the Japanese were about to strike us once more in the mid-Pacific. King was especially concerned that "attempts at long-range bombing of the Hawaiian Islands may be planned."[2]

But our estimates of the same decrypts pointed to an opposite conclusion. Japan appeared committed to the southward movement through New Guinea and was sending her main striking forces into the Indian Ocean. Confirmation of this came on 12 March from the British at Station Anderson in Colombo. Their analysis had ascertained the arrival of a carrier at Singapore to cover the invasion of the Andaman Islands south of Burma. The analysis reported that Japanese "operations now appear a full-scale one, and possibly a prelude to further western advance."[3]

None of the Allied intercept stations, however, revealed the extent to which the Indian Ocean operation, originally scheduled to begin on 15 March, had been delayed by a month after the Combined Fleet sortied in response to the false report of American carriers off Wake. So the Cincpac intelligence bulletin that I issued the next day reported that Car-

378

rier Division 5 and two submarine squadrons were "expected to operate in Malay area and Indian Ocean."[4]

This was the first of the daily summaries of enemy movements that King had authorized Nimitz to issue. Other bulletins superseded the Hypo summary and they were radioed in code to all commands. They were intended to convey the gist of our latest radio intelligence estimates without making direct reference to the sources of the information. This information was confined to the exchanges among our stations in cipher on the Copek circuits; derivative information for other commands and task forces was confided to less secure ciphers without disclosing the source, as and when appropriate.

Guarding the security of our radio intelligence network now became a major concern. During the final stages of the battle for the Philippines, as the Japanese relentlessly drove MacArthur's forces down to the dead end of the Bataan Peninsula, Cominch ordered the evacuation of all members of Station Cast. If any one of these men fell into enemy hands he would be tortured to reveal details of American code breaking. King regarded the unit to be "of such importance to the successful prosecution of the war in the Far East" that "to preserve its continuity" advanced plans had been made for its safe withdrawal by "any means of transportation."[5] A three-stage evacuation by submarine was planned so that each unit—consisting of linguists, cryptanalysts, radiomen, and equipment—could continue to operate independently of the others.

The first group of four officers, thirteen enlisted men, and equipment left Corregidor on 5 February 1942 in submarine *Seadragon*. On 11 March thirty more left for Australia on board *Permit*. (This was five days after General Douglas MacArthur put to sea from embattled Corregidor to make his escape by PT boat.) Three officers and eighteen men remained working without respite in the Malinta Tunnel until the early hours of 8 April. Under merciless bombardment that caused the American forces on Bataan to surrender later that day, they were ferried out to *Seadragon* and survived a prolonged depth-charge attack en route to Fremantle on the west coast of Australia.

On 16 March, while the second group of cryptanalysts was awaiting its turn to be evacuated, Station Cast relayed a worrying decrypt indicating that Tokyo naval intelligence was disseminating the call signs of our units. The call signs were so accurate we feared that they might have captured one of our call-sign books. The following day Hypo confirmed the bad news that "enciphered calls as given by Tokyo for the 16th indicate he has a copy of our Call Sign Publication #1161."[6]

This dispatch caused a real flap. It reinforced the principle laid down by the office of naval operations of "maintaining maximum security by minimum distribution."[7] Postwar evidence confirmed that the Japanese had obtained a copy of one of our old communications manuals that spelled out the three-tier system of our letter-numeral-letter designators for commanders and the three-letter indicators for our principal shore bases. From the manual the Owada analysts had been able to work out the structure of our naval communications system and were almost as good at keeping track of our call signs as we had become at keeping up with theirs.

Call signs were one thing, but intensive checking at Hypo and Negat provided no evidence that they were breaking any substantive messages in our ciphers. We, however, were making steady progress penetrating theirs. That is why Nimitz was able to endorse my bulletin of 18 March dismissing Washington's week-old alert against Japanese attacks in the mid-Pacific. It stated, "No indication of immediate major offensive action except in Malaya area."[8]

While Nimitz's steadfast confidence in his intelligence outfit saved the fleet from dashing off in response to every one of Washington's nervous twitches, he could not ignore the strategic directions of Cominch. On 19 March he learned for the first time that he was expected to assign one third of our entire Pacific carrier forces to a risky operation that had been cooked up in the navy department. That Thursday, Captain Donald B. Duncan arrived at Pearl Harbor on a top-secret mission. King's air officer had come to tell Nimitz that he had been given charge of one of America's biggest gambles of the war—an operation to bomb Tokyo itself.

The plan to strike the Japanese homeland had its genesis in a discussion two months earlier in which Admiral King reviewed, with Duncan and his war plans officer, Captain Francis F. "Froggie" Lowe, ways to hit back at the Japanese. Nimitz had been directed to make carrier strikes against Japan's forward island bases. But King wanted a more dramatic demonstration that the navy was able to counter Japan's cataract of victories. Something was needed to shake enemy morale and provide a boost for sagging American morale. The ideal thing, they agreed, would be some kind of attack on Japan's sacred home soil.

Radio intercepts and American submarine sightings had shown that Japan had land-based planes reconnoitering to seaward, and a string of picket boats on patrol, as much as five hundred miles off her southeastern coasts. Our navy Dauntless bombers lacked sufficient range for a seaborne launch, because the carriers would have to be brought so close that they ran the risk of being sunk, like *Repulse* and *Prince of Wales*, by a massive land-based air attack. The army's B-25 medium bombers had range enough, but could they be launched from carrier decks?

King directed Duncan and Lowe to look into the possibilities and discuss them with General Hap Arnold. Within a week they reported that B-25s could do it, and that Arnold was willing and eager to organize and equip the necessary planes and crews. Preparations of B-25s and crews from the 17th Bombardment Group, USAAF, were begun under Lieutenant Colonel James H. Doolittle at Eglin Field, Florida. Lieutenant Henry F. Miller, USN, instructed the pilots in short-takeoff techniques, using an airstrip on which the outline of a carrier flight deck was painted, somewhat elongated to allow for the wind generated by the forward motion of the ship.

Specially modified medium-range bombers would cross the Pacific by aircraft carrier to a point close enough for them to launch, strike targets in Japan, and cross the East China Sea to airfields in eastern China. While the crews trained, negotiations were carried on for Chiang Kai-shek's approval and cooperation. The secrecy of the mission was so tight that the Chinese were not given specific details and no part of the planning was committed to writing.

The B-25 crews were still in training at Eglin Field on 19 March when Captain Duncan arrived at Pearl Harbor to brief Nimitz on the plan, which had just been endorsed by the newly instituted Joint Chiefs of Staff, whose responsibility was the overall military direction of the war. With army bombers filling *Hornet's* flight deck her own planes could not be used for air patrol, so Nimitz was directed to assign that job to carrier *Enterprise* of Halsey's Task Force 8.

When Duncan had completed his presentation, Nimitz spoke to Halsey. "Do you think it will work, Bill?"

"They'll need a lot of luck."

"Are you willing to take them out there?"

"Yes, I am."

"Good!" said Nimitz. "It's all yours,"[9]

Task Force 8 sailed from Pearl Harbor 8 April for an ocean rendezvous with *Hornet,* which had left San Francisco six days earlier, carrying sixteen B-25s lashed down on her deck. Code-named Task Force Mike, the combined group plowed through heavy North Pacific seas on the final leg to reduce the chance of detection. Once the carriers had rendezvoused without a hitch, Nimitz's enthusiasm for the operation increased, encouraged by intelligence intercepts that detected no signs of increased air activity off Japan's east coast.

The gamble of risking two precious carriers to this venture, at a time when we had so few, still made him uneasy. But his fears were lessened by Rochefort's radio intelligence briefs, which indicated that the Japanese were preparing to resume operations in the southwest Pacific for an "RZP" campaign. Rochefort tentatively identified the RZP target as being in the Port Moresby area at the southern tip of New Guinea. "Numerous indications which point to impending offensive from Rabaul Base," Joe reported on 3 April. Four days later we knew that repairs on *Kaga* were being rushed ahead so that the carrier could "participate in the RZP campaign."[10]

The locations of American and Japanese carriers were of critical importance in the strategic picture at this juncture. With two carriers in the North Pacific committed to the Tokyo raid, and *Lexington* in dry dock for overhaul at Pearl, Nimitz had only one carrier task force left, and it was cruising in the Coral Sea. Its mission was to prevent southward advances by the Japanese in that area. For the present there was no doubt that the main enemy naval power was being committed to the Indian Ocean. On 5 April the *Kido Butai* raided the British Far East naval base at Colombo, and Trincomalee four days later, sinking a carrier and cruiser. The Japanese occupation of the Andaman Islands and cruiser strikes against merchant shipping in the Bay of Bengal forced the numerically inferior British fleet to beat a strategic retreat from Ceylon to the African port of Mombasa. It left the Japanese in total control of the Indian Ocean.

The American army suffered the biggest defeat in its history when Bataan fell on 9 April. In the midst of these gloomy events, Nimitz's burdens were vastly increased in March by the Joint Chiefs' reorganization of the command structure in the Pacific, which divided responsibility between Nimitz and General Douglas MacArthur in Australia, who assumed the additional title of Commander in Chief of the Southwest Pacific Area (Cincsowespac). MacArthur was put on a par with Admiral Nimitz, whose official designation now was Commander in Chief Pacific Ocean Areas (Cincpoa) as well as Commander in Chief Pacific (Cincpac).

The 160th meridian marked the official dividing line between the two Allied commanders; accordingly, Cincpac was assigned the Allied naval forces in the eastern approaches to Australia, including the Coral Sea. On 14 April, Nimitz informed Admiral Fletcher that he had assumed command of the South Pacific area from King. Task Force 17 was to proceed to our Tongatabu base south of Samoa for replenishment in order to be back on station in the Coral Sea by the end of the month when the RZP operation against Port Moresby was anticipated to commence.

The need for haste was endorsed by the relay of a British decrypt on 15 April which indicated that the Japanese striking forces were leaving the Indian Ocean and that Carrier Division 5 was to be detached "proceeding to Truk, arriving about 28 April."[11] This message, and Rochefort's report of continual southward movement of Japanese air units and supplies, revealed to Nimitz that "an offensive in the southwest Pacific is shaping up."[12] At his 17 April staff conference, Nimitz reviewed the intelligence picture in great detail. What concerned him was when Japan's southward operation could be expected to resume, and how far it would extend. Station Belconnen, the code name assigned to the evacuated Cast cryptanalysts now in Melbourne where they had joined forces with the Australian navy's radio intelligence team, gave one estimate of 21 April. But we considered this to be too early, since we judged that the Japanese could not have all their forces in place until early May. Australian reports of intensifying air attacks on Port Moresby clearly showed that it was the main Japanese objective. Nimitz was determined to block them.

"We are trying to get together a force to oppose [it]," Nimitz reported to King. "Task Force 17 [Fletcher] will be ready; Task Force 11 [Fitch] and Task Force 8 [Halsey] are otherwise committed." With *Yorktown* in the Coral Sea vicinity; *Lexington* just two days out of Pearl, heading south; and *Hornet* and *Enterprise* on their way to raid Tokyo, Nimitz regarded it as essential to remind Cominch of the possibility that our carrier forces would find themselves outnumbered two to one. It was a measure of King's concern that he took the unusual step of directly requesting Station Hypo's analysis of the situation. King's request was unprecedented. It was the only time he ever went directly to Rochefort for information. "We were a little surprised," Joe was to recall, "that he would ask us what our views were. I personally felt that he was not even aware of our existence."[13] Rochefort later joked about King's having gone over my head.

Rochefort's reply was completed and on its way within six hours, with an information copy to Cincpac. The Hypo team consensus made five main points: (1) Indian Ocean operations by the Japanese were now concluded. (2 and 3) There were two other offensives planned for eastern New Guinea and the Coral Sea. (4) No evidence had emerged that Japan intended to invade Australia. (5) Another Pacific operation was being planned whose objective and details had yet to become clear. The same day Rochefort's team discovered that the light carrier whose name we were erroneously reading as *Ryukaku* (actually it was *Shoho*) was assigned, along with a cruiser division, to cover movements into the Rabaul area.[14] This further increased the tense atmosphere in Washington, and Nimitz warned King that "Cincpac will probably be unable to send enough force to be sure of stopping the Jap offensive."[15]

The enemy operation that was causing us so much concern marked the opening of the *second* phase of Japan's grand strategy. It was really a compromise that resulted from a long-running debate about how Japan was going to achieve her war objectives. The first phase, which had called for the surprise attack on Pearl Harbor as a diversion to the capture of the Philippines, Malaya, and the Dutch East Indies, was well on the way to being fulfilled. However, the American carrier strikes had demonstrated the fallacy of the hoped-for "invincible strategic position for Japan."

The original goal of the second phase had been the consolidation of Japan's island defense system in the Pacific for operations against the American fleet. After "a strategic situation of long-term invincibility" had been established according to the Japanese strategic master plan, the plan's ambitious third phase called for the "capture of Hawaii and the outlying islands, attack on the United States, Canada, Panama Canal, as well as against Central America until the United States loses its fighting spirit and the war can be brought to a conclusion."[16]

Yamamoto, who had always regarded the original war plan's "wait-in-ambush" policy for the American fleet as self-defeating, had wanted to cash in on the supposed success of Pearl Harbor by revising the second phase. He wanted to remove the threat posed by Allied bases in Australia. But in January the army staff had opposed the plan to invade the northern and eastern part of Australia because of the tremendous resources of shipping and troops this would demand. They compromised on a plan that was intended to achieve the same effect by strangling the lines of communication between Hawaii and Australia by seizing the islands of Fiji, Samoa, and New Caledonia.

Yamamoto and his Combined Fleet staff, after concluding that it was necessary to knock out only the Allied bases in the southwest Pacific islands, proposed opening the second phase with the capture of Ceylon, New Guinea, and Port Darwin in northern Australia. The army staff refused to yield on the Australian adventure and opposed the invasion of Ceylon as premature. But imperial general headquarters agreed to extend the first phase in their 29 January directive. It authorized the Combined Fleet to assault and occupy, as soon as feasible, the Lae and Salamaua bases in New Guinea, Tulagi in the Solomon Islands, to be followed by the capture of Port Moresby.

Yamamoto, however, refused to give up. He interpreted these operations as "preliminary moves to the invasion of Australia or interruption of communications between the United States and Australia."[17] The American carrier strikes of February and March burned the fingers, but not the ambitions, of the Combined Fleet staff. But the raids provided them with the rationale for a makeshift plan of attacking Midway: It would entice the American carriers out from Pearl Harbor to their destruction. Yamamoto's staff argued that such an operation would not only be feasible for the second phase but that a "continued initiative," including an assault on Hawaii, was now essential to ensure "a short decisive war."[18]

On 3 April Yamamoto sent Commander Yasuji Watanabe, his persuasive staff gunnery officer, to sell his draft to the naval staff in Tokyo. The war plans section charged that the Midway operation would be too dangerous. It might not succeed in luring out the American carriers. They insisted on the occupation of the southwest Pacific islands to cut Australia off from the United States. Commander Watanabe, seeing no hope of changing the mind set at headquarters, appealed over the heads of his opponents directly to Vice Admiral Seiichi Ito, the deputy chief of the naval staff. Yamamoto's former chief of staff agreed to intercede. The wrangling continued for three more days until Watanabe phoned his chief to report the impasse. Yamamoto's mind was "firmly made up," however, and there was no change in his views. Admiral Shigeru Fukudome took Yamamoto's implicit threat of resignation as the signal for him to capitulate. He turned to Ito. "Since the CinC is so set on it, shall we leave it to him?" The deputy chief nodded without speaking and a compromise was hammered out that same day.[19]

Yamamoto got his Midway operation, and Fukudome got his occupation of Fiji and New Caledonia, but only the destruction of facilities on Samoa. Japan's second operational phase was scheduled to begin on 7 May with the capture of Port Moresby. Midway and the Aleutians were slated for assault a month later. By the third week in July the operations to secure the southwest Pacific islands were to be completed. After reaching agreement with the Combined Fleet, the naval staff managed to persuade the initially reluctant army leaders that the Midway operation did not necessarily commit them to the occupation of the Hawaiian Islands. But the capture of the Aleutians was deemed essential to prevent their being used as bases for long-range air strikes against Tokyo.

Imperial general headquarters gave its final approval to the operational schedule on 15 April after the chief of the naval general staff, Admiral Nagano, obtained the emperor's sanction for the second-phase objectives. Any lingering dissension over the Midway operation was quelled three days later when, for the first time in her long history, an enemy force struck at the heart of Japan.

The Combined Fleet was now about to pay the price for its previous bouts of jumpiness. This time there was not even a false alarm that two American carriers were less than a thousand miles off the Japanese coast. And this time Japanese radio intelligence failed to appreciate evidence that *was* available.

On the day *Enterprise* set sail to rendezvous with *Hornet,* Tokyo radio intelligence reported, "Many patrol aircraft appeared in the Pearl Harbor area on 9 April." Nothing was made of this, nor was any increased alert ordered after analysis of patrol plane traffic indicated that "a strong enemy surface force" was apparently operating south of the Aleutians. Also overlooked or ignored was another radio intelligence warning that "there has been steadily increasing activity of enemy submarines off the approaches to our main islands."[20] Both Combined Fleet flagship and the headquarters of the Fifth Fleet, which had the prime responsibility for defending the home islands, received these reports. But after the recent siege of jitters neither command was ready to order another false alert on such slender evidence.

Nevertheless, Halsey's plan, to launch bombers on the afternoon of 18 April at a distance of five hundred miles from the coast, was knocked into a cocked hat when his radars pierced the early-morning blackness 700 miles off the Japanese coast to detect two vessels of the naval picket line. The task force altered course to avoid them, and launched scout planes at first light. Some 40 miles ahead of the task force they sighted a picket boat which, before being sunk, reported to Tokyo that she had spotted the planes.

Halsey knew that full surprise was probably lost but decided, with Doolittle's concurrence, to launch as soon as the B-25s could be readied. "Good luck and God bless you!" Halsey flashed to *Hornet,* just before Doolittle lifted his twin-engine bomber off the bucking carrier's flight deck at 0725. Within an hour the last of the sixteen planes were Tokyo-bound. Halsey hauled course 90 degrees and, still keeping radio silence, raced northeastward at twenty-five knots.

Our intercept stations heard a Japanese picket boat reporting, "THREE ENEMY PLANES, COURSE SOUTHWEST."[21] Four hours later, when Doolittle's bombers roared in over noontime Tokyo, our radio listening posts actually picked up the wail of air raid sirens on the civilian Radio Tokyo broadcast. The planes stirred up a hornet's nest of plain-language contact reports and a flurry of alert orders to warships. Cincpac informed Halsey of "considerable 5th Fleet activity," including Japanese warships ordered out in search of "three U.S. carriers and two cruisers."[22] Halsey's own radio intelligence unit in the flagship also kept him informed of Japanese stirrings, and he was able to show his furious pursuers a clean pair of heels.

"Abruptly the air became tense at headquarters," recorded Admiral Matome Ugaki with uncharacteristic understatement after the picket boats had raised the alarm.[23] Yamamoto immediately grasped the urgency of the situation and made the urgent signal, "ENEMY TASK FORCE CONTAINING THREE AIRCRAFT CARRIERS AS MAIN STRENGTH SIGHTED 0630 THIS MORNING 730 MILES EAST OF TOKYO. . . . OPERATE AGAINST AMERICAN FLEET."[24]

A submarine squadron en route to Truk was diverted to make a sweep to the north of the Bonin Islands. Another patrol five hundred miles out from Honshū was ordered to intercept and attack the enemy carriers. In the Combined Fleet home anchorage at Hashirajima, boiler-room gangs in battleships, cruisers, and destroyers labored to raise steam and head out through the Inland Sea to give chase. A thousand miles to the northwest, Admiral Nobutake Kondo ordered his cruiser force out of Yokosuka.

The nearest warships were two armed merchant cruisers. They raced out into the Pacific, but failed to make any contact, and poor visibility hampered the land bombers that by midmorning were scouring the seas hundreds of miles offshore. So great was Japanese optimism about this massive air search's making contact that the one flight of thirty bombers that took off shortly after midday was ordered "AT APPROXIMATELY 1600 . . . MAKE TORPEDO ATTACKS."[25]

Nerves at Japanese headquarters were frayed that evening after all planes returned to base without reporting any sightings. Six months earlier Admiral Yamamoto had written to the navy minister of his fears that a surprise air attack on Tokyo would turn public opinion against the navy. So the next day almost every warship that Japan could muster, from the home islands to the Marianas and the Marshalls, was committed to the hunt. It even included the carrier striking force returning from the Indian Ocean. Even Soviet freighters north of Japan were stopped and boarded in case they had picked up ditched American fliers. Not until darkness fell over the northern Pacific two days after the raid did Yamamoto issue the order, "CEASE OPERATIONS AGAINST AMERICAN FLEET."[26]

The effects of the raid were not momentous, nor commensurate with the American risk of two of our four precious aircraft carriers in the Pacific. Military and utility installations in four Japanese cities were targeted. But the modest load of four five-hundred-pound bombs carried by each of the thirteen B-25s assigned to Tokyo could not inflict any really significant damage. The other three planes assigned to Nagoya, Kobē, and Osaka carried only incendiary bombs.

A school had been inadvertently struck, and a total of twelve people killed, fifty houses and shops demolished, and the bow of a warship in dry dock damaged. There was no significant military damage. The real impact of the attack was psychological: to boost American morale and dent that of the Japanese. That it succeeded was indicated by such triumphant headlines in the United States as JAPAN BOMBED, DOOLITTLE DOOED IT and the outrage expressed in Japanese newspapers that innocent schoolchildren had been "murdered" by the enemy fliers. Four American airmen were killed in crash landings of our planes in China, and three who were captured were later tried and executed after a show trial in Tokyo.

The frantic air and sea searches had not produced so much as a single clue concerning the size of or the direction taken by the American carrier task force. The Japanese embarrassment was greatly enhanced and the cataclysmic emotional shock the raid inflicted on the naval staff was aggravated because, as Ugaki put it, "we were not able to strike one blow in retribution."

"Even though there wasn't much damage, it's a disgrace that the skies over the imperial capital should have been defiled without a single enemy plane shot down," Yamamoto wrote. "It provides a regrettably graphic illustration of the saying that a bungling attack is better than the most skillful defense."[27]

It was not only Yamamoto and his immediate Combined Fleet staff who were mortified by the raid. So were the upper echelons of the Japanese naval staff in Tokyo, who shared the sense of personal disgrace that resulted from the public having witnessed enemy planes winging over the imperial palace. Most important of all, the naval staff resolved that they must save face. First by tightening up defenses to prevent any repetition, but also by some retributive mission against the United States carrier task forces that had poked such a painful thorn in the national pride. As Ugaki saw it: "This brings up the necessity for fundamental changes, from now on, in our plans and countermeasures."[28]

Those fundamental changes were to have such a far-reaching impact on the future course of the Pacific war that the Halsey-Doolittle raid must never be dismissed as having been militarily useless. This is borne out by the official history published by the Japan Defense Agency that assigns the raid a far greater impact than any of us at Cincpac could have calculated. The record said the raid:

1. Caused great morale problems to the Japanese.
2. Caused the military to lose face, for they had said that Tokyo would *never* be bombed.
3. Caused diversions of Japanese forces—a fact that most historians overlook.
4. Caused the Japanese army to jump on the bandwagon for *Midway*.
5. Aligned the imperial general headquarters unreservedly behind Combined Fleet's Midway-Aleutian operation plan.

It was the eventual failure of Japan's Midway plan that put the Japanese navy on the strategic defensive (with the sinking of their four finest front-line carriers), and cost them the initiative in the war.

29
Fog of Battle

A S HALSEY WITHDREW from Japanese waters, we were able to follow the frantic air and sea search for his task force. Since we knew the Combined Fleet's objective, and because every available ship was pressed into the futile hunt, the radio traffic brought a bonus of intercepted messages that updated and confirmed the latest call signs of ships and shore stations.

Once we knew that Halsey's carriers were safe, Nimitz's staff conferences were occupied with considering how best to deploy our forces to meet the impending Japanese offensive in the southwest Pacific. One unexpected outcome of the Tokyo raid was that so many enemy units would have to return for replenishment after chasing Halsey that their next operation would be delayed.[1]

"We are taking steps to oppose Japan's expected move in the southwest Pacific," Nimitz recorded in the daily headquarters summary. His main worry was whether we would "be able to send enough forces to be *sure* of stopping the expected Jap offensive [emphasis added]."[2] The delay, however, brought our evaluation into line with Washington's estimate that the attack would commence in the first week in May. Admiral King was breathing down our necks. Hardly a day passed without some chivvying message.

On 20 April, Nimitz discussed "ways and means to deal with the expected Japanese offensive in the southwest Pacific." Australian naval intelligence had reported an intensification of air surveillance in the northern sector of the Coral Sea. Orders were flashed out to *Lexington* for Admiral Fitch's Task Force 11 to make for the southwest Pacific. That evening a dispatch from Washington informed us that a joint army-navy committee was studying Pacific logistics. "So are we," Nimitz noted laconically in his daily log.[3]

The next day the British reported that a cruiser division, and a carrier whose name ended in *kaku,* were scheduled to be in Truk by 25 April.[4] A Belconnen decrypt from Australia alerted us that the Japanese had scheduled 1 May for the introduction of a new operational cipher. This was sure evidence that major operations would soon follow.[5]

I summarized the intelligence picture on 22 April at one of the most critical Cincpac staff meetings of the war by saying: "There are many indications that the enemy will launch an offensive in the New Guinea-New Britain-Solomon area." All the signs showed that it would "start very soon."[6] I believed that our chance was coming to turn the tables on the enemy. As long as they were flushed with victory, their efficiency would remain high. But I predicted from my experience with the Japanese character that once they had suffered a major setback, they would be forced to improvise, and morale and fighting efficiency would fall.

According to my estimate, the enemy's plan was an amphibious operation to complete the takeover of New Guinea and the adjacent islands. I warned the staff not to underestimate what it would take to stop this offensive. Excellence of naval planning and training had been demonstrated in the attack on Pearl Harbor. Their army was no less effective. Their long war in China had shown that it had been trained to reach its objectives against fierce opposition, over impossible terrain. Their soldiers were able to survive on a few handfuls of rice a day. Malaya and the Philippines had shown that the Japanese were able to accept heavy losses from gunfire and drownings during an assault and still achieve their goals.[7]

Radio intelligence had as yet revealed only sketchy details of the impending operation. But I was able to tell Nimitz and his staff that they might deploy as many as 5 carriers, 1 battleship, 5 heavy cruisers, at least 4 light cruisers, 12 destroyers, and more than a dozen submarines. In addition, their air strength in the southwest Pacific might run to 135 land-based bombers, plus the same number of fighter planes and at least 100 reconnaissance aircraft. The springboard of the southward thrust appeared to be their heavily fortified base at Truk in the Carolines where I estimated that as many as twenty-thousand troops were ready to sail.

Against the Japanese advantages of superior carrier strength and land-based airpower, we could count on radio intelligence to reveal direction and deployment. This was the crucial factor that persuaded Nimitz to commit his outnumbered forces to stopping the Japanese advance toward Australia. But since his primary duty was to guard the Hawaiian Islands and protect the Pacific route to Australia, Nimitz needed to be certain about the direction and scale of the enemy offensive before deploying all of our task forces against it. Would they go for Port Moresby only, or would they go for Port Moresby and the Solomons at this time? There was also the possibility that they would ignore Port Moresby and the Solomons for a direct advance on New Caledonia and Fiji.[8]

Our intelligence could not provide a categorical answer at the time. It was clear, however, that there were no signs of Japanese movements toward the Hawaiian Islands. "Past performance indicates that the enemy much prefers to make his moves under protection of land-based aircraft," I told the conference that Wednesday. "Our immediate problem as being an attack for the capture of Moresby is correct."[9]

"To know your enemy's intentions is fine but such knowledge does not always mean you can stop him" was how naval historian Samuel Eliot Morison would sum up the dilemma that Nimitz faced. But like Kimmel three months earlier, Nimitz appreciated that carrier-borne airpower was the decisive naval weapon in the vast Pacific theater. He therefore concluded that the best chance of stemming the Japanese tide in the southwest was to concentrate all our available task forces against it.

Lexington with Fitch's Task Force 11 was ordered to rendezvous with *Yorktown,* which was then replenishing at Tongatabu in order to make the thousand-mile trip into the Coral Sea. There they would join Rear Admiral John Crace, RN, and his Anzac cruisers. *Enterprise* and *Hornet* were not due to return to Pearl until 25 April, so it was unlikely that Halsey could make the ten-day trip to the Coral Sea before the Japanese offensive began. But Fitch and Fletcher could count on the support of the land-based planes of MacArthur's forces in northeast Australia and New Guinea. We could only hope that our intelligence estimates were correct and that the Japanese would not consider it necessary at the last minute to commit more than three carriers to the Port Moresby operation.

Nimitz decided that "we should be able to accept odds in battle if necessary."[10] His belief was based on my prediction that the enemy would—contrary to Captain Mahan, the American naval strategist who had articulated the doctrine of the concentration of naval forces—divide their strength in an ambitious effort to cover both the Moresby landing and an occupation of the Solomon Islands. Nimitz was required, nonetheless, to embark on a colossal strategic gamble, the enormity of which justified his decision to fly to San Francisco on 25 April to brief Admiral King.

Somewhat to Nimitz's surprise, his "calculated risk" for meeting the Japanese in the Coral Sea proved less of a concern to King than the "desirability of ridding Pearl Harbor of pessimists and defeatists."[11] He was principally concerned that Frank Jack Fletcher had not shown himself aggressive enough to conduct operations until Halsey could arrive in the southwest Pacific in the second week of May. King was one of those who held the Task Force 17 commander partly to blame for the debacle that cost us Wake Island, an impression that had not been erased later when Fletcher failed to push home his carrier raids in the Marshalls with the resolution and tenacity demonstrated by Halsey.

Nimitz, who was known for his loyalty to subordinates, expressed his confidence in Fletcher's capability. After calling for precautionary reinforcement of the Midway garrison, King approved the overall Cincpac strategy. But he also required that a carrier task force was henceforth to remain in the southwest Pacific. King considered protecting our route to

Australia so strategically important that on 20 April a South Pacific Area had been established. Vice Admiral Robert L. Ghormley was designated its commander in chief, but until he could depart from Washington to set up his headquarters in New Zealand, it was agreed that Nimitz would maintain direct control of operations in the area.

Nimitz returned to Pearl Harbor on 28 April, and, the next day, issued "Cincpac Operation Plan No. 23-42," outlining our Coral Sea strategy. We still needed to fill in critical details of the Japanese plan and it was a blessed relief when Rochefort reported that the Japanese were not changing their JN-25 cipher as an earlier intercept had foreshadowed. Apparently the distribution and delivery of the new code books had been delayed and a decrypt revealed that the changeover was being postponed until 27 May.

We heaved a deep sigh of relief when we realized that the old version of the Japanese JN-25 naval cipher was to continue for another three and a half weeks. This was to prove to be one of the most critical periods of the war. Our ability to eavesdrop on the enemy's main operational traffic enabled us to discover the details of Yamamoto's Port Moresby operation. More important, it simultaneously made us aware that there was an even bigger offensive in the making: Midway.

Unknown to us, our hit-and-run carrier raids had forced the Japanese navy to recast their entire Pacific strategy. First, the raids had forced a delay in the enemy's southward advance to secure New Guinea until after the end of April, when carriers could be detached from Admiral Nagumo's striking force as it returned from raiding operations in the Indian Ocean. Second, Yamamoto was obliged to extend his palisade of island defenses by ordering the simultaneous capture and occupation of Nauru and Ocean to plug the gap between the Gilberts and Solomons. Third, the urgent need to protect the eastern flank of Japan's southward advance had been Yamamoto's principal justification for the Midway operation. But by scheduling it for the first week in June, he forced the naval staff to advance the date for completing the Port Morseby and Solomons operations.

At Fourth Fleet headquarters in Rabaul, Admiral Inouye was dismayed when he was told that he had only until the second week of May to secure Port Moresby. This was long before he was due to receive the land-based air cover in New Guinea he needed to ensure the success of the landing. Next he was informed that fleet carrier *Kaga* could not be repaired in time and that he would have to rely only on the planes from *Shokaku* and *Zuikaku*. The relatively inexperienced pilots of Rear Admiral Chuichi Hara's Carrier Division 5 were no substitute for the crack pilots of Carrier Division 2; nor was it much consolation that light carrier *Shoho* was assigned to operate as close escort for the four heavy cruisers of Rear Admiral Aritomo Goto's main force.

In addition to providing mobile cover for the Port Moresby invasion, Carrier Division 5 would also be overstretched. Its planes were scheduled to provide distant support for the assaults on Tulagi in the Solomons and the Deboynes—the group of small islands flanking the northern neck of the Coral Sea. Their capture was considered essential; they were needed for use as seaplane bases from which to fly patrols that could give early warning of any American task forces steaming to interdict the invasion as it threaded its way from Rabaul through the treacherous shoal waters of the Louisade Islands off New Guinea's southernmost tip.

In addition to these complex operations, Admiral Hara's carriers were also expected to carry out preliminary raids on the Allied airfields in northern Australia. So when Hara sailed into the imposing sweep of Truk lagoon on 25 April he was appalled to learn the potential for disaster in the number of tasks assigned him, and that he would be subordinate commander of the Port Moresby striking force. He appealed over the head of Vice Admiral Takeo Takagi, the cruiser force commander, objecting to Inouye's instructions ordering him to risk his carriers to make the Australian raid within range of Allied land-based bombers.[12]

Fourth Fleet headquarters dithered. Not until the eve of the intricately balanced operation was Hara given the discretion to abandon the Australian raids. But Inouye responded by adding yet another complication. He requested that Hara's carriers ferry additional Zeros to reinforce Rabaul during their run south. This was to prove the straw that broke the camel's back.

Unaware of these last-minute changes, our radio intelligence analysts were having difficulty unraveling the various objectives of the Japanese operation from the complex orders flying among the three forces involved. Less than 20 percent of the intercepted JN-25 traffic was eventually made readable, and Nimitz was also having to cope with King's second-guessing about Japan's real intentions. After a bombing raid on Port Darwin, these fears appeared to be confirmed on 25 April by a decrypted message requesting a thousand copies of maps of northern Australia.[13] Washington appears to have been panicked by the thought that the enemy would not stop at New Guinea.

Rochefort, however, was able to prove that these fears were exaggerated by an unfortunate error in decryption made by Belconnen and Negat. Their discovery of a new "RO" operation turned out to be a misreading of the "MO" for the Moresby campaign.[14] The same day—27 April—Hypo picked up an order for the so-called Mandates Force to sail from Truk to join with another group for "operations against an enemy in RX area."[15] It was Joe's belief that "RX" was an island in the western Solomons—probably Bougainville—and this was consistent with our prediction of Japan's forthcoming operations in the northern sector of the Coral Sea.

On 28 April, Rochefort found another indication that the Japanese plan involved the Solomons with the identification of "RXB" as the island of Tulagi, which lay in the northeasterly bight of Guadalcanal in the middle of the island chain. This was important. But Rochefort really struck paydirt the following day when Hypo decrypted a message from Tokyo that referred to the dispatch of maps covering the Aleutian Islands. This was the first hint we received that Yamamoto was contemplating another, more ambitious, operation.[16] The value of Hypo's product was now so essential to Nimitz that he made a request to Cominch that Rochefort's team concentrate on "reading today's traffic today while it is of value to forces afloat," while Washington's cryptanalysts "undertake code recovery on back traffic,"[17]

King gave immediate approval for this practical division of effort. Evidently he did so without asking the opinion of Commander John R. Redman, the head of OP-20-G, whose feathers were ruffled by the independence that Rochefort had achieved. This victory for Hypo made the Redman brothers more determined than ever to centralize the control of radio intelligence in their own hands. It was another score to be settled with Joe and myself in the long term. And it added fuel to the rivalry that was developing between Negat and Hypo over which unit best evaluated intelligence.

Fortunately for us, Nimitz's intervention with King made Hypo's supremacy a fait accompli. Washington accepted our broad estimate of both the timing and objective of the Japanese advance to Port Moresby and the Solomons. The opening moves were being made in what would become known as the Battle of the Coral Sea.

On 1 May local time, as the two Japanese covering forces headed south from Truk, *Yorktown* joined up with *Lexington* at Point Buttercup, some three hundred miles due south of the tiny island of Tulagi. Lying in the middle of the Solomons, it was the target of another enemy force that was bearing down from the northwest. Since all the warships involved were observing radio silence, they had not revealed themselves yet to the radio intelligence units (RIU) on board our carriers. (Each unit consisted of one of Hypo's Japanese language officers and two or three radiomen; their responsibility was to monitor local enemy broadcasts for tactical information.)

Halsey had been the first task force commander to profit from the RIU teams. But Fletcher, who had never been properly indoctrinated in radio intelligence, did not have much use for his RIU officer. For any admiral of the old school, it all came down to a question of prestige and the reluctance to take the word of a junior lieutenant on important tactical information. To build up the trust of an admiral often demanded considerable tact and diplomacy by the intelligence officer. But in Fletcher's case, establishing this mutual confidence, so essential for getting important tactical intelligence across during an action, had been prejudiced when he had tried to browbeat Lieutenant Forrest R. Biard over his strict security regulations.[18]

"I want you to tell me and my staff all about your communications intelligence organization and the code breaking it does," Fletcher demanded of Biard during a lunch in the wardroom. Aware that most of the admiral's staff had not been cleared, Biard flatly refused to explain the details of his work, thereby incurring his admiral's extreme displeasure.

But his regard for the value of *Yorktown's* RIU nose-dived on 1 May when Biard could not confirm whether a Japanese submarine, which was depth-charged thirty miles north of the carrier, had radioed a sighting report.[19] Later that afternoon Fitch had been flown over to *Yorktown* for a conference with the news that *Lexington's* RIU officer, Lieutenant Commander Ranson Fullinwider, had heard the submarine signaling.[20] Biard was hauled before the admiral and chewed out for his failure.

If such a signal was made, it evidently failed to reach Rabaul—and we did not pick it up at Pearl Harbor. But Fletcher and Fitch did not know that. They quite properly had to assume that the Japanese knew their position. It became an imperative factor governing their decision after they received our dispatch a few hours later alerting them that the enemy operation was "now under way" and that it "involves New Guinea and the Louisade Archipelago." The message summarized the air and sea forces involved and gave a general summary of objectives as we had been able to piece them together. Included was a reference to an intercept mentioning Townesville and advice that we "do not believe Australia involved in immediate future except for submarine operations."[21]

Fletcher evidently inferred that the Japanese carriers would make this northern Australian port one of their targets. He concluded that the main enemy force was, therefore, at least nine hundred miles away to the northwest. Despite the enemy submarine reports, refueling was conducted at a leisurely pace the next day. When Task Force 11 had still not finished with the oilers that afternoon, Fletcher—contrary to specific orders from Nimitz—split his forces and headed off west after instructing Task Force 11 to rendezvous forty-eight hours later after Crace's cruisers had topped up their fuel tanks.

The following morning the Japanese occupied Tulagi, but Fletcher and Fitch remained ignorant of the unopposed landing. Not until 1900 that day, when they were more than a hundred miles apart, did they receive a radio relay from MacArthur's headquarters informing them that troop transports and five or six enemy warships had been spotted in the sound between Guadalcanal and Tulagi.

To Fletcher the tempting target was less than five hundred miles away and "just the kind of opportunity we have been waiting two months to receive." He could not break radio silence and considered it too late to send a plane off to *Lexington.* So he dispatched a destroyer, *Sims,* and oiler, *Neosho,* to meet Fletcher and Crace the next morning to instruct them to head for a new rendezvous point three hundred miles south of Guadalcanal on 5 May. Then he ordered *Yorktown*'s task force to steam north at twenty-four knots in order to be off Guadalcanal to launch a dawn strike on Tulagi the next day.

As Fletcher raced north, through a night punctuated by tropical squalls, he received a Cincpac intelligence dispatch that appeared to justify his risky decision to rush into the attack with only half his forces. This was the impression conveyed by a mistranslated four-day-old decrypt suggesting that the Japanese carriers would divide their attention between countering American naval forces and raids on the airfields of northern Australia.

Fletcher was luckier than he knew. Only the bad weather preventing Hara from flying off the Zero reinforcements to Rabaul had prevented Carrier Division 5 from being within striking distance of Tulagi that afternoon. But for this two-day delay, *Yorktown*'s pilots would have taken off the next morning into well-defended air space and Task Force 17 would have found itself outnumbered two to one by enemy carrier planes.

Fortunately for us, when *Yorktown*'s dive bombers came screaming down over Tulagi an hour after sunrise on 4 May, there was no resistance. The Japanese garrison commander radioed the alarm, but Hara's carriers were out of air strike range, and refueling off Rabaul some four hundred miles away. News of the attack brought a hasty disconnection of oiling hoses as Hara's two carriers charged southward off the eastern Solomons. Admiral Goto detached light carrier *Shoho* from escorting the Port Moresby invasion transports. But none of the Japanese forces could get within striking distance of Tulagi before darkness brought an end to the first day of action in the Coral Sea.

Round one of the battle had gone to Fletcher as Task Force 17 retreated undetected into the two-hundred-mile curtain of bad weather that hung east to west across the Coral Sea. Three waves of planes had been launched, but the strikes against Tulagi had not been well coordinated. Although *Yorktown*'s exuberant pilots reported they had totally destroyed the enemy forces, only two minesweepers and a transport had been sunk, a destroyer beached, and five floatplanes sent up in flames. Fletcher was so fired up that afternoon that he ordered his two cruisers in to polish off any survivors. But his innate sense of caution prevailed and they were recalled before nightfall, saving them from what would have been certain destruction from the bombs and torpedoes of the Japanese carrier planes that arrived over Tulagi the next morning.

At 1945 on 5 May, *Yorktown*'s combat air patrol shot down a four-engine Mavis flying boat that had been picked up by the carrier's radar shortly before Fletcher reached the rendezvous point with Fitch and Crace. A simultaneous submarine sighting by a scout plane convinced our admirals that their positions were again known to the Japanese. But Fletcher, on the basis of the intelligence he had received, had no reason to believe that enemy carriers were only four hundred miles to the north, so he spent most of the day refueling on a southerly course.

That afternoon an Allied reconnaissance flight spotted a Japanese convoy steaming down the Louisades toward the Jomard Passage. This was the route through the shoals that the enemy was expected to take. The pilot mistakenly identified a heavy carrier escorting the transports, further reinforcing Fletcher's belief that the main Japanese force was at that moment heading for the archipelago that trailed from the southern tip of New Guinea.

At dusk at 5 May when Fletcher hauled his combined task force around to head for the Jomard Passage, he still believed that the enemy carriers were over 400 miles ahead. In fact, Carrier Division 5 had that day looped around the southern Solomons and was that evening just astern less than 250 miles off his starboard quarter. That night the wakes of the two protagonists carved phosphorescent tracks up the dark waters of the Coral Sea.

Fletcher was so certain that the enemy lay ahead of him that it prejudiced any chance of his making a correct reading of the situation from a Cincpac intelligence dispatch, which provided him with a partial decrypt of the 4 May order to Carrier Division 5. But at Hypo we had slipped up too. By mistranslating the word "pass"[22] as "proceed" in the instruction telling Hara to "pass north-northeast of Bougainville thence to southward" the impression given was that the two Japanese carriers immediately entered the Coral Sea.[23] As Fitch's action report makes only too plain, this was read as an indication that Carrier Division 5 "would run southward from the vicinity of Bougainville and might be within striking distance on the morning of 7 May."[24]

In making this assumption, however, both Fletcher and Fitch appear to have discounted the second part of the dispatch, which clearly ordered the Japanese carriers to "go to Tulagi." But this did not square with the information in the second dispatch he received during the night of 6 May. It referred to a three-day-old decrypt stating that the Japanese carriers "will launch attacks on Allied bases in the Port Moresby area."[25] This suggested that if the enemy force had indeed entered the Coral Sea on 5 May as the first dispatch indicated, they would already have hurried westward to support the invasion force.

Unaware that Hara's two carriers were to the northeast of Fletcher's task force and sending out air patrols in search of them, our task forces spent 6 May holding course on the Coral Sea heading up toward the Louisades. But Fletcher's hopes of surprising the enemy force vanished the next day when they were spotted by a Japanese flying boat.

"Discovered what appears to be a large enemy force bearing 190 degrees" the Tulagi-based "Emily" flashed out just after 1000. The report caught Hara's carriers refueling south of New Georgia. Once again hose connections were broken as Takagi ordered Carrier Division 5 ahead of his cruisers to try for a strike that afternoon. But Hara's scouts, who headed south along the vector given by the flying boat, ran smack into the heavy weather and turned back. Had they been just a little more persistent they would have penetrated the southern curtain of squalls to discover our two carriers steaming serenely under clear skies.

When Hara decided late that afternoon to reverse course to rejoin Takagi's cruiser force to prepare for a dawn strike the next day, he did not know that less than a hundred miles separated his pilots from a stunning chance victory. Nor had Fletcher realized just how close to disaster he was sailing that afternoon when he completed another refueling of his destroyers before ordering oiler *Neosho* to fall back with an escorting destroyer to keep out of range of enemy bombers from Rabaul.

While our task forces were engaged in this deadly round of blind man's buff, Pacific Fleet plotting room at Pearl Harbor was also in the dark about the precise location of the opposing forces in the Coral Sea. Because Fletcher and Fitch were observing radio silence, our only clue to their whereabouts came from the decrypt of the seaplane sighting, which had been relayed by Jaluit radio. When no further action reports had been picked up by nightfall, we could only assume that Carrier Division 5 had given up its chase and was now heading for the Jomard Passage to cover the most critical phase of the Port Moresby operation. I put "Cardiv 5 and Crudiv 5 with enemy forces to south of Rabaul" in my daily intelligence bulletin. Nimitz and his staff retired early, anticipating an early start to the clash the next day, which we believed would be fought on relatively even terms.

Dawn on 7 May in the northern quarter of the Coral Sea was disturbed by ten scout planes roaring off from *Yorktown*. At 0618 they fanned out into gusty squalls, and a sky fluffy with cumulus clouds that obscured horizon visibility to the northeast where the Japanese were expected to appear. Fletcher, who could not count on the static weather front as an ally, decided to fight a carrier duel without Crace's cruisers. They were sent ahead to guard the southern exit of the Jomard Passage.

Confirmation that the Japanese were also out searching for our carriers came at 0815 when a *Yorktown* scout shot down an enemy floatplane some 250 miles away over Misima Island, which marked the northern side of the Jomard Passage. Within half an hour another scout radioed that two enemy carriers and two cruisers had been sighted off Misima, heading south.

Fletcher was so confident that this must be the main enemy force that, without awaiting confirmation, he ordered a full air attack launched from *Yorktown* and *Lexington*. At 1015 when the ninety-three-plane strike went roaring off to the northwest, Biard came to inform Fletcher that a Japanese carrier aircraft had been spotted nearby. He was still in the Cincpac plot when the *Yorktown* scout pilot came to report that he had made an unfortunate coding error. What he had actually sighted were not two carriers, but two heavy cruisers and two destroyers.

"Young man, do you know what you have done? You have just cost the United States two carriers!" roared Admiral Fletcher. Disaster loomed with the realization that our task forces had shot their bolt. The awful dimension of his mistake caused the admiral to lose control. According to Biard, "Here was the commander of a vital naval task force shouting in the presence of officers and several enlisted men that we had already lost a battle we were yet to fight!"[27]

Leaving Fletcher and his staff to debate whether to recall the air strike, Biard withdrew to the RIU shack behind flag plot. He was full of apprehension that any moment he would hear that a Japanese pilot was making a sighting report that could seal the fate of our task forces. But fate appeared to be forgiving of Fletcher that week. At 1022 MacArthur's headquarters in Brisbane relayed a B-17 pilot's report of a Japanese carrier north of Misima.

The roller-coaster emotion on *Yorktown*'s flag bridge hurtled up again as Fletcher ordered the strike redirected thirty miles to the north of its original target. Then hope plunged down minutes later when oiler *Neosho* radioed from three hundred miles astern that enemy bombs were raining down. Since the hapless tanker and her escorting destroyer were well out of range of any Japanese land base, Fletcher faced his moment of truth: His task force was boxed in by enemy carriers fore and aft.

Fortunately for Fletcher, his potentially disastrous error had been duplicated by his opponent. When Hara ordered his seventy-six-plane strike launched at 1015, after a reconnaissance patrol had spotted an enemy carrier force some 200 miles south of flagship *Zuikaku*, he was convinced that it was the quarry he had been hunting for the previous day. But less than five minutes after he had watched his aircraft disappearing over the southern horizon, Hara was informed that another Japanese patrol had sighted an American task force 350 miles to the west of him off Deboyne Island. Then came a report that there was another force on the same bearing less than 200 miles away heading for the Louisades.

"We will join battle with the enemy in the west after we have attacked to the south," Hara decided after a brief discussion with his staff.[28] Just after midday he found out how badly he had called his shots. The target of the air strike turned out to be nothing more substantial than an oiler and destroyer. While one bomber group bombed *Neosho* into a drifting wreck and sank destroyer *Sims,* the other planes responded to the urgent recall signal.

Hara hauled his carriers around 180 degrees after concluding that the "enemy in the west" must be the American flattops. But he had to let his returning planes know where to find their flight decks. In his cramped RIU space on board *Yorktown,* Biard picked up *Zuikaku*'s repeated homing signal giving course "280 degrees speed 20 knots." Fletcher was immediately informed that the enemy carrier force was closing from astern. But he dismissed Biard's intelligence. Fletcher preferred to believe the message flashed from Fitch. It interpreted the same signals as "enemy course and speed as 280 degrees 20 knots," because Fullinwider, the RIU officer on board *Lexington,* had mistranslated the Japanese. "The explanation was easy," Biard recalled having tried to point out to Fletcher. "We had not recently been on any course even approximating to 280 degrees, and our steaming speed was nothing like 20 knots."[29]

Fletcher, however, "just would not accept it." The admiral was soon diverted from the significance of what Biard was trying to tell him by reports that our air strike had finally connected with an enemy carrier northeast of Misima Island.

From ten thousand feet the American dive bombers dropped like hawks out of clear skies. Japan's light carrier struggled to launch additional fighters. In what one *Yorktown* pilot described as "a spectacular and convincing pageant of destruction," the defending Japanese Zeros were swept aside. Bombs plummeted through *Shoho*'s flight deck as torpedoes ripped into the small carrier's flanks. At 1210 *Lexington*'s air group leader sent the prearranged message that was cheered in the radio rooms of our ships as loudly as it was at Pearl: "Scratch one flattop!"[30]

The light carrier had been sunk against the loss of a single dive bomber—the same price paid by the Japanese for our oiler and destroyer. Fletcher and Fitch ended the second round of the Coral Sea battle ahead on points. The appearance of Admiral Crace's cruisers south of the Jomard Passage had succeeded in forcing Admiral Inouye to stand off the invasion transports to the north until the carrier duel had been decided. The Anzac cruisers, which had escaped two hours of continuous bombing by land-based aircraft by skillful helmsmanship, had also diverted attacks from the carrier task force. But no sooner had the enemy been beaten off than three American B-26s mistakenly made an attack run. "Fortunately," Crace sardonically reported, "their bombing, in comparison with that of the Japanese a few minutes earlier, was disgraceful."[31]

When the morning strike returned to report that they had sunk only a light carrier, Fletcher knew that his priority must be to locate Carrier Division 5. Shortly after 1400 Task Force 17's planes were again ranged on the flight decks, refueled, bombed up, and ready to take off. But although the attack on *Neosho* and *Sims* indicated that the enemy carriers were somewhere astern, the precise whereabouts were hidden by the curtain of heavy weather. Incredibly, considering his predicament, Fletcher turned a deaf ear to Biard who had been plotting the course of Hara's carriers from the radio transmissions until 1400.

Biard tried again to explain his intelligence to Fletcher and asked if a search-and-strike mission was planned on the two enemy carriers he and his radiomen "knew to be within fighting distance and looking for us."[32] But the admiral remained unconvinced. Chastened by his earlier miscalculation, Fletcher ruled out launching a search-and-destroy mission, to preserve maximum fighter cover against the Japanese attack that he anticipated would materialize at any moment. He was especially reluctant to risk losing planes in the heavy weather, preferring to "rely on shore-based aircraft to locate the enemy carriers."[33] He later attributed his lack of action that afternoon to "insufficient daylight for an attack following an extensive search."[34]

In a strikingly parallel predicament, Hara was also paralyzed by caution and hesitation. Long before the afternoon grew old, he had effectively given up the hunt because "there is no possibility for an attack today."[35] He changed his mind just after 1600, when a floatplane reported that the American carriers could be close to within striking distance before nightfall. The most experienced aircrews volunteered for a hazardous dusk raid and twelve bombers and fifteen torpedo planes took off from *Shokaku* and headed out through the squall line.

The sun was setting two hours later at 1830 when the Japanese strike ran into the combat air patrols guarding Task Force 17. Bombs and torpedoes were jettisoned in a fight that cost the enemy seven aircraft for three of our fighters. But in the twilight some of the Japanese pilots managed to get a close look at an American flattop for the first time in the war. As they buzzed low over *Yorktown* they were at first mistaken for our own planes coming in to land, until it was realized that they were circling counterclockwise which was contrary to our navy's flight routine.

Fletcher did not relish Biard's report that the enemy planes had radioed very precise reports of our task force's position before they headed off to the northeast into the gathering darkness. In his action report Fletcher stressed that the direction and distance of the Japanese carriers was still uncertain, even though he discussed with his staff whether to detach his cruisers for a night attack. He abandoned the idea when advised of the enemy's night-fighting capabilities, deciding to commit himself to the main engagement the following day.

Less than two hundred miles away to the northeast, Admiral Hara's staff was making the same preparations.

At first light on 8 May, round three of the battle opened with American and Japanese scouts probing for each other's carriers. Hara had the advantage of the weather. His ships remained under cover. Task Force 17, on the other hand, was steaming in near-perfect visibility on the south side of the squall line. But thanks to radar Fletcher avoided premature discovery around 0800 when *Lexington*'s combat patrol fighters chased off a Japanese scout before it sighted the American ships.

The first actual contact was made fifteen minutes later when the *Shokaku* and *Zuikaku* were spotted 175 miles east-northeast of Fletcher's force. Minutes later a Japanese plane was heard radioing, "Have sighted enemy carriers."[36]

The American first strike of seventy-five aircraft roared off to the northeast just after 0900, when sixty-nine Japanese planes started their flight southward. To reduce signaling between carriers, and to allow "complete freedom of action for his carriers and air groups," Fletcher handed over tactical command of the task force to Admiral Fitch, in recognition of his greater experience in handling air operations.[37]

Yorktown's dive bombers reached the target first. At 1100 they came hurtling through a clear patch in the overcast onto *Shokaku,* while *Zuikaku* dodged away into the cover of a convenient squall. Our first strike on a large, well-defended carrier task force lacked the necessary coordination between the dive bombers and the torpedo planes, which made their low-level run in without fighter protection.

The defending Zeros easily broke up the attack and torpedoes went splashing wide of *Shokaku.* Antiaircraft fire disrupted the bombers and three were downed. But fifteen of our pilots managed to fight their way through to score three hits. *Shokaku* was set ablaze and flight operations were interrupted for an hour. Undamaged below the waterline, the carrier withdrew northward, trailing a long column of smoke.

"When last seen, about fifteen minutes after the attack, fires were burning fiercely," one *Yorktown* pilot reported optimistically. "It is believed that this carrier was so badly damaged that it finally sank."[38] But it was not until our aircrew rendezvoused with Task Force 17 around 1300 that Friday that they discovered how much more accurately their Japanese opponents had executed their attack.

Two hours earlier, *Lexington*'s radar had picked up "bandits" seventy miles away to the northeast. Fitch had sufficient warning to send up the twenty-three remaining dive bombers to augment his weak fighter screen. But this was not enough to break up the well-coordinated Japanese attack that erupted twenty minutes later. With no squalls to dodge into, the two carriers and their escorts were forced to weave like skaters. *Yorktown* answered her helm more adroitly than the larger *Lexington.*

Like a stately dowager, "Lady Lex" turned ponderously until two torpedoes slammed into her port side, letting in thousands of tons of water that caused a dangerous list. Damage-control parties struggled to right *Lexington* by counterflooding, but without maneuverability the large carrier became an easy target for a series of bombs that set fires raging belowdecks. Meanwhile, *Yorktown* suffered a hit near her island, which caused a temporary shutdown of her boilers and loss of way. The confusion was compounded in the closing stages of the action when *Lexington*'s fighters, low on fuel, came in for pancake landings on her battered deck and several went skidding over the side.

In less than a quarter of an hour the Japanese departed, jubilantly radioing that the loss of *Shoho* the previous day had been avenged two to one. Accepting at face value their reports of sinking one large and one medium carrier, Admiral Hara believed that both American carriers had been sent to the bottom.

Fletcher's preliminary report was almost as optimistic as Hara's. "First enemy attack completed, no vital damage our force," he radioed

Nimitz. "*Yorktown* now making thirty knots. I propose retire tonight, fill *Yorktown* complement planes as far as possible from *Lexington,* and send that ship to Pearl."[39]

At Pacific Fleet headquarters Fletcher's early after-action report made it appear that we had indeed won a significant victory. "This was a red-letter day for our forces operating in the Coral Sea," Nimitz had already recorded in the official diary.[40] Later Fletcher's initial optimism evaporated.

"Congratulations on your glorious accomplishments" from Nimitz had already been handed to Fletcher when disaster struck *Lexington.* The wounded carrier's list had been corrected and her fires brought under control, enabling her to recover her returning strike aircraft. Then just after 1245 the carrier was riven by a tumultuous explosion set off by sparks from a generator that ignited fuel vapor escaping from damaged internal tanks. The resulting inferno was to defeat the fire-fighting parties belowdecks even as the aircraft controllers aloft were rounding up the tail-end Charlies.

At 1507 it was clear that "Lady Lex" was doomed. Her captain gave the order to abandon ship. Five hours later *Lexington* was still afloat, her hull plating glowing cherry red in places from fires raging inside. The miserable spectacle ended only when destroyer *Phelps* was ordered to finish her off with torpedoes. As the great warship slid hissing and roaring to her final berth on the bottom of the Coral Sea, Fletcher was now facing a tactical defeat. To add to his predicament, his air commander alerted him to the "strong indications that an additional carrier had joined the enemy forces."[41] Plans for a night destroyer attack on the retreating enemy were abandoned and the order was given for Task Force 17 to withdraw to the southeast.

Hara, who could have pursued his victory with his undamaged carrier, also decided to leave the field of battle. Lack of fuel and planes was the reason he would give for not following Combined Fleet orders "to extend the gains of the battle and destroy the remaining enemy forces."[42] Whatever the reason, his failure to follow orders turned a tactical victory for Japan into a strategic defeat.

Admiral Inouye was to blame Hara's retreat for his decision to recall the invasion force the next morning. His dispatch informed Yamamoto, "Port Moresby attack will be postponed to a later date. Your approval is requested. Nauru-Ocean operation, however, will most likely be carried out as scheduled."

Lexington's loss was a terrible blow to Nimitz. He was visibly jolted and muttered several times that they should have saved her. But he was always self-possessed when things looked bleakest. He immediately tried to buoy us. "Remember this," he told us that night. "We don't *know* how *badly* he's hurt. You can bet your boots he's hurt too! Remember this—the enemy has got to be hurt, his situation is not all a bed of roses."[43]

Nimitz's optimism was infectious—and was justified, as we soon learned. Rochefort that evening sent over the decryption of Hara's afternoon battle summary, and although we were disappointed that *Shokaku* had suffered only "slight damage" and was steaming to Truk, by the following morning we knew that the Port Moresby operation had been postponed. Nimitz might have lost one of our most valuable carriers, but Task Force 17 had succeeded in its objective of halting Japan's southward advance. If this delay proved permanent, Nimitz would indeed be justified in claiming the Coral Sea as "a victory with decisive and far reaching consequences."[44]

For the first time since Pearl Harbor an important psychological defeat had been inflicted on the previously invincible Japanese navy. According to General MacArthur, who was loath to praise the navy, the Battle of the Coral Sea was "the real safeguard of Australian independence."[45] It provided him with a timely measure of revenge for Bataan, which had fallen on 6 May.

If the Coral Sea action had not yet put Japan on the defensive, it served Admiral Yamamoto with notice that despite our numerical inferiority, the Pacific Fleet could muster its forces at long range to check the Combined Fleet. The battle also marked the first naval engagement in history to be fought without the rival warships ever catching sight of one another. Radio intelligence had proved itself a crucial factor in turning the strategic outcome in our favor. But the action had shown how a commander who was inexperienced in the use of tactical radio intelligence could make egregious errors. Nonetheless a secret wartime navy department assessment concluded: "It takes nothing from the achievements of the fleets of the U.S. Navy at Coral Sea to say that they had been brought to the right spot at exactly the right time by the work of radio intelligence."[46]

30

"Science and Skill"

I F IT HAD NOT BEEN FOR radio intelligence, the first we would have heard about the Coral Sea probably would have been a victory announcement by the Tokyo *Domei* news agency. Only Nimitz and a few close aides knew, however, that our strategic success in the action was largely the result of Joe Rochefort's unique abilities to smell out "something fishy" in the intercepts. He had demonstrated a sixth sense when it came to assembling seemingly unrelated information in partially decrypted enemy messages and turning the puzzle into an accurate picture of enemy plans and intentions.

The Coral Sea was an important victory for Hypo because it persuaded Nimitz to trust Rochefort over and above the often conflicting assessments being made by naval intelligence in Washington. Perhaps more important, as I have said earlier, Joe had smelled out indications that another and bigger Japanese offensive was in the making before the first shots were fired in Coral Sea. On 27 April he had revealed Tokyo's interest in maps of the Aleutians.[1] On 4 May he discovered that a battleship had signaled that a 21 May schedule for completion of her refit made it impossible "to accompany you in the campaign."[2] The next day Joe reported that Yamamoto's flagship had ordered Tokyo to "expedite delivery" of a large quantity of refueling hose because it was needed for "scheduled operations."[3]

Just what "the campaign" might be was still unclear, but it was evidently something much bigger than Admiral Inouye's declared intention to capture Ocean and Nauru islands. A strike against the Aleutians would account for the Combined Fleet requesting more hoses for seagoing refueling operations, but Rochefort had a hunch. Based on a subtle shift in radio traffic, he believed that the main Japanese objective was in the mid-Pacific. Specific ship-movement decrypts, while individually insignificant, were creating a pattern that pointed to an impending operation in the area. Units began exchanging messages with Saipan at an increasing rate, an indication that the ports in the Marianas were becoming the focus of a Combined Fleet movement unconnected with the current operation in the south.[4]

"While the Japanese offensive in the south Pacific continues, it is noted they now have sufficient forces in the central Pacific to raid in the central and north Pacific area," Nimitz logged on 6 May, reflecting Hypo's current intelligence estimates.[5] That Wednesday, Rochefort uncovered the first clue to one of the elements in the Japanese operation. A decrypted message from Sixth Fleet submarine force headquarters on Kwajalein requested a new set of transmitter crystals "for use in aircraft in the second K campaign." The crystals had to reach Sixth Fleet headquarters by 17 May.[6]

Since submarines at the French Frigate Shoals had refueled flying boats for the first "K" Operation, Joe believed that the Japanese intended to duplicate that 5 March flight over Oahu, because "AK" was their designator for Pearl. On the strength of this information Nimitz ordered that a minelayer be stationed at the French Frigate Shoals.

It had been the unexpected appearance of our second carrier task force in the Coral Sea that had prompted Yamamoto to order a second long-range reconnaissance of Pearl Harbor. It was necessary as a prelude to the Combined Fleet's big offensive to know where our fleet was. But by ordering the reconnaissance Yamamoto had unwittingly dealt himself a losing card. So far he had been on a hot roll, the dice had been falling his way. But when he drew up the final plans for his Midway strategy he unwisely relied too much on his lucky streak continuing. The Japanese, who are adept at turning an appropriate phrase to explain the tides of fate that govern human affairs, were to attribute their reverses after five months of triumph to shōribyō—"victory disease."

While the battle was being fought in the Coral Sea, Yamamoto and his staff appear to have been afflicted with a bad case of shōribyō during the tabletop maneuvers in which they rehearsed the Midway operation. The heat of battle was absent in the calculations that were made by the principal naval commanders of the Combined Fleet during their five-day conference in Hashirajima Bay.

"The Combined Fleet cannot assume a long drawn-out defense," Yamamoto told the conference, which assembled on 1 May in superbattleship Yamato's cavernous wardroom.[7] He outlined his grand design for a massive attack on Midway, and a diversionary assault on the Aleutians, which was intended to lure the Pacific Fleet carriers out to be smashed.

The trap was to be sprung by deploying every available warship in the Combined Fleet that could be spared. Operation MI—for Midway, as it had been code-named—was the most ambitious operation ever mounted by the Japanese navy. It was also one of the most complex naval operations ever planned, depending for its success on the simultaneous cooperation of five tactical groups.

Admiral Nagumo's carrier striking force was to play the key role. The *Kido Butai* was to support amphibious landings on Midway, while a northern force including two carriers covered the capture of Kiska and Attu at the western end of the Aleutian chain. An advance force of submarines was to interpose a patrol line west of the Hawaiian Islands to provide early warning and launch underwater attacks on the anticipated American sortie to defend Midway. Yamamoto himself would then lead the Combined Fleet's main force into the final action, springing the jaws of the gigantic trap shut, with the northern force advancing south from the Aleutians to cut off the Pacific Fleet's line of retreat.

For four days the Japanese admirals and captains rehearsed the complex operation that involved the interlocking moves of over seven hundred planes and two hundred ships—including eleven battleships, eight carriers, twenty-three cruisers, sixty-five destroyers, and twenty submarines. The objective of Operation MI was to eliminate the American carrier threat and advance Japan's defensive perimeter another two thousand miles eastward into the Pacific. This was the preliminary step prior to the third phase of Yamamoto's grand design: to invade Hawaii and force the United States to sue for peace.

The war games, however, did not always produce the desired result. Instead they exposed a disturbing number of flaws. The Combined Fleet staff had calculated that the American carriers could not reach Midway before it had been captured and a strong Japanese air umbrella established on the atoll. If this condition was not met, disastrous results were demonstrated. In one run-through, the attacking force suffered two carriers sunk, a third bombed into retreat, and a whole division of destroyers lost for lack of fuel, while the actual capture of Midway was delayed for more than a week. But "victory disease" had infected the umpires. They permitted all three of the supposedly "sunken" carriers to be miraculously refloated to participate in the next stage of the operations!

In the critique that followed the tabletop maneuvers, Yamamoto was taxed by some of his subordinate commanders. They were so concerned at the complexity of the operation that they wanted a postponement for more preparations and training. There was considerable worry about how the commander in chief was going to personally coordinate so many scattered forces when he intended to be at sea himself, and would be obliged to maintain radio silence until the fleet action began.

But Yamamoto would allow no alterations to the plan which would delay the launch of his mid-Pacific offensive. He was boxed in by imperial general headquarters' inflexible timetable of conquest and by immovable meteorological considerations. Midway could be invaded only during the first days of the month, when slack high water after dawn would allow the assault craft to get over the atoll's reef. The weather forecast for July predicted the Aleutians would be locked in by impenetrable fog banks. These two factors dictated that the twin phases of the MI operation had to be set for the first week in June.

To pull off his Midway strategy, Yamamoto needed luck. His intricate battle choreography also required that his opponents move according to predicted positions; one false step or foreknowledge of the plan could throw the entire operation into disarray.

Imperial general headquarters issued the final orders for the "occupation of Midway and strategic points in the western Aleutians" on the 5 May national festival known as Boys Day, celebrating future achievement. But an inauspicious prelude to his big campaign came within forty-eight hours when Yamamoto received news from the Coral Sea that cost his Midway operation the services of two carriers and many skilled aircrews. It was at this point that he unwittingly drew a second losing card by ordering the flying boat reconnaissance of Pearl Harbor.[8]

The plan for a second "K" operation was spotted almost at once by Rochefort. On 7 May he learned that many Combined Fleet commanders were being summoned to Kagoshima in Japan for a mid-month briefing.[9] The next day a destroyer division announced that it would be unable to "participate in your forthcoming campaign."[10] On 9 May a large number of destroyers that were to screen the carriers and battleships involved in "the forthcoming campaign" were ordered to "to depart Yokosuka on 17 May."[11]

Decrypt by decrypt, Rochefort began peeling away the cover to reveal the extent and direction of Yamamoto's grand design. Joe was the ideal combination of intelligence-officer-cum-cryptanalyst. But his idiosyncratic ways and fierce independence were already irritating the new regime running naval intelligence in Washington. They wanted everything cut and dried. They wanted everyone assigned to a particular section of analysis so that the end product could be fit into a neat picture of Japanese intentions. But Rochefort and his team did not work that way, and, during the month of May, their method produced the results that Washington failed to achieve. The record bears out that most of the significant decrypts were made by Hypo. This was galling to the Redman brothers in Washington, who wanted to prove to Admiral King how effectively they had shaken up and reorganized naval intelligence.

"The war actually was being fought out yonder," Captain McCollum was to admit later. The head of naval intelligence's Far East section was succinct in his comments. He went on to say: "Whatever we did around here in Washington would be more or less in the category of toting buckets of water out there. The strategic setup and concepts were discussed here, but on the plane of commanders-in-chief and their staffs. The actual concept of the operations was largely left in the hands of Admiral Nimitz."[12]

McCollum might have been content to leave Cincpac to evaluate the concept of enemy operations, but this did not square with the ideas of naval communications director Captain Joseph R. Redman, or his younger brother, Commander "Jack" Redman, who was head of the restructured OP-20-G. They also had the ear of Admiral King, who was fighting his own battle with the Joint Chiefs to restore the priority of the Pacific theater. On 5 May, King warned the Joint Chiefs of the "disastrous consequences if we are unable to hold the present position in the Pacific."[13] But General Marshall persuaded Roosevelt that "it was impossible to make every point in the island chain impregnable." King was told that he would have to fight the Japanese with the ships and planes already assigned to the Pacific.

Nimitz had already made a flying visit to Midway on 2 May. This was in response to King's mounting concern about the defense of our Pacific island outposts and not, as many historians have wrongly suggested, because of his anticipation of the Japanese attack, which had yet to be revealed. On Nimitz's return he ordered the atoll's reinforcement with more planes and ammunition. But his principal concern was how to "make our position secure and provide for an adequate striking force" to deal with the new Japanese offensive.[14] Although *Saratoga* would complete her refit by the beginning of June, the loss of *Lexington,* plus *Yorktown*'s estimated three months for repairs, left our carrier forces outnumbered nearly five to one.

Distance may lend enchantment, but in King's case it produced a bout of strategic jitters in terms of the Pacific defense. The sinking of *Lexington* had been an almost personal blow. The carrier had once been his flagship. He knew as well as Nimitz that the loss of another flattop would cripple our ability to hold advanced positions between Alaska and Australia. It was this concern that prompted him to place impossible restrictions on Nimitz.

Halsey's orders to foil the Japanese move to Ocean and Nauru were hamstrung when Nimitz received King's dispatch directing that "operations of Task Force 16 inadvisable in forward areas beyond shore-based air cover and within range enemy shore-based air." Cominch went even further, suggesting that to "preserve our carriers . . . it may be better to operate one or more carrier [air] groups from shore."[15]

This proposal from a former flattop skipper—that carrier aircraft should be operated from land bases at New Caledonia and Fiji—was as disturbing to Nimitz as the revelation that King apparently believed that Japan's next campaign would be against our island bases in the South Pacific. If Nimitz was going to regain control of the carriers, he would have first to convince King of the error in his potentially disastrous miscalculation about the direction the next enemy offensive would take.

"If we listen to Washington," one Hypo staff officer warned Rochefort, "we will all end up as Japanese POWs."[16]

Joe and I faced a difficult task. We had the confidence of Nimitz, but now we had to demonstrate beyond any doubt that the evaluations being made in Washington were wrong. And this had to be done at a time when we had only a vague notion of the Japanese intentions. Our problem was made more complex by Washington's deductions, which were based on the same decrypts we were using, that the enemy had begun a buildup at Truk and not Saipan. If this was true, it would indeed indicate a Japanese advance south into New Caledonia, Port Moresby, and Fiji. Washington was dismissing Rochefort's estimate of a movement to the Marianas (Midway) as a feint—like the Aleutians—and claiming instead that four carriers and seven battleships were about to head southward.

We tried to understand why Washington had come up with such a contradictory evaluation of similar intelligence. Joe and I could conclude only that being so distant from operational headquarters they were more concerned with "enemy capabilities," while we concentrated on what the Japanese *were doing,* could do, and would probably do. Then there was the question of King's domineering personality. Like Turner, he over-awed his subordinates. They tended to feed him information that reinforced his convictions, and every officer in Washington knew that King was struggling to get more resources for the Pacific war. Raising the level of the alarm about the Japanese threat to our lifeline to Australia evidently was more likely to evoke the support of General Marshall than asking for reinforcements for Midway or the Aleutians.

The different priorities of Washington and Pearl Harbor inevitably colored the estimates that were made by the two intelligence staffs. But once positions are taken, they are difficult to reverse, especially at a time when the communications intelligence outfit in the navy department was fighting to reassert Washington's authority over Station Hypo. But none of us at Pearl Harbor had forgotten what had happened six months earlier. Rochefort and his team were determined never again to be suckered by complacent evaluations of the type that had contributed to disaster. Joe particularly resented any attempt to confine his activities to any one area of additive or code recoveries. He remembered all too well how Washington had denied him access to the vital intelligence in the Japanese consular traffic that had been totally ignored by the navy department.

What had happened was that Washington had combined three partial messages and misinterpreted the results. They had confused the Midway phase of Yamamoto's plan with the third phase, which did indeed include a strike to the south toward Fiji, Samoa, and New Caledonia. The three signals involved included a Belconnen decrypt of a 2 May signal directing that carrier *Kaga* "upon completion of repairs will depart Sasebo and anchor at _____ in Truk."[17] Washington read this in conjunction with another message that assigned berths in Truk to Battleship Division 3.[18] Then there was a third signal that placed the First Air Fleet commander on board *Kaga*. This final message was misinterpreted in Washington to mean that Nomura's striking force must be heading southward for Truk.

Rochefort, however, assembled the pieces differently. First, he said that the air commander on board *Kaga* was ordering the other air commanders of the carrier strike force to a 17 May conference aboard *Kaga* in Kagoshima, the southernmost harbor in Japan. Second, Rochefort saw that Washington had misread the additive group and misidentified Kagoshima as being Truk.[19] Furthermore, other decrypts suggested that intensive operational exercises were being conducted off the southern coast of Japan, and it was only logical that these exercises would be followed by a staff conference. After ten more days of working on the additives, Rochefort was able to circulate the correct decrypt of the original message intercepted by Belconnen. It directed that the "striking force may be in Truk for a period of about two weeks after ((94539)), please arrange for _____ and designate anchorages."[20]

The date represented by the numerals "94539" was superenciphered and although it could not be broken out—it was later discovered to be 20 June—the reference to a two-week stay suggested that the Combined Fleet's main force would reassemble at Truk *after* the mid-Pacific operation. But the analysts of OP-20-G stuck to their guns, trying to justify their contention that the main force was heading south on the basis of the recent increase in traffic to Rabaul. Although this traffic was unreadable, Rochefort was able to point out that it had the characteristics of administrative rather than operational traffic.

While the navy department analysts were busily trying to bolster their case, systematic analysis of traffic by Hypo revealed that virtually every destroyer command in the Combined Fleet had been assigned to the mid-Pacific operation. We were positive that wherever the Japanese might be heading, it was not south. (No new destroyer assignments had been detected on the Truk radio circuits by the end of the second week in May.) Yet what appeared obvious to us was ignored or dismissed in Washington.

Decrypts of 11 May assigning the Second Fleet anchorages at Saipan prompted Rochefort to remind Washington: "Do not believe Japanese are carrying out a drill in Saipan area at this time. Suggest possibility that this and preceding message all refer to campaign or operation."[21] Three days later Joe made the big break that Nimitz had been waiting for.

"I've got something so hot here it's burning the top of my desk" was how Joe told me about it that Thursday. When I asked what it was he said, "You'll have to come over and see it. It's not cut and dried, but it's hot! The man with the blue eyes will want to know your opinion of it."

When I reached his underground headquarters, Rochefort was ebullient as he showed me a partially decrypted message. It contained the words "*koryaku butai.*" It was the proven value for "invasion force" and it was followed by the geographic designator "AF" in a signal referring to the "forthcoming campaign." The term "*koryaku butai,*" Joe pointed out, had been used during the invasions of Rabaul, Java, Sumatra, and Bali.[22]

Now we knew that the Japanese intended to invade "AF." By a brilliant piece of detective work, Rochefort then convinced me that the objective was Midway. The clinchers were two messages sent out by the Second Fleet command to its associated air units. The first went to the "AF occupation force," which was ordered to "proceed direct to the Saipan-Guam area and wait for the forthcoming campaign." The second one ordered another unit to "load its base equipment and ground crews and advance to AF . . . everything in the way of base equipment and military supplies which will be needed for the K campaign will be included."[23]

Joe was jubilant. He had finally tied the mysterious "K" operation to the Japanese forces concentrating at Saipan. From there his deduction that AF must be Midway was simple and convincing. We knew that AH was Oahu and that AK was probably the French Frigate Shoals. Now that the base supplies for an air unit were being readied for shipment into "AF" with the occupation forces, it had to be one of our island bases within striking distance of Pearl Harbor. Midway was the obvious target, since it was nearly 150 miles nearer the Japanese on Wake than the alternative, Johnston Island.

I immediately reported Rochefort's analysis to Nimitz. He asked Captain Lynde V. McCormack, his war plans chief, to go down to Hypo with me for confirmation. McCormack was quickly convinced. From that afternoon on, despite all that has been written, there was never any doubt in Nimitz's mind that Midway was the main objective of the Japanese operation. But Washington changed its mind about the identity of AF even though the "Decryption Intelligence Bulletin" circulated earlier by naval intelligence in Washington on 30 April had listed AF as being Midway.

"It required no exceptional stretch of intelligence to appreciate that AF would have to be Midway," Rochefort pointed out.[24] But it was not such a simple deduction for the analysts in the navy department.[24] They challenged Hypo's analysis.

"The amazing part of the whole thing was that many people could not accept this line of reasoning," Rochefort was to say later while reflecting on the bitter dispute that broke out over the secure Copek cable circuit. "We were quite impatient at Station Hypo that people in Washington could not agree with our rationale, because they had the same information and should, without any particular stress on their brain, have come up with the same answer."[25]

The issue was not simply the correct interpretation of the first and sixth letters of the alphabet, but the question of whether or not radio intelligence evaluations were to be made in Washington or Pearl Harbor. Since the whole course of the Pacific war turned on the correct evaluation—and Washington made the wrong deductions—it is significant to note that the daily records of Cominch's decryption intelligence are missing from 8 May 1942 onward at this point. Furthermore there are extensive deletions in the summaries that survive from the White House map room.

One of the last of the navy department evaluations that has been located reveals the bones of the dispute: "An actual landing may be attempted on Midway or possibly on Johnston Island. Every effort is being made to determine more exactly the reliability of this report and which of the two locations is correct."[26] The OP-20-G head, Commander John R. Redman, evidently chose to conclude that the Japanese were heading for Johnston Island. One factor that apparently influenced his decision was a refusal to believe that by the most incredible coincidence the Japanese should have selected the same two letters as our own code designator for Midway—AF.[27]

"There was no doubt that Washington was totally in error," recalled Tommy Dyer, Rochefort's chief cryptanalyst. "There was never a question in our minds about AF being Midway."[28] According to Hypo's analysis the Japanese designator for Johnston Island was AG, but Washington got around that by claiming that Rochefort's JN-25 additives were unreliable and that what we were reading as AF in the intercept should have been correctly decrypted as AG. The fight was therefore not about whether AF was Midway, but about whose additives were to be accepted. This went right to the heart of the competence issue.

"It was a mess" was how Ham Wright, Dyer's chief assistant, recalled the adversarial relationship. "We would fight with OP-20-G all the time; we could not get together."[29] Rochefort had little respect for the abilities of Jack Redman who was not a trained cryptanalyst. His experience had been less important than his brother's influence in his becoming head of OP-20-G and gaining control of the "correlation and interpretation of all radio intelligence."[30] The feud between the two men exacerbated the natural rivalry of the two intelligence outfits. It became a veritable war of words, which was carried on even in the "padding"—the junk sentences inserted by enciphering officers before and after the actual message text as an additional measure of security.[31]

"Some of it was not too polite," Wright observed laconically. "Washington wanted to take complete charge and tell us what to do in detail, but Rochefort would have no part of it."[32] To the members of Hypo it seemed that the Redman brothers were determined to impose their intelligence evaluations and recoveries of the JN-25 additives on Hypo regardless of whether they were right or wrong. Each combat intelligence unit had been assigned a particular area to concentrate on in the additive recoveries and their results were shared daily on the secure interstation Copek line. The Coral Sea estimates had proved the Hypo cryptanalysts had the edge. This further rankled the Redmans and their allies in Washington.

"It boiled down to who was going to do the work and who was going to get the credit," said Wright, who was later sent to Washington to negotiate a truce. "The Negat cryptanalysts did not want to trust our additives and would not use them. This attitude reached down to OP-20-G's radio operators and the lists we sent in would often wind up in the waste basket. It was very easy to get additives wrong. We were certainly most reluctant to trust theirs, so we worked out our own."[33]

When Rochefort challenged Washington's additives on the "AF" issue, Jack Redman accused him of being uncooperative and getting out of his assigned area of additive recovery. Joe replied by referring curtly to King's recent authorization that Hypo was to deal with all current decrypts. Admiral Nimitz, moreover, had directed him (through me) to try to break *any* messages concerning the air fleet on board the Japanese carriers.[34]

This implicit challenge to Jack Redman's authority infuriated him. He wanted to bring Hypo into his preserve. So instead of utilizing Rochefort's unique cryptanalytic abilities, Redman dug his heels in about his own estimates. He became more and more irritated by some of Joe's tart replies to the estimates from Washington that Japan was preparing to raid Panama or California.

"I was trying to see it from the point of view of the Japanese general staff and was not at all interested in what our own assessments were" was how Rochefort dismissed the fear that the enemy might also be planning to attack the west coast. "I have never been able to understand why Cominch gave any more than a couple of thoughts to the idea that this operation might be directed against the mainland, because it was simply beyond the capability of the Japanese transport and supply operation."[35]

Washington might have raised every conceivable objection to Rochefort's Midway analysis, but after carefully reviewing his conclusions with McCormack, on 14 May Nimitz was firmly convinced that Joe was right. Any doubts about the direction of Japan's offensive he might have had were dispelled later that same day when Hypo decrypted a message from Tokyo listing the American charts to be sent to Saipan. Of the seven reference numbers given, all but one were sections of the Hawaiian Islands.[36]

Although we still had no clear idea of just what forces were being committed to the invasion of Midway, one decrypt revealed that battleship *Hiei*, and Carrier Division 3, were sharing escorts and would depart from Sasebo to take part in the operation. When Nimitz reviewed the situation with me on the evening of Thursday, 14 May, he was in a strategic bind.

On the assumption that our estimates were correct, and that the Japanese would launch their mid-Pacific campaign in about two weeks, there was no time to be lost before retrieving Halsey's two carriers, so that every available task force could be concentrated off Midway. But this had to be effected against Admiral King's express instructions—and at a time that King was still being wrongly advised by his own intelligence staff that the enemy was going south instead of east.

"Evidently Cominch believes the enemy will strike at 'Poppy' and 'Roses' after 25 May" was how Nimitz reacted to King's blast that the

Japanese were intending to seize New Caledonia and Fiji.[37] Nimitz played a tactful devil's advocate by hinting that Japanese forces might even be heading as far east as the west coast. He reassured King that seaplane tender *Tangier* had been dispatched to Noumea, and was able to reject as unnecessary the idea of stranding *Lexington*'s surviving air groups down in New Caledonia. King was assured that Halsey would remain outside the range of land-based bombers but it would be difficult for him to keep his distance from long-range flying boat patrols. Nimitz stressed that Japan's precise plan was still uncertain so it was essential to maintain "our striking forces in a state of maximum mobility to act against advancing enemy forces or to conduct offensive operations as opportunity presents."[38]

The most difficult problem that Nimitz faced was how to free Halsey's two carriers from King's standing order that would keep them down in the southwest Pacific. He proposed that Task Force 16 "may be retained or moved in accordance with information received," and that if the "enemy drive to the southeast is not indicated," it should be recalled to the central Pacific area. A decision was needed because of the "time and distances involved."[39]

Time was indeed the most critical factor. Nimitz recognized this that Thursday evening by setting in motion a stratagem to force King's prompt agreement. He fell in with my suggestion for sending a personal private message to Halsey to let his force be sighted steaming north toward Ocean and Nauru.

Halsey, who was "mad as hell" at the Cincpac relay of King's instruction that it was "inadvisable" for Task Force 16 to operate within enemy air range, fully grasped the situation when he got the second, "eyes only" message. We knew we could count on him to make good use of his on-board radio intelligence unit to confirm he had been spotted before high-tailing south under cover of darkness. Since Halsey was effectively being told to ignore Cominch orders to comply with his secret instructions from Cincpac, Nimitz wanted no copies of the dispatch filed.[40]

The next morning Halsey played his assigned role to perfection. Task Force 16 was spotted steaming north 450 miles due east of Tulagi at 1015 by a Japanese flying boat making its patrol report. By late that afternoon he was satisfied he had persuaded the Japanese that he was heading full tilt for the Phosphate Islands, some 700 miles to the north, but he waited until dusk before altering course to the east. Nimitz received almost instantaneous confirmation that our ruse had worked. Decrypts from Fourth Fleet headquarters on Rabaul revealed that Admiral Inoue had mobilized his warships to guard the invasion transports from anticipated attack the following day and orders were issued for "wiping out the enemy striking force."[41]

Halsey managed to slip away to the east, but his very appearance had the desired effect. On the evening of 15 May, I was able to hand to

Nimitz a decrypt reading, "Occupation of Ocean and Nauru postponed indefinitely."[42] Indications of future activities now all pointed to the mid-Pacific. My Enemy Activities File the next day concluded from the map information and a spate of sub sightings off Midway that the Japanese were preparing an "advance to Midway (AF) via Saipan." It predicted, "The occupation of Midway is a necessary step toward an assault on Oahu."[43]

That Friday evening, after reviewing his options, Nimitz issued two dispatches that were to have far-reaching strategic implications. "Desire you proceed to Hawaiian area," he signaled Halsey in the early hours of 16 May. At the same time he sent off a long message to Admiral King—with Halsey as information addressee—justifying his decision to recall Task Force 16 in defiance of the intelligence estimates in Washington.

While Nimitz conceded the possibility of another Japanese thrust in the southwest toward Port Moresby, as well as the probable diversionary raid on the Aleutians, he predicted that the main enemy offensive would be "against Midway-Oahu line, probably involving initially a major landing attack against Midway, for which it is believed the enemy's main striking force will be employed." The timing of these offensives was not yet clear, but Nimitz advised King that "sighting Halsey in south yesterday caused postponement of Ocean and Nauru operations and will expedite northern and central operation."[44]

Since the Pacific Fleet did not have the necessary strength to counter all three offensives, Nimitz believed it essential that Halsey be recalled to Pearl Harbor for the defense of "the most vital area." "Unless the enemy is using radio deception on a grand scale, we have a fairly good idea of his intentions," he concluded, adding that it was possible that Japan would "attack Midway and raid Oahu in the first part of June."[45]

While Joe and I were impressed by this vote of confidence in our estimates, we were aware that by challenging King and his intelligence staff head on, Nimitz had put himself out on a limb—and we were clinging onto it behind him. On the basis of another review the following day, Nimitz considered it advisable to send a follow-up cable to King that addressed the issue dividing Hypo and Negat.

"Considerable difference in estimates probably on the same data is noted," Nimitz admitted. But he insisted that his latest information "does not confirm future enemy concentration at Truk."[46] That Saturday the Cincpac staff met to discuss ways to match our thin offensive and defensive resources. Reassuring news was received from our New Caledonia naval base. After *Yorktown* limped into Noumea, Fletcher reported that a preliminary damage inspection indicated that his carrier could be patched up at Pearl Harbor without the need for dry-docking on the west coast.

Nimitz received his second and even more important break the next evening in an "urgent and confidential" cable in our most secret flag officers code. Washington had made a remarkable turnabout. It now accepted our strategic evaluation. "Differences in estimate due to earlier receipt by you of decryption intelligence" was the face-saving formula that King employed to agree with Nimitz's assessment of the Japanese plan. Evidently Jack Redman had been hauled over the coals and made to eat his previous predictions.[47] It must have been an uncomfortable twenty-four hours spent reviewing and revising intelligence estimates. King did not appreciate being made anyone's fall guy, but now he had admitted that Hypo had been right and his staff wrong. He did not have to, but he did. And that was a remarkable tribute to Hypo.

"I have somewhat revised my estimate and now generally agree with you," King informed Nimitz. Concerned that Memorial Day and the emperor's birthday coincided, he added the caveat "except I believe enemy attempt to capture Midway and Unalaska will occur about May 30th (note the double holiday [sic]) or shortly thereafter." Washington apparently had discovered how their estimates had gone astray, because King now accepted that "enemy south Pacific campaign will be started middle or later part of June and will be strong attempt to capture Moresby plus northeast Australia, or New Guinea and Fijis."[48]

Washington now agreed that Midway was Yamamoto's immediate objective, and that the "enemy intention included effort to trap and destroy a substantial portion of the Pacific Fleet." King concluded by laying down that the "appropriate strategy" for the Pacific Fleet would be "to make a strong concentration" in the Hawaiian areas and "employ strong attrition tactics and not repeat not allow our forces to accept such decisive action as would be likely to incur heavy losses."[49]

These were the guidelines that Nimitz set before his staff at his 18 May strategic review. While I still could not provide a firm timetable for the Japanese offensive, all the indications were that enemy units would be heading east from Saipan in the final days of May. So Nimitz set a 25 May deadline for completing the reinforcement of Midway with planes and submarines, and for sending a North Pacific force to Alaskan waters. Halsey was expected back in Pearl Harbor by 26 May, and Fletcher by 27 May. Nimitz announced that if we could expedite *Yorktown*'s repairs we would have three carriers on station in the critical area off Midway by the first of June.

It did not need any mathematical wizardry to know that even if this near miracle was achievable, our forces would still be perilously outnumbered. Everything now depended on Rochefort's being able to balance the odds by discovering the details of the Japanese battle plan.

31

"You Don't Have to Be Crazy to Work Here —But It Helps"

W E DID NOT KNOW it at the time, but our whole intelligence effort—and the course of the war itself—had been put in jeopardy. It was an incident that I logged in my Enemy Activities File as being "possible raider activity 10 May at 26-43 south, 89-56 west." This pinpointed the location of distress signals we had picked up from a British steamer in the Indian Ocean that had reported being attacked by a German surface raider.[1]

Forty years were to pass before I was to understand the significance of the capture of a five-thousand-ton freighter by the armed merchant cruiser *Thor*. The whole picture emerged from declassified German records and the wartime intelligence records released recently by the New Zealand government. The facts were simple, the results complex. The freighter *Nankin* was seized by the raider *Thor* two days out of Freemantle en route from Wellington to Ceylon. On board were top-secret Royal Navy mail bags.

Fortunately for us the mail bags were not properly examined until they reached Japan more than two months later. When *Thor*'s supply ship *Regensberg* docked at Yokohama on 18 July, the mail was sent to Tokyo where Admiral Wenneker, the German naval attaché, at once realized the importance of the documents. Of special interest were the weekly summaries of the Combined Operations Intelligence Center (COIC) of the New Zealand armed forces. After cabling details of them to Berlin, Wenneker received authority to pass the documents to the Japanese.[2]

Pearl Harbor had supplied COIC with a great amount of sensitive data. Some of it was even referred to as being from "Ultra" sources in "Most Secret" summaries that were circulated on an officers-only basis to twenty-two recipients—including Admiral Nimitz. The intelligence digests were a treasure trove of information for the enemy. They gave the positions of all Allied warships as well as our best estimates of the Japanese dispositions throughout the Pacific, based on my own daily bulletins.

Any Japanese intelligence officer worth his salt would immediately be aware of the success of our radio intercept operation from reading these COIC summaries. They might have suspected that such details as the transfer of flags, and the location of individual seaplane units in the mandates, could have come only from code breaking.[3]

If the Germans had given the *Nankin*'s secret mail to the Japanese as promptly as they had communicated the minutes of the British war cabinet captured eighteen months earlier, it would have blown our intelligence advantage before the most critical battle of the Pacific war. For if the Japanese had changed their operational codes even a week earlier, we would have been deprived of date and final details of their deployment at Midway. Or if Yamamoto had been alerted to the accuracy and detail of the information we had obtained, he might well have reconsidered his strategy. At the very least the Japanese forces would have steamed out to battle on the alert. The surprise that was so essential to our ability to ambush superior forces would have been lost, and the Battle of Midway—if it had been fought at all—might have been the decisive naval victory for Japan that Yamamoto intended.

Years later, another aspect of the situation still gave me sleepless nights. If the Japanese had received the New Zealand summaries before the end of May, and if we were stripped of our intelligence advantage, we would never have been aware of the reasons for it. The British *never* warned us then, or later, that this freighter was carrying a consignment of secret mail to the Royal Navy's Station Anderson in Colombo. My daily bulletins had been sent to the Australian and New Zealand naval boards under strictest secrecy at the express direction of Admiral King. This was against the better judgment of Admiral Nimitz, who was increasingly disturbed about how they were being used by Australia's prime minister. The day after the Cincpac bulletin had reported that the Japanese had called off their Port Moresby operation, for example, reassuring reports appeared in every Australian newspaper to that effect. The prime minister had then announced that there would be plenty of warning of any invasion attempt.

"If I were you, I would not put anything in your intelligence bulletin about the possibility of an attack on Midway," Nimitz told me. "I think the thing to do is to hold this one really close, so there will be no leaks."

We could not afford to raise the enemy's suspicions about their communications. Their radio security was better than before the Coral Sea action. No intercepts were being made that contained complete operational orders. Rochefort was trying instead to put together an outline of their plan from seemingly unrelated instructions that were being issued to the different units. Orders involving Saipan, the Aleutians, the "K" operation, and "AF" were the only guidelines he had to work on in sifting through the decrypts. Another problem was that Hypo was intercepting less than 60 percent of the total Japanese traffic, and less than 40 percent of those messages could be broken. Many of them were only partial translations, so it was like trying to assemble a jigsaw puzzle with lots of missing pieces.[4]

After Rochefort had discovered the key "AF" piece, which locked Midway into the center of the picture, he began the search for leads to the other units that might be involved, and for the date the operation was to begin. The date was the most critical piece of intelligence, and Joe called me on 19 May with an important pointer. That Tuesday he had broken out from a dispatch, sent by a member of Admiral Nagumo's *Kido Butai* staff, references to the attacks "from a northwesterly direction from N-2 day inclusive until N day."[5] Since N minus two was clearly forty-eight hours before the N-date of the invasion—and it specified an indecipherable map reference "50 miles northwest of AF"—this message confirmed that Japan's main carrier striking force was to play a pivotal role in the capture of Midway. Now all we needed to know was what date N-day represented.

Rochefort's cryptanalyst team, led by Dyer and Wright, began a marathon review of every intercept. They carefully checked even unimportant routing instructions to transports for hints of the date. Nimitz, who could not afford to miss the boat on this one, had flashed Task Force 16 an "expedite return" dispatch on 18 May. "That could only mean one thing" was Halsey's reaction to such an urgent summons. "Trouble was brewing somewhere else in the Pacific."[6]

At the beginning of the third week in May, the current decrypts and traffic analysis indicated that the Combined Fleet was still on operational maneuvers south of Japan. But a 20 May decrypt contained instructions for the prebattle conference on Saipan for 26 May. And it contained the vitally important clue "to depart on 27th."[7] Saipan was 2,191 miles from Midway, or five days' steaming at twenty knots. This suggested that N-day could be 2 or 3 June. This was two weeks before the mid-June date that King had predicted, and nearly a week earlier than our original estimates.

Washington refused to buy this new date. And Rochefort just did not have enough of the current additives to break the date-time code out of the superenciphered groups in which the Japanese transmitted them for additional security. What was needed at this crucial juncture was an all-out cooperative effort. But the cryptanalysts at Negat in Washington were not only reluctant to supply the correct additives (which would have proved their estimates wrong), but naval intelligence dug up their own justifications for sticking with the mid-June date.

"All evidence indicates that the Midway attack plans have brought a number of problems which are giving responsible commanders considerable concern, and causing delays," McCollum reported to Admiral King on 23 May. "Although the so-called occupation force is now principally in the Saipan-Guam area, there are indications that the 2nd Fleet striking force may proceed to Truk for some two weeks . . . it is an indication that the main attack is now planned for about the middle of June."[8]

There were even those in Washington who suggested that their Hypo rivals had been taken in by an elaborate Japanese deception. They believed that the real Japanese objective was an attack on the west coast.[9] It was to silence the skeptics in Washington that Rochefort embarked on a brilliant piece of deception that has been celebrated and misinterpreted by every historian who has ever written about Midway.

When he cooked up the stratagem for sending a fake message about a water shortage on Midway, Joe's intention was *not* to persuade Nimitz he was *right*, but to prove Washington *wrong*. The idea came from one of Joe's assistants, Lieutenant Commander Jasper Holmes. He had studied the Midway Pan Am facility before the war when he was with the engineering school at the University of Hawaii, and he had been impressed that the island's entire freshwater supply was obtained from an evaporator plant. On 19 May, after receiving Admiral Bloch's preliminary approval Rochefort brought the scheme over to me.[10]

I took the proposal to Nimitz, who authorized the transmission by submarine cable to Midway of a dispatch that ordered the garrison commander to immediately radio a plain-language emergency request for water. At the same time the report was to be made by one of the strip-cipher code systems we knew the Japanese had captured on Wake. This would make a convincing detailed follow-up to the emergency first-flash report of an explosion in their water distillation system.

The instructions were duly sent out to the Midway commander that same Tuesday. Midway broadcast the messages soon afterward. They were picked up by the Japanese listening post at Kwajalein and flashed to the Owada headquarters of the Special Duty Radio Intelligence Group the same day.

The American emergency report electrified the Special Duty unit, to the surprise of Lieutenant Kenichi Nakumuta who had just joined the staff as a language student-reservist. "It was puzzling to me," he was later to recall, "knowing nothing of the impending assault on Midway, why such a 'shortage of fresh water' should be so important."[11] Later, he was "mortified" when he discovered how his superiors had fallen for the ruse and radioed the intelligence to the units involved. For within hours, the commander of the air unit destined for Midway was signaling headquarters to supply his force with emergency water supplies.

When that message was intercepted at Pearl, it surprised even Rochefort's second-in-command, who had not been let in on our secret. "I happened to read the Japanese interception of the water message," Captain Dyer recalled, "and I was so ignorant of the whole affair that I told Rochefort, 'Those stupid bastards on Midway. What do they ever mean by sending out a message like this in plain language.'"[12]

Tactfully, Rochefort decided to let Station Belconnen in Melbourne be the first to break the news to Washington. They obliged the next day with their translation: "The AF air unit sent following radio message to commandant 14th Naval district. AK (Pearl Harbor) of 20th. With reference to this unit's report dated 19th. At present time we have only enough water for two weeks. Please supply us immediately."[13]

To keep up the deception, Fourteenth Naval District headquarters at Pearl Harbor had also radioed the Midway garrison that barges of fresh water were on the way. It was essential that Washington did not suspect that they were the main objects of our little piece of deception. Belconnen stated, "This will confirm identity of AF." Rochefort tactfully waited until Friday morning to send his reminder: "As stated previously AF confirmed here as Midway."[14]

Our deception about water produced an unexpected bonus—and another black eye for Hypo's detractors in Negat. The Japanese air unit's request for a two-week water reserve revealed that the Japanese planned the Midway assault to be completed *before* Washington's predicted date of 15 June. Rochefort set about trying to pin down his hunch that N-day, when the Japanese carrier force would be northwest of the atoll, would be 2 or 3 June. With Midway being only three days of hard steaming away from Pearl, and with Halsey's task force due on 26 May, and Fletcher anticipated a day later, Nimitz had no margin for error if he was going to concentrate our forces for an ambush.

Rochefort now put his phenomenal power of recall, and all his cryptanalysts, to the test. With less than a week remaining before Nimitz had to issue his final orders, decrypts were being processed at the rate of five hundred to a thousand a day. Each one had to be scanned, although many of them were reports of transport movement. Others were so badly garbled, or incomplete, that valuable hours might be taken up trying to make sense of a word or two. Just processing the intercepts was a demanding physical effort, because each one had its five-digit groups punched into IBM cards. A single message might require anywhere from sixty to seventy of the slim, manila three-by-seven, eighty-column IBM cards. A lengthy signal could easily consume two hundred of them. Each one had to be hand-punched and sorted by the former band members of battleship *California,* who manned the IBM machines that they kept chattering around the clock.

In the frantic but meticulous search for the key that would unlock the final piece of the Midway puzzle, Hypo was consuming nearly three million punch cards a month. Just keeping Hypo supplied without arousing the suspicion of outsiders created a security risk. And storing all the cards in hundreds of open boxes for future reference created severe problems. For the printouts produced from the tabulating process, from which the

Japanese messages could be translated, were piled up on desks, floors, and every available space. Each analyst working on current decrypts needed his own stack of acco binders containing the printouts of past messages for reference.

"We didn't have time to cross-file or cross-index, and it was one reason why people thought we were crazy" was how Rochefort recalled that hectic week of effort. "You'd mention something and someone would recall a previous message and they'd look in this pile of junk—all the previous messages that had come in—and were able to locate it."[15]

To outsiders like myself, who had the necessary security clearance to get past the armed marine door guard, the Hypo "dungeon" was organized chaos. Over his desk the enigmatic Captain Dyer had hung a sign reading, YOU DON'T HAVE TO BE CRAZY TO WORK HERE—BUT IT HELPS! Under the glass on his desk resided what was reputed to be the best collection of pin-ups in the Pacific Fleet, which added its own touch to an unbelievably cluttered appearance. But Tommy Dyer knew exactly where everything was on it. A new yeoman once made the mistake of tidying up the legendary "Dyer's desk" and it brought down Dyer's wrath after he was unable to locate a critical decrypt.[16]

What saved the whole system from collapsing was the team's overall easygoing lack of hierarchy and its remarkable ability to recall and relate details of decrypts made months earlier. "People might not believe that this was how it was done, because we had no machinery other than the IBM punches, sorters, and tabulators," Joe later recalled, noting how he "kept everything in his head."[17]

"I would receive the decrypted messages, in Japanese but not in full," Rochefort explained. "They might say, 'From Commander in Chief Sixth Fleet to Commander in Chief Striking Force: You will . . .' and then a bunch of blanks. 'Upon completion of this, you will proceed . . .' and then some more blanks. My job was to fill it in. I could remember back three or four months when that command had sent a similar message."[18]

In this way Rochefort personally reviewed and filled in the blanks of some 140 messages a day. New decrypts often enabled him to make new connections and after as many gaps as possible had been filled in, the cryptanalysts' work sheets had to be collated. Donald M. Showers, who had joined the Hypo team as an ensign in February 1942, stayed with the unit until January of 1945 when I took him to Cincpac advance headquarters in Guam as my assistant. He eventually became a rear admiral and a chief of staff of the Defense Intelligence Agency.

"When we read a partially decrypted message we would always try to mentally fill in the blanks with the help of our accumulation of similar examples. Often the meaning of an unknown code group would then materialize."[19] Showers recalled the work he did as an assistant to Holmes. "We typed the translated decrypts onto a five-by-eight card, the entire message: call signs, date-time groups, frequency of transmission when known, and then the text," Showers recalled. "We underlined everything that was meaningful. Then we used a multilith duplicator to make twenty or thirty copies of each, depending on the number of underlined items. The cards were then placed in racks of open boxes in date sequence with a special set for each underlined item, such as all abbreviations and designators. When one of the cryptanalysts recalled some earlier decrypt, I would break out a stack of cards for the day in question and search through them by the underlinings. Each of our recoveries was valued from A to D, according to reliability."[20]

Much was to be written after the war about Rochefort's eccentric dress, because he wore a battered smoking jacket and slippers to combat the frigidity of the temperamental air-conditioning system. The pressure of work was so great during the first six months of the war that Joe went into Honolulu only twice. And during the critical weeks of May he virtually lived in the Hypo office. He had a cot installed so that he could be on call around the clock. The other members of the team also put in long hours, fighting mental and physical fatigue with Benzedrine tablets that were passed around like jellybeans.

Slowly but surely, the enormous effort inspired by Rochefort began to pay off. On 21 May, Hypo decrypted an order for a *maru* transport to load munitions and supplies for the Occupation Force and Striking Force and "June 2nd (or 3rd) depart Kurē for Truk." This bracketed the possible dates for the Midway invasion, because it was an indication that the second phase of Yamamoto's campaign "starts from Truk about 15 June."[21]

In best crossword puzzle tradition, some of the clues were misleading. A partial translation of a 21 May message listed "small craft which are to proceed to Truk by unknown date." Hypo cryptanalysts failed to break out the superencipherment dates, so it was forwarded to Washington with the comment that the 34839 group was "the date the forthcoming campaign gets under way." Negat replied that additives made this 15 June. Rochefort then realized that the message referred to the planned movement *after* Midway had been captured. But Washington seized on it as further proof that Japan's campaign would not begin until 15 June![22]

Mid-June did not, however, square with Hypo's intercept of orders to an oiler, previously identified as being part of the Japanese carrier striking force, which was to carry out refueling on 30 May.[23] Nor did it fit a Belconnen decrypt of a revision in the instructions transmitted to the submarine force commander at Kwajalein that his patrol "prior to _____ will be 150 miles more or less to the westward of AI."[29] We knew that AI was the designator for the Hawaiian Islands, so this clearly referred to the line of submarines that were intended to give warning of our forces heading out from Pearl for Midway, and which were to be in place *before* the invasion was launched.

These and other decrypts were read in conjunction with more signals that detailed the time and place of the prebattle conference, like the one to be held on board flagship *Akagi* "at 0830 26 May, regarding air operations of Striking Force."[25] Another confirmation that the Midway occupation was set for 2 or 3 June came from a signal summoning the Aleutians task force for a 26 May conference, from which Rochefort concluded from fragments, "date departure Ominato commencement of operations is 27th at the earliest."[26]

While the Hypo team were laboring through the decrypts to fit together the precise time sequence of the complex Japanese operation, Nimitz was pressing me for information. I sensed from his controlled impatience that he was weighing the magnitude of the risk that he was willing to run against the pressure from King to accept the mid-June date for the Japanese operation. But I knew that he had faith in us and that he would probably back Rochefort's estimate against the conflicting information that he was receiving from Washington. Joe and I were acutely aware we had to be certain of the date of Japan's N-day. We used the secure line to discuss every new clue forty or more times a day.

When Nimitz called his staff together on 26 May, on the eve of Halsey's return to Pearl, I could still not name the day with absolute certainty. My best calculation was that one attacking force would depart for the Aleutians from Ominato in northern Japan on 25 or 26 May, and that the Midway invasion force would sail from the Saipan area a day or so later. If my assumptions were correct, this meant that our forces would have to be in position in the Alaskan sector by 1 June, and off Midway by 3 June at the very latest.

Reviewing the options open to him, Nimitz was under no illusions. As he put it: "Common sense dictates that we cannot now afford to slug it out with the probably superior approaching Japanese forces." He reminded his staff of King's directive "to employ strong attrition tactics and not allow our forces to accept such decisive action as would be likely to incur heavy losses in our carriers and cruisers."[27] On the assumption that *Yorktown* could be repaired and turned around in four days—and that was a capital "IF" until the carrier had been dry-docked—Nimitz hoped to be able to get three task forces to the waters off Midway by "about 1 June." Carrier *Saratoga* was not scheduled to leave San Diego until 5 June and so "could be in the critical area of the Central Pacific only if the Japanese are considerably later than now expected." Every plane that could be spared was being rushed to reinforce Midway. A northern Pacific force of heavy cruisers was being formed of "all the forces which can reach Alaskan waters during the first week in June." Our submarines would concentrate in the waters off Midway with orders to attack "with regard to assigned sectors."[28]

Attrition tactics, however, required detailed knowledge of "enemy intentions." So Nimitz announced that he was counting on our "ability to detect changes in enemy intentions." Everything had to be done to preserve our tactical advantage: "Extreme care will be used to prevent the enemy from gaining information of our deployment by radio or otherwise."[29] It was essential that the Japanese believe that Task Force 17's two carriers were still in the southwest Pacific, and he had already alerted them, "Do not break radio silence to report position." Their pilots were instructed not to use their radios at any time, even when coming in to land.[30] Halsey and Fletcher had been informed that a search plane would be sent out to meet them with harbor entry instructions.[31]

"More information of the enemy is expected," Nimitz told his staff, and that his operations plan would be issued "prior to the departure of major forces."[32] With the sailing of the Japanese invasion force less than two days away, it had already been drafted on the assumption that his own intelligence staff had correctly estimated the date when the enemy would commence operations. Nimitz reasoned that this was the most prudent course of action. If Washington was right and the Japanese did not invade Midway until two weeks later, our only loss would be fuel. Waiting, however, could lead to disaster. And Nimitz had no desire to suffer the fate of Admiral Kimmel, who had been made a scapegoat for the miscalculations of the navy department in Washington.

Nimitz was too much of a realist not to take very serious account that the Japanese might be deceiving us. He questioned me closely about the possibility after receiving a personal warning the previous day from the Hawaiian Army commander. General Delos C. Emmons had evidently been alerted to naval intelligence's concerns by Admiral King.

"Japs may be practicing deception with radio orders intercepted by us," Emmons had cautioned Nimitz. "Estimates should be directed at capabilities rather than probable intentions. Forces reported in Cominch dispatch 21st have sufficient strength to make damaging raid on Oahu with view to wrecking facilities Pearl Harbor and Honolulu."[33]

Although Emmons was principally alarmed at losing control of his B-17, long-range bombers that Nimitz was urging be sent to help defend Midway, it was galling that Washington had backhandedly enlisted the army's support to try to turn Nimitz against Hypo. Apparently they shared Marshall's uneasiness that "one Japanese unit gave Midway as its post office address, and that seemed a little bit too thick."[34]

"If it sounds too good to be true, it probably is." This old saying may have been one of the factors that caused the naval staff in Washington to continue in its attempts to cast doubts on Hypo's analysis of both the timing and the objective of the impending enemy operation. "While all available information indicates that attack and occupation of Midway is the objective of the force assembled at Saipan," the Cominch intelligence summary of 24 May stated, "attention is invited to the fact that from this base a force can move with almost equal facility southward in the direction of Australia."[35]

This astonishing volte-face by Washington defied the logic of their own analysis. That very day a Hypo decrypt referring to the transport of American weapons that had been captured on Wake in a *maru* that would depart from the atoll "on N-3 day for Midway"[36] was connected to an earlier message arranging to have the captured "terror guns" sent by tender "on 4 June to be transported to AF."[37] The OP-20-G analysts had therefore made the logical deduction that if these guns were the same ones, then "N-3 days is at the earliest June 4th."[38] Yet, the very same day, Captain McCollum was advising Admiral King and the president's map room that "the forces involved in the attack are still scattered and not ready to move."[39]

The inability of naval communications and naval intelligence to adjust their preconceptions to factual information had proved fatal before the Pearl Harbor attack. The same clouded evaluations were again being made in Washington. Fortunately for the navy, the Pacific Fleet was not going to be trapped a second time by such wooden thinking and complacency. That Monday, Rochefort called me with a partially decrypted message referring to "Occupation Force Operational Order No. 4." It directed a unit to "depart Kuré on N-5," on a date that was given in the code group 74448, in order to "join main body of occupation force."[40] It was hardly necessary for Rochefort to advise Negat "this date important," because it was self-evident that adding five days would give the date of the Midway invasion.

The battle with Washington over Midway, and their insistence that the Japanese had delayed their operation until mid-June, persuaded Rochefort that Hypo must make an all-out effort to break the recalcitrant Japanese date-time groups—with or without Negat's help. Their objective was to break through to discover the key to unlock the superenciplerment of the date-time information which had been preencoded before the message was put into the JN-25B cipher. The Hypo staff searched back through their memories and the stacks of printouts and punch cards for similar five-digit number sequences. They found that all possible ones were only of C and D grades, not the most reliable. But at least they now had a starting point. Next they had to unravel the cipher itself. It was Lieutenant Joseph Finnegan, a linguist-cryptanalyst, who finally hit upon the method that the Japanese had used to lock up their date-time groups.

It was a neat, simple substitution cipher, with garble check, involving a 12 × 31 (12 rows for months, 31 columns for days) garble table. The 31 kana of the first row were A, I, U, E, O, KA, KI . . . . HA, HI, FU, HE, HO. The second row was I, U, E, O, ... HE, HO, A; the third, U, E, O . . . . . . HO, A, I, and so on, for 12 rows. At the left, representing the 12 months, was a column of 12 kana, different from those in the table—SA, SI, SU, SE, SO, TA, TI, TU, TE, TO, NA, NI (SA for January, NI for December). To encipher, for example, 27 May, one picked the 5th line (May=SO), ran across to the twenty-seventh column, HA, and recorded the kana at that intersection, HO. The encipherment, then, was SO HA HO, the third kana providing the garble check.[41]

This simple table allowed Rochefort to break out the dates from a Combined Fleet intercept of 26 May that contained the orders for two groups of destroyers escorting the invasion transports to Midway. This signal really clinched the pivotal date of the operation, because they were to leave Saipan on 28 May and proceed at eleven knots for a 1 June rendezvous at an indecipherable location, then "at 1900 6 June arrive at AF."[42] This meant that the actual attack would occur a day earlier at least. There could no longer be any doubt that N-day was to be either 4 or 5 June.

Joe kept me posted by telephone on the progress the Hypo team made throughout 26 May. I informed Nimitz, who needed the information for the staff conference he had called for the next day as a final review of what he called "the Midway problem." At this time it was originally intended that I should brief Admiral Halsey. But the previous day Nimitz had received a shock for which he was unprepared.

When Task Force 16 had docked, the commander we were counting on to lead our outnumbered forces in the most critical action of the war reported to headquarters. He was worn, haggard, and ready only for a hospital bed. Unknown to us, Halsey had been suffering for weeks from a progressive skin irritation that was to be diagnosed as dermatitis. He vigorously protested when Nimitz ordered him to the base medical facility. Halsey called it "the most grievous disappointment of my career." But he insisted that the man to take his place on *Enterprise*'s flag bridge was his cruiser commander, Rear Admiral Raymond A. Spruance.

Nimitz did not demur. Spruance's intellectual capacity and readiness to take advice were qualities that had already marked him out for a place at Cincpac headquarters. Although he had no experience as a carrier tactician, the cruiser admiral was familiar with Halsey's staff, and he had the quickness of mind essential for a task force commander. His lack of seniority, however, would require him to defer to Admiral Fletcher if *Yorktown* could be repaired in time to join the action. Meanwhile, Nimitz counted on Spruance's proven ability as an administrator to dispel friction between the two commands.

Any apprehension on Nimitz's part about Spruance not being the right choice was dispelled by the rapidity with which he set about briefing himself for the next day's staff discussion. General Emmons had also been invited to attend so as to calm the army's fears that our carriers were not chasing a wild goose to Midway. Also attending was General Robert C. Richardson, who had been sent out to Hawaii by Marshall. The conference, therefore, was an occasion at which Nimitz wanted to present the whole intelligence picture. It was one of the rare occasions when he summoned Rochefort to attend.

Joe naturally wanted to be as certain as he could of the accuracy of the information on which the Pacific Fleet would be sent out to do battle. He was fully aware that the Pacific war might be lost on a miscalculated code break. So when the staff assembled at the appointed hour and Rochefort had not appeared, I checked my watch and wondered what had happened to him.

Joe finally turned up half an hour late, looking disheveled and bleary-eyed from lack of sleep. Well aware that he had kept the commander in chief waiting, he could not escape the icy gaze that greeted his brief apology. He explained that he had been reviewing all the intelligence details that we had assembled on the Midway invasion and he handed Nimitz the information about the escort forces, with a brief comment about its significance.

"The atmosphere was very impersonal," Rochefort would later remember.

> Admiral Nimitz asked me a question, and I would look over there and see four stars. I would answer that to the best of my ability I was sure of my facts, but stressed that they were only deductions. I could not have blamed him if he had not accepted my estimates. I think, looking back, that it was obvious when Nimitz sent for me that he had already decided on his course of action. His operational orders were set and the matter closed. My appearance at this final staff meeting was to ensure that everyone was thinking alike.[43]

In a sense, Rochefort was correct. Nimitz had decided to put his own staff intelligence above the conflicting estimates being made in Washington. On the previous day I had spent many hours at the Cincpac plot, calculating and tracing the possible elements of the Japanese strategy as they were revealed by traffic analysis and the decrypts.

The latest Hypo information had enabled me to make a more precise estimate of the distance-time factors by applying the rule that when you don't know things, you had to try to see them as if you were a Jap. Working backward from the sailing dates, and the decrypted orders for the 6 June arrival of the invasion force transports, I reconstructed a tentative plot that was accurate enough to predict when and where the transports carrying the assault troops should be sighted by search planes from Midway.

This was relatively simple to calculate, because transports had to take a pretty direct route from Guam. When it came to the carrier striking force, which would set out from Saipan, I could not be so certain. They had the speed to make the kind of detour they had made to reach Oahu undetected. I estimated that they would probably do so again, but one thing was certain, they would have to be within air-strike distance of Midway on 3 or 4 June to carry out the scheduled softening-up raids set for N minus 2.

This was when Nimitz asked me for the all-important information: Name the dates and dispositions the enemy intends to take up around Midway. I told him that it was still very difficult for me to be specific.

"I want you to be specific," Nimitz said, fixing me with his cool blue eyes. "After all, this is the job I have given you—to be the admiral commanding the Japanese forces, and tell me what is going on."

It was a tall order, given that so much was speculation rather than hard fact. I knew that I would have to stick my neck out, but that was clearly what he wanted. Summarizing all my data, I told Nimitz that the carriers would probably attack on the morning of 4 June, from the northwest on a bearing of 325 degrees. They could be sighted at about 175 miles from Midway at around 0700 local time.

On the strength of this estimate Admiral Nimitz crossed his Rubicon on 27 May 1942. At the staff conference, which set the seal on our Midway defense plan, he gave the impression of being thoroughly confident that the Japanese would appear when and where I had predicted. But the next seven nights were sleepless ones for me. I knew very well the extent to which Nimitz had staked the fate of the Pacific Fleet on our estimates, and his own judgment, against those of Admiral King and his staff in Washington.

32

"A Glorious Page in Our History"

I T WOULD BE a week and a half before Nimitz received proof that the intelligence estimates on which he had staked the fate of the Pacific Fleet were correct. Those days seemed more like years to the staff. Rochefort, however, was relaxed and confident.

"If we get ready for this attack on June 3 and it does not come off, we may look silly," Joe was saying, "but there will be time for our ships to refuel and get back on station. If we are not prepared and the Japs strike, it will be a case of Pearl Harbor all over again—and the Navy will have no excuse."[1]

Nimitz was also quietly confident. After the crucial staff conference on 27 May, at which the plans for Midway had been approved, he visited carrier *Enterprise* and told one of the three pilots he decorated with the Distinguished Flying Cross, "I think you'll have a chance to win yourself another medal in the next few days."[2]

A few hours later *Yorktown* limped into Pearl, trailing a ten-mile-long oil slick from her leaking tanks. Tugs nudged the carrier through the open caisson gates of the flooded number 1 dry dock and powerful pumps roared into action. The last of the water was still being drained late that Wednesday afternoon when Nimitz donned waders to lead an inspection party of shipwrights and engineers under the dripping hull. After seeing for himself where the carrier's plates had been sprung by the near misses of Japanese bombs, he ordered the minimum repairs necessary to make her seaworthy. A giant steel patch was to be welded to the hull; weakened internal bulkheads were to be shored up with timber. Time did not permit anything fancier. All that mattered was that *Yorktown* be made ready for battle in the shortest possible time.

"We must have the ship back in three days," Nimitz told his engineers.[3] Within an hour the cranes were swinging the steel plates into position. As darkness fell, fifteen hundred dockyard workers were as-

sembled from less-urgent tasks and lights were rigged for work to continue through the night in spite of the blackout.

When Nimitz returned to headquarters, he found Fletcher waiting in
his office. He was prepared to make a preliminary oral report on the
Coral Sea action. Reluctantly, Nimitz informed him that he needed to
submit a detailed analysis by the next day to answer Admiral King's criticism of Task Force 17's tardy refueling and failure to conduct its operations with sufficient aggression. Admiral Spruance joined them briefly;
then he and Fletcher got down to the afternoon's most important business. The conference included the task force's operational and intelligence staffs and Nimitz's own staff. It continued into the evening as we
hammered out the final details of the battle plan.

"In carrying out the tasks assigned in OP Plan 29-42, you will be
governed by the principle of calculated risk," read the ten-page-long Midway operational orders. Fletcher and Spruance's objective would be to
"inflict maximum damage on the enemy by employing strong attrition
tactics."[4] Our blueprint for the forthcoming action spelled out the estimated disposition of the Japanese. This included the mustering of their
carrier striking force northwest of Midway for preliminary raids during
the approach of their invasion force, while a diversionary attack was to be
made on the Aleutians. Since not all of those attending had comint clearance, security considerations prevented me from revealing to the conference how we could be so certain of the enemy plans other than by stating
that my confidence derived from information I had obtained from a "very
reliable source."

"That man of ours in Tokyo is worth every cent we pay him,"
Enterprise's navigating officer, Commander Richard Ruble, commented.[5]
Like many of the other officers who were briefed on our plan, he assumed that our detailed knowledge of the enemy intentions must have
come from espionage. I could only hope that our intelligence would not
betray their confidence, because the following morning both Rochefort
and I would have dearly loved it if we had our mythical man in Tokyo.
During the night the Japanese put a new version of their naval code system into action, effectively blacking out our ability to detect last-minute
changes in the enemy's battle plan.

Although we had been anticipating this revision in the JN-25 naval
operational code (it had been postponed twice), the change from the B
version of the cipher to the C version was a body blow. It meant that
eighteen months of hard work had to be abandoned overnight, and the
grueling labor of assembling additive groups had to begin all over again.
It was some consolation to know that the blackout would have been even
more disastrous had it occurred a few days earlier, for in the week prior
to the forthcoming battle we decrypted only four enemy signals and none
of these pertained to the Midway operation.

As the navy's top secret 1942 evaluation of our radio intelligence put it, in a report that remained classified for forty years: "It was all over but the shooting!"[6] We had certainly done our best. But we still had to wait and hope that our best was good enough for the sailors and airmen on whom everything now depended.

Even if we could no longer eavesdrop directly on the Japanese moves, we could fool Admiral Yamamoto into believing that our carriers were still in the South Pacific. So as Task Force 16 slipped out of Pearl Harbor on 28 May, and Spruance set course for the aptly named Point Luck some 350 miles northeast of Midway, we began an elaborate radio deception to disguise our own movements. At Efate, 1,500 miles to the southwest in the New Hebrides, seaplane tender *Tangier* pretended to be a full-fledged carrier making transmissions in a pattern similar to that of a task force flying routine air operations. The same ploy was used by heavy cruiser *Salt Lake City* on patrol in the Coral Sea. The idea was to persuade Japanese traffic analysts at the Owada intelligence center outside Tokyo that Halsey's two carriers were more than 1,000 miles away from Midway.[7]

The major units of the Japanese Combined Fleet began their eastward sorties the same day. First to sail was Admiral Nagumo's Striking Force, the *Kido Butai*. This time it was composed of Carrier Divisions 1 and 2, plus two battleships escorted by two heavy cruisers and a dozen destroyers, and accompanied by five oilers. Also, the main force of three battlewagons, a light carrier, two seaplane carriers, and nine destroyers left tranquil Hashirajima anchorage through the Bungo Strait. Our radio intelligence had not revealed this latter and vital part of Yamamoto's operation. Nor did we know that it would be led by the commander in chief himself in superbattleship *Yamato*.

According to the elaborate choreography of Yamamoto's plan, twelve *maru* transports, carrying the five-thousand-strong Midway occupation force, departed from Saipan the next morning. They were escorted by a light cruiser and ten destroyers. Also setting sail from nearby Guam were the two battleships, four heavy cruisers, one light cruiser, and seven destroyers of the Midway covering force, together with the four heavy cruisers and two destroyers of the support force.

As for the attack on the Aleutians, that striking force of two light cruisers, two heavy cruisers, two seaplane tenders, and four destroyers was already plowing its way across the northern Pacific when the eight transports carrying the Kiska and Attu invasion force sailed from Ominato in northern Japan on 29 May. Their close escort of two cruisers and six destroyers was to rendezvous with another cruiser squadron off the Kurile Islands.

By 30 May, 145 Japanese warships were at sea. Their boilers were devouring more fuel than the imperial navy had consumed during the previous year. The tiny patch of Pacific coral sand whose two thousand acres was the object for their invasion represented less dry land than the total deck area of the Japanese ships involved in the operation.

The thirty-five surface ships that Nimitz had mustered to oppose this armada were insignificant by comparison. Spruance's Task Force 16 included only five heavy cruisers, one light cruiser, and nine destroyers with carriers *Enterprise* and *Hornet*. That Saturday morning Fletcher sailed from Pearl to rendezvous with Spruance at Point Luck with *Yorktown* and the two heavy cruisers and six destroyers of Task Force 17.

A few hours later, Rear Admiral Robert A. Theobald headed north from Pearl in command of two heavy cruisers, three light cruisers, and four destroyers. Theobald had been briefed that our "reliable sources" indicated the enemy intended to capture Kiska and Attu and raid Dutch Harbor. But without telling us, he decided to ignore our intelligence estimate. He believed it was an enemy ruse. Instead he decided to follow his own hunch that the Japanese intended to attack Alaska. Accordingly he headed out to ambush them four hundred miles south of Kodiak Island. This blunder put Theobald's force a thousand miles east of the position we had anticipated for him. As a result, his force was helpless to intervene when the Japanese attacked three days later exactly where and when we had predicted.[8]

Fortunately, Fletcher and Spruance did not duplicate Theobald's total disregard of intelligence. If they had, Nimitz's strategy would have been in ruins. As it was, shortly after midday, 31 May, we sent out to all task force commanders our updated "Estimate of Midway Force Organization." This listed *Akagi, Kaga, Hiryu,* and *Soryu* as the four Japanese carriers in the striking force. We predicted they would be accompanied by two battleships, four heavy cruisers, and twelve destroyers. The support force would include one carrier, two battleships, four heavy cruisers, two light cruisers, and ten destroyers. We were less certain about the number and type of escorts for the four *maru* transports of the occupation force, but we predicted that at least fourteen enemy submarines would be on patrol off Midway.

Our final estimate omitted entirely Yamamoto's main force that was bringing up the rear. Therefore, it did not appear on the large-scale maps on which we laid out the courses of the opposing forces converging on Midway. At that time the Cincpac operation plotting room was a rather primitive affair that consisted of a large chart of the Pacific laid over plywood across a pair of sawhorses.[9] On top of the chart was tracing paper on which plotting officers laid down the movements of our ships in blue crayon, with the estimated tracks of the Japanese forces in orange. Every midnight we replaced the overlays with fresh ones, incorporating the latest intelligence data and predictions.

Apart from our serious omission of Yamamoto's main force, another bit of data that did not find its way onto the Midway plot was the presence of John Ford and his film crew on the atoll. At the time the Hollywood director was at Pearl Harbor on attachment as a lieutenant commander in the navy, and it seemed to me a good idea to get some morale-boosting footage of the upcoming action. I called Ford into my office and, without disclosing any details, asked if he was interested in a trip "somewhere in the Pacific" that might produce some interesting shots.

"Can you guarantee action?" Ford asked.

"As near as I can guarantee anything," I told him. Ford agreed and I went to see Nimitz. He approved the plan and asked me to have Ford and his cameraman flown out to Midway. He insisted on absolute secrecy, so I called Ford into my office after putting everyone else out.

"Where you are going, you won't know till you get there, and you won't be able to send any messages," I told him. "It's so secret and the United States is right on the line. If you want this assignment we'll put you on an airplane and fly you there this afternoon."

"You wouldn't kid me," Ford said.

I assured him I would not. He promised me honorary membership in the Hollywood drinking club he had formed with John Wayne, so I swore on my nomination that what I was telling him about a major battle was true. "It's a chance for a scoop that no one else is going to have and it may even get you an Oscar." He was finally convinced. By 1500 he and his cameraman reported to Kaneohe air station where two PBYs were waiting to take them to Midway.

When Ford returned two weeks later with his remarkable shots of Midway under attack, he thanked me. After the war he gave me a bit part in a movie called *Big Jim McClean*. Still, the fact remains that had it not been for three critical blunders by the Japanese during the last forty-eight hours of May, Ford might have become a prisoner of war. His film footage would then have ended up in a Japanese victory documentary celebrating their capture of the island "Minazuki"—the classical Japanese name for the month of June—the mailing address that they had overconfidently assigned to the Midway occupation force. (The characters for it translate "no water month," an interesting coincidence of our "AF" ruse.)

The first setback to Yamamoto's Midway campaign came with the cancellation of the 30 May reconnaissance flight over Pearl Harbor. This occurred when the submarines detailed to refuel the "K" operation seaplanes arrived off the French Frigate Shoals and found one of our patrol boats anchored in the lagoon. The next error was a two-day delay in getting all their submarines on station west of the Hawaiian Islands, which allowed our two task forces to slip by undetected. The third lapse was Yamamoto's decision not to break radio silence to ensure that Admiral Nagumo had picked up signals indicating that an American carrier task force might be in Hawaiian waters.

Three hundred miles ahead of the main force, the four carriers of the

Kido Butai continued steaming toward Midway ignorant of the possibility that the Americans might be within striking distance. *Akagi*'s radio operators had failed to pick up the suspicious radio transmissions that had alerted Yamamoto's communications officer, and Nagumo relied on the reassuring reports that were relayed from Tokyo reporting that the only two American carriers afloat were a thousand miles away in the South Pacific. It had apparently not occurred to the Japanese intelligence analyst that *Yorktown* might not only have survived the trip back from the Coral Sea, but that it would be possible for us to get her back into action in any less time than the three months needed to repair the damaged *Shokaku*.

The Japanese were completely taken in by our radio deception scheme. We, however, were not fooled by their elaborate efforts to divert our attention. They materialized on 1 June with reports of midget-submarine attacks on a British battleship at Madagascar, and the torpedoing of a ferryboat in Sydney Harbor. Although we had not picked up any advance warning of these diversions, they failed to arouse Washington's fears that Japan might be preparing to invade Australia.

We knew too much about Yamamoto's operation to be taken in on 3 June, when an urgent dispatch was received just after 0800 that Wednesday, informing us that Japanese carrier planes had just bombed Dutch Harbor on Unalaska Island off the western tip of Alaska. The message that really galvanized Pacific Fleet headquarters had come in a hour earlier. It was the electrifying sighting report of a Midway-based PBY reconnaissance plane: "Main Body . . . bearing 262, distance 700 miles. . . . Eleven ships, course 090, speed 19 knots."[10]

I happened to be in Nimitz's office when this message came in. His eyes lit up like searchlights.

"Layton," he said excitedly, "have you seen this?"

"What is it, sir?"

"The sighting of the Japanese forces," Nimitz replied, giving me a dazzling smile. "It ought to make your heart warm."

The admiral was positively beaming as he waved the PBY dispatch reporting the invasion force west of Midway. The Japanese were exactly where we had put them on our plot. "This will clear up the doubters now," Nimitz declared. "They just have to see this to know that what I told them is correct."

To avoid any chance that Fletcher and Spruance would be confused, Nimitz immediately sent them an urgent dispatch: "Main body . . . that is not, repeat not, the enemy striking force."[11]

The invasion force was attacked that afternoon from ten thousand feet by nineteen army B-17s flown from Midway. The unpracticed bombardiers failed to score a single hit, despite enthusiastic claims that they had sunk several "*Normandie*-type" transports. Later that evening, Navy PBY pilots swooped down on the convoy to make a low-level torpedo attack and managed to damage an oiler. But they failed to halt the convoy's eastward march toward Midway.

Admiral Yamamoto was apparently unconcerned about the reports of the two bombing attacks. According to the calculations made by his staff, our discovery of the intention to invade Midway would hasten any possible sortie from Pearl Harbor by only a few noncritical hours.

Confidence was building, too, at Pacific Fleet headquarters that evening. Nimitz flashed out an encouraging dispatch to the task force commanders. "The situation is developing as expected. Carriers, our most important objective, should soon be located. Tomorrow may be the day you can give them the works." That day's entry in the Cincpac Command Summary concluded with the prophetic words: "The whole course of the war in the Pacific may hinge on the developments of the next two or three days."[12]

That night our armed forces were on maximum alert on the west coast and in the Hawaiian Islands. California's radio stations closed down early to prevent enemy bombers from homing in on their transmitters. Standing out to sea from Seattle to San Diego, a long line of requisitioned motor yachts and fishing boats, manned by naval reservists, patrolled the dark waters to give early warning of any Japanese attempt to raid the mainland.

The defenders of Midway had no doubt that they were the objective of enemy forces bearing down on them. As the first gray streaks of light over the eastern horizon signaled the dawn of 4 June, the atoll was at the point of an invisible four-hundred-mile-long V, with the opposing fleets closing on each other as they advanced down its sides. Nagumo's carriers were off to the northwest. Our own task forces were four hundred miles away to the northeast. Unknown to the Japanese, the distance between them and three hostile carriers was steadily decreasing as the pilots, bombardiers, and navigators of both sides breakfasted, were briefed and clambered into their cockpits.

The opposing aircrews, awaiting signals to take off, had very different targets in mind. Shortly after dawn, the Japanese planes began taking off to raid Midway. They had been armed with high-explosive bombs. At their briefings the pilots of their seventy-six bombers and thirty-six escorting fighters had been reassured by the latest Tokyo intelligence estimate: "There is no evidence of an enemy task force in our vicinity."[13] Nagumo nonetheless prudently retained thirty-six Zeros to fly combat air patrol over his four carriers. He made the mistake, however, of not ordering out all of his ten floatplanes for a dawn reconnaissance. Only four were catapulted off the heavy cruisers, and fate decreed that the launch of the scout assigned to patrol the eastern sector was delayed a critical half hour by a faulty catapult.

Meanwhile, Fletcher's scouts flew off to the west at dawn, across the V, to concentrate their search for the Japanese in an area two hundred miles northwest of Midway whence Cincpac operation orders had predicted that the enemy carriers would be making their run in to Midway. The same patch of Pacific was also being scoured by PBY patrols from the atoll's airstrip, and it was one of the Catalinas that first sighted enemy planes flying south. Then, at 0545 local time, Lieutenant Howard Ady nosed his PBY through a cloud bank and saw "the curtain rise on the Biggest Show on Earth."[14]

"ENEMY CARRIERS" was all that Ady managed to get off before taking evasive action to avoid being jumped by a pair of Japanese fighters. Once inside the safety of some clouds, he completed the report that we had all been waiting for: "PLANE REPORTS TWO CARRIERS, TWO BATTLESHIPS, BEARING 320 DEGREES, DISTANT 180 MILES, COURSE 135 DEGREES, SPEED 25 KNOTS."[15]

It was shortly after 0600 at Pearl when we went to the Operations Room. The position of the enemy carrier force, which I was certain numbered at least four, was marked on the plot 180 miles northwest of Midway.

"Well, you were only five minutes, five degrees, and five miles out," Nimitz remarked to me with a smile.

The position of the striking force, and the report of enemy planes heading toward Midway, made it obvious that Nagumo must still be unaware that our carriers were in the vicinity. Otherwise, he would not have been holding steady to his course down the west leg of the V toward Midway. While Fletcher and Spruance might still be too far away to launch an air strike, we were confident that after receiving the PBY report they would be steaming hard to close the range.

We assumed that every land-based plane on Midway had been scrambled and was either preparing to beat off the raid or heading northwest to attack the Japanese carriers. Our task forces had been instructed to maintain radio silence to ensure that their ambush achieved the maximum element of surprise, so Nimitz relayed the latest reports out to them, the implication being that they were to launch a strike as soon as practical. Although he retained operational command, Nimitz had announced that he would not interfere with the conduct of the action unless he felt that the task force commanders were being led astray.

"AIR RAID MIDWAY" came by submarine cable from the garrison commander at 0625. While this informed us that the Japanese attack had begun, we were to learn nothing more until 0830 when Midway reported, "ONLY 3 FIGHTING PLANES REMAIN. NO CONTACT DIVE BOMBING PLANES."[16] Another two hours went by before the exaggerated reports of the returning Midway pilots were relayed to us. Based on their past performance, we were very skeptical of their claims to have hit several carriers, leaving one of them ablaze. Unfortunately, we could believe that the Japanese Zeros had taken a heavy toll of our planes, including all but one of the marines' slow torpedo bombers.

Still no word came from Fletcher and Spruance. This was a good sign, because we assumed that it meant that the enemy had yet to spot them. But this assumption did not reduce the tension. Nimitz had retreated to his office and I followed his example. There I could use my private telephone line to keep in touch with Rochefort. Hypo's main source of news came from the Japanese as its radio operators monitored the progress of the Japanese end of the battle, picking up the voice and Morse circuits being used by Nagumo's pilots.

Thanks to their reports I was able to tell Nimitz just after 0800 that a Japanese carrier scout plane had been heard radioing that it had spotted "TEN SURFACE SHIPS" 240 miles northeast of Midway heading south at twenty knots.[17] He took the message out to the plot to see whether it coincided with our estimated position for the task forces. When it agreed, he wanted to know if the pilot had sighted our carriers yet. I checked with Rochefort. Not yet. I was able to confirm that they were still undetected. But eleven minutes later Rochefort called me with the news that the Japanese plane had just made the signal, "Enemy is accompanied by what appears to be a carrier bringing up the rear."[18]

It was both bad and good news. Nagumo now knew about *Yorktown*, but he was still unaware of Spruance's two carriers. As we studied the operations plot, it was clear to us that the outcome of the impending clash depended on the urgent decision that was even then being made by Admiral Nagumo. The discovery of our carrier put him in a dilemma. Either he launched his remaining planes against this contact, or he waited until his planes returning from the Midway strike had been recovered to send off a full attack. Either way, a golden opportunity had opened up for Spruance and Fletcher to strike the first blow and catch the enemy carriers with their flight decks crowded with refueling aircraft.

We could only wait. But we need not have worried. As Nimitz predicted, Spruance had reacted to the news of the Midway raid by seizing the chance that fate handed him. Calculating that the enemy was just within reach of the two-hundred-mile range of his aircraft, he advanced by two hours the launch of his first strike.

Spruance had decided to risk his torpedo planes, which had a combat radius of only 175 miles and might not have enough gas to get back to the carriers. But Midway was an alternative landing site. Only thirty-six fighters were held back for combat air patrol when the strike headed off to the southwest just after 0730 local time. Spruance's caution was soon justified. Task Force 16's sixty-seven Dauntless dive bombers and twenty-seven Devastator torpedo bombers, escorted by twenty-seven Wildcats, were winging their way to their targets when a lone enemy floatplane appeared over the horizon. *Enterprise*'s radio intelligence unit reported that the pilot could be heard radioing the task force's position.

Admiral Fletcher, following sixteen miles astern of Task Force 16, now decided that the time had come to launch seventeen Dauntlesses, sixteen Devastators, and six Wildcats. The memory of his near fatal error at the Coral Sea persuaded him to retain half his planes in case another Japanese force appeared.

Our strike of 155 planes was therefore well on its way across the open arms of the V before Admiral Nagumo began wrestling with his tactical problem. The shocking news that American carriers were within striking range of the *Kido Butai* also coincided with the arrival of our land-based bombers from Midway. These were easily beaten off, but the carriers had to weave and dodge. Adding to the problems on the flag bridge were additional evasive measures adopted to counter the attack made by submarine *Nautilus*. Although her torpedoes also failed to find a target, Nagumo's tight defensive formations were disrupted as the debate about what to do continued.

On the *Akagi*'s hangar deck, a second strike against Midway had been prepared. The planes, armed with high-explosive, impact-fused bombs, were already starting to be arranged on deck. To rearm the aircraft with armor-piercing bombs and torpedoes would require an extensive delay, and so Nagumo reluctantly complied with the impatient request flashed to *Akagi* from the Carrier Division 2 commander: "CONSIDER IT ADVISABLE TO LAUNCH ATTACK FORCE IMMEDIATELY."[19]

Assuming that only a single American carrier was in the area, and assured by Commander Genda and his air staff that refueling could be completed in less than an hour, Nagumo finally decided to give priority to landing and refueling the planes that had attacked Midway rather than hitting the opposing naval force. This meant removing those aircraft already on the flight deck. More valuable minutes were lost as they were shuttled below and disarmed, while the returning aircraft began circling overhead for permission to land.

Nagumo and his staff knew that they had made a fatal miscalculation when, half an hour later, a scouting Zero radioed "TEN ENEMY TORPEDO PLANES HEADING TOWARD YOU."[20] The decks of their carriers were covered with planes, snaking gasoline hoses, and trolley loads of bombs and ammunition. Belowdecks lay rows of torpedoes and high-explosive bombs, which, in the frenzy of rearming the second strike, had not been returned to the protected magazines.

The Japanese air commanders urgently signaled "SPEED PREPARATIONS FOR IMMEDIATE TAKEOFF," as a fierce antiaircraft barrage opened up against the *Hornet*'s torpedo bombers.[21] The slow and ungainly Devastators, led by Lieutenant Commander John C. Waldron, made a courageous attempt at low-level runs although they lacked the cover of their fighters. "He went straight for the Japanese fleet as if he had a string tied to them," reported Ensign George Gay, who was the sole survivor of the attack as every one of the torpedo bombers fell victim to gunfire and the forty Zeros flying protective cover for the *Kido Butai*.[22] Following hard on the tails of Waldron's gallant band, Lieutenant Commander Eugene

E. Lindsey lost nine of *Enterprise*'s fourteen Devastators without scoring a single hit. And only two of *Yorktown*'s twelve torpedo bombers managed to make it back after fighting through a curtain of antiaircraft fire. Out of those slow-running torpedoes dropped by the American planes, none found a target.

The slaughter of the first wave of the American attack gave Nagumo and his staff temporary respite. At Pearl, where we calculated that the climax of the battle must be fast approaching, tension was running high. We had heard nothing. Admiral Nimitz was frantic; I mean as frantic as I have ever seen him. He appeared agitated and called for his communications officer, Commander Curts, to know why we were not getting any messages or hearing something. Although they must have known by now that they could break radio silence, it seemed that our task force commanders were neglecting to keep Nimitz informed of what was going on. Germany Curts, however, advised against requesting information that might distract Fletcher and Fitch at what might be a critical juncture of the action.

Not until 1008 did the communications center at Pacific Fleet headquarters report hearing *Enterprise*'s air officer yelling, "Attack! Attack immediately!"[23] This frenzied order, and the tantalizing reply to it, only added to our apprehension.

"Wilco, as soon as I can find the bastards!" Lieutenant Commander Clarence W. McClusky[24] radioed *Enterprise*. Like the other leaders, he was unaware that the enemy carriers had swung about onto a more northerly course to recover their first strike. *Hornet*'s thirty-five dive bombers were to hunt for their quarry fruitlessly for more than an hour before giving up to refuel at Midway. Fortunately, Clarence McClusky followed his nose north and discovered the Japanese destroyer which had dropped behind to depth-charge *Nautilus,* and was now hightailing it to the northwest to rejoin the strike force.

The fortune that had deserted our torpedo bombers that morning now smiled on the dive bombers. McClusky sighted the four enemy carriers after all their patrolling fighters had been drawn to deck height to prepare to chase off the last of *Yorktown*'s torpedo planes. Not even the high-performing Zeros could climb back up to ten thousand feet in time to disrupt *Enterprise*'s sixty-seven Dauntlesses. Picking the two largest carriers, they came hurtling down in a 70-degree dive, their bombsights locked on the red deck roundels of *Akagi* and *Kaga*.

"Hell divers!" was how Captain Fuchida recalled that awful moment when the attack alarms sounded. The man who had led the attack on Pearl Harbor, who had risen to watch flight operations from his berth in sick bay after undergoing an appendectomy, was now forced to crawl for cover. "The terrifying scream of the dive bombers reached me first, followed by a direct hit," Fuchida wrote. "I was horrified at the destruction that had been wrought in a matter of seconds. There was a huge hole in the flight deck just abaft the amidships elevator. The elevator itself, twisted like molten glass, was drooping into the hangar. Deck plates reeled upward in grotesque configurations. Planes stood tail up belching livid flames and jet-black smoke."[25]

The flight deck was turned into an inferno by detonating torpedoes and bombs. Within the hour, Nagumo was forced to take refuge from the blazing *Akagi* and transfer his staff to a destroyer. Off the flag carrier's starboard quarter, four direct hits made short work of *Kaga*. Then *Yorktown*'s dive bombers arrived to concentrate their attack on *Soryu*. Two of their bombs hurled the elevator against the bridge, setting parked planes ablaze, as a third detonated in the hangar. Later that afternoon the blazing carrier's fate was sealed by two torpedoes from *Nautilus*.

At the cost of forty-seven planes, we had wiped out, at a single blow, three quarters of the vaunted *Kido Butai*. All of *Yorktown*'s dive bombers escaped unscathed. McClusky's flight was not so lucky. Sixteen of his planes were shot down by the pursuing Zeros and others had to ditch when they ran out of fuel looking for *Enterprise*, which had not updated her position by radio to avoid homing in a Japanese attack.

At Pacific Fleet headquarters, however, we still had no definite news of how the battle was going. I was in constant touch with Rochefort. He was making every effort to try to break into an action report that appeared to have been sent from Admiral Nagumo. But he could get nothing solid, except for an important clue that the flagship's call sign had been shifted from *Akagi* to a cruiser. I hoped this meant that *Akagi* had been hit, but I cautioned Nimitz that we could not yet be certain.

Then Hypo reported picking up a plain-language order made to a Japanese plane: "Inform us of position of enemy carriers." Another plane radioed a sighting report, and an air group commander gave them a "STAND BY," followed shortly by "ATTACK! ATTACK! ATTACK!"[26] We did not know which of our task forces was being attacked, nor how many enemy carriers were still able to respond to Nagumo's desperate signal, "ATTACK ENEMY CARRIERS."[27]

Fortunately for us it turned out that Rear Admiral Tamon Yamaguchi of *Hiryu* was evidently under the impression that the earlier floatplane sighting represented the sum total of our task forces, because he sent only eighteen dive bombers and six fighters. Nor did he tell Nagumo how small a strike he had launched when he radioed confirmation that his planes had departed "for purpose of destroying enemy carrier."[28]

Yamamoto also believed that his operation was being opposed by a single carrier task force. After receiving the devastating report that Nagumo was retiring to the north leaving three of his carriers ablaze, he attempted to snatch a victory from the jaws of defeat. He began urgently summoning the carriers in the northern force back from the Aleutians. They were to join the Midway covering force while the main force raced in from the west. Too late, Yamamoto discovered the peril of ignoring

Mahan's dictum on the need to concentrate forces before a major battle. The overwhelmingly superior forces of the Combined Fleet, which might have proved decisive if they had been marshaled off Midway on that day, were scattered far and wide over the Pacific.

Yamamoto's hopes of winning a decisive surface engagement now depended entirely on *Hiryu*'s pilots. They found *Yorktown* around noon as she was recovering her dive bombers. Although Fletcher's position was now known to the enemy, he did not break radio silence until he received a reminder from Nimitz.

Only then did we learn that our task forces had successfully attacked two or three enemy carriers. But Fletcher reported, "NO INDICATION OF ADDITIONAL CARRIERS WHICH HAVE SIGHTED THIS FORCE."[29] Then twenty minutes after we had picked up the Japanese planes being vectored in by voice, Fletcher sent a further dispatch, "HAVE BEEN AT-TACKED BY AIR 150 MILES NORTH MIDWAY."[30]

Three direct hits were scored, but the precautionary flooding of the gasoline refueling lines with inert carbon dioxide averted the conflagration that had doomed the three Japanese carriers. One bomb detonated in the smokestack and put five of *Yorktown*'s six boilers temporarily out of commission. It also swept away all the communications aerials, and Fletcher was obliged to transfer his flag to cruiser *Astoria* and turn over tactical command of our task forces to Spruance.

Before 1400 that day, damage-control parties succeeded in dousing the flames, and *Yorktown*'s engine room staff nursed the carrier's speed up so that she could recover her remaining planes. The Japanese strike leader, however, had radioed that they had left *Yorktown* a blazing wreck.

This report led Yamaguchi to believe that his strike had evened the score. Now Yamamoto's main force had a fighting chance of victory. Then a lone scouting plane, which had suffered a radio failure, landed on *Hiryu* shortly after 1300 to report the presence of at least one more carrier. Only ten torpedo planes and six fighters were available until the first strike returned, but Yamaguchi decided the situation demanded that he immediately send them on to hunt for the second American carrier.

An hour later the leader of *Hiryu*'s second strike reported that he had sighted the target. What he did not realize was that they had spotted the supposedly sunk *Yorktown*. The attack went in and the Japanese pilots skillfully sent two torpedoes into her port side, jamming the rudder and ripping open her patched-up hull. The list increased so alarmingly that *Yorktown*'s captain decided, prematurely as it turned out, to abandon ship. A destroyer was ordered alongside to take off the crew.

From Fletcher's urgent message requesting that tugs be sent out from Pearl, we knew that *Yorktown* had become a salvage operation at best. But the crippled carrier's Dauntless scouts, which had been sent off an hour earlier, now located *Hiryu* 110 miles to the northwest. Their urgent sighting reports were what Spruance had been waiting for. At 1530 he ordered *Enterprise* around into the wind to launch another strike of twenty-four dive bombers, including ten of *Yorktown*'s Dauntlesses, which had taken refuge on the flagship of Task Force 16 when their own flattop was being bombed.

Even with no Wildcat fighters for escorts, Lieutenant W. Earl Gallagher, who lead the strike, was eager to chalk up a second enemy carrier after his earlier successful attack on *Kaga*. An hour and a half later, he was able to claim that distinction as his bombs tore into the bowels of *Hiryu*. Yamaguchi's flagship was soon transformed into a floating torch. She was to burn through the night, long after the diminutive admiral had ordered his crew to abandon ship as he remained on board his doomed command.

That was a fate that some of Yamamoto's staff felt would have been appropriate for Admiral Nagumo when he radioed he was "retiring" in the face of at least five enemy carriers that were advancing westward. Nagumo's action was in direct defiance of Yamamoto's rallying order: "THE ENEMY FLEET HAS BEEN PRACTICALLY DESTROYED AND IS RETIRING TO THE EASTWARD."[31] Chief of Staff Ugaki took this to mean that Nagumo "has no stomach for a night action." He was therefore relieved of his command after being ordered to reverse course and prepare his battleships and cruisers to "PARTICIPATE IN THE NIGHT ENGAGEMENT."[32]

The night action that Yamamoto so desperately sought never took place. A reconnaissance at dusk by B-17s based at Midway reported being attacked by the Zeros that were buzzing around the blazing *Hiryu*. Spruance interpreted this as meaning there might yet be another Japanese carrier in the vicinity. Lacking a clear picture of the forces still opposing him, he decided not to risk our victory by making a stern chase through the hours of darkness.

Spruance then radioed his battle report, claiming a fourth enemy carrier had been sunk as well as hits on an escorting battleship and a heavy cruiser. Following reports by his pilots, he also informed us: "THREE SHIPS BELIEVED CARRIERS PREVIOUSLY ATTACKED WERE OBSERVED TO SOUTHEASTWARD STILL BURNING." On the strength of this Nimitz prepared a dispatch to be radioed to all units and Admiral King: "You who have participated in the battle of Midway today have written a glorious page in our history. I am proud to be associated with you. I estimate that another day of all-out effort on your part will complete the defeat of the enemy."[33]

When this victory message was flashed out on the early evening of 4 June, Nimitz still believed that the day's actions were "the start of what may be the greatest sea battle since Jutland."[34] Such hopes proved to be premature, because we had not yet discovered the presence of Admiral Yamamoto's powerful surface force. Also, as the night wore on, successive dispatches from Task Force 16 indicated that Spruance was not in hot pursuit, but was actually backing off to the east.

"I did not feel justified in risking a night encounter with possibly superior enemy forces," Spruance was to explain. "But on the other hand I did not wish to be too far away from Midway next morning."[35] It was not at first clear to us why Spruance had chosen to be so cautious. The Monday morning quarterbacks at Pacific Fleet headquarters thought that this was not the way to do it. But Nimitz was very reluctant to intervene, even when the issue was raised in his staff meeting during the early hours of Friday morning. "I am sure that Spruance has a better sense of what's going on there than we have here," he told us. "I'm sure he has a very good reason for this. You must remember that he's there and knows what's going on. From here we can't 'kibbitz' a commander on the field of action."

But it was already becoming apparent that Spruance had made the proper tactical decision. Late on Thursday evening, radio intelligence had come up with the ominous indications that Yamamoto in the Combined Fleet flagship was racing toward the action with two battleship divisions.

When Yamamoto finally broke radio silence and began rallying his scattered forces, Rochefort's On the Roof Gang was able to identify the unmistakable "fist" of Yamamoto's chief radioman tapping out messages from *Yamato*. This was so surprising to us that at first we thought the radio direction finder bearings, obtained from the same transmissions, were way off and that the fleet flagship could not be closer than the Bonin Islands south of Japan. But as Hypo obtained more fixes during the night, *Yamato* was confirmed heading into the western approaches to Midway.

"What do we make of that. How do you account for his getting here so suddenly?" Nimitz said to me. "I thought you said that they would remain as they did at Pearl Harbor, in home waters."

"Well, that's part of this radio intelligence game and I'm sorry," I had to admit.

"But they are apparently out there and they didn't show up previously."

Contrary to what some historians have written, and as I have said earlier, Yamamoto's main force was not part of our prebattle estimate of enemy forces engaged in the Midway operation. Rochefort had been able to make only one association of Yamamoto's call signs with the forces involved in the Midway operation. And we had dismissed it as being "accidental." In truth, it could have cost us the battle if Task Force 16 had ventured too far west, and had been lured under the guns of Yamamoto's battle fleet that Thursday night.

This was a chilling reminder that radio intelligence, which had provided us with the key to victory, could just as easily have been our undoing. If Spruance had not exercised the caution he did, our victory could have been shot to pieces before dawn. And Hypo and I would rightfully have been blamed for failing to identify two battleship divisions in the Japanese order of battle.[36]

The discovery that Yamamoto's battlewagons were bearing down on

Midway from the northwest raised Nimitz's concern that they intended to push ahead with the invasion. These fears became very real at 0130 on 5 June when the Midway garrison cabled that an enemy submarine was lobbing shells ashore.

""'Do you think that the Japs still intend to land despite their damage?" Nimitz wanted to know.

"Well, they are pretty stubborn," I replied. "If they have plans, they always try to carry them out until it's obvious that they can't."

Nimitz was worried that the enemy's main forces had retired only temporarily. For a time, it looked as though he might be right. We knew that a bombardment by cruisers and submarines would be the preliminary to any assault on Midway, but as the night wore on without more shelling, I grew increasingly confident that the enemy had retreated. My estimate was that four carriers had been sunk, and because a large oil slick had been reported by our air patrols, that one was badly damaged and limping away.

During the small hours of 5 June, while Nimitz was concerned that the Japanese might still press on with their invasion, the feasibility of doing just that was being debated by staff of the Combined Fleet. Those who urged a face-saving occupation of Midway were finally silenced by Yamamoto's reminder: "In battle as in chess [*shogi*], it is the fool who lets himself be led into a reckless move through desperation."[37]

It was not until 0300, after Yamamoto had concluded that our surviving carriers were not going to be suckered into a night action, that he finally swallowed the bitter pill of defeat. "MIDWAY OPERATION CANCELED" was the signal that caused the transports to head back for Saipan. The covering force was ordered to join up with the remnants of Nagumo's Striking Force and rendezvous with the main force northwest of Midway. Only the invasion of the Aleutian Islands was to go ahead as scheduled.

It was not until late the next day, when Rochefort had been able to partially decrypt these messages, that Nimitz had confirmation that the Midway operation had been abandoned. Throughout the night of 5 June, however, plain-language Japanese messages continued to be picked up by Hypo that indicated that one of Yamamoto's battleships was damaged and sinking. This was deception pure and simple, aimed at luring our carrier force into a nighttime gunnery duel. "Keep an eye on this," Nimitz told me. "I may have to caution Spruance not to be drawn off in that direction."

A message to this effect was sent out to Spruance, warning him that while the Japanese were apparently retiring to the northwest, they were trying to draw him after them. Spruance didn't bite, but the deception continued. When I informed Nimitz of this he smiled. "Sometimes they can be quite transparent, can't they?"

I agreed. "Yes, and sometimes they can be pretty obtuse."

At 0300 we decided that the Japanese must be more obstinate than obtuse when we received a report from one of our submarines of "MANY UNIDENTIFIED SHIPS"[38] some ninety miles northwest of Midway. The four heavy cruisers of the close support were not preparing to invade, but responding to Yamamoto's orders to retreat when they spotted the unmistakably sinister profile of a submarine. In their hasty maneuvers to avoid any torpedoes as USS *Tambor* submerged, cruiser *Mogami* collided with cruiser *Mikuma*.

Two hours later *Tambor* surfaced to report that one of the heavy cruisers was damaged and leaking oil. But Nimitz was not taking any chances. He radioed all our submarines to gather west of Midway and be ready to disrupt any invasion attempt. He told his commanders, "There are strong indications the Japanese will attempt assault and occupation Midway regardless past losses."[39]

Early in the morning, search planes from Midway reported that the enemy was, in fact, retreating to the west. Dive bombers and B-17s managed to find the two damaged cruisers and reported two hits. After reversing course back to the east during the night, as the enemy activity appeared to increase around Midway, Spruance was also less than fifty miles north of the island when he radioed an alert to our submarines that Task Force 16 was resuming the westerly pursuit. But it was not until afternoon, after a report that the main Japanese force was still northwest of the island, that he launched a search-and-strike mission.

Spruance discovered that day, however, that there is truth in the old naval adage that "a stern chase is a long one." On the evening of 5 June, when his planes returned after failing to make any contact, he decided to give up trying to overtake the main enemy units. He was concerned that to do so would bring his task force within range of the Japanese land-based bombers at Wake. Instead, he decided to concentrate his efforts on locating the damaged cruisers.

When *Enterprise*'s dive bombers found the pair of cripples in the midmorning on 6 June, it was like shooting fish in a barrel. After three successive strikes from Task Force 16, *Mikuma* sank. But *Mogami*, although ablaze and badly mauled, managed to limp away and make good an escape to Truk.

The final round of the epic battle of Midway, however, was not entirely ours. For a day and a half, the captain and volunteers from her crew had been struggling to save *Yorktown*. They had reboarded the ravaged carrier and brought her under tow with an accompanying destroyer supplying electric power for the pumps that kept her afloat. But one of the last acts of a floatplane from the retreating heavy cruisers had been to make a sighting report that brought a Japanese submarine stalking the crippled flattop.

On the afternoon of 6 June a salvo of torpedoes split destroyer *Hammann* in two, and opened up a new gash in *Yorktown*'s hull. As thousands of tons of green water poured in, for the second time in two days, the abandon-ship order was given. Without power to keep her pumps running, *Yorktown* succumbed, capsizing before making her death plunge shortly before dawn on 7 June.

While not unexpected, the news that *Yorktown* had foundered was made harder to bear by the reports that Sunday morning that the Japanese had landed on the westernmost Aleutian Islands of Attu and Kiska. Expectation that the American public would demand an immediate response prompted Nimitz to order Task Force 16 north to dislodge these embarrassing new outposts of the Japanese empire. But Spruance was relieved to be recalled the following day. This was after the Pacific Fleet staff had had time to reflect on the enormous risks involved in allowing our precious carriers to venture into the zone of northern storms where they would be easy prey to ambush by enemy battleships and submarines.

Despite Tokyo's crowing propaganda, the capture of the two barren outposts of the United States could not undo the ringing triumph that our carriers had won three days earlier. The eventual loss to Japan was to prove far greater than material casualties: four carriers, one cruiser, 2,500 men, and 322 aircraft. Although the Combined Fleet still outnumbered our Pacific Fleet, Yamamoto's grand strategic design for bringing about a quick Japanese victory through a decisive naval engagement had been wrecked. We had paid the considerable price of 347 lives, a carrier, a destroyer, and 147 aircraft. But during the months that followed, Midway proved to mark the beginning of the ebb tide for Japanese naval power in the Pacific.

"Pearl Harbor has now been partially avenged," Admiral Nimitz's communiqué of 6 June announced. "Vengeance will not be complete until Japanese seapower is reduced to impotence."[40]

Admiral King's congratulatory message and promise "to make the enemy realize that war is hell" was broadcast to the fleet in plain language to add to the discomfiture of the Japanese.

"The Battle of Midway was the first decisive defeat suffered by the Japanese Navy in 350 years," King was to write. "Furthermore it put an end to the long period of Japanese offensive action, and restored the balance of naval power in the Pacific."[41]

Admiral King's dispatch persuaded General Emmons to make a gracious gesture for having doubted our intelligence estimates. He arrived at Pacific Fleet headquarters that Sunday morning with a jeroboam of champagne, wrapped up navy-style in blue and gold ribbons. As glasses were handed around, Nimitz accepted Emmons's apologies. The admiral insisted on sending his car to fetch Commander Rochefort. But Joe took so long changing from his informal attire into uniform whites that the champagne had run dry by the time he arrived. Nimitz, nevertheless, magnanimously declared to his assembled staff, "This officer deserves a major share of the credit for the victory at Midway."[42]

It was typical of Joe that he waited another couple of days before giving his exhausted staff a two-day break so they could hold what can only be described as a great big drunken brawl.[43]

33

"One Unforgivable Sin"

IN THE MONTHS AFTER Midway, when the success of our intelligence operation at Pearl Harbor should have been recognized, you can imagine our dismay when Washington launched a bitter attack against us.

We knew that more fighting was about to break out in the southwest Pacific, and we knew how good our operation was with Rochefort running Station Hypo. There was no doubt in our minds that if Nimitz had listened to Washington's forecasts about Midway, there would have been no victory to celebrate.

As it turned out, Washington believed differently. Neither Captain Joseph Redman nor his younger brother, John, who was head of OP-20-G, was inclined to recognize that Hypo had made any contribution to the victory. They were determined to hide the facts about how badly they had blundered by predicting the wrong date and target of the Japanese operation.

The director of naval communications was also taking his share of the credit for the "remarkable intelligence work" that had ensured that our outnumbered forces had achieved tactical surprise. As he put it: "It is not believed that the enemy knew the whereabouts of our carriers until after radio silence was broken."[1] And the Redman brothers, thanks to their ready access to senior members of the naval staff in Washington, circulated the word that Midway was the result of their outfit's work, and not that of Rochefort's team. Furthermore, the Redmans claimed that their operation was the one that had broken out the 3 June date from the Japanese ciphers that allowed Nimitz to get his carriers on station. They were soon boasting that without the efforts of the Negat cryptanalysts in Washington, Midway and the Hawaiian Islands would have been captured by the Japanese. Their campaign of disinformation worked: Within two months the elder brother was promoted to rear admiral, while the younger brother was given a leg up to captain.

We knew something of what was going on, but not enough. Just how successful the Redmans were at perpetrating their fraud didn't come to light for more than a year, when Commander John S. Holtwick reported to Rear Admiral Joseph R. Redman in October 1943. Redman was six months into his second tour of duty as director of naval communications at the time—for which he was awarded the Distinguished Service Medal—and he remarked that "Pearl Harbor had missed the boat at the battle of Midway but the Navy Department had saved the day."[2]

The assuredness with which the lie was told "took the breath away" from Commander Holtwick. As one of Rochefort's traffic analysts, he had played a key role in providing the intelligence that proved OP-20-G wrong about Midway. Although "boiling mad," Holtwick managed to state that Admiral Nimitz believed the reverse was true. Redman dismissively insisted that he "must have been misinformed."[3] Then Holtwick respectfully pointed out that he had received a letter of commendation from the commander in chief of the Pacific Fleet for the part he had played in the Hypo intelligence breakthrough that had been instrumental in securing our victory on 4 June.

When he found that other members of the department appeared to have been taken in by the Redman version, Holtwick was determined to "tell the truth about the Midway tip-off."[4] But with the elder Redman so firmly entrenched in the hierarchy of the navy department, Holtwick's campaign resulted in an anonymous monograph that was written by another ranking officer in the naval intelligence community who, understandably, chose to remain anonymous.

The memo was headlined: *The Inside Story of Midway and the Ousting of Commander Rochefort,* and it set down in precise detail how a clique of officers in league with the Redman brothers had conspired to cast slurs on Rochefort to deny him and the Hypo team their proper credit. The memorandum also stated that there had been a move in Washington during the spring of that year to shift some of the blame for Pearl Harbor onto Hypo by falsely accusing Rochefort of allowing himself to become the victim of a nonexistent Japanese radio deception.

By the end of 1943, a number of copies of the memo appear to have been circulated in Washington confidentially and unofficially. Each of the twenty pages that exposed "the dirty work that went on in the Navy Department" was stamped SECRET. Although this was not an official stamp, because the monograph contained a classified listing of the sequential changes in the Japanese naval codes, it was to remain locked in the safes of the naval intelligence establishment for forty years. Another reason why it was quarantined and kept from declassification was the fact that it washed the navy department's dirty linen.

Although recently released records indicate that some of the memo's charges are overstated, the memo itself is a telling indictment of how self-serving officers advanced their careers and authority by distorting—and in some cases rewriting—the historical record. That the Redmans and their associates rose to the most senior rank in the naval establishment is perhaps another reason why their successors wanted to conceal this indictment. Fortunately, it was "officially" declassified and released in late 1984 after a navy security review determined that it contained "no currently classified information."[5]

The memo contains startling revelations that are supported by the most recently released radio intelligence records and copies of official reports discovered among the papers of Captain Rochefort. Statements made by Captain Dyer before his death have added to the revelations that demonstrate how the power play by the Redman brothers to further their own careers had an immediate and deleterious impact on the conduct and consequences of the war. The charge that they pursued a vendetta against Rochefort is confirmed by the recent declassification of two memoranda of 20 June 1942. These prove how the Redmans worked hand in glove to distort the facts, to ensure Rochefort's ouster from Hypo, and how they tried to bring the Pacific Fleet combat intelligence unit directly under their control.

These two memos were addressed to Vice Admiral Frederick J. Horne, King's deputy chief of naval operations, who appears to have been a willing assistant, if not an active promoter of the Redman cause. One memo is signed by Captain Joseph Redman, although it is clear that both were drafted so as to be mutually supportive, and it argued that "radio intelligence cannot thrive and function efficiently except under the direct control of naval communications."[6] To this end Joseph Redman charged that Hypo "has been, by virtue of seniority, in the hands of an ex-Japanese language student" who was "not technically trained in Naval Communications" and that the navy's own war effort against the Japanese was "suffering because the importance and possibilities of the phases of Radio Intelligence are not fully realized."[7]

This was an outrageous accusation. Rochefort not only had been present at the birth of the navy's radio intelligence effort, but he had demonstrated only three weeks earlier what it could achieve by setting the stage for our victory at Midway.

Captain Joseph Redman also complained that the "realization of combined radio intelligence unit objectives worked out more smoothly in the Melbourne unit [Belconnen] than in the Com 14 unit [Hypo]." He argued that this was because the officer in Belconnen was more experienced and attuned to the needs of naval intelligence in Washington! He further charged that "administration was weak" at Hypo, and he said that Rochefort should be replaced by "a senior officer trained in radio intelligence rather than one whose background is in Japanese language."[8] To support this charge, he enclosed a detailed list of Hypo's omissions and errors prepared by his younger brother, and he recommended that Commander John Redman "make a quick trip to Honolulu to get first hand information on which to base recommendation *for remedial action* [emphasis added]."⁹

The younger Redman's memorandum was an even more self-serving document. It implicitly accused Rochefort of insubordination and belittled his ability to achieve results. "Experience has indicated," Commander Redman disingenuously concluded, "that units in combat areas cannot be relied upon to accomplish more than the business of merely reading enemy messages and performing routine work necessary to keep abreast of minor changes in the cryptographic systems involved."¹⁰

Now that historians have access to the revealing record for the first time, it is extraordinary to find that immediately after Midway, the head of OP-20-G was asserting that only Washington had the "large numbers of skilled persons and expensive, complicated machinery" for the "extremely complex" task of "obtaining intelligence from enemy communications." Yet Redman, whose supposedly more talented and experienced team had got it so wrong, was able to get away with his claim that "a properly qualified officer" should be put in charge of Hypo "in order that proper relations between the intelligence activities and the operational staff may be maintained."¹¹

The charges made by the Redmans were contradicted by reality. As Captain Dyer observed years later, the Redmans' "slur" against Hypo's achievements was "more than amply refuted by the record."¹² Rochefort's former deputy drew attention to some particular examples that give the lie to the Redmans' suggestion that Hypo had been incapable of serious cryptanalytic effort.

"In April 1942," Dyer pointed out, "it was suggested to Washington that a solution of JN-20 might be helpful. Their reply was, 'It cannot be done.' In May of same year Pearl did it! [And] the same month, Wright and Finnegan came up with a brilliant solution of the internal time-date code which was vitally important in determining when the attack on Midway should be expected."¹³

The Redmans' memoranda confirm what many of us have suspected for so long. The two brothers led a conspiracy, knowing that they could count on a receptive audience in Admiral King's staff for their contention that radio intelligence had "worked well," and that it should continue "under the control and administration of the Chief of Naval Operations" with the director of naval communications in immediate charge.¹⁴ While we were busy fighting for our country out at Pearl, the Redmans were more concerned with winning bureaucratic turf.

"I have given a great deal of thought to the Rochefort affair, and I have been unwillingly forced to the conclusion that Rochefort committed the one unforgivable sin," Dyer wrote shortly before his death in 1985. "To certain individuals of small mind and overweening ambition, there is no greater insult than to be proved wrong. I have rather a bitter personal memory of having been threatened with reprisal for being right when Washington was wrong."¹⁵

It was especially ironic that Rochefort, who kept a notice on his desk saying "We can accomplish *anything* provided no one cares who gets the credit," found himself the target of the Redmans' campaign for self-aggrandizement. But we now know that they were prepared to stop at nothing to effect his recall as part of their plan to centralize control of radio intelligence in Washington. Yet this private war was also to lead to the Japanese being sent an alert about our code-breaking successes at one of the most critical junctures of the war.

The opportunity for that damaging betrayal surfaced with the headlines of the *Chicago Tribune* on Sunday, 7 June:

JAP FLEET SMASHED BY U.S.

2 CARRIERS SUNK AT MIDWAY. NAVY HAD WORD OF JAP PLAN TO STRIKE AT SEA

KNEW DUTCH HARBOR WAS A FEINT

The sensational story, which also appeared simultaneously in the *New York Daily News,* the *Washington Times-Herald,* and four other midwestern newspapers associated with the *Chicago Tribune,* was attributed to "reliable sources in the navy department."[16] While the story stopped short of saying that the information had been obtained by code breaking, it was clear that unless Admiral Nimitz had a personal spy in the enemy camp, there was no other way that he could have known the names of the four carriers, two battleships, two heavy cruisers, and twelve destroyers that were listed as part of the striking force. The article went on to name the classes of warships that made up support and occupation forces. And it detailed how we had worked out the broad objectives of Yamamoto's plan to invade Midway in order not to be taken in by the feint attack on Dutch Harbor.

Nimitz and I were dismayed when we learned about the newspaper articles in a dispatch from Washington on 8 June. My personal horror of the situation was greater, because it appeared that the information on which the story was based had been taken directly from our Cincpac bulletin, which had been sent to all task force commanders on 31 May. We launched an investigation and found that the fleet public relations officer had not insisted the *Tribune*'s Johnson sign a security pledge before he went on board *Lexington.*[17]

Admiral King was furious. He moved swiftly to have the office of naval censorship hush up the story. As a former newspaperman, Secretary of the Navy Knox pulled out all the stops to have the seven newspapers involved drop the coverage voluntarily. Even though characters in the comic strips would soon be portrayed busily stealing Japanese codes and solving ciphers, it was hoped that if Tokyo did pick up the story, the fact that it was a one-time item would persuade them that it was nothing more than sensationalistic speculation.

The Redmans, however, were determined to run the culprits to the ground. They may well have concluded that Rochefort or I must have been involved in the leak. Commander Redman knew as well as we did that the story could have been written only from the 31 May Cincpac intelligence bulletin and his suspicions were evidently aroused because the story carried the by-line of war correspondent Stanley Johnson, who had passed through Pearl Harbor a week earlier after his rescue from *Lexington* during the Coral Sea action.

For over a month Secretary Knox managed to prevent a full-scale investigation of Johnson, which, he predicted, would lead to more unfortunate publicity. Commander John Redman, however, refused to let the matter rest. Along with his brother he continued to urge that "something ought to be done about it."[18]

The chance to "do something" came after newspaper columnist Walter Winchell made a radio broadcast on 5 July in which he made reference to Coral Sea and Midway, asserting: "When the history of these times is written it will be revealed that *twice* the fate of the civilized world was changed by intercepted messages." Winchell claimed, moreover, that he "could not enlarge on that as it is military information."[19]

Two days later Winchell apparently abandoned any such scruples he might have had by dropping another juicy morsel in his "On Broadway" gossip column in the *New York Daily News*. In it he accused Colonel McCormick, the anti-Roosevelt proprietor of the *Chicago Tribune*, of having "tossed safety out of the windows" when he "allegedly printed the lowdown on why we won at Midway—claiming that the U.S. Navy decoded the Japs' secret messages." Winchell pointed out the irony that his "deadliest enemy in Chicago, publisher Frank Knox," had saved McCormick from being brought to account for his disregard for military secrecy.[20]

Commander Redman never raised any protest about who was leaking Winchell his inside information. But the columnist's revival of the issue gave Redman the excuse to send Admiral King a trenchant memorandum on "Security of Radio Intelligence Activities."

In it Redman charged, "Such statements are considered to be extremely prejudicial to our interests."[21] The memorandum was backed up by personal word of mouth when Captain Joseph Redman took up the campaign and succeeded in getting King and his staff so stirred up that they prevailed on Knox to reverse his decision not to move against the *Chicago Tribune*.

A naval investigation was launched. The managing editor of the *Chicago Tribune* was summoned to the navy department to testify to investigators on 9 July. He maintained that his correspondent Johnson had obtained the information legally from naval sources. But when Johnson was examined four days later he sought to protect the identity of the officer who had communicated the top-secret information. He claimed, moreover, that he had never been required to sign a written pledge agreeing to submit to strict security regulations and was therefore free to publish information freely volunteered to him.

Had the matter been allowed to rest there, the curse would have been taken off the whole incident. But the Redmans were out for blood. Evidently they smelled Rochefort's. They would not be stopped, even though the issue was now alarming the ranking officers of naval intelligence. Captain McCollum, who had by this time got wind of their vendetta, warned Admiral Wilkinson of the serious damage that the affair could do to our code-breaking effort if the Japanese got wind of it. But the Redmans had the bit between their teeth and were determined to resort to the public courts to force Johnson to reveal his sources. The Judge Advocate General's Office, which had investigated the case, informed Knox that there were some grounds for legal action.

On 29 July, the day after receiving the attorney general's express warning of "the possibility of disclosure of our naval code and the means by which the Navy obtains its information concerning the enemy,"[22] the secretary of the navy reluctantly asked the attorney general to prosecute Johnson and the *Chicago Tribune* under the 1917 Espionage Act.[23] The affair now became public property. A Chicago grand jury heard testimony from seven of *Lexington*'s officers, as well as Johnson and the newspaper's managing editor. It quickly emerged that the source of the story was our 31 May estimate. Johnson had been shown the copy addressed to Admiral Fitch by *Lexington*'s executive officer while the party was on board cruiser *Chester* en route to the west coast. This violated every security rule in the book, but the grand jury refused to return an indictment. The *Chicago Tribune* beat the rap because the intelligence estimate had been volunteered to Johnson without any injunction about its being secret.

Barrages of publicity surrounded the case. They could not possibly have escaped the watchful eyes and ears of Tokyo. Just as McCollum and Wilkinson had warned, the prosecution backfired and the welter of accusations and denials made good newspaper copy. Less than a week after the story broke on 8 August 1942, the Japanese adopted a brand-new version of the JN-25 code. All the progress we had made in breaking into the C version of the operational cipher was made worthless when the new D books came into use on 14 August.[24]

This was a double setback. Our cryptanalytic effort had to begin all over again. And it would take almost four months of grueling intellectual effort to rebuild the "dictionary" and recover sufficient additives and cipher keys before we could regain any real penetration of the Japanese navy's principal operational system. (Some of the minor administrative systems, such as the one used for weather reports, were not changed.) Hypo was forced to fall back on traffic analysis to keep Nimitz informed during the bitterly fought Solomons campaign, which involved some of the fiercest naval actions of the war.

Such a drastic revision of their main code only a week after the Midway publicity indicated that the Johnson affair must have triggered concerns in Tokyo about the security of their naval ciphers. What really upset Rochefort was that the change came just at the time he had his hands on a complete copy of the current JN-25 C code and additive books. These had been recovered from a cache of Japanese documents discovered by our marines after their landing in the Solomons on 6 August. (Many other cryptographic aids had also been discovered buried near the partially completed airstrip on Guadalcanal Island.)

The Japanese did not suspect that our invasion of Guadalcanal had prejudiced their security; this is clear from one of the last decrypts made in the old system, which revealed that the local Japanese commanders had radioed that all confidential material had been destroyed.[25] There were only two other reasons that could have led them to believe that a cipher had been prejudiced after being in use for less than two and a half months. One was the revelations, which I mentioned earlier, of the advanced state of our naval intelligence as betrayed by documents captured two months earlier on board *Nankin*. But according to German records these were not handed over to the Japanese until 29 August.[26] The other reason was the publicity resulting from the Johnson case.

Rochefort had suspected that the Johnson leak had something to do with the JN-25 code change on 8 August. But when the news reached him that the Redmans had been the prime instigators of the second round of undesirable publicity, the Hypo team was filled with a burning resentment. The blackout could not have come at a more unfortunate juncture for Nimitz, because we had gone onto the offensive despite our very limited resources of ships, men, and aircraft. The whole Guadalcanal campaign was to be bedeviled by our failure to get up-to-date radio intelligence.

34
Guadalcanal

A T THE JUNE SUMMIT in Washington between Roosevelt and Churchill, the Joint Chiefs of Staff blocked any increase in the forces assigned to the Pacific theater. Admiral King then conceived a campaign to seize control of the Solomons as the starting point for the navy's offensive against the Japanese. In the optimistic afterglow of Midway, he anticipated a rapid advance up the strategically placed chain of islands, which would lead to an early capture of Rabaul, followed by an advance to Truk, Guam, Saipan, and a smash up through the underbelly of the enemy's southern defensive perimeter.

At the same time, General MacArthur was to begin a northward drive up New Guinea from the Allied base at Port Moresby. To avert a dispute between MacArthur and Admiral Ghormley, who had assumed control of the South Pacific Area under Nimitz, the Joint Chiefs had shifted the Cincpac boundary of control west of Guadalcanal.

The Japanese were equally determined to consolidate their position and continue their advance. Although Yamamoto's defeat at Midway had forced imperial general headquarters to abandon their plan to seize American bases in Samoa and Fiji, they pressed on with the plan to capture Port Moresby. This time they would do it overland, with a punishing trek across the precipitous, jungle-clad peaks of the Owen Stanley mountain range. At the same time preparations were made to nail down their hold on the Solomons by building an airfield on Guadalcanal. This ominous development had been monitored earlier as intercepted signals of the C version of the JN-25 code began to yield up its additives.

This was the intelligence that Admiral Nimitz brought with him on 3 July to a strategic conference with King in San Francisco. The capture of the Santa Cruz Islands, south of the Solomons, had been the original objective of Operation Watchtower, as it had been code-named in deference to King's intention that it should be the curtain raiser to a full-scale

457

naval campaign in the Pacific. But news of the progress of the airfields on Guadalcanal brought a major revision in the plan. It meant abandoning the Santa Cruz operation in favor of invading Guadalcanal, and the seaplane base at Tulagi, before the enemy could achieve air superiority over the Coral Sea, which, in turn, would threaten our bases in Fiji and New Caledonia.

Admiral Richmond Kelly Turner was to be in charge of the landing, exercising his new responsibility as commander of Amphibious Forces South Pacific. (He had been cooling his heels for six months following his replacement as war plans chief, because of his inability to work with army planners.) He and Admiral Ghormley therefore had less than five weeks to plan and execute our first major amphibious operation. Because of the demands of the Allied agreement to commit their major effort to the invasion of North Africa in the fall, King had been assigned only the 1st Marine Division for Watchtower—an operation whose commanders called it Shoestring because of its makeshift nature.

The first wave of our assault splashed ashore on the beaches of Tulagi and Guadalcanal shortly before dawn on 6 August. The Japanese were completely taken by surprise. After some sharp fighting the marines captured the seaplane base and took over the half-finished airfield. But it was not just the hostile reception that made these steamy jungle-clad islands very different from the tropical paradise which many of the leathernecks had been expecting.

In the six months that were to follow, a bitter campaign of attrition developed for control of the island that was the strategic key to the Solomons. Within forty-eight hours of the landings, Yamamoto issued urgent orders to the Fourth Fleet to intervene, and then erupted the first of six savage naval battles that were to cost us and the Japanese twenty-four warships apiece.

The enemy force of seven cruisers that came charging south from Rabaul was spotted by Australian coast watchers as it entered the northern Solomons on 7 August. An Allied air patrol was sent up to the Bougainville area, but when the Japanese ships knew they had been spotted they turned around to mislead our pilots. Hypo's ability to read the JN-25 C traffic was running a week or more behind current intercepts. Vice Admiral Gunichi Mikawa's heavy cruisers came rushing south in response to our landing. But because they kept radio silence their advance was not picked up from our traffic analysis.

Admiral Fletcher, who was in overall command of the naval forces, was determined not to lose any more carriers. Admiral Leigh Noyes, in immediate command of the air support force, which included carriers *Saratoga, Wasp,* and *Enterprise,* also favored an early withdrawal. His defenses had already been weakened by the loss of one fifth of his fighter aircraft in dogfights with Japanese land-based planes for control of the airspace over Guadalcanal. On the afternoon of 8 August, Fletcher made the independent decision to withdraw his task forces to the south for refueling.

Fletcher's decision to withdraw *all* our air cover simultaneously, instead of removing one carrier at a time, enormously increased the vulnerability of Turner's transports. They were still unloading supplies. Also jeopardized was the covering cruiser force. As usual, Turner had insisted, as he had before the attack on Pearl Harbor, that he would be his own intelligence officer. So while he protested Fletcher's decision, he nonetheless decided from his reading of the intelligence that no enemy surface force could arrive to interfere with his landing until late the following day.[1]

Given the information that he had received on enemy movements, Turner's error was understandable. But he might have saved himself and his ships if he had not refused to have one of Hypo's mobile radio intelligence units on board his headquarters ship. If he had not been so pigheaded, Turner could have received an early warning that enemy forces were approaching that evening when the Japanese cruisers sent a floatplane to radio a reconnaissance report. It succeeded in reporting the disposition of our transports off the beachhead, and that of the ships guarding the entrance to the sound between Tulagi and Guadalcanal.

As a result, Mikawa achieved total surprise when his force swept in from the darkness north of Savo Island and set the night ablaze in a twenty-minute gunnery duel that sank four Allied cruisers and a destroyer. Turner's transports were saved from complete destruction only by the Japanese decision to withdraw because they believed our carrier task force was still in the vicinity and might catch them in a dawn counterstrike.

After suffering one of the worst naval defeats in our history, Turner withdrew his transports and a surviving cruiser after the enemy stepped up their bombing raids from Rabaul the next morning. Major General Alexander Vandegrift's force of six thousand marines on Tulagi and ten thousand on Guadalcanal were then left stranded. They had lost their one-thousand-man reserve, and their heavy weapons. They had only a few entrenching tools and less than a months' rations and medical stores.

"It was as if the Marines held Jones Beach and the rest of Long Island were loosely dominated by the enemy" was how my old Annapolis classmate Hanson Baldwin summed it up for *The New York Times*.[2] But in a remarkable feat of bravery, and despite their lack of resources, the marines managed to complete the airstrip within a week using the single bulldozer that the Japanese had abandoned.

The arrival of marine fighter planes was the signal for the contest for Guadalcanal to begin in earnest. Now it was the Japanese who were faced with the strategic necessity for eliminating the airfield. On 20 August they made their first attempt to drive through the jungle to dislodge the marines who had dug themselves in around the airstrip perimeter. The attacks collapsed in a bloody series of banzai charges against machine guns. The Japanese then began a series of nighttime destroyer runs from Rabaul, which we dubbed "the Tokyo Express," to land troop reinforcements for a major offensive. Our fighters fought the enemy bombing raids as replacement aircraft were ferried in from our carrier task forces south of the Solomons.

- As the level of attrition escalated, more and more units of the Combined Fleet were sucked into the struggle. This raised Yamamoto's hopes for a decisive naval engagement. Nimitz realized that with Fletcher's task forces outnumbered by more than two to one, we had to avoid a major confrontation at all costs, especially when the odds worsened after the 23 August carrier duel off the eastern Solomons. *Saratoga* was sent limping back to the west coast after a torpedo hit. Although his planes sank an enemy light carrier, Fletcher was forced to retreat southward when *Enterprise* was also damaged. It was another tactical defeat for the Pacific Fleet.

The naval setback in the Guadalcanal campaign was partially offset when MacArthur's tough Australian troops finally halted the stubborn Japanese assault on Port Moresby in the first week of September. The imperial general headquarters ordered the army to retreat from the Moresby front and concentrate all its efforts on regaining control of Guadalcanal. Fortunately, the Japanese were less effective at achieving results on land than they were at sea. On 13 September the marines beat off a second major attack on the airfield's perimeter, but enemy submarines torpedoed, in short order, a carrier, a destroyer, and a battleship.

Wasp and her destroyer escort foundered. *North Carolina* managed to make it back to Pearl with a thirty-foot gash in her hull. This was a major blow to Nimitz. He could not understand why Admiral Leigh Noyes had confined his task force to operating in a narrow patch of water south of the Solomons when our intelligence bulletin had warned that the area was heavily patrolled by enemy submarines. Later we found that Noyes had misinterpreted his operational orders. He had assumed that he was to confine his operations to the Cincpac area and that he was not allowed to stray into the waters that were technically under the command of MacArthur.

The next major clash came a month later. The Tokyo Express of 11 October was derailed south of Savo Island by Fletcher's heavy cruiser squadron, which sank an enemy cruiser and destroyer in what was the first-ever defeat of the Japanese navy in a night action. But Yamamoto promptly raised the stakes in the naval war of attrition. He sent down battleships to escort the nightly reinforcement runs and bombard our marine defenses with fourteen-inch shells. The climax was fast approaching. We estimated that much of the Combined Fleet had been sent south. Yamamoto had now concentrated four battleships, five carriers, ten

cruisers, and twenty-nine destroyers in a massive blockade and bombardment operation.

"It now appears that we are unable to control the sea in the
Guadalcanal area" was how Nimitz's headquarters diary summed up the
grim situation. "Thus our supply of the position will only be done at great
expense to us. The situation is not hopeless but it is certainly critical."[3] It
was evident to all of us at Pearl that Commander in Chief South Pacific
Admiral Ghormley was faltering. His actions—or lack of them—had ab-
dicated command of the sea to the enemy. The marines were undersup-
plied and having a very hard time under the daily air raids and nighttime
battleship bombardment. Their aviators were suffering from lack of fuel,
from attrition, and fatigue as their planes were being shot out of the skies
faster than our remaining carriers could ferry in replacements.

It was now clear to Nimitz that unless we could fight more reinforcements through, we were in danger of losing the campaign. During a full
meeting of his staff, his eyes turned from sunny blue to a very grim gray.
"I don't want to hear, or see, such gloom and such defeatism," he
snapped. "Remember the enemy is hurt too, but our job here is to provide them with everything they need on Guadalcanal to fight this battle.
We aren't going to do any good sitting here moaning or wailing or wringing our hands."

After the meeting was over, Nimitz kept a few of his staff, including
myself, for a further review of the worsening situation. We sat around the
admiral's desk. He asked each one of us for recommendations as to what
we would do to improve the situation. His principal concern was that the
navy was obviously not in control of the approaches to Guadalcanal. Although he did not say so directly, it was obvious that he felt that
Ghormley had handed over command of the sea to the Japanese. We
proposed that personalities should be set aside and that the commander
South Pacific should be replaced by someone who could do a more effective job. Nimitz would not hear of it, saying that this was "mutiny."

After several more days, during which the situation on Guadalcanal
grew even bleaker, a number of the staff, me included, got together one
evening to chew over the matter. As a result of our discussion, we agreed
that we should see Admiral Nimitz right away—it was then about 2200.
We phoned his orderly, who told us that the admiral was ready to go to
bed, but that he would give us five minutes. We arrived at his Makalapa
quarters to find Nimitz in pajamas and dressing gown. We wasted no time
spelling out what was on our minds. Halsey was on a tour of the South
Pacific preparatory to relieving Fletcher as carrier task forces commander. Thus Halsey was on the spot to take over from Ghormley. We
tried to assure the admiral that we were aware of his appreciation of
personnel problems from his time spent at the Bureau of Navigation. In
our view, however, the situation was so grave that he could not allow any
thought of kindness or sympathy for a brother officer to stand in the way.

Nimitz thanked us. He said he understood entirely why we had spoken so frankly. There was no further discussion of the painful issue, which he resolved on 18 October by a dispatch sent out ordering Halsey to "take command of the South Pacific and South Pacific Forces immediately."[4] The news that America's preeminent fighting admiral was taking over command at this critical juncture in the campaign put new heart into the marines on Guadalcanal.

"One minute we were too limp with malaria to crawl from our foxholes, the next we were whooping it up like kids," General Vandegrift was to record. He flew to Halsey's New Caledonia headquarters for a straight-talking conference with the new commander South Pacific, who promised to do whatever was possible to get more supplies and reinforcements through. With only carrier *Hornet* available, Halsey admitted that the situation appeared "almost hopeless." Then on 23 October the patched-up *Enterprise* task force sailed back to Noumea accompanied by battleship *South Dakota*. Halsey was guardedly optimistic: "Now we had a fighting chance," he later recalled.[5]

The marines on Guadalcanal were battling off another attempt by the Japanese to break through their defenses on 26 October. Meanwhile, Admiral Thomas C. Kinkaid, with *Enterprise* and *Hornet* in his task force, was playing an equally desperate round of hide-and-seek with Admiral Kondo's Second Fleet south of Santa Cruz Island. During the night less than two hundred miles separated the opposing fleets. We knew that the Japanese battleships were out. So did Kinkaid.

Hypo was still lagging behind the current JN-25 decrypts, so we could not provide Kinkaid with an accurate intelligence picture. But that morning we had picked up and relayed to him the familiar "TE TE TE" used by Japanese carrier scouting planes when radioing a sighting report. We did not know that Kinkaid had already launched a strike against three enemy carriers to the north. Two of the enemy carriers were damaged in the duel. But the Japanese came out ahead. Their planes mauled *Hornet* so badly that Kinkaid ordered the carrier sunk rather than trying to save her and risking his task force to a superior enemy.

We knew from partial decryption of the intercepts that evening that Kondo was charging south with his battleships in hope of capturing the crippled carrier and engaging our task force in a night action. I think that Nimitz felt better when he realized this and appreciated that if *Hornet* had not been sunk and Kinkaid had not withdrawn, our forces might have been overwhelmed. But there was no getting away from the disappointment that the Battle of the Santa Cruz Islands, as the action was called, had been another tactical defeat. We could take some consolation that although he left Halsey with only *Enterprise* to keep on fighting supplies through to Guadalcanal, two of Japan's big carriers were now on their way home for repairs. The main question was how long Yamamoto would be willing to go on accepting this level of attrition to the Combined Fleet.

The answer came after a fierce three-day naval action fought in the narrow channel off Guadalcanal. Those waters had been dubbed Ironbottom Sound because they had become the graveyard of so much naval tonnage. Two of our cruisers were lost on 12 November in a head-on collision with a Tokyo Express that was escorted by two Japanese battleships. But the score was evened up when battleship *Hiei* was sunk the following morning as the retreating Japanese force was caught by dive bombers from Guadalcanal and *Enterprise*.

Halsey judged that the odds and time were now ripe for challenging the Tokyo Express with his battlewagons, despite the risks they would run maneuvering in such narrow waters. *Enterprise*'s aircraft smashed up a Japanese cruiser force the next day, and the night action fought on 14 November was to prove that our new radar and our big-gun superiority were decisive. When *Washington* and *South Dakota* came crashing up Ironbottom Sound to trade their sixteen-inch salvos with the fourteen-inch guns of *Kirishima* at close range, the enemy battleship was pounded into a blazing wreck.

The victory that our naval forces had won coincided with the failure of an all-out bid by the Japanese army to capture the Guadalcanal airstrip. This was the excuse Yamamoto used to withdraw the Combined Fleet the next day from its close support role. The loss of twenty-four warships, including a carrier and two battleships, had finally proved unacceptable to the imperial navy. This was the decisive turning point. Although destroyers continued to supply the remaining Japanese troops until they were evacuated three months later, the Guadalcanal campaign had, for all intents and purposes, been won. As Halsey was to observe of the enemy's crushing defeat: "Until then he had been advancing at his will. From then on he retreated at ours."[6]

35

"I'm Not Coming Back"

T HE STRUGGLE FOR Guadalcanal was raging toward its climax at the same time that the feud between Hypo and Negat reached its unhappy conclusion. The bad blood between the two camps was made worse by the refusal of Admiral King to accept Nimitz's recommendation that Rochefort should receive the Distinguished Service Medal for Joe's contribution to the Midway victory. While Joe was flattered that his name had been put forward, he had advised Nimitz against it, saying that it would only aggravate the opposition of the Redmans. Joe was right. The Redmans were among those who strongly advised King against singling out Rochefort for the decoration. For him to have received it would have been a tacit admission that the principal intelligence breakthrough had been made by Hypo. Worse, it would not have squared with the Redmans' claims that their Negat team was responsible for the crucial cryptanalytic success. The 22 June memorandum to Admiral King advised that he "disapprove" Rochefort's recommended decoration because "equal credit is due to the Cominch planning section for the correct evaluation of enemy intelligence. . . ."[1]

Relations were further strained when Rochefort discovered that the Redman brothers had been instrumental in pressing the investigation of the Stanley Johnson case, and how they had caused the public discussion that had warned the Japanese that we had been reading their naval messages.

Joe held the Washington clique responsible for the arduous struggle that he and his cryptanalysts were waging to get back into the new D version of the JN-25 code. This in turn brought to a head the touchy debate about which station was producing the most accurate additive recoveries. There were some nasty exchanges, and Joe took increasing exception to what he described as "the bullying tactics to try to make us conform to their way of thinking."[2]

464

There was so much questioning and arguing going back and forth that it began to interfere with our efforts to get back into the Japanese operational traffic. Joe had also been warned by a friend in the navy department that a "special agent" was being sent out by an officer on King's staff to investigate us both. This would be done under a cover of making arrangements for a survey of the office equipment needed to set up a new interservice intelligence center.

The snooper, who turned out to be a chief yeoman who had been a mail orderly in *West Virginia* when I was on board the battleship in 1924, appeared less interested in the number of desks, chairs, and telephones the new facility needed than about how well I got on with Hypo. Thanks to Joe's alert we agreed to give the impression that our relationship was strictly professional and that we were not the best of friends. Even this was to be turned against Joe later with accusations that I found him difficult to work with. After the snooper had departed, Rochefort and I concluded that we were being targeted for removal by the Redmans and their allies in OP-20-G. We could assume only that they were determined to remove us before we again made them look like fools as we had over the "AF" issue before Midway. Then there was the matter of the new intelligence facility for which Nimitz had won King's approval, and which evidently appeared to Washington to be another bid for independence by Hypo.

The new operation, Intelligence Center Pacific Ocean Area, or Icpoa as it was to be known, had its origins in a proposal that I had made to Nimitz shortly after the Battle of Midway for increasing the size of our intelligence operation. Nimitz was adamantly opposed to expanding his own staff. Instead, he proposed to Washington that a new intelligence facility be attached to the Fourteenth Naval District as an adjunct to Rochefort's combat intelligence unit.

Captain Joseph Redman, anticipating that this was an attempt to carve off a piece from his naval communications empire, tried to pour cold water on the scheme in his June memorandum. But the scheme had been strongly supported by the director of naval intelligence, who saw it as an extension of his turf. Captain McCollum had also come out strongly in favor because he had observed firsthand how successfully the British had integrated their interservice intelligence operations. With King's blessing the new outfit was established on 24 June 1942 and Joe was appointed the first commanding officer of Icpoa.[3]

Although the duties that Rochefort shouldered in addition to Hypo were not onerous, his responsibility for Icpoa opened another front in his confrontation with the Redmans. They immediately renewed their efforts to bring Hypo under the direct control of OP-20-G. When the newly promoted Captain John Redman arrived to become Nimitz's communications officer on 15 September, Rochefort suspected that an attempt was being made to box him in. This appeared confirmed, because the younger

Redman's sudden transfer to Pearl came hard on the heels of his elder brother's promotion, which required that he perform six months' sea duty with a Pacific Fleet cruiser force before resuming his former post as director of naval communications.

The appointment of Captain William B. Goggins as OP-20-G in Washington on 3 September also made nonsense of John Redman's insistence two months earlier that only those "properly qualified" should command radio intelligence units. Although Goggins had been in the radio division of the Bureau of Engineering, the new head of Station Negat lacked any extensive experience in code breaking, traffic analysis, or intelligence evaluation. The principal factor behind his selection appears to have been that he was a close friend of the Redmans. And the fact that his appointment was approved was yet another indication of the lack of emphasis that the navy bureaucracy—even in wartime—placed on seeing that intelligence officers were properly qualified for their jobs.

When Captain John Redman arrived at fleet headquarters in mid-September, his first mission appears to have been to make good on the brothers' June promise to take "remedial action" as far as Hypo was concerned.[4] This translated into effecting the removal of Rochefort as rapidly as possible. There can be little doubt that this was a carefully planned conspiracy. Before John Redman left Washington for Pearl, he had arranged with Commander Wenger to open up a secret line of private communications by using a strip cipher and one of the navy radio circuits. Redman had not been at fleet headquarters for more than a couple of weeks before he was using this channel to report that Rochefort was uncooperative and that Wenger should arrange for his transfer to be requested.

Joe had already picked up what was in the wind: that Redman's arrival at Cincpac headquarters was another attempt to chip away at the measure of independence that Hypo had achieved from Washington with Nimitz's blessings. With the Guadalcanal campaign reaching its critical phase, he complained to Nimitz that the repeated petty disputes with Washington had become counterproductive to our intelligence effort.

The final straw came in the second week of October when Goggins arrived at Pearl Harbor. After less than seven weeks as OP-20-G, he had been replaced by Captain Earl E. Stone, another officer who was equally inexperienced in radio intelligence. Neither Cincpac nor the Fourteenth Naval District had been given any official or unofficial notice of Goggins's arrival. His orders merely indicated that he was taking up duties as "executive officer" of Icpoa. But it was soon evident that he had another mission, because of his insistence on advising Rochefort how to reorganize the combat intelligence unit. There was an embarrassing incident when Goggins made his first attempt to get past the armed guard and was denied admission to Hypo until he had established his identity and shown the proper written security clearance.

Rochefort, naturally, resented Goggins's intrusion. Joe suspected that the new arrival was really trying to undermine his position when he began to receive directions on how Hypo and Icpoa were to collaborate in radio intelligence work. One of Joe's team suggested that he should "just tell Washington to go to hell."[5] After seeking assurances from Nimitz's chief of staff, then Admiral Spruance, that is precisely what Joe tried to do. He drafted a cablegram to that effect. I showed it to Nimitz, who personally approved that it should be sent. Diplomatically but firmly it told Negat in effect, "I'm working for Admiral Nimitz so get off my back!"

Captain Redman evidently found out about Rochefort's protest, and that Nimitz was entirely sympathetic to it. He sent a second coded alert to Wenger: "Get rid of Rochefort at all costs."[6] Captain Stone of OP-20-G was shown this message. He tried to wash his hands of the affair, because he recognized the illegality of using navy cipher systems for private communications. Wenger was then obliged to take it up himself with Captain C. F. Holden, the new director of naval communications.

Holden's first action was to order his ambitious subordinate to destroy his private cipher and report the whole affair to Admiral Horne, who was King's deputy chief of naval operations. Horne, who already had been primed with misinformation by the Redmans' June memoranda, concluded that despite the questionable methods that Captain Redman had employed, he was right. The obstructive Rochefort must be removed. After obtaining King's authorization—but without consulting either the Fourteenth Naval District commandant, Cincpac, or the director of naval communications—the necessary arrangements were made with the Bureau of Personnel.[7]

Exactly a week after Goggins arrived at Pearl, Joe received orders on 22 October 1942 detaching him from Hypo for "temporary additional duty" in Washington. Admiral Nimitz immediately protested to King. Nimitz said that while he had nothing against Goggins, he did not want Joe detached. Nimitz's communication stressed that Rochefort had been instrumental in effecting the Pacific Fleet's Midway victory. "I will do all that I can," King cabled back in a "Personal" message that Nimitz showed me. King promised to intervene to get Rochefort's detachment order canceled.

King, however, was apparently caused to change his mind by those members of his staff, such as Admiral Horne who had been persuaded by the Redmans' memoranda that Rochefort was insubordinate and uncooperative and in need of direct supervision. Nimitz received a second message from King that said that Rochefort was to return to Washington for ten days of temporary duty. This made it appear that they wanted Joe's specialist advice on restructuring of Negat's radio intelligence organization. Nimitz could hardly refuse what, on the face of it, was a reasonable proposal.

Rochefort, however, realized that he had lost. "When I leave Pearl,

I'm not coming back," he told a number of us, and he sadly turned over a package of personal papers and the keys to his desk before leaving Pearl Harbor on 25 October.[8]

Two weeks after Joe's departure, Captain Goggins was introduced to the Hypo team as "your new boss."[9] This came as a surprise to his deputy, Captain Dyer, as it did to the other officers.

"It was another blow to our morale," wrote Lieutenant Jasper Holmes, who would shortly receive a melancholy letter from Rochefort. It conveyed his "sincere regrets on leaving under such circumstances" and thanked "the best damn intelligence organization the U.S. Navy or any other navy has seen."[10]

On 15 November Nimitz received notice that Rochefort's "temporary orders" had been "modified to permanent duty." Since this dispatch had been deliberately sent by surface mail rather than cable, it was too late for him to intervene. Nimitz was furious, and it was said that he refused to speak to John Redman for two weeks. His communications officer, however, was an adept politician who was able to mend his fences and remain on the Cincpac staff for the next two and a half years.

Rochefort arrived in Washington, exhausted, and justifiably resentful at the shabby treatment he had received. "I made several mistakes in a great big hurry, one of which compounded the other," he was to admit later. "And the net effect was that I flatly refused the offer of special work in Washington."[11] This confirmed rather than dispelled the slurs that the Redmans had spread about him. No consideration was given to making him head of OP-20-G, the one other post besides Hypo in which Rochefort's talents could have continued assisting our war effort.

Joe insisted on sea duty, although he knew that it was against standing regulations to send anyone with knowledge of our work on the Japanese codes into the war zone. After a series of minor intelligence postings on the west coast, Rochefort was finally granted his wish—in a backhanded way—when he was assigned the command of a floating dry dock on San Francisco. But it was conditional that he would not take it to sea, merely supervise its fitting out. Not until April 1944 were Rochefort's real talents again tapped when he returned to Washington to work on Pacific Fleet Strategic Intelligence studies and on plans for the anticipated invasion of Japan.[12]

It was very disturbing for me, his friend of many years, to see how Rochefort was speared like a frog and hung out to dry for the rest of the war when he could have done so much more to help us win it. When it was apparent that Joe had been spirited away over the personal protests of Nimitz, I tried to persuade the admiral to back up his request that Rochefort be awarded the Distinguished Service Medal.

"When the time comes, I hope to take this up," Nimitz promised. But he reminded me, "Layton, if you know anything about Admiral King, you know that when he has made his mind up, it is made up. I've got enough to do to fight this war right now." Unlike the Redmans, he was not one to elevate a personal feud above struggle with the enemy.

About ten days later Nimitz sent for me. He showed me a personal letter on Admiral King's hand-laid bond and told me to read the paragraph he pointed out. It began, "Now that I have taken care of Rochefort, I will leave it up to you to take care of Layton."

"Layton, you've got an enemy there in Washington," the admiral said. "Why do they want to get rid of you?" I was dumbfounded because I had not at the time appreciated the machinations of the Redman clique. I suggested that maybe he might like to find a nice destroyer for me to command.

"Go back to your office and don't think any more about it," Nimitz told me with a reassuring chuckle. With that he pulled from his desk a portrait photograph, which he signed then and there: "To Commander Edwin T. Layton. As my intelligence officer you are more valuable to me than any division of cruisers."

Epilogue: On to Tokyo Bay

"THE FATE OF THE NATION quite literally depended upon about a dozen men who had devoted their lives and their careers, in peace and war, to radio intelligence."[1]

That was how Captain Jasper Holmes, then deputy director of Jicpoa, summed it up in a postwar assessment that Nimitz enthusiastically endorsed. Actually, the intelligence war had been won by the end of 1942, so you can imagine the blow to Hypo's morale, to say nothing of my own disappointment, when Rochefort left Pearl Harbor just before the tide turned in the campaign for Guadalcanal.

After Joe left, and the fleet shifted to the offensive in 1943, radio intelligence remained the cornerstone of our effort in the Pacific. The concepts remained the same. But it was inevitable that major changes would be made in our operations at Pearl. The Intelligence Center Pacific Ocean Area (Icpoa) increasingly acted as the middleman between fleet headquarters and Hypo, especially after Icpoa received its first large group of translators in February 1943. These twenty reserve officers were graduates of an eleven-month crash course in Japanese at the naval language school at the University of Colorado in Boulder. They were the first of a growing stream of linguists and analysts necessary to meet the demands of our expanding amphibious operations.[2]

A major reorganization of intelligence was made seven months later when Nimitz was named commander in chief Pacific Ocean Area. In September 1943, almost a year after Rochefort's replacement, Joe's plans for Hypo were finally vindicated. Its code-breaking and traffic analysis function was placed directly under Cincpac command as the Fleet Radio Unit Pacific Fleet or Frupac. The new Icpoa became Jicpoa, reflecting the "Joint" nature of Nimitz's command, and its staff continued to grow. By the final year of the war it was almost two thousand strong. Members of the army, navy, air force, marines, and coast guard all helped make it one of the most effective intelligence organizations in military history.

Jicpoa's task was to prepare strategic estimates for our major operations by drawing together information from every source of intelligence: from radio intercepts to prisoner of war interrogations. One new role was combat intelligence, which proved most effective. Intelligence teams would go ashore with the first wave of our landings to collect any documentation that would assist with the assault.

While Jicpoa provided the clearinghouse for assembling and disseminating other intelligence, our principal source throughout the war remained the radio intelligence units. Especially important were the Hypo team. Dyer, Wright, Finnegan, and the other men, who had been inspired by Rochefort, continued their brilliant work of penetrating the enemy code traffic. So well did their operation function that despite temporary setbacks as a result of the Japanese introducing new additives or code books, there was never a sustained period when we were not able to read communications in the principal JN-25 operational system.

"During the whole war the enemy's traffic was consistently read in detail and in great volume," stated an official wartime naval appraisal. "After the battle of the Coral Sea, most of his moves were disclosed through this source alone. Whenever the main code was not being read, a feeling of frustration and exasperation permeated the radio intelligence organization and spurred them on to each new success."[3]

The road to Tokyo was to be bitterly fought. Its route was to be disputed among our own commands, but the intelligence obtained from enemy radio traffic provided Admiral Nimitz with the tactical and strategic key to his Pacific campaign. Even General MacArthur was to concede that radio intelligence "saved us many thousands of lives and shortened the war by no less than two years."[4]

Twelve months of fighting on the defensive after Pearl Harbor had helped us forge radio intelligence into a potent, war-winning weapon. But the Japanese never remedied the fundamental flaws in their communications security, which should have been exposed by our success at Midway. They also failed to make any serious penetration of our own code systems, perhaps on the fatalistic assumption that our ciphers, like theirs, were too complex to admit any sustained eavesdropping. Fortunately for us, our enemy paid no heed to the injunction made a century earlier by Edgar Allan Poe: "It may be roundly asserted that human ingenuity cannot concoct a cipher which human ingenuity cannot resolve."

While the Japanese never read our ciphers, we were able to maintain our penetration of their principal naval operational ciphers from early 1943 onward. This included the four-digit code used by their merchant shipping. The breakthrough into the so-called *maru* cipher used by the Japanese transports was the product of five months' sustained effort by the Hypo team led by Captain Dyer and Commander Wright.[6] The Japanese modeled their merchant ship communications system on British "reporting and routing" practice. So our ability to read the *maru* code allowed us to plot the Japanese convoy routes from their daily noon position reports. Their merchant skippers obligingly and methodically transmitted reports at 0800 and 2000 each day. Our ability to know exactly where their convoys were heading was to become the vital factor in running our successful submarine war, which, by late 1944, had effectively severed the seaborne lifelines of Japan's scattered empire.

Only after the *maru* code had been broken early in 1943 was it possible for Nimitz to begin the undersea war in earnest. Until then we had tried to use radio intelligence to direct our submarines against enemy warships. It had been my duty to keep the commander of our submarine force posted with the movements of major Japanese warships. A simple code was used to disguise the source of the information by which our boats were directed to map references where they could expect "whales" (carriers) or "bears" (cruisers). Enemy carriers were given high priority, but at long distance it proved difficult to direct our submarines in attacking fast-moving and well-protected naval units.

Radio intelligence, however, did eventually provide an explanation of some of our more notable failures, such as the ten torpedoes that submarine *Tunny* successfully fired at close range into an enemy task force south of Truk on 10 April 1943. After her skipper's report, we had high hopes that two out of three Japanese carriers had been hit.[7] But within a few hours, I was reluctantly reporting to Nimitz that we had decrypted a message from Truk's port director reporting the safe arrival of all of the task force. Such disappointments were all too frequent. They culminated on 11 June in a string of failures by our submarines in Tokyo Bay to sink any fleet units, although *Trigger*'s skipper reported explosions after a full salvo successfully fired at carrier *Hiryu*.

Following my radio intelligence report that *Hiryu* had signaled that she was only slightly damaged, Nimitz summoned Rear Admiral Charles Lockwood, his submarine force commander, for an emergency conference on 23 June. After I had given my evidence to support the long list of our attack failures, they concluded that the magnetic detonators on our torpedoes were probably defective.

"I think that we ought to deactivate the magnetic exploders," Nimitz proposed.

"I can't order that," Lockwood said, "but I wish that you would."

"I can and will," Nimitz declared. He promptly ordered that the magnetic detonators on the torpedoes in all ships and airplanes under his command were to be deactivated.

The Bureau of Ordnance at first refused to believe that their torpedoes were at fault. But they could not argue with the submarine skippers' action reports, or my list of decrypts confirming the failure to inflict any major damage in most of their attacks despite some hits. An investigation revealed that there were indeed design faults with a poorly tested exploder, as well as other defects that caused our torpedoes to run deeper than their set depth. Until an improved design was manufactured, temporary measures were ordered to correct the defects, and the sinking of Japanese ships by our submarines increased through the summer of 1943 on a satisfyingly rising curve.[8]

While radio intelligence was helping to uncover the eccentricities of our torpedoes, the ability to read the *maru* code system enabled us to redirect our submarines economically and effectively against the slow-moving, poorly escorted enemy convoys. (As an old submariner, Nimitz was an enthusiastic advocate of unrestricted warfare against Japan's most vulnerable line of supply and communications.) Commander Jasper Holmes, who was later promoted to captain and made deputy director of Jicpoa, was chosen by Nimitz to mastermind this offensive. He soon established a routine that began at 0900 each day when he met with the operations officer of the Pacific Fleet submarine force to update their plot of Japanese convoys and decide which targets would be allocated to each submarine patrol.

Orders would be flashed out with up-to-date information on the courses of Japanese convoys. This made for a very efficient use of our forces, because it eliminated long and fruitless searches for likely targets. It was not unusual for all of our submarines on patrol in the central Pacific to be occupied simultaneously in an attack directed on the basis of information supplied by radio intelligence. Sometimes it was only a matter of hours between decryption of a *maru* message and one of our submarines reporting a sinking. A hand-powered telephone link with the commander of the submarine force and Jicpoa completed what Holmes described as "the basis of almost perfect coordination between operations and intelligence."[9]

The breaking of the *maru* code was a major factor in sending the annual sinking rates up by the end of 1943 to a million and a half tons. By January 1944 our submarines were sending enemy merchantmen to the bottom at the rate of almost a third of a million tons a month. There was no way for the Japanese shipbuilding industry to keep pace. Over eight and a half million tons of enemy shipping had been sunk by 1945, an attrition that made a significant strategic contribution to winning the war.

In the early months of 1943, Hypo also broke the Japanese navy's main weather code. Later, this played an important part in our strategic bombing offensive. But it was our ability to keep eavesdropping on the Japanese JN-25 fleet operations code which continued to make the biggest contribution of our war effort. Hypo's ability to keep track of the changed editions of the cipher's additive groups was greatly assisted by our salvage of confidential documents from Japanese submarine *I-23*, which had been sunk on 29 January in shallow water off Guadalcanal. Although the current JN-25 code book was buried when the crew escaped ashore, we recovered a red-covered code book, and additive tables from earlier versions, that yielded valuable intelligence data.[10]

The Japanese navy's main operational JN-25 D code system remained substantially unchanged except for the regular key changes until 31 May, when it was succeeded by the E version. By then it had been in use for over nine months, three months longer than the maximum prewar period. Their failure to change their main ciphers more frequently had permitted us to make the Midway code breaks a year earlier. In April 1943 a similar lapse of cryptographic security enabled us to strike another deadly blow. The target this time was not enemy ships or bases, but the irreplaceable commander in chief of the Combined Fleet.

We knew from the call sign intercepts that Admiral Yamamoto had arrived in Rabaul at the beginning of April to direct an all-out naval air offensive, code-named I-Go, against our bases in the lower Solomons and New Guinea. On 7 April, he had waved good luck to the first two hundred fighters and bombers that took off to blast Guadalcanal in the biggest air raid since Pearl Harbor. Four days later he decided to make a personal tour of the Japanese air bases in the northern Solomons. His staff gunnery officer, Captain Yasuji Watanabe, had planned Yamamoto's itinerary and ordered that it be transmitted only by naval communications because he did not trust the security of army codes. Contrary to his request it was sent by both systems and we picked up both of them. Major Alva B. Lasswell had the duty at Hypo that day and was first to break the message.

Ever since Combined Fleet headquarters had moved south, we were keeping a special watch on the Rabaul radio circuits. This attention paid off in the early hours of 14 April when a signal was intercepted. The partial decrypt was to prove to be Yamamoto's death warrant:

> On 18 April CinC Combined Fleet will visit RYZ, R—— and RXP in accordance with the following schedule:
>
> 1. Depart RR at 0600 in a medium attack plane escorted by 6 fighters. Arrive at RYZ at 0800. Proceed by minesweeper to R—— arriving at 0840.
>
> 2. At each of the above places commander in chief will make a tour of inspection and at —— he will visit the sick and wounded but current operations should continue.[11]

Although Tommy Dyer and Ham Wright had not been able to recover all of the area designator code groups, we knew that RR was Rabaul, RXZ was Ballale, and RXP was Buin on the southern tip of Bougainville. Since the message was addressed to the garrison commander at nearby Ballale island, it was clear that the first part of this trip would bring his plane within range of our fighters from Guadalcanal. The question that confronted me, when Jasper Holmes called me on our private telephone line that Wednesday morning, was what action to take. After he hand-carried the text of the message to Cincpac headquarters, I hurried down the corridor to consult with Nimitz.[12]

It was shortly after 0800 when Commander H. Arthur Lamar, Nimitz's flag secretary, told me, "Zero Zero is in and will see you now."[13] After the admiral had studied the message and checked his wall chart to confirm that Yamamoto's itinerary would bring him within range of our fighters, his question was: "Do we try to get him?"[14]

There was no doubt in my mind that shooting down Yamamoto would be a vital and serious blow to the Japanese. There was no one of the same stature to replace him. Admiral Yamaguchi had gone down with carrier *Hiryu* at the Battle of Midway, and during our review of who might succeed to the command of the Combined Fleet, Nimitz proved surprisingly well informed of the reputations and qualifications of the senior Japanese naval staff. In a final summary I assured him that there was indeed only one Yamamoto. "You know, Admiral Nimitz, it would be just as if they shot you down," I said. "There isn't anybody to replace you."

After our meeting Nimitz sent Admiral Halsey an "eyes only" message telling him that Yamamoto himself would arrive at Buin at 0600 on 18 April in two "Betty" bombers escorted by six Zeros. Halsey responded by confirming that the army air commander on Guadalcanal could arrange for his shootdown by long-range P-38 fighters. But he expressed his concern that such an operation might alert the Japanese that we were breaking their codes.

In anticipation of this reply I had already prepared a draft for Nimitz that "authorized and directed" them to go ahead "provided all personnel concerned, particularly the pilots, are briefed that the information comes from Australian Coastwatchers near Rabaul." Nimitz, who had already received the president's approval for the operation via the secretary of the navy, read my message carefully. He initialed it for release after adding "Best of luck and good hunting."

There were some qualms of conscience on my part. I was signing the death warrant of a man whom I knew personally. It was impossible for me not to feel for Admiral Yamamoto with a certain amount of fondness. It was not as though we were involved in the shooting of somebody whom I had never met. Although he had been my "official friend" four years ago, however, I could not dismiss the fact that he was now my sworn enemy. War, in essence, involves the destruction of your enemy. As the leader and inspiration for the Japanese navy, Yamamoto was an important foe whose death would benefit the Allied cause.

That was very much my reaction on the Sunday afternoon when Nimitz showed me the signal that Halsey had relayed to him:

P-38s led by Major John W. Mitchell, U.S.A., visited Kahili area about 0930. Shot down two bombers escorted by Zeros flying close formation. One shot believed to be test flight. Four Zeros added to score sum total six. One P-38 failed to return. April 18 seems to be our day.[15]

"Sounds as though one of the ducks in their bag was a peacock," Halsey added.

"It seems probable that CinC Combined Fleet was shot down in a place over the Buin area today by Army P-38s" was the epitaph Nimitz accorded Yamamoto in the Cincpac war log.[16] Any public reaction had to wait another month until Tokyo Radio on 21 May announced that their fallen leader's ashes had been returned to Tokyo and that Yamamoto had been killed "while directing general strategy at the front line in April of this year, engaged in combat with the enemy and met a gallant death in a war plane."[17]

The shooting down of Yamamoto was a trauma for most Japanese. His death also struck at the fighting morale of their navy, not the least because Admiral Mineichi Koga, his chosen successor, was a conservative strategist who lacked flair and charisma. Yamamoto's distraught friend and gunnery chief, Watanabe, was mortified when he discovered that his chief's itinerary had also been broadcast in army cipher to the Buin garrison. Although Watanabe was never able to confirm his suspicions, he always remained convinced that we obtained our tip-off from army rather than from navy communications.[18] That was also the scuttlebutt opinion of our army pilots who had carried out the operation. But fortunately for us the newspapers back home did not pick up this story or Watanabe's suspicions might have prompted another major code change.

The impact of Yamamoto's death was intensified a month later when eleven hundred men of the Seventh U.S. Army landed on Attu on 11 May and recaptured our Aleutian island by the end of the month. The operation was not carried out without considerable difficulty. Surprising as it may seem, we lacked any detailed maps.

The assault had to be planned on the basis of aerial reconnaissance missions. The photographs provided the troops with accurate dispositions of the enemy's installations and order of battle. But they did not warn us how hard an enemy outnumbered five to one would fight. Instead of surrendering when their predicament became hopeless, they launched a suicidal banzai charge on 30 May, which left the slopes of Chicagof Harbor strewn with corpses. Only twenty-eight Japanese were left alive out of the garrison of nearly twenty-five hundred, and the recapture of this inhospitable scrap of rock and tundra cost us a thousand dead.[19]

It became clear that the only easy way to overcome the Japanese on neighboring Kiska Island was to kill as many of them as possible before our troops went in. But when our assault landed on 15 August after a two-day air-and-sea bombardment, there were no Japanese on the island. Undetected by our intelligence, they had executed a skillful evacuation operation three weeks earlier. Nimitz was greatly relieved at the lives saved, but there were some red faces in the Pearl Harbor intelligence organizations when an examination of photographic intelligence records showed that we had overlooked one picture on which the photo interpreter had noted "things strewn around beaches and other places as if the island had been abandoned."

While the Japanese were being dislodged from their toeholds in the Aleutians, Halsey's campaign was driving them back up the Solomons as he advanced from Guadalcanal to New Georgia at the end of June. Intelligence provided a timely alert that a big Tokyo Express was heading down from Rabaul to land enemy reinforcements behind our newly established beachhead.

Halsey promptly dispatched a task group of three light cruisers and four destroyers under Rear Admiral Walden L. "Pug" Ainsworth to guard the entrance to the Kula Gulf off the northern tip of New Georgia. Shortly after midnight on 5 July the Tokyo Express of ten destroyers collided with our force. The Japanese managed to land their reinforcements although they lost two destroyers, and our cruiser *Helena* was torpedoed and sunk. Admiral Ainsworth, however, reported that he had sunk two enemy cruisers and he claimed additional destroyers, which had "vanished" from his radar screens during the action.

On the day following the action, Nimitz asked for my assessment. A year earlier, after too many "sinkings" had turned up in our after-action radio reports, Nimitz had determined Cincpac would make no official action reports until they had been reviewed by fleet intelligence. Nimitz was very enthusiastic when he asked me to check up on how many cruisers Ainsworth had sunk at Kula Gulf.

"Admiral, we did not get any cruisers," I reported. "There were no Japanese cruisers within five hundred miles of the action." He was reluctant at first to believe that one of his admirals could have made such an exaggerated claim. The following day I was able to tell him that the Japanese decrypts indicated that only one destroyer had been sunk by naval gunfire; the other had run aground on a reef. When Ainsworth flew in to Pearl to make a personal report, Nimitz, very uncharacteristically for him, put me in the firing line by calling me in to confront Ainsworth with the facts.

"How can you sit here on your fat ass, thousands of miles from the action and make such a statement," a furious Ainsworth demanded. "How can you say this, it's absolutely preposterous!"

"All I can do is report what we get from radio intelligence," I tried to explain. "I have no stake in this matter personally, but I have a stake in the war."

Ainsworth continued to berate me after Nimitz had passed the matter to Soc McMorris, for arbitration. We went around and around on the issue but Ainsworth remained unconvinced. Twelve days later, I had hard evidence proving that my version was correct. It reached Halsey's headquarters from a Japanese survivor of another destroyer sinking. He was carrying a folder whose red border designated it a top-secret Japanese document. It was the Japanese action report for the Kula Gulf action.

The report was flown to Pearl, and I showed it to Nimitz to confirm that there had been no cruisers involved and that only two enemy destroyers had been lost. He ordered it translated immediately—and I assigned the task to Commander Alwin Kramer, who had just arrived to join the Cincpac intelligence staff. In checking on his progress with this urgent project, I discovered that Kramer had left it half translated and had gone off to Honolulu, where he was finally located in a pool hall. I did the translation myself, with my yeoman doing the tracing of the action chart.

Nimitz had already drafted a covering letter to convey the translation to Admiral Ainsworth, saying that it would be "grievous to you to hear that our intelligence was found to be more accurate than your report," but as commander in chief he had to rely on intelligence and "not be carried away by overoptimistic estimates of enemy losses." I heard no more from Ainsworth—and Kramer shortly found himself posted to Halsey's headquarters in the southwest Pacific.

While our admirals sometimes became carried away with their action reports, more often it was our carrier pilots. There was a spate of overestimates after the Bougainville landings in the first week of November. Radio intelligence had alerted us that major units of the Combined Fleet were being rushed to Rabaul to threaten our Empress Augusta Bay beachhead. Halsey decided to take a calculated risk by sending his carriers north to launch a series of raids against the enemy forces assembling in the heavily defended fleet base at Simpson Harbor. Starting on 11 November, five carrier air groups began a series of massive air strikes to "change the name from Rabaul to Rubble," as Halsey graphically put it.[20]

We knew from the radio decrypts that Admiral Koga had made the too-cautious decision not to challenge our cruiserless task forces, and had withdrawn the Combined Fleet units to Truk. Our fliers, nevertheless, were soon claiming to have sunk five or six Japanese carriers. Although there were no longer any large warships at Simpson Harbor, they were still reporting hits on battleships and carriers. Nimitz became very concerned.

"There is nothing that we can do about this," I told him, explaining that they were probably mistaking landing craft for capital ships. "It is my assessment that when these boys drop a bomb, they are under great mental stress. They see a big explosion and they figure they must have sunk a large warship."

Nimitz's concern was, however, justified. We could not afford to underestimate the enemy strength at this critical point of the war when the final phase of the Solomons campaign coincided with the launch of the navy's long-awaited central Pacific offensive. This offensive had originally been intended to follow the Rainbow war plan strategy for seizing a major base in the Marshalls. Our intelligence estimates, however, had revealed that enemy air strength was being built up in anticipation of our assault on the outer islands of their Pacific defense perimeter.

Nimitz was a careful strategist. He was able to convince Admiral King that we should advance into the heavily defended Marshalls by way of the island stepping-stones in the Gilberts. These were within bombing range of our air bases at Canton Island and Funafuti in the Ellice group. The northernmost atolls of Tarawa and Makin were selected for capture, after the Cincpac staff had ruled out Ocean and Nauru because their steep bluffs would make them difficult to assault. The capture of the enemy airfield at Betio, the largest of the pair of islands that composed Tarawa, along with that of the Makin airfield, would then afford us the land-based air cover for a northwest advance into the Marshalls.

Admiral Spruance was designated as the overall commander. Turner was in charge of the amphibious force with marine General Holland M. Smith commanding the actual landing. These two officers both held strong opinions about how to conduct such an operation. But the warfare that erupted during the planning sessions between Terrible Turner and Howlin' Mad Smith was only a foretaste of the reception awaiting their forces on the narrow beach at Tarawa.

Carrier raids the month before the scheduled landing date of 20 November had softened up the enemy defenses. But the strikes had also alerted the enemy. When the marines hit the beach at Betio on 20 November 1943, despite a heavy predawn bombardment from the battleships, the Japanese kept up a concentrated fire from their fortified bunkers. A tragic miscalculation from the tide tables stranded the second wave of amphibious tanks and landing craft hundreds of yards from the beach, forcing the marines to wade ashore under a murderous hail of gunfire.

Jicpoa intelligence estimates had put the Tarawa garrison at fewer than 4,000, but they had been reinforced by a contingent of Japanese marines of the Special Naval Landing Force who had been exhorted to fight to the last man. Only 150 Japanese and Korean noncombatant laborers survived the three-day battle for the 291 acres of battered palm and coral that cost the lives of 1,027 of our marines with 2,292 wounded. Makin was weakly garrisoned by comparison, and the army lost only 64 men, but it nevertheless took almost as long to secure as Tarawa.

Nimitz flew in to inspect the devastation at Tarawa. Deeply shocked, he compared it to the terrible slaughter at the Battle of Ypres in World War I. The gallantry and courage of the assault was in the finest tradition of the marine corps, but our commanders returned to Pearl determined to avoid such costly landings in the future. One of the "Lessons Learned at Tarawa," according to a special report prepared by Turner, was the

need for much heavier and more accurate bombardment of enemy for-
tifications.[21]

After "Bloody Tarawa," the task force commanders assumed that we
would crack the outer shell of the Marshalls first. But radio intelligence
revealed that this was precisely what the enemy anticipated. They were
moving army units and artillery from their Kwajalein headquarters to the
outer atolls. Nimitz instructed me to keep track of this movement and
draw up a new order of battle for each of the island groups. This was kept
up on a day-to-day basis and cross-checked against such intelligence as
the latest intercepted ration reports and the routine lists of sick and hospitalized personnel. By the end of the first week in December it was
indisputable that Jaluit, Wotje, Maloelap, and Mili had been heavily reinforced at the expense of the defenses of the inner islands.

"Are you sure of this information?" Nimitz asked me. To convince
him that our intelligence was right, I brought him actual decoded messages and showed him the traffic analysis. By this time the admiral was
familiar with all the technical data and the special language used in the
decrypts. After making a careful study of the raw decrypts, he called his
task force commanders to a conference at fleet headquarters on 14 December.

Admiral Spruance, General Smith, and Admiral Turner assembled,
along with their chiefs of staff and planning officers. Just before the meeting began, Nimitz again reviewed my order of battle. He told me to bring
along my intelligence summary to the meeting, and to be prepared to
answer any questions.

Carefully avoiding any revelation as to how we had obtained the details, Nimitz reviewed the new intelligence on the enemy order of battle
in the Marshalls. He then polled each of his commanders individually
in turn to determine whether they still thought it advisable to proceed
with their plans to assault the outer islands. Mili and Maloelap emerged
as their preferred targets. No one mentioned Kwajalein. Nimitz heard all
their discussion patiently, and then dropped his bombshell.

"No, gentlemen, we are not going to any of your islands," Nimitz
declared. "I have decided we are going to Kwajalein. The Japanese
aren't going to know this and they're going to be just as surprised as you
are."

The admirals and the general looked at him as if he had lost his mind.
They argued that all of their plans were complete, down to the details of
the landing areas, troop deployments, and resupply. They unanimously
favored the original objectives.

"I don't care what you've done; just go back and redo it for Kwajalein," Nimitz stated firmly. "That's the enemy's weakest point and they
won't expect us."

The point was then made that Japanese air strength, which was deployed along the outer perimeter, would make a penetration of their de-

fenses all the way to Kwajalein too hazardous. It seemed to me that since their original plans were practically complete, they did not want to change them, despite solid intelligence against them.

Some of the commanders wanted to know what would be done about the outer islands. "We're going to bypass them," Nimitz said, smiling benignly. "We'll just let them wither on the vine."

"I think we should go the other way," General Smith objected for a third time. But Nimitz was quite firm, telling them in effect, "We are going to take Kwajalein and if you don't want to, I'll just replace you."

Majuro was the only concession that Nimitz would make to seizing an atoll in the outer Marshalls—and that was only because radio intelligence and aerial reconnaissance showed that it was almost undefended. When he insisted that this island be captured by a single army battalion, General Smith protested that there must be "a couple of thousand Japs there."

"Layton, you tell General Smith how many Japs are there," Nimitz said, addressing me for the first time since our morning meeting.

"Six."

Smith jumped up and said, "*Six*! You mean six thousand, don't you?"

When I insisted that there were indeed six, according to their ration reports for the past few months, Howlin' Mad Smith growled, "I'll bet you the best bottle of bourbon there is in the Pacific against anything you name that there's at least six hundred on Majuro when we go ashore." Just before the operation I upped my predicted figure to a dozen, because a Japanese sub chaser had been sunk off the atoll and we had intercepted a radio message reporting that some of the crew had managed to get ashore. But I had no doubt about winning the bet.

When Majuro was captured on 31 January 1944, it turned out that there was only one Japanese on the island. He had been left as the so-called police chief when the others were taken off just before the start of Operation Flintlock, as our Marshalls campaign was code-named. The name was singularly inappropriate for an operation involving the largest amphibious force yet marshaled by the navy. Spruance's fleet consisted of 375 ships and 700 carrier aircraft. Their mission was to put ashore fifty-three thousand troops under the air umbrella of another 475 land-based planes from the Gilberts. Additional air and sea bombardment was to be supplied by Rear Admiral Marc Mitscher's task force of 12 carriers, 8 fast battleships, 6 cruisers, and 36 destroyers. This force was also to guard the two invading forces against any attempt by the enemy to send units east from Truk.

Yet even after three days of sustained battering from sea and air, Kwajalein resisted. It took four days of fierce skirmishing until the last of the garrison was overcome. Across the largest coral lagoon in the Pacific, the opposition on Roi and Namur islands was more quickly overcome. Overwhelming force might not have accelerated Kwajalein's capture, but it certainly saved the lives of our men. Fewer than four hundred were killed crushing the enemy defenders.[22]

A fortuitous minor error in the Flintlock plan produced an intelligence bonanza. It proved to be of inestimable value for the next stages in the so-called atoll war. One army raider unit missed its intended landing and went ashore on an islet too far to the west, off the southeast entrance to the Kwajalein lagoon. There a Japanese officer was captured who was carrying a roll of red-edged charts. Standing instructions identified all red-bordered documents as top-secret, so the haul was rushed to Turner's command ship. This windfall provided us with detailed charts of all the mandate islands, showing which areas were mined and which lagoons had been cleared of coral heads.

These charts proved to be invaluable aids in planning our future operations, and I was not the only one on Nimitz's staff to wonder if that army unit had not made their wrong landing as a result of some divine "misguidance." The chart for Kwajalein, for example, enabled us to quickly clear the lagoon of minefields, while possession of the details of the approach to Eniwetok was a great advantage when we put into effect stage two of Operation Flintlock.

Even before we received the captured charts, our intelligence estimates had assured Nimitz that our large troop reserves allocated to the Kwajalein and Majuro assaults would enable Turner to move on directly to capture Eniwetok, 360 miles to the northwest. The atoll was captured within forty-eight hours of our 18 February 1944 landing. But this was only after a last-minute revision of the assault plan, following the capture of yet another set of enemy documents, which indicated that the garrison was stronger than we had predicted. At the same time, Mitscher's carriers completed two and a half days of almost continuous raids on Truk and destroyed 275 Japanese planes and a quarter of a million tons of auxiliary shipping.

Admiral Koga had ordered all his warships west to the Palaus immediately after the Kwajalein attack. But the auxiliaries were scheduled to leave later, however, and the delay was fatal. When our pilots arrived over Truk, they were disappointed not to find the carriers, battleships, and cruisers that they had expected in Japan's "Gibraltar of the Pacific." They nevertheless sank many oilers, submarine tenders, and supply ships.

The destruction of the fleet supply train proved just as effective in curtailing Combined Fleet operations as would have the sinking of its capital ships. Without these support vessels, Japan's ability to mount offensive operations was ended. After the war, the Japanese admirals I talked to always referred to the raid on Truk as the one that broke their back. They had "endured" Midway and the loss of the carriers and their skilled aircrews, but our two-day air strike in the second week of February 1944 was the body blow that had caused them to abandon any hope of forward operations thereafter.

The evacuation of Truk meant that we had successfully cracked through the outer shell of Japan's defensive perimeter and that the enemy bases in the Carolines could be left to "wither on the vine." Truk was safe to bypass. The road to Tokyo could now be opened by breaking through the Marianas to the north, and Palaus to the west, and capturing Formosa as the springboard for an invasion of Japan.

While this was the strategic picture of operations that opened up for Nimitz and Admiral King, it did not agree with MacArthur's grand design. His forces were still battling up the northern coast of New Guinea. He had just secured a foothold in the Admiralty Islands as a prelude to capturing Rabaul, which would serve as a forward base for "a big piece of the fleet"[23] that he anticipated being put under his command. This would enable him to fulfill his promise to liberate the Philippines. MacArthur was determined that any road to Tokyo should pass through Manila. He saw the rapid progress of Nimitz's mid-Pacific campaign as a threat to his strategic concept, and he feared King would sabotage his plans if the navy succeeded in persuading the Joint Chiefs in Washington that the Philippines should be bypassed.

MacArthur and his supporters began a bitter campaign in Washington that lasted throughout the spring and summer of 1944. He was determined to persuade the president, and the Joint Chiefs, to agree to his commanding a single line of advance through the Philippines. Nimitz was under no illusions. The general had sent his key staff members to argue his case that spring at Pearl Harbor. But Nimitz knew that MacArthur could not make any large-scale amphibious assault without the Pacific Fleet. Nor would Admiral King ever agree to putting major naval forces under the control of any general. Although Halsey was technically subject to MacArthur's authority in the southwest Pacific area, he stoutly rejected the general's offer to make him "a greater man than Nelson ever dreamed of being."[24]

In March, however, the Joint Chiefs postponed a final decision on the route to Tokyo by authorizing MacArthur to begin preliminary planning for a fall invasion of the Philippines, while, at the same time, they endorsed Nimitz's plan for an assault on the Marianas (as a first step to a tentative Formosan invasion the following February). Much to his chagrin, MacArthur was denied Rabaul. But Nimitz was also directed to send the Fifth Fleet south. This was to support MacArthur's ambitious plan to bring the New Guinea campaign to a swift conclusion by leapfrogging assaults up the north coast toward the Philippines.

When members of MacArthur's staff arrived at Pearl shortly afterward with their concept of an eight-hundred-mile leapfrog to capture the strategic port of Hollandia, it was agreed the Fifth Fleet would be in support after its carrier task forces had been detached to launch strikes to keep enemy planes from interfering from their bases to the north in the Palaus. Tension between the two staffs was running high, because Mac-

Arthur's headquarters had bombarded Nimitz with a series of communications that should have been written on asbestos.

MacArthur told Nimitz later that his chief of staff had issued these dispatches without his knowledge. Even so, I always wondered why Nimitz kept a picture of the general prominently displayed in his office. It was an unsigned rotogravure clipped from a magazine. One day when I asked about the general's perpetual presence, Nimitz gave me one of his smiles: "Layton, I'll tell you. It's to remind me not to be a horse's ass."

For one of these March sessions with MacArthur's staff Nimitz asked me to play the role of the Japanese command and plot the expected movements of the Japanese land-based air forces in response to the reports of our operation that we assumed Combined Fleet headquarters would receive.

My principal observation was that most of their planes were now piloted by army fliers who lacked overwater navigational experience. Thus, they seldom ventured more than 150 miles to seaward. As a result our carrier task forces were directed to advance on a southerly route close to the New Guinea coast. This enabled them to reach their destination off Palau on 29 March undetected. Our carrier planes destroyed 150 enemy aircraft and sank 70 auxiliary vessels before heading south to cover the Hollandia landings.

The total surprise achieved by this tremendous leap forward encouraged MacArthur to advance, by almost a month, the capture of the Japanese bases at New Guinea's northern tip. The success of his leapfrogging strategy depended on our ability to read the Japanese army ciphers, which we had broken for the first time the previous year. As the army intelligence division put it: "Never has a commander gone into battle as did the Allied Commander Southwest Pacific, knowing so much about the enemy."[25]

After lending a helping hand to MacArthur in New Guinea, the Pacific Fleet staff turned their attention to the June assault on the Marianas. Like the Jicpoa analysts we were heavily dependent on the enemy radio traffic for intelligence, because Saipan, Guam, and Tinian were beyond the range of our reconnaissance flights. The Fifth Fleet was also sent up to make a preliminary raid and to obtain photographs of the Japanese defenses. But our biggest break came not from our reconnaissance flights or enemy radio transmissions, but from another batch of captured documents.

One unforeseen result of the Hollandia operation was that the carrier strikes on the Palaus forced Admiral Koga and his staff to abandon the islands as their fleet headquarters. It was the third time that the Combined Fleet staff had been forced into an evacuation in less than a year. This time the number one flying boat carrying the commander in chief vanished in a typhoon. The number two plane, carrying his chief of staff, Admiral Shigeru Fukudome, was forced down in the water off the island of Cebu in the southern Philippines. Fukudome was still clutching his waterlogged briefcase when he was rescued by Filipino guerrillas. Although he was later released after threats of reprisals, his documents were confiscated. Word was sent to MacArthur that important Japanese papers had been captured. A submarine was sent to collect them.

The Japanese linguists at MacArthur's headquarters were unfamiliar with naval terminology. From their gist translation, however, it was evident to me that the captured documents were the Combined Fleet's operational plans for concentrating its total sea and air strength against our next advance into their island defense system.

As our Fifth Fleet and the Marianas invasion forces were already assembling at Eniwetok, I urged Nimitz to get a photographic copy of this plan sent to Pearl as soon as possible. When it arrived we stayed up all night translating the enemy's so-called A-Go operational strategy. It was plain that their tactical effort to hurl everything they had against us would remain in effect. The next day, a flying boat rushed the copies of my translation of the A-Go plan with Nimitz's final instructions out to the task force at Eniwetok.

Spruance and Mitscher, who commanded the Fifth Fleet carrier task forces, were therefore well aware of the enemy strategy when they set course north across the Philippine Sea for the Marianas. The combined force of 535 ships and 127,571 troops made Operation Forager the largest amphibious assault yet mounted in the Pacific. It began with an air strike on Saipan on 15 June.

This attack caught the Combined Fleet completely off balance, with their battleships poorly disposed to intervene. This was because of faulty intelligence estimates. They had concluded from MacArthur's attack two weeks earlier on the island of Biak, off the northwest tip of New Guinea, that our next objective would be in the Palaus. At his Borneo headquarters, Admiral Soemu Toyoda, the new commander in chief, had to recast their A-Go strategy to deal with our attack on the Marianas. He had already sent superbattleships *Yamato* and *Musashi* charging south to Biak. Now they had to be turned around and redirected northeast into the Philippine Sea where Toyoda hoped that the decisive naval battle could be fought under skies controlled by his land-based aircraft.

Sighting reports from our submarines on patrol off Luzon on 16 June alerted Nimitz that two large naval forces were heading westward from the Philippines. The frantic scale of enemy naval and air activity was confirmed by radio intelligence. Spruance was warned accordingly. That afternoon he cautioned his staff that the Fifth Fleet was to make ready for action because the Japanese were coming after them.

The Fifth Fleet could send nearly nine hundred planes up from its fifteen carriers. This outnumbered by more than two to one the air power that could be flown off the six Japanese carriers. But Toyoda intended to even up the odds by using the airfields on Tinian and Guam for shuttle bombing while he rushed in his reserve of land-based planes from Japan using the Bonin Islands as way stations.

An elaborate decoy operation was supposed to lure our forces westward, but Spruance did not take the bait on 17 June when our radio direction finding put the approaching Japanese warships some six hundred miles west of Guam. Spruance's primary task was to protect the Saipan beachhead. He also knew from the captured Japanese plan that if he went after them full tilt, the enemy carrier planes would be able to multiply their effectiveness by using the other airfields in the Marianas for shuttle-bombing runs. It would also expose him to attack from a stream of land-based planes flying south from Japan.

Spruance, therefore, did not give chase as the Japanese intended—he waited for the enemy to come for him. On 18 June Mitscher's fifteen carriers and light carriers gained the tactical advantage by whittling down the land-based air force in the Marianas before the main enemy air attack.

Then on 19 June when the Japanese carriers launched nearly three hundred planes against our forces from the southwest, Mitscher's radio intelligence unit came into its own by monitoring the voice circuit of the Japanese pilot who coordinated the strikes from high above the swirling air battles. The stream of orders issued by Coordinator "Jo," as he was dubbed by Mitscher's air commander, enabled our fighters to be vectored onto the incoming enemy attack waves long before they reached our task forces. When he was eventually heard radioing for his relief to take over, it was suggested that one of our fighters should be directed up to shoot down Coordinator Jo.

"No indeed," said Captain Arleigh A. Burke, who was then Mitscher's chief of staff. "He's done us too much good this day!"

Mitscher concurred. Thanks to radio intelligence our pilots had won what they jubilantly dubbed the Great Marianas Turkey Shoot in which they had bagged 243 Japanese aircraft.

Toyoda's A-Go plan was already falling into a shambles that afternoon when our submarines torpedoed and sank carriers *Shokaku* and *Taiho.* Another carrier, *Hiryu,* was sunk and two more were badly damaged by a Fifth Fleet air strike late the following afternoon. Spruance was to be criticized by the Monday morning quarterbacks at Fleet headquarters for not keeping up his hot pursuit westward during that night. But his primary duty to guard the beachhead justified his reluctance to expose his carriers to a night action with the five enemy battleships.

Although he denied himself an overwhelming triumph at the Battle of the Philippine Sea, Spruance nevertheless had won one of the most decisive victories of the Pacific war. The Combined Fleet had lost half of its remaining carriers and *all but thirty-six of its aircraft.* While the enemy still maintained a powerful naval presence in theory, in practice Toyoda now commanded an enfeebled fleet. Without carrier air power for its protection, and lacking the auxiliaries to sustain itself for long-range sea-going operations, the Combined Fleet was never again to pose a threat to our command of the Pacific Ocean area.

The Philippine Sea battle also wiped out a large part of the Japanese land-based air power. It also ensured the success of the Saipan operation that followed. During the assault phase, a Jicpoa intelligence team discovered a hastily abandoned Japanese command post in a schoolhouse. After a night spent translating captured documents by flashlight, our forces possessed the enemy battle plan, including precise locations of their batteries and tanks, in time to thwart the counterattack when it came on the following evening.

Yet despite our early success, the battle for Saipan turned into a bloody slugging match. Three more weeks of fighting were required to bring the island under our control. When the firing ceased, three thousand Americans were dead in addition to the more than forty-five thousand enemy killed. Thousands of Japanese chose to commit suicide in the caves of their embattled redoubt, and on the northern peninsula of Saipan many others hurled themselves from cliffs rather than face the disgrace of surrendering.

The loss of Saipan, however, drained the fight from the less-determined defenders on Guam and Tinian. The islands were secured within three weeks of our landings. By the final week of July work was under way to extend their airfields for the launching of the strategic air offensive against Japan.

Meanwhile, Roosevelt journeyed to Pearl Harbor by sea on 26 July. In a well-publicized demonstration of his authority as commander in chief, carefully timed to kick off his bid for reelection to a fourth term in the White House, he was to adjudicate the strategic issue of the Philippines invasion. The army and navy staffs were still divided on whether bypassing or capturing the occupied commonwealth would accelerate the end of the war. While MacArthur had campaigned vigorously behind the scenes for the invasion, Admiral King was opposed to it. Nimitz was stranded somewhat uncomfortably between the two.

MacArthur had arrived on time at Oahu that Wednesday afternoon after his long flight from Australia, but somehow he contrived to be an hour late for his dockside rendezvous with heavy cruiser *Baltimore*, which had carried the president from the mainland. He finally rolled up in a presidential-style motorcade like a conquering hero, a gesture that was no doubt calculated to overawe his totally unflamboyant rival Pacific commander as much as to impress the assembled newsmen.

Nimitz knew that he was in for a tough battle. That evening the two Pacific commanders plunged right into the debate with presentations of their differing strategic views of the next phase of the Pacific war. We had prepared a battery of charts to support the Cincpac contention that it was necessary only to neutralize the Japanese air bases in the Philippines before moving to invade Formosa as the final springboard to Japan. By contrast MacArthur spoke without a map or a note, delivering an impassioned appeal intended to remind the president that any attempt to bypass the Philippines would be militarily and politically disastrous. "American public opinion will condemn you," he concluded. "And it will be justified."[27]

After the general's masterfully eloquent histrionics, Nimitz sensed that Roosevelt's mind had already been made up. When MacArthur left by air the next day for Australia he told his staff on board his plane that he had "sold it." The victory that he won owed more to the political realities of Roosevelt's reelection campaign than to sound military calculation—as evidenced by the fact that it took a month before Admiral King and the naval staff were persuaded to give their reluctant endorsement of the Philippine invasion. On 8 December the Joint Chiefs of Staff issued their directive for the campaign. It was to be launched Christmas week, with a major amphibious assault on the southern island of Mindanao.

At Pacific Fleet headquarters, preparations were already in their final stages for the occupation of Peleliu in the Palaus and the capture of Yap and Ulithi to the north to provide air cover and an advanced base for the fleet. After Nimitz's decision to rotate the fleet's commander's in chief to keep up the pace of our offensive, Admiral Halsey was to take charge of the next round of operations.

The Fifth Fleet was therefore renamed the Third Fleet on 11 September when Halsey arrived in battleship *New Jersey* to lead a series of carrier strikes on airfields in the Philippines. The raids had no sooner begun than the reports of his pilots prompted an enthusiastic dispatch advising Nimitz that enemy air strength on Mindanao had been wiped out. The Philippines defenses appeared to be wide open. Halsey therefore urged that his fleet's intended assault on the Palaus be abandoned in favor of advancing the Philippines invasion. This, he contended, should go in at Leyte. He claimed the change would shorten the war by "many months" by making our initial assault one step nearer the main island of Luzon.[28]

Our intelligence, however, did not make us quite so sanguine as Halsey about the weakness of Japanese air defenses in the Philippines. Nonetheless, Nimitz forwarded Halsey's proposal to the Joint Chiefs. When they approved the Leyte operation for the end of November, Nimitz dropped the Yap assault. But he held fast to the Palaus operation to provide nearby support and repair bases if enemy resistance proved more formidable than Halsey predicted.

A week later, while Third Fleet task forces stood guard, MacArthur's troops captured the island of Morotai off the northeastern extremity of New Guinea and the marines went into the Palaus. Ulithi fell within a matter of minutes; Angaur was in our hands in three days. But the struggle for the nearby island of "Bloody Peleliu," as it came to be called, raged on for over two months. The Japanese had dug themselves into well-fortified positions in the hilly interior of the island. They had to be fought out, cave by inaccessible cave, in hand-to-hand combat whose ferocity exceeded the worst days of the Guadalcanal campaign. Almost two thousand Americans died securing an island which, despite Nimitz's predictions, made little strategic contribution to the winning of the war itself. As one of Halsey's admirals was later to observe, "If military leaders were gifted with the same accuracy of foresight as they are with hindsight, undoubtedly the assault of the Palaus would never have been attempted."[29]

While the struggle for Peleliu was raging in its second month, a thousand fighters and bombers from Third Fleet carriers were carrying out raids on the Japanese airfields on Okinawa and the Ryukyu Islands. More than five hundred enemy planes were shot down, like "so many eggs thrown against the stone wall of indomitable enemy formations," as the now reinstated Admiral Fukudome reported.[30]

With the enemy now battering the inner ring of Japan's defenses, Admiral Toyoda decided that it was time for desperate measures. He submitted his Sho (victory) plan for the emperor's approval. It represented the navy's supreme and final strategic gamble to hurl the remaining strength of the Combined Fleet against the anticipated American assault on the Philippines. To bolster the efforts of the navy's 150 surviving carrier planes, pilots with only basic training had volunteered to make one-way suicide missions against the enemy. They had taken the name *kamikaze,* after the "divine wind" typhoon that had saved Japan in 1281 from invasion by the Mongol fleet.

Divine intervention of some kind was certainly going to be needed if the 7 battleships, 4 carriers, 2 hybrid battleship-carriers, 20 cruisers, and 29 destroyers remaining to the Combined Fleet were going to stop the invasion. Halsey now had the kind of overwhelming naval superiority that few admirals in history have commanded. He could muster 32 carriers, 12 battleships, 23 cruisers, 100 destroyers, and 1,400 planes in the Third Fleet's air umbrella. The Leyte operation was under the joint command of Halsey and MacArthur. Their 430 transports were to be covered by Admiral Kincaid's Seventh Fleet. The scale of the invasion was such that it rivaled the armada that five months earlier had landed the Allied armies in Normandy.

The 20 October invasion date was designated "A-Day" by MacArthur to distinguish his triumphant return to the Philippines from "D-Day." The landings on Leyte were executed with clockwork precision against almost no enemy interference. By the evening of A-Day MacArthur's troops had secured a seventeen-mile front against little enemy ground resistance.

The real opposition came forty-eight hours later, when Toyoda's

Sho-1 started to roll and the surviving and still-formidable might of the Combined Fleet came steaming out of the Borneo port of Brunei. As they headed northeast, the main force led by five battleships set course for the San Bernardino Strait, which separates Luzon from Leyte. The second force, led by two battleships, headed for the Surigao Strait off the southern tip of Leyte. Their intention was to debouch north and south and smash our invasion beachhead in a pincer movement. They were counting on the main strength of our Third Fleet being lured away to the northeast of the Philippine Sea by a decoy force of aircraft carriers that was already heading toward Cape Engaño from the north.

A major change in the Japanese naval code and the observation by their forces of strict radio silence had denied us advance intelligence of the Sho-1 plan. But early on the morning of 23 November, we received some inkling of what was afoot. Two of our submarines sighted and attacked the main force, sinking two heavy cruisers and damaging a third.

The next day, the main force was subjected to heavy air attacks from Third Fleet planes as it headed northwest across the Sulu Sea toward the San Bernardino Strait. After superbattleship *Musashi* had been sunk and *Yamato* damaged, the force turned around to await the cover of night before attempting to force the straits. Halsey therefore assumed that the enemy battle force was in full retreat when he received reports late in the afternoon from his other scouting planes that enemy carriers had been spotted 190 miles northeast of Luzon's Cape Engaño.

"Central force heavily damaged according to strike report," Halsey radioed Cincpac headquarters that evening. "Am proceeding north with three groups to attack carrier force at dawn."[31] This dispatch, however, failed to make it clear to Nimitz, or any of our task force commanders, that the Third Fleet battleships were no longer standing guard off the San Bernardino Strait.

Admiral Kinkaid was also unaware that his force guarding the beachhead was now wide open to attack from the north. He naturally assumed that Halsey would have left at least some of his Task Force 34 battleships as a precaution against an enemy breakthrough. Kinkaid deployed his six old battlewagons off Surigao Strait that evening after sporadic air attacks had failed to halt the advance of the enemy's southern force. When the Japanese made a desperate attempt to fight their way through the Surigao Strait, they were wiped out in the only battleship action of the Pacific war.

An evening air patrol reported that the first Japanese force had reversed course and was again heading for the San Bernardino passage. But Halsey appears to have misread, or ignored, the danger during his dash to the north.

The magnitude of this blunder was not appreciated until the following morning when superbattleship *Yamato* was spotted leading the enemy force racing down the coast toward the beachhead. At Pearl we just could not understand how all these Japanese battleships and cruisers with their

destroyer screen had broken through the San Bernardino Strait undetected and unmolested. They would have smashed the invasion beachhead, too, but for the stark heroism of Rear Admiral Clifton S. Sprague,
the commander of a group of escorts. His "Jeep" carriers were all that
stood between the wolves and the fold. For more than an hour Sprague's
pilots fought off the enemy battleships. Such a fierce fight was put up by
our planes that in the fog of battle the Japanese commander, believing
that he was confronting the Third Fleet carriers, ordered a retreat. The
action fought by the "Jeep" carriers that morning saved the invasion. It
was one of the most magnificent displays of gallantry in the Pacific war.

Nimitz was pretty perturbed when he realized that Halsey had taken
all his forces off to the north and left the gate open for the wolves to
jump the sheep. After we had picked up Sprague's urgent report, followed by Kinkaid's plain-language call for Halsey to send back the fast
battleships, Nimitz decided to intervene. But the Third Fleet commander
in chief was racing full tilt to finish off the carriers, which were under
attack from his air strikes, when the Cincpac dispatch reached him on the
flag bridge of battleship *New Jersey*. Nimitz's message appeared even
more of a rebuke than he intended, because Halsey's decipher had failed
to strip off the padding at the end of the message.

"Where is repeat where is Task force 34? The world wonders"[32] was
what Halsey read. Choking with rage at this apparent rebuff from Nimitz,
the four-star admiral hurled his famous cap onto the deck and stomped
on it. Then, after debating the tactical situation with his staff, Halsey
turned flagship *New Jersey* about to lead his battleships back to Leyte,
leaving his quarry to the mercies of Mitscher's air strikes. The planeless
carriers were sunk, but two battered hybrid battleship-carriers, two
cruisers, and six destroyers managed to get away. It added to Halsey's
chagrin when he learned that the enemy's main force, including superbattleship *Yamato,* had also made good their escape through the San Bernardino Strait.

The Japanese never realized how close they had come to achieving a
punishing victory as the three-day Battle of Leyte Gulf came to a close
with the planes of the Special Attack Force making their fiery debut. The
first group of kamikazes made their suicidal crashes on Sprague's unfortunate Jeep carriers, inflicting heavy damage and sinking *St. Lo.* But even if
"rotten communications," as Halsey described them, had denied him the
total naval victory he had anticipated, by disrupting the imperial navy's
suicidal banzai charge, he and Kinkaid had inflicted a terrible defeat on
the imperial navy. The largest naval battle in history, which had swirled
around Leyte Gulf, cost the Japanese more than a hundred aircraft in
addition to the sinking of four carriers, three battleships, six cruisers, and
twelve destroyers. It had reduced the Combined Fleet to an impotent
force; it was now too weak to defend the approaches to Japan.

The naval war in the Pacific effectively ended with the Battle of Leyte

Gulf. But there still remained nine more months of hard fighting for the Pacific Fleet. It had to battle against the growing menace of the kamikazes at Iwo Jima in February 1945, and the four-month-long struggle for Okinawa that began in April.

The only attempt that the Japanese made at another surface engagement was the suicidal death ride of *Yamato,* which ended on 7 April when the superbattleship was pounded beneath the waves off Okinawa by our carrier planes. Our marines and soldiers continued fighting the bloody battles ashore, while our submarines sank Japanese ships until no enemy merchantman dared venture to sea during daylight. By the late spring of 1945 our carrier air power was increasing and it turned to raiding mainland ports and defense installations. From the end of 1944, Japan had been blockaded by sea and air as swarms of B-29 Flying Fortresses from the airfields of Saipan and Tinian began a systematic destruction of Japan's centers of production and fire-bombed her major cities.

Yet the Japanese fought on with a fanatic zeal. For the majority at home and overseas there could be no question of surrender. The high casualty rates that we had suffered during the landing at Iwo Jima and during the grueling Okinawa campaign were terrible harbingers of the cost we would have to pay as we began planning an invasion of Japan proper.

Nimitz had moved the Cincpac advance headquarters to Guam at the end of January. It was there that I first learned of the weapon that promised hope for our deliverance. I was brought into the secret of the atomic bomb because Nimitz insisted that his intelligence officer be fully briefed as to what was going on. This occurred when Major General Leslie Groves, the Manhattan Project's director, arrived with representatives of the secretary of war's ad hoc committee shortly after the first atomic bomb had been exploded in Alamogordo, New Mexico, on 16 July.

After we had watched the movies of the Alamogordo test, I was convinced that if the bomb worked, it could give the Japanese a psychological "out" from the terrible dilemma they were facing. Although they were defeated and knew it, they just could not surrender. I told the team from Washington that it was my firm opinion that only a decisive intervention from the emperor would end the war. The atomic bomb represented a new kind of warfare. It would give the emperor the chance to "turn off the faucet" on the slaughter and end the war without loss of face. When I was asked my opinion of an appropriate target, I named Okura, an army arsenal city that had not yet been raided.

Hiroshima, however, was selected. When Nimitz was given the top-secret alert that the superfortress carrying the first atomic bomb would take off from Tinian in the early hours of 6 August, I called in Jasper Holmes and told him that we wanted all the army air force radio networks covered, even at the expense of the loss of fleet circuits. After we received the news that the B-29 named *Enola Gay* was airborne, I had nothing more to relay to Nimitz until we picked up the "Bombs away" message the next morning. Minutes later it was followed by the word "Bingo!"

I did not know that there was a second bomb ready to go, but I was disappointed when the Japanese did not accept our surrender ultimatum after Hiroshima. Four days later another atomic blast flattened Nagasaki. I was in my office on 15 August when my special cipher teletype sprang to life with a message from the chief of naval operations at 0720. It clattered away, typing out the actual decrypt of the Japanese acceptance of surrender message. I tore off the top sheet and dashed into Nimitz's outer office.

"This is the hottest thing we've had," I told his flag secretary and went directly in to see Nimitz.

"Here it is," I said, handing over the message.

He read it, beamed one of his searchlight smiles, and announced, "I've just got one from Admiral King."

That morning he issued a dispatch to all ships: "This is a peace warning." But not until the next day did Cincpac send the dispatch to "Suspend all operations," which ended the fighting in the Pacific.

When Nimitz told me two weeks later that I would be accompanying him as his guest to the formal surrender ceremony in Tokyo Bay, he wanted to know if he would face any trouble from right-wing extremists during his intended visit to the Yokosuka naval base. I told him that I did not think so. But I hoped that he would take a marine orderly who was a crack pistol shot "just in case."

"They wouldn't attack me," the admiral said with surprise. "They'd attack MacArthur."

"Not the Japanese," I replied. "MacArthur didn't win this war as far as the Japanese are concerned. It's been your carriers that have been attacking their port cities and it's been the B-29s based in your command area that have carried the bombs to Japan, including the two atomic bombs. They know that it was our naval power that has brought Japan to its knees because they have no shipping. You're the one they would kill, not MacArthur, if anyone were to try such a thing."

Nimitz then asked me if I was a good shot, since I was to accompany him, and there would be no marine orderly. To improve my skills, he took me down to the personal shooting range, which he had set up at Guam headquarters. There we practiced with Colt .45s every day until we left for Japan. So it was with a heavy pistol in a shoulder holster that I accompanied Nimitz when he went ashore at Yokosuka with Admiral Halsey. Fortunately, there were no incidents.

The afternoon of the surrender ceremony, Admiral Nimitz suggested that we take ashore the Chevrolet sedan we had brought with us, and I proposed a trip to Kamakura. This beautiful town had never been bombed. It was a historic enclave full of aged cryptomeria trees and ancient shrines, including the *daibatsu,* or great buddha, and the Tsurugaoka-hachimangu, which had been built by the first shōgun, Yoritomo Minamoto, in the twelfth century. It struck me as particularly appropriate, on the day that marked the formal beginning of peace, that Admiral Nimitz should see for himself the shrine which for so many Japanese had symbolized their god of war.

THE RAID ON PEARL HARBOR: 7 December 1941

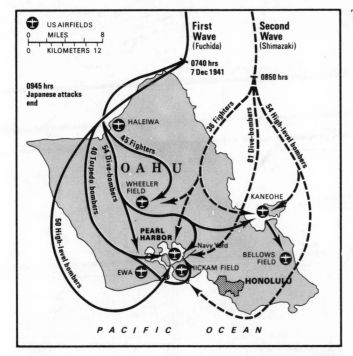

The Attack on Oahu

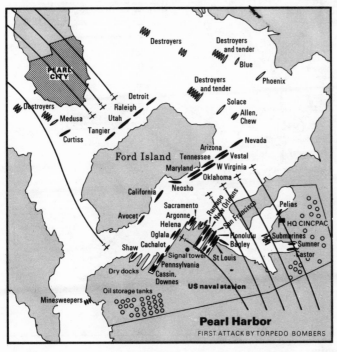

The Strike on Battleship Row

JAPAN INVADES THE PHILIPPINES: December 1941–May 1942

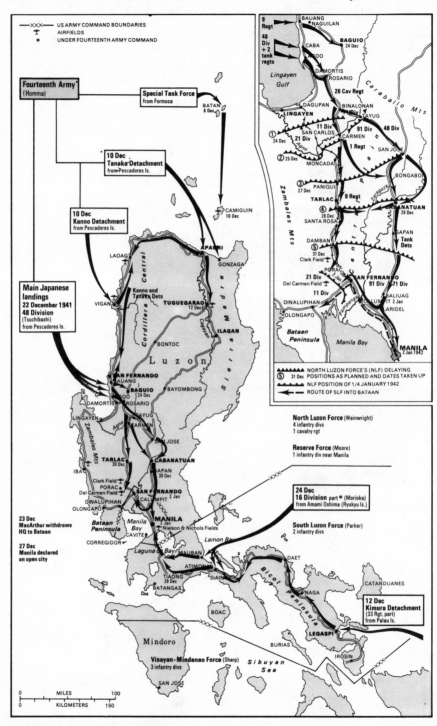

The Luzon Campaign

THE BATTLE OF THE CORAL SEA: 3–7 May 1942

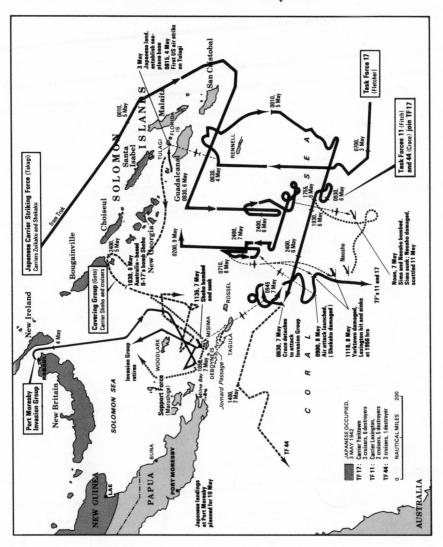

THE BATTLE OF MIDWAY: 3–5 June 1942

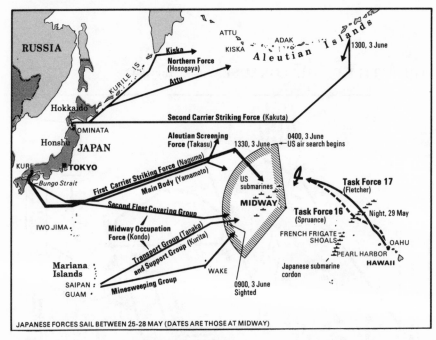

Admiral Yamamoto's Operational Plan

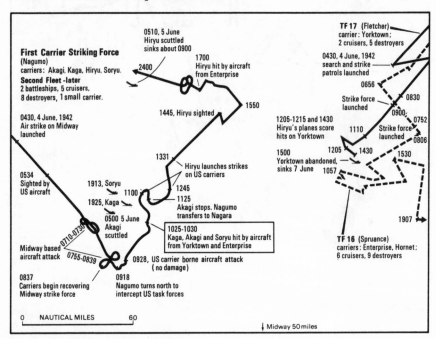

The U.S. Pacific Fleet's Victory

THE SOUTHWEST PACIFIC THEATER CAMPAIGNS: 1942–1944

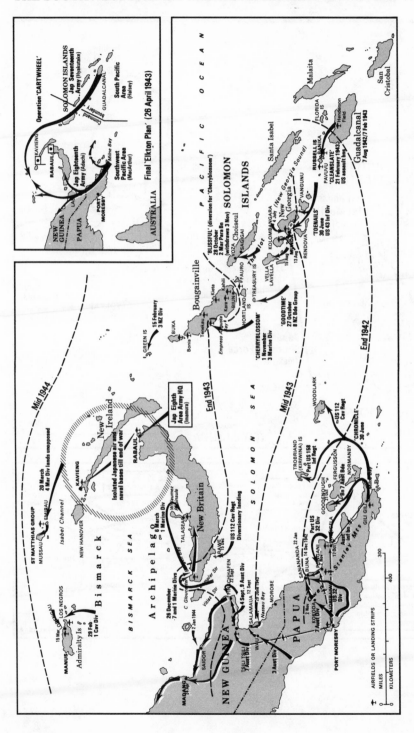

THE BATTLE OF THE PHILIPPINE SEA: 13–16 June 1944

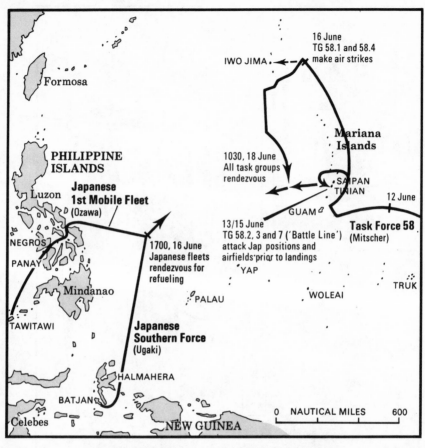

16 June
TG 58.1 and 58.4
make air strikes

IWO JIMA

Formosa

Mariana
Islands

1030, 18 June
All task groups
rendezvous

PHILIPPINE
ISLANDS

Japanese
1st Mobile Fleet
(Ozawa)

Luzon

SAIPAN
TINIAN

12 June

GUAM

NEGROS

1700, 16 June
Japanese fleets
rendezvous for
refueling

13/15 June
TG 58.2, 3 and 7 ('Battle Line')
attack Jap positions and
airfields prior to landings

Task Force 58
(Mitscher)

PANAY

YAP

Mindanao

TRUK

PALAU

WOLEAI

TAWITAWI

Japanese
Southern Force
(Ugaki)

HALMAHERA

BATJAN

0   NAUTICAL MILES   600

Celebes

NEW GUINEA

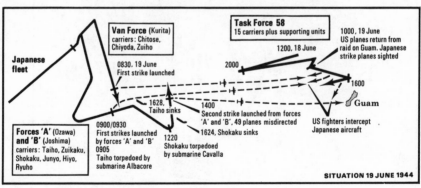

Van Force (Kurita)
carriers: Chitose,
Chiyoda, Zuiho

Task Force 58
15 carriers plus supporting units

1000, 19 June
US planes return from
raid on Guam. Japanese
strike planes sighted

Japanese
fleet

0830, 19 June
First strike launched

1200, 18 June

2000

2000

1628,
Taiho sinks

1400

1600

Guam

Forces 'A' (Ozawa)
and 'B' (Joshima)
carriers: Taiho, Zuikaku,
Shokaku, Junyo, Hiyo,
Ryuho

0900/0930
First strikes launched
by forces 'A' and 'B'
0905
Taiho torpedoed by
submarine Albacore

1220
Shokaku torpedoed
by submarine Cavalla

Second strike launched from forces
'A' and 'B', 49 planes misdirected

1624, Shokaku sinks

US fighters intercept
Japanese aircraft

SITUATION 19 JUNE 1944

THE BATTLE OF LEYTE GULF: 23–25 October 1945

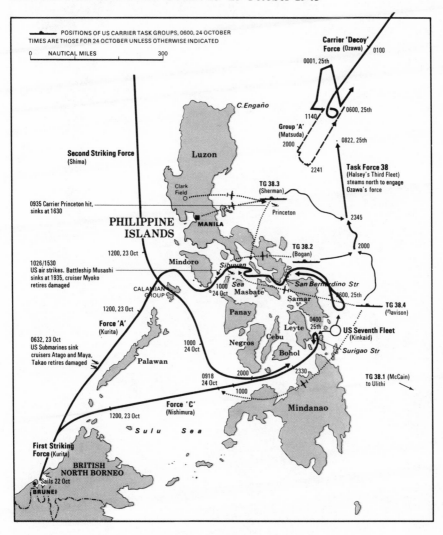

POSITIONS OF US CARRIER TASK GROUPS, 0600, 24 OCTOBER
TIMES ARE THOSE FOR 24 OCTOBER UNLESS OTHERWISE INDICATED

0   NAUTICAL MILES   300

Carrier 'Decoy' Force (Ozawa)   0100

0001, 25th

1140

0600, 25th

Group 'A' (Matsuda)

2000

0822, 25th

2241

Task Force 38 (Halsey's Third Fleet) steams north to engage Ozawa's force

2345

2000

Second Striking Force (Shima)

Luzon

C. Engaño

Clark Field

0935 Carrier Princeton hit, sinks at 1630

TG 38.3 (Sherman)

Princeton

PHILIPPINE ISLANDS

MANILA

1200, 23 Oct

Mindoro

Sibuyan

TG 38.2 (Bogan)

1026/1530 US air strikes. Battleship Musashi sinks at 1935, cruiser Myoko retires damaged

CALAMIAN GROUP

Sea

1000 24 Oct

Masbate

San Bernardino Str

0600, 25th

TG 38.4 (Davison)

1200, 23 Oct

Samar

Force 'A' (Kurita)

Panay

Leyte

0400, 25th

US Seventh Fleet (Kinkaid)

0632, 23 Oct US Submarines sink cruisers Atago and Maya, Takao retires damaged

Cebu

Negros

1000 24 Oct

Palawan

Bohol

2000

2330

Surigao Str

TG 38.1 (McCain) to Ulithi

0918 24 Oct

1000

Force 'C' (Nishimura)

Mindanao

1200, 23 Oct

Sulu   Sea

First Striking Force (Kurita)

BRITISH NORTH BORNEO

Sails 22 Oct

BRUNEI

AUTHORS' NOTES

While Controversy Rages, Lessons to Be Learned

I. A CASE FOR REVISION

EDWIN THOMAS LAYTON was a naval intelligence officer who cared deeply about his craft and its application in defense of the United States. He saw a need to establish precisely what went wrong before the disaster of 7 December 1941, and to explain what happened in the following six months that enabled us to halt the Japanese at Midway and end any hope of their winning the Pacific war. He also believed that the nation needed a final explanation of the intelligence failures of 1941 to reduce the possibility of a nuclear Pearl Harbor in the 1980s and beyond.

When we first considered the possibility that Layton might agree, at the age of eighty, to undertake an account of his World War II experiences, we discussed the idea with Admiral Arleigh Burke. He said that he knew Layton to be a "one channel man, nicely stubborn, who realized the importance of a job to be done, and did not transfer that importance to himself." He added: "If Eddie Layton would publish his story, it could be one of the most important books to come out of the war in the Pacific."

A native of Nauvoo, Illinois, Layton was born in 1903 and after high school he entered the Naval Academy in 1920 and graduated and was commissioned an ensign in June 1924. After serving in battleship *West Virginia* and destroyer *Chase,* he went to Japan in June 1929 for three years of language study. In October 1932 he served in Peiping as assistant naval attaché at the American legation.

In February 1933 Lieutenant Layton returned to the United States for duty in the office of naval intelligence. He joined battleship *Pennsylvania* in June 1933 for a three-year stint as a main turret captain. He returned to ONI Washington in June 1936 and was shortly thereafter assigned as officer in charge of the Japanese translation section (OP-20-GZ) of the cryptanalytic section of naval communications.

Lieutenant Layton went to our embassy in Tokyo as assistant naval attaché in April 1937. Two years later, he was given command of destroyer-minesweeper *Boggs* based on the west coast and then Hawaii. On 7 December 1940 Lieutenant Commander Layton reported for duty as intelligence officer on the staff of commander in chief, U.S. Fleet (Cincus), Admiral James O. Richardson. Two months later he stayed on as intelligence officer to Admiral Husband E. Kimmel—a post in which Admiral Chester W. Nimitz retained him throughout the war.

Detached from Pacific Fleet duty in February 1946, Captain Layton next commanded the naval net depot at Tiburon, California, before returning to Washington in October 1948 and founding the naval intelligence school. He returned to Pearl Harbor, again as intelligence officer on the staff of the commandant Fourteenth Naval District, and also on the staff of commander naval forces Far East. In July 1953, Rear Admiral Layton was assigned to the office of the Joint Chiefs of Staff as assistant director for intelligence. He was assistant chief of staff to the commander in chief of the Pacific Fleet from September 1956 to April 1958. He then resumed duty as director of the naval intelligence school until his retirement on 1 November 1959. His decorations include the Distinguished Service Medal and the Navy Commendation Medal.

In 1959, Layton established Far East headquarters for the Northrop Corporation in Japan, and served as its director until 1963. He continued to write and lecture extensively on naval intelligence, World War II, and Japan.

Captain Roger Pineau was a Japanese linguist during World War II. As a junior officer he served with the code-breaking section of naval communications at the Nebraska Avenue annex that is today the Washington, D.C., headquarters of the Naval Security Group Command. During the final year of the war he was an assistant to Captain Joseph J. Rochefort in Pacific Strategic Intelligence Studies. Immediately after the war, he had duty in Japan with the U.S. Strategic Bombing Survey interviewing Japanese leaders.

At that time Pineau made contacts that were to prove invaluable when he later became assistant to Admiral Samuel Eliot Morison, when the Harvard professor was preparing and writing much of his fifteen-volume *History of United States Naval Operations in World War II*. During his ten years with Morison, Pineau had access both to the navy's operational archives and to the captured records of Japan's naval headquarters.

The Japanese source material had never been properly studied by American historians, and except for the small fraction that Pineau did for Morison, was shipped back to Tokyo untranslated. This documentation forms the basis for the works of naval history in the hundred-volume

Senshi Sōsho—War History Series—published in the 1970s by the historical section of Japan's Self-defense Force. It has yet to be published in English.

Layton was initially helpful to Morison in his volumes III (*Rising Sun in the Pacific*) and IV (*Coral Sea, Midway, and Submarine Actions*). Throughout 1948, Pineau consulted frequently with Layton, who was director of the navy's intelligence school in Washington. Layton retained a vivid personal interest in, and memory of, his service as fleet intelligence officer to Admiral Kimmel and then Admiral Nimitz. Pineau found that Layton was especially intrigued by the new information that was revealed by the Japanese naval staff records. A warm personal friendship grew out of these meetings.

In 1949 Pineau made his second extended visit to Japan, this time to conduct interviews with Admiral Yamamoto's surviving naval commanders for Morison's volumes covering the battles of Coral Sea, Midway, and Guadalcanal. En route to Tokyo, he stopped off in Honolulu for research and consultation with officers including Layton, who was beginning yet another tour of duty as Pacific Fleet intelligence officer. The cooperation Pineau received at Pearl Harbor contrasted with the obstacles encountered when he reached Japan.

General MacArthur, the supreme commander for the Allies, had his intelligence chief, Major General Charles Willoughby, assembling material for a "definitive" history of the Pacific campaign. It was to be based not on the captured Japanese records, still in Washington, but on a series of monographs. These were generalized accounts prepared under U.S. Army direction.

Pineau had difficulty in getting Willoughby's historians to let him interview Japanese officers. Neither Pineau nor his mentor Morison agreed with what they termed MacArthur's "military approach to history." It was obviously aimed at emphasizing and enshrining the general's role as the American commander who had done the most to win the war in the Pacific.

The chief civilian historian attached to MacArthur's headquarters was Dr. Gordon W. Prange, who volunteered, "as one naval officer to another," that he would help Pineau all he could. But all interviews were to be conducted under his auspices. Prange, who neither spoke nor wrote Japanese, was following orders to restrict all questioning to the type of "intensive interrogations"[1] he conducted through army interpreters. These provided material for *The Reports of General MacArthur* and appear to form the basis for much of Prange's own writings on Pearl Harbor and Midway.

Pineau found this military historical procedure unsatisfactory. It blocked the easy flow of information, and he readily accepted the direct help of such Japanese as Captain Yasuji Watanabe (Yamamoto's friend and staff officer), headquarters planning officer Captain Toshikazu

Ohmae, and many others. They invited Pineau to their homes for relaxed interviews. Through them Pineau was able to meet informally with a range of Japanese: from kamikaze pilots to commanders in chief of the Combined Fleet, Soemu Toyada and Jisaburo Ozawa.

These sessions included Pineau's invitation to a select dinner party at the old navy club in Tokyo. Rear Admiral Sadatoshi Tomioka, who had been instrumental in the planning of the Pearl Harbor attack, was the host. On this occasion he questioned Pineau about Morison's judgment that "one can search military history in vain for an operation more fatal to the aggressor. On a tactical level, the Pearl Harbor attack was wrongly concentrated on ships rather than port installations and oil tanks. On a strategic level it was idiotic."[2] Tomioka said, "We thought we did a pretty good job."

Pineau thereupon asked Tomioka how long Yamamoto's staff had predicted it would take for the Pacific Fleet to recover and begin offensive operations after the Pearl Harbor raid.

"Twelve to eighteen months," Tomioka answered almost instantaneously.

"And how long was it before we did make an offensive move?"

There was a long pause as they sat cross-legged at the low dining table. Tomioka sucked in his breath, deep in thought. Simultaneously the others, captains and commanders, dutifully did the same, as though helping him to ponder the matter.

Tomioka eventually looked up and said, with a touch of astonishment, as though it were occurring to him for the first time: "The carrier strikes on the Gilberts and Marshalls at the beginning of February 1942."

Pineau then produced Morison's volume on the Pearl Harbor attack. The Japanese officers smiled when he pointed out the familiar photograph taken from one of their attacking planes over Ford Island. When he asked them to identify the small white circles in the corner of the picture, they all said confidently, "Fuel tanks."

"How many bombs had been dropped on them?" Pineau asked.

"None," said Tomoika. "Only your capital ships and airfields were assigned as targets."

Pineau then pointed out that since Japan wanted to immobilize our fleet, the surest way to have done this would have been to have bombed the fuel tanks. Every drop of fuel used by our warships at Pearl Harbor had to be brought from the west coast. If Japan had knocked out the oil farm, no ships could have moved until tankers arrived with more fuel. By stationing submarines east of Oahu the Japanese could have interdicted any attempt to resupply Pearl Harbor. Had Yamamoto's staff done this, then Tomioka's "twelve to eighteen months" would have been closer to reality.

The former staff officers sat in stunned silence. Pineau then diplomatically assured Tomioka that if he had promoted the bombing of the fuel tanks, he would have earned another star on his shoulder marks. The admiral said with a wry smile, "Pineau-san, you should have been in the Japanese navy."

Pineau's diplomatic skills and his oath of secrecy were to be tested later in his visit. Watanabe, with whom he by now had established a warm rapport, asked if it was because the U.S. Navy had intercepted the Japanese army's message about Yamamoto's itinerary that we had been able to shoot down his "chief." Pineau tactfully told him that Morison's historical research had not yet reached April 1943.

While Pineau was establishing his own contacts with the Japanese admirals, Willoughby's staff tried to prevent him from contacting the leaders held in Sugamo prison for war crimes. But thanks to a personal intervention of the prison commandant, Pineau managed to interview several of the key detainees, including Lord Keeper of the Privy Seal Koichi Kido and Mamoru Shigemitsu, the one-legged former foreign minister who had signed the formal surrender document on board battleship *Missouri.*

The following year Pineau returned to Japan with Morison. They conducted further interviews in Sugamo and also had a long session with MacArthur. During the course of this meeting, the general surprised them with his sincerity and conviction in assuring Morison that the strategy of bypassing Japanese strongholds and letting them wither on the vine had been his idea. MacArthur's claims certainly did not agree with the recent study Pineau had prepared. Wartime staff records showed how the general's representatives had argued for a frontal assault on Rabaul, and that it was Admiral Nimitz who had proposed bypassing the Japanese strongholds.

Morison and Pineau were also concerned to find that MacArthur was still unaware of the outcome of the March 1943 Battle of the Bismarck Sea. He assured Morison that the original claim that twenty or more destroyers and transports had been sunk by his bombers off the New Guinea coast was correct. However, captured documents, translated soon after the action by Layton at Cincpac, had revealed that only eight destroyers and eight transports participated in the operation—and four destroyers survived. After seeing the evidence, Nimitz had sent a cautionary dispatch to MacArthur's headquarters about accepting air force claims at face value. The general had angrily fired back that such a remark impugned his integrity and should be resolved by court-martial if the official report was to be altered. Nimitz let the matter drop.

MacArthur, to assure Morison that there had been no mistake, summoned his intelligence chief for corroboration. Willoughby, as usual, agreed with the general, and promised Morison proof the following morning. When Pineau dropped into the history section that afternoon he found Prange in a conference with his staff. Willoughby had ordered them to substantiate MacArthur's point, but they were at a loss about how to do so. Pineau reminded Prange of the photostatic copies of the official Japanese record on the subject, which he had sent two months earlier. Prange then pulled the report from his office file, and he acknowledged that it was a sensitive point that he had not yet raised in preparing the manuscript of *MacArthur's War Against Japan.*

The challenge that this incident presented to the chief of MacArthur's history team evidently worried Prange. Shortly afterward Pineau was summoned to Willoughby's office. The general announced that Pineau's activities had "displeased many officers in the command" and he would have to leave Japan within forty-eight hours. When pressed, Willoughby conceded that Prange had complained to him that Pineau was "being a nuisance." By now it was clear to Pineau that MacArthur's historical team was anxious to limit "outsiders" in search of information in Japan. Thanks to Admiral C. Turner Joy, our commander of naval forces in Japan, Willoughby's whimsical order was nullified. Pineau stayed to complete his research. In 1952, Pineau returned to Japan to complete his work and discovered the conditions easier. MacArthur had returned to the United States, along with his historians Willoughby and Prange.

The Morison volumes were completed in 1962 and remain unchallenged for their narrative insight and accurate accounting of the naval war against Japan. But in one vitally important aspect they are lacking— *they include no mention of the key role played by radio intelligence.* The 1945 congressional investigation had produced sensational revelations about our ability to read Japan's secret diplomatic exchanges, but the extent to which we had penetrated the Japanese naval ciphers remained classified. Neither Pineau nor Layton—nor even Nimitz himself—was permitted to hint at the real source of the "various bits of information"[3] to which Morison attributed our success at Midway. Pineau eventually arranged officially for Morison to be let in on the secret—but he could never write about it.

Not until 1967 did the public begin to learn the extent to which code breaking contributed to the Battle of Midway in Walter Lord's stirring account *Incredible Victory,* and David Kahn's landmark study *The Codebreakers: The Story of Secret Writing.* The same year also saw the publication of *The Broken Seal: The Story of Operation Magic and the Pearl Harbor Disaster.* Written by Ladislas Farago, a former civilian employee of the office of naval intelligence, the book detailed some of the undocumented background that Roberta Wohlstetter had been unable to include in her scholarly study *Pearl Harbor: Warning and Decision.*

Published five years earlier, when it had been hailed as "the definitive book" on Pearl Harbor, Professor Wohlstetter's book was less concerned than other writers' with apportioning blame for the disaster. Relying principally on the evidence contained in the record of the 1945 congressional investigations, which Layton and McCollum helped her interpret, her scholarly account set out to show how "relevant signals, so clearly audible after the event, will be partially obscured before the event by surrounding noise. . . ."[4]

Prior to these works, the fifties had seen a spate of books by so-called revisionist historians. Their principal champions were Charles Callan Tansill in *Back Door to War: The Roosevelt Foreign Policy 1933–41* and by Rear Admiral Robert A. Theobald, *The Final Secret of Pearl Harbor: The Washington Contribution to the Japanese Attack.* As their titles suggest, these polemics sought to demonstrate that Roosevelt deliberately provoked Japan—then denied Pearl Harbor intelligence—so that the United States would have a *casus belli* for joining Britain's struggle against Hitler.

Wohlstetter's articulate reconstruction of the evidence then available revealed just how insubstantial was the foundation on which the revisionist edifice had been constructed. But reexamining Pearl Harbor, as Wohlstetter has acknowledged, had already become something of a preoccupation for historians. To date the Library of Congress computer lists over a hundred and two titles on the subject that have been published so far. The need to establish precisely what went wrong before 7 December 1941 clearly reflects the nervous uncertainty of an age that needs a final explanation to reassure the nation that the United States could not fall victim to a nuclear Pearl Harbor.

Layton had continued to keep up with the latest publications in the final years of his service career, during which he was a ranking intelligence officer to the Joint Chiefs of Staff. Pineau corresponded regularly with him, including the three years Layton spent in Japan as representative of the Northrop Corporation. It was during this time that Layton renewed his acquaintance with some of Yamamoto's staff officers with whom he had become acquainted as assistant naval attaché in Tokyo.

After his retirement in 1962 to the picturesque tranquillity of his home overlooking the restless Pacific at Carmel, Layton finally found the time to start assembling the full evidence about Pearl Harbor. He began to make meticulous handwritten translations of the *Senshi Sōsho* war histories in school exercise books. He also started the laborious task of reconstructing the Pacific Fleet's wartime radio intelligence communications from microfilmed message files he was able to study at the navy's language school in nearby Monterey.

Meanwhile, Pineau, encouraged by Layton, had begun his own retirement project: to compile a history of Japanese language officers in the U.S. Navy. The admiral's knowledge was so extensive that Pineau urged him to write his own story, but Layton always maintained that this would be impossible without the release of the wartime intelligence records. During the course of the sixties many historians such as Nimitz's biographer, Professor E. B. Potter, and Prange—then a professor at the University of Maryland—consulted Layton. But he was able to give them only general information, in keeping with the constraints imposed by the oath of secrecy he had taken as an intelligence officer. At the same time, Layton turned his hand to writing insightful articles and book reviews for *Proceedings,* the journal of the U.S. Naval Institute.

Layton was dismayed that his foray into print multiplied the number of inquiries he received soliciting information about Pearl Harbor, from naval cadets to distinguished historians from all over the world. If he had answered every one, it would have left him no time to pursue his other interests, which ranged from ship modeling and scrimshaw to bird and whale watching. But he would always find the time to encourage diligent young historians to take their research in fresh directions. One such was John B. Lundstrom, whose thesis *The First South Pacific Campaign* was the first published work on Midway and Coral Sea to make use of Cincpac's so-called Gray Book, the running estimate and summary kept at Nimitz's headquarters.

John Costello, a former BBC producer who had co-authored a best-selling book, *D Day,* first met Layton at the 1977 Naval History Symposium at the U.S. Naval Academy, Annapolis. Costello had just published *The Battle of the Atlantic,* and the admiral offered to help him on a comprehensive history of the Pacific war.

Three years later *The Pacific War* was in its final stages when a massive amount of hitherto classified naval records became available in the National Archives. President Jimmy Carter had effected the release of the World War II communications intelligence records, and it meant that all previous histories were to a degree rendered obsolete.

While Costello was completing his book, Layton was learning about the hundred thousand unindexed Japanese navy and diplomatic messages that were steadily building up in the National Archives. Costello could use only a small part of the documents to meet the publication schedule for *The Pacific War.* It was then that John Taylor of the National Archives introduced Costello to Pineau, who generously agreed to help with the interpretation of the new material.

Published simultaneously with *The Pacific War* in the fall of 1981 was Professor Gordon W. Prange's work *At Dawn We Slept.* The latter book drew heavily on the thirty years of interviewing effort that had commenced with Prange's "intensive interrogations" of the Japanese for Mac-Arthur's history project. He illustrated with minute anecdotal detail Japan's massive expertise at planning the Pearl Harbor attack. But he devoted proportionally less effort to uncovering the underlying intelligence failure that ensured the success of the Japanese attack.

Although widely praised for its apparently exhaustive research, Prange's account did nothing to provide any new understanding of what had really gone wrong in Washington. *At Dawn We Slept* merely served to reinforce the politically loaded thirty-five-year-old report produced by the congressional investigating committee.

"One cannot fault the logic," Prange explained, of the majority report that had apportioned the major blame for the disaster on the Hawaiian commanders.[5] Kimmel and Short, according to Prange, were correctly charged with a "devastating list of failures." Principal among them was their failure "to discharge their responsibilities in the light of the warning received from Washington, other information possessed by them, and the principle of command by mutual cooperation."[6] Prange believed that Washington's miscalculations were insignificant compared to the failures of the Hawaiian commander—although magnanimously agreeing that this constituted "errors of judgement and not dereliction of duty. . . ."[7] Prange therefore affirms that the "verdict of history" demands that we leave the inequitable judgments of 1946 undisturbed.

Layton, who had been one of Prange's interviewees, was particularly concerned by some of the erroneous charges made in *At Dawn We Slept*, but most especially with the renewed attack on his former commander in chief. Layton had always suspected that Kimmel had been given a "raw deal" by Washington, but it was not until after the war that he discovered just how Kimmel had been framed. Layton knew that the fundamental cause of the Pearl Harbor disaster was Washington's failure to properly evaluate and disseminate radio intelligence information. He was especially angered to read Prange's charge that when deciding in which sectors to send out long-range aerial patrols that Kimmel did not "seek the advice and professional judgment of . . . Layton, his Fleet intelligence officer."[8]

This was a distortion of the facts as they had been made available to Prange. But it was also evident to Layton that in spite of Prange's claims that "my scholarship and credibility are unimpeachable,"[9] that *At Dawn We Slept* took no account of new documentation from General Marshall's declassified files, which appeared to indicate that the Hawaiian commanders were made scapegoats not simply for Washington's intelligence failure, but also for the collapse of the entire American Pacific strategy.

The declassification of the most secret files of the U.S. Army chief of staff now reveals that the decision to switch the entire output of B-17 bomber production from England to the Philippines was a key factor in establishing an Anglo-American Far East deterrent force. We can now see that by November 1941 MacArthur was making preparations to threaten the Japanese with preemptive bombing raids. The Hawaiian commanders were not made aware of the extent to which our Pacific strategy had been dramatically revised in the fall of 1941. But MacArthur was—and he enthusiastically encouraged it. The need to get the bombers out to the Philippines explains why Washington so recklessly stripped Pearl Harbor's aerial defenses and long-range reconnaissance capabilities. The bomber strategy also explains why Washington was caught flat-footed on 7 December 1941. Not only was the attack being anticipated from the wrong direction, but the debacle that overtook the intended strategic bombing force in the Philippines the same day was a humiliating coup de grâce to Washington's ill-founded deterrent posture against Japan.

Worse, for reasons that have never been fully or properly examined or explained, MacArthur failed to respond to the Japanese threat facing him for nine hours after the attack on Pearl Harbor. And while Kimmel and Short were pilloried for a failure that was unfairly blamed on them, Mac-Arthur was never called to account. The flamboyant general was not even hinted at as a target of blame when Washington had to produce scapegoats to cover its strategic and intelligence blunders to assuage an outraged American public.

Significantly, *At Dawn We Slept* makes no mention of the army chief of staff's reports that clearly demonstrate that MacArthur had received 250 maps of industrial targets in and around Tokyo in the final weeks before war broke out. Whether this was because Prange's researches were less exhaustive than he claimed or because he was unduly influenced by his five-year supervision of the MacArthur histories is a matter for speculation. But Prange's failure to take the intended role of the bomber force in the Philippines into account certainly contributes to his erroneous claims that "Kimmel's primary problem on December 2 continued to be the proposed moving of Marine Corps aircraft to outlying islands."[10] We now know that it was a direct request from General Marshall that resulted in Admiral Stark's 27 November order to Kimmel to use his two carriers to ferry fighter reinforcements to Wake and Midway. This was to cover the impending flight of forty-eight more B-17 bombers from the west coast to the Philippines.

Prange endorsed navy secretary Forrestal's 1945 charge that Kimmel's "most grievous failure was his failure to conduct long-range air reconnaissance in the more dangerous sectors from Oahu during the week preceding the attack."[11] He does not explain that Forrestal's endorsement was the result of a systematic effort by the administration to shift the blame for Pearl Harbor back onto the Hawaiian commands after the secret 1944 Navy Court of Inquiry had exonerated Kimmel of any failure. But then Prange errs in claiming that Kimmel failed "by rejecting long-distance aerial reconnaissance."[12]

Kimmel did *not* reject aerial reconnaissance. The record of the Pearl Harbor hearings shows that in the first week of December, as Layton has pointed out, extensive deep-ocean aerial reconnaissance *was* being conducted to the west and southwest of Oahu. This was the one sector—according to radio intelligence—from which the main danger threatened in the shape of a Japanese striking force sortie from the Marshalls.

Prange appears to have completely disregarded that the Pacific Fleet's war orders required an immediate advance to capture a forward base in the mandates. In spite of his misrepresentation that Kimmel did not take Layton's advice, his decision to concentrate available long-range reconnaissance west of Oahu was the result of his intelligence officer's detailed reports on the Japanese buildup in the Marshalls. Layton makes it clear that the "nearest snake" was a recurring subject of their daily briefing sessions.

By accepting Forrestal's politically motivated second-guessing of Kimmel, Prange condemned the admiral, showing none of the "special advantage" he professed to possess as a result of having been a naval officer. Had he done so, a few simple calculations with a protractor and chart would have shown him that Kimmel did all that he was told to do—and more. In the final week before the attack Kimmel even rotated some of his scarce long-range air capability to patrolling the northern approaches to Oahu. But since this was not possible on a daily basis, not even Forrestal—who *did* know the facts—went as far as to suggest that Kimmel should have sent patrols out to the north on Sunday.

In spite of what Prange and others have asserted, in the prewar American fleet exercises, strikes were launched from the *northwest* but not from due north, which leaves an awfully large expanse of ocean to be covered. But it stretches credulity to argue that Kimmel should have second-guessed both Washington's guidance and the Japanese threat from the Marshalls.

Another of Prange's conclusions is that Kimmel should have "taken the possibility of aerial torpedo strikes on his ships as seriously as the Japanese took the possibility of antitorpedo nets protecting the American vessels."[13]

Prange claims that if he had been Pacifc Fleet commander, he would have spent 1941 "hounding the Navy Department" to provide the fleet with net defenses. But he neglects to inform us that this issue was thoroughly aired in the 1945 congressional hearings. The navy department, it emerged, had examined the question and had assured fleet headquarters that net defenses were unnecessary. Kimmel was reassured by the chief of naval operations that Pearl Harbor was too shallow for a successful Taranto-style raid. Until it was realized on 7 December that the Japanese had overcome this problem by boxing in the fins, it was assumed torpedoes dropped from aircraft would simply plunge harmlessly into the mud.

Another of Prange's confusions shows in his interpretation of the radio intelligence record. It is as faulty as his characterization of Kimmel as wandering "blindly as any dark-starred hero of Greek or Elizabethan drama."[14] Prange asserts that "blackout of the task force, the dummy message traffic, and American complacency effectively canceled out the possibility of locating Japan's First Air Fleet by this means."[15] But neither Layton, Rochefort, nor Kimmel was at all complacent about the lack of information they were receiving after the 1 December change in Japanese call signs. Nor, as the archival records now show, was there any concerted Japanese radio deception plan that led a "blindly" wandering Kimmel and his staff astray. It was the *absence of any radio messages* to and from the First Air Fleet (the *Kido Butai*) that so successfully concealed their progress across the north Pacific toward Hawaii.

The facts are a matter of record. They negate Prange's allegations that culminate with his assertion that Kimmel "lacked the perception to read the meanings of the warnings and events of those last ten days before the disaster." Ironically, as Layton has pointed out, this charge *would* have been true *if* applied to the navy department rather than Kimmel.

"Mistakes at Washington level were many and varied, but it seems most unlikely that any one of them in itself was a decisive factor."[16] Prange's conclusion, as Layton has demonstrated, could not be more wrong. How did the real explanation of the disaster evade one who asserts so confidently that he "burrowed more deeply into published and unpublished materials on Pearl Harbor than anyone in the historical and writing professions?"[17]

The simple answer is that Prange died before he had a chance to examine the vast amount of newly declassified intelligence documentation. In that case the fault may lie with his collaborators, who prepared the voluminous manuscripts for publication after his death. They declare that in "a thorough search of more than thirty years, including all publications released up to May 1, 1981, we have not discovered one document or one word of testimony that substantiates the revisionist position."[18]

Could they have repeated Prange's own mistake of confusing revisors of history for revisionists? By doing so they evade the major flaw in his researches. Neither he nor they take account of the vast new body of documentary evidence that became available before the publication of *At Dawn We Slept* and its sequel, *Miracle at Midway*, which relies so heavily on the accounts of Fuchida, Lord, and Morison.

Significantly, while acknowledging his indebtedness to Captain Safford, Prange took little notice of his account. He wrote that Safford had "something of a guilt complex about Kimmel and as a result became a rabid revisionist, so I had to be cautious in evaluating his material."[19] Like many historians who had studied Pearl Harbor, Prange felt obliged to protect his "unimpeachable" scholarship from being tainted. In doing so he failed to distinguish the flexibility that conscientiously seeks to revise our understanding of historical events as new facts become available. The revisionist school of historians was championed by Harry Elmer Barnes, who in his edition of *Perpetual War for Perpetual Peace* set out to "prove" that Roosevelt goaded Japan into war and then denied Pearl Harbor access to advance intelligence of the attack.

A more recent revisionist recruit, John Toland, charged that the navy department in Washington actually plotted on a chart the course of the Japanese carriers as they advanced toward Pearl Harbor. His "new" evidence was based on mysterious radio signals picked up northwest of Hawaii that could have been made by a Russian freighter or Japanese submarine. Toland supported his thesis by quoting an erroneous translation of an entry in the diary of the Dutch naval attaché in Washington. That material was withdrawn from subsequent editions of *Infamy* without explanation by the author.

Prange did not live to challenge the revisionist revival led by Toland. But by denying Safford's credibility and failing to research the collection of papers that the National Archives list as the "Navy Pearl Harbor Liaison Office" in record group 80, Prange missed important documentation that the former head of OP-20-G had been assembling from early 1943. These would have alerted him to the truth in Safford's charges of incompetence and conspiracy in the upper reaches of the navy department. Another important reason why Prange did not get to the real heart of the Pearl Harbor failure was that those who suspected, or knew, what had gone wrong in Washington—like Layton, Rochefort, and McCollum—did not feel free to talk.

Prange's reliance on the interviews and monographs he supervised while a member of MacArthur's headquarters historical section also suggests that an important caveat has to be applied when making a final evaluation of the conclusions reached in *At Dawn We Slept*. Prange himself admitted that he owed his "once in a lifetime opportunity" to his position on MacArthur's staff.[20]

New documentation has revealed the reason for the concentration of American strategic air power in the Philippines in the months before the Japanese attack. Given what we now know about his intention to make preemptive raids on Tokyo, MacArthur's failure to heed the clear warnings he received both before and after the attack on Pearl Harbor must raise questions about his own dereliction of duty. *At Dawn We Slept* devotes fewer than a dozen lines to what Prange terms the "undeniable irony which made a hero of one surprised and defeated commander and drove two others off active duty."

Yet MacArthur's culpability for the destruction of his air force and our military defeat in the Philippines is largely uncriticized by Prange. Compared to this strategic disaster, the loss of the five battleships at Pearl Harbor had relatively little influence on the course of the war. The Japanese learned this when the Pacific Fleet was able to take the offensive almost immediately after Pearl Harbor and was able to win a major victory at Midway only six months later.

Prange's special pleading is evident in his unsupported assertion that "few Americans with the interests of their country at heart can regret that MacArthur remained on the job."[21] The convenient destruction of all but a few of MacArthur's headquarters files in the retreat to Bataan, and the carefully groomed accounts prepared by MacArthur's history section—eventually to be headed by Prange—have left us with a lopsided view of the American Caesar.

Layton certainly did not agree with Prange's adulation of Mac-

Arthur—nor would Admiral Nimitz, or any of the "Battling Bastards of Bataan" who composed the disparaging verses about "Dugout Doug." For years it has been known how MacArthur inflated his victories by means of self-laudatory communiqués, but only recently has a formerly secret wartime intelligence history revealed that MacArthur won battles because his advance knowledge of his enemy's intentions made him the "best informed general in history."[22]

As Layton shows, MacArthur's running feud with Nimitz brought the naval war against Japan to a dead stop in 1943. A year later, MacArthur employed political blackmail to pressure Roosevelt into overriding the navy department's strong recommendation that a Philippine invasion was unnecessary to secure the defeat of Japan. MacArthur's determination to vindicate his earlier defeat by fulfilling his pledge to return to Manila can now be seen to have been a costly diversion of naval and military resources that prolonged the war in the Pacific by as much as six months.

MacArthur never once—even after the war—raised his voice in defense of his fellow Pacific commanders Kimmel and Short, who were made the scapegoats for Pearl Harbor. This was presumably another one of those sensitive subjects like the glaring discrepancy over the results of the Battle of the Bismarck Sea. For any exoneration of Kimmel and Short would inevitably open the way to bring in a new verdict of history on MacArthur.

The willingness of the public to accept *At Dawn We Slept* as the definitive word on Pearl Harbor, followed by the sensational charges against the navy made by Toland in *Infamy,* persuaded Layton that there was an urgent need for a surviving insider to set the record straight before it was too late. But first he wanted to assure himself that the documentation he needed to prove his case was available. In the fall of 1982 Pineau, Costello, and Layton spent several days in the National Archives with John Taylor, examining the latest releases of wartime radio intelligence summaries and Japanese naval intercepts.

As a preliminary step, Layton decided to work up a paper on Admiral Halsey's early carrier raids for delivery to the 1983 Naval History Symposium. The Naval Academy had also invited Costello to give a paper on Pearl Harbor, so the admiral and he spent a March weekend comparing their documentation and research. It was then that the admiral decided to speak more frankly than he had ever done before. Layton's account of how an intelligence blunder by Washington similar to Pearl Harbor almost lost the Battle of Midway so impressed Costello that he contacted his publisher.

By coincidence, Costello's editor, Bruce Lee, had also been Prange's editor for *At Dawn We Slept.* Lee knew the strengths and weaknesses of the Prange book. Years earlier he recalled having been told by Admiral Thomas C. Kinkaid, a longtime friend of the family, that he should publish the full story of Pearl Harbor and that one day the documentation would be available to establish the true story. Accordingly, Lee went to the National Archives with Costello and wrote to Pineau to enlist his help in persuading Layton that the time was now ripe to write his book. "I am not interested in looking for scapegoats, nor in protecting the good name of various services," Lee declared. "I want a book that tells the facts within the limits of national security."[23]

So after Costello and Pineau had visited Layton at Carmel to assure him of their willingness to assist in the research and writing, the admiral finally agreed. Many hours of tape recordings resulted in an agreed outline; work began in the summer of 1983 to marry the information gathered by Layton in his collection of notebooks and in the translations he had made of Japanese publications. The object was to weave his personal narrative into the contemporary story of how radio intelligence was developed in the twenties and thirties, and how it was applied—and misapplied—during the Pacific war.

From the outset the project received the fullest cooperation from the history section of the National Security Agency thanks to the personal interest shown in the project by Rear Admiral Paul W. Dillingham. By September, when Layton and Costello presented their papers to the Naval History Symposium, the first chapters were already being drafted. Layton felt that the project was proceeding well enough to announce publicly that he was working on his memoirs. The news was enthusiastically received and his surviving contemporaries volunteered their accounts, confident that the full story of Pearl Harbor and Midway was at last going to be told by someone from the inside who knew the truth.

The admiral prepared his longhand drafts, which were assembled and typed by Mrs. Layton. Between trips to Carmel, Pineau and Costello concentrated on excavating and assembling, at the admiral's direction, the new documentary material. This involved the preparation of a computer finding aide for the decrypts of more than a third of a million Japanese naval messages that are boxed in random order in the National Archives. Such was the progress made that by April 1984 when the admiral suffered his fatal stroke, the first draft of the manuscript up to the Battle of Midway was approaching completion.

Costello and Pineau were immediately invited by Mrs. Layton to come to Carmel to box up all the papers, notebooks, and memorabilia that the admiral had been working on the afternoon he was taken ill. They were shipped to Pineau's home in Bethesda and after a detailed review, the co-authors and their publisher were agreed that the project should be continued.

In the year that it has taken to complete and edit the manuscript much new information has surfaced from declassified documentation and personal testimony. Where appropriate it has been incorporated to reinforce the narrative left by Layton. Bringing such a complex project to publication would not have been possible but for the support that Pineau and

Costello have received from many of those who knew and worked alongside Layton during the war. In particular the late Captain Thomas Dyer,
Captain Wesley A. Ham Wright, and Rear Admiral Donald M. Showers
devoted generous amounts of time to answering many questions when it
came to interpreting the details of Layton's voluminous notes. Captain
Raymond P. Schmidt, U.S.N.R., formerly naval cryptologic historian and
now serving on active duty, gave unstinting assistance with many details
in the manuscript.

   In completing the book, Pineau and Costello are confident that *And I
Was There* tells Layton's story in the way that he began it. No reputations
have been spared for the sake of modesty. The blame for Pearl Harbor
and the credit for Midway are accordingly laid where he wanted them to
be, wherever possible supported by new documentation and research.
The same applies to the evidence of possible Soviet involvement in Pearl
Harbor and the disastrous consequences of the code losses that the British have never officially admitted.

   Layton's testimony and the declassified documents demonstrate the
strength of his central assertion: that he and Kimmel were "shortchanged" of intelligence information by Washington before the attack. It
should now be indisputable that the information that might have averted
the disaster *had been received* by the navy department by 6 December
1941. There is now convincing evidence that the bomb plot messages, or
even the eleventh-hour "lights code" message, could have alerted Pearl
Harbor to the threat.

   Prange merely attributed "the gap between knowledge of possible
danger and belief in its existence"[24] as the "root of the whole tragedy."
But Layton's blow-by-blow account shows how the real cause of the tragedy was the internal feuding in the navy department that limited Washington's ability to evaluate and disseminate intelligence. Supported by
documents never before made public, Layton reveals how this war within
a war raged on through the first half of 1942 while the Pacific Fleet was
locked in deadly struggle with the Japanese.

   Layton breaks the forty-three-year-old silence on how Japan was
really checked at Midway. He relates the never-before-told story of the
fight that was waged between Pearl Harbor and Washington over Midway
three weeks before the actual battle. The fight over who had made the
right intelligence evaluation of Japanese objectives was every bit as fierce
and vital as the battle itself was to prove. Layton reveals how Nimitz and
he had to resort to subterfuge to get our carriers to Midway in time to
fight, and how Pearl Harbor's code breakers were right and Washington
was wrong about the date for the projected battle. For a week in May,
the entire course of the war turned on the outcome of a struggle fought
by cablegram and intercept within the navy department.

   Layton tells how Washington then successfully covered up their second
major intelligence blunder to take credit for the code breaks and intel-

ligence evaluation that rightfully belonged to Commander Rochefort. A report that has until now remained locked in a navy safe details the shocking story of how a few ambitious naval officers in the navy department put their careers before their country to wage a vendetta against Rochefort. Their campaign succeeded, and in the fall of 1942, the fleet was denied the services of its most brilliant radio intelligence officer. One of its unintended results was the Japanese code change that brought a four-month blackout of our intelligence during the close-run Guadalcanal campaign.

Writing from his unique position, Layton reviews the major contributions that radio intelligence made to winning the war in the Pacific. He discusses the shootdown of his old bridge partner Admiral Yamamoto, "The Great Marianas Turkey" shoot during the Battle of the Philippine Sea, and the staggering success of our submarine war against Japan. Nimitz's ability to outmaneuver both Washington and MacArthur so that he could effectively deploy his forces made him one of the war's most effective commanders. Layton's account shows that while MacArthur was more adept at public relations, it was Nimitz's effective application of radio intelligence that made him the understated and unsung hero of the Pacific war.

Of this account we can be certain only that it will not be the last word. But while new information may surface to adjust the perspective, it is unlikely that there will be any dramatic alteration in the scene. Layton did not subscribe to Samuel Taylor Coleridge's view of history—that "the light which experience gives is a lantern at the stern which shines only on the ways behind." Layton's hope was that by shattering old myths, illumination might also be cast on the way ahead with its lurking peril of a nuclear Pearl Harbor.

—ROGER PINEAU
—JOHN COSTELLO

Bethesda, Maryland
July 1985

II. THE FLAWS IN THE OFFICIAL INVESTIGATIONS

1. The Roberts Commission

18 December 1941–23 January 1942

Convened: By presidential executive order to establish the facts relating to the Japanese attack on Pearl Harbor. The prime object was to determine whether any dereliction of duty or errors of judgment had contributed to the enemy success.

Members: Associate Justice Owen J. Roberts, U.S. Supreme Court, chairman; Admiral William H. Standley, U.S.N. (Ret.); Rear Admi-

ral Joseph M. Reeves, U.S.N. (Ret.); Major General Frank R. Mc-
Coy, U.S. Army (Ret.); Brigadier General Joseph T. McNarney, U.S.
Army.

Proceedings: The first critical days of Washington testimony were unsworn and unrecorded. Magic was discussed, but who received it and
what it contained were not detailed. No actual intercepts were introduced into evidence, but the impression was given by the senior officers of the war and navy departments that the Hawaiian commands
were receiving *all* the intelligence available to Washington.

Findings: The secretaries of state, war, and navy as well as General
Marshall and Admiral Stark had discharged their duties. Admiral
Kimmel and General Short were severely censured for their failures
to take appropriate action in light of the warnings they had received.

2. The Hart Inquiry

15 February 1944–June 15 1944

Convened: By order of the navy department to take evidence pertinent to the Pearl Harbor attack so that important testimony should
not be lost by hazard of war.

Composition: A one-member inquiry conducted by Admiral Thomas
C. Hart, U.S.N. (Ret.).

Proceedings: Collected statements of parties concerned. It did not
consider Magic but Hart, who had been Asiatic Fleet commander at
the outbreak of war, was fully aware of the extent of radio intelligence
about Japanese naval and diplomatic activity.

Findings: Hart was not required to make specific recommendations
since the purpose of this inquiry was ostensibly to forestall the statute
of limitations that would prevent the trial by court-martial of officers
considered to be guilty of serious derelictions of duty.

3. The Army Pearl Harbor Board

20 July 1944–20 October 1944

Convened: By the adjutant general in response to the Act of Congress
13 July 1944, which directed the secretaries of navy and war to investigate the Pearl Harbor catastrophe. Directed to ascertain and report
the facts and make such recommendations as deemed proper.

Composition: Lieutenant General George Grunert, U.S. Army, president; Major General Henry D. Russell, U.S. Army; Major General Walter H. Frank, U.S. Army; Colonel Charles W. West, U.S. Army, recorder (without vote); Colonel Harry A. Toulmin, U.S. Army, executive officer (without vote); Major General Henry C. Clausen, U.S. Army, recorder (without vote).

Proceedings: The board heard evidence in Washington, San Francisco, and Hawaii from 151 witnesses. The voting members of the board were advised of the existence of the radio intelligence intercepts, but considered evidence of Magic only in the final week of testimony.

Findings: The report was published, without reference to Magic. It therefore appeared unduly critical of General Short, but General Marshall and the war department were also censured for the first time.

Marshall failed in his duty: (1) to keep Short fully advised of the worsening situation with Japan; (2) to reply to Short's "sabotage alert" report; (3) by not forwarding to Short on the evening of 6 December and the morning of 7 December the critical information; (4) by not determining the state of readiness of the Hawaiian command.

General Gerow, chief of war plans division, failed in his duty: (1) by not keeping the Hawaiian command informed with the substance of Magic; (2) by not making the 27 November warning a clear, concise directive and for approving the confusing dispatch that was sent; (3) by not taking steps to see that the joint plans agreed between the army and navy were properly effected.

General Short was held to have failed in his duties: (1) by not placing his command in a higher state of alert; (2) by not implementing the Joint Army-Navy Coastal Frontier Defense Plan; (3) by not informing himself of the partial effectiveness of the navy's aerial reconnaissance; (4) by not replacing inefficient staff officers.

4.   The Naval Court of Inquiry

24 July 1944–19 October 1944

Convened: By the secretary of the navy in response to the same congressional act as the army board, and its hearings ran parallel to the other inquiry.

Composition: Admiral Orin G. Murfins, U.S.N. (Ret.), president; Admiral Edward C. Kalbfus, U.S.N. (Ret.); Vice Admiral Adolphus Andrews, U.S.N. (Ret.).

Proceedings: The naval court was the first inquiry to take full consideration and testimony on the role of radio intelligence and decryption.

All testimony on Magic was suppressed in its public report. Evidence was heard in Washington and at Pearl Harbor, but no account was taken—as the army board did—of the failures in the navy department to effect the Joint Army-Navy Coastal Frontier Defense Plans for all Pacific commands or send a precise, specific war warning to Pearl Harbor.

Findings: The report of the navy inquiry was a complete exoneration for Admiral Kimmel. It found that he had conferred adequately with Short and each "was informed of the measures being undertaken by the other in defense of the Base to a degree sufficient for all useful purposes."[25] Kimmel's plan of defense was held to be "sound" but it depended on "advance knowledge that an attack was to be expected." Kimmel was held to have conducted the proper long-range aerial reconnaissance appropriate to the intelligence he received and the planes available.

Admiral Stark, however, was severely criticized for the first time. He was censured for sending a war warning that "standing alone could not convey to the commanders in the field the picture as it was seen in Washington."[26] He was criticized for failing to relay to Kimmel information that had come into his possession, "especially on the morning of 7 December." No further proceedings, however, were recommended against any officer because the court concluded that the attack, "delivered under the circumstances then existing, was unpreventable. When it would take place was unpredictable."[27]

The secretaries of war and navy—and their departments—were understandably unhappy with the opinions of the Army Pearl Harbor Board and the Naval Court of Inquiry, which shifted the responsibility back to Washington. Stimson and Forrestal decided on the ploy of keeping the findings secret until additional investigations could be made to redirect the burden of failure back onto the Hawaiian commanders.

5. The Clausen Investigation

23 November 1944–12 September 1945

Convened: By the personal direction of the secretary of war to supplement the investigation of the Army Pearl Harbor Board.

Composition: A one-man inquiry by Major Henry C. Clausen, the assistant recorder of the Army Pearl Harbor Board.

Proceedings: This was a secret inquiry that relied on affidavits rather than direct testimony.

Findings: No public report, but Clausen later testified before the congressional investigating committee.

6. The Hewitt Inquiry

14 May 1945–11 July 1945

Convened: By the secretary of the navy to continue the investigation of the Navy Court of Inquiry.

Composition: Admiral W. Kent Hewitt, U.S.N., with John F. Sonnet, special assistant to the secretary of the navy as counsel.

Proceedings: Magic and radio intelligence were discussed in detail. Witnesses testified and were cross-examined in secret proceedings by Sonnet, whose conduct of the inquiry, especially in off-the-record questioning, was later to be criticized. Admiral Kimmel was denied the right of an interested party to be present and conduct his own cross-examination of witnesses.

Findings: No separate report was published. But as a result of Hewitt's findings and the Naval Court of Inquiry, the secretary of the navy, James P. Forrestal, issued an announcement on 29 August 1945 that "the Admiral Husband E. Kimmel and Admiral Harold R. Stark, particularly during the period 27 November to 7 December, 1941, failed to demonstrate the superior judgment necessary to exercising command commensurate with their rank and assigned duties."[28]

7. The Clarke Investigation

14–16 September 1944, and 13 July 1945–4 August 1945

Convened: Ordered by the war department to investigate the handling of top secret communications by the military intelligence division before the Pearl Harbor attack.

Composition: Conducted by Colonel Carter W. Clarke, then chief of the military intelligence division.

Proceedings: The top secret investigation was reconvened to investigate testimony given to the Hewitt inquiry by Safford and others to the effect that war department signal archives relating to the Winds code messages had to be destroyed on the orders of General Marshall.

Findings: No evidence was adduced to support the destruction of radio intelligence documents.

8. The Joint Congressional Committee

15 November 1945–31 May 1946

Convened: By a concurrent resolution of Congress to make a full investigation of the events and circumstances connected with the Japanese attack on Pearl Harbor and to report the results to Congress with such recommendations as deemed advisable.

Composition: Six Democrats and four Republicans: Senator Alben W. Barkley, (D) Kentucky, chairman; Representative Jere Cooper, (R) Tennessee; Senator Walter F. George, (D) Georgia; Senator Scott W. Lucas, (D) Illinois; Senator Owen Brewster, (R) Maine; Senator Homer Ferguson, (R) Michigan; Representative J. Bayard Clark, (D) North Carolina; Representative John W. Murphy, (D) Pennsylvania; Representative Bertrand W. Gearhart, (R) California; Representative Frank B. Keefe, (R) Wisconsin. The legal staff consisted of a general counsel and three assistants.

Proceedings: Witnesses were called and cross-examined, but the politics of the day inevitably intruded and the democratic majority effectively managed the course of the proceedings to divert criticism from the Roosevelt administration. The principal surviving participants were called and examined, except for the ailing Stimson. Magic was discussed exhaustively to the concern of the military intelligence officers. But any mention of the extent of the penetration of the Japanese naval code systems was severely restricted.

The evidence of the seven previous Pearl Harbor inquiries was not introduced until three months into the hearings. The findings of the earlier investigations also remained secret until the entire forty-volume congressional report with its eleven volumes of evidence, ten volumes of exhibits, seventeen volumes of hearings, and one-volume report was published.

Findings: A summary of the six-member majority concludes that:

(1) Japan's attack was unprovoked.
(2) the attack had been skillfully planned.
(3) American policies had provided no provocation for the attack.
(4) there was no evidence that Roosevelt's cabinet had provoked the attack to facilitate a declaration of war from Congress.
(5) the president had made every effort to avoid war with Japan.
(6) the disaster was due to the Hawaiian commanders' failure to effect adequate measures to detect the attack and to go to a state of readiness commensurate with the imminence of war.
(7) the Japanese attack was a total surprise although the possibility

of an air raid and the imminence of war was appreciated as a possibility at Pearl Harbor and Washington.

(8) the Hawaiian commanders failed to make disposition commensurate with the warnings and intelligence received, but the errors made by the Hawaiian commanders were of judgment, not derelictions of duty.

(10) the war department failed in its duty to warn Short that a sabotage was an inadequate state of alert.

(11) army and navy intelligence had failed to evaluate the significance of the bomb plot and 1 P.M. deadline messages and communicate them to the Pacific commands.

(12) during the final forty-eight hours before the attack, the war and navy departments were not sufficiently on alert to the imminence of war.

The two-member minority report also censured Roosevelt for not taking "quick and instant executive action on Saturday night, December 6th and Sunday morning."[29] Apart from the president they concluded that Secretary Stimson, Secretary Knox, General Marshall, Admiral Stark, General Gerow, as well as the two Hawaiian commanders, had failed to discharge their responsibilities.

III. THE EAST WINDS RAIN ENIGMA

Was a genuine winds alert message ever received? If so, when was it picked up? These questions became a *cause célèbre* of the 1945 congressional hearings when conflicting testimony denied admissions made in the secret wartime investigations. A furiously partisan public debate erupted that has smoldered ever since. Safford charged that a winds alert did come in, that it was later removed from the records, and that officers who had earlier claimed to have seen and handled it were pressured into changing their accounts.

The controversy refused to go away, because the postwar interrogations of Japanese officials failed to produce clear-cut answers on whether Tokyo had or had not transmitted a winds alert broadcast in the prescribed form. Many historians, such as Wohlstetter and Prange, have sidestepped the issue by pointing out that Japan's 2 December codes-destruct messages—which Kimmel had received—were a more accurate indication of Japan's intention of going to war.

The fact is, however, that Washington believed that the east winds rain message would be the ultimate signal that war would break out. They were the ones who considered it even more important after 2 December, when it was assumed that an "east winds rain" phrase in Tokyo radio's daily weather broadcast would be the final war warning. Safford's

1944 testimony, supported by Kramer and Sadtler until they modified their recollections in 1945, suggests that some message that was taken to be that warning was received toward the end of the first week of December. Safford claimed that when he tried to locate the "east winds rain" alert in the fall of 1943, it was missing from the OP-20-G files. Up till then he had been unable to understand why the Pacific Fleet commander had ignored the warning. When Safford discovered that none had been sent to Pearl Harbor as a result of this message, he began his campaign to "expose the people who had framed Admiral Kimmel and General Short."[30]

The navy department went to great lengths to contradict Safford's charges. Witnesses and affidavits were produced to deny that a "*Higashi No Kaze Ame*" ("East Winds Rain") message had ever been picked up. But the newly declassified records do show that Safford was correct in claiming that there is a suspiciously blank page in the OP-20-G Japanese diplomatic message file. Whether or not it contained a now-missing "east winds rain" intercept, the records show that a colossal amount of navy department bureaucratic effort was exerted in 1945 to proving that no such message had ever existed. The "no message, no case" argument certainly succeeded in drawing a very large red herring across the congressional hearings—to confuse the real issue of Washington's failure to pass on to the Hawaiian commanders other more important and specific intelligence such as the "bomb plot" and "lights" intercepts.

Certainly if an "east winds rain" message had been produced at the congressional hearing, it would have provided irrefutable indication of Washington's failure to communicate such a warning to Pearl Harbor. But as Safford discovered to his cost and credibility, trying to prove his case without that vital message challenged the institution and integrity of the navy department. It brought a collective closing of ranks in the navy that lasted for over forty years.

Safford's testimony rested largely on the blank page in the run of serial numbers in the running record by Kramer's translation section. As each decrypt of an intercepted Japanese diplomatic message was typed up, it was assigned a serial number—and after it had been circulated to naval intelligence, it was returned to be refiled.[31] The one that Safford claims was originally "east winds rain" is now a blank page with the notation "7001-Cancelled."[32] Safford repeatedly affirmed under cross-examination that the number had originally been assigned to a true winds execute message that had been intercepted by Station M in Maryland, which had been relayed from the Cheltenham teleprinter to OP-20-G on the morning of either 4 or 5 December 1941.

Although Safford's case was not helped by his confusion over the date, his recollection of the intercept's appearance was impressively precise. He described it as "a teletype copy (typed on yellow paper) of the entire Japanese broadcast about 200 or 300 words long. Three significant words (*Kita, Higashi,* and *Nishi*) appeared and they were in Japanese. Kramer's translation appeared in pencil, or colored crayon, at the bottom of the sheet. There was very little chance of confusion."[33]

In a November 1943 letter to Safford from Kramer—which predates the first official inquiry—Kramer admitted that he had only "a hazy recollection of being called down to the office" because of the "arrangements to handle it expeditiously." But at the 1944 Navy Court of Inquiry Kramer unhesitatingly answered yes when asked whether he had seen Safford's teleprinter sheet with the winds message containing the Japanese code words indicating relations with the United States were in danger.

"'*Higashi no kaze ame*,' I am quite certain," Kramer testified: "The literal meaning of '*Higashi no kaze ame*' is 'East wind, rain.' That is plain Japanese language. The sense of that, however, meant strained relations or a break in relations, possibly even implying war with a nation to the eastward, the United States." But by April 1945, however, Kramer "was less positive" in his testimony before Admiral Hewitt's inquiry. Now he was "under the impression that the message referred to England and possibly the Dutch rather than the United States." By February 1945 when he came before the congressional hearings, Kramer's recollection was that there had been "a false alarm on the winds system," which he thought at the time was authentic and which referred to only one country: "To the best of my recollection, it was England."[34]

Kramer's contradictory evidence was the result of "being instructed on orders from above to deny delivering the message," according to Mrs. Eunice Willson Rice, longtime OP-20-G staff member who used to type up and file the Japanese diplomatic messages.[35] She has recently confirmed that no copies were ever made, but the originals were kept in a sequentially numbered file.[35]

Although Mrs. Rice was away visiting her sister in Maine the week before the Pearl Harbor attack, she recalled that after her return she noticed that one message appeared to be missing from the numerical sequence. She asked Kramer about it. He said that it was one indicating that war was imminent and that he himself had turned it over to the duty officer in the chief of naval operations office and called attention to its importance. When it had not come back after the Japanese attack after the usual period of time, Kramer had asked about it, only to receive a noncommittal answer.[36]

Mrs. Rice was not the only one to claim she believed that considerable pressure was put on Kramer to change his testimony before the congressional investigating committee in 1945. His Arlington neighbor and friend at the time, Lieutenant Commander (now rear admiral retired) Robert F. Weeks, recalls Kramer's telling him that he had been directed to "speak right or undergo more mental treatment."[37]

This was a reference to the fact that Kramer had been in the neuropsychiatric ward of Bethesda Naval Hospital in November, two months before he was called to testify. The story made newspaper headlines after Representative Keefe, a member of the congressional investigating committee, had charged that Kramer was being held there "under orders" and that his uniform had been taken away. When he testified, Kramer denied that he had been "beset and beleaguered" or badgered in any way.[38]

Kramer did, however, make a substantial change in his story. Safford was in no doubt that it was a result of the strong pressure Kramer was under to support the navy department contention that no winds message had been received. According to his friend Weeks, Kramer was a man of character whose arm was twisted. On the eve of his appearance in the Capitol Hill committee room, Weeks recalled, "He said he would have to lay it on the line next day."[39]

One witness, who also claimed to have seen a winds alert, was apparently not allowed to give testimony in 1945. Ralph T. Briggs believed that he was deliberately prevented from appearing before the congressional hearings to corroborate Safford's story. In 1977 this former On the Roof Gang radioman asserted that he was the one who intercepted the actual message when he was on duty at the navy's Cheltenham Station M in Maryland in December 1941.

Briggs, experienced in taking kana Morse, went on to become a chief warrant officer with the staff of naval intelligence command. In 1960, Briggs made a thorough search of the wartime microfilm records. But like Safford and the 1945 team of navy investigators, Briggs found that all the Cheltenham station signal sheets for the first week in 1941 were missing. Unable to locate the original "Higashi no kaze ame" intercept, he settled for writing on one of the original duty personnel log sheets that "all transmissions intercepted by me between 0500 thru 1300 on the above date are missing from these files and that these intercepts contained the 'Winds message warning code.'"[40]

Sixteen years later Briggs recounted his story to the Naval Security Group. Historian Raymond Schmidt, who took his deposition, recorded Briggs's statement that the winds alert, which Briggs claimed to have taken down on 4 December 1941, could not be picked up by any other overseas listening post because of atmospheric conditions. Briggs also told how Safford had contacted him in 1945 during the congressional hearings but that his commanding officer had ordered him not to give any testimony. Briggs regarded this as "a definite effort to cover up the truth of the matter" and put to rest what had happened to the missing winds execute message.[41]

A puzzling inconsistency, however, must be noted in Briggs's testimony. Apart from the length of time that elapsed before he decided to give his version of the story to posterity, Briggs claimed to have picked up the winds message on 4 December. But the duty log that bears his 1960 inscription is for 2 December.

If it was the intercept that Briggs made that set alarm bells ringing in OP-20-G, apart from the fact that there is no east winds rain message on the intercept file, his account further confuses the issue of when it was supposed to have been received. Much was made of this confusion to cast doubt on Safford's testimony and to suggest that he was confused by a number of false alarms.

According to Kramer, the watch officers were inundated by "reams, yards of teletype paper covering the plain-language broadcasts of the Japanese."[42] Every message from the navy's listening posts had to be translated and checked. More winds alerts arrived from the Federal Communications Commission whose monitoring stations had also been instructed to listen in to Tokyo radio weather reports. False alarms were raised, such as one on the afternoon of 4 December, by a weather report that stated:

> Tokyo today north wind, slightly stronger; may become cloudy tonight; tomorrow slightly cloudy and fine weather. Kanagawa prefecture today north wind cloudy from afternoon more clouds.
>
> Chiba prefecture today *north wind clear* may become slightly cloudy ocean surface calm.[43]

This particular message appeared so similar to one on the prompt cards that the Thursday afternoon GY watch officer checked it with a translator before telephoning the director of naval communications the winds message was in.[44] By the time it had been realized that it was an innocent weather forecast, news of the alert had spread throughout the navy department. Turner, however, recalled how he had been able to discount the "north wind clear" phrase as "obviously not matching" the prearranged Japanese code words.[45]

Turner made a great point, during the congressional hearings, of dismissing this and other false winds alerts. Yet it's difficult to believe that Safford, with his long experience in radio intelligence, would have put his career on the line for a *deus ex machina* that was as obviously incorrect as the one Turner cited. But testimony volunteered in 1980 by another GY watch officer, George W. Linn, confirms that "this episode established that an execute had not been received prior to late on December 4."[46] Linn's 1983 deposition to the Navy Security Group historian asserts he did not see any genuine winds message. But it could have arrived when he was not on duty, the following morning—which is precisely when Sadtler, in his persuasive testimony to the 1944 army board of inquiry, claims that it did come in.[47]

Further corroboration that the Japanese transmitted a winds code was provided by Brigadier General R. Thorpe, who in 1941 was lend-lease commissioner and military observer with the Dutch command on Java. Thorpe, who did not testify at any of the Pearl Harbor investigations, later claimed that the commander of the Dutch army in the East Indies—

General Hein ter Poorten—showed him a winds execute message. It was contained in a decrypt of "an intercepted and decoded dispatch from the Foreign Office in Tokyo addressed to the Japanese ambassador in Bangkok."[48] Thorpe took it to the American consul general in Batavia, who forwarded it to Washington—but with a comment to the effect that it was not to be taken seriously.[49] Not content with Dr. Walter Foote's assessment, Thorpe—whose own code books were a hundred miles away in his Bandoeng office— took his message to the senior naval attaché, Commander Paul S. Slawson, who sent it off in navy cipher.

When this message was produced for the 1945 congressional inquiry it contained only details of the winds code setup, but *not* the text of the actual Tokyo radio "east winds rain" execute phrase.[50] According to the written recollection of General ter Poorten, he had called in the American and British liaison officers and he also had sent a teletype of the winds message to the Dutch embassy in Washington.[51]

The Dutch consulate in Honolulu also received a copy of this same message warning of "an imminent attack somewhere in the Pacific." Ter Poorten notes, "I did not specifically mention Pearl Harbor."[52] He also reports that when the winds execute was hand-delivered by the Dutch military attaché in Washington to the war department, the only response from General Marshall was to ask for the source of the information.[53]

The Dutch intelligence records were all destroyed before their evacuation of Bandoeng. So Ter Poorten's written postwar confirmation of Thorpe's account—while convincing—still does not prove that an "east winds rain" alert was transmitted by Tokyo. But Thorpe also claimed that while stationed in Japan after the war he eventually located a Japanese who had actually transmitted the message. Thorpe's account is supported with information that has recently surfaced in the Royal Netherlands archives. Dutch army headquarters in Bandoeng, Java, maintained throughout 1941 a small but highly successful cryptanalytic unit that had succeeded in breaking into the Japanese diplomatic codes independently of the American or British efforts. Although they had not penetrated Purple, they were reading the messages in the Red machine cipher and also the J-19 consular traffic.

According to Captain J. W. Henning, then chief cryptanalyst of the so-called *Kamer 14* at Bandoeng, they were "doing business on a mutual basis" with their potential allies and "all Japanese coded telegrams, which were decoded by us, were subsequently passed to the British, Americans and Australians." Henning confirmed that Bandoeng headquarters had indeed been aware of the winds code setup and that an execute broadcast was intercepted. "From a deciphered teletype of the beginning of December 1941, we concluded that a Japanese attack was to be expected at short notice."[54]

In spite of what Toland has claimed in *Infamy* about Washington receiving a *specific* warning from the Dutch about Pearl Harbor, it is pertinent to note that Henning's evidence denies this completely. "When and where the first Japanese attack would explode could not be concluded from the telegram."[55]

Yet another piece of the "east winds rain" jigsaw puzzle was provided in the spring of 1985 by Lieutenant Commander Cedric Brown, a British naval officer who in 1941 was in charge of ciphers at R.N. headquarters in Hong Kong. After his capture by the Japanese, he encountered in a prisoner of war camp a New Zealand naval officer, Lieutenant H. C. Dixon. He had served at the Hong Kong naval base signal's intelligence intercept unit on Stonecutter's Island, known by its secret designation "Q." Dixon told Brown that he could not understand how the Americans had been caught so unprepared for the Japanese attack because, several weeks before war broke out, the Royal Navy cryptanalysts at "Q" had intercepted and decoded the preliminary winds alert setup and that they had subsequently picked up the Tokyo weather broadcast "a few days before the attack on Pearl Harbor."[56]

The new evidence must add to the presumption that the Japanese did send out the winds alert and that it was picked up by the British as well as the Dutch. Since such intelligence was being freely exchanged, it would indicate that Washington did receive the warning from two other sources besides the intercept that Safford claimed arrived through OP-20-G.

This may be another reason why the British are so reluctant to release any of their Japanese intercepts. Until an east winds rain message turns up, however, there can be no final proof that Safford and Sadtler were correct in asserting that one was received and that it was later removed by ranking officers in the Washington cover-up. The new evidence must tip the scale of probability to indicate that some alert was received on the morning of 5 December. The suspicious blank page in the Japanese diplomatic signal log, the large volume of paperwork generated to deny Safford's charge, and the pressure brought to bear on Kramer and others to amend their testimony are also factors that point toward this conclusion.

IV. THE COMINT FEUD

The peremptory ousting of Joe Rochefort in October 1942 from his position as officer in charge of Hypo caused strong feelings in the comint community. A harbinger of that action can now be seen in the lateral displacement of Laurence F. Safford, which took place the preceding February. Safford was shunted aside as head of OP-20-G to take charge of the less important OP-20-Q cryptography office. The other half of his former duties—cryptanalysis—was turned over to Commander John R. Redman, as OP-20-G, with Commander Joseph N. Wenger as his deputy.

Captain Joseph R. Redman, John's older brother, was then assistant director of naval communications and therefore largely instrumental in effecting these arrangements. Commander Wenger, who had been serving in Negat at the outbreak of war, was "directed by Captain Redman to make an investigation of OP-20-G and submit recommendations for any corrective measures considered advisable."[57] He spent "about a month" preparing his critique and "naturally consulted Safford with a view towards ascertaining if he had any special problems that needed attention or ideas that he had not been able to implement."[58]

According to Wenger, he "offered me no suggestions" but Safford, as we have seen, on 23 January 1943, submitted his memorandum urging that the status quo be maintained. Three days later Wenger put in his recommendations for a radical reorganization that separated the day-to-day operational effort from the administrative and code-security functions of OP-20-G. It appears that these were immediately approved, over Safford's head, by Admiral King as part of his administrative shake-up of the office of naval operations. By mid-February, John Redman, who was "regarded as a forceful administrator," had assumed full control of OP-20-G and Wenger was given authority to "reorganize it according to my proposals."[59] His task was facilitated because shortly afterward the elder Redman replaced Admiral Leigh Noyes as head of the office of naval communications.

Safford had been promoting a decentralized radio intelligence operation, based on a vertical division by tasks, with Negat assigned to a particular enemy cipher system while Hypo specialized on another and Cast on a third. By contrast, the so-called Redman-Wenger plan envisaged that Negat would manage the entire radio intercept and analysis operation centrally. A greatly expanded cyrptanalytic operation in Washington was intended to perform the basic solution and recovery in the whole range of enemy ciphers. This called for a horizontal division of functions by which Hypo would be directed in the exploitation of Negat's results to some of its own recoveries to provide the fleet with basic combat intelligence.

Views vary among the World War II veterans of the communications and intelligence service as to the proprieties of this reorganization. But there is general agreement that Safford would probably not have been the most effective of managers under wartime pressures. The organization that he founded in 1924, and directed for seventeen years except for two tours of sea duty, had grown up in response to a hit-or-miss, crisis-reaction style of operation that was a product of prewar budgetary constraints and the lack of understanding of the importance of the intelligence function by gunnery club admirals. In the wake of Pearl Harbor trauma Safford faced criticism for the intelligence failure and charges that his unmethodical ways might lead to future disasters.

With the advantage of 20/20 hindsight it can be argued that if the Redman-Wenger concept had been operative throughout 1941, the Pacific

Fleet might have received proper intelligence that would have warned of Japan's impending attack. But such a hypothesis does not take into consideration the extent to which Admiral Turner had imposed his own stranglehold on operational intelligence throughout 1941. Nor does it take into account the long-running feud for control of the OP-20-G between the offices of naval intelligence and communications.

Safford had also come under suspicion for drifting into increasing collaboration with ONI and the Redmans' perception of Rochefort's independence might well have been colored by his 1932 memorandum advocating "that the Cryptographic Section be removed from the Office of Naval Communications and placed under the Office of Naval Intelligence."[60]

Comint, as its name implies, combines elements of communications and intelligence in both staffing and end product. To give the entire operation to either specialization would have left the other in the lurch. In the navy department, as in any institution, sectional rivalry and personalities played a role in determining how intelligence was evaluated and disseminated. The events leading up to Pearl Harbor had underlined the importance of radio intelligence just as Midway demonstrated its war-winning potential. A stake in its operation was therefore regarded as a cap-feather for those officers who controlled the flow of information to the fleet.

So while Safford was a highly intelligent, if undisciplined prodigy, the Redman brothers were quick to spot the importance of the organization he had created. They were down-to-earth, practical, ambitious bureaucrats who seized the main chance. They enlisted an ally in Wenger, a communications officer of proven abilities who was also a farsighted opportunist. Although he lacked Safford's intuitive flair for code breaking, Wenger—perhaps more clearly than the Redmans—anticipated the importance that intelligence would play in military operations. His foresight led to the creation of the Navy Security Group, which he later ably commanded, and it presaged the postwar growth of comint at the National Security Agency.

It was Safford who singlehandedly had conceived, founded, and built the navy's comint entity. It was Wenger who harnessed the power and drive of the Redmans to organize radio intelligence for the navy's, and the nation's, long-term goals.

At the same time the Hypo team of Rochefort-Dyer-Wright was to prove the Redman-Wenger philosophy of a centrally controlled and directed radio intelligence operation was not applicable to a tactical command. The Hypo contribution was to show what could be achieved by an extremely competent, well-motivated team working in close liaison with the Pacific Fleet command. It was Rochefort who made one element of the organization work superbly at a crucial time in a crucial place, thereby justifying Safford's vision, regardless of any previous or subsequent performance. It was Layton who avoided direct involvement in the

Negat-Hypo feud to remain the conduit and analyst to Nimitz of comint. Captain Jasper Holmes, a member of the Cincpac-Hypo organization throughout the war, observed, "If Admiral Nimitz had not had Eddie Layton as his intelligence officer, he might not have had the confidence to risk everything on the conclusion of what many other senior officers considered to be a bunch of nuts, in a basement, dreaming up wild hallucinations." As Admiral Burke has said, "Layton, by keeping his job above his personality, contributed the necessary rapport that someone else might not have been able to provide."

Growth of United States Navy Radio Intelligence

		OFFICER	ENLISTED	CIVILIAN	TOTAL
	1924	1		1	2
	1925	1	2	4	7
	1936	11	88	10	109
June	1940	12	121	15	147
January	1941	44	489	10	543
December	1941	75	645	10	730*
July	1942	114	496	110	720
December	1942	234	784	170	1188
July	1943	365	2175	116	2656
December	1943	734	2622	96	3452
February	1944	780	2854	88	3722
October	1945	1499	6908	47	8454

Geographic Distribution, December 1941

	OFFICER	ENLISTED	CIVILIAN	TOTAL
Negat	52	351	10	413**
West Coast	3	99		102
Hypo	18	128		146
Cast	9	61		70
Port Darwin	1	8		9
	83	647	10	740*

Officer in Charge, Research Desk (OP-20-G)

January 1924–February 1926	Lt. Laurence F. Safford
February 1926–September 1927	Lt. John J. Rochefort
November 1927–March 1929	Lt. Bern Anderson
August 1929–April 1932	Lt. Cdr. Laurence F. Safford
April 1932–May 1933	Lt. Cdr. J. W. McClaran
May 1933–June 1935	Cdr. H. F. Kingman
September 1935–May 1936	Cdr. J. W. McClaran
May 1936–February 1942	Cdr./Capt. Laurence F. Safford
February 1942–	Capt. John R. Redman

*Discrepancy accountable to new arrivals and departures during December.
**Total does not include translators, who were furnished by ONI. These were Lt. Cdr. Alwin D. Kramer, U.S.N., and six civilians: Phillip H. Cate, B. T. Hoffman, Fred C. Woodrough, Jr., Ralph Cory, C. F. Thurston, and Dorothy Woodrough Edgers.

Officer in Charge, Translation Section (OP-20-GZ)

June 1934–mid-1936	Lt. Thomas D. Birtley
mid-1936	Lt. Edward S. Pearce
August 1936–February 1937	Lt. Edwin T. Layton
March 1937–February 1939	Lt. Redfield Mason
February 1939–May 1942	Lt./Lt. Cdr. Alwin D. Kramer
May 1942–December 1945	Lt. Cdr./Capt. Redfield Mason
December 1945–	Capt. John G. Roenigk

—SOURCE: SRH 355

TRANSLATION Date	By	JD#	SIS#	OTHER #	BRIEF
**Dec. 1	A	6943	(25552) (25553)	Tokyo 985	The conversations between Tokyo and Washington now stand ruptured - broken. Say very secretly to Hitler and Ribbentrop that there is extreme danger that war may suddenly break out between the Anglo-Saxon nations and Japan, and this war may come quicker than anyone dreams. Will not relax our pressure on the Soviet, but for the time being we would prefer to refrain from any direct moves in the north. Impress on the Germans and Italians how important secrecy is. (Nov. 30, 1941.) /Note: Coded message forwarded by Com 16 as OYROP Ø1ØØØ1, Ø1ØØ14, or Ø1ØØ27. Also forwarded from London as Admiralty #104 and #105. Admiralty Ø1153Ø advised "Tokyo to Berlin #985 of immediate interest."/
*Dec. 1	A	6944	(25554) (25555)	Tokyo 986	The Imperial Govt. can no longer continue negotiations with the U.S. The proposal presented by the U.S. on the 26th contains one insulting clause. It is clearly a trick. The U.S. has decided to regard Japan as an enemy. (Nov. 30, 1941.) /Forwarded by Com 16 as OYROP Ø1ØØØ1, Ø1ØØ14, or Ø1ØØ29./
*Dec. 1	N	6983	—	Tokyo 865	To prevent the United States from becoming unduly suspicious we have been advising the press and others that the negotiations are continuing. The above is for only your information. (OY Log #6428.)
**Dec. 1	N	6984	—	Tokyo 2444	The four offices in London, Hongkong, Singapore, and Manila have been instructed to abandon the use of the code machines and to dispose of them. The machine in Batavia has been returned to Japan. (OY Log #6432.)
*Dec. 2	N	6985	25609	Tokyo 2409	Hidden Word Code (Nov. 27, 1941 - J19). For later additions see:

	JD#	SIS#	OTHER #
	7122	25830	Tokyo 2432
			Tokyo 2433 (?)
	7214	25943	Tokyo 2450
	7360		Tokyo 2431

TRANSLATION Date	By	JD#	SIS#	OTHER #	BRIEF
***Dec. 4	N	7001	—	—	JD #7001 is believed to be the (missing) translation of the Winds Message.
**Dec. 3	A	7017	25640	Tokyo 867	Washington burn all codes except one copy of "Oite" (Pa-K2) and "L" (LA). Stop using the code machine and destroy it completely. When you have finished this, wire back "HARUNA." Destroy all message files and other secret documents. (Dec. 2, 1941.)

1944 OP-20-G listing of Japanese diplomatic intercepts—asterisks indicated that this intelligence was of critical importance. ROCHEFORT PAPERS

SECRET

WAR DEPARTMENT
OFFICE OF THE CHIEF OF STAFF
WASHINGTON

WDCSA/351 Philippines (12-4-41)

November 21, 1941.

MEMORANDUM FOR THE SECRETARY, GENERAL STAFF:
      (For inclusion in special <u>Philippine</u> file)

           Subject: Air Offensive Against Japan.

      While talking informally on November 19, General Marshall directed that information be obtained referring to an air offensive against the Japanese Empire.

      Specifically, he wanted answers to the questions--what General MacArthur would attack in Japan (from bases in the Vladivostok area) if war were declared December 1, 1941; what data we have assembled in Washington on the subject; what appears to us to be profitable systems of objectives, and how much of our data was presented to and was taken to the Philippines by General Brereton.

      As of this date, the following data have been assembled:

      1. Before General Brereton's departure for the Philippines, all of his discussions were based on the employment of the Philippine Air Force on the strategic defensive. With the very small offensive force projected for the Philippine Air Force (never over two heavy bombardment groups), a sustained air offensive against the Japanese Empire was never discussed. The conception of the employment of the offensive Air Force at that time was limited to operations against lines of communication from Japan proper. Specific objectives for this attack would obviously consist almost wholly of shipping in the northern approaches to the China seas. Japanese naval bases in the islands off Formosa and at the mandated islands (from bases in New Britain) were discussed, but no data are available as to the details of those naval bases.

      2. General Brereton did take with him, however, separate Air Staff studies on the steel and petroleum industries and on the electric power establishment in Japan.

      3. Shortly after General Brereton's arrival in the Philippines, G-2 received cable requests for data on objectives in Japan. In reply thereto there have been mailed to General MacArthur a series of maps showing the location of approximately 600 industrial objectives, in Japan proper. He has also been informed that objectives folder data to support these maps are in preparation and will be forwarded to him at the earliest possible date. The present status of this project (now under way in the Chief of Air Corps branch office at Bolling Field) indicates that about one-third of the total projected number of objective folders may be completed and prepared for shipment to the Philippines

SECRET

Map and memorandum detailing the extent of preparations for a strategic-bombing offensive against Japan. NATIONAL ARCHIVES, SECRETARY OF WAR SECRET FILE

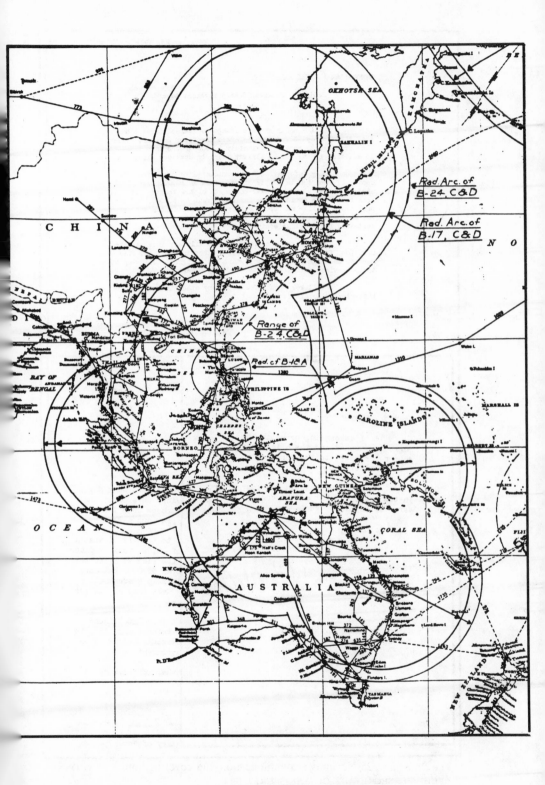

November 25, 1941

MEMORANDUM FOR THE PRESIDENT:

Subject: Japanese Convoy Movement towards
Indo-China.

About a month and a half ago we learned through Magic
that the Japanese Government informed the Vichy Government that
they proposed to move approximately 50,000 troops into Indo-China
in addition to the 40,000 already there by previous agreement.

Today information has accumulated to the effect that a
convoy of from ten to thirty ships , some of 10,000 tons displacement, has been assembled near the mouth of the Yangtse River below
Shanghai. This could mean a force as great as 50,000, but more
probably a smaller number. Included in this ship concentration
was at least one landing-boat carrier. The deck-load of one vessel
contained heavy bridge equipment.

The officers concerned, in the Military Intelligence
Division, feel that unless we receive other information, this is
more or less a normal movement, that is, a logical follow-up of
their previous notification to the Vichy Government.

I will keep you informed of any other information in
this particular field.

Henry L Stimson
Secretary of War.

November 27, 1941.

Dear Mr. Secretary:

I am sending herewith the
English estimate and the original of
your report sent to the President
Tuesday afternoon.

We found this in due course
in the inside pocket of the coat of a
very distinguished gentleman.

I am,

Very sincerely yours,

Pa Watson
EDWIN M. WATSON.

Honorable Henry L. Stimson,
The Secretary of War.

The "missing" 25 November communication and covering note. NATIONAL
ARCHIVES, SECRETARY OF WAR SECRET FILE

259

P.M. approved of draft of this telegram 8.30 p.m 7.12.41. Subsequently in view of news of Japanese commencement of hostilities instructions were given to cancel it. [initials] 7.12.41

Draft Telegram to Lord Halifax, Washington.

Most Immediate.   Most Secret.

1.   From your recent telegrams we understand we can rely on armed support of United States if we become involved in hostilities with Japan in the following circumstances:-

(a)   Japanese invasion of Malaya or Netherlands East Indies.

(b)   Action on our part in the Kra Isthmus to forestall or repel Japanese landing in that Isthmus.

(c)   Action on our part in Kra Isthmus in event of Japanese encroachment on Thailand by force or threat of force (President's 3rd hypothesis in your Telegram No. 5519 of December 1).

2.   We read your Telegram 5653 (of December 6) as meaning that in President Roosevelt's view we should be justified in attacking at sea any Japanese expedition sailing in direction of Thailand or Malaya (and presumably East Indies).   We ourselves should desire to have this latitude.

Telegram drafted half an hour before the Pearl Harbor attack by Churchill confirming that Roosevelt *had* guaranteed U.S. armed support even if Britain made a preemptive attack on the Japanese. PUBLIC RECORDS OFFICE, PRIME MINISTER'S FILES

(ed)

U WO 2   All Fleets
DE
HA FU 6   TOKYO Radio
- SU U   N 90

- - - - - - - - - - - - - -

From: TU HI 017.   Secty, COMBINED FLEET.
Action: YA MI 9   C/S COMBINED FLEET
Info: Missing.   (Probably Chief Tokyo Comm. Office)

2300/24 November 1941   (TOI 11/2500JG WE H155A) H

████   Serial   616██

Additions to Call List "RA TO YO"

1. Additions to the "surface force" section (pages 1 and 2).

CALL	UNIT
SE TA to HI TE (6 calls)	E (British Malay) Force. H (Dutch Indies) Force. M (Philippine) Force. N (Japan) Force. AA (Wake) Occupation Force. G (Guam) Occupation Force.
HI SE to WU FU	Main Force.
FO I to N RE	Flagship of Maru Force.
B NO to HO A	Striking Force.
SE WI to NU HU	Flagship of Striking Force.
NI HI to WU KU	Air Force (Southern Force).
SI YO to FU RO	Ship-shore administrative offices of Commander Air Force (Southern Force).
WI SO to KO WU	Advance Expeditionary Force.
EE WI to SI NU	Flagship of Advance Expeditionary Force.
HO FU to G NA	Submarine Force (Southern Force).
KI NU to HA SO	Flagship of Submarine Force (Southern Force).
FO HE to SE WU	Southern Force.
JN 5 0063 Z	(crown) Navy Trans 11/29/45

JN-25 intercepts of Japanese operational orders before war broke out. Although not fully decrypted until 1945 they reveal clear signs of the scale and direction of the impending attack. NATIONAL ARCHIVES, SRN SERIES

(cb)

- - - - - - - - - - - - - -

From: YO MI Ø/   Combined Fleet, CinC.
Action: SE TU 7   Combined Fleet.

1?/0-1500/I 1941   (TOI 14/022100 & XT 4155 A) - H

Serial 676

This despatch is Top Secret.

This order is effective at 1730 on 2 December:

Combined Fleet Serial) # 10.

Climb NIITAKAYAMA 1208, repeat 1208!

Comment: Interpreted freely, above means "Attack on 8 December". Explanation:
This was undoubtedly the prearranged signal for specifying the date for opening
hostilities. However, the significance of the phrase is interesting in that it
is so appropriately used in this connection.

NIITAKAYAMA is the highest mountain in the Japanese Empire. To
climb NIITAKAYAMA is to accomplish one of the greatest feats. In other words
undertake the task (of carrying out assigned operations). 1208 signifies the
12th month, 8th day, Item time.

GI Comment: Intercepted 2100, 2
Dec. 1941.

LBH   F

(JAPANESE)

JN 5   0012 Z   (KK) Navy from TOP SECRET ULTR

NAVAL MESSAGE   NAVY DEPARTMENT

			MESSAGE PRECEDENCE
PHONE EXTENSION NUMBER		ADDRESSEES	
FROM **OPNAV**	FOR ACTION	CINCAF CINCPAC	**PRIORITY** ROUTINE DEFERRED
RELEASED BY **ADM INGERSOLL** **27 NOV 1941** DATE			
TOR CODEROOM _____ DECODED BY _____ PARAPHRASED BY	INFORMATION	CINCLANT SPENAVO *Signed for by McDowry - Op-12B*	PRIORITY ROUTINE DEFERRED

INDICATE BY ASTERISK ADDRESSEES FOR WHICH MAIL DELIVERY IS SATISFACTORY

262337   (CR0921)

UNLESS OTHERWISE DESIGNATED THIS DISPATCH WILL BE TRANSMITTED WITH DEFERRED PRECEDENCE.

ORIGINATOR FILL IN DATE AND TIME FOR DEFERRED AND MAIL DELIVERY

DATE   TIME   GCT

TEXT THIS DISPATCH IS TO BE CONSIDERED A WAR WARNING X NEGOTIATIONS WITH JAPAN LOOKING TOWARD STABILIZATION OF CONDITIONS IN THE PACIFIC HAVE CEASED AND AN AGGRESSIVE MOVE BY JAPAN IS EXPECTED WITHIN THE NEXT FEW DAYS X THE NUMBER AND EQUIPMENT OF JAPANESE TROOPS AND THE ORGANIZATION OF NAVAL TASK FORCES INDICATES AN AMPHIBIOUS EXPEDITION AGAINST EITHER THE PHILIPPINES THAI OR KRA PENINSULA OR POSSIBLY BORNEO X EXECUTE AN APPROPRIATE DEFENSIVE DEPLOYMENT PREPARATORY TO CARRYING OUT THE TASKS ASSIG ED IN WPL46X INFORM DISTRICT AND ARMY AUTHORITIES X A SIMILAR WARNING IS BEING SENT BY WAR DEPARTMENT X SPENAVO INFORM BRITISH CONTINENTAL DISTRICTS GUAM SAMOA DIRECTED TAKE APPROPRIATE MEASURES AGAINST SABOTAGE

*Signed for by
McDowry - Op-12B*

SEE ART 76(4)
NAV REGS

MAKE ORIGINAL ONLY, DELIVER TO COMMUNICATION WATCH OFFICER IN PERSON

The navy's 27 November 1941 alert that was phrased to warn both the Asiatic and Pacific fleet commanders of impending war, but clearly applied primarily to the former. NATIONAL ARCHIVES, PEARL HARBOR LIAISON OFFICE

FROM	SECRET	FOR ACTION	CINCAF	ROUTINE
RELEASED BY	RADM BRAINARD			DEFERRED
DATE	2 DEC. 1941			
TO & CODEROOM	2356	INFORMATION		PRIORITY
DECODED BY	CALLAN			ROUTINE
PARAPHRASED BY	GLUNT			DEFERRED

INDICATE BY ASTERISK ADDRESSEES FOR WHICH MAIL DELIVERY IS SATISFACTORY

Ø12356CRØ313

UNLESS OTHERWISE DESIGNATED THIS DISPATCH WILL BE TRANSMITTED WITH DEFERRED PRECEDENC

ORIGINATOR FILL IN DATE AND TIME FOR DEFERRED AND MAIL DELIVERY

| | DATE | TIME | GCT |

TEXT

PRESIDENT DIRECTS THAT THE FOLLOWING BE DONE AS SOON AS POSSIBLE

AND WITHIN TWO DAYS IF POSSIBLE AFTER RECEIPT THIS DESPATCH. CHARTER 3 SMALL VESSELS TO FORM A "DEFENSIVE INFORMATION PATROL" MINIMUM REQUIREMENTS TO ESTABLISH IDENTITY AS U.S. MEN-OF-WAR

ARE COMMANDED BY A NAVAL OFFICER AND TO MOUNT A SMALL GUN AND 1 MACHINE GUN WOULD SUFFICE. FILIPINO CREWS MAY BE EMPLOYED WITH NUMBER MINIMUM/NAVAL RATINGS TO ACCOMPLISH PURPOSE WHICH IS TO OBSERVE AND REPORT BY RADIO JAPANESE MOVEMENTS IN WEST CHINA SEA AND GULF

OF SIAM. 1 VESSEL TO BE STATIONED BETWEEN HAINAN AND HUE. ONE VESSEL OFF THE INDO-CHINA COAST BETWEEN CAMRANH BAY AND CAPE ST.

JAQUES AND ONE VESSEL OFF POINTE DE CAMAU. USE OF ISABEL AUTHORIZED BY PRESIDENT AS ONE OF THE THREE BUT NOT OTHER NAVAL VESSELS.

REPORT MEASURES TAKEN TO CARRY OUT PRESIDENTS VIEWS. AT SAME TI INFORM ME AS TO WHAT RECONNAISSANCE MEASURES ARE BEING REGULARLY

PERFORMED AT SEA BY BOTH ARMY AND NAVY WHETHER BY AIR SURFACE VE SELS OR SUBMARINES AND YOUR OPINION AS TO THE EFFECTIVENESS OF

THESE LATTER MEASURES.   FILES...CNO...GENERAL...2Ø 0 DISTRIBUTION...38...ORIGINATOR...RECORD COPY..12

MAKE ORIGINAL ONLY, DELIVER TO COMMUNICATION WATCH OFFICER IN PERSON

The president's order to the Asiatic Fleet to send out three expendable vessels on what appears to have been a "fishbait" mission. NATIONAL ARCHIVES, PEARL HARBOR LIAISON OFFICE

I KA MI (GUADALCANAL Oper. For.)
DE: SO SU FU (RABAUL Comm. Unit)
U TU 785 W 176
- - - - - - - - - - - - - - - - - -

From: ?
Action: RO HI 2 · | (SOLOMONS Defense Force)
           HO KO 8 · | ?   '
           KU TA 2 | (Air Group #204)
           YU YO 2 _ _ | (Air Flotilla #26)

           (Ballale Garrison Comdr.)
Info: NO KA 1   ?

4/131755/I &943   (TCI 4/140009/I on 4990 A kcs) bt

#?   From: CinC Southeastern Air Fleet.

          On 18 April CinC Combined Fleet will visit
RXZ, R___ and RXP in accordance following schedule:

          1. Depart RR at 0600 in a medium attack
plane escorted by 6 fighters. Arrive RXZ at 0800.
Proceed by minesweeper to R__ arriving at 0840.
(___ have minesweeper ready at #1 Base). Depart R____
at 0945 in above minesweeper and arrive RXZ at 1030?
(- - - - - - - -). Depart RXZ at 1100? ◄ in medium
attack plane and arrive RXP at 1110. ~~xxxxxxx~~
- - - - - - - -. Depart RXP at 1400 in medium attack
plane and arrive RR at ~~x~~ 1540.

          2. At each of the above places the Commander-
in-Chief will make short tour of inspection and at _____
he will visit the sick and wounded, but current
operations should continue. Each force commander - - - -'

JN-3: 2825 (MR)   (Japanese)
                        (S) Navy Trans. 4/141705/Q(?)

The decrypted intercept of Admiral Yamamoto's scheduled tour of Bougainville bases that became his death warrant. Note five-minute disparity in
minesweeper trip, because of tides. NATIONAL ARCHIVES, SRN SERIES

II

The Navy Department Decrypting Unit had been assisting Pearl Harbor in the solution of the Jap Naval Operations Code for about a year, and had handled solution single-handed before this "project" was assigned to Pearl Harbor in 1941. The British C.I. Unit in Singapore had been evacuated to Ceylon and then withdrawn to East Africa, so that it was temporarily in a state of "suspended animation" so far as its cryptanalytical efforts were concerned. The Asiatic C.I. Unit had been evacuated (by submarine) from Corregidor to Australia during March, April, and early May, 1942: there they joined the enthusiastic but inexperienced Australian C.I. Unit at Canberra and were just getting on their feet again when Midway was fought. So the whole burden of communication intelligence (in the Pacific) fell on Pearl Harbor and Washington. It is true that the Navy Department was turning out more "key recoveries" and "code values" than Pearl Harbor. (They had more personnel to assign to this project.) However, Pearl Harbor was always several days ahead in its information—because it was adjacent to the Intercept Station—and in this instance made a correct evaluation of available evidence while the Navy Department busted cold.'

Neither John Redman nor Wenger were inclined to share credit with anyone else, let alone admit a blunder, so they proceeded to bluff their way through. They told the Director of Naval Communications (Capt. Joseph R. Redman) that they had spotted the change of date, that Pearl Harbor had missed the boat on this occasion, and that without the warning from Washington, Midway and parts of the Hawaiian Islands would have been captured! It is presumed that Captain Redman told this to Vice Admiral Horne, to Vice Admiral Willson, and to Admiral King. This could be verified by questioning these Admirals - if they still remember the incident.

The exposure of the above-mentioned fraud did not come until October, 1943, when Commander J. S. Holtwick was ordered to the Navy Department for a short period of temporary duty prior to going to Chungking for liaison duty with the Chinese Government. Holtwick called on the D.N.C. (Rear Admiral Joseph R. Redman) to pay his respects. In the course of conversation, Admiral Redman casually remarked that Pearl Harbor had missed the boat at the Battle of Midway but the Navy Department had saved the day. This took Holtwick's breath away, but he managed to say that Admiral Nimitz thought the reverse was true. Admiral Redman then said that the Commander in Chief must have been misinformed, to which Holtwick replied:

> "Admiral Nimitz read the official dispatches and drew
> his own conclusions. Also, he has just given me a
> letter of commendation for my part in the work."

(Incidentally, Admiral Nimitz gave similar letters of commendation to Dyer, Wright, Rochefort (*), and others.)

-4-

A page from the anonymous wartime memorandum accusing certain members of the navy department of conspiring to sack Rochefort. ADMIRAL SHOWERS

UNITED STATES FLEET
HEADQUARTERS OF THE COMMANDER IN CHIEF
NAVY DEPARTMENT, WASHINGTON, D. C.

S E C R E T

June 22, 1942.

MEMORANDUM FOR: The Admiral.

Subject: Commander Rochefort Recommendation for Medal
Award.

     1.   I do not concur in the recommendation that
Commander Rochefort be awarded a Distinguished Service
Medal.

     2.   This officer is not the originator of this
particular service, though he has been very active in it,
and, while he has apparently performed his present duties
in a highly successful manner, he has merely efficiently used
the tools previously prepared for his use.

     3.   Ground-work, prepared over a period of many
years, is the result of the efforts of many officers and
it would seem hardly befitting to award a medal only to
the officer who happens to be in a position to reap the
benefits, at a particular time, unless in actual combat
operation with the enemy.

     4.   The work of Corregidor, Belconnen and the
Navy Department has been, I think, of as high an order
as that done in Honolulu. However, these Officers in
Charge performed a more or less mechanical, technical job
in utilizing a tool already forged to their use.

     5.   I consider that equal credit is due to the
COMINCH Planning Section for the correct evaluation of enemy
intentions, based upon all sorts of intelligence, and
strategical application of that intelligence. In this particular case radio intelligence was invaluable.

OK
K
     6.   I recommend that you disapprove this recommend-
ation ation and other similar ones which may be received,
particularly at this time.

Done
K
     7.   I do recommend, however, that a "Well Done" be
sent from COMINCH to the stations and units concerned in
their particular private cipher system. Despatch attached
for your release if you approve.

Respectfully,

RUSSELL WILLSON
Chief of Staff.

King rejected the recommended award to Rochefort. Notations indicate King's
acceptance of the advice of his chief of staff. ROCHEFORT PAPERS

Notes

Essentially this book is the autobiographic memoir of Admiral Edwin T. Layton. He determined with his co-authors that where his recollections were the primary source there was no need for references and footnotes. The basis for these recollections are derived from a wide variety of his writings contained in dozens of school exercise books and the notes with which he filled hundreds of pieces of paper. These include translations from Japanese books and documents, transcriptions from message file marginal notes, and the notations in the books from his personal library. Layton's correspondence files, his tape-recorded interviews and reminiscences conducted with his co-authors are primary sources. So too are the oral history produced by the United States Naval Institute in Annapolis and Professor E. B. Potter's detailed interview with Layton conducted for the biography of Admiral Nimitz. Among other important sources are Layton's published papers and writings, and his verbatim testimony and cross-examinations recorded in the following official hearings into the attack on Pearl Harbor:

Roberts Commission	Part 23	pages 657–672
Hart Inquiry	Part 26	pages 225–240
Army Board	Part 28	pages 1577–1595
Navy Inquiry	Part 33	pages 832–839
Clausen Investigation	Part 35	pages 49–51
Hewitt Inquiry	Part 36	pages 111–173
Joint Congressional	Part 10	pages 4829–4909

Detailed citations of the author's personal quotations and references are all incorporated in the Edwin T. Layton Collection held by the U.S. Naval War College, Newport, Rhode Island. This collection includes the original notebooks, pencil drafts, tape recordings, and correspondence as well as the admiral's own collection of documents and microfilms.

Chapter 1 (pages 17–22) "I Was There"

1. *Hearings Before the Joint Committee on the Investigation of the Pearl Harbor Attack, Congress of the United States, Seventy-ninth Congress* (Washington, 1946), Part 4, page 1976, (hereafter PHH 4/1976).
2. PHH 4/1975.
3. PHH 26/22; 28/1594.
4. PHH 23/663.

Chapter 2 (pages 23–37) The Undeclared War

1. Capt. Wesley A. Wright conversation, 9 January 1985.
2. Kenichi Nakamuta, *Joohoo shikan no kaisoo* (Reflections of an intelligence officer) (hereafter Nakamuta) (Tokyo: Daiya Mendosha, 1947), p. 74.
3. National Archives of the United States (Record Group 457, Modern Military Branch, Military Archives Division) SRH histories. SRH 355: "Naval Security Group History to World War II," compiled by Captain J. S. Holtwick, Jr., June 1971; Volume II as quoted on page 19 (hereafter SRH 355).
4. Laurence F. Safford, "History of Radio Intelligence: The Undeclared War," 15 November 1943, SRH 305, p. 11.
5. Laurence F. Safford, "A Brief History of Communications Intelligence in the United States," 21–27 March 1952, SRH 149, p. 1.
6. David Kahn, *The Codebreakers* (hereafter Kahn), pp. 352–54.
7. SRH 355, pp. 26–27.
8. Ibid., p. 28.
9. SRH 305, p. 1.
10. Henry L. Stimson and McGeorge Bundy, *On Active Service in Peace and War* (hereafter Bundy), p. 188.
11. SRH 305, p. 1.
12. Kanya Miyauchi *Niitakayama nobore 1208* (hereafter Miyauchi), p. 481.
13. Ibid.
14. SRH 355, p. 30.
15. Ibid., p. 23.
16. Mrs. Eunice Willson Rice letter to Pineau, 23 June 1985.
17. SRH 355, pp. 18–19, 29, 160, 341.
18. Rice letter.
19. SRH 305, p. 3.
20. SRH 355, p. 72, Capt. Raymond Schmidt interview, 1970.
21. SRH 305, p. 8.
22. SRH 149, p. 5.
23. SRH 305, p. 8.
24. Ibid.
25. Ibid.
26. Ibid.
27. Ibid., p. 10.
28. Ibid.
29. Ibid., pp. 4–6.
30. SRH 305, p. 5.
31. Private papers of Capt. J. J. Rochefort (hereafter Rochefort papers): "Memorandum for Captain Ogan [acting director of naval intelligence] re Cryptographic Section," dated 21 December 1932.
32. SRH 305, p. 6.
33. Rochefort memo, 21 December 1932.
34. Ibid.
35. Ibid.
36. SRH 305, p. 5.

Chapter 3 (pages 38–51)   Keep the Dogs Yapping

1. Herbert O. Yardley, *The American Black Chamber,* pp. 163–65, 187–211.(Republished by Ballantine Books.)

2. Japanese Foreign Ministry Files: Memorandum of 10 June 1931.

3. Elting E. Morison, *A Study of the Life and Times of Henry L. Stimson* (Boston, 1960), p. 382.

4. Grew to Stimson, 23 February 1933, *Foreign Relations of the United States, Diplomatic Papers* (hereafter FRUS-DP) (Department of State, 1949) Vol. 3, p. 195.

5. SRH 305, p. 4.

6. U.S. Naval Institute Oral History Program, transcript of 1969 interviews with Capt. J. J. Rochefort, p. 30 (hereafter Rochefort OH).

7. Dyer interview, 27 June 1984.

8. SRH 355, pp. 80, 88.

9. SRH 305, p. 12.

10. Nakamuta, pp. 83–84.

11. Rochefort papers: "Memorandum for Lieutenant Curts," 25 September 1934.

12. Toshiyuki Yokoi, *Nihon no kimitsu shitsu* ("The Japanese Version of the Black Chamber") (hereafter Yokoi), draft article, English translation 1953, p. 6.

13. Ibid., p. 7.

14. Ibid., p. 9.

15. Ibid., p. 12.

16. SRH 305, p. 14.

17. Rochefort papers, letter from Adm. J. M. Reeves dated 22 April 1935.

18. Ibid.

19. Wright interview, 24 May 1984.

20. Ibid.

Chapter 4 (pages 52–69)   Codebreaking and Kabuki

1. Vice Admiral George C. Dyer, U.S.N. (Ret.), *On the Treadmill to Pearl Harbor: The Memoirs of Admiral James O. Richardson U.S.N. (Retired)* (hereafter Dyer, *Richardson),* p. 10.

2. Ibid., p. 320.

3. Ibid., p. 332.

4. Ibid.

5. Ibid., p. 435.

6. *Webster's Third New International Dictionary of the English Language* (Springfield, Mass.: G. & C. Merriam Co., 1964), p. 1174.

7. SRH 355, p. 40.

8. Ibid., p. 147.

9. Ibid., pp. 40–41.

10. SRH 305, p. 13.

11. Ibid.

12. SRH 355, p. 19.

13. Ibid., pp. 353–55.

14. Yokoi, p. 7.

15. SRH 355, pp. 115–16.

16. Yokoi, p. 7.

17. Ibid., p. 8.

18. PHH 7/3251.

19. Ibid., pp. 3355–58.

20. Ibid., p. 3356.

Chapter 5 (pages 70–81) When We Fight

1. Shinsaku Hirata, *Warera moshi tatakawaba (When We Fight)* (Tokyo: Kodansha, 1933), Chapter I.

2. Shigeru Fukudome, *Shikan: Shinjuwan koogeki* (Tokyo: Jiyu Ajiya 1955), p. 137.

3. Dorothy Borg and Shumpei Okamoto, eds., *Pearl Harbor as History*, p. 167.

4. Hiroyuki Agawa, *The Reluctant Admiral: Yamamoto and the Imperial Navy* (hereafter Agawa), p. 158.

5. Ibid.

6. Ibid., p. 189.

7. Ibid., p. 219.

8. PHH 14/1402.

9. U.S. Navy Operational Archives, Strategic Plans Division Records (hereafter NWPD), secretary of navy to secretary of war, January 1941 [reference (SC) A7-2(2)/FF1]

10. Ibid.

11. PHH 22/330.

12. Ibid., p. 332.

13. Ibid., p. 334.

14. PHH 15/1437; and PHH 22/350.

15. Ibid.

16. PHH 22/351.

17. PHH 4/1941.

18. SRH 355, p. 395.

19. Ibid., p. 319*n*.

20. Ibid., p. 329.

21. Dyer interview, Rochefort papers "Top Secret Ultra" memorandum, dated 15 August 1944; and SRH 355, pp. 396–99.

22. Captain E.S.L. Goodwin letter, 1 April 1985.

23. Ibid.; and SRH 355, p. 398.

24. Ibid.

25. Ibid., p. 396.

26. SRH 355, pp. 161, 247–49, 401; and SRH 149, pp. 8–9.

27. SRH 355, p. 161.

28. Ibid.

29. Ibid., pp. 160–163.

30. Ibid., p. 159.

31. Ibid., p. 8.

32. SRH 159, "Preliminary Historical Report on the Solution of the 'B' Machine," William F. Friedman, December 1945; and Theodore M. Hannah, "Frank Rowlett," in *Cryptologic Spectrum,* Spring 1981, p. 16.

33. Ibid., p. 18.

34. Ibid., p. 15.

Chapter 6 (pages 82–91) Pacific Overtures

1. FRUS-Japan, 1941, Vol. II, pp. 387–89.

2. FDR Lib., Hyde Park, New York, Complete Press Conferences #702, 17 December 1940.

3. NA/RG 457: SRA individual translations, Japanese military attaché messages, No. 1848, Washington-Tokyo, 16 April 1941, tr. 1945.

4. Ibid.

5. NA/RG 457: SRDJ individual translations, Japanese diplomatic messages. See in particular: SRNA 000001, Tokyo-Washington, 5 May 1940, concerning meeting at Nipponese Club, New York, between agent Katoo and German agent Steamer (probably phonetic spelling of "Sthaemer"); and SRDJ 011811, JD-1 2360, Washington-Tokyo, 14 May 1941 re a request for half a million Yen for intelligence operations in the United States. It details the assistance given spy chief Terasaki by Senator "G" and his links with the America First Committee and Charles Lindbergh who "according to W [name deleted) has been cautioned by the German Embassy."

SRDJ 011769, JD-1 2598, Washington-Tokyo, 9 May 1941 (tr. 19 May 1941) re cultivation of contacts among "very influential Negro leaders" to stir racial discontent "to stall the program the US plans for national defense and the economy, as well as for sabotage." This report also referred to a network of informants among "our second generation workers in airplane plants."

SRDJ 16637, SIS 24538, Washington-Tokyo, 6 November 1941 (tr. 8 November 1941) reporting liaison with Lindbergh through C. K. Armstrong and the America First Committee.

6. Cordell Hull, *The Memoirs of Cordell Hull* (hereafter Hull *Memoirs*), p. 982.

7. Hajime Sugiyama, *Sugiyama Memo (Sugiyama's Memoranda)* (Tokyo: Hara Shebo, 1967) Vol. 1, p. 1201.

8. NA/RG:457 SRNA, individual translations, Japanese naval attaché messages, No. 0020, Berlin-Tokyo, 12 December 1940.

9. NA/RG 242: Collection of foreign records seized 1941: *Oberkommando der Kriegsmarine: Marine Attaché Gruppe: "Kriegstagebuch des Marinesattaches und des Militarischen Leiters der Gross-Etappe Japan/China,"* 28 August 1939–31 March 1943 (hereafter Wenneker diary), entry 3 July 1940.

10. Wenneker diary, 13 August 1940.

11. *Senshi Soosho* [War history series] (Tokyo: Defense Headquarters History Office) (hereafter SSS) Vol. 91, *Daihonei kaigun bu—rengokantai*, pp. 420–31.

12. Ibid.

13. SSS, Vol. 91, p. 496n.

14. Public Records Office, Kew, England, War Cabinet records 66/10 (hereafter PRO CAB), "Situation in the Far East in the Event of Japanese Intervention Against Us," Chiefs of Staff Committee (hereafter COS), 31 July 1940.

15. Wenneker diary, 7 December 1940, Telegram No. 209–212; SRNA 0020: "Forty Years On—The Imperial Japanese Navy, The European War and the Tripartite Pact," Professor J.M.W. Chapman in 1980 Proceedings of British American Japan Society, Vol. 1, Part 1; *see also* "The Sinking of The *Nankin* and the Capture of the *Aretimedon*," James Rushbridger, *Encounter*, May 1985, Vol. LXIV, No. 5

16. CAB 66/10; COS "Appreciation" covering letter, 15 August 1940.

17. Wenneker diary, 12 December 1940.

18. Warren Kimball, *Churchill-Roosevelt: The Complete Correspondence* (Princeton, 1984), Vol. 1, "Alliance Emerging" (hereafter Kimball WSC/FDR), C-60X 15 February 1941, pp. 135–36.

19. Maurice Matloff and Edwin M. Snell, *Strategic Planning for Coalition Warfare: 1941–1942* (hereafter Matloff and Snell) (Washington, D.C.: Office of the Chief of Military History, U.S. Army, 1953), p. 75.

20. Ibid.

21. Kimball WSC/FDR, C Box, 5 February 1941, pp. 135–36.

22. PHH 16/2151.

23. Ibid., p. 2163.

24. Ibid., pp. 2164–65.

25. Knox-Stimson letter, 24 January 1941.

26. PHH 20/4300.

27. PHH 15/1635.

28. Ibid.
29. Henry L. Stimson diary, 24 April 1941 (manuscript in Stimson papers) (Yale) (hereafter Stimson diary).
30. PHH 16/2160–61.
31. Ibid., p. 2229.
32. Ibid., p. 2160.
33. PHH 10/4846.

Chapter 7 (pages 92–102)   On the Mat

1. Rochefort papers, "High Frequency Direction Finding in the Pacific Ocean Prior to December 7, 1941," 9 August 1944; "RI Activities, 14th Naval District," confidential memorandum of 14 August 1940; also SRH 355, pp. 343–47.
2. Rochefort papers, top secret Ultra memoranda, 5 August 1944 and 15 August 1944.
3. Ibid.
4. Ibid.
5. Ibid., and SRH 149, p. 14 and SRH 355, pp. 297–399, which state in general terms that JN-25 was being decrypted to some extent throughout 1941. The precise amount of JN-25 traffic which could be read in December 1941 is a matter of some debate—and considerable historical importance—which may be why no contemporary decrypts have yet been released either by American or British sources. Admiral Layton, despite repeated efforts, was unable to obtain any official records or specific examples of messages that would clarify the issue. The British foreign office, shortly before this manuscript went to press, again insisted that it was not its policy ever to release any documents that would indicate that Britain decrypted the communications of a foreign power which was officially at peace.

The anonymous and undated "secret" memorandum "The Inside Story of the Battle of Midway and the Ousting of Commander Rochefort" (hereafter A Memo) asserts that JN-25 was "50 % readable" but provides no details. This was an exaggeration—at least as far as the U.S. navy was concerned—according to the postwar opinions of Captains Rochefort, Dyer and Wright. They estimated that Washington's success at reading JN-25B in November was probably on the order of 10 to 15 percent. This would agree with Safford's 1945 assessment of the extent of JN-25 penetration given in a secret 17 May 1945 memorandum to the Hewitt investigation (RG 80, PHLO Box 49). For details of his discussion see Chapter 21, note 27.
6. PHH 15/1864.
7. Ibid.
8. Julius A. Furer, *Administration of the Navy Department in World War II* (hereafter Dyer, *Admin.*), p. 123.
9. Ibid.
10. A. A. Hoehling, *The Week Before Pearl Harbor* (hereafter Hoehling), p. 54.
11. Ibid., p. 56.
12. Dyer, *Admin.*, p. 129.
13. PHH 4/1915.
14. Robert Sherrod, *On to Westward*, p. 250.
15. PHH 4/1914.
16. U.S. Navy Operational Archives, General Board file 429.
17. PHH 4/1926.
18. "The Reminiscences of RADM Arthur H. McCollum USN (Ret.)," an oral history (hereafter McCollum OH) (Annapolis, 1973), p. 309.

19. Ibid., p. 310.
20. Ibid., p. 311.
21. Ibid., pp. 311–12.
22. Ibid., p. 311.
23. Hoehling, p. 56.
24. PHH 4/1926.
25. Ibid.
26. PHH 4/1926.
27. Stimson diary, 6 May 1941.
28. PHH 4/1926.
29. Dyer, *Admin.,* p. 186.
30. McCollum OH, p. 112.
31. Ibid., p. 312.
32. Ibid., p. 313.
33. Ibid., p. 314.
34. Ibid., pp. 324–25.
35. SRH 305, p. 15.
36. Yokoi, p. 10.
37. Ibid.

Chapter 8 (pages 103–111)   The Biggest Rattlesnake

1. Samuel I. Rosenman, ed., *The Public Papers and Addresses of Franklin Delano Roosevelt* (New York: Random House, 1938–1950), 4 Vols., year of 1941, pp. 181–94.

2. NA/RG: 181, Records of the 14th Naval District, "Investigation Report: Japanese Consulate, Honolulu—Espionage Activities," 6 and 9 February 1942 (hereafter Com-14-espionage report).

3. Ibid.

4. SRNA 000006, Tokyo-Washington, 29 September 1940, tr. 11 October 1945 arranging agents' meeting in New York; similarly SRNA 000010, Berlin-Washington, 10 October 1940; SRNA 000015, Berlin-Tokyo, 13 December 1940; SRNA 00078, Washington-Tokyo, 27 June 1940 reporting Okada-Tachibana operations; and SRNA 000083, Tokyo-Washington, 7 June 1940 on precautions for undercover operations.

5. J. F. Bratzel and L. B. Rout, Jr., "Pearl Harbor, Microdots, and J. Edgar Hoover," *The American Historical Review,* Vol. 87, No. 5, pp. 1342–48; also Dusko Popov, *Spy/Counterspy* (New York: G&D, 1974).

6. NA/State Department, RG 59, State Department Decimal Intelligence File: 862.20210 Engles, Albrecht Gustav/71.

7. FDR-Lib. letter, Hoover-Gen. Watson, 3 September 1941 plus enclosures.

8. FDR-Lib., Hoover-Gen. Watson, "Memorandum Re: Japanese Activities," 13 November 1941.

9. SRDJ 012780, JD-1 3490, Washington-Tokyo, 4 July 1941, Tr. 8 July 1941.

10. SRNA 00007 and 8, op. cit.

11. Sources for Blake Account: "Me, Jap Agent—for Uncle Sam" by Al Blake in *Official Detective Stories* February-June 1942 and *Honolulu Advertiser,* 1 May 1941, p. 1.

12. SRDJ 012485, SIS 18626, Hollywood-Washington, 10 June 1941, tr. 25 June 1941.

13. NA/RG 181, Records of the 14th Naval District, District Intelligence Office, Sumner Welles—secretary of navy, 7 July 1941; FDR-Lib. H. R. Stark letter to secretary of state, 23 June 1941, ser. no. 0498416.

14. *The "Magic" Background of Pearl Harbor* (hereafter *"Magic" Back-*

ground), Appx. II, (Washington, D.C.: Department of Defense, 1977), message No. 85, p. A-46.

15. SRH 255, "Interview with Robert D. Ogg," 14 November 1983, pp. 12–20; see also RG: 181, Records of 12th Naval District memo "Coordination of FBI, ONI and MID," 5 June 1940 and subject index to box 8, "Japanese Individuals—Investigation of Japanese Organizations in the United States," 1941.

16. Mrs. William L. Magistretti interview, 6 August 1984.

17. SRH 255, pp. 28–30.

18. PHH 35/84.

19. Com 14 espionage report.

20. SSS, Vol. 10, pp. 14–22; Agawa, p. 253.

Chapter 9 (pages 112–122)   Dropping the Ball

1. PHH 16/2237–38.

2. Ibid.

3. Edwin T. Layton Oral History (hereafter ETL OH), U.S. Naval Institute, p. 48.

4. Rochefort papers, reports on Orange Naval Maneuvers, August 1940; PHLO Box 40, Layton reports on Orange Naval Maneuvers in mandates, May 1941.

5. PHH 10/4829.

6. PHH 6/2502.

7. Ibid.

8. PHH 33/693.

9. PHH 11/5475.

10. SRDJ 011563, JD-09, Tokyo-Washington, 5 May 1941, Tr. 5 May 1941.

11. NA/RG 80: "Records of the Navy Liaison Office to the Joint Congressional Committee Investigating the Attack on Pearl Harbor" (PHLO), Box 62: Japanese diplomatic intercepts JD-1 2372, 2368, 2346, 2367—these are 1945 photocopies of the originals and unlike the SRDJ file, which deletes the cipher identifier, those called JD cite precisely the Purple code in which they were transmitted.

12. Ibid., p. 2636.

13. Dr. Ruth Harris, "The 'Magic' Leak of 1941 and Japanese-American Relations," *Pacific Quarterly*, Vol. LX1, February 1981, pp. 77–96.

14. SRH 154, pp. 31–32.

15. PHH 11/5476.

16. SRDJ 012722, SIS 19018, Tokyo-Berlin, 2 July 1941, tr. 3 July 1941.

17. Ibid.

18. SRDJ 012724, SIS 19033, Berlin-Tokyo, 2 July 1941, tr. 5 July 1941.

19. Harold L. Ickes, *The Secret Diary of Harold L. Ickes: The Lowering Clouds, 1939–1941*, (hereafter Ickes diary), pp. 552–60.

20. Ibid., pp. 564–68.

21. Ibid.

22. PHH 20/4018–19.

23. SRDJ 012722, op. cit., p. 204.

24. PHH 14/1398.

25. Ibid.

26. Ibid.

27. Ibid., p. 1399.

28. PHH 6/2512.

29. Ibid., p. 2513.

30. PHH 16/2173.

31. PHH 5/2384.

32. PHH 14/1399.
33. Ickes diary, pp. 583–84.

Chapter 10 (pages 123–130)   A Ridiculous Situation

1. PHH 14/1327.
2. McCollum OH, p. 321.
3. Ibid., p. 315.
4. Ibid., p. 320.
5. PHH 14/1398.
6. PHH 36/113–14.
7. PHH 16/2322, 36/116.
8. PHH 36/132.
9. PHH 16/2276–77.
10. Ibid.
11. PHH 7/3130.
12. PHH 16/2239.
13. Ibid., p. 2174.
14. Ibid.
15. Ibid., p. 2242.
16. Ibid., p. 2176.
17. FDR Lib.: Frankfurter papers, Box 98, 11 March 1943.
18. Public Record Office, Kew, England (hereafter PRO), Prime Minister's Files (hereafter PREM) 4, 27/9, 13 March 1941.
19. Kimball FDR/WSC R-52X, p. 229.
20. PHH 12/9.

Chapter 11 (pages 131–137)   Deceptive Deterrents

1. FRUS-DP 1941, Vol. 1, pp. 351–54.
2. NA/RG 18: Records of the Army Air Forces, entry 293, Series II classified files, 337 B Memo for Chief of Staff, "Notes on Staff Conference, 11–12 August 1941, on board *Prince of Wales*" (hereafter Argentia notes), p. 4.
3. Ibid.
4. Library of Congress, Manuscript Division, papers of General Henry H. "Hap" Arnold, transcribed diary notes (hereafter Arnold diary), 10 August 1941 entry, p. 9 and 14 August 1941 entry, p. 15.
5. Argentia notes, p. 4.
6. Arnold diary, entry 14 August 1941, p. 15.
7. FRUS-JAPAN 1941, Vol. II, p. 355.
8. NA/RG 225, records of Joint Army and Navy Boards and committees, 301 minutes (hereafter J-Bd. Min.), 4 September 1941.
9. Ibid., 13 November 1941.
10. Ibid., Statement of Admiral Ingersoll before Joint Board, November 3, 1941.
11. PRO F13114/86/32, Halifax-Foreign Secretary, 1 December 1941.
12. Hansard, 27 January 1941, p. 607.
13. Ibid.
14. FDR-Lib., Hopkins papers, Hopkins-FDR, 21 February 1942.
15. PHH 6/2513.
16. Ibid., p. 2503.

Chapter 12 (pages 138–145)   Shortchanged

1. SRDJ 014086, JD-1 21045, Washington-Tokyo, 7 August 1941, tr. 15 September 1941.

2. SRDJ 014134, SIS 2116, London-Tokyo, 8 August 1941, tr. 18 September 1941.
3. SRA 17353, Washington-Tokyo, 9 August 1941, tr. 4 May 1945.
4. SRDJ 013967, Washington-Tokyo, 9 August 1941, tr. 12 September 1941.
5. PHH 10/4832.
6. J-Bd. Min., 25 July 1941.
7. PHH 33/889.
8. PHH 9/4594.
9. PHH 3/1210.
10. PHH 5/2176.
11. Ibid., p. 2175.
12. PHH 33/883.
13. Hoehling, p. 54.
14. Ibid., p. 56.
15. PHH 33/897.
16. Ibid., p. 898.
17. PHH 4/1976.
18. Ibid., p. 1975.
19. Ibid., p. 1976.
20. Ibid.
21. Ibid.
22. McCollum OH, p. 311.
23. Ibid.
24. Ibid.

Chapter 13 (pages 146–160)   Waves of Strife

1. PHH 17/2870.
2. *Colliers,* 14 June 1941, pp. 11–78 passim.
3. Dyer papers, letter, 6 June 1983.
4. PHH 17/2874.
5. NWPD memo to Leahy, 10 August 1936, SPDR, Box 89.
6. *Washington Times-Herald,* 21 September 1941.
7. Congressional Record, Vol. 67, Pt. 7, 2 October 1941, p. 7592.
8. Carl J. Pritchard letter to Pineau, 12 January 1985.
9. PHH 16/2244.
10. PHH 14/1401.
11. NA/RG 18, Entry 293, Series II, Central Decimal Files 1939–1942, p. 281; D War Plans 1941 classified files.
12. PHH 14/1021–30.
13. Ibid., p. 1031.
14. Ibid.
15. NA/RG 18, Entry 293, Series II, WPD Classified 381.D, memorandum "Aircraft Requirements for Defense of the Western Hemisphere and American Interests in Asia," 26 August 1941.
16. PHH 3/1119.
17. Masanobu Tsuji, *Singapore: The Japanese Version* (New York: St. Martin's Press, 1960), p. 22.
18. SRDJ 014152, SIS 21151, Washington-Tokyo, 16 August 1941, tr. 19 August 1941.
19. FRUS-Japan, Vol. 1, pp. 559–65.
20. SRDJ 014203 JD-1 502, 26 August 1941, tr. 29 September 1941.
21. Takushiro Hattori, *Dai-Toa Senso Zenshi (A Complete History of the Greater East Asia War)* (hereafter Hattori), Vol. 1, pp. 178–82. This is a translation done for the U.S. Army military intelligence in 1953, Document 77510, 500th Military Intelligence Group, NA: AF-8-5.1, Vol. 1.

22. Ibid.
23. Nobutake Ike, ed., *Japan's Decision for War* (hereafter Ike), pp. 95–96.
24. Ibid., pp. 133–63.
25. PHH 20/4004.
26. Hattori, pp. 176–82.
27. PHH 20/4005.
28. Ibid.
29. Ibid.
30. Joseph C. Grew, *Ten Years in Japan* (hereafter Grew), p. 426.
31. Ibid.
32. PHH 20/4214.
33. PHH 16/2209.
34. SSS, Vol. 10, pp. 101–4.
35. Agawa, pp. 228–29.
36. Pineau interview with Fuchida, May 1950.
37. Agawa, p. 230.
38. Ibid., p. 229.
39. Hattori, Vol. 1, pp. 190–96, 281–82; and see also Robert J. C. Butow, *Tōjō and the Coming of the War* (hereafter Butow *Tōjō*), (Princeton, N.J.: Princeton University Press, 1961), p. 263.
40. SRDJ 015229, SIS 22819, Tokyo-Washington, 28 September 1941, tr. 29 September 1941.
41. SRDJ 015178, SIS 22753, Tokyo-Washington, 26 September 1941, tr. 26 November 1941.
42. SRDJ 015491, Washington-Tokyo, 3 October 1941, tr. 7 October 1941 following full report of Hull meeting in SRDJ 015436, SIS 301, 2 October 1941, tr. 6 October 1941 and Tokyo reply in SRDJ 015450, Tokyo-Washington, 3 October 1941, tr. 6 October 1941.
43. Hattori, p. 191.
44. Ibid.
45. Stimson diary, 6 October 1941.
46. SRDJ 01539, SIS 23384, Tokyo-Washington, 10 October 1941, tr. 13 October 1941.
47. Ibid.
48. Grew, p. 456.
49. SRDJ 01552 JD-1 5779, Tokyo-Washington, 13 October 1941, tr. 13 October 1941.
50. Hattori, p. 197.
51. PHH 14/1402.
52. PHH 16/2212.
53. Ibid., p. 2213.
54. PHH 32/191.
55. Ibid.
56. PHH 16/2249.
57. Ibid., p. 2219.

Chapter 14 (pages 161–168)   Affirmative Misrepresentation

1. Interview with Tachibana cited by Gordon W. Prange, *At Dawn We Slept* (hereafter Prange), p. 248.
2. PHH 12/261.
3. Ibid., p. 262.
4. SRH 012, "The Role of Communications Intelligence in the American Japanese Naval War," 4 Vols., Vol. 1, "Diplomatic Background to Pearl Harbor," 1 August 1942 (hereafter SRH 012), pp. 137–202.

5. SRDJ 014545, SIS 21769, Tokyo-Washington, 2 September 1941, tr. 4 September 1941.

6. SRH 012, p. 141.

7. SRDJ 015132, SIS 22697, Honolulu-Tokyo, 4 September 1941, tr. 26 September 1941.

8. PHH 9/4196.

9. Ibid.

10. PHH 2/795.

11. Ibid.

12. PHH 9/4534.

13. Ibid.

14. PHH 5/2175.

15. PHH 4/1922.

16. RADM Alan G. Kirk Oral History transcript, Columbia University (hereafter Kirk OH), p. 179.

17. Rochefort papers, Wilkinson-Rochefort, 14 November 1941.

18. Kimmel papers, "The Bomb Plot Revised," draft apparently prepared from Safford's information by Commander C. C. Hiles.

19. PHH 4/1747.

20. Ibid., p. 1749.

21. SRDJ 017188, JD-1 6991, Tokyo-Honolulu, 15 November 1941, tr. 3 December 1941.

22. SRDJ 017270, JD-1 7063, Tokyo-Honolulu, 18 November 1941, tr. 5 December 1941.

23. SRDJ 017331, JD-1 17086, Tokyo-Honolulu, 20 November 1941, tr. 5 December 1941; SRDJ 017311, JD-1 17086, Tokyo-Honolulu, 29 November 1941, tr. 5 December 1941.

24. J-Bd. Min., 12 July 1941; letter from secretary of war-president, 27 September 1941 endorsed "Not Used."

25. PHH 2/911.

26. PHH 34/59.

27. PHH 6/2543.

28. Ibid., p. 2540.

29. Ibid.

Chapter 15 (pages 169–180) Imperfect Threats

1. PHH 16/2214.

2. PHH 12/76.

3. PHH 4/1946.

4. PHH 16/2216.

5. Ibid., pp. 2214–15.

6. PHH 3/1120.

7. J-Bd. Min., 19 September 1941.

8. PHH 3/1119.

9. Ibid., p. 1167.

10. NA/RG 107: Formerly top secret correspondence of Secretary of War Stimson ("Safe File") July 1940-September 1945; Folder: White House Correspondence, Stimson to president, 21 October 1941 (hereafter Stimson Safe File).

11. FDR-Lib., Private Secretary's File (hereafter PSF), Stimson file.

12. NA/RG 165: Army Chief of Staff, memorandum for secretary of war from acting assistant chief of staff, "Strategic Concept of the Philippine Islands," 8 October 1941.

13. Ibid., memorandum "Strategic Air Offensive Against Japan" for General Marshall, 19 November 1941 (hereafter SAO-Japan).

14. Stimson memo to president, 21 October 1941, op. cit.
15. PHH 3/1167.
16. Ibid.
17. Stimson memo to president, 21 October 1941, op. cit.
18. Agawa, p. 232.
19. Ibid., p. 235.
20. Ibid., p. 237.
21. Ibid.
22. SSS, Vol. 10, pp. 225–26.
23. PHH 35/63.
24. Ibid.
25. Com 14 Japan-espionage investigation.
26. Ibid.
27. SRDJ 016190, SIS 24292, Tokyo-Washington, 2 November 1941, tr. 3 November 1941.
28. PHH 14/1052.
29. J-Bd., Min., 3 November 1941.
30. Ibid.
31. Ibid.
32. Ibid.
33. PHH 16/2222.
34. Ibid.
35. SRDJ 015226, SIS 22814, Washington to San Francisco, Los Angeles, Seattle consulates, 4 September 1941, tr. 29 September 1941. For Tokyo's concern about American bombers see also SRDJ 016786, Washington-Tokyo, 19 October 1941, tr. 20 November 1941 querying bombers sent to Russia via Persia. SRDJ 016587, SIS 24850, Manila-Tokyo, 10 November 1941, tr. 17 November 1941 reporting the arrival of more four-engine bombers, and SRDJ 016890, Tokyo-Manila, 15 November 1941, tr. 24 November 1941 "ascertain what route large bombers went to Philippines."
36. SAO-Japan, op. cit.
37. PRO Prem 3, 183/2, memo first Sea Lord, 29 August 1941.
38. Kimball WSC/FDR, c-125X, p. 265.
39. Ibid.
40. PRO Prem 3, 163/3, prime minister South Africa to WSC, 16 November 1941.
41. PHH 12/97.
42. Ibid., p. 92.
43. Ibid., p. 94.
44. Ibid., p. 98.
45. Ibid., pp. 99–100.
46. Ibid., p. 100.
47. PHH 2/429.
48. PHH 16/2219.
49. PHH 14/1403.
50. PHH 16/2220.

Chapter 16 (pages 181–188)   "What Will We Do?"

1. PHH 16/2251.
2. Ibid., p. 2252.
3. PHH 17/2607.
4. Ibid., p. 2606.
5. Ibid., pp. 2608, 2615.
6. Ibid., p. 2614.

7. Ibid., p. 2616.
8. Ibid., p. 2620.
9. Ibid., p. 2621.
10. NA/RG 80: PHLO, and originals of Layton intelligence summaries and original reports located in boxes 40, 41, 42, 48, 49, and 63 (hereafter PHLO-ETL).
11. Ibid., and PHH 10/4834.
12. Ibid.
13. Ibid., p. 4836.
14. Ibid.
15. PHH 10/4834–35.
16. Ibid.
17. Ibid., p. 4834.
18. PHH 17/2623.
19. PHLO-ETL, and PHH 17/2623.
20. PHH 10/4836.
21. PHH 16/2220.
22. Ibid., p. 2223.
23. Ibid., p. 2253.
24. Ibid., p. 2223.
25. PHH 10/4886.
26. PHH 14/1405.
27. PHH 36/144.
28. Ibid., p. 145.
29. PHH 14/1106.
30. PHH 5/2306, 2319.
31. PHH 16/2224–25.
32. Ibid.

Chapter 17 (pages 189–197)   Negotiations On

1. *The New York Times,* 10 November 1941.
2. SRDJ 016641, SIS 168, Tokyo-San Francisco, 10 November 1941, tr. 18 November 1941.
3. SRDJ 016514, JD-1 6417, Tokyo-Washington, 11 November 1941, tr. 12 November 1941.
4. SRDJ 016626, JD-1 6559, Washington-Tokyo, 13 November 1941, tr. 17 November 1941.
5. SRDJ 016772, JD-1 1106, Washington-Tokyo, 15 November 1941, tr. 19 November 1941.
6. SRDJ 016598, JD-1 6553, Washington-Tokyo, 14 November 1941, tr. 17 November 1941.
7. SRDJ 016576, JD-1 6254, Tokyo-Washington, 15 November 1941, tr. 15 November 1941.
8. SRDJ 016617, JD-1 6556, Tokyo-Washington, 15 November 1941, tr. 17 November 1941.
9. SRDJ 016844, JD-1 6721, Washington-Tokyo, 17 November 1941, tr. 22 November 1941.
10. Ibid.
11. FDR-Lib. PSF 141: COI, Donovan—Whitney-Donovan telegram 5392, 12 November 1941.
12. PRO Foreign Office 12475, 86/23, Halifax-foreign office, 17 November 1941.
13. FRUS-DP 1941, Vol. IV, pp. 606–13.
14. Ibid., Vol. II, p. 755*f.*

15. SRDJ 016777, SIS 25806, Washington-Tokyo, 18 November 1941, tr. 21 November 1941.
16. SRDJ 016823, JD-1 6735, Tokyo-Washington, 18 November 1941, tr. 22 November 1941, and SRDJ 016875 of 19 November 1941, tr. 24 November 1941.
17. PHH 12/155.
18. Ibid., p. 158.
19. SRDJ 016855, SIS 25716, Washington-Tokyo, 24 November 1941, tr. 24 November 1945.
20. Ibid.
21. SRDJ 016816, JD-1 6742, Tokyo-Washington, 22 November 1941, tr. 22 November 1941.
22. Ibid.
23. PHLO Hull written testimony, p. 114 Hull; and PHH 2/554.
24. FRUS-DP 1941, Vol. II, p. 755.
25. Kimmel papers, the text of Hornbeck-Hull and Hull-Hornbeck exchange given in letter to Joseph C. Grew, 14 October 1955 from Max Bishop (before he became U.S. ambassador to Thailand). He had been attached to U.S. embassy Tokyo and in 1941 was a State Department aide who "kept the files of all American-Japanese conversations during the summer and fall of 1941." Bishop records how he was "directed" to "return to Hornbeck his 'personal' memoranda. . . . These two were included in that category. However, because of their historical significance I felt they should not disappear into the incinerator. Virginia Collins, who you will recall used to be with us in Tokyo, was in the Department at the time and made copies for me. The original [sic] were given to Hornbeck and are either in his files or destroyed. They were seen by Max Hamilton, by Joe Ballantine and myself in addition to, of course, Hornbeck and Secretary Hull."
26. Ibid.
27. Ibid.
28. SRDJ 016851, SIS 25177, Tokyo-Washington, 24 November 1941, tr. 24 November 1941.
29. Kimball WSC/FDR, R-69X, pp. 275–76.
30. PHLO: Contains two typewritten drafts of the Stimson diary: (1) A running abbreviated version (hereafter PHLO-Stimson A) and (2) full version similar to the Yale collection (hereafter PHLO-Stimson B). Gist the same, although wording sometimes differ. (A) 25 November 1941, p. 46.
31. Ibid., p. 47.
32. Ibid.
33. PHLO-Stimson B, p. 15.
34. PHLO-Hull-Hornbeck memorandum of conversation 24 November 1941 dated 25 November 1941.
35. PHH 14/1194.
36. PHLO-Hull memo of conversations with Chinese ambassador, 25 November 1941.
37. Ibid.
38. Ibid.

Chapter 18 (pages 198–207)   Negotiations Off

1. SRDJ 017036, Washington-Tokyo, 26 November 1941, tr. 28 November 1941.
2. PHLO-Stimson A, 26 November 1941, p. 49.
3. PRO Prem 3, 156/6, Minute-Foreign Secretary, 23 November 1941.
4. Ibid.
5. PRO FO 371, file 35957, Sir Robert Craigie's report, file dockets 22 August 1943.

6. Ibid.; and WSC Secret Minute-Foreign Secretary, 19 September 1943.

7. Winston Churchill, *The Second World War: The Grand Alliance* (hereafter WSC-Vol. III), p. 502.

8. Kimmel papers: Bishop-Grew letter of 14 October 1955 quoting information given him "the other day" by Landreth Harrison (until July 1941, he was second secretary at U.S. embassy Berlin): "It was just a day or so before November 26 when Harrison was in Mr. Hull's office and Hull was summoned by private telephone to the White House. He asked Harrison to wait in the office for he, Secretary Hull, expected to return immediately. The Secretary was gone only 15 minutes or so and came back in a very agitated frame of mind. He said something like this:

> Those madmen over there (White House—he may have used the [sic] term "madmen" but Harrison doesn't want to go that far) do not believe me when I tell them that the Japs will attack us. . . . You cannot give an ultimatum to a powerful and proud people and not expect them to react violently.

For contemporary confirmation of Hull's determination to achieve a *modus vivendi* see Robert Sherwood, *Roosevelt and Hopkins,* p. 428 quoting Hopkins's memorandum of events: "It is true that Hull told the Secretaries of War and Navy that he believed Japan might attack at any moment. On the other hand, up to the very last day, he undoubtedly had hopes that something could be worked out at the last moment. Hull had always been willing to work out a deal with Japan. . . . Hull wanted peace above everything, because he had set his heart on making an adjustment with the Japanese and had worked on it night and day for weeks. There was no question that up until the last ten days prior to the outbreak of war he was in hopes that some adjustment could be worked out."

9. Kimmel papers: Bishop letter quoting Hull-Hornbeck exchange of 27 November 1941.

10. Ibid.

11. Ibid.

12. PHLO-Stimson A, 26 November 1941 entry, p. 49.

13. Ibid., p. 50.

14. Ibid.

15. Ibid., 25 November 1941, p. 48.

16. Ibid.

17. Stimson Safe File, 25 November 1941 letter to White House, Watson 27 November 1941 note, and British 21 November 1941 Joint Intelligence Committee enclosed with same fold creases in Philippines folder.

18. Ibid.

19. Ibid., and White House folder, copy marked "For complete file see White House" was "hand delivered by Sergeant Quick 1225 Nov 26 1941." Original in FDR-Lib. Stimson correspondence file.

20. Ibid.

21. Ibid.

22. PHH 3/1444.

23. PHH 32/732.

24. Ibid.

25. PHH 3/1404–14.

26. PHH 5/2304.

27. H. Montgomery Hyde, *Room 3603* (London, 1962), p. 293; and Sir W. Stephenson-Costello telegram, 28 February 1982.

28. PRO Prem 3/469, and WSC-FDR and covering letters.

29. PRO Prem 3/2526/6B, closed index note; correspondence: minister of state for defense-Anthony Grant MP, 7 December 1979; and Cabinet office-J. Costello, 1 and 29 September 1983.

30. SRA 17952, Tokyo-Bangkok, 25 November 1941, tr. 20 June 1945.
31. SRH 154: "Signal Intelligence Disclosures in the Pearl Harbor Investigation," p. 33, and PHH 11/5179.
32. Michael Montgomery, *Who Sank the Sydney* (London, 1982), *q.v.* details, accounts and references.
33. RAAF reports as cited p. 173.
34. SRN 115385, Tokyo-AU Fleets, 20 November 1941.
35. F. H. Hinsley et al., *British Intelligence in the Second World War* (hereafter Hinsley), Vol. 1, p. 53*n.*
36. Robert Haslach, *Nishi no Kaze Hare* (*West Wind Clear*) (Netherlands: Urieboek, 1985) for background on Dutch intelligence in Far East prior to World War II. Royal Netherlands Army Archives (hereafter NAA), Captain J. W. Henning, chief cryptanalyst, Kamer 14, Bandoeing (hereafter Henning report), dated 11 March 1965.
37. NAA Ter Poorten letter, 23 July 1960.
38. Dr. L.G.M. Jaquet, *Aflossing van de Wacht* (Rotterdam, 1980) and letter to James Rushbridger, 22 June 1985.
39. PHH 13/414–18.
40. Henning report.

Chapter 19 (pages 208–213) "Future Action Unpredictable"

1. FDR-Lib., Morgenthau diary, 26 November 1941, p. 1020 (hereafter Morgenthau diary).
2. PHH 5/2319–22.
3. NA/RG 165: WDCSA/381 minutes, "Conference in the Office of the Chief of Staff 10:40 am, November 29, 1941."
4. Ibid.
5. Ibid.
6. J-Bd.-Min., 26 November 1941.
7. Ibid.
8. Nav. Op. Archives: Hart papers—handwritten "Private Diary Dec. 29, 1940-Dec. 26, 1941":
    25 November: Today, I learn from Washington—straight from the horse's mouth—that the tension between the Japanese and ourselves is very far from having eased up. It's quite the reverse and I'm told that the barometer is so very low that the storm pretty much *must* break, somewhere. . . .
    27 November: The plot grows thicker and thicker—today our communication system brought Sayre *his* war warning right straight from the very biggest horse's mouth [Hart's testimony referred to Philippine Commissioner Francis Sayre's cable from Roosevelt warning "that this next Japanese aggression might cause an outbreak of hostilities between the United States and Japan" (PHH 11/5214)].
9. Opnav 271442 November 1941, PHLO box 45, and *Magic Background* A, p. 109.
10. Ibid.
11. PHLO Stimson diary A, 27 November 1941, p. 51.
12. PHH 14/1083.
13. Ibid.
14. PHLO Stimson diary A, 27 November 1941, p. 52.
15. Ibid.
16. PHH 14/1407.
17. PHH 32/234.
18. Ibid.
19. PHH 4/1916, 2001.

20. SRDJ 016976, JD-1 6843, transpacific telephone call transcript, 26 November 1941.

21. Ibid.

22. SSS, Vol. 10, p. 269, and Onishi diary, entry 28 November 1941.

23. Ibid., and Fujita diary, entry 28 November 1941.

24. Agawa, p. 244.

25. Ibid.

26. SSS, Vol. 10, p. 268.

Chapter 20 (pages 214–221)   Going to Be a Fight

1. PHH 6/2519.

2. William F. Halsey and Joseph Bryan III, *Admiral Halsey's Story* (hereafter *Halsey's Story*), pp. 73–75.

3. Opnav, 27 November 1941, PHLO box 45.

4. PHH 14/1407.

5. PHH 36/115.

6. PHH 7/2943.

7. Ibid., p. 3029.

8. PHH 10/4938.

9. PHH 14/1328.

10. PHH 11/5429.

11. PHH 14/1329.

12. Ibid.

13. PHH 3/1421.

14. PHH 14/1405.

15. PHH 26/280.

16. PHH 14/407.

17. PHH 16/2278.

18. PHH 14/1405.

19. PHH 6/2518.

20. PHH 32/234.

21. Ibid.

22. PHH 16/2223.

23. PHH 12/154.

24. Ibid., p. 155.

25. PHH 17/2659.

26. SRDJ 017048, JD-1 6895, Tokyo-Washington, 28 November 1941, tr. 28 November 1941.

27. PHLO-Stimson diary A, p. 53.

28. Ibid.

29. Ibid.

30. Ibid.

31. SSS, Vol. 10, p. 269.

32. Ibid.

33. Robert Haslach: Paper delivered to 1983 naval history symposium at Annapolis, citing research and information from Record Group 36: Bureau of Customs, Los Angeles Collection, International Port of Los Angeles, "Records of Entrances and Clearances of Vessels Engaged in Foreign Trade 1897–1957," box 67. See also evidence of Russian sailing from San Francisco in the transportation section of *The San Francisco Chronicle* for 26-28 November 1941 citing 27 November 1941 for mail for vessel departing Soviet Union.

34. SRH 012, p. 162.

Chapter 21 (pages 222–235)   Self-Deception

1. *Halsey's Story*, pp. 75–76.
2. PHH 16/2276.
3. PHH 23/1137.
4. PHH 16/2276.
5. PHLO-ETL.
6. PHH 36/149; Com 14 260110 November 1941.
7. PHH 36/159–60.
8. PHH 6/2431.
9. Ibid., p. 2535.
10. PHH 33/709.
11. PHH 6/2535.
12. Ibid., pp. 2535–36.
13. PHH 17/2632.
14. PHH 36/126.
15. *The New York Times*, 13 March 1982: "We kept absolute radio silence," said the former Commander Genda who helped plan the attack. For about two weeks before the attack the thirty-one ships "used flag and light signals," Mr. Genda, seventy-seven, said in an interview. Former Lieutenant Commander Chuichi Yoshoka, seventy-three, who was the communications officer on the flagship *Akagi*, said he did not recall any ship dispatching a radio message before the attack.
16. PHH 17/2666.
17. Ibid., p. 2667.
18. PHH 36/37.
19. A memo, pp. 14–15, referring to Navy Department Secret Publication CSP 1494A, which appeared under signature of Vice-Admiral F. J. Horne, sponsored by the Redmans, dated 15 April 1942, especially pp. 6–8 captioned: "Did the Japanese Paint Us a 'Picture.'" According to the well-informed author of the A Memorandum:

> The main effect (if not the intended purpose) of this particular story was to make the service believe that the old lie was actually true—that Rochefort, Huckins and Williams had been sucked in by Japanese radio deception. . . . Rochefort and the other officers at Pearl Harbor took offense at the contemptible way in which their reputations had been smeared. . . . There were *no* dummy messages on Japanese naval radio circuits *at any time* during 1941. There was one "High Command Cipher" used throughout 1941 and most of 1942 that neither we nor the British ever succeeded in solving. (Otherwise Cincpac would have had a tipoff of the Pearl Harbor raid that *no one* in Washington would have blocked.) No responsible person in the C. I. Organization ever believed that the messages in this system were "dummies." A partial solution by the British confirmed our earlier estimate. The Japs sometimes sent test or drill messages (their alphabet, for instance) but these were readily identified by our intercept operations.

20. PHH 36/128.
21. PHLO-ETL papers, Radio Intelligence Summaries, p. 18.
22. Ibid.
23. W. J. Holmes, *Double-Edged Secrets* (hereafter Holmes), p. 18; Wright interview, 15 March 1985.
24. SSS, Vol. 10, p. 270.
25. SRN 115428, Com Fleet to all flagships, 17 November 1941.
26. Dundas P. Tucker, "Rhapsody in Purple," *Cryptologia*, July 1982, p. 223.
27. The A Memorandum indicates that 50 percent of JN-25 was being read in 1941, but both Dyer and Wright believed that their opposite numbers in Washington and Cavite could not decipher more than 15 percent of the traffic. In the

absence of any actual decrypts, the most accurate record is that of Safford himself, who in May 1945 (PHLO box 49) produced a memorandum for Lieutenant Commander John F. Sonnet, the investigator of Admiral Hewitt's inquiry: "Evaluation of Messages, 26 November 1941":

> Com 16's estimates were more reliable than Com 14's not only because of better radio interception but because *Com 16 was currently reading messages in the Japanese Fleet's Cryptographic System ("5 number code" or "JN-25") and was exchanging technical information and translations with the British CI Unit at Singapore.* . . . The major project of the 14th Naval District CI Unit in November 1941 was to attack the Japanese Flag Officers Cryptographic system (transposition cipher) superposed [sic] on a 4 character code—I think we called it "AD"—in which they were being backed up by a similar attack in the Navy Department. This system (its earlier editions) had been our main source of information on the Japanese navy from 1926–27 up until November 1940. It was the most difficult, as well as the most important, system the Japanese navy was using and our most skilled and most experienced officers and men were attempting its solution.
>
> If we could have solved the flag-officers' system, Admiral Kimmel would probably have known of the Japanese plans and the Pacific fleet would not have been surprised on 7 December 1941. Unfortunately, neither the US navy nor the British cryptanalysts ever succeeded in cracking this system. The "5 numeral" system yielded no information which would arouse even a suspicion of the Pearl Harbor raid, either before or afterward. The Japanese abandoned the "AD" system in 1942 or 1943, apparently because of extensive delays and unreadable messages. As regards the "JN-25" or "5-numeral" system, the current code (JN-25B) had been in effect since 1 December 1940, remaining in effect until 27–31 May 1942, and *was partly readable in November 1941.* A new system of keys was introduced on 4 December 1941 and reported by Com 16 041502, but the carry-over of the old code made their solution quite simple, and we were reading messages again by Christmas, Corregidor getting the actual break on 8 December 1941. The Hawaiian CI unit did not commence work on the Japanese navy's "5-digit" system until 10 December 1941, at which date they discontinued their attack on the "flag officers" system. (The Navy Department continued its attack on the flag officers system as long as it remained in use.) [Emphases added].

28. Goodwin letter, 22 May 1985.
29. SRN 115380, Min. Navy to All Ships, 14 November 1941.
30. SRN 115491, Tokyo to Section, 15 November 1941.
31. SRN 115468, Comb. Fleet Sec. to All Fleet Secs., 16 November 1941.
32. SRN 115478, Desdiv 34 Com to Comb. Fleet Sec., 19 November 1941.
33. SRN 115491, Cardivs. Comb. Fleet to Comb. Fleet COS, 19 November 1941.
34. SRN 115375, *Shiya* to COS Cardivs Comb. Fleet, 20 November 1941.
35. SRN 115438, Hainan Guard District to Takao (Formosa), report of "factual case of leakage of secret information," 20 November 1941.
36. SRN 115385, Comb. Fleet CinC to Cardivs and expeditionary fleets: "At 000 on 21 November, repeat 21 November, carry out second phase of preparations for opening hostilities," 20 November 1941.
37. SRN 115435, 4th Fleet CinC to Crudiv 6, 29 November 1941.
38. SRN 115404–5, 115419–20, 115428–34.
39. SRN 115561, Kita to Tokyo, 27 November 1941.
40. PHH 10/4885.

Chapter 22 (pages 236–298)   Countdown to War

1. SSS, Vol. 10, p. 269.
2. Ibid., p. 270.
3. Ibid.
4. Ibid.
5. PHH 17/2664.
6. SRDJ 017113, SIS 2553, Tokyo-Berlin, 30 November 1941, tr. 1 December 1941.
7. SRDJ 017159, JD-1 6903, Tokyo-Washington, 1 December 1941, tr. 1 December 1941.
8. PHH 12/266.
9. SRDJ 017106, JD-1 6939, Tokyo-Washington, 1 December 1941, tr. 1 December 1941.
10. PHH 15/1840.
11. Ibid., p. 1842.
12. PHH 8/3385.
13. FDR-Lib., Morgenthau diary, p. 1036.
14. PRO Prem 3, 156/5, London-Halifax, 29 November 1941.
15. Ibid.
16. Ibid., Halifax-London, 1 December 1941, F13114.
17. Sugiyama 1:539–44; Ike, pp. 162–268.
18. Ibid.
19. Hattori, p. 457.
20. SRN 115376, CinC Comb. Fleet to Comb. Fleet 12/021500 December 1941.
21. SSS, Vol. 10, p. 267.
22. Ibid., p. 272.
23. PHLO-ETL, RI summary, 2 December 1941.
24. Rochefort papers; handwritten letter, envelope marked "SECRET To be opened only by Lt. Commander Rochefort, District Communications Officer."
25. PHH 26/336.
26. Dyer letter was of 4 June 1983.
27. PHH 26/226.
28. PHH 35/206; and R. T. Crowley interview, 1984.
29. PHH 16/2255.
30. Ibid., p. 2256.
31. Ibid.
32. PHH 11/5427.
33. Hoehling, p. 101.
34. Gallup survey as quoted in Robert Dallek, *Franklin D. Roosevelt and American Foreign Policy* (hereafter Dallek), p. 310.
35. PHLO box 45: Dispatches: Opnav-Cincaf 2 December 1941.
36. Ibid.
37. PHLO box 45, Opnav-Cincaf, 300419 November 1941.
38. PHLO box 45, CNO, 012358 December 1941.
39. PHLO box 45, Cincaf, 021320 December 1941.
40. Kemp Tolley, *The Cruise of the Lanikai* (Annapolis, Md.: USNIP, 1973), pp. 268–80.
41. Ibid., p. 71.
42. PRO Prem 3,165/5, Halifax-London.
43. Ibid., mins. of War Cabinet Defense Committee (Operations), 3 December 1941.
44. Ibid., London-Halifax, 3 December 1941, FO 1316/56/23.
45. International Military Tribunal for the Far East, "Transcript of Proceedings," pp. 420–21 (hereafter IMTFE).

46. Ibid., pp. 10830–49.

47. SRN 116741, Navy min. to commanders, 2 December 1941.

48. PHLO box 45, Opnav 031855, which derived from Magics: SRDJ 017160, JD-1 6984, Tokyo-Washington, 1 December 1941, tr. 1 December 1941; SRDJ 017287, JD-1 7091, Tokyo-London, 1 December 1941, tr. 5 November 1941, and SRDJ 017184, JD-1 7017, Tokyo-Washington, 3 December 1941, tr. 3 December 1941.

49. PHH 36/137.

50. Ibid.

51. PHH 6/2764.

52. PHH 36/137.

53. PHH 22/379.

54. PHH 5/2131.

55. PHH 9/4233.

56. PHH 4/2002.

57. McCollum OH, p. 384; PHH 9/4240.

58. McCollum OH, p. 329.

59. PHH 26/3921.

60. Ibid.

61. PHH 36/283.

62. PHH 11/5284.

63. Ibid.

64. PRO F113114/86/23, 3 December 1941 telegram, Halifax-London.

65. FDR-Lib., Morgenthau diary, p. 1067.

66. Gwen Terasaki, *Bridge to the Sun,* pp. 66–69.

67. SRDJ 017324, JD-1 017324, Rome-Tokyo, 3 December 1941, tr. 6 December 1941.

68. SRDJ 01732, JD-1 017323, Berlin-Tokyo, 3 December 1941, tr. 6 December 1941.

69. Agawa, p. 246.

70. SSS, Vol. 10, p. 273.

71. Ibid.

72. Ibid., p. 274.

73. Rochefort papers: "Station H Chronology," dated 1 December 1943 [sic].

74. SRH 012, p. 184: Opnav-Cincpac, 042017.

75. PHH 6/2765.

76. PHH 8/3413.

77. McCollum OH, p. 335.

78. PHH 10/4637.

79. PRO Halifax to FO 4 December 1941, F13114/86/32.

80. Nav.Op. Archives, Hart papers, private diary, entry 26/27 November 1941.

81. Ibid.

82. PHH 10/5083.

83. Opnav 124.

84. PHH 10/4802.

85. Ibid.

86. PHH 10/4812.

87. SSS, Vol. 10, p. 275.

88. Agawa, p. 251.

89. Haslach op. cit.

90. Ibid.

91. Matson Navigation Company Collection: Leslie E. Grogan journal, and see also *Ships in Gray,* the story of the Matson Line in World War II (*Infamy,* p. 351).

92. SRH 255, interview with Robert D. Ogg.

93. Ibid., p. 54.

94. Ibid., pp. 35–36.

95. Ibid., p. 53.

96. Haslach op. cit.

97. PHH 36/139.

98. PHH 26/345.

99. SRH 210: "Collection of Papers Related to 'Winds Execute' Message, US Navy 1945," p. 65.

100. SRDJ 017025, JD-1 6875, Tokyo-Washington, 19 November 1941.

101. PHLO Safford/Kramer correspondence; letters dated 22 December 1943 and questionnaire of 22 December 1943 with Safford's comments, 22 January 1944.

102. Rochefort papers: carbon copy of "Streamlined Index of Translations and Memoranda Re Pearl Harbor (1941)," marked SECRET and evidently compiled from the existing OP-20-G diplomatic file in September 1944 when Rochefort, then attached to OP-20-G, made a personal search for this material at the orders of the Director of Naval Communications in compliance with a War Department request for "any written record of the winds execute message." (Memorandum prepared by Safford dated 1 February 1945 in PHLO: Safford file.) See also in PHLO Top Secret-Ultra memorandum, "JD-1: 7001, special studies concerning," dated 8 November 1941 and attachments. These detail conclusions of Lieutenant Sally T. Lightle to find the "missing" winds message at the behest of congressional investigators. "From this study it would appear that JD-1: 7001, if it was assigned to a translation, was for a message dated 28 November 1941, translated on either 2 December 1941 or 3 December 1941 by the Army." Her investigation supported the navy department's "official" contention that the number was not used, or if it was, could not have been assigned on 4 or 5 December 1941. The testimony of Mrs. Eunice Willson Rice, however, who was responsible for keeping the JD intercept file for Kramer (see Authors' Notes on east winds rain controversy), suggests it was.

103. SRH 081: "US Army Investigations into the Handling of Certain Communications Prior to the Attack on Pearl Harbor." See transcript of testimony of Colonel Otis K. Sadtler to Clarke Investigation, 15 September 1944, p. 2:

> The first information that I had regarding any new developments on that message [east wind rain] was on the morning of December 5, when Adm. Noyes called me and said, "Sadtler, the message is in" or words to that effect.

For more details see Authors' Notes on "east wind rain" controversy.

104. PHLO: Memorandum Safford to Admiral Hewitt, subject "Pearl Harbor Investigation—My testimony given this date" 22 June 1945:

> The winds "execute" message which passed through my hands on the morning of 4 December 1941 was a teletype copy (typed on yellow teletype paper) of the entire Japanese broadcast about 200 or 300 words long. Three significant words (Kita, Higashi, and Nishi) appeared and they were in Japanese. Kramer's translation appeared in pencil, or colored crayons, at the bottom of the sheet. There was very little chance of confusion.

See Authors' Notes on "east wind rain" and Sadtler's testimony for the rationale that Safford must have confused 4th and 5th.

105. PHLO-Safford: comment by Safford on Kramer questionnaire dated 22 January 1944, p. 10.

106. Ibid.

107. PHH 26/394.

108. PHH 33/905.

109. Ibid.

110. PHH 10/4629.
111. Ibid.
112. Ibid.
113. Ibid., p. 3646.
114. Ibid.
115. Ibid., p. 4630.
116. Ibid., p. 4635.
117. Ibid., p. 4637.
118. PHH 9/4347.
119. PHH Turner 4/1963.
120. PHH 9/4269.
121. Hoehling, pp. 106–7.
122. Ibid.
123. PHH 26/393.
124. Ibid.
125. Ibid.
126. PHLO-Kramer/Safford correspondence, letter dated 22 January 1941.
127. PHH 8/3390.
128. Hoehling, p. 107.
129. PHH 8/3388.
130. McCollum OH, p. 333.
131. PHH 8/3388.
132. PHH 4/1970.
133. Ibid., and Hoehling, p. 106.
134. PHH 8/3388.
135. PHLO east wind rain message investigation for answers given to navy investigators by radiomen in charge of the intercept stations when asked "Did you know anything about the "winds message?":

"No, I did not know anything about this message until I read about it in the newspapers": Truett C. Lusk, Port Blakely, Washington.

"No, not until I read about it in the newspapers": P. W. Wigle, Cheltenham, Maryland.

"I did not know about this 'winds' code until I read about it in the newspapers": Max C. Gunn, Winter Harbor, Maine.

"No, I did not know about this 'winds' code until I read about it in the newspapers": W. J. Edens, Jupiter, Florida.

"No, I did not know about this 'winds' code until I read about it in the newspapers": E. J. Fowles, Jupiter, Florida.

This surprisingly uniform ignorance of the "winds" code conflicts with the specific instructions that had been issued to all these radiomen in charge to listen out for all weather broadcasts.

136. PHLO Lieutenant Baecher to SecNav, 13 February 1946, SO/1083A.
137. SRDJ 017328, JD-1 7136, Washington-Tokyo, 5 December 1941, tr. 6 December 1941.
138. SRDJ 017332, JD-1 7141, Washington-Tokyo, 5 December 1941, tr. 6 December 1941 in reply to SRDJ 017331, JD-1 7140, Tokyo-Washington, 5 December 1941.
139. SRDJ 107355, SIS 25848, Washington-Tokyo, 3 December 1941.
140. Ibid.
141. Hoehling, p. 102.
142. SRDJ 017334, JD-1 7139, Washington-Tokyo, 5 December 1941, tr. 6 December 1941.
143. Ibid.
144. Hull memoirs, p. 1093.
145. University of Columbia Oral History Project, interview with Frances Perkins (hereafter Perkins OH).

146. Ibid.

147. NA/RG 59: State Department; secretary of state confidential file (711-94); typewritten draft of thirty pages, pencil note "About Dec 5, 1941," p. 14.

148. Ibid., p. 30.

149. Ibid., pp. 23, 24.

150. SRN 115371, CinC Comb. Fleet-Comb. Fleet, 7 December 1941.

151. SRN 115367, CinC 6th Fleet relayed from Submarine *I-72,* 12/07 1450.

152. SSS, Vol. 10, p. 277.

153. SRN 115377, Chief of Naval Section IHQ-Commands 12/07 1800.

154. PHH 36/141.

155. PHH 10/4896.

156. Ibid., and PHH 14/1409.

157. PHH 35/274–75.

158. PHH 29/1666.

159. PHH 31/3188–89.

160. PHH 28/1542, and PHH 27/738.

161. PHH 36/350.

162. PHH 23/674.

163. Capt. Wesley A. Wright interview, 20 April 1985.

164. SRH A 012, p. 1941 as noted against Tokyo-Honolulu, 2 December 1941 translated by army on 30 December 1941: "This message was received in Washington on December 23."

165. SRDJ 017616, JD-1 7370, Honolulu-Tokyo, 3 December 1941, tr. 11 December 1941.

166. SRDJ 017633, JD-1 7381, Tokyo-Honolulu, 6 December 1941, tr. 12 December 1941.

167. SRDJ 017383, JD-1 7179, Honolulu-Tokyo, 6 December 1941, tr. 8 December 1941.

168. SSRDJ 017305, JD-1 7062, Tokyo-Honolulu, 18 November 1941, tr. 6 December 1941.

169. SRDJ 017188, JD-1 6991, Honolulu-Tokyo, 15 November 1941, tr. 3 December 1941.

170. SRDJ 017270, JD-1 7063, Tokyo-Honolulu, 18 November 1941, tr. 5 December 1941.

171. SRDJ 017209, JD-1 7029, Tokyo-Honolulu, 20 November 1941, tr. 4 December 1941; and SRDJ 017311, JD-1 7086, Tokyo-Honolulu, 29 November 1941, tr. 29 November 1941.

172. SRH 012, pp. 186–87.

173. PHH 36/303–4.

174. Fred C. Woodrough, Jr., interview, 8 June 1984.

175. Ibid.

176. PHH 36/304.

177. Woodrough interview.

178. PHH 9/4171.

179. Ibid.

180. Woodrough interview.

181. Ibid.

182. Ibid.

183. PHLO-Kramer file, Kramer memo dated 16 January [1946] to "Baecher re my N.Y. activities"; and Rear Admiral Robert Weeks interview, June 1983.

184. Ibid.

185. Ibid.

186. SRDJ 017350, JD-1 7144, Tokyo-Washington, 6 December 1941, tr. 6 December 1941.

187. PHH 14/1413–15.

188. PHH 29/2399.

189. Hoehling, p. 130.

190. Vice Admiral Frank E. Beatty, "The Background of the Secret Report," *National Review,* 13 December 1966, p. 1261 (hereafter Beatty report); and Hoehling, p. 59.

191. PHH 29/2395–2400.

192. SRH 012, p. 185, Opnav-Cincpac 06 17.43., 4 December 1941.

193. PHH 36/356.

194. Hoehling, p. 130.

195. PRO Prem 3, 158/6, Halifax-Foreign Office #5653, 6 December 1941; prime minister's minute for foreign secretary and chiefs of staff, 7 December 1941, "Noon."

196. Ibid.

197. PHH 2/931.

198. PHLO-Stimson diary A, 6 December 1941, p. 58.

199. FDR-Lib., Harold D. Smith diary, 6 December 1941.

200. Sherwood, p. 427.

201. Ibid.

202. PHH 11/5166.

203. Ibid.

204. PHH 14/1243–45.

205. Ibid., p. 1238; and Joseph P. Lash, *Eleanor and Franklin* (New York: W. W. Norton, 1971), p. 646.

206. Hoehling, p. 148.

207. PHLO-Safford/Kramer correspondence, "Memorandum for Captain Safford" from Kramer, dated 28 December 1943 (hereafter Kramer memo).

208. SRDJ 017336, JD-1 7143, Tokyo-Washington, 6 December 1941, Navy tr. 6 December 1941.

209. Ibid.

210. Ibid.

211. PHH 10/4662.

212. Ibid., p. 4663.

213. Ibid., p. 4664.

214. Kramer memo.

215. PHH 8/3905.

216. Kramer memo.

217. PHH 8/3903.

218. Kramer memo.

219. PHH 11/5545.

220. PHH 4/4026–30.

221. PHH 9/4513–18.

222. PHH 10/4608.

223. Ibid., pp. 4608–9.

224. Ibid., p. 4612.

225. PHH 9/4473.

226. PHH 10/4611.

227. Ibid., p. 4616.

228. Ibid., p. 4612.

229. Kimmel papers: "George Marshall's Actions in the Pearl Harbor Attack December 7, 1941," signed "Certified a true copy of the original statement made by Colonel Raymond Orr, USAF (Ret)" and dated 17 October 1941. The authenticity of Orr's claim that Bratton had told him he had gone to Marshall's headquarters around nine o'clock in the evening on 6 December 1941 with the thirteen parts of the Japanese message only to be "ordered . . . from the house, and severely reprimanded . . . for such a rude intrusion on a private dinner party" conflicts with the *Washington Times Herald* report that the chief of the army was at a veterans reunion. Marshall himself testified that he spent all evening at Fort Myer with his wife. There also appears to be a serious flaw in Orr's secondhand retelling of Bratton's account that "early the next morning" Bratton had again made the trip to Fort Myer. When informed that the general was "horseback riding in Rock Creek Park" he drove there and "found Marshall on horseback, and in company with a woman."

In fact Marshall testified that he was riding along the Potomac on the Virginia shore and there has never been any other corroboration of his mysterious female companion.

More reliance, however, may be accorded Bratton's account of Marshall's attitude on the afternoon of 6 December 1941 because it offers a credible explanation for the army chief's admitted and surprising determination to remain aloof from the onrush of events:

> Colonel Bratton, as Marshall's G-2, had numerous messages, especially on December 5 and 6, all pointing to an early Japanese attack on Hawaii. All this information was quickly given Marshall along with reminders of General Short's unanswered request. Finally, about noon December 6, Colonel Bratton suggested to Marshall that General Short's request be answered, giving General Short permission to move his forces into a defensive position, and allow Admiral Kimmel permission to move his ships out of Pearl Harbor. Marshall promptly refused Colonel Bratton's suggestion. During the afternoon of Saturday, December 6, Marshal left his office, telling Colonel Bratton he was going to his quarters at Fort Myer, Virginia, and that he did not want to be disturbed.

According to a report in the next day's *Washington Herald Tribune,* Marshall had attended a reunion of World War I veterans who had "made a pilgrimage to Fort Myer, Va., scene of part of their training. . . . Later at a dinner in University Club, they honored their former 'CO,' Brig. Gen. Joseph A. Atkins, who came from San Antonio, Tex., for the celebration. *Gen. George C. Marshall, Chief of Staff, attended and was given a vote of confidence."* The reunion might explain why Marshall was so anxious to leave the war department early that afternoon— but it is surprising when he was cross-questioned at the 1945 congressional hearings that he could not recall attending the dinner in the University Club that evening.

230. PHH 2/968.

231. SRDJ 01726, SIS 25764, Manila-Tokyo, 28 November 1941, tr. 5 December 1941.

232. PHH 3/1429.

233. Ibid., p. 1430.

234. PHH 2/925.

235. Ibid.

236. Ibid., p. 926.

237. Ibid., p. 942.

238. Kimmel papers: James G. Stahlman to Professor Preston Slosson, Vanderbilt University, dated 28 April 1975. The credibility of this firsthand account is vouchsafed by his unique access and relationship to the secretary of the navy:

> I was on duty in the Navy from 20 January '41, eleven months before Pearl, until the war was practically over in 1945. I was in Naval Intelligence most of that time as Chief of the Navy Section of the Joint Intelligence Collection Agencies, embracing A-2, G-2, ONI, OSS, BEW(?) [sic] and State Department Intelligence. . . . Frank Knox was my close personal friend, by reason of our long service together in the newspaper business. I had entree to his office as a junior reserve which irritated the hell out of some of the regular USN boys.

239. Sherwood, p. 428.
240. Ibid.
241. B. Berle and T. Jacobs, eds., *Navigating the Rapids* (hereafter Berle), p. 382.
242. Ibid.
243. Ibid.
244. PHH 2/942.
245. J-Bd. Min., 22 October 1941 op. cit.; see also PRO Prem 3,158/6, especially draft telegram to Halifax from Churchill 8:30 P.M. 7 December 1941: "From your recent telegrams we understand we can rely on armed support of United States if we become involved in hostilities with Japan. . . ."
246. PHH 3/1121.
247. Donald G. Brownlow, *The Accused,* p. 127.

Chapter 23 (pages 299–324)   Day of Infamy

1. 1st Destroyer Div. diary, as quoted in Prange, p. 776.
2. PHH 12/584.
3. PHH 8/3393.
4. Ibid.
5. McCollum OH, p. 411.
6. PHH 11/5274.
7. PHH 37/1299.
8. Ibid., p. 1283.
9. Mitsuo Fuchida, "I Led the Air Attack on Pearl Harbor" (hereafter Fuchida), *U.S. Naval Institute Proceedings* (hereafter *USNIP*), September 1952, Vol. 78, No. 9, p. 945.
10. SRDJ 017357, JD-1 7145, Tokyo-Washington, 7 December 1941, tr. 7 December 1941.
11. PHH 9/4527.
12. Ibid., p. 4571.
13. Ibid., p. 4539.
14. Butow, *Tōjō,* p. 392.
15. PHH 9/4524.
16. PHH 11/5175–76.
17. PHH 8/3910.
18. PHH 9/4048.
19. PHH 8/3909.
20. PHH 9/4043.
21. PHH 36/26.
22. Ibid.
23. Hoehling, p. 172; and McCollum OH, p. 411.
24. McCollum OH, p. 411.
25. PHH 33/859–60.
26. PHH 9/4518.
27. PHH 14/1410.
28. PHH 9/4518.
29. Ibid.
30. PHH 5/2132.
31. Ibid., p. 2184.
32. Ibid.
33. PHH 29/2313.
34. PHH 9/4519.
35. Ibid.
36. PHH 14/1334.

37. PHH 9/4519.
38. PHH 36/57.
39. PHH 32/444.
40. Hoehling, p. 178.
41. PHLO-Stimson diary A, 7 December 1941 entry, p. 59.
42. Ibid.
43. Ibid.
44. PHH 27/520.
45. Ibid., p. 531.
46. Ibid., p. 532.
47. Ibid.; and PHH 27/569.
48. Hoehling, p. 179.
49. J. Leasor, *Singapore, The Battle That Changed the World,* pp. 166–67.
50. Fuchida, p. 947.
51. Ibid., p. 949.
52. Ibid., p. 950.
53. PHLO box 45: Cincpac-Cinclant Cincaf Opnav (reference NPM 1516 1850), 7 December 1941.
54. Fuchida, p. 950.
55. Interview as quoted in Prange, p. 507.
56. Wright conversation, April 1985.
57. Fuchida, p. 949.
58. PHH 8/3829.
59. Ibid.
60. Sherwood, pp. 430–31.
61. Hull, p. 106.
62. Ibid.
63. Hull's oath quoted but unattributed by John Toland, *The Rising Sun,* p. 357.
64. Walter Karig and Wellborn Kelly, *Battle Report: Pearl Harbor to Coral Sea* (New York: Farrar and Rinehart, 1944), p. 79.
65. PHH 23/899.
66. PHH 32/426.
67. PHH 37/1250.
68. Samuel Eliot Morison, *History of United Sates Naval Operations to World War II,* Vol. III, *The Rising Sun in the Pacific* (hereafter SEM III), p. 215.
69. SEM III, p. 212.
70. Churchill, Vol. III, p. 510.
71. J. J. Beck, *MacArthur and Wainwright* (Albuquerque: University of New Mexico Press, 1974), p. 11; William Manchester, *American Caesar,* p. 205; and D. MacArthur, *Reminiscences,* p. 117.
72. D. Clayton James, *The Year of MacArthur, Vol. 11, 1941–45* (hereafter James, *MacArthur)* (Boston: Houghton-Mifflin, 1975), p. 10.
73. Fuchida, p. 971.
74. SEM III, p. 126.
75. Joseph K. Taussig, Jr., "I Remember Pearl Harbor," *USNIP,* December 1972, p. 20; Prange, p. 568; and PHH 35/212.
76. Fuchida, p. 952.
77. Prange, p. 546.
78. Matome Ugaki, *Sensōroku (War Diary)* (hereafter Ugaki diary), p. 34.
79. PHH 6/2812.
80. Perkins OH, Vol. 8, pp. 70, 87–88.
81. PHH 19/3503-4.
82. PHLO-Stimson diary A, p. 62; and Hull, Vol. II, pp. 199–1100.
83. Alexander Kendrick, *Prime Time: The Life of Edward R. Murrow* (Boston: Little, Brown, 1969), p. 239.

84. Edgar G. Whitcomb, *Escape from Corregidor* (Chicago: Regnery, 1958), p. 23.

Chapter 24 (pages 325–337)   Hard for Us to Take

1. Ernest Saftig letter, 1985.
2. The Congressional Record, Vol. 87, Pt. 9, p. 9504 for 8 December 1941.
3. Arthur Bryant, *The Turn of the Tide,* p. 282.
4. William L. Shirer, *Rise and Fall of the Third Reich* (New York: Simon and Schuster, 1960), p. 1173.
5. Samuel I. Rosenman, *Working with Roosevelt* (New York: Harper, 1952), p. 156.
6. Library of Congress, Knox papers, box 1, letter to Paul S. Mowrer, 18 December 1941.
7. Beatty report, p. 1262.
8. Ibid.
9. Nav.Op. Archives Cincpac message, file 1941: Opnav 09 1812, 1941.
10. Ibid.
11. University of Wyoming, papers of Harry E. Barnes, box 61, letter Safford-Barnes.
12. FDR Lib. Map Box, Box 31.
13. SEM III, p. 220.
14. Ibid.
15. SEM III, p. 222.
16. Beatty report, p. 1263.
17. Ibid.
18. Ibid.
19. Ibid.
20. Ibid.
21. Ibid.
22. Ibid.
23. Ibid.
24. Ibid.
25. Ibid.
26. Stimson diary, 11 December 1941.
27. SEM III, p. 232.
28. Paul S. Dull, *A Battle History of the Imperial Japanese Navy, 1941–1945,* p. 25.
29. SEM III, p. 235.
30. Beatty report, p. 1264.
31. Kimmel papers, Stahlman, op. cit.
32. FDR-Lib., Morgenthau diary, 15 December 1941.
33. PHH 6/2749–60.
34. E. B. Potter, *Nimitz* (hereafter Potter), p. 9.
35. Stimson diary, 15 December 1941.
36. *The New York Times,* 16 December 1941.
37. Ibid.
38. Ibid.
39. Stimson diary, 15 December 1941.
40. Potter, p. 9.
41. *The New York Times,* 18 December 1941.

Chapter 25 (pages 338–352)   Sold Down the River

1. Edwin P. Hoyt, *How They Won the War in the Pacific,* p. 15.
2. PHH 17/2733.

3. Hoehling, p. 211.

4. Ibid.

5. Kimmel papers: "Memorandum of Interview with Admiral King in Washington on Thursday, 7 December 1944," signed by Admiral Kimmel, p. 6.

6. SEM III, p. 250.

7. Rochefort papers: Opnav-Com 14, 17 December 1941.

8. Ibid.; and copy Copek Com 16-Opnav, 15 December 1941.

9. Nav.Op.Archives: NWPD, chief of war plans copy of "SECRET Memorandum for The Chief of Naval Operations, Subject: Proceedings of President's Investigating Committee, 1000 to 1200, December 19, 1941," signed T. S. Wilkinson, dated 19 December 1941 (hereafter Wilkinson report).

10. Ibid., p. 1.

11. Ibid.

12. Ibid.

13. Ibid., p. 2.

14. Ibid., p. 3.

15. Ibid., p. 4.

16. Ibid., p. 3.

17. PHH 7/3280.

18. SEM III, p. 240.

19. Ibid. (November 1960 reprint by Little, Brown), p. 243.

20. SEM III, p. 248.

21. Ibid., p. 252.

22. Ibid., p. 106.

23. Ibid., p. 253.

24. PHH 7/3155.

25. PHH 23/987.

26. Wilkinson report, p. 1.

27. Husband E. Kimmel, *Admiral Kimmel's Story,* p. 151.

28. Prange interview as quoted in *At Dawn We Slept,* p. 594.

29. PHH 7/3268.

30. Kimmel papers: William H. Standley and Arthur A. Ageton, "The Pearl Harbor Debacle," unpublished manuscript, p. 84 (hereafter Standley); and *Infamy,* pp. 33, 338*n.*

31. PHH 23/657.

32. PHH 23/663.

33. Ibid.

34. Standley ms., p. 88.

35. PHH 7/3266.

36. PHH 39/1–21.

37. Ibid.

38. Kimmel papers, letter of retirement dated 18 February 1942.

39. Ibid.

40. King papers, LoC.

Chapter 26 (pages 353–363)   Heaven's Admonition

1. Potter, p. 16.

2. Ibid., p. 17.

3. Ibid., p. 19.

4. SEM III, p. 257.

5. RG 165: Minutes of Arcadia ABC Conference, 24 December 1941–14 January 1942.

6. Ernest J. King and Walter M. Whitehill, *Fleet Admiral King: A Naval Record,* pp. 144–45.

7. Com 16, 190215 January 1942.

8. SSS, Vol. 80, *Dai honei kaigunbu-rengokantai* (Imperial naval general headquarters and Combined Fleet) (hereafter SSS, Vol. 80), Vol. 2, p. 176.

9. Ibid.

10. SSS, Vol. 38, *Chubu taiheiyo homen kaigun sakusen* (Central Pacific naval operations) (hereafter SSS, Vol. 38), Vol. 1, p. 486.

11. Brigadier General Bankson T. Holcomb interview, 8 May 1983 (hereafter Holcomb interview).

12. Com TF 8-Cincpac, 9 February 1942, "Report of Action in the Marshall Islands, 1 Febuary 1942."

13. Ibid.

14. SSS, Vol. 43, p. 25.

15. Ugaki diary, p. 75.

16. Ibid.

Chapter 27 (pages 364–377)   Where and When?

1. Nav.Op. Archives: *Enterprise* log, 5 February 1942.

2. Holcomb interview.

3. Cominch-Cincpac, 061513 February 1942.

4. Potter, p. 41.

5. Cincpac-Cominch, 9 February 1942.

6. SRH 355: "Memorandum for Admiral Noyes," dated 23 January 1942, signed L. S. Safford, pp. 451–52.

7. Ibid., pp. 453–57, Memorandum for 20-A; Subject: Reorganization of Section 20-G, Reference (A) Captain Safford's memo of 23 January 1942, dated 26 Jan. 1942, signed J. N. Wenger.

8. Ibid.

9. SRH 279: "Communication Intelligence Organization, 1942–1946." See also John Redman memorandum in SRH 355, "Naval Security History," p. 458.

10. SRH 279, passim.

11. *Nanto homen kaigun sakusen* (*Southeast Asia Naval Operations*) (hereafter SSS, Vol. 49), pp. 88–89.

12. Ugaki diary, p. 87.

13. Ibid.

14. Ibid., p. 91.

15. SSS, Vol. 38, No. 1, p. 489.

16. Com 14, 021113 March 1942.

17. Cominch, 032230 March 1942.

18. Com 16, 040630 March 1942.

19. SSS, Vol. 38, p. 503, Layton, "Rendezvous in Reverse," *USNIP,* May 1953.

20. Ibid.

21. Cincpac-CTF 9, 05001 March 1942.

22. Cominch-Cincpac, 042227 March 1942.

23. SEM III, p. 388.

24. SSS, Vol. 38, p. 517.

25. SSS, Vol. 26, *Ranin-Bengare Wan homen kaigun shinko sakusen (Netherlands East Indies-Bengal Bay naval operations)* (hereafter SSS, Vol. 26), p. 123.

26. Ibid.

27. Ibid.

28. SSS, Vol 38, p. 93.

Chapter 28 (pages 378–388)   A Bungling Attack

1. Cominch (AIDAC), 111620 March 1942.

2. Cominch, 102313 March 1942, Orange intelligence, Vol. 36.

3. SRH 209: "OP-20-G Traffic and Decryption Charts, Japanese Navy," p. 53.
4. Cincpac 160615 and Cominch 140815 March 1942.
5. Cominch-Cincaf 011500 February 1942 (signal to Cincpac).
6. Com 14, 180922 March 1942.
7. SRH 012: "Coral Sea, Midway Appendix" (hereafter SRH 012 (B)), pp. 209–10.
8. Cincpac, 182359 March 1941.
9. Potter, p. 66.
10. Com 14, 030217 April 1942.
11. Opnav to Cincpac, 152049 April 1942.
12. "Captain Steele's Running Estimate and Summary, 7 December 1941–31 August 1942" (hereafter Cincpac Gray Book), 15 April 1942.
13. Gray Book: 17 April 1942.
14. Com 14, 172343 April 1942.
15. Cincpac Gray Book, 18 April 1942.
16. SSS, Vol. 43, *Middue-kaissen (Midway Sea Battle)* (hereafter SSS, Vol. 43), p. 23.
17. SSS, Vol. 80, pp. 64–75.
18. SSS, Vol. 43, p. 40.
19. Ibid., p. 44.
20. SSS, Vol. 29, *Hokuto homen kaigun sakusen (Northeast area naval operations)* (hereafter SSS, Vol. 29), p. 155.
21. Com 14, 170305 April 1942; and SSS, Vol. 85, p. 82.
22. Cincpac to all TF commanders 181807, 181957, 181147 April 1942.
23. SSS, Vol. 29, p. 116.
24. SSS, Vol. 85, p. 82.
25. Ibid., pp. 85–86.
26. Ibid., p. 95.
27. Agawa, p. 300.
28. SSS, Vol. 85, p. 171.

Chapter 29 (pages 389–404)   Fog of Battle

1. Gray Book, 18 April 1942; and Cincpac, 180153 April 1942.
2. Gray Book, pp. 371–442.
3. Ibid.
4. Admiralty, 211552 April 1942.
5. Melbourne, 211306 April 1942.
6. Cincpac, 220109 April 1942.
7. Gray Book, 22 April 1942.
8. Ibid.
9. Ibid.
10. Ibid.
11. John B. Lundstrom, *The First South Pacific Campaign: Pacific Fleet Strategy December 1941–June 1942* (hereafter Lundstrom, *South Pacific*), p. 87.
12. SSS, Vol. 1, p. 18.
13. Com 14, 260052 April 1942.
14. Belconnen, 250110 April 1942.
15. Com 14, 261208 April 1942.
16. Com 14, 271032 April 1942.
17. Com 14, 291010 April 1942.
18. When Captain Arleigh Burke joined Admiral Mark Mitscher in the spring of 1944 as chief of staff, he was surprised to find that a lieutenant jg—Charles A. Sandy Sims, U.S.N.R.—had access to the admiral at any hour, and often took him aside for discussions. Burke inquired of the young officer why he conferred with the admiral in private so frequently. Sims answered politely, but firmly, that

he was not free to divulge the subject of their talks. "I'm his chief of staff and I want to know what you tell him," he insisted. Sims referred him to the admiral. Mitscher agreed, but Sims had to check with his superior at Pearl. It was only after the necessary authority had been radioed from Frupac that Burke was initiated into the intricacies of comint [Burke interview, July 1985].

19. Forrest R. Biard, unpublished manuscript, "Some Notes on Radio Intercept Work in the Coral Sea Action," 20 June 1984, pp. 26–27 (hereafter Biard ms.).

20. Ibid., p. 27.
21. Com 14, 011145, 011138, 011108 May 1942.
22. SRH 012 (B), p. 243.
23. Cincpac, 052329 May 1942.
24. N-OpA: CTF 17, afteraction report.
25. Cincpac, 050345 May 1942.
26. SSS, Vol. 49, *Nanto homen kaigun sakusen,* Vol. 1 (Until Guadalcanal counteroffensive) (hereafter SSS, Vol. 49), p. 239.
27. Biard ms., p. 34.
28. SSS, Vol. 49, pp. 276–77.
29. Biard ms., p. 35.
30. Lundstrom, *The First Team,* p. 205.
31. James, *MacArthur,* p. 161.
32. Biard ms., p. 38.
33. N-OpA: CTF 17 report, action report (May 1942), p. 6.
34. Ibid.
35. SSS, Vol. 49, pp. 291–92.
36. CTF 17, p. 7.
37. Ibid.
38. Ibid.
39. Potter, p. 75.
40. Gray Book, p. 443.
41. CTF 17, p. 9.
42. SSS, Vol. 49, p.299.
43. Potter, p. 76.
44. Ibid., p. 77.
45. SRH 012(B), p. 254.

Chapter 30 (pages 405–417)   Science and Skill

1. Com 14, 271032 April 1942.
2. Com 14, 040816 May 1942.
3. Com 14, 051014 May 1942.
4. Rochefort OH, pp. 189–91.
5. Gray Book, 6 May 1942.
6. Com 14, 060526 May 1942.
7. SSS, Vol. 43, pp. 87–88.
8. Ibid., p. 96.
9. Com 14, 070205 May 1942.
10. Com 14, 092236 May 1942.
11. Com 14, 090114 May 1942.
12. McCollum OH, p. 484.
13. Lundstrum, *South Pacific,* p. 134.
14. Gray Book, 12 May 1942.
15. Cominch 121945, 121950 May 1942.
16. Dyer interview, 27 June 1984.
17. Belconnen, 050202 May 1942.

18. SRNM: "Miscellaneous Records Pertaining to Japanese Naval Communications 13 March–4 June 1942 OP-20-G," p. 778.

19. Com 14, 070205 May 1942.

20. Ibid., 170614 May 1942.

21. Com 14, 140945, 141020, 141022 May 1942.

22. ETL letter to RADM D. M. Showers, 5 November 1982, and see Com 14, 140945 May 1942.

23. SRH 012, pp. 271–72, and see Com 14, 140700 May 1942.

24. Rochefort OH, p. 203.

25. Ibid.

26. SRNS: "Japanese Naval Intelligence Summaries," p. 31, and SRNM 0697.

27. SRH 355, p. 432.

28. Dyer interview, June 1984.

29. Wright interview, July 1984.

30. SRH 279: "OP-20-G File Communication Intelligence Organization, 1942–1946," p. 1. Memorandum for Admiral Noyes via OP-20-A, "Reorganization of OP-20-G," dated 23 January 1942, signed L. Safford, and p. 4 memorandum on same subject dated 26 January 1942, signed J. N. Wenger.

31. Ibid.

32. Wright interview, July 1984.

33. Ibid.

34. Layton OH, p. 137.

35. Rochefort OH, pp. 190–93.

36. Com 14, 142136 May 1942.

37. Gray Book, 13 May 1942.

38. Cincpac, 140639 May 1942.

39. Gray Book, 14 May 1942.

40. Layton letter to Lundstrom, 12 June 1974.

41. Com 14, 160638 May 1942; SSS, Vol. 49, p. 255.

42. Cincpac, 161921 May 1942.

43. SRH 272: "CINPAC Enemy Activities File, April–May 1942," 15 May 1942, p. 66.

44. Cincpac, 160325 May 1942.

45. Ibid.

46. Cincpac, 170407 May 1942 and Gray Book p. 490.

47. Cominch, 172220 May 1942.

48. Ibid., and Gray Book, p. 489.

49. Ibid.

Chapter 31 (pages 418–430)   You Don't Have to Be Crazy

1. SRH 272, p. 68.

2. Captain's loss report, Pro ADM 202/10/1854, MP 1185/8, and Wenneker diary op. cit.

3. New Zealand National Archives, Navy Series, List 11, Intelligence Summaries, 21–30 March, 6 April 1942.

4. PHH 10/4855.

5. Com 14, 161900 May 1942.

6. *Halsey's Story,* p. 106.

7. Opnav, 201630 May 1942.

8. SRNS 0062, 23 May 1942.

9. E. B. Potter interview of Admiral Layton (hereafter Layton/Potter OH), p. 49.

10. Layton letter to Showers, 5 November 1982.

11. Nakumuta, p. 23.

12. Dyer interview, 27 June 1984.

13. Belconnen, 212245 May 1942.

14. Com 14, 220732 May 1942.

15. Rochefort OH, p. 132.

16. Dyer interview, and Showers interview, June 1984.

17. Rochefort OH, p. 131, passim.

18. Ibid.

19. Showers interview.

20. Ibid.

21. Various decrypts, significantly *not* attributed to Com 14 (the *were* decrypted by Rochefort), cited pp. 293–95 SRH 012(B).

22. Com 14, 212245 May 1942.

23. SRH 012, p. 291.

24. Belconnen, 220238 May 1942.

25. SRH 012, p. 297.

26. Com 14, 23/1922 May 1942.

27. Cincpac, 172220 May 1942.

28. Ibid.

29. Ibid.

30. Cincpac, 220135 May 1942.

31. Gray Book, 26 May 1942, "Estimate of Situation."

32. Ibid., p. 521.

33. Cominch to Comgenhaw, 251930 May 1942.

34. PHH 3/1158.

35. SRNS, p. 64, 24 May 1942.

36. Com 14, 252140 May 1942.

37. Ibid., and Com 14, 222350 May 1942.

38. SRH 012, p. 303.

39. SRNS, p. 66, 25 May 1942.

40. Com 14, 252140 May 1942.

41. Ibid., Com 14, 272118, 272158 May 1942, and Goodwin letters.

42. Ibid., and Com 14, 272058 May 1942.

43. Rochefort OH, pp. 223–24; 230–31.

Chapter 32 (pages 431–448)   A Glorious Page in Our History

1. A memorandum, "The Inside Story of the Battle of Midway and the Ousting of Commander Rochefort," op. cit., p. 3.

2. Potter, *Nimitz*, p. 85.

3. Ibid.

4. Ibid., p. 87.

5. Ibid.

6. SRH 012, p. 320.

7. Lundstrom, *South Pacific*, p. 180.

8. SEM *Coral Sea, Midway, and Submarine Actions* (hereafter Vol. IV), pp. 170–72.

9. Potter, *Nimitz*, p. 70.

10. RG 181: Com 14 Midway Battle dispatches (hereafter Midway dispatches).

11. Ibid.

12. Ibid.

13. Fuchida and Okumiya, *Midway*, p. 144.

14. SEM IV, p. 103.

15. ETL-Potter OH, p. 45.

16. Midway dispatches.

17. Ibid.

18. Ibid.
19. Ibid.
20. Fuchida and Okumiya, *Midway,* pp. 170–73.
21. Ibid.
22. S. L. James and G. H. Gay, eds., "Torpedo Squadron 8: The Heroic Story of 30 Men Who Attacked the Japanese Fleet," *Life* magazine, 31 August 1942, pp. 70–72.
23. SEM IV, p. 122.
24. Ibid.
25. Fuchida and Okumiya, *Midway,* p. 177.
26. Potter-Layton OH, p. 41.
27. Fuchida, p. 178.
28. SEM IV, p. 132.
29. Potter, p. 97.
30. Ibid.
31. Fuchida and Okumiya, *Midway,* p. 213.
32. Ibid., p. 214.
33. Midway dispatches.
34. Potter, p. 98.
35. SEM IV, p. 142.
36. Potter, pp. 99–101.
37. Fuchida and Okumiya, *Midway,* p. 216.
38. Midway dispatches.
39. Ibid.
40. Potter, p. 107.
41. King and Whitehill, p. 171.
42. Rochefort OH, p. 234.
43. Ibid., p. 266.

Chapter 33 (pages 449–456)   One Unforgivable Sin

1. The A Memorandum, op. cit., p. 7.
2. Ibid.
3. Ibid.
4. Ibid.
5. Letter covering formal release of A Memorandum by Naval Security Group Command, 9 August 1984.
6. SRH 279: "OP-20-G File, Communications Intelligence Organization 1942–46," pp. 9–14.
7. Ibid.
8. Ibid.
9. Ibid.
10. Ibid.
11. Ibid.
12. Dyer letter, *Cryptalog,* Summer, 1984.
13. Ibid.
14. Ibid.
15. Ibid.
16. *The Chicago Tribune,* 7 June 1942.
17. Rochefort papers: memorandum for secretary of the navy signed by Lieutenant Waldo Drake, public relations officer, Cincpac, and dated 18 June 1942.
18. A Memo, p. 8.
19. *The New York Daily Mirror,* 7 July 1942.
20. A Memo, p. 8.
21. A Memo reproducing memorandum "Security of Radio Intelligence Ac-

tivities" for Admiral King, signed "Respectfully John R. Redman" 6 July 1942.

22. Rochefort papers: Copy of confidential letter from attorney general to secretary of the navy dated 28 July 1942.

23. Ibid.: Secretary of the navy to attorney general, 29 July 1942: "The Navy Department believes that the evidence in its possession is sufficient to convict. . . ."

24. A Memo, pp. 9–10.

25. Wenneker diary, op. cit.; and PRO: ADM 223/51 supplied by James Rusbridger.

Chapter 34 (pages 457–463)   Guadalcanal

1. SEM V, pp. 19–28.

2. Heinl, *Soldiers of the Sea* (Annapolis: USNIP, 1962) (hereafter Heinl), p. 353.

3. SEM V, p. 178.

4. James M. Merrill, *A Sailor's Admiral: A Biography of William F. Halsey* (New York: Crowell, 1976), p. 52.

5. Ibid., p. 120.

6. Ibid., p. 131.

Chapter 35 (pages 464–469)   "I'm Not Coming Back"

1. Rochefort OH, pp. 251–52.

2. Ibid., p. 52.

3. Rochefort papers: Bupers orders "Temporary additional duty" dated 24 June 1942.

4. SRH 268: "Advanced Intelligence Centers in the US Navy, 1942." Memoranda for Vice Admiral F. J. Horne: (1) "Establishment of advanced intelligence centers," signed John R. Redman, OP-20-G, dated 20 June 1942. (2) "Radio Intelligence Organization," signed Joseph R. Redman, dated 20 June 1942.

5. Rochefort OH, p. 136.

6. A Memo, pp. 19–21.

7. Ibid.

8. Rochefort OH, p. 258.

9. Holmes, p. 115.

10. A Memo, p. 21.

11. Rochefort OH, p. 158.

12. Ibid., p. 272.

Epilogue (pages 470–494)

1. SRH 306, "OP-20-G, Exploits and Commendations World War II, 1942–1948," p. 30; and JICPOA 8 November 1945.

2. Holmes, p. 125.

3. SRH 306, p. 30, DOIC JICPOA 8 November 1945.

4. Ibid.

5. As quoted SRH 213: "Office of Naval Operations Bulletins," p. 30.

6. Dyer, *Cryptalog* letter, op. cit.

7. Holmes, p. 134.

8. Clay Blair, *Silent Victory,* pp. 275–78.

9. Holmes, p. 126.

10. Ibid., p. 125.

11. SRN 006430 13 April 1941.

12. Holmes, p. 135.

13. Potter, p. 233.

14. Ibid.
15. Potter, p. 233.
16. Gray Book, 17 April 1943.
17. Potter, p. 234.
18. Pineau interview with Watanabe, 1950.
19. SEM VII, pp. 37–51.
20. Halsey, p. 183.
21. Potter, p. 262.
22. SEM VII, pp. 264–72.
23. Halsey, p. 186.
24. Ibid.
25. SRH 035: "History of the Special Branch, MIS, War Department, 1942–45."
26. Interview with Admiral Arleigh Burke, July 1985.
27. Potter, p. 318.
28. SEM XII, pp. 12–15.
29. Heinl, p. 473.
30. Shigeru Fukudome, "Strategic Aspects of the Battle off Formosa," in *USNIP,* December 1952.
31. Potter, p. 335.
32. Ibid., p. 340.

Authors' Notes (pages 495–529)

1. *Reports of General MacArthur—Japanese Operations in the South West Pacific Area,* compiled from Japanese Demobilization Bureau records, 2 Vols., 4 Pts. (Washington, D.C.: Department of the Army, GPO, 1966–67).
2. SEM III, p. 132.
3. SEM IV, pp. 79–80.
4. Roberta Wohlstetter, *Pearl Harbor—Warning and Decision,* p. 397.
5. Prange, p. 723.
6. PHH report of Joint Committee, p. 252.
7. Prange, p. 723.
8. Ibid., p. 733.
9. Ibid., p. 796.
10. Ibid., p. 443
11. Ibid., p. 733.
12. Ibid.
13. Ibid.
14. Ibid., p. 734.
15. Ibid.
16. Ibid.
17. Ibid., p. 802.
18. Ibid., p. 850.
19. Ibid., p. 799.
20. Ibid., p. 796.
21. Ibid., p. 591.
22. SRH 035: "History of the Special Branch, MIS, War Department, 1942–45."
23. Lee to Pineau, 10 March 1983.
24. Prange, p. 736.
25. PHH 39/299.
26. Ibid., p. 317.
27. Ibid., p. 308.
28. Robert A. Theobald, *The Final Secret of Pearl Harbor,* p. 166.

29. PHH report of Joint Committee.

30. PHLO-Safford/Kramer correspondence: Safford 26 November 1943.

31. Ibid.; and see official report, op. cit.

32. Eunice Willson Rice letter, op. cit., and Rochefort papers analysis of Japanese diplomatic messages, op. cit.

33. PHLO: Safford letter to Adm. Hewitt, 22 June 1945, op. cit.

34. PHH 9/3936.

35. Rice letter.

36. Ibid.

37. Admiral Weeks interview, op. cit.

38. PHH 9/4009.

39. Weeks interview.

40. Copy of Briggs entry provided by Navy Operational Archives.

41. SRH 051: "Interview with Mr. Ralph T. Briggs by the Historian of the Naval Security Group Command," 13 January 1977.

42. PHH 9/3934.

43. PHH 4/1960.

44. SRH 81: "Information from George W. Linn, Captain USNR (Ret.) 23/10/80" (hereafter Linn), pp. 1-3, "The Winds Message."

45. PHH 4/1969.

46. Linn, p. 3. In his epilogue, Linn's statement added yet another mystery to the whole winds controversy:

> Early in the afternoon [7 December] GZ [Kramer] came into the watch office and motioned me to one side. I was floored when he asked if we could encrypt a message in the Purple system for transmission. This was a requirement I had never even considered and had to do some fast thinking before saying we could but it would be a very slow process. Next, I can remember saying something along the following lines (probably needlessly): I hope that whatever this message is supposed to accomplish is of the highest importance. Ultimately, the Japanese will discover our ruse and certainly will re-evaluate all of their crypto-systems, including military. Years of work will go down the drain and we may not be reading Japanese traffic for months or years. GZ nodded and left, saying he would let me know. . . . I have no knowledge of the addressee or content of the contemplated message. I sensed it was not GZ's idea; it came from higher up. I did not question GZ about it then or later. I doubt that he would have told me—I had no need to know.

This astonishing revelation by Linn aroused Admiral Layton's intense curiosity. But after much discussion neither he nor his co-authors were able to come up with an explanation which satisfied him. The obvious deduction is that the director of war plans or communications, or intelligence, briefly considered a madcap scheme that involved sending some false message to Tokyo, perhaps purporting to come from their Washington envoys. If so, it was quickly realized that any such transmission would threaten the whole Allied comint operation. Given this, another hypothesis was that the "fake" Purple message was *never intended to be transmitted*, but merely to reside on the diplomatic files to cover up or confuse any investigation—but even this requires a farfetched conspiracy. The explanation—as Linn's testimony indicates—depended on who was the ranking officer who initiated the request?

47. PHH: Sadtler testimony, op. cit. Clarke.

48. Kimmel papers: Thorpe letter.

49. Ibid.

50. PHH 33/757.

51. Royal Netherlands Army Archives (hereafter RNAA), Thorpe-Long, 23 July 1960, File DC 40/8 (courtesy James Rushbridger).

52. Ibid.
53. Ibid.
54. RNAA 40/8, Henning letter, 11 May 65.
55. Ibid.
56. Rushbridger interview with Brown, 9 May 1985.

Radio Intelligence: Personalities and Principles

57. SRH 355: p. 460.
58. Ibid.
59. Ibid.

Selected Bibliography

Books

Agawa, Hiroyuki. *The Reluctant Admiral: Yamamoto and the Imperial Navy.* New York: Harper & Row, 1979.

Allen, Louis. *Singapore, 1941–1942.* Newark, Delaware: University of Delaware Press, 1979.

Army Times, eds. *Attack on Pearl Harbor,* Washington D.C., 1941.

Arnold, Henry H. *Global Mission.* New York: Harper, 1949.

Baker, Leonard. *Roosevelt and Pearl Harbor.* New York: Macmillan, 1970.

Baldwin, Hanson W. *Battles Lost and Won: Great Campaigns of World War II.* New York: 1966.

Bamford, James. *The Puzzle Palace.* Boston: Houghton Mifflin, 1982.

Barker, Arthur J. *Pearl Harbor.* New York: Ballantine Books, 1969.

———. *Midway: The Turning Point.* New York: Macmillan, 1971.

———. *Midway.* Englewood Cliffs, N.J.: Prentice-Hall, 1983.

Barkley, Alben W. *That Reminds Me.* Garden City, N.Y.: Doubleday, 1954.

Barnes, Harry E., ed. *Perpetual War for Perpetual Peace.* Caldwell, Idaho: The Caxton Printers Ltd., 1953.

———. *Pearl Harbor After a Quarter of a Century.* New York: Arno Press, 1972.

Bartlett, Bruce R. *Cover-up.* New Rochelle, N.Y.: Arlington House, 1978.

Beard, Charles A. *American Foreign Policy in the Making, 1932–1940.* New Haven, Conn.:Yale University Press, 1948.

———. *President Roosevelt and the Coming of the War.* New Haven, Conn.: Yale University Press, 1941.

Belote, James H., and William M. Belote. *Titans of the Seas: The Development and Operations of Japanese and American Carrier Task Forces During World War II.* New York: Harper and Row, 1975.

Bergamini, David. *Japan's Imperial Conspiracy.* New York: William Morrow, 1971.

Berle, Beatrice, and Travis Jacobs, eds. *Navigating the Rapids: From the Papers of Adolf A. Berle.* New York: Harcourt Brace, 1973.

Blair, Clay. *Silent Victory.* Philadelphia: J. B. Lippincott, 1975.

Blum, John M. *From the Morgenthau Diaries: Years of War, 1941–1945.* Boston: Houghton-Mifflin, 1959–1967.

———. *Roosevelt and Morgenthau.* Boston: Houghton-Mifflin, 1970.

———. *The Price of Vision: The Diary of Henry A. Wallace, 1942–1946.* Boston: Houghton-Mifflin, 1973.

Borg, Dorothy. *The United States and the Far Eastern Crisis of 1933–1938.* Cambridge, Mass.: Harvard University Press, 1964.

———, and Shumpei Okamoto, eds. *Pearl Harbor as History: Japanese-American Relations, 1931–1941.* New York: Columbia University Press, 1973.

Boyle, John H. *China and Japan at War 1937–1945.* Stanford, Calif.: Stanford University Press, 1972.

Braisted, William R. *The United States Navy in the Pacific, 1897–1909,* Vol. I., Austin, Tex.: University of Texas Press, 1958.

———. *The United States Navy in the Pacific, 1909–1922,* Vol. II., Austin, Tex.: University of Texas Press, 1971.

Brownlow, Donald G. *The Accused: The Ordeal of Rear Admiral Husband Edward Kimmel, U.S.N.* New York: Vantage, 1968.

Buell, Thomas B. *The Quiet Warrior: A Biography of Admiral Raymond A. Spruance.* Boston: Little, Brown, 1974.

Burns, James MacGregor. *Roosevelt, The Soldier of Freedom.* New York: Harcourt Brace, 1970.

Burtness, Paul S., and Warren U. Ober, eds. *The Puzzle of Pearl Harbor.* Evanston, Ill.: Row, Peterson, 1962.

Busch, Noel F. *The Emperor's Sword: Japan vs. Russia in the Battle of Tsushima.* New York: Funk & Wagnalls, 1969.

Butow, Robert J. C. *The John Doe Associates: Backdoor Diplomacy for Peace, 1941.* Stanford, Calif.: Stanford University Press, 1974.

———. *Tojo and the Coming of the War.* Princeton, N.J.: Princeton University Press, 1961.

———. *Japan's Decision to Surrender.* Stanford, Calif.: Stanford University Press, 1954.

Byas, Hugh. *Government by Assassination.* New York: Alfred A. Knopf, 1942.

Caffrey, Kate. *Out in the Midday Sun: Singapore 1941–1945.* New York: Stein & Day, 1973.

Calvocoressi, Peter, and Guy Wint. *Total War.* New York: Pantheon Books, 1972.

Carver, Michael, ed. *The War Lords: The Military Commanders of the Twentieth Century.* Boston: Little, Brown, 1976.

Castillo, Edmund L. *Midway: Battle for the Pacific.* New York: Random House, 1968.

Chihaya, Masataka. *Teikoku Rengo Kantai (Imperial Combined Fleet).* Tokyo: Kodansha, 1969.

———. *Nihon kaigun senryaku hassō (Strategic Concepts of the Japanese Navy).* Tokyo: Purejidento sha, 1985.

Churchill, Winston L. S. *The Second World War.* Vols. I–VI. Boston: Houghton-Mifflin, 1948–1953.

Clark, Blake. *Remember Pearl Harbor!* New York: Modern Age Books, 1942.

Clark, Ronald W. *The Man Who Broke Purple: The Life of the World's Greatest Cryptologist, Colonel William F. Friedman.* Boston: Little, Brown, 1977.

Coffey, Thomas M. *Imperial Tragedy: Japan in World War II, the First Days and the Last.* New York: World Publishers. 1970.

Coggins, Jack. *The Campaign for Guadalcanal: The Battle That Made History.* Garden City, New York: Doubleday, 1972.

Cole, Wayne S. *Charles A. Lindbergh and the Battle Against American Intervention in World War II.* New York: Harcourt Brace, 1974.

Collier, Basil. *The War in the Far East, 1941–1945.* New York: Morrow, 1969.

Collier, Richard. *The Road to Pearl Harbor—1941.* New York: Atheneum, 1981.

Corson, William R. *The Armies of Ignorance: The Rise of the American Intelligence Empire.* New York: Dial Press, 1977.

Costello, John. *The Pacific War.* New York: Rawson & Wade, 1981.

Craigie, Sir Robert Leslie. *Behind the Japanese Mask.* London: Hutchinson, 1945.

Craven, Wesley Frank, and James Lea Cate, eds. *The Army Air Forces in World War II, Vol. 1.* Chicago: University of Chicago Press, 1948.

Crowley, James B., ed. *Modern East Asia: Essays in Interpretation.* New York: Harcourt Brace, 1970.

Current, Richard N. *Secretary Stimson: A Study in Statecraft.* New Brunswick, N.J.: Rutgers University Press, 1954.

Dallek, Robert. *Franklin D. Roosevelt and American Foreign Policy, 1932–1945.* New York: Oxford University Press, 1979.

David, Jules. *America and the World of Our Time: U.S. Diplomacy in the Twentieth Century.* New York: Random House, 1960.

Davis, Kenneth Sydney. *Experience of War: The United States in World War II.* Garden City, N.Y.: Doubleday, 1965.

Deacon, Richard (aka Donald McCormack). *Kempeitai: A History of the Japanese Secret Police.* New York: Berkley Edition, 1985.

Deane, John R. *The Strange Alliance.* Toronto: Viking, 1947.

Dorwart, Jeffery M. *Conflict of Duty.* Annapolis, Md.: U.S. Naval Institute Press, 1983.

Drury, Allen. *A Senate Journal, 1943–1945.* New York: McGraw-Hill, 1961.

Dull, Paul S. *A Battle History of the Imperial Japanese Navy (1941–1945).* Annapolis, Md.: U.S. Naval Institute Press, 1978.

Dyer, VADM. George C. *On the Treadmill to Pearl Harbor: The Memoirs of Admiral James O. Richardson, U.S.N. (Retired).* Washington, D.C.: Naval History Division, Department of the Navy, 1973.

———. *The Amphibians Came to Conquer: The Story of Admiral Richmond Kelly Turner.* Washington, D.C.: Naval History Division, Department of the Navy, 1971.

Farago, Ladislas. *The Broken Seal: Operation Magic and the Pearl Harbor Disaster.* New York: Random House, 1967.

Feis, Herbert. *The Road to Pearl Harbor.* Princeton, N.J.: Princeton University Press, 1950.

Flynn, John T. *The Truth About Pearl Harbor.* New York: privately printed pamphlet, 1944.

Fuchida, Mitsuo, and Masatake Okumiya. Tr. Masataka Chihaya; Clarke H. Kawakami and Roger Pineau, eds. *Midway, The Battle That Doomed Japan.* Annapolis, Md.: U.S. Naval Institute Press, 1955.

Furer, RADM. Julius Augustus. *Administration of the Navy Department in World War II.* Washington, D.C.: Naval History Division, Department of the Navy, 1959.

Geneki kaigun shikan meibo [Directory of active duty naval officers]. 1939.

Goldston, Robert C. *Pearl Harbor: 7 December 1941.* New York: Watts, 1972.

Grenfell, Russell. *Main Fleet to Singapore.* London: Faber and Faber, 1951.

Grew, Joseph C. *Ten Years in Japan.* New York: Simon & Schuster, 1944.

———. *Turbulent Era: A Diplomatic Record of Forty Years, 1904–1945, Part II.* Walter Johnson, ed. Boston: Houghton-Mifflin, 1952.

Halsey, Fleet Adm. William F., U.S.N., and Lt. Cmdr. Joseph Bryan III, U.S.N.R., *Admiral Halsey's Story.* New York: McGraw-Hill, 1947.

Hara, Captain Tameichi, with Fred Saito and Roger Pineau. *Japanese Destroyer Captain.* New York: Ballantine Books, 1961.

Harada, Kumao. *Saionji Ko to Seiyoku.* Tokyo: Iwanami Shoten, 1950–56.

Hashimoto, Mochitsura. *Sunk: The Story of the Japanese Submarine Fleet.* Tr. Cmdr. E.H.M. Colegrave, RN (Ret.). New York: Henry Holt, 1954.

Hattori, Takushiro, *Dai-toa senso zenshi (A Complete History of the Greater East Asia War).* Tokyo: Hara Shobo, 1953.

Heinl, Lt. Col. Robert D., Jr. *The Defense of Wake.* Washington, D.C.: Historical Section, Division of Public Information, Headquarters U.S. Marine Corps, 1945.

————. *Marines at Midway.* Washington, D.C.: Historical Section, Division of Public Information, Headquarters U.S. Marine Corps, 1948.

Hinsley, Francis A., et al. *British Intelligence in the Second World War,* 3 Volumes. Cambridge, Eng.: Cambridge University Press, 1979–1983.

Hoehling, A. A. *The Week Before Pearl Harbor.* New York: W. W. Norton, 1963.

Holmes, Wilfred J. *Double-Edged Secrets.* Annapolis, Md.: U.S. Naval Institute Press, 1979.

————. *Undersea Victory.* Garden City, N.Y.: Doubleday, 1966.

Hough, Richard A. *The Battle of Midway.* New York: Macmillan, 1969.

Howarth, Stephen. *The Fighting Ships of the Rising Sun.* New York: Atheneum, 1983.

Hoyt, Edwin P. *How They Won the War in the Pacific: Nimitz and His Admirals.* New York: Weybright & Talley, 1970.

Huie, William B. *The Fight for Air Power.* New York: L. B. Fisher 1942.

Hull, Cordell. *The Memoirs of Cordell Hull.* New York: Macmillan, 1948.

Ickes, Harold L. *The Secret Diary of Harold L. Ickes, Vol. III, The Lowering Clouds 1939–1941.* New York: Simon & Schuster, 1954.

Ike, Nobutake, ed. *Japan's Decision for War: Records of the 1941 Policy Conferences.* Stanford, Calif.: Stanford University Press, 1967.

Ito, Masanori, with Roger Pineau and Andrew Y. Kuroda. *The End of the Imperial Japanese Navy.* New York: W. W. Norton, 1962.

Jones, Ken, and Hubert Kelley. *Admiral Arleigh ("31-Knot") Burke.* Radnor, Pa.: Chilton Book Co., 1962.

Kahn, David. *The Codebreakers.* New York: Macmillan, 1967.

Kaigun shikan meibo [Directory of naval officers]. 1 July 1944.

Kase, Toshikazu. *Journey to the "Missouri."* New Haven, Conn.: Yale University Press, 1950.

Kato, Masuo. *The Lost War.* New York: Alfred A. Knopf, 1946.

Kennett, Lee B. *For the Duration.* New York: Charles Scribner's Sons, 1985.

Kimball, Warren F. *Churchill and Roosevelt: The Complete Correspondence.* Princeton, N.J.: Princeton University Press, 1984.

Kimmell, Husband E. *Admiral Kimmel's Story.* Chicago: Henry Regnery Co., 1955.

King, Ernest J. *U.S. Navy at War, 1941–1945* (Official Report to the Secretary of the Navy). Washington, D.C.: Government Printing Office, 1946.

————, and Walter Muir Whitehead. *Fleet Admiral King: A Naval Record.* New York: W. W. Norton, 1952.

Langer, William L., and S. Everett Gleason. *The Undeclared War: 1940–1941.* New York: Harper & Brothers, 1953.

Lash, Joseph P. *Roosevelt and Churchill 1931–1941: The Partnership That Saved the West.* New York: W. W. Norton, 1976.

Leasor, James. *Singapore: The Battle That Changed the World.* Garden City, N.Y.: Doubleday, 1968.

Lewin, Ronald. *The American Magic.* New York: Farrar Straus Giroux, 1982.

Lord, Walter. *Day of Infamy.* New York: Holt, Rinehart & Co., 1957.

————. *Incredible Victory.* New York: Harper & Row, 1967.

Lundstrom, John B. *The First South Pacific Campaign: Pacific Fleet Strategy December 1941–June 1942.* Annapolis, Md.: U.S. Naval Institute Press, 1976.

————. *The First Team.* Annapolis, Md.: U.S. Naval Institute Press, 1984.

MacArthur, Douglas. *Reminiscences.* New York: McGraw-Hill, 1964.

McGowen, Tom. *Midway and Guadalcanal.* New York: F. Watts, 1984.

McIntire, VADM. Ross T. *White House Physician.* New York: G. P. Putnam's Sons, 1946.

Manchester, William. *American Caesar: Douglas MacArthur, 1880–1964.* Boston: Little, Brown, 1978.

Melosi, Martin V. *The Shadow of Pearl Harbor.* College Station, Tex.: Texas

A & M University Press, 1977.

Middleton, Drew. *Crossroads of Modern Warfare*. Garden City, N.Y.: Doubleday, 1983.

Millis, Walter. *This Is Pearl! The United States and Japan—1941*. New York: William Morrow, 1947.

Mitchell, Joseph B., and Sir Edward Creasy. *Twenty Decisive Battles of the World*. New York: Macmillan, 1964.

Miyauchi, Kanya. *Niitakayama nobore 1208 (Climb Mount Niitaka 8 December)*. Tokyo: Rokko Shuppan, 1975.

Morgenstern, George E. *Pearl Harbor: The Story of the Secret War*. New York: Devin-Adair Co., 1947.

Morison, Samuel Eliot. *The Rising Sun in the Pacific*. Boston: Little, Brown, 1948.

———. *Coral Sea, Midway and Submarine Actions, May 1942–August 1942*. Boston: Little, Brown, 1950.

———. *The Struggle for Guadalcanal August 1942–February 1943*. Boston: Little, Brown, 1954.

Morton, Louis. *United States Army in World War II: The War in the Pacific: Strategy and Command: The First Two Years*. Washington, D.C.: Department of the Army, Office, Chief of Military History, 1962.

Mosley, Leonard. *Hirohito, Emperor of Japan*. Englewood Cliffs, N.J.: Prentice-Hall, 1966.

Nakamuta, Kenichi. *Jihō shikan no kaisu (Recollections of an Intelligence Officer)*. Tokyo: Daiya Mendosha, 1947.

Nihon rikukaigun no seido, soshiki, jinji (The System, Organization, and Personnel of the Japanese Army and Navy). Tokyo: Tokyo daigaku shiryo kenkyuukai, 1971.

Okumiya, Masatake. *Nihon kaigun no senryaku hasso (Strategic Ideas of the Japanese Navy)*. Tokyo, 1982.

———, and Jiro Horikoshi. *Zero!* New York: E. P. Dutton, 1956.

Pantzer, Eric F. *The Debacle at Pearl Harbor*. Indianapolis, Ind.: Thesis, Indiana University, 1965.

Perkins, Frances. *The Roosevelt I Knew*. New York: Viking Press, 1946.

Pogue, Forrest C. *George C. Marshall: Education of a General*. New York: Viking Press, 1963.

———. *George C. Marshall: Ordeal and Hope, 1939–1942*. New York: Viking Press, 1966.

———. *George C. Marshall, Organizer of Victory, 1943–1945*. New York: Viking Press, 1973.

Potter, Elmer B. *Nimitz*. Annapolis, Md.: U.S. Naval Institute Press, 1976.

———. *Bull Halsey*. Annapolis, Md.: Naval Institute Press, 1985.

Potter, John Deane. *Yamamoto, the Man Who Menaced America*. New York: Viking Press, 1965.

Prange, Gordon W. *Tora! Tora! Tora!* Tokyo: Reader's Digest (in Japanese), 1966.

———. *At Dawn We Slept*. New York: McGraw-Hill, 1981.

Reynolds, David. *The Creation of the Anglo-American Alliance 1937–41*. London: Europa, 1981.

Roscoe, Theodore. *United States Destroyer Operations in World War II*. Annapolis, Md.: U.S. Naval Institute Press, 1953.

———. *United States Submarine Operations in World War II*. Annapolis, Md.: U.S. Naval Institute Press, 1949.

Sakamaki, Kazuo. *I Attacked Pearl Harbor*. New York: Association Press, 1949.

Sanson, G. B. *The Western World and Japan*. New York: Alfred A. Knopf, 1950.

Schlesinger, Arthur M., Jr., and Roger Bruns, eds. *Congress Investigates: A Doc-*

umented History, 1792–1974, Vol. 5. New York: Chelsea House, 1975.

Sherrod, Robert. *Tarawa*. New York: Duell, Sloan and Pearce, 1944.

———. *On to Westward*. New York: Duell, Sloan, and Pearce, 1945.

———. *History of Marine Corps Aviation in World War II*. Washington, D.C.: Combat Forces Press, 1952.

Sherwood, Robert E. *Roosevelt and Hopkins*. New York: Harper & Brothers, 1948.

Smith, Chester L. *Midway, 4 June 1942*. London: Regency, 1962.

Smith, Peter C. *The Battle of Midway*. London: New English Library, 1976.

Smith, William W. *Midway, Turning Point of the Pacific*. New York: Crowell, 1966.

Sontag, Raymond Japme, and James Stuart Beddie, eds. *Nazi-Soviet Relations, 1939–1941*. Washington, D.C.: Department of State, 1948.

Spector, Ronald H. *The Eagle Against the Sun: The American War with Japan*. New York: The Free Press, 1985.

Standley, William H., and Arthur A. Ageton. *Admiral Ambassador to Russia*. Chicago: Henry Regnery Co., 1955.

Stillwell, Paul, ed. *Air Raid: Pearl Harbor!* Annapolis, Md.: U.S. Naval Institute Press, 1981.

Stimson, Henry L., and McGeorge Bundy. *On Active Service in Peace and War*. New York: Harper & Row, 1947.

Tansill, Charles C. *Back Door to War*. Chicago: Henry Regnery Co., 1952.

Taylor, Theodore. *Air Raid—Pearl Harbor*. New York: Crowell, 1971.

———. *The Magnificent Mitscher*. New York: W. W. Norton, 1954.

Terasaki, Gwen. *Bridge to the Sun*. Chapel Hill, N.C.: University of North Carolina Press, 1957.

Theobald, Robert A. *The Final Secret of Pearl Harbor*. New York: Devin-Adair Co., 1954.

Thorne, Christopher. *Allies of a Kind: The United States, Great Britain and the War Against Japan 1941–43*. New York: Oxford University Press, 1978.

Thorpe, Elliott R. *East Wind, Rain*. Boston: Gambit, Inc., 1969.

Togo, Shigenori. *The Cause of Japan*. New York: Simon & Schuster, 1956.

Toland, John. *The Rising Sun*. New York: Random House, 1970.

———. *Infamy*. Garden City, N.Y.: Doubleday, 1982.

Toyama, Isao. *Rikukaigun shookan jinji sookan* [A collection of army and naval officers]. Tokyo: Fuyo shobo, 1981.

Trefousse, Hans L. *What Happened at Pearl Harbor?* New York: Twayne Publishers, 1958.

———. *Pearl Harbor, the Continuing Controversy*. Malabar, Fla.: Krieger, 1982.

Tuleja, Thaddeus V. *Climax at Midway*. New York: W. W. Norton, 1960.

Tully, Grace. *F.D.R., My Boss*. New York: Charles Scribner's Sons, 1949.

Ugaki, Matome. *Sensōroku* [war record]. Tokyo: Nihon Shuppen Kyodo, 1952–1953.

United States Department of State. *Papers Relating to the Foreign Relations of the United States: Japan, 1931–1941*, 2 Volumes. Washington, D.C.: GPO, 1943.

United States Naval War College. *Battle of Midway Including the Aleutians Phase 3–14 June 1942: Strategic and Tactical Analysis* (NAVPERS 91067). Newport, R.I.: 1946.

———. *Battle of the Coral Sea 1–11 May 1942: Strategic and Tactical Analysis* (NAVPERS 91050). Newport, R.I.: 1947.

United States Office of Naval Intelligence. *The Japanese Story of the Battle of Midway*. Tr. Fred C. Woodrough. Washington, D.C.: Government Printing Office, 1947.

Van Der Rhoer, Edward. *Deadly Magic: A Personal Account of Communication*

Intelligence in World War II in the Pacific. New York: Charles Scribner's Sons, 1978.

Waller, George M. *Pearl Harbor: Roosevelt and the Coming of the War.* Boston: Heath, 1965.

————. *Pearl Harbor.* Lexington, Mass.: Heath, 1976.

Wallin, Homer N. *Pearl Harbor: Why, How, Fleet Salvage, and Final Appraisal.* Washington, D.C.: Naval History Division, 1968.

Whitehead, Don. *The FBI Story.* New York: Random House, 1956.

Wilson, Rose Page. *General Marshall Remembered.* Englewood Cliffs, N.J.: Prentice-Hall, 1968.

Willmott, H. P. *The Barrier and the Javelin.* Annapolis, Md.: U.S. Naval Institute Press, 1983.

Wohlstetter, Roberta. *Pearl Harbor—Warning and Decision.* Stanford, Calif.: Stanford University Press, 1962.

Yardley, Herbert O. *The American Black Chamber.* New York: Ballantine Books, 1981.

Yokoi, Toshiyuki. *Nihon no kimitsu shitsu [Japan's Secret Chamber].* Tokyo: Rokumaisha, 1951.

Zacharias, Ellis M. *Secret Missions.* New York: G. P. Putnam's Sons, 1946.

Series

"Magic" Background of Pearl Harbor. Washington, D.C.: Department of Defense, 1977.
>   Vol. I, 14 February–12 May 1941.
>   Vol. II, 12 May–6 August 1941.
>   Vol. II, Appendix.
>   Vol. III, 5 August–17 October 1941.
>   Vol. III, Appendix.
>   Vol. IV, 17 August–7 December 1941.
>   Vol. IV, Appendix.
>   Vol. V, Index.

Reports of General MacArthur. Washington, D.C.: Government Printing Office, 1966.
>   Vol. I, *The Campaigns of MacArthur in the Pacific,* prepared by his general staff.
>   Vol. II, parts I and II, *Japanese Operations in the Southwest Pacific Area,* compiled from Japanese Demobilization Bureau records.

Senshi Sōsho [War History series]. Tokyo: Defense Headquarters History Office. Dates indicated.
>   Vol. 10, *Hawai sakusen [Hawaii operation],* 1967.
>   Vol. 12, *Marianas oki kaisen [Sea Battles off the Marianas],* 1968.
>   Vol. 24, *Philippines-Marei hoomen kaigun shinkoo sakusen [Philippines-Malay Area Naval Attack Operations],* 1969.
>   Vol. 26, *N.E.I.-Bengaru wan hoomen kaigun shinkoo sakusen [N.E.I.-Bengal Bay Area Naval Attack Operations],* 1969.
>   Vol. 29, *Hokutoo hoomen kaigun sakusen [Northeast Area Naval Operations],* 1969.
>   Vol. 38, *Chuubu taiheiyoo hoomen kaigun sakusen [Central Pacific Naval Operations],* 1970.
>   Vol. 39, *Daihonei kaigunbu-rengoo kantai (4) [Imperial General Headquarters–Combined Fleet],* 1970.
>   Vol. 43, *Midooei kaisen [Midway Sea Battle],* 1971.
>   Vol. 46, *Kaijō bōei sen [Surface Defensive Actions],* 1971.
>   Vol. 49, *Nantoo hoomen kaigun sakusen [Southeast Area Naval Actions Until Guadalcanal Reinforcement],* 1971.

Vol. 62, *Chuubu taiheiyoo hoomen kaigun sakusen [Central Pacific Area Naval Operations* (after June 1942)]*, 1973.

Vol. 83, *Nantoo hoomen kaigun sakusen [Southeast Area Naval Operations Until Guadalcanal evacuation]*, 1975.

Magazine and Newspaper Articles

Adair, RADM. Charles, U.S.N. (Ret.), "As I Recall . . . End of Peace in the Philippines," *USNIP*, August 1985.

Costello, John E., "Remember Pearl Harbor," *USNIP*, September 1983.

Cressman, Robert J., "That Gallant Ship: A History of USS *Yorktown* (CV-5)," *The Hook*, Spring 1981, pp. 11–24.

D'Andrea, Thomas M., "Marines at Midway," *Marine Corps Gazette*, November 1964, pp. 27–31.

Davenport, Walter, "Impregnable Pearl Harbor," *Colliers*, 14 June 1941.

Forrest, Jerome, and Clarke H. Kawakami, "General MacArthur and His Vanishing War History," *The Reporter*, 14 October 1952, pp. 20–25.

Frank, Larry J., "*The United States Navy* v. *the Chicago Tribune*," *Historian*, February 1980, pp. 284–303.

Hannah, Theodore M., "Frank B. Rowlett—A Personal Profile," *Cryptologic Spectrum*, Spring 1981, pp. 4–22.

Harris, Dr. Ruth M., "The Purple Code," *Pacific Quarterly*, Vol. LXI, February 1981.

"Hawaii: Sugar-Coated Fort," *Fortune*, August 1940, pp. 30–82, passim.

Layton, RADM, Edwin T., "Rendezvous in Reverse," *USNIP*, May 1953.

———, "24th Sentai, Japan's Commerce Raiders," *USNIP*, June 1976.

———, "America Deciphered Our Code," *USNIP*, June 1979, pp. 98–100.

Meigs, LCOL Montgomery C., USA, "This Must Mean the Philippines," *USNIP*, August 1985.

Nagumo, Chuichi, "The Japanese Story of the Battle of Midway," tr. Fred C. Woodrough, Jr., *ONI Review*, May 1947, pp. 3–72.

Nubser, RADM. J.F.W., "A History of Adeling I (Intelligence) Naval Staff, Batana, NEI," *The Cryptogram*, Vol. XLVII, No. 2, Summer 1985.

Robinson, Walton L., "*Akagi*, Famous Japanese Carrier," *USNIP*, May 1948, pp. 578–95.

Rushbridger, James, "The Sinking of the *Nankin* and the Capture of the *Automedon*," *Encounter*, May 1985, Vol. LXIV, No. 5.

Tucker, Dundas P., "Rhapsody in Purple: A New History of Pearl Harbor," *Cryptologia*, July (pp. 193–229) and October (pp. 346–67), 1982.

Vogel, Bertram, "Japan's Navy and the Battle of Midway," *Marine Corps Gazette*, December 1947, pp. 36–41.

Unpublished Sources

Unlike previous analysts, Layton insisted, wherever possible, in returning to the actual message files for both signals and intercepts. Although this confronts the researcher with a daunting task of having to sift through thousands of randomly filed intercepts in the SRN and SRDJ records in addition to the Cincpac message files, it provides a unique access to primary sources.

Researchers are urged to resist the temptation of some recent writers to rely only upon the SRH histories. Although these provide a digest of radio intelligence materials, they are not primary sources. In the case of SRH 012, Layton was to demonstrate how its interpretation of the comint account of Pearl Harbor and Midway was slanted to reflect the bias of the navy department. It provides the historian only with Washington's view by omitting the errors of misevaluation made by OP-20-G while claiming the credit for the correct analyses.

So too does the interpretation so given the Purple intercepts in the so-called *Magic Background to Pearl Harbor*. Like the selected records presented in the congressional hearings, the decrypts are incomplete and presented out of context. In the SRDJ files, we now have the ability to analyze how the intercepts were perceived as they were actually decrypted. In the sequential pattern that emerges, it is evident that the "noise" of similar messages should have reinforced as much as some historians have argued that it confused the evaluations being made in 1941. As an anonymous wartime navy analyst pointed out, the concentration pattern of the Honolulu consulate traffic that was being decrypted in Washington ought to have triggered a special alarm to the fleet.

Even with an expert guide like Layton, who was familiar with many of the intercepts, his co-authors had to employ a computer data base to bring order to the chaos of the SRN files. After months of sifting through the intercepts they developed a finding aid that could locate individual Japanese intercepts by date-time group. This resulted in the discovery of two blocks of JN-25 intercepts that were received—but not decrypted—in the three months before Pearl Harbor. This finding aid will be made available to the National Archives to help researchers to tap more deeply into this rich lode of material on the intelligence war in the Pacific.

All of the following cryptologic documents are available in Record Group 457, Records of the National Security Agency, on file in the National Archives of the United States.

Japanese Military Attaché Messages (SRA)
    SRA 1 through 16401

Translations of Japanese Naval Messages (SRN)
    SRN   1–125,093   1942–1946
    SRN 125,094–129,615   1942–1946
    SRN 129,616–133,367   5 December 1941–25 March 1942
    SRN 133,368–165,038 19 December 1942–31 December 1943
                                       (Cincpac)

Translations of Japanese Naval Attaché Messages (SRNA)
    SRNA 1–5,308   1942–1946

Japanese Naval Radio Intelligence Summaries (SRNS)
    SRNS 1–1,289   1942–1946

Miscellaneous Records of Japanese Naval Communication (SRNM)
    SRNM 1–1,292   March–June 1942

Japanese Diplomatic Messages (SRDJ)
    SRDJ   1–2,204   (1940–March 1941)
    SRDJ   9,361–19,978   (April 1941–January 1942)
    SRDJ   19,979–32,199   (February 1942–February 1943)

SRDJ   32,201–43,166   (February 1943–September 1943)
SRDJ   43,167–113,784   (September 1943–March 1945)
SRDJ 113,785–114,197   (September 1940–April 1941)

Where cited, the chapter notes provide an SRDJ number, which in general represents when the intercept was decrypted, followed by the JD-1 number (Japanese diplomatic number according to the OP-20-G filing system—or the Army SIS number), from-to, date transmitted, and the date that the translation was made.

Example: SRDJ 012780, JD-1 3490, Washington-Tokyo, 4 July 1941, tr. 8 July 1941.

Cincpac Message File: The dispatches received and sent from Pacific Fleet headquarters have been assembled from the microfilm records of the navy's operational archives and the so-called Gray Book. They are cited in the following form:
    Cominch 092245 May 1942
    This indicates a dispatch from the commander in chief U.S. Fleet transmitted on 9 May at 2245 hours.

Histories (SRH)

SRH 012 Role of Radio Intelligence in the American-Japanese naval war. Four vols., August 1941–September 1942 (2,128 pages).
        Appendix II, Coral Sea.
        Appendix III, Midway.
SRH 029 A Brief History of the Signal Intelligence Service, by William F. Friedman 29 June 1942 (18 pages).
SRH 035 History of the Special Branch, MIS, war department 1942–1944 (63 pages).
SRH 036 Radio Intelligence in World War II Tactical Operations, Pacific Ocean Areas, January 1943 (688 pages).
    136 Pacific Ocean Areas, December 1942 (707 pages).
    144 Pacific Ocean Areas, Parts I & II, February 1943 (639 pages).
SRH 041 MIS Contribution to the War Effort, December 1945 (22 pages).
SRH 043 Comment on Marshall-Dewey exchange concerning Pearl Harbor, September 1944 (14 pages).
SRH 051 Interview with Mr. Ralph T. Briggs, January 1977 (17 pages).
SRH 081 Information from George W. Linn, Capt. U.S.N.R. (Ret.), October 1980 (15 pages).
SRH 106 Special Intelligence, Specific Instructions for Handling and Dissemination, 25 January 1941, G2, DA, DNI, USN.
SRH 115 U.S. Army Investigations into the Handling of Certain Communications Prior to the Attack on Pearl Harbor 1944–45 (387 pages).
SRH 125 Certain aspects of "Magic" in cryptological background of various investigations into Pearl Harbor attack, by William F. Friedman (74 pages).
SRH 128 Study of Pearl Harbor Hearings, MIS, 1947 (39 pages).
SRH 136 Radio Intelligence in World War II, Tactical Operations, Pacific Ocean Areas, December 1942 (707 pages).
SRH 149 Communications Intelligence in the United States, a brief history, by Laurence F. Safford, Captain U.S.N. (Ret.) (22 pages).
SRH 150 Birthday of Naval Security Group (6 pages).
SRH 152 History Review of OP-20-G (13 pages).

SRH 154 Signal Intelligence Disclosures in the Pearl Harbor Investigations (147 pages).
SRH 159 Preliminary Historical Report on the Solution of the "B" Machine (10 pages).
SRH 177 Interrogation of Japanese Concerning Possible Broadcast of the Winds Message, October–November 1945 (15 pages).
SRH 207 Evacuation of U.S.N. Comint Personnel from Corregidor in World War II (99 pages).
SRH 209 Decryption Intelligence Charts, OP-20-G, 20 January–May 1942 (250 pages).
SRH 210 Collection of papers relating to the "Winds Execute" Messages (80 pages).
SRH 211 Japanese Radio Communications and Radio Intelligence, Cincpac-poa Bull, May 1945 (34 pages).
SRH 222 Japanese grand fleet maneuvers, May–June 1930, OP-20 report (211 pages).
SRH 223 Japanese grand fleet maneuvers, June–August 1933, various reports (278 pages).
SRH 224 Japanese grand fleet maneuvers, August–October 1934 (119 pages).
SRH 225 Japanese grand fleet maneuvers, July–September 1935 (78 pages).
SRH 230 The Role of Comint in the Battle of Midway (9 pages).
SRH 231 Japanese reports on monitoring of Allied wireless communications in Philippines, January–December 1943 (113 pages).
SRH 235 Comint contributions, Submarine Warfare in World War II (4 pages).
SRH 239 Japanese army signal centers and officer lists, MIS, war department, 1 September 1945 (27 pages).
SRH 254 Japanese Intelligence System, MISWDGS, 4 September 1945 (171 pages).
SRH 255 Robert D. Ogg, history interview (82 pages).
SRH 268 Advance Intelligence Centers in U.S. Navy [Redman memos] (2 pages).
SRH 272 Cincpac enemy activities file, April–May 1942 (122 pages).
SRH 275 Fleet Radio Unit, Melbourne (Frumel), 28 June 1943–2 September 1945 (24 photos and 130 pages).
SRH 278 War diary, combat intelligence unit (Pacific), 1942 (190 pages).
SRH 279 Communications Intelligence Activities, OP-20-G, 1942–1946 [including reorganization memos] (82 pages).
SRH 287 Radio Intelligence in World War II, Tactical Operations in the Pacific Ocean Areas, March 1943 (444 pages).
SRH 289 Mobile radio intelligence units (RIU), by commands afloat in World War II (151 pages).
SRH 305 History of Radio Intelligence, the Undeclared War, Captain Laurence F. Safford (29 pages).
SRH 306 OP-20-G, Exploits and Commendations, World War II (82 pages).
SRH 309 Mobile RIU reports, Pacific, 1945, Pt. I (236 pages).
Mobile RIU reports, Pacific, 1945, Pt. II (274 pages).
Mobile RIU reports, Pacific, 1945, Pt. III (338 pages).
SRH 313 Mobile RIU reports, Pacific, 1942 (39 pages).
SRH 314 Mobile RIU reports, Pacific, 1944 (116 pages).
SRH 317 Mobile RIU reports, Pacific, 1943 (304 pages).
SRH 355 Naval Security Group History to World War II, prepared by Captain J. S. Holtwick, Jr., U.S.N. (Ret.), June 1971 (464 pages).

Among other collections in the National Archives, which include RG 165, RG 187 and RG 80 and which have yielded new primary source material, is the so-called Pearl Harbor Liaison Office File containing many thousands of documents pertaining to the navy's investigations for the congressional hearings in 1945. Its 136 boxes contain a trove of original documentation, from Layton's contemporary notes and reports to a complete set of Purple decrypts still bearing the code notations that have been sanitized from the SRDJ series.

Documents, statements, and memoranda collected by Admiral Kimmel during more than two decades are available in the University of Wyoming library. They provide some revealing insights into the character of the commander who was made a scapegoat by Washington and the methods of his accusers. Rochefort's papers, by contrast, are mainly copies of official documents, many of which are not readily accessible or have been destroyed.

The most intriguing document of all is the anonymous SECRET memorandum entitled "The Inside Story of the Battle of Midway and the Ousting of Commander Rochefort," which we had designated "A." While unable to establish its authorship, from the secrecy with which it has been accorded for nearly forty years and the information it contains—much confirmed by recently declassified documentation—must make it a significant primary source. Whoever wrote it appears to have been a ranking officer on the naval intelligence staff and it appears several copies were clandestinely circulated in the navy department sometime after 1943. It would be out of keeping for Rochefort himself to have been either the instigator or the author of the A Memorandum, but the marginal comments appear to be in his handwriting.

Copies of the memorandum and many of the other documents that have provided the authors with their primary sources will be incorporated into the Edwin T. Layton Collection and be available for research at the Naval War College.

Index